HUMBER COLLEGE LIBRARY

HUMBER COLLEGE LIBRARY
205 HUMBER COLLEGE BLVD.
P.O. BOX 1900
REXDALE, ONTARIO, CANADA
M9W 5L7

www.wadsworth.com

wadsworth.com is the World Wide Web site for Wadsworth and is your direct source to dozens of online resources.

At *wadsworth.com* you can find out about supplements, demonstration software, and student resources. You can also send email to many of our authors and preview new publications and exciting new technologies.

wadsworth.com
Changing the way the world learns®

SIXTH EDITION

HUMAN EVOLUTION AND PREHISTORY

William A. Haviland

University of Vermont

With the assistance of
Harald Prins and Dana Walrath
Technical Consultants

160101

THOMSON

™

WADSWORTH

AUSTRALIA • CANADA • MEXICO • SINGAPORE • SPAIN
UNITED KINGDOM • UNITED STATES

THOMSON

WADSWORTH

Anthropology Editor: Lin Marshall
Assistant Editor: Analie Barnett
Editorial Assistants: Amanda Santana, Reilly O'Neal
Technology Project Manager: Dee Dee Zobian
Marketing Manager: Diane McOscar
Project Manager, Editorial Production: Jerilyn Emori
Print/Media Buyer: Barbara Britton
Permissions Editor: Sandra Lord
Production Service: Robin Lockwood Productions

Photo Researcher: Sandra Lord
Copy Editor: Jennifer Gordon
Illustrators: Carol Zuber-Mallison, Magellan Geographix
Cover Designer: Hiroko Chastain/Cuttriss & Hambleton
Cover Image: National Geographic
Cover Printer: Phoenix Color Corp.
Compositor: New England Typographic Service, Inc.
Printer: Transcontinental/Interglobe

COPYRIGHT © 2003 Wadsworth, a division of Thomson Learning, Inc. Thomson Learning™ is a trademark used herein under license.

ALL RIGHTS RESERVED. No part of this work covered by the copyright hereon may be reproduced or used in any form or by any means—graphic, electronic, or mechanical, including but not limited to photocopying, recording, taping, Web distribution, information networks, or information storage and retrieval systems—without the written permission of the publisher.

Printed in Canada
2 3 4 5 6 7 06 05 04 03

For more information about our products, contact us at:
Thomson Learning Academic Resource Center
1-800-423-0563

For permission to use material from this text, contact us by:
Phone: 1-800-730-2214
Fax: 1-800-730-2215
Web: http://www.thomsonrights.com

ExamView® and ExamView Pro® are registered trademarks of FSCreations, Inc. Windows is a registered trademark of the Microsoft Corporation used herein under license. Macintosh and Power Macintosh are registered trademarks of Apple Computer, Inc. Used herein under license.

COPYRIGHT 2003 Thomson Learning, Inc. All Rights Reserved. Thomson Learning WebTutor™ is a trademark of Thomson Learning, Inc.

Library of Congress Control Number 2002105834

ISBN 0-534-61011-0

Wadsworth/Thomson Learning
10 Davis Drive
Belmont, CA 94002-3098
USA

Asia
Thomson Learning
5 Shenton Way #01-01
UIC Building
Singapore 068808

Australia
Nelson Thomson Learning
102 Dodds Street
South Melbourne, Victoria 3205
Australia

Canada
Nelson Thomson Learning
1120 Birchmount Road
Toronto, Ontario M1K 5G4
Canada

Europe/Middle East/Africa
Thomson Learning
High Holborn House
50/51 Bedford Row
London WC1R 4LR
United Kingdom

Latin America
Thomson Learning
Seneca, 53
Colonia Polanco
11560 Mexico D.F.
Mexico

Spain
Paraninfo Thomson Learning
Calle/Magallanes, 25
28015 Madrid, Spain

To my three sons:

Thomas Philip Haviland

Wallace de Laguna Haviland

Theodore William John Haviland

Wᴵᴸᴸᴵᴬᴹ A. Hᴀᴠᴵᴸᴬɴᴅ, Pʀᴏꜰᴇꜱꜱᴏʀ Eᴍᴇʀᴵᴛᴜꜱ ᴏꜰ Aɴᴛʜʀᴏᴘᴏʟᴏɢʏ ᴀᴛ ᴛʜᴇ Uɴᴵᴠᴇʀꜱᴵᴛʏ ᴏꜰ Vᴇʀᴍᴏɴᴛ, earned his BA, MA and PhD degrees at the University of Pennsylvania. He began his career as a physical anthropologist at the Philadelphia Center for Research in Child Growth and as a research assistant for its director, Dr. Wilton M. Krogman. He subsequently went on to teach at Hunter College and Barnard College in New York City, and then at The University of Vermont, Burlington, VT, where he founded the anthropology department.

Dr. Haviland's first field experience was as a member of a Smithsonian Institution field crew doing archaeology on the Lower Brule Indian Reservation in South Dakota. A year later, he became a member of the University of Pennsylvania's archaeological project at the ancient Maya city of Tikal, Guatemala, where he explored prehistoric settlement and served as physical anthropologist. After six seasons there, he helped establish a program of Cultural Resource Management in Vermont, where he also began research on the archaeology, ethnography, and ethnohistory of the region's Native American inhabitants. In 1989, he served as expert witness for Vermont's Abenakis in a landmark case involving aboriginal fishing rights, and has frequently testified before legislative committees on their behalf. During this same period, he also investigated Anglo-American settlement in a Maine coastal community over the 200 years since the community was established.

Dr. Haviland is a member of several professional societies and has served on the board of the American Anthropological Association's general Anthropology Division. He has published many research articles in North American, British, and Mexican journals. Besides his three college texts published by Harcourt College Publishers, he has several other books to his credit, including technical monographs on his work at Tikal and *The Original Vermonters,* of which he is senior author. His professional publications cover three of the four subfields of anthropology.

Now retired, Dr. Haviland is heavily involved in writing and continues as co-editor of the University of Pennsylvania Museum's series of Tikal Reports. He spends much of his spare time in his wooden lobster boat on the waters of Penobscot Bay with his wife, sons, and grandchildren.

TABLE OF CONTENTS

PREFACE   XV

ACKNOWLEDGMENTS   xxi

PUTTING THE WORLD IN PERSPECTIVE   xxii

PART I

THE STUDY OF HUMANKIND   2

CHAPTER 1 THE NATURE OF ANTHROPOLOGY   4

THE DEVELOPMENT OF ANTHROPOLOGY   7

FRANK HAMILTON CUSHING (1857–1900),
MATILDA COXE STEVENSON (1849–1915)   7

ANTHROPOLOGY AND THE OTHER SCIENCES   8

THE DISCIPLINE OF ANTHROPOLOGY   8

ANTHROPOLOGY APPLIED: FORENSIC ANTHROPOLOGY   9

PHYSICAL ANTHROPOLOGY   10

CULTURAL ANTHROPOLOGY   10

ARCHAEOLOGY   13

LINGUISTIC ANTHROPOLOGY   14

ETHNOLOGY   14

ANTHROPOLOGY AND SCIENCE   17

FRANZ BOAS (1858–1942),
FREDRIC WARD PUTNAM (1839–1915),
JOHN WESLEY POWELL (1834–1902)   18

ORIGINAL STUDY: THE STRANGE CASE OF PILTDOWN MAN 19

DIFFICULTIES OF THE SCIENTIFIC APPROACH   21

COMPARISON IN ANTHROPOLOGY   22

GEORGE PETER MURDOCK (1897–1985)   23

ANTHROPOLOGY AND THE HUMANITIES   25

QUESTIONS OF ETHICS   25

ANTHROPOLOGY AND CONTEMPORARY LIFE   26

CHAPTER SUMMARY   30

CLASSIC READINGS   31

CHAPTER 2 METHODS OF STUDYING
THE HUMAN PAST   32

METHODS OF DATA RECOVERY   34

THE NATURE OF FOSSILS   35

ORIGINAL STUDY: WHISPERS FROM THE ICE   36

SITES AND FOSSIL LOCALITIES   40

SITE AND LOCALITY IDENTIFICATION   41

SITE AND LOCALITY EXCAVATION   43

Archaeological Excavation   43

ANTHROPOLOGY APPLIED: CULTURAL
RESOURCE MANAGEMENT   44

Excavation of Fossils   46

STATE OF PRESERVATION OF
ARCHAEOLOGICAL AND FOSSIL EVIDENCE   47

SORTING OUT THE EVIDENCE   48

DATING THE PAST   51

METHODS OF RELATIVE DATING   52

METHODS OF CHRONOMETRIC DATING   52

CHANCE AND THE STUDY OF THE PAST   54

CHAPTER SUMMARY   56

CLASSIC READINGS   57

CHAPTER 3 BIOLOGY AND EVOLUTION   58

THE CLASSIFICATION OF LIVING THINGS   60

THE DISCOVERY OF EVOLUTION   61

    CHARLES R. DARWIN (1809–1882)   63

ORIGINAL STUDY: THE UNSETTLING NATURE
OF VARIATIONAL CHANGE   64

HEREDITY   65

    THE TRANSMISSION OF GENES   65

    Genes   66

    GREGOR MENDEL (1822–1884)   68

    Chromosomes   68

ANTHROPOLOGY APPLIED: THE ETHICAL, LEGAL,
AND SOCIAL IMPLICATIONS OF THE HUMAN
GENOME PROJECT   69

    Cell Division   70

    Polygenetic Inheritance   72

POPULATION GENETICS   73

    THE STABILITY OF THE POPULATION   73

EVOLUTIONARY FORCES   74

    MUTATION   74

    GENETIC DRIFT   76

    GENE FLOW   76

    INTERSPECIES GENE TRANSFER   77

    NATURAL SELECTION   77

ADAPTATION   79

    THE CASE OF SICKLE-CELL ANEMIA   80

CONCLUSION   83

CHAPTER SUMMARY   84

CLASSIC READINGS   85

PART II

**PRIMATE EVOLUTION AND THE
EMERGENCE OF THE HOMININES**   86

CHAPTER 4 MONKEYS, APES, AND HUMANS:
    THE MODERN PRIMATES   88

THE PRIMATE ORDER   90

CHARACTERISTICS   92

    THE PRIMATE BRAIN   92

    PRIMATE SENSE ORGANS   93

    PRIMATE DENTITION   94

    THE PRIMATE SKELETON   95

    REPRODUCTION AND CARE OF YOUNG   98

    ESTABLISHING EVOLUTIONARY
    RELATIONSHIPS   99

MODERN PRIMATES   100

    STREPSIRHINES   100

    HAPLORHINES   100

    Tarsiers   101

    New World Monkeys   101

    Old World Monkeys   101

    Small and Great Apes   102

THE SOCIAL BEHAVIOR OF PRIMATES   104

    THE GROUP   104

    JANE GOODALL (B. 1934)   105

    INDIVIDUAL INTERACTION   105

    SEXUAL BEHAVIOR   106

    PLAY   109

    COMMUNICATION   109

    HOME RANGES   109

ANTHROPOLOGY APPLIED: PRIMATE CONSERVATION   110

  LEARNING   110

  USE OF OBJECTS AS TOOLS   111

  HUNTING   112

THE QUESTION OF CULTURE   113

ORIGINAL STUDY: THE CULTURE OF CHIMPANZEES   113

  PRIMATE BEHAVIOR AND HUMAN EVOLUTION   115

CHAPTER SUMMARY   116

CLASSIC READINGS   117

CHAPTER 5   MACROEVOLUTION AND THE EARLY PRIMATES   118

SPECIATION   120

  ISOLATING MECHANISMS   120

  DIVERGENCE AND CONVERGENCE   122

  LINEAR EVOLUTION   123

  THE NONDIRECTEDNESS OF EVOLUTION   123

EARLY MAMMALS   125

RISE OF THE PRIMATES   126

  PALEOCENE PRIMATES   127

  EOCENE PRIMATES   128

  OLIGOCENE MONKEYS AND APES   129

  MIOCENE APES   130

ORIGINAL STUDY: WILL THE REAL HUMAN ANCESTOR PLEASE STAND UP?   133

MIOCENE APES AND HUMAN ORIGINS   137

  HOMINOID ADAPTATIONS AND LATE MIOCENE CLIMATIC CHANGE   138

EARLY APES AND HUMAN EVOLUTION   141

EARLY PRIMATE EVOLUTION: AN OVERVIEW   141

CHAPTER SUMMARY   142

CLASSIC READINGS   143

CHAPTER 6   THE EARLIEST HOMININES   144

AUSTRALOPITHECUS   146

  GRACILE AUSTRALOPITHECINES   147

  ROBUST AUSTRALOPITHECINES   154

  LOUIS S. B. LEAKEY (1903–1972), MARY LEAKEY (1913–1996)   155

AUSTRALOPITHECINE PREDECESSORS   157

ENVIRONMENT, DIET, AND AUSTRALOPITHECINE ORIGINS   159

  HUMANS STAND ON THEIR OWN TWO FEET   161

ORIGINAL STUDY: THE NAKED AND THE BIPEDAL   162

CHAPTER SUMMARY   166

CLASSIC READINGS   167

PART III

EVOLUTION OF THE GENUS HOMO AND THE DEVELOPMENT OF EARLY HUMAN CULTURE   168

CHAPTER 7   HOMO HABILIS AND CULTURAL ORIGINS   170

EARLY REPRESENTATIVES OF THE GENUS HOMO   172

  RELATIONS BETWEEN HOMO HABILIS AND AUSTRALOPITHECUS   174

LOWER PALEOLITHIC TOOLS   176

  OLDUVAI GORGE   176

  OLDOWAN TOOLS   178

  TOOLS, MEAT, AND BRAINS   181

ORIGINAL STUDY: CAT IN THE HUMAN CRADLE   181

ADRIENNE ZIHLMAN (B. 1940)   185

THE EARLIEST SIGNS OF CULTURE: TOOLS   187

COOPERATION AND SHARING   189

LANGUAGE ORIGINS   190

CHAPTER SUMMARY   190

CLASSIC READINGS   191

CHAPTER 8   *Homo erectus* AND THE EMERGENCE OF HUNTING AND GATHERING   192

HOMO ERECTUS FOSSILS   194

Homo erectus FROM JAVA   194

Homo erectus FROM CHINA   195

Homo erectus FROM AFRICA   197

Homo erectus FROM EUROPE   198

PHYSICAL CHARACTERISTICS OF *Homo erectus*   199

RELATIONSHIP BETWEEN *Homo erectus* AND *Homo habilis*   200

THE CULTURE OF *HOMO ERECTUS*   200

THE ACHEULEAN TOOL TRADITION   201

ORIGINAL STUDY: *HOMO ERECTUS* AND THE USE OF BAMBOO   203

USE OF FIRE   208

OTHER ASPECTS OF *HOMO ERECTUS'* CULTURE   209

THE QUESTION OF LANGUAGE   212

CHAPTER SUMMARY   214

CLASSIC READINGS   215

CHAPTER 9   ARCHAIC *Homo sapiens* AND THE MIDDLE PALEOLITHIC   216

THE APPEARANCE OF *HOMO SAPIENS*   218

LEVALLOISIAN TECHNIQUE   220

ARCHAIC *Homo sapiens*   221

AFRICAN, CHINESE, AND JAVANESE POPULATIONS   223

THE CULTURE OF ARCHAIC *HOMO SAPIENS*   224

MIDDLE PALEOLITHIC   224

The Mousterian Tradition   224

THE SYMBOLIC LIFE OF NEANDERTALS   226

ANTHROPOLOGY APPLIED: FORENSIC ARCHAEOLOGY   227

NEANDERTALS AND SPOKEN LANGUAGE   228

ARCHAIC *HOMO SAPIENS* AND MODERN HUMAN ORIGINS   230

THE MULTIREGIONAL HYPOTHESIS   230

FRANZ WEIDENREICH (1873–1948)   231

THE "EVE" OR "OUT OF AFRICA" HYPOTHESIS   233

ORIGINAL STUDY: AFRICAN ORIGIN OR ANCIENT POPULATION SIZE DIFFERENCES?   235

CHAPTER SUMMARY   238

CLASSIC READINGS   239

CHAPTER 10   *Homo sapiens* AND THE UPPER PALEOLITHIC   240

UPPER PALEOLITHIC PEOPLES: THE FIRST MODERN HUMANS   242

UPPER PALEOLITHIC TOOLS   243

ANTHROPOLOGY APPLIED: STONE TOOLS FOR MODERN SURGEONS   245

UPPER PALEOLITHIC ART   247

ORIGINAL STUDY: PALEOLITHIC PAINT JOB   252

OTHER ASPECTS OF UPPER PALEOLITHIC
CULTURE   256

THE SPREAD OF UPPER PALEOLITHIC PEOPLES   256

WHERE DID UPPER PALEOLITHIC PEOPLE
COME FROM?   260

MAJOR PALEOLITHIC TRENDS   262

CHAPTER SUMMARY   264

CLASSIC READINGS   265

PART IV

HUMAN BIOLOGICAL AND CULTURAL EVOLUTION SINCE THE OLD STONE AGE   266

CHAPTER 11   CULTIVATION AND
DOMESTICATION   268

THE MESOLITHIC ROOTS OF FARMING
AND PASTORALISM   270

MESOLITHIC TOOLS AND WEAPONS   270

CULTURAL DIVERSITY IN THE MESOLITHIC   271

THE NEOLITHIC REVOLUTION   273

DOMESTICATION: WHAT IS IT?   273

EVIDENCE OF EARLY PLANT
DOMESTICATION   274

EVIDENCE OF EARLY ANIMAL
DOMESTICATION   276

BEGINNINGS OF DOMESTICATION   276

WHY HUMANS BECAME FOOD PRODUCERS   277

V. GORDON CHILDE (1892–1957)   278

OTHER CENTERS OF DOMESTICATION   283

ANTHROPOLOGY APPLIED: ARCHAEOLOGY FOR
AND BY NATIVE AMERICANS   286

THE SPREAD OF FOOD PRODUCTION   287

CULTURE OF NEOLITHIC SETTLEMENTS   289

EARLIEST FULL-FLEDGED FARMING
SETTLEMENTS   289

JERICHO: AN EARLY FARMING COMMUNITY   290

NEOLITHIC TECHNOLOGY   290

POTTERY   291

HOUSING   292

CLOTHING   292

SOCIAL STRUCTURE   293

NEOLITHIC CULTURE IN THE NEW WORLD   293

THE NEOLITHIC AND HUMAN BIOLOGY   294

ORIGINAL STUDY: HISTORY OF MORTALITY AND
PHYSIOLOGICAL STRESS   294

THE NEOLITHIC AND THE IDEA OF PROGRESS   296

CHAPTER SUMMARY   298

CLASSIC READINGS   299

CHAPTER 12   THE RISE OF CITIES
AND CIVILIZATION   300

WHAT CIVILIZATION MEANS   302

TIKAL: A CASE STUDY   306

SURVEYING THE SITE   306

EVIDENCE FROM THE EXCAVATION   307

ANTHROPOLOGY APPLIED: ECONOMIC DEVELOPMENT
AND TROPICAL FORESTS   309

CITIES AND CULTURAL CHANGE   309

AGRICULTURAL INNOVATION   310

DIVERSIFICATION OF LABOR   311

CENTRAL GOVERNMENT 313

Evidence of Centralized Authority 313

The Earliest Governments 315

SOCIAL STRATIFICATION 316

Evidence of Social Stratification 317

ORIGINAL STUDY: FINDING THE TOMB OF A MOCHE PRIESTESS 317

THE MAKING OF CIVILIZATION 322

THEORIES OF CIVILIZATION'S EMERGENCE 323

Irrigation Systems 323

Trade Networks 323

Environmental and Social Circumscription 324

Religion 324

CIVILIZATION AND ITS DISCONTENTS 326

CHAPTER SUMMARY 328

CLASSIC READINGS 329

CHAPTER 13 MODERN HUMAN DIVERSITY 330

VARIATION AND EVOLUTION 332

PHYSICAL VARIABILITY 332

THE MEANING OF RACE 333

ASHLEY MONTAGU (1905–1999) 335

RACE AS A BIOLOGICAL CONCEPT 336

ORIGINAL STUDY: RACE WITHOUT COLOR 336

THE CONCEPT OF HUMAN RACES 341

SOME PHYSICAL VARIABLES 343

SKIN COLOR: A CASE STUDY IN ADAPTATION 344

THE SOCIAL SIGNIFICANCE OF RACE: RACISM 347

RACE AND BEHAVIOR 348

RACE AND INTELLIGENCE 348

INTELLIGENCE: WHAT IS IT? 350

CONTINUING HUMAN BIOLOGICAL EVOLUTION 352

ANTHROPOLOGY APPLIED: STUDYING THE EMERGENCE OF NEW DISEASES 357

CHAPTER SUMMARY 358

CLASSIC READINGS 359

GLOSSARY 361

BIBLIOGRAPHY 366

PHOTO CREDITS 372

LITERARY CREDITS 374

INDEX 375

PURPOSE

Human Evolution and Prehistory is designed for college-level introductory anthropology courses that combine physical anthropology and archaeology. The text presents the key concepts and terminology from these two subfields of anthropology that apply to the interrelated subjects of human biological and cultural evolution.

A textbook that combines archaeology and physical anthropology cannot by itself hope to be an adequate introduction to either subdiscipline, but it does provide more of the biological background than one would get in a course in archaeology alone. Alternatively, it provides more of the cultural context than one would get in a course restricted to physical anthropology. The first and most obvious aim of the text, therefore, is to give students a comprehensive introduction to each subfield as it bears on the related topics of the origin of humanity, the origin of culture, and the development of human biological and cultural diversity. In the process the student will come to understand the ways human culture and biology are interdependent, with each having an impact on the other.

If most students have little substantive concept of anthropology, they often have less clear—and potentially more destructive—views of the primacy of their own culture and its place in the world. A secondary goal of the text, then, is to persuade our students to understand the true complexity of our evolution and that our presence is *not* the outcome of a process that led inexorably and predictably to where we are today. Indeed, "debunking" is an important function of anthropology, and questioning beliefs in the superiority of humans over other forms of life, farming over food foraging, or complex civilizations over cultures based on subsistence farming is something that anthropologists do especially well. Anthropology is, in this sense, a tool to enable students to rethink their place in the world and their responsibilities to it.

ORGANIZATION OF THE BOOK

A Unifying Theme

I have found in my own teaching that introductory students lack a sense of the bigger picture in their studies of human beings. The best solution seems to be the use of a common theme that unifies chapters but that also allows students to make sense of each chapter and part introduction, regardless of the order in which they are read. For want of a better term, I refer to this common theme as one of *adaptation,* although not in the sense of simple behavioral responses to environmental stimuli. The fact is that people do not react to an environment as a given; rather, they react to it as they perceive it, and different groups of people may perceive the same environment in dramatically different ways. People also react to things other than the environment: their own biological natures, for one, and their beliefs, attitudes, and the consequences of their behavior, for others. All of these factors present them with problems, and people maintain cultures to deal with problems or matters that concern them. To be sure, their cultures must produce behavior that is generally adaptive, or at least not maladaptive, but this is far from saying that cultural practices necessarily arise because they are adaptive in a particular environment.

Many Messages, Many Media

For most of the discipline's history, anthropologists have relied upon print resources to share information, especially the very linear genre of ethnography, occasionally supplemented with photographs and, in fewer cases, film and analog recordings. However, humans, as primates, rely heavily on visual input for information, and so it is not surprising that people today depend heavily on media other than print for much of their information. Moreover, in conveying descriptive information about a fossil, an artifact, or other archaeological feature, a picture is often worth more than words alone. Given this, and our students' level of comfort with nonprint media, the art program is an important part of the sixth edition's narrative, and a selection of videos (discussed in more detail below) brings action and life to the ideas presented in the book, while Web links (also discussed below) build skills for analysis and research and move the content of *Human Evolution and Prehistory* away from standard linear textbook format to a multimedia package. Instructors will find the PowerPoint® slides and overhead transparencies helpful in bringing the ideas and art of the text into the classroom. And, of course, the classic readings and bibliography continue to provide students with a rich library of anthropological resources. Anthropology has served as an archive of human behavior, and it is important that the discipline continue to show the richness and diversity of humanity through the appropriate media.

SPECIAL FEATURES OF THE BOOK

Readability

The purpose of a textbook is to present ideas and information, much of which is new, in a way that encourages readers to see old things in new ways and to think about what they see. A book may be the most elegantly written, most handsomely designed, most lavishly illustrated text available on the subject, but if it is not interesting, clear, and comprehensible to the student, it is valueless as a teaching tool. The key is not just to present facts and concepts, but to make them *memorable.*

The readability of a text is enhanced by the writing style. *Human Evolution and Prehistory* presents even the most difficult concepts with prose that is clear, straightforward, and easy for today's first- and second-year students to understand, without making them feel that they are being "spoken down to." Where technical terms are necessary, they appear in bold-faced type, are carefully defined in the text, and defined again in the running glossary in simple, clear language.

Integration of Physical Anthropology and Archaeology

A major feature of this textbook is that the findings of physical anthropology and archaeology are presented together, rather than in separate sections. This format recognizes that no organism can survive unless it is able to adapt to some available environment. Adaptation requires the development of behavior patterns that help the organism utilize the environment to its advantage; in turn, organisms need to have the biological equipment that makes possible the development of such behavior. Obviously, the biology of an organism cannot be understood apart from the way the organism behaves and vice versa. To understand human evolution, then, we must consider biology and behavior together rather than separately.

Maps, Photographs, and Other Illustrations

In this text, numerous four-color photos have been used to help make important anthropological points that engage the eyes and minds of students. Many illustrations are unusual in the sense that they are not standard anthropological textbook photographs; each has been chosen because it complements the text in some distinctive way. And many photographs are shown paired so that students can contrast and compare their messages. In the sixth edition, for instance, Chapter 8 has two photos that compare a modern human and a Neandertal. The success of the visuals can be measured in the number of comments I have received from students and other instructors over the years about the vividness of particular selections.

In addition, the line drawings, maps, charts, and tables were selected especially for their usefulness in illustrating, emphasizing, or clarifying particular anthropological concepts; these have also proved to be valuable and memorable teaching aids. Maps, in particular, have been a popular aid through each edition of *Human Evolution and Prehistory,* and the sixth edition builds on this success. Many of the marginal locator maps are new or have been revised.

Original Studies

A special feature of this text is the Original Study that appears in each chapter. These studies consist of selections from original works by women and men who have done, or are doing, work of anthropological significance. Each study, integrated within the flow of the text, sheds additional light on an important anthropological concept or subject area found in the chapter. Their content is not extraneous or supplemental. The Original Studies bring specific concepts to life through specific examples. And a number of Original Studies also demonstrate the anthropological tradition of the case study, albeit in abbreviated form.

The idea behind the Original Studies is to present material so that the two halves of the human brain, which have different functions, are engaged. Whereas the left (dominant) hemisphere is logical and processes verbal inputs in a linear manner, the right hemisphere is creative and less impressed with linear logic. Psychologist James V. McConnell described the human brain as "an analog computer of sorts—a kind of intellectual monitor that not only handles abstractions, but also organizes and stores material in terms of Gestalts [that] include the emotional relevance of the experience." Logical thinking, as well as creative problem solving, occurs when the two halves of the brain cooperate. The implication for textbook writers is obvious: To be truly effective, they must reach both sides of the brain. The Original Studies help to do this by conveying some "feel" for humans and their behavior and how anthropologists actually study them. For example, in Chapter 4's Original Study, by A. Whitten and C. Boesch, students learn that culture is not a uniquely human possession, but something that arises out of our primate heritage. As with other Original Studies, the firsthand experiences of the authors drives the discussion of a host of issues deeply relevant to students and anthropology.

Integrated Gender Coverage

Unlike many introductory texts, the sixth edition of *Human Evolution and Prehistory* integrates rather than separates gender coverage. Thus, material on gender-related issues is included in *every* chapter. This approach gives the sixth edition a very large amount of gender-related material: the equivalent of one full chapter. This much content far exceeds that in most textbooks that combine physical anthropology and archaeology.

Why is the gender-related material integrated? Anthropology is itself an integrative discipline; concepts and issues surrounding gender are almost always too complicated to remove from their context. Moreover, spreading this material through all of the chapters emphasizes how considerations of gender enter into virtually everything people do. Much of the new content for the sixth edition (listed below) relates to gender in some way. These changes generally fall into at least one of two categories: changes in thinking about gender within the discipline and examples that show the important ramifications of gender of the human species as well as nonhuman primates. Examples of new material range from an expanded discussion of homosexual identity and same-sex marriage to current thinking on the role of females in ape societies. By consistently covering gender throughout the text, the sixth edition avoids "ghettoizing" gender and relegating it to a single chapter that is preceded and followed by resounding silence.

Previews and Summaries

An old and effective pedagogical technique is repetition: "Tell 'em what you're going to tell 'em, tell 'em, and then tell 'em what you've told 'em." To do this, each chapter begins with preview questions that set up a framework for studying the contents of the chapter. At the end of the chapter is a summary containing the kernels of the more important ideas presented in the chapter. The summaries provide handy reviews for students without being so long and detailed as to seduce students into thinking they can get by without reading the chapter itself.

Web Links

The Internet has proved to be an increasingly important means of communication and will no doubt continue to grow in relevance and complexity. The sixth edition draws upon the World Wide Web both as an instructional tool and as a vehicle for providing new examples of culture and cultural change. Every chapter contains two to three Cyber Road Trips that refer the student and instructor to the book's companion Web site, found at **http://www.wadsworth.com/product/053461020X,** where Web links and accompanying interactive exercises can be found for each chapter.

Classic Readings and Bibliography

Each chapter includes a list of classic readings that will supply the inquisitive student with further information about specific anthropological points. The books suggested are oriented toward the general reader and the interested student who wishes to explore further the more technical aspects of the subject. In addition, the bibliography at the end of the book contains a listing of more than 200 books, monographs, and articles from scholarly journals and popular magazines on virtually every topic covered in the text that a student might wish to investigate further.

Glossary

The running glossary is designed to reinforce the meaning of each newly introduced term. It is also useful for chapter review, as the student may readily isolate the new terms from those introduced in earlier chapters. A new, complete glossary is also included at the back of the book for easy reference. In the glossaries each term is defined in clear, understandable language. As a result, less class time is required going over terms, leaving instructors free to pursue matters of greater interest.

THE SIXTH EDITION

Every chapter in the sixth edition has been thoroughly updated, edited, and fine-tuned with the help of Dana Walrath, an expert consultant. Major changes for the sixth edition include:

CHAPTER 1

New discussion of anthropology's relevance illustrated with discussion of racism in the United States, the issue of same-sex marriage, *and* the common confusion of "nation" with "state." There is a revised discussion of ethics illustrated by the author's work.

CHAPTER 3

Completely rewritten with greatly expanded coverage of human genetics.

CHAPTER 4

New discussion of chimpanzee culture.

CHAPTER 5

Extensive revision; material on macroevolution moved to this chapter and simplified discussion of fossil primates.

CHAPTER 6

Revised discussion of *Australopithecus* and new material on *Ardipithecus, Kenyanthropus,* and *Orrorin tugenensis.*

CHAPTER 7

Revised discussion of Oldowan tools.

CHAPTER 8

Revised discussion of Acheulean tools; new discussion of comparable technology from China; new material on implications of stone tool technology for language origins.

CHAPTER 9

New material on Neandertal DNA; new discussion of the controversial "Neandertal flute"; expanded section on Neandertals and spoken language.

CHAPTER 10

New emphasis on difficulty of defining "anatomically modern"; rewritten and expanded discussion of the peopling of the Americas; removal (to Chapter 11) of section on the Mesolithic.

CHAPTER 11

Placement of section on the Mesolithic at the start of the chapter; new material on early domestication of goats.

CHAPTER 12

Expanded discussion of Çatalhöyük; new material on early writing; expanded section on "Civilization and its Discontents," including material on genetic diseases (cystic fibrosis and Tay-Sachs).

New Original Studies

Four of the 13 Original Studies are new to the sixth edition:

> *Chapter 1* The Strange Case of "Piltdown Man," abstracted from J. S. Weiner (1995)
>
> *Chapter 3* The Unsettling Nature of Variational Change, by Stephen Jay Gould (2000)
>
> *Chapter 4* The Culture of Chimpanzees, by A. Whitten and C. Boesch (2001)
>
> *Chapter 5* Will the Real Human Ancestor Please Stand Up?, by Dana Walrath (2002)

New Anthropology Applied and Bio Boxes

One new Anthropology Applied box is:

> *Chapter 3* Anthropology and the Ethical, Legal, and Social Implications of the Human Genome Project, by Dana Walrath

In addition, the Anthropology Applied boxes for Chapters 1 and 13 have been updated and revised.

Two new Bio Boxes are:

> *Chapter 3* Gregor Mendel
>
> *Chapter 13* Ashley Montagu

SUPPLEMENTS FOR INSTRUCTORS

In keeping with the sixth edition's recognition that the use of many messages requires many media, the selection of ancillaries accompanying *Human Evolution and Prehistory* should meet most instructor's needs.

Technology Demo CD-ROM for Anthropology

The Technology Demo CD-ROM introduces and demonstrates all of the key technology supplements that Wadsworth offers. The demos provide instructors with an overview of each supplement and a more detailed demonstration of exactly how to use each product. The Technology Demo CD-ROM comes in each Instructor's Edition of the text.

Instructor's Manual

This supplement provides student learning objectives, a chapter review, brief descriptions of chapter feature pieces, key terms, lecture and class activity suggestions, as well as a list of additional resources that correspond to each chapter of the textbook. Concise user guides for InfoTrac® College Edition, an online database of over 4,000 journals, and WebTutor are provided as appendices.

Test Bank

Each chapter of the Test Bank features approximately 40–70 multiple-choice questions; 10–15 true/false questions; matching, and many short-answer, and essay questions. In addition to answers and page references, all test questions are followed by codes that indicate the type of question, whether the question focuses on the main narrative of the text or on a feature piece, and if a similar question can be found in the Study Guide and Workbook.

ExamView Computerized and Online Testing

Create, deliver, and customize tests and study guides (both print and online) in minutes with this easy-to-use assessment and tutorial system. *ExamView* offers both a Quick Test Wizard and an Online Test Wizard that guide you step by step throughout the process of creating tests, while its unique "WYSIWYG" capability allows you to see the test you are creating on screen exactly as it will print or display online. Using *ExamView*'s complete word processing capabilities, you can enter an unlimited number of new questions or edit existing questions.

Classroom Presentation Tools for Instructors

Wadsworth's Cultural Anthropology Transparency Acetates 2003

A set of four-color acetates from Wadsworth's cultural anthropology texts is available to help prepare lecture presentations.

Wadsworth's Physical Anthropology Transparency Acetates 2003

A set of four-color acetates from Wadsworth's physical anthropology texts is available to help prepare lecture presentations.

Multimedia Manager for Anthropology: A Microsoft PowerPoint Link Tool for 2003

This CD-ROM contains digital media and PowerPoint presentations for all of Wadsworth's 2003 introductory anthropology texts, placing images, lectures, and video clips at instructors' fingertips. Start with our pre-assembled Power-Point presentations, which include chapter outlines and key terms. Then easily add video and images from Wadsworth's anthropology texts, all included on the CD-ROM. Instructors can also add their own lecture notes and images to create a custom-made PowerPoint presentation. The Wadsworth Multimedia Manager also includes new lecture launchers from exciting Earthwatch Institute research expeditions.

Wadsworth Anthropology Video Library

Qualified adopters may select full-length videos from an extensive library of excellent educational video sources drawn from *Films for the Humanities and Sciences.*

CNN Today Anthropology Video Series, Volume I

CNN Today Cultural Anthropology Video Series, Volumes I–V

CNN Today Physical Anthropology Video Series, Volumes I–IV

The *CNN Today Anthropology* video series is an exclusive series jointly created by Wadsworth and CNN for the anthropology course. Each video in the series consists of approximately 45 minutes of footage originally broadcast on CNN within the last several years. The videos are broken into short 2–7 minute segments, which are perfect for classroom use as lecture launchers or to illustrate key anthropological concepts. An annotated table of contents accompanies each video with descriptions of the segments and suggestions for their possible use within the course.

SUPPLEMENTS FOR STUDENTS

Study Guide and Workbook

This guide includes chapter synopses, chapter goals, lists of key terms and people, and questions to guide students in their reading of chapter material. Each chapter also includes practice tests consisting of fill-in-the-blank, multiple-choice, matching, true/false, and essay questions.

Researching Anthropology on the Internet, Second Edition

Written by David Carlson, this useful guide is designed to assist anthropology students in all of their needs when doing research on the Internet. Part One contains general information necessary to get started and answers questions about security, the type of material available on the Internet, the sites with information that is reliable and the sites that are not, the best ways to find research, and the best links to take students where they want to go. Part Two looks at each main discipline in anthropology and refers students to sites where the most enlightening research can be obtained.

WEB RESOURCES AND SUPPLEMENTS FOR INSTRUCTORS AND STUDENTS

Anthropology Online: Wadsworth's Anthropology Resource Center

The Wadsworth Anthropology Resource Center contains a wealth of information and useful tools for both instructors and students. After logging on to the Wadsworth home page at **http://anthropology.wadsworth.com,** click on Course Materials, Anthropology, and the *Haviland* book cover. Proceed to the Student Resources section by clicking For Students. There, students will find many exciting chapter specific resources such as CNN video clips, crossword puzzles, Internet exercises, Info-Trac College Edition exercises, practice quizzes that calculate results that can then be emailed to instructors, and much more. Instructors too will find a wealth of materials such as an online Instructor's Manual and PowerPoint lecture slides.

A Virtual Tour of Applying Anthropology

This special section of the Web site serves as an online resource center for the anthropology student. Students will find Applied Anthropologists at Work, Graduate Studies Info, Job Boards, Internships and Fieldwork, and an Essay on Careers with video.

InfoTrac College Edition

Ignite discussions or augment lectures with the latest developments in anthropology and societal change. InfoTrac College Edition (available as a free option with newly purchased texts) gives instructors and students 4-months' free access to an easy-to-use online database of reliable, full-length articles (not abstracts) from hundreds of top academic journals and popular sources. Among the journals that are available 24 hours a day, seven days a week, *American Anthropologist, Current Anthropology, Canadian Review of Sociology and Anthropology.* Contact your Wadsworth/Thomson learning representative for more information.

WebTutor Advantage™ on WebCT and Blackboard

For students, WebTutor Advantage offers real-time access to a full array of study tools, including chapter summaries, flashcards (with audio), practice quizzes, interactive maps and timelines, online tutorials, and Web links. Professors can use WebTutor Advantage to provide virtual office hours, post syllabi, set up threaded discussions, track student progress with quizzing material, and more. WebTutor Advantage provides rich communication tools, including a course calendar, asynchronous discussion, "real-time" chat, a whiteboard, and an integrated email system.

ACKNOWLEDGMENTS

The sixth edition of *Human Evolution and Prehistory* has its beginnings in the 10th edition of my book, *Anthropology,* and so it owes a great deal to those anthropologists who helped me in one way or another with that edition: Jeffrey A. Behm, University of Wisconsin, Oshkosh; Gregory R. Campbell, University of Montana; James G. Flanagan, University of Southern Mississippi; Jim Merryman, Wilkes University; H. Lyn Miles, University of Tennessee, Chattanooga; and William H. Thomas, Marquette University. Others who helped with this book specifically are: Joanna Casey, University of South Carolina; Joseph W. Ball, San Diego State University; Orlando Correa, Hartford Community College; Christopher Howell, Red Rocks Community College; Karen Rosenberg, University of Delaware; and Suzanne Walker, Southwest Missouri State University.

Their prerevision comments were all helpful and carefully considered; how I have made use of them has been determined by my own perspective on the human past, as well as by my experience with undergraduate students. Therefore, they should not be held responsible for any shortcomings this book may have.

My own particular perspective on the human past owes a good deal to a number of anthropologists under whom I was privileged to study archaeology and physical anthropology. I learned my archaeology at the University of Pennsylvania from William R. Coe, Carleton S. Coon, Robert Ehrich, J. Louis Giddings, Ward H. Goodenough, Alfred V. Kidder II, Froelich Rainey, and Linton Satterthwaite; and in the field, first from Warren W. Caldwell in South Dakota and then William R. Coe in Guatemala. My physical anthropology I learned from Carleton S. Coon, Loren Eisley, and especially Wilton M. Krogman, for whom I worked while a graduate student at the Philadelphia Center for Research in Child Growth. My debt to all these people, many of whom are now gone, is enormous. None, however, should be held responsible for the final product, despite their important contributions to my thinking.

I have taught introductory courses in physical anthropology from 1962 until 1999 and archaeology from 1964 until the mid-1970s, and I must acknowledge the contribution made by the students who enrolled in these courses over the years. My experience with them and their reactions to various textbooks has been important in determining what has and what has not gone into this book. Although I no longer teach the introduction to archaeology, I have continued my interest in the course, through discussions with my colleague Marjory Power, who taught it until her retirement, and James Petersen, Deborah Blom, and Peter Mills, who have taught it since then; through review of new textbooks for such courses; and as a member of the national advisory board for an archaeology course funded by the Annenberg/CPB Project.

The sixth edition owes a special debt to anthropologists Harald E. L. Prins of Kansas State University and Dana Walrath of the University of Vermont College of Medicine. Harald worked closely with me on the revision of *Anthropology* 10th edition, and Chapter 1 of this book shows his influence. Dana wrote the Anthropology Applied box in Chapter 3, the Original Study for Chapter 5, prepared the timelines for Chapters 5 through 10, and supplied the Cyber Road Trips. She also did a careful review of my initial revisions, certainly strengthening the final product. Harald, Dana, and I share some common research interests, as well as similar visions of what anthropology is (and should be) all about, and I look forward to their expanded participation in future editions of this book.

It has been my great good fortune to work with a supportive, friendly group of people at Wadsworth. These include senior acquisitions editor Lin Marshall, development editor Reilly O'Neal, and production editor Robin Lockwood. A special thanks goes to Sandra Lord, photo researcher, who has been phenomenally helpful for several editions of this book. I also wish to thank the skilled editorial, design, and production team headed by Jerilyn Emori. The greatest debt of all is owed my wife, Anita de Laguna Haviland, who not only has put up with my preoccupation with this revision but has taken care of all of the word processing as well. Her suggestions for topics to include and ways to express concepts have enormously benefited the book.

*A*lthough all humans that we know about are capable of producing accurate sketches of localities and regions with which they are familiar, CARTOGRAPHY (the craft of mapmaking as we know it today) had its beginnings in 13th century Europe, and its subsequent development is related to the expansion of Europeans to all parts of the globe. From the beginning, there have been two problems with maps: the technical one of how to depict on a two-dimensional, flat surface a three-dimensional spherical object, and the cultural one of whose worldview they reflect. In fact, the two issues are inseparable, for the particular projection one uses inevitably makes a statement about how one views one's own people and their place in the world. Indeed, maps often shape our perception of reality as much as they reflect it.*

In cartography, a PROJECTION refers to the system of intersecting lines (of longitude and latitude) by which part or all of the globe is represented on a flat surface. There are more than 100 different projections in use today, ranging from polar perspectives to interrupted "butterflies" to rectangles to heart shapes. Each projection causes distortion in size, shape, or distance in some way or another. A map that shows the shape of land masses correctly will of necessity misrepresent the size. A map that is accurate along the equator will be deceptive at the poles.

Perhaps no projection has had more influence on the way we see the world than that of Gerhardus Mercator, who devised his map in 1569 as a navigational aid for mariners. So well suited was Mercator's map for this purpose that it continues to be used for navigational charts today. At the same time, the Mercator projection became a standard for depicting land masses, something for which it was never intended. Although an accurate navigational tool, the Mercator projection greatly exaggerates the size of land masses in higher latitudes, giving about two-thirds of the map's surface to the northern

hemisphere. Thus, the lands occupied by Europeans and European descendants appear far larger than those of other people. For example, North America (19 million square kilometers) appears almost twice the size of Africa (30 million square kilometers), while Europe is shown as equal in size to South America, which actually has nearly twice the land mass of Europe.

A map developed in 1805 by Karl B. Mollweide was one of the earlier equal-area projections of the world. Equal-area projections portray land masses in correct relative size, but, as a result, distort the shape of continents more than other projections. They most often compress and warp lands in the higher latitudes and vertically stretch land masses close to the equator. Other equal-area projections include the Lambert Cylindrical Equal-Area Projection (1772), the Hammer Equal-Area Projection (1892), and the Eckert Equal-Area Projection (1906).

The Van der Grinten Projection (1904) was a compromise aimed at minimizing both the distortions of size in the Mercator and the distortion of shape in equal-area maps such as the Mollweide. Allthough an improvement, the lands of the northern hemisphere are still emphasized at the expense of the southern. For example, in the Van der Grinten, the Commonwealth of Independent States (the former Soviet Union) and Canada are shown at more than twice their relative size.

The Robinson Projection, which was adopted by the National Geographic Society in 1988 to replace the Van der Grinten, is one of the best compromises to date between the distortion of size and shape. Although an improvement over the Van der Grinten, the Robinson projection still depicts lands in the northern latitudes as proportionally larger at the same time that it depicts lands in the lower latitudes (representing most third-world nations) as proportionally smaller. Like European maps before it, the Robinson projection places Europe at the center of the map with the Atlantic Ocean and the Americas to the left, emphasizing the cultural connection between Europe and North America, while neglecting the geographical closeness of northwestern North America to northeast Asia.

The following pages show four maps that each convey quite different "cultural messages." Included among them is the Peters Projection, an equal-area map that has been adopted as the official map of UNESCO (the United Nations Educational, Scientific, and Cultural Organization), and a map made in Japan, showing us how the world looks from the other side.

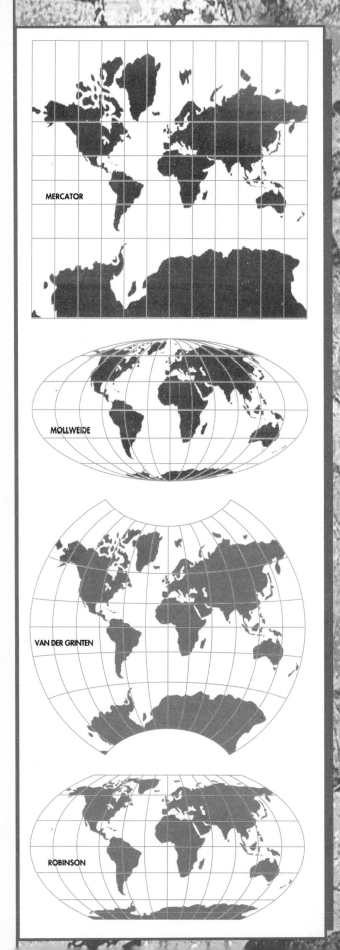

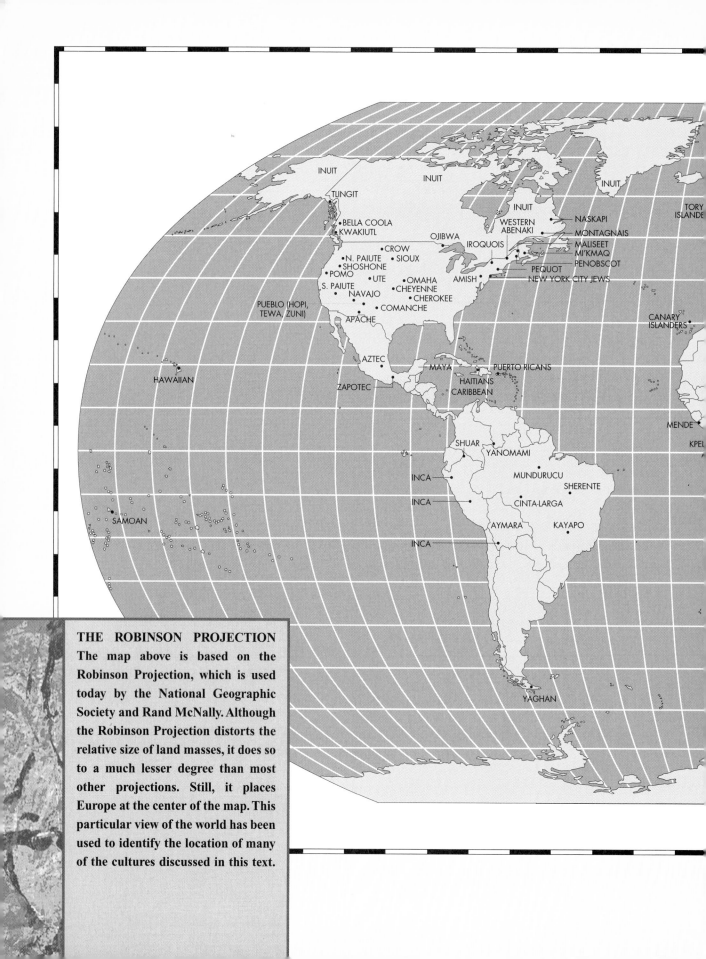

INUIT

TLINGIT

INUIT

INUIT

INUIT

BELLA COOLA
KWAKIUTL

WESTERN
ABENAKI

NASKAPI

TORY
ISLANDE

OJIBWA

IROQUOIS

MONTAGNAIS

MALISEET

MI'KMAQ

CROW

N. PAIUTE   SIOUX

SHOSHONE

PENOBSCOT

POMO

UTE

PEQUOT

S. PAIUTE

OMAHA

AMISH

NEW YORK CITY JEWS

NAVAJO

CHEYENNE

CHEROKEE

PUEBLO (HOPI,
TEWA, ZUNI)

COMANCHE

APACHE

CANARY
ISLANDERS

HAWAIIAN

AZTEC

MAYA

PUERTO RICANS

ZAPOTEC

HAITIANS

CARIBBEAN

MENDE

SHUAR

YANOMAMI

KPEL

INCA

MUNDURUCU

SHERENTE

INCA

CINTA-LARGA

SAMOAN

AYMARA

KAYAPO

INCA

YAGHAN

THE ROBINSON PROJECTION
The map above is based on the Robinson Projection, which is used today by the National Geographic Society and Rand McNally. Although the Robinson Projection distorts the relative size of land masses, it does so to a much lesser degree than most other projections. Still, it places Europe at the center of the map. This particular view of the world has been used to identify the location of many of the cultures discussed in this text.

SAAMI (SKOLT LAPPS)

INUIT

CROATS — SERBS
BOSNIANS

CHECHENS

JAPANESE

KURDS

ISRAELIS

BAKHTIARI

TIBETANS
MELEMCHI

CHINESE

AWLAD ALI
BEDOUINS

EGYPTIANS

CHENCHU

KAREN

TAIWANESE

TRUK

YORUBA

NUER

NAYAR

KAPAUKU

BENIN

AFAR &
TEGREANS

KOTA AND
KURUMBA

WAPE

IBIBIO

AZANDE

ENGA

U.

MBUTI

TURKANA
NANDI

TSEMBAGA

AKO

MONGO

SOMALI

TODA AND
BADAGA

MINANGKABAU

HUTU
AND TUTSI

GUSII

MASAI
TIRIKI

MELANESIANS

HADZA

ARAPESH

BALINESE

TROBRIANDERS

DOBU

JU/'HOANSI

SHMEN

SWAZI

ABORIGINES

TASMANIANS

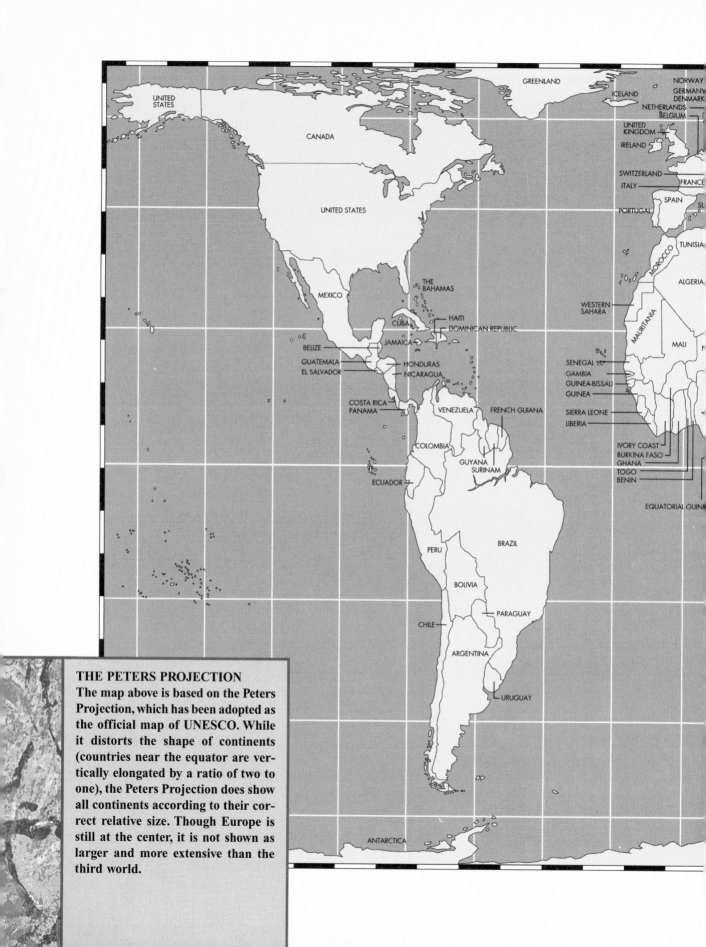

THE PETERS PROJECTION
The map above is based on the Peters Projection, which has been adopted as the official map of UNESCO. While it distorts the shape of continents (countries near the equator are vertically elongated by a ratio of two to one), the Peters Projection does show all continents according to their correct relative size. Though Europe is still at the center, it is not shown as larger and more extensive than the third world.

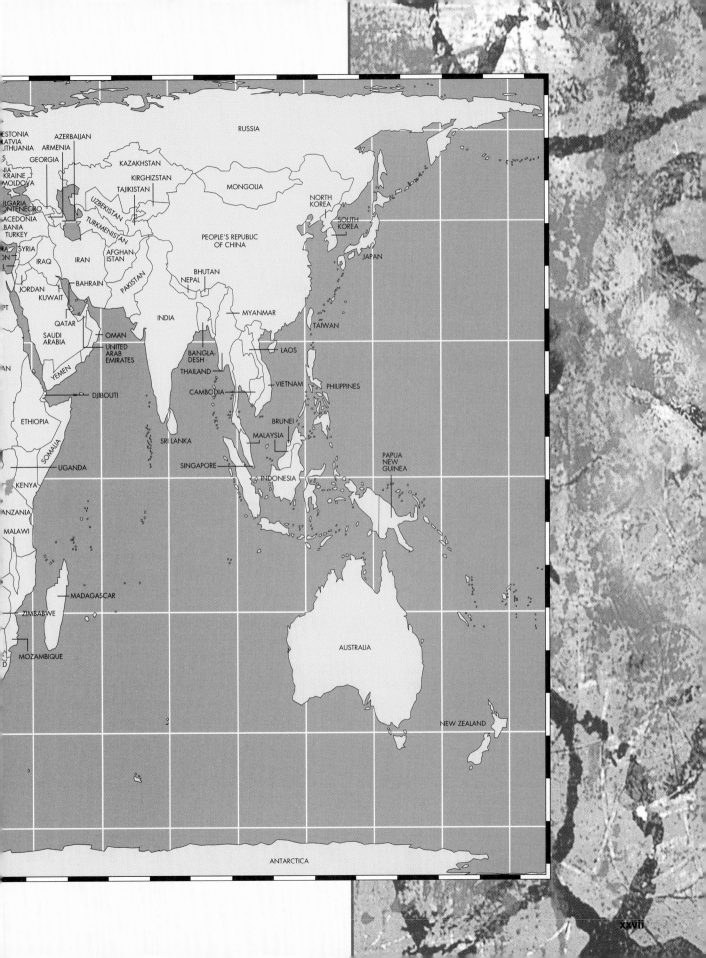

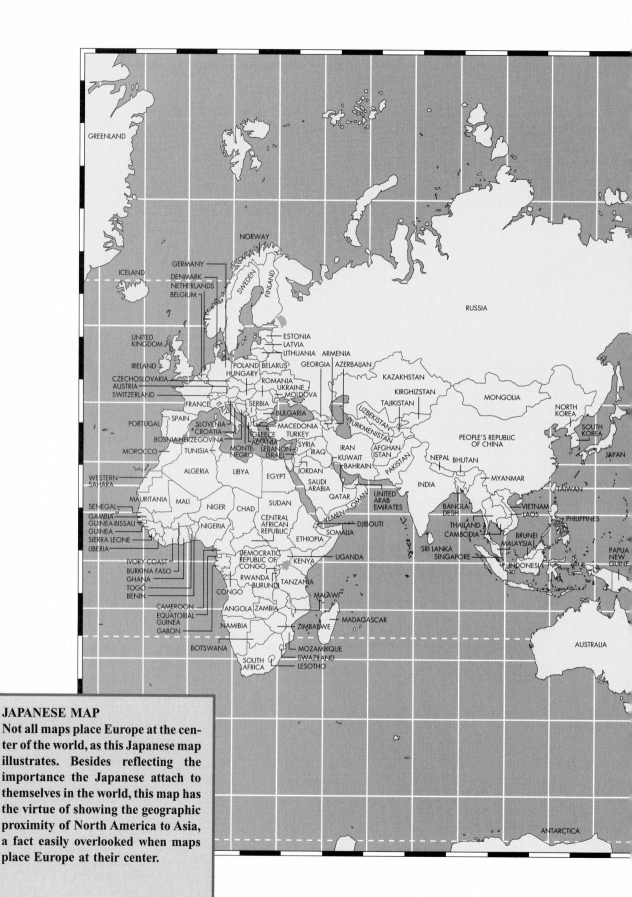

JAPANESE MAP
Not all maps place Europe at the center of the world, as this Japanese map illustrates. Besides reflecting the importance the Japanese attach to themselves in the world, this map has the virtue of showing the geographic proximity of North America to Asia, a fact easily overlooked when maps place Europe at their center.

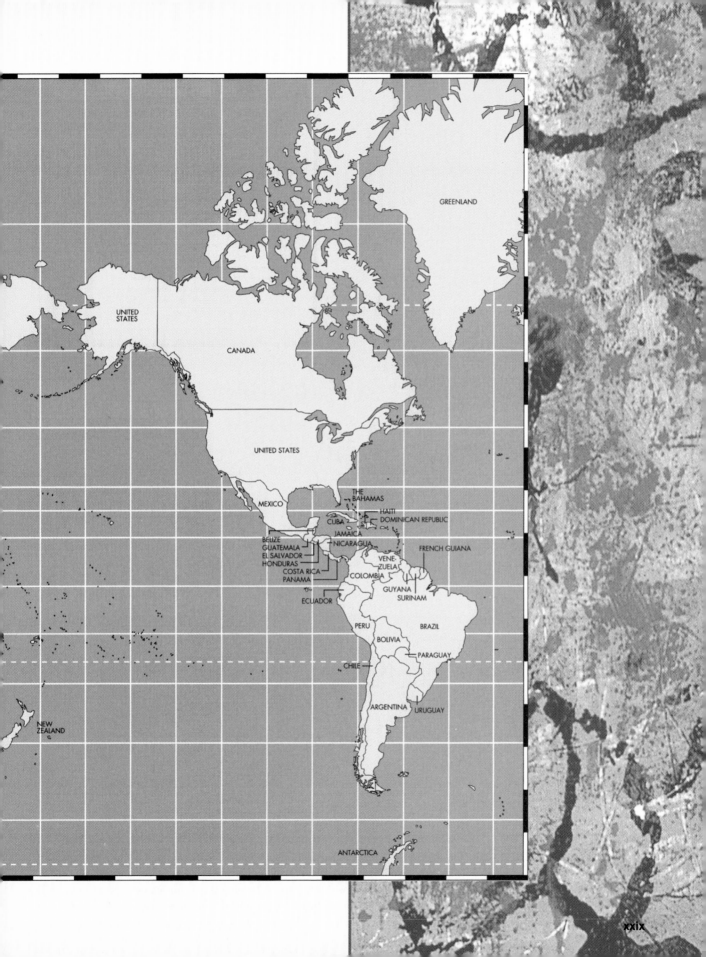

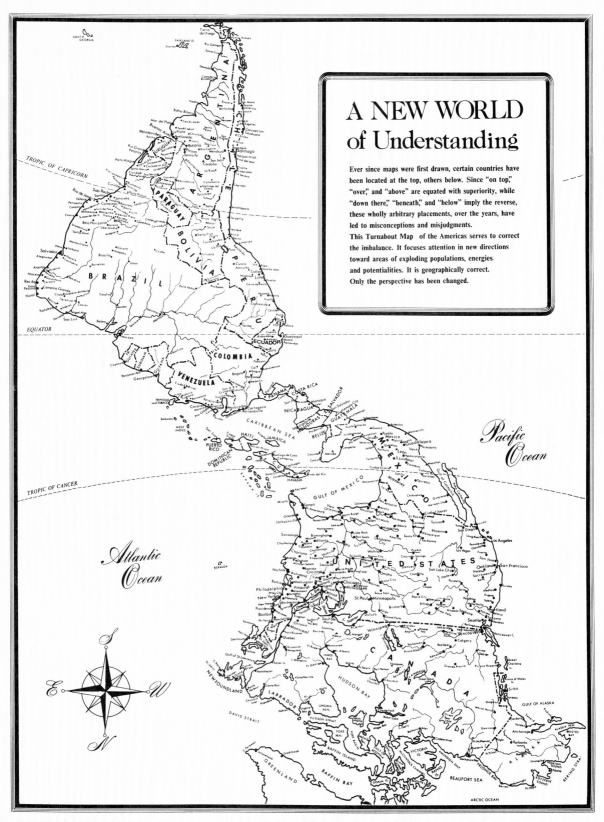

A NEW WORLD of Understanding

Ever since maps were first drawn, certain countries have been located at the top, others below. Since "on top," "over," and "above" are equated with superiority, while "down there," "beneath," and "below" imply the reverse, these wholly arbitrary placements, over the years, have led to misconceptions and misjudgments.

This Turnabout Map of the Americas serves to correct the imbalance. It focuses attention in new directions toward areas of exploding populations, energies, and potentialities. It is geographically correct. Only the perspective has been changed.

THE TURNABOUT MAP The way maps may reflect (and influence) our thinking is exemplified by the "Turnabout Map," which places the South Pole at the top and the North Pole at the bottom. Words and phrases such as "on top," "over," and "above" tend to be equated by some people with superiority. Turning things upside down may cause us to rethink the way North Americans regard themselves in relation to the people of Central America. © 1982 by Jesse Levine Turnabout Map™ —Dist. by Laguna Sales, Inc., 7040 Via Valverde, San Jose, CA 95135

HUMAN EVOLUTION AND PREHISTORY

THE STUDY OF HUMANKIND

Chapter 1   The Nature of Anthropology

Chapter 2   Methods of Studying the Human Past

Chapter 3   Biology and Evolution

INTRODUCTION

Anthropology is the most liberating of all the sciences. Not only has it exposed the fallacies of racial and cultural superiority, but also its devotion to the study of all peoples, everywhere and throughout time, has cast more light on human nature than all the reflections of sages or the studies of laboratory scientists. If this sounds like the assertion of an overly enthusiastic anthropologist, it is a statement made by philosopher Grace de Laguna in her 1941 presidential address to the Eastern Division of the American Philosophical Association.

The subject matter of anthropology is vast, as we shall see in this book: It includes everything that has to do with human beings, past and present. Of course, many other disciplines are concerned in one way or another with human beings. Some, such as anatomy and physiology, study humans as biological organisms. The social sciences are concerned with the distinctive forms of human relationships, while the humanities examine the great achievements of human culture. Anthropologists are interested in all of these things, too, but they try to deal with them all together, in all places and times. It is this unique, broad perspective that equips anthropologists so well to deal with that elusive thing called human nature.

Needless to say, no single anthropologist is able to investigate personally everything that has to do with humanity. For practical purposes, the discipline is divided into various subfields, and individual anthropologists specialize in one or more of these. Whatever their specialization, though, they retain a commitment to a broader, overall perspective on humankind. For example, cultural anthropologists specialize in the study of human behavior, while physical anthropologists specialize in

the study of humans as biological organisms. Yet neither can afford to ignore the work of the other, for human behavior and biology are inextricably intertwined, with each affecting the other in important ways. We can see, for example, how biology affects a cultural practice such as color-naming behavior. Human populations differ in the density of pigmentation within the eye itself, which in turn affects people's ability to distinguish the color blue from green, black, or both. Consequently, a number of cultures identify blue with green, black, or both. We can see also how a cultural practice may affect human biology, as exemplified by abnormal forms of hemoglobin, the substance that transports oxygen in the blood. In certain parts of Africa and Asia, when humans took up the practice of farming, they altered the ecology in a way that, by chance, created ideal conditions for the breeding of mosquitoes. As a result, malaria became a serious problem (mosquitoes carry the malarial parasite), and a biological response to this was the spread of certain genes that, in those people who inherit the gene from only one parent, produced a built-in resistance to the disease. Although those who inherit the gene from both parents contract a potentially lethal anemia, such as sickle-cell anemia, those without the gene are apt to succumb to malaria. (We will take up this topic in Chapter 3.)

To begin our introduction to the study of anthropology, we will look closely at the nature of the discipline. In Chapter 1 we will see how the field of anthropology is subdivided, how the subdivisions relate to one another, and how they relate to the other sciences and humanities. Chapter 1 introduces us as well to the methods anthropologists use to study human cultures, especially those of today, or the very recent past. However, because the next two parts of the book take us far back into the human past to see where we came from and how we got to be the way we are today, Chapter 2 deals with the very different methods used to find out about the ancient past. Here we discuss the nature of fossils and archaeological materials, where they are found, how they are (quite literally) unearthed, and how they are dealt with once unearthed. From this, one can begin to appreciate what the evidence can tell us if handled properly, as well as its limitations. In order to understand what fossils have to tell us about our past, we need some knowledge of how biological evolution works. Unlike flesh-and-blood people, fossils do not speak for themselves, and so they must be interpreted. If we are to have confidence in an interpretation of a particular fossil, we must be sure the interpretation is consistent with what we know about the workings of evolution; therefore, Chapter 3 is devoted to a discussion of evolution. With this foundation, we will have set the stage for our detailed look at human biological and cultural evolution in Parts II, III, and IV. ■

THE NATURE OF ANTHROPOLOGY

In 1534, Jacques Cartier explored the St. Lawrence River for France, bringing him in contact with members of several native groups. Such contacts sparked the curiosity about other peoples that led to the development of anthropology.

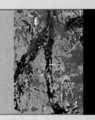

1

WHAT IS ANTHROPOLOGY?

Anthropology, the study of humankind everywhere, throughout time, seeks to produce reliable knowledge about people and their behavior, both about the things that make them different and the things they all have in common.

2

WHAT DO ANTHROPOLOGISTS DO?

Physical anthropologists study humans as biological organisms, tracing the evolutionary development of the human animal and looking at biological variation within the species, past and present. Cultural anthropologists are concerned with human cultures, or the ways of life in societies. Within cultural anthropology are archaeologists, who seek to explain human behavior by studying material objects, usually from past cultures; linguists, who study languages, by which cultures are maintained and passed on; and ethnologists, who study cultures as they have been observed, experienced, and discussed with people whose culture they seek to understand.

3

HOW DO ANTHROPOLOGISTS DO WHAT THEY DO?

Anthropologists are concerned with the description and explanation of reality. By formulating and testing hypotheses, they hope to develop reliable theories, although they recognize that no theory is ever completely beyond challenge. To frame objective hypotheses that are as free of cultural bias as possible, anthropologists typically develop them through fieldwork that allows them to become so familiar with the minute details of the situation that they can recognize patterns inherent in the data. It is also through fieldwork that anthropologists test existing hypotheses and explain what is going on.

Acommon part of the mythology of all peoples is a legend that explains the appearance of humans on earth. Such myths, for example, are the accounts of creation recorded in the Bible's Book of Genesis. Another vastly different example, which nonetheless serves the same function, is the belief of the Nez Perce (a people native to the American Northwest) that humanity is the creation of Coyote, one of the animal people that inhabited the earth before humans. Coyote chased the giant beaver monster, Wishpoosh, in an epic chase whose trail formed the Columbia River. When Coyote caught Wishpoosh, he killed him and dragged his body to the riverbank. Ella Clark retells the story:

> With his sharp knife Coyote cut up the big body of the monster.
>
> "From your body, mighty Wishpoosh," he said, "I will make a new race of people. They will live near the shores of Big River and along the streams which flow into it."
>
> From the lower part of the animal's body, Coyote made people who were to live along the coast. "You shall live near the mouth of Big River and shall be traders."
>
> "You shall live along the coast," he said to others. "You shall live in villages facing the ocean and shall get your food by spearing salmon and digging clams. You shall always be short and fat and have weak legs."
>
> From the legs of the beaver monster he made the Klickitat Indians. "You shall live along the rivers that flow down from the big white mountain north of Big River. You shall be swift of foot and keen of wit. You shall be famous runners and great horsemen."
>
> From the arms of the monster he made the Cayuse Indians. "You shall be powerful with bow and arrows and with war clubs."
>
> From the ribs he made the Yakima Indians. "You shall live near the new Yakima River, east of the mountains. You shall be the helpers and the protectors of all the poor people."
>
> From the head he created the Nez Perce Indians. "You shall live in the valleys of the Kookooskia and Wallowa rivers. You shall be men of brains, great in council and in speech making. You shall also be skillful horsemen and brave warriors."

> Then Coyote gathered up the hair and blood and waste. He hurled them far eastward, over the big mountains. "You shall be the Snake River Indians," said Coyote. "You shall be people of blood and violence. You shall be buffalo hunters and shall wander far and wide."[1]

For as long as they have been on earth, people have sought answers to questions about who they are, where they came from, and why they act as they do. Throughout most of their history, though, people relied on myth and folklore for their answers to these questions, rather than the systematic testing of data obtained through careful observation. Anthropology, over the last 200 years, has emerged as a scientific approach to answering these questions. Simply stated, **anthropology** is the study of humankind in all places and throughout time. The anthropologist is concerned primarily with a single species—*Homo sapiens*—the human species, its ancestors, and its near relatives. Because anthropologists are members of the species being studied, it is difficult for them to maintain a scientific detachment toward those they study. This, of course, is part of a larger problem in science. As one leading U.S. scientist puts it,

> Nature is objective, and nature is knowable, but we can only view her through a glass darkly—and many clouds upon our vision are of our own making: social and cultural biases, psychological preferences, and mental limitations (in universal modes of thought, not just human stupidity).
>
> The human contribution to this equation of difficulty becomes ever greater as the subject under investigation comes closer to the heart of our practical and philosophical concerns."[2]

Because nothing comes closer to the heart of our practical and philosophical concerns than ourselves and others of our kind, can we ever hope to gain truly objective knowledge about peoples' behavior? Anthropologists worry about this a great deal; but they have found that by maintaining a critical awareness of their assumptions, and constantly testing their conclusions against new

---

[1]Clark, E. E. (1966). *Indian legends of the Pacific Northwest* (p. 174). Berkeley: University of California Press.

[2]Gould, S. J. (1996). *Full house* (p. 8). New York: Harmony Books.

Anthropology.   The study of humankind, in all times and places.

FRANK HAMILTON CUSHING (1857–1900)
MATILDA COXE STEVENSON (1849–1915)

In the United States anthropology began in the 19th century when a number of dedicated amateurs went into the field to gain a better understanding of what many European Americans still regarded as "primitive people." Exemplifying their emphasis on firsthand observation is Frank Hamilton Cushing, who lived among the Zuni Indians for 4 years (he is shown here in full dress as a war chief).

Among these founders of North American anthropology were a number of women, whose work was highly influential among those who spoke out in the 19th century on behalf of women's rights. One of these pioneering anthropologists was Matilda Coxe Stevenson, who also did fieldwork among the Zuni. In 1885, she founded the Women's Anthropological Society, the first professional association for women scientists. Three years later, she was hired by the Bureau of American Ethnology, making her one of the first women in the United States to hold a full-time position in science. The tradition of women being active in anthropology continues, and since World War II more than half the presidents of the American Anthropological Association have been women.

sources of data, they can achieve a useful understanding of human behavior. By scientifically approaching how people live, anthropologists have learned an enormous amount, about both human differences, and about the common humanity underlying those differences.

THE DEVELOPMENT
OF ANTHROPOLOGY

Although works of anthropological significance have a considerable antiquity—two examples are the accounts of other peoples by the Greek historian Herodotus (written in the fifth century B.C.) or by the North African scholar Ibn Khaldun (written in the 14th century A.D.)—anthropology as a distinct field of inquiry is a relatively recent product of Western civilization. In the United States, for example, the first course in general anthropology to carry credit in a college or university (the University of Rochester) was not offered until 1879. If people have always been concerned about themselves and their origins, and those of other people, why then did it take such a long time for a systematic discipline of anthropology to appear? The answer to this is as complex as human history. In part, it relates to the limits of human technology. Throughout most of their time on earth, people have been restricted in their geographical horizons. Without the means of traveling to distant places, observation of cultures and peoples far from one's own was a difficult—if not impossible—venture. Extensive travel was usually the exclusive prerogative of a few; the study of foreign peoples and cultures was not likely to flourish until adequate modes of transportation and communication could be developed.

This is not to say that people have always been unaware of the existence of others in the world who look and act differently from themselves. The Old and New Testaments of the Bible, for example, are full of references to diverse peoples, among them Jews, Egyptians, Hittites, Babylonians, Ethiopians, Romans, and so forth. The differences between these people pale by comparison to those between any of them on the one hand and, for example, indigenous people of Australia, the Amazon forest, or arctic North America. With the means to travel to truly faraway places, it became possible to meet for the first time such radically different people. It was the massive encounter with hitherto unknown peoples, which came as Europeans sought to extend their trade and political domination to all parts of the world, that focused attention on human differences in all their glory.

Another significant element that contributed to the slow growth of anthropology was that Europeans only gradually came to recognize that beneath all the differences, they might share a basic humanity with people everywhere. Societies that did not share the fundamental cultural values of Europeans were labeled "savage" or "barbarian." It was not until the mid-18th century that a significant number of Europeans considered the behavior of such people to be at all relevant to an understanding of themselves. This growing interest in human diversity, coming at a time when there were increasing efforts

to explain things in terms of natural laws, cast doubts on the traditional explanations based on authoritative texts such as the Torah, Bible, or Qu'ran.

Although anthropology originated within the context of Western civilization, it has long since gone global. Today, it is an exciting, transnational discipline whose practitioners are drawn from diverse societies all across the globe. Even societies that have long been studied by European and North American anthropologists—several African and Native American societies, for example—have produced anthropologists who continue to make their mark on the discipline. Their distinctive perspectives help shed new light not only on their own cultures, but on those of others including Western societies.

ANTHROPOLOGY AND THE OTHER SCIENCES

It would be incorrect to conclude from the foregoing that serious attempts were never made to analyze human diversity before the 18th century. Anthropologists are not the only scholars who study people. In this respect they share their objectives with the other social and natural scientists. Anthropologists do not think of their findings as something quite apart from those of psychologists, economists, sociologists, or biologists; rather, they welcome the contributions these other disciplines have to make to the common goal of understanding humanity, and they gladly offer their own findings for the benefit of these other disciplines. Anthropologists do not expect, for example, to know as much about the structure of the human eye as anatomists or as much about the perception of color as psychologists. As synthesizers, however, they are better prepared to understand how these relate to color-naming behavior in different human societies than any of their fellow scientists. Because they look for the broad basis of human ideas and practices without limiting themselves to any single social or biological aspect, anthropologists can acquire an especially broad and inclusive overview of the complex biological and cultural organism that is the human being.

Anthropologists are not all men, nor are they all European or European American. Mamphela Ramphele is a native South African anthropologist who studied the migrant labor hostels of Cape Town before moving on to high administration positions at the University of Cape Town and the World Bank.

THE DISCIPLINE OF ANTHROPOLOGY

Anthropology is traditionally divided into four fields: physical anthropology and the three branches of cultural anthropology: archaeology, linguistic anthropology, and

Anthropology Applied

Forensic Anthropology

In the public mind, anthropology is often identified with the recovery of the bones of remote human ancestors, the unearthing of ancient campsites and "lost cities," or the study of present-day "tribal" peoples whose way of life is erroneously seen as being something out of the past. What people are often unaware of are the many practical applications of anthropological knowledge. One field of applied anthropology—known as **forensic anthropology**—specializes in the identification of human skeletal remains for legal purposes. Forensic anthropologists are routinely called upon by police and other authorities to identify the remains of murder victims, missing persons, or people who have died in disasters such as plane crashes or the recent terrorist attacks on the World Trade Center and the Pentagon. From skeletal remains, the forensic anthropologist can establish the age, sex, population affiliation, and stature of the deceased, and often whether they were right- or left-handed, exhibited any physical abnormalities, or had evidence of trauma (broken bones and the like). In addition, some details of an individual's health and nutritional history can be read from the bones.

One well-known forensic anthropologist is Clyde C. Snow, who has been practicing in this field for over 35 years, first for the Federal Aviation Administration and more recently as a freelance consultant. In addition to the usual police work, Snow has studied the remains of General George Armstrong Custer and his men from the 1876 battlefield at Little Big Horn, and in 1985, he went to Brazil where he identified the remains of the notorious Nazi war criminal Josef Mengele. He was also instrumental in establishing the first forensic team devoted to documenting cases of human rights abuses around the world. This mission began in 1984, when he went to Argentina at the request of a newly elected civilian government as part of a team to help with the identification of remains of the *desaparecidos,* or "disappeared ones," the 9,000 or more people who were eliminated by government

Forensic anthropologist Laura Fulginiti gives advice on a human skull to an artist with the Maricopa County Sheriff's Department in Phoenix, Arizona.

death squads during 7 years of military rule. A year later, he returned to give expert testimony at the trial of nine junta members and to teach Argentineans how to recover, clean, repair, preserve, photograph, x-ray, and analyze bones. Besides providing factual accounts of the fate of victims to their surviving kin and refuting the assertions of "revisionists" that the massacres never happened, the work of Snow and his Argentinean associates was crucial in convicting several military officers of kidnapping, torture, and murder.

Since Snow's pioneering work, forensic anthropologists have become increasingly involved in the investigation of human rights abuses in all parts of the world, from Chile, to Guatemala, to Haiti, to the

Forensic anthropology. Field of applied physical anthropology that specializes in the identification of human skeletal remains for legal purposes.

Philippines, to Iraqi Kurdistan, to Rwanda, to (most recently) Bosnia, Kosovo, and East Timor. Meanwhile, they continue to do important work for regular clients in the United States. Snow, for example, is regularly consulted by the medical examiners' offices of Oklahoma; Cook County, Illinois; and the Federal Bureau of Investigation. Although not all cases he investigates involve abuse of police powers, when this is an issue, evidence provided by forensic anthropologists is often crucial for bringing the culprits to justice. To quote Snow: "Of all the forms of mur-

der, none is more monstrous than that committed by a state against its own citizens. And of all murder victims, those of the state are the most helpless and vulnerable since the very entity to which they have entrusted their lives and safety becomes their killer."[*] Thus, it is especially important that states be called to account for their deeds.

*Joyce, C. (1991). Witnesses from the grave: the stories bones tell. Boston: Little, Brown.

---

ethnology. **Physical anthropology** is concerned primarily with humans as biological organisms, while **cultural anthropology** deals with humans as a culture-making species. Both, of course, are closely related; we cannot understand what people do unless we know how people are made. And we want to know how biology does and does not influence culture, as well as how culture affects biology.

Physical Anthropology

Physical anthropology (or, alternatively, biological anthropology) is the branch of anthropology that focuses on humans as biological organisms, and one of its many interests is human evolution. Whatever distinctions people may claim for themselves, they are mammals—specifically, primates—and, as such, they share a common ancestry with other primates, most specifically apes and monkeys. Through analysis of fossils and observation of living primates, physical anthropologists try to reconstruct the ancestry of the human species in order to understand how, when, and why we became the kind of animal we are today.

Another major concern of physical anthropology is the study of present-day human variation. Although we are all members of a single species, we differ from each other in many obvious and not so obvious ways. We differ not only in such visible traits as the color of our skin or the shape of our nose, but also in such biochemical

factors as our blood type and our susceptibility to certain diseases. The physical anthropologist applies all the techniques of modern molecular biology to achieve fuller understanding of human variation and the ways in which it relates to the different environments in which people have lived and to different cultural practices.

Cultural Anthropology

Because the capacity for culture is rooted in our biological nature, the work of the physical anthropologist provides a necessary background for the cultural anthropologist. In order to understand the work of the cultural anthropologist, we must clarify what we mean when we speak of culture. For our purposes here, we may think of *culture* as the often unconscious standards by which societies—structured groups of people—operate. These standards are socially learned rather than acquired through biological inheritance. Because they determine, or at least guide, the day-to-day behavior of the members of a society, human behavior is above all cultural behavior. The manifestations of culture may vary considerably from place to place, but no person is "more cultured" in the anthropological sense than any other.

Just as physical anthropology is closely related to the other biological sciences, cultural anthropology is closely related to the other social sciences. The one to which it has most often been compared is sociology, since the business of both is the description and expla-

---

Physical anthropology.   The systematic study of humans as biological organisms.   •   **Cultural anthropology.** The branch of anthropology that focuses on humans as a culture-making species.

nation of behavior of people within a social context. Sociologists, however, do not examine cultural and biological factors together. Moreover, they have concentrated heavily on studies of people living in industrialized North American and European societies, thereby increasing the probability that their theories of human behavior will be **culture-bound:** that is, based on assumptions about the world and reality that are part of the sociologists' own Western culture. Since cultural anthropologists, too, are largely products of the culture with which they grew up, they are also capable of culture-bound theorizing. However, they constantly seek to minimize the problem of bias by studying the whole of humanity in all times and places and do not limit themselves to the study of recent Western peoples; anthropologists have found that to fully understand the complex of human ideas and behavior, all humans, past and present, must be studied. More than any other feature, this absolutely unique cross-cultural and long-term historical perspective distinguishes cultural anthropology from the other social sciences. It provides anthropology with a far richer body of data than that of any other discipline that studies humankind, and it can also be applied to any current issue. As a case in point, consider the way infants in the United States are routinely made to sleep apart from their parents, their mothers in particular. To most North Americans, this may seem quite normal, but cross-cultural studies show that "co-sleeping" is the rule. Only in the past 200 years, generally in Western indus-

trialized societies, has it been considered proper for mother and infant to sleep apart. In fact, it amounts to a cultural experiment in child rearing.

Recent studies have shown that this unusual degree of separation of mother and infant in Western societies has important consequences. For one thing, it increases the length of the infant's crying bouts, which may last in excess of 3 hours a day in the child's second and third month. Some mothers incorrectly interpret the cause as a deficiency in breast milk and switch to less healthy bottle-fed formulas, but in extreme cases, the crying may provoke physical abuse, sometimes with lethal effects. But the benefits of co-sleeping go beyond significant reductions in crying; infants also nurse more often and three times as long per feeding; they receive more stimuli (important for neurological development); and they are apparently less susceptible to sudden infant death syndrome ("crib death"). But there are benefits to the mother as well: Frequent nursing prevents early ovulation after childbirth, and she gets at least as much sleep as mothers who sleep apart from their infants.[3]

The emphasis cultural anthropology places on studies of ancient and more recent non-Western cultures has often led to findings that run counter to existing beliefs derived from Western studies. Thus, cultural anthropologists were

---

[3]Barr, R. G. (1997, October). The crying game. *Natural History,* 47. Also McKenna, J. J. (1997, October). Bedtime story. *Natural History,* 50.

Sociologists conduct structured interviews and administer questionnaires to *respondents,* whereas psychologists experiment with *subjects.* Anthropologists, by contrast, *learn* from *informants.*

Culture-bound.   Theories about the world and reality based on the assumptions and values of one's own culture.

the first to demonstrate "that the world does not divide into the pious and the superstitious; that there are sculptures in jungles and paintings in deserts; that political order is possible without centralized power and principled justice without codified rules; that the norms of reason were not fixed in Greece, the evolution of morality not consummated in England.... We have, with no little success, sought to keep the world off balance; pulling out rugs, upsetting teatables, setting off firecrackers. It has been the office of others to reassure; ours to unsettle."[4] Although the findings of cultural anthropologists have often challenged the conclusions of sociologists, psychologists, and economists, anthropology is absolutely indispensable to them, as it is the only consistent check against culture-bound assertions. In a sense, anthropology is to these disciplines what the laboratory is to physics and chemistry: an essential testing ground for their theories.

Cultural anthropology may be divided into the areas of archaeology, linguistic anthropology, and ethnology (often called sociocultural anthropology; see Figure 1.1).

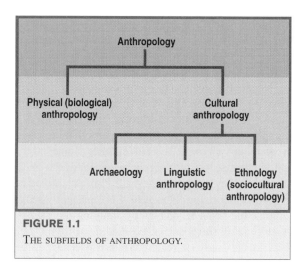

FIGURE 1.1
THE SUBFIELDS OF ANTHROPOLOGY.

---

[4]Geertz, C. (1984). Distinguished lecture: Anti anti-relativism. *American Anthropologist, 86,* 275.

Although each has its own special interests and methods, all deal with cultural data. The archaeologist, the linguist, and the ethnologist take different approaches to the subject, but each gathers and analyzes data that are useful in explaining similarities and differences between human cultures, as well as the ways that cultures everywhere develop, adapt, and continue to change.

The discovery by geologists in the 18th and 19th centuries that the world was far older than most Europeans thought paved the way for the anthropological exploration of past cultures and peoples.

Although history tells us something of the horrors of slavery in North America, the full horror is revealed only by archaeological investigation of the African burial ground in New York. Even young children were worked so far beyond their ability to endure that their spines actually fractured.

Archaeology

Archaeology is the branch of cultural anthropology that studies material remains in order to describe and explain human behavior. Traditionally, it has focused on the human past, for material products and traces of human practices, rather than practices themselves, are all that survive of that past. The archaeologist studies the tools, pottery, and other enduring features such a hearths and enclosures that remain as the legacy of earlier cultures, some of them as many as 2.5 million years old. Such objects, and the way they were left in the ground, reflect aspects of human behavior. For example, shallow, restricted concentrations of charcoal that include oxidized earth, bone fragments, and charred plant remains, and near which are pieces of fire-cracked rock, pottery, and tools suitable for food preparation, are indicative of cooking and associated food processing. From such remains much can be learned about a people's diet and subsistence practices. Thus the archaeologist is able to find out about human behavior in the past, far beyond the mere 5,000 years to which historians are ultimately limited by their dependence upon written records. But archaeologists are not limited to the study of prehistoric societies; they may also study those for which historical

documents are available to supplement the other material remains that people left behind. In most literate societies, written records are associated with governing elites rather than with people at the "grass roots." Thus, while they can tell archaeologists much that they might not know from archaeological evidence alone, it is equally true that archaeological remains can tell historians much about a society that is not apparent from its written documents.

Although most have concentrated on the human past, significant numbers of archaeologists are concerned with the study of material objects in contemporary settings. One example is the University of Arizona's Garbage Project, which, by a carefully controlled study of household waste, continues to produce information about contemporary social issues. Among its accomplishments, the project has tested the validity of interview-survey techniques, upon which sociologists, economists, other social scientists and policymakers rely heavily for their data. The tests clearly show a significant difference between what people say they do and what garbage analysis shows they actually do. For example, in 1973, conventional techniques were used to construct and administer a questionnaire to find out about the rate of alcohol consumption in Tucson. In one part of town, 15 percent of respondent households affirmed

Archaeology.   The study of material remains, usually from the past, to describe and explain human behavior.

consumption of beer, but no household reported consumption of more than eight cans a week. Analysis of garbage from the same area, however, demonstrated that some beer was consumed in over 80 percent of households, and 50 percent discarded more than eight empty cans a week. Another interesting finding of the Garbage Project is that when beef prices reached an all-time high in 1973, so did the amount of beef wasted by households (not just in Tucson, but in other parts of the country as well). Although common sense would lead us to suppose just the opposite, high prices and scarcity correlate with more, rather than less, waste. Obviously, such findings are important, for they show that ideas about human behavior based on conventional interview-survey techniques alone can be seriously in error. Likewise, they show that what people actually do does not always match what they think they do.

In 1987, the Garbage Project began a program of test excavations in landfills in different parts of the country. From this work came the first reliable data on what materials actually go into landfills and what happens to them there. And once again, common beliefs turn out to be at odds with the actual situation. For example, biodegradable materials such as newspapers take longer to decay when buried in deep, compacted landfills than anyone previously expected. Needless to say, this kind of information is vital if the United States is ever to solve its waste-disposal problems.

Linguistic Anthropology

Perhaps the most distinctive feature of humanity is its ability to speak. Humans are not alone in the use of symbolic communication. Studies have shown that the sounds and gestures made by some other animals—especially by apes—may serve functions comparable to those of human speech; yet no other animal has developed a system of symbolic communication as complex as that of humans. Ultimately, language is what allows people to preserve and transmit their culture from generation to generation.

The branch of cultural anthropology that studies human languages is called **linguistic anthropology.** Linguists may deal with the description of a language (the

way a sentence is formed or a verb conjugated) or with the history of languages (the way languages develop and change one another with the passage of time). Both approaches yield valuable information, not only about how people communicate but also about how they understand the world around them. The everyday language of North Americans, for example, includes a number of slang words, such as *dough, greenback, dust, loot, cash, bucks, change,* and *bread,* to identify what an indigenous native of Papua New Guinea would recognize only as "money." Such phenomena help identify things that are considered of special importance to a culture. Through the study of language in its social setting, anthropologists are able to understand how people perceive themselves and the world around them.

Anthropological linguists may also make a significant contribution to our understanding of the human past. By working out the genealogical relationships among languages and examining the distributions of those languages, they may estimate how long the speakers of those languages have lived where they do. By identifying those words in related languages that have survived from an ancient ancestral tongue, they can also suggest both where, and how, the speakers of the ancestral language lived.

Ethnology

As the archaeologist has commonly concentrated on cultures of the past, so the **ethnologist,** or sociocultural anthropologist, concentrates on cultures of the present. And unlike the archaeologist, who focuses on the study of material objects to learn about human behavior, the ethnologist concentrates on the study of human behavior as it can be seen, experienced, and even discussed with those whose culture is to be understood.

Fundamental to the ethnologist's approach is descriptive **ethnography.** Whenever possible, the ethnologist becomes ethnographer by going to live among the people under study. The intent of such fieldwork is not just to describe their culture but to explain as well relationships among its various aspects. Through **participant observation**—eating a people's food, speaking their lan-

---

Linguistic anthropology. The branch of cultural anthropology that studies human language. • **Ethnologist.** An anthropologist who studies cultures from a comparative or historical point of view, utilizing ethnographic accounts. • **Ethnography.** The systematic description of a particular culture based on firsthand observation. • **Participant observation.** In ethnography, the technique of learning a people's culture through direct participation in their everyday life for an extended period of time.

guage, and personally experiencing their habits and customs—the ethnographer seeks to understand their way of life to a far greater extent than any nonparticipant anthropologist or other social scientist ever could; one learns a culture best by learning how to behave acceptably in the society in which one is doing fieldwork. To become a participant observer in the culture under study does not mean that the ethnographer must join in a people's battles in order to study a culture in which warfare is prominent; but by living among a warlike people, the ethnographer should be able to understand how warfare fits into the overall cultural framework. He or she must be a careful observer in order to be able to get an in-depth overview of a culture without placing undue emphasis on one of its parts at the expense of another. Only by discovering how all cultural institutions—social, political, economic, religious—relate to one another can the ethnographer begin to understand the cultural system. Anthropologists refer to this as the **holistic perspective,** and it is one of the fundamental principles of anthropology. Robert Gordon, an anthropologist from Namibia, speaks of it in this way: "Whereas the sociologist or the political scientist might examine the beauty of a flower petal by petal, the anthropologist is the person that stands on the top of the mountain and looks at the beauty of the field. In other words, we try and go for the wider perspective."[5]

In participating in an unfamiliar culture, the ethnographer does not just blunder about blindly but enlists the assistance of individual **informants.** These are members of the society in which the anthropologist as ethnographer is working, with whom she or he develops close relationships, and who help the anthropologist as a newcomer in the community unravel whatever activities are taking place. As a child learns proper behavior from its parents, so do informants help the anthropologist in the field unravel the mysteries of what is, at first, a strange culture.

So basic is ethnographic fieldwork to ethnology that the British anthropologist C. G. Seligman once asserted, "Field research in anthropology is what the blood of the martyrs is to the church."[6] The popular image of ethnographic fieldwork is that it takes place among far-off, exotic peoples. To be sure, much ethnographic work has been done in places like Africa, the islands of the Pacific Ocean, the deserts of Australia, and so on. One very good reason for this is that non-Western peoples have been ignored too often by other social scientists. Still, anthropologists have recognized from the start that an understanding of human behavior depends

---

[5]Gordon, R. (1981, December). [Interview for Coast Telecourses, Inc.]. Los Angeles.

[6]Lewis, I. M. (1976). *Social anthropology in perspective* (p. 27). Harmondsworth, England: Penguin.

In Cartagena, Colombia, an ethnographer interviews local fishermen.

Holistic perspective.   A fundamental principle of anthropology, that the various parts of culture must be viewed in the broadest possible context to understand their interconnections and interdependence. • **Informants.** Members of a society in which the ethnographer works who help interpret what she or he sees taking place.

upon knowledge of all cultures and peoples, including their own. During the years of the Great Depression and World War II, for example, many anthropologists in the United States worked in settings ranging from factories to whole communities. One of the landmark studies of this period was W. Lloyd Warner's study of "Yankee City" (Newburyport, Massachusetts). Less well known is that it was Philleo Nash, an anthropologist who was working on the White House staffs of Presidents Roosevelt and Truman, who was instrumental in desegregating the armed forces and moving the federal government into the field of civil rights. Nash put his anthropological expertise to work to accomplish a particular goal, an example of **applied anthropology.** Later on, he served as lieutenant governor of Wisconsin and as Indian Affairs Commissioner in President Kennedy's administration. Today, numerous anthropologists work outside of academic settings as applied anthropologists, and examples of their work are provided in succeeding chapters of this book.

In the 1950s, the availability of large sums of money for research in foreign lands diverted attention from work at home. Later, as political unrest made fieldwork increasingly difficult to carry out, there was renewed awareness of important anthropological problems that need to be dealt with in North American society. Many of these problems involve people whom anthropologists have studied in other settings. Thus, as people from South and Central America have moved into the cities and suburbs of the United States, or as refugees have arrived from Haiti, Southeast Asia, and other places, anthropologists have been there not just to study them but to help them adjust to their new circumstances. Simultaneously, anthropologists are applying the same research techniques that served them so well in the study of non-Western peoples to the study of such diverse things as street gangs, corporate bureaucracies, religious cults, health care delivery systems, schools, and how people deal with consumer complaints.

An important discovery from such research is that it produces knowledge that usually does not emerge from the kinds of research done by other social scientists. For example, the theory of cultural deprivation arose during the 1960s as a way of explaining the educational failure of many children of ethnic minorities. In order to account for their lack of educational achievement, some social scientists proposed that such children were "culturally deprived." They then proceeded to "confirm" this idea by studying children, mostly from Native American, African American, and Hispanic populations, interpreting the results through the protective screen of their theory. By contrast, ethnographic research on the cultures of "culturally deprived" children reveals a different story. Far from being culturally deprived, they have elaborate, sophisticated, and adaptive cultures that are simply different from the ones espoused by the educational system. Although some still cling to it, the cultural-deprivation theory is merely a way of saying that people are "deprived" of "my culture." One cannot argue that such children do not speak adequate Spanish, African American vernacular English (sometimes called Ebonics or Black English), or whatever; clearly they do well the things that are considered important in *their* cultures.

Much though it has to offer, the anthropological study of one's own culture is not without its own special problems. Sir Edmund Leach, a major figure in British anthropology, once put it this way:

> Surprising though it may seem, fieldwork in a cultural context of which you already have intimate firsthand experience seems to be much more difficult than fieldwork which is approached from the naive viewpoint of a total stranger. When anthropologists study facets of their own society their vision seems to become distorted by prejudices which derive from private rather than public experience.[7]

Although the ethnographer strives to get an inside view of another culture, he or she does so very self-consciously as an outsider. And the most successful anthropological studies of their own culture by North Americans have been done by those who first worked in some other culture. Lloyd Warner, for example, had studied the Murngin aborigines of Australia before he tackled Newburyport, Massachusetts. The more one learns of other cultures, the more one gains a different perspective on one's own. Put another way, as other cultures come to be seen as less exotic, the more exotic one's own seems to become. In addition to getting ourselves outside of our own culture

---

[7]Leach, E. (1982). *Social anthropology* (p. 124). Glasgow, Scotland: Fontana Paperbacks.

Applied anthropology. The use of anthropological knowledge and methods to solve practical problems, often for a specific client.

before trying to study it ourselves (so that they may see ourselves as *others* see us), much is to be gained by encouraging anthropologists from Africa, Asia, and South America to do fieldwork in North America. From their outsiders' perspective come insights all too easily overlooked by an insider. This is not to say that the special difficulties of studying one's own culture cannot be overcome; what is required is an acute awareness of those difficulties.

Although ethnographic fieldwork is basic to ethnology, it is not the sole occupation of the ethnologist. Largely descriptive in nature, ethnography provides the basic data the ethnologist (who is more theoretically oriented) may then use to study one particular aspect of a culture by comparing it with that same aspect in others. Anthropologists constantly make such cross-cultural comparisons, and this is another hallmark of the discipline. Interesting insights into one's own beliefs and practices may come from cross-cultural comparisons, as when one compares the time that people devote to what North Americans consider to be "housework." In the United States, there is a widespread belief that the ever-increasing output of household appliance consumer goods has resulted in a steady reduction in housework, with a consequent increase in leisure time. Thus, consumer appliances have become important indicators of a high standard of living. Anthropological research among food foragers (people who rely on wild plant and animal resources for subsistence), however, has shown that they work far less at household tasks, and indeed less at all subsistence pursuits, than do people in industrialized societies. Aboriginal Australian women, for example, devote an average of approximately 20 hours per week to collecting and preparing food, as well as other domestic chores. By contrast, women in the rural United States in the 1920s, without the benefit of laborsaving appliances, devoted approximately 52 hours a week to their housework. One might suppose that this has changed over the decades since, yet some 50 years later, urban U.S. women who were not working for wages outside their homes were putting 55 hours a week into their housework—this despite all their "laborsaving" dishwashers, washing machines, clothes dryers, vacuum cleaners, food processors, and microwave ovens.[8]

Cross-cultural comparisons highlight alternative ways of doing and thinking about things and so have much to offer North Americans—large numbers of whom, opinion polls show, continue to worry about the effectiveness of

their own ways of doing things. In this sense, one may think of ethnology as the study of alternative ways of doing things. At the same time, by making systematic cross-cultural comparisons of cultures, ethnologists seek to arrive at valid conclusions concerning the nature of culture in all times and places.

ANTHROPOLOGY AND SCIENCE

The foremost concern of all anthropologists is the detailed and comprehensive study of humankind. Anthropology has been called a social or a behavioral science by some, a natural science by others, and one of the humanities by still others. Can the work of the anthropologist properly be labeled scientific? What exactly do we mean by the term *science*?

Science is a carefully honed way of producing knowledge to explain or understand the underlying logic, the structural processes, that make the world tick. Science is

To many people, a scientist is someone (usually a White male) who works in a laboratory, carrying out experiments with the aid of specialized equipment. Contrary to the stereotypical image, not all scientists work in laboratories, nor is experimentation the only technique they use (nor are scientists invariably White males in lab coats).

[8]Bodley, J. H. (1985). *Anthropology and contemporary human problems* (2nd ed., p. 69). Palo Alto, CA: Mayfield.

FRANZ BOAS (1858–1942)
FREDRIC WARD PUTNAM (1839–1915)
JOHN WESLEY POWELL (1834–1902)

In North America, anthropology among the social sciences has a unique character, owing in large part to the natural science (rather than social science) background of the three men pictured here. Franz Boas (top), educated in physics, was not the first to teach anthropology in the United States, but it was he and his students, with their insistence on scientific rigor, who made such courses a common part of college and university curricula. Putnam (middle), a zoologist specializing in the study of birds and fishes, and permanent secretary of the American Association for the Advancement of Science, made a decision in 1875 to devote himself to the promotion of anthropology. Through his efforts many of the great anthropology museums were established: at the University of California (now the Phoebe Hearst Museum), Harvard University (the Peabody Museum), and the Field Museum in Chicago; in New York he founded the anthropology department of the American Museum of Natural History. Powell (bottom) was a geologist and founder of the United States Geological Survey, but he also carried out ethnographic and linguistic research (his classification of Indian languages north of Mexico is still consulted by scholars today). In 1879, he founded the Bureau of American Ethnology (ultimately absorbed by the Smithsonian Institution), thereby establishing anthropology within the U.S. government.

a creative endeavor that seeks testable explanations for observed phenomena, ideally in terms of the workings of hidden but universal and immutable principles, or laws. Two basic ingredients are essential for this: imagination and skepticism. Imagination, though capable of leading us astray, is required in order that we may recognize unexpected ways phenomena might be ordered and think of old things in new ways. Without it, there can be no science. Skepticism is what allows us to distinguish **fact** from fancy, to test our speculations, and to prevent our imaginations from running away with us.

In their search for explanations, scientists do not assume that things are always as they appear on the surface. After all, what could be more obvious than that the earth is a stable entity, around which the sun travels every day? And yet, it isn't so. Religious and metaphysical

---

Fact.   An observation verified by several observers skilled in the necessary techniques of observation.

explanations are rejected, as are all explanations and appeals to any authority that are not supported by strong empirical (observational) evidence. Because explanations are constantly challenged by new observations and novel ideas, science is self-correcting; that is, inadequate explanations are sooner or later shown up as such, to be replaced by more reliable explanations.

The scientist begins with a **hypothesis** or hunch about the possible relationship among certain observed facts. By gathering various kinds of data that seem to support such generalizations, and, equally important, by showing that alternative hypotheses may be proved wrong or eliminated from consideration, the scientist arrives at a system of validated hypotheses, or **theory.** Thus a theory, contrary to popular use of the term, is more than mere speculation; it is a carefully checked-out explanation of observed reality. Even so, no theory is ever considered to be beyond challenge. Truth in science is not considered to be absolute but rather a matter of varying degrees of probability; what is considered to be true is what is most probable. This is just as true in anthropology as it is in biology or physics. But while nothing can be proved to be absolutely true, incorrect assumptions can be proved false. Indeed, if a theory (or hypothesis) is not potentially falsifiable, it cannot be considered scientific. So it is that, as our knowledge expands, the odds in favor of some theories over others are generally increased, even though old "truths" sometimes must be discarded as alternative theories are shown to be more probable.

To illustrate how scientific methodology works, the following Original Study presents a famous case from physical anthropology.

The Strange Case of "Piltdown Man"[9]

Original Study

In 1910, parts of a human skull and an almost intact lower jaw were found in the Piltdown gravels in Sussex, England. Although the gravels were thought to be quite ancient, the skull was remarkably modern in appearance. The jaw, however, was exceedingly apelike. The find, Piltdown I, was named *Eoanthropus dawsoni,* Dawson's "dawn man," after its discoverer Charles Dawson, an amateur archaeologist, paleontologist, and practicing lawyer. In 1913 an apelike canine tooth was found to go with the jaw, and in 1915 Piltdown II, fragments of skull plus a molar tooth, were found 2 miles from Piltdown I. So much for the facts, but what to make of them? Two hypotheses come to mind. The first is that the remains are just what they seem: an ape jaw found in proximity to human skull remains. The other is that skulls and jaw belong to some kind of "missing link" with a modern-sized human brain but primitive, apelike jaws. It was the second hypothesis, even though it aroused occasional dissension, that was generally accepted until the early 1950s.

---

[9]Based on Weiner, J. S. (1955). *The Piltdown forgery.* New York: Oxford University Press.

Hypothesis.   A tentative explanation of the relations among certain phenomena.   •   **Theory.**   In science, an explanation of natural phenomena, supported by a reliable body of data.

Original Study

The reasons for widespread acceptance of hypothesis 2 are as follow. With the publication in 1859 of Darwin's theory of evolution by natural selection, intense interest developed in finding traces of prehistoric human ancestors. Accordingly, predictions were made as to what those ancestors looked like. Darwin himself, on the basis of his knowledge of embryology and the comparative anatomy of living apes and humans, suggested in his later book *The Descent of Man* that early humans had, among other things, a large brain and an apelike face and jaw.

Although the tools made by prehistoric peoples were forthcoming, their bones were not. To be sure, a few Neandertal and Cro-Magnon skeletons came to light in Europe, but they weren't at all like the predicted missing link. Moreover, more ancient and primitive *Homo erectus* fossils found in Java were the subject of a heated debate. Their discoverer reacted to this controversy by burying the fossils beneath his dining room floor, where no one could examine them. Given this state of affairs, the Piltdown finds could not have come at a better time. Here at last was the long-awaited missing link, and it was almost exactly as predicted. Even better, so far as English-speaking scientists were concerned, it was found in English soil!

In the context of the evidence available in the early 1900s, the idea of an ancient human with a large brain and an apelike face could become widely accepted as valid. A reexamination of this theory, however, was forced by the discovery of more and more fossils, primarily in Africa, China, and Java. These seemed to show that modern-looking human jaws preceded the development of large-sized brains, rather than the other way around. Thus, the Piltdown remains became more and more of a problem. This led one physical anthropologist, J. S. Weiner, to reconsider the Piltdown fossils, and this is what he found:

1. The only actual human characteristic of the jaw was the apparent tooth wear; otherwise, it was just like the jaw of an ape.

2. The muscle attachments indicate an apelike arrangement of jaw muscles, which would not produce a human wear pattern.

3. The heavy wear of the canine tooth is inconsistent with other features of the tooth that clearly indicate it came from an immature individual.

4. The parts of the jaw that would give it away as surely that of an ape were missing.

5. When drilling for a dentine sample from a tooth, it was found that this was pure white beneath a thin surface stain—not what one would expect in a very ancient fossil.

On the basis of these findings, Weiner returned to the first of our two original plausible hypotheses—that the remains were human skulls and an ape jaw. But now there was a corollary hypothesis that someone had faked the evidence, causing widespread acceptance of the "big-brained human with apelike jaws" hypothesis. Specifically, Weiner proposed that someone had stained the jaw of an ape, destroyed the parts that would give it away for what it was, filed the teeth, and then planted them together with the human skull parts in the Piltdown gravels. He and two of his colleagues then devised a series of appropriate procedures to test the logical consequences of his hypothesis. For example, microscopic examination revealed the presence of abrasion on the teeth, as would be produced by filing. Chemical tests revealed significant differences in chemical content between jaw and skull; these would be expected if they were from different sources but not if they belonged together. In short, Weiner and his colleagues were able to conclusively falsify the "big-brained human with apelike jaws" hypothesis and to confirm Weiner's version of the "ape jaw with human skull" hypothesis.

The End

Difficulties of the Scientific Approach

Straightforward though the scientific approach may seem, there are serious difficulties in its application in anthropology. One problem is that once one has stated a hypothesis, one is strongly motivated to verify it, and this can lead to unwittingly overlooking negative evidence, as well as other mistakes. This is a familiar problem in science; as paleontologist Stephen Jay Gould puts it: "The greatest impediment to scientific innovation is usually a conceptual lock, not a factual lock."[10] In the fields of cultural anthropology there is a further difficulty: In order to arrive at useful theories concerning human behavior, one must begin with hypotheses that are as objective and as little culture-bound as possible. And here lies a major—some people would say insurmountable—problem: It is difficult for someone who has grown up in one culture to frame hypotheses about others that are not culture-bound.

As one example of this sort of problem, we may look at attempts by archaeologists to understand the nature of settlement in the Classic period of Maya civilization. This civilization flourished between A.D. 250 and 900 in what is now northern Guatemala, Belize, and adjacent portions of Mexico and Honduras. Today much of this region is covered by a dense tropical forest of the sort that people of European background find difficult to manage. In recent times this forest has been inhabited by few people, who sustain themselves through slash-and-burn farming. (After cutting and burning the natural vegetation, crops are grown for 2 years or so before fertility is exhausted and a new field must be cleared.) Yet numerous archaeological sites featuring temples sometimes as tall as modern 20-story buildings, other sorts of monumental architecture, and carved stone monuments are to be found there. Because of their cultural bias against tropical forests as places to prosper and against slash-and-burn farming as a means of raising sufficient food, North American and European archaeologists asked the question: How could the Maya have maintained large, permanent settlements on the basis of slash-and-burn farming? The answer seemed self-evident: They couldn't; therefore, the great archaeological sites must have been ceremonial centers inhabited by few, if any, people. Periodically a rural peasantry, living scattered in small hamlets over the countryside, must have gathered in these centers for rituals, or to provide labor for their construction and maintenance.

This view dominated for several decades, and it was not until 1960 that archaeologists working at Tikal, one of the largest of all Maya sites, decided to ask the simplest and least biased questions they could think of: Did anyone live at this particular site on a permanent basis? If so, how many, and how were they supported? Working intensively over the next decade, with as few preconceived notions as possible, the archaeologists were able to establish that Tikal was a large settlement inhabited on a permanent basis by tens of thousands of people, who were supported by forms of agriculture more productive than slash-and-burn alone. It was this work at Tikal that proved wrong the older culture-bound ideas and paved the way for a new understanding of Classic Maya civilization.

By recognizing the potential problems of framing hypotheses that are not culture-bound, anthropologists have relied heavily on a technique that has proved successful in other fields of the natural sciences. As did the archaeologists working at Tikal, they immerse themselves in the data to the fullest extent possible. By doing so, they become so thoroughly familiar with the minute details that they can begin to see patterns inherent in the data, many of which might otherwise have been overlooked. These patterns are what allow the anthropologist to frame hypotheses, which then may be subjected to further testing.

This approach is most easily seen in ethnographic fieldwork, but it is just as important in archaeology. Unlike many social scientists, the ethnographer usually does not go into the field armed with prefigured questionnaires; rather, he or she recognizes that there are probably all sorts of unguessed things, to be found out only by maintaining as open a mind as one can. This does not mean that anthropologists never use questionnaires, for sometimes they do. Generally, though, they use them as a means of supplementing or clarifying information gained through other methods. As the fieldwork proceeds, ethnographers sort their complex observations into a meaningful whole, sometimes by formulating and testing limited or low-level hypotheses, but as often as not by making use of intuition and playing hunches. What is important is that the results are constantly scrutinized for consistency, for if the parts fail to fit together in an internally consistent manner, then the ethnographer knows that a mistake has been made and that further work is necessary.

---

[10]Gould, S. J. (1989). *Wonderful life* (p. 226). New York: Norton.

Two studies of a village in Peru illustrate the contrast between the anthropological and other social-science approaches. One was carried out by a sociologist who, after conducting a survey, concluded that people in the village invariably worked together on one another's individually owned plots of land. By contrast, an anthropologist who lived in the village for over a year (during which the sociologist did his study) observed the practice only once. Although a belief in exchange relations was important for the people's understanding of themselves, it was not an economic fact.[11]

This is not to say that all sociological research is bad and all anthropological research is good; rather, reliance on questionnaire surveys is a risky business, no matter who does it. The problem is that questionnaires all too easily embody the concepts and categories of outsiders rather than those of the people under study. The misfit between the concepts of professionals from industrialized societies and those of a different people is likely to be great, and the questions asked often construct artificial chunks of knowledge that bear little relation to the reality experienced by other people. Even where this is not a problem, questionnaire surveys alone are not good ways of identifying causal relationships. Correlations alone say nothing definite about cause, nor do they effectively explore such social relationships as reciprocity, dependence, exploitation, and so on. They tend to concentrate on what is measurable, answerable, and acceptable as a question, rather than probing less tangible and more qualitative aspects of society. Moreover, for a host of reasons—fear, prudence, wishful thinking, ignorance, exhaustion, hostility, hope of benefit—people may give slanted or false information. Finally, to the degree that extensive questionnaire surveys preempt resources, using up staff as well as funds, they prevent other approaches.

Another problem in scientific anthropology is the matter of validity. In the other natural sciences, replication of observations and/or experiments is a major means of establishing the reliability of a researcher's conclusions. The problem in ethnology is that observational access is far more limited. As anthropologist Paul Roscoe notes,

In the natural sciences, the ubiquity of the physical world, coupled with liberal funding, traditionally has furnished a comparatively democratic access to observation and representation: The solar spectrum, for example, is accessible to, and describable by, almost any astronomer with access to the requisite equipment.[12]

Thus, one can see for oneself if one's colleague has "gotten it right." Access to a non-Western culture, by contrast, is constrained by the difficulty of getting there and being accepted, the limited number of ethnographers, often inadequate funding, the fact that cultures change so what's observed at one time in one particular context may not be at others, and so on. Thus, one cannot easily confirm for oneself the reliability or complete-ness of the ethnographer's account. For this reason, an ethnographer bears a special responsibility for accurate reporting.

In the final record, the ethnographer must be clear about three things: What did he or she do in the field and why? Who did he or she talk to and learn from? And, what was brought back to document it? Without these, one cannot judge the validity of the account.[13]

COMPARISON IN ANTHROPOLOGY

The end result of archaeological or ethnographic fieldwork, if properly carried out, is a coherent statement about a culture that provides an explanatory framework for understanding the ideas and actions of the people who have been studied. And this, in turn, is what permits the anthropologist to frame broader hypotheses about human behavior. Plausible though such hypotheses may be, however, the consideration of a single society is generally insufficient for their testing. Without some basis for comparison, the hypothesis grounded in a single case may be no more than a historical coincidence. On the other hand, a single case may be enough to cast doubt on, if not refute, a theory that had previously been held valid. The discovery in 1948 that aborigines living in Australia's northern Arnhem Land put in an average workday of less than 6 hours, while living well above a bare sufficiency level, was enough to call into question the widely accepted

[11]Chambers, R. (1983). *Rural development: Putting the last first* (p. 51). New York: Longman.

[12] Roscoe, P. B. (1995). The perils of "positivism" in cultural anthropology. *American Anthropologist, 97,* 497.

[13] Sanjek, R. (1990). On ethnographic validity. In R. Sanjek (Ed.), *Fieldnotes* (p. 395). Ithaca, NY: Cornell University Press..

GEORGE PETER MURDOCK (1897–1985)

Modern cross-cultural studies in anthropology derive from efforts of this man to develop a rigorous methodology. Educated at Yale University, he was strongly influenced by the firm belief of his mentor, Albert Keller, in history's "lawfulness" (in the sense of scientific laws). Influenced as well by a pioneering attempt at statistical comparison by the early British anthropologist Sir Edward B. Tylor, in 1937 Murdock instituted the Cross Cultural Survey in Yale's Institute of Human Relations. This later became the Human Relations Area File (HRAF), a catalogue of cross-indexed ethnographic data filed under uniform headings. In the landmark book *Social Structure* (published in 1949) he demonstrated the utility of this tool for researching the ways in which human societies were structured and changed. Later in life, Murdock used HRAF as the model for his *World Ethnographic Sample* (1957) and (after he moved to the University of Pittsburgh) *An Ethnographic Atlas.* The latter is a database of over 100 coded cultural characteristics in almost 1,200 societies.

The value of HRAF (now available at many colleges and universities) and other such research tools is that they permit a search for causal relationships, utilizing statistical techniques to provide testable generalizations. To cite one example, anthropologist Peggy Reeves Sanday examined a sample of 156 societies drawn from HRAF in an attempt to answer such questions as these: Why do women play a more dominant role in some societies than others? Why, and under what circumstances, do men dominate women? Her study, published in 1981 *(Female Power and Male Dominance),* besides disproving the common myth that women are universally subordinate to men, shed important light on the way men and women relate to one another in human societies, and ranks as a major landmark in the study of gender. (So important is this topic, because gender considerations enter into just about everything people do, that it is included in every single chapter of this book.)

Valuable though HRAF is, the files are not without their problems. Although they permit blind searches for correlations among customs, such correlations say nothing about cause and effect. All too easily they are rationalized by construction of elaborate causal chains that may amount to little more than "just so" stories. What is required is further historical analysis of particular practices. The strength of Sanday's study is that she did not ignore the particular historical contexts of the societies in her sample.

Other problems consist of errors in the files from inadequate ethnographies or unsystematic sources; from the nonrandom nature of the sample (cultures are included or rejected in accordance with the quality of available literature); and from the fact that items are wrenched out of context. In short, HRAF and similar databases are useful tools, but they are not foolproof; they can lead to false conclusions unless carefully (and critically) used.

notion that food-foraging peoples are so preoccupied with finding food that they lack time for any of life's more pleasurable activities. Even today, economists are prone to label such peoples as "backward," even though the observations made in the Arnhem Land study have since been confirmed many times over in various parts of the world.

Hypothetical explanations of cultural phenomena may be tested by the comparison of archaeological and/or ethnographic data for several societies found in a particular region. Carefully controlled comparison provides a broader context for understanding cultural phenomena than does the study of a single culture. The anthropologist who undertakes such a comparison may be more confident that the conditions believed to be related really are related, at least within the region that is under investigation; however, an explanation that is valid in one region is not necessarily so in another.

Ideally, theories in cultural anthropology are generated from worldwide comparisons. The cross-cultural researcher examines a worldwide sample of societies in order to discover whether or not hypotheses proposed to explain cultural phenomena seem to be universally applicable. Ideally the sample should be selected at random, thereby enhancing the probability that the conclusions of the cross-cultural researcher will be valid; however, the greater the number of societies being compared, the less likely it is that the investigator will have a detailed understanding of all the societies encompassed by the study. The cross-cultural researcher depends upon other ethnographers for data. It is impossible for any single individual personally to perform in-depth analyses of a broad sample of human cultures throughout the world.

In anthropology, cultural comparisons need not be restricted to ethnographic data. Anthropologists can, for example, turn to archaeological data to test hypotheses about cultural change. Cultural characteristics thought to be caused by certain specified conditions can be tested archaeologically by investigating situations where such conditions actually occurred. Also useful are data provided by the ethnohistorian. **Ethnohistory** is a kind of historical ethnography that studies cultures of the recent past through oral histories; the accounts of explorers, missionaries, and traders; and through analysis of such records as land titles, birth and death records, and other archival materials. The ethnohistorical analysis of cul-

tures, like archaeology, is a valuable approach to understanding change. By examining the conditions believed to have caused certain phenomena, we can discover whether or not those conditions truly precede those phenomena.

Ethnohistoric research is also valuable for assessing the reliability of data used for making cross-cultural comparisons. For example, anthropologists working with data from such resources as the Human Relations Area Files (see the biography on George Peter Murdock on page 23) have sometimes concluded that among food foragers it is (and was) the practice for married couples to live in or near the household of the husband's parents (anthropologists call this *patrilocal residence*). To be sure, this is what many ethnographers reported. But what this fails to take into account is that most such ethnographies were done among food foragers whose traditional practices had been severely altered by pressures set in motion (usually) by the expansion of Europeans to all parts of the globe. For example, the Western Abenaki people of north-western New England are asserted to have practiced patrilocal residence prior to the actual invasion of their homeland by English colonists. What ethnohistorical research shows, however, is that their participation in the fur trade with Europeans, coupled with increasing involvement in warfare to stave off incursions by outsiders, led to increased importance of men's activities and a change from more flexible to patrilocal residence patterns.[14] Upon close examination, other cases of patrilocal residence among food foragers turn out to be similar responses to circumstances associated with the rise of colonialism. Far from wives regularly going to live with their husbands in proximity to the latter's male relations, food-foraging peoples originally seem to have been far more flexible in their postmarital residence arrangements.

Ethnohistorical research, like the field studies of archaeologists, is valuable for testing and confirming hypotheses about culture. And like much of anthropology, it has practical utility as well. In the United States, ethnohistorical research has flourished, for it often provides the key evidence necessary for deciding legal cases

---

[14]Haviland, W. A., & Power, M. W. (1994). *The original Vermonters* (Rev. and exp. ed., pp. 174–175, 215–216, 297–299). Hanover, NH: University Press of New England.

Ethnohistory. The study of cultures of the recent past through oral histories; accounts left by explorers, missionaries, and traders; and through analysis of such records as land titles, birth and death records, and other archival materials.

involving Native American land claims. And here again is an example of a practical application of anthropological knowledge.

ANTHROPOLOGY AND THE HUMANITIES

Although the sciences and humanities are often thought of as mutually exclusive approaches to learning, they share common methods for critical thinking, mental creativity, and innovation.[15] In anthropology, both come together, which is why, for example, anthropological research is funded not only by such hard science agencies as the National Science Foundation, but also by such organizations as the National Endowment for the Humanities. To paraphrase Roy Rappaport, a past president of the American Anthropological Association, the combination of scientific and humanistic approaches is and always has been a source of tension. It has been crucial to anthropology because it truly reflects the condition of a species that lives and can only live in terms of meanings that it must construct in a world devoid of intrinsic meaning, yet subject to natural law. Without the continued grounding in careful observation that scientific aspects of our tradition provide, our interpretive efforts may float off into literary criticism and speculation. But, without the interpretive tradition, the scientific tradition that grounds us will never get off the ground.[16]

The humanistic side of anthropology is perhaps most immediately evident in its concern with other cultures' languages, values, and achievements in the arts and literature (including oral literature among peoples who lack writing). Beyond this, anthropologists remain committed to the proposition that one cannot fully understand another culture by simply observing it; as the term *participant observation* implies, one must *experience* it as well. Thus, ethnographers spend prolonged periods of time living with the people they study, sharing their joys and suffering their deprivations, including sickness and, sometimes, premature death. They are not so naive as to believe that they can be, or even should be, dispassionate about the people whose trials and tribulations they

share. As Robin Fox puts it, "Our hearts, as well as our brains, should be with our men and women."[17] Nor are anthropologists so self-deceived as to believe that they can avoid dealing with the moral and political consequences of their findings. Indeed, anthropology has a long tradition of protecting and promoting the rights of indigenous peoples.

The humanistic side of anthropology is evident as well in its emphasis on qualitative, as opposed to quantitative, research. This is not to say that anthropologists are not aware of the value of quantification and statistical procedures; they do make use of them for various purposes. Nevertheless, reducing people and the things they do to numbers has a definite dehumanizing effect (it is easier to ignore the concerns of impersonal numbers than it is those of flesh-and-blood human beings) and keeps us from dealing with important issues less susceptible to numeration. For all these reasons, anthropologists tend to place less emphasis on numerical data than do other social scientists.

Given their intense involvement with other peoples, it should come as no surprise that anthropologists have amassed as much information about human weakness and greatness—the stuff of the humanities—as any other discipline. Small wonder, too, that above all they intend to avoid allowing a coldly scientific approach to blind them to the fact that human societies are made up of individuals with rich assortments of emotions and aspirations that demand respect. Anthropology has sometimes been called the most human of the sciences, a designation in which anthropologists take considerable pride.

QUESTIONS OF ETHICS

The kinds of research carried out by anthropologists, and the settings within which they work, raise a number of important moral questions about the use and abuse of our knowledge. Who will make use of the findings of anthropologists, and for what purposes? Who, if anyone, will profit from them? In the case of a hostile minority, for example, will governmental or corporate interests use anthropological data to suppress that minority? And what of traditional communities around the world? Who is to decide what changes should or should not be introduced for community "betterment"? By whose definition is it betterment—the community's, that of some remote govern-

---

[15]Shearer, R. R., & Gould, S. J. (1999). Of two minds and one nature. *Science, 286,* 1093.

[16]Rappaport, R. A. (1994). Commentary. *Anthropology Newsletter, 35,* 76.

[17]Fox, R. (1968). *Encounter with anthropology* (p. 290). New York: Dell.

ment, or an international agency like the World Bank? Then there is the problem of privacy. Anthropologists deal with people's private and sensitive matters, including things that people would not care to have generally known about them. How does one write about such matters and at the same time protect the privacy of informants? Not surprisingly, because of these and other questions, there has been much discussion among anthropologists over the past two decades on the subject of ethics.[18]

Anthropologists recognize that they have obligations to three sets of people: those whom they study, those who fund the research, and those in the profession who expect us to publish our findings so that they may be used to further knowledge. Because fieldwork requires a relationship of trust between fieldworker and informants, the anthropologist's first responsibility clearly is to his or her informants and their people. Everything possible must be done to protect their physical, social, and psychological welfare and to honor their dignity and privacy. In other words, *do no harm.* Although early ethnographers often provided colonial administrators with the kind of information needed to control the "natives," they have long since ceased to be comfortable with such work and regard as basic a people's right to their own culture.

As an example of how these issues play out, I turn to my own work with the Western Abenakis of northwestern New England. In writing a book about them, I made a point of having them see the manuscript to ensure that I did not violate anyone's confidences or privacy, or misrepresent them in any way. I also had to be sensitive to legal matters having to do with federal recognition, traditional hunting and fishing rights, and potential land claims. I had to be careful to present information in such a way that the state could not use it unfairly against them. Recognizing an obligation to "give back," I have done this in various ways. These include signing over the book's royalties to the Abenakis, responding to their requests in various ways, giving countless presentations to a wide range of schools, public and civic organizations, testifying on the Abenaki's behalf before legislative committees, and providing expert testimony in court over native fishing rights. Truly this has been a long-term relationship. With regard to those funding my work—the National Endowment for

the Humanities, the Vermont Historical Society, and the University of Vermont—publication of the book satisfied their requirements. Finally, my obligations to the profession have been met not only through the book but by publication of supplementary articles in specialist journals as well.

ANTHROPOLOGY AND CONTEMPORARY LIFE

Anthropology, with its long-standing commitment to understanding people in all parts of the world, past and present, coupled with its holistic perspective, is better equipped than any other discipline to grapple with a problem of overriding importance for all of humanity at the beginning of the 21st century. An inescapable fact of life is that North Americans—a small minority of the world's people—live in a global community in which all of those people are interdependent. There is now widespread awareness of this in the business community, which relies on foreign sources for raw materials, sees the non-Western world as its major area for market expansion, and more and more is manufacturing its products abroad. Nevertheless, citizens of the United States are on the whole as ignorant about the cultures of the rest of the world as they have ever been. This is true not just of average citizens but highly educated people. In Guatemala, for example, where over half the population is made up of Maya Indians, U.S. Foreign Service personnel are largely ignorant of the literature—most of it by anthropologists—pertaining to these people.[19] As a result, too many of us are poorly equipped to handle the demands of living in the modern world.

The relevance of anthropological knowledge for the contemporary world may be illustrated by three quite different examples. In the United States today, discrimination based on notions of race continues to be a serious problem affecting economic, political, and social relations. What anthropology has shown, as we shall see in Chapter 13, is the fallacy of racial categories themselves. Far from being the biological reality it is thought to be, the concept of race emerged in the 18th century as a device for justifying the dominance of Europeans and their descendants over Africans, American Indians, and other

---

[18]American Anthropological Association. (1998). Code of ethics of the American Anthropological Association. *Anthropology Newsletter, 39* (6), 19–20.

[19]Nance, C. R. (1997). Review of Haviland's *Cultural Anthropology* (p. 2).

Ignorance of other cultures can have serious consequences. When President George W. Bush responded to attacks on targets in New York and the Pentagon, he spoke of a "crusade" against terrorism, which the Department of Defense dubbed "Operation Infinite Justice." These choices of language caused problems with Islamic countries, where the word *crusade* reminds people of Christian invasions of Muslim lands, where only Allah can dispense "infinite justice."

"people of color." In fact, differences of skin color are adaptations to differing amounts of ultraviolet radiation and have nothing to do with other abilities. Nor do they covary with other biological characteristics; a northern European, for example, may have more in common with a "black" from southern Africa than with someone from Greece or Italy, depending on what genetically based characters other than skin color are considered. Moreover, one finds far more biological variation within any given human population than between them. In short, human races are nothing more than folk categories, and the sooner this is recognized, the better off we will all be.[20]

---

[20]American Anthropological Association. (1998). Statement on "race." Available: *www.ameranthassn.org.*

A second example involves the issue of same-sex marriage. As this is written, two countries have moved toward allowing such unions: Brazil, by recognizing "stable unions" between same-sex partners, and the Netherlands, which is about to recognize same-sex marriages called *homohuwelijk* by national law. In the United States, California is debating and Vermont has legalized "civil unions" between same-sex couples. Those opposed to same-sex unions frequently argue that marriage has always been between one man and one woman, and that only heterosexual relations are natural. Yet, neither assertion is true. Anthropologists have documented same-sex marriages in many human societies in various parts of the world, where they are regarded as perfectly acceptable under appropriate circumstances. As for homosexual behavior, it is quite common in the animal world (see, for

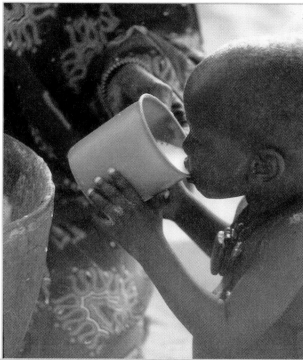

Though their skin colors differ, this northern European and East African share the genetically based ability to digest milk, something that sets them apart from many central Europeans and central Africans. Because their differences are distributed independently, humans cannot be classified into races having any biological validity.

These people are protesting Vermont's civil union legislation. Their objections are based on beliefs that anthropologists have shown are without foundation.

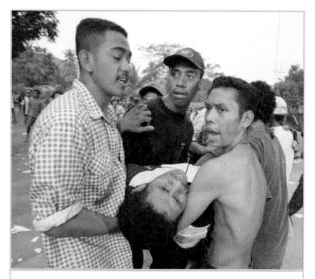

Violence triggered by East Timor's vote for independence exemplifies the problem of multinational states in which members of one nationality try to control those of another through all possible means.

HIGHWAY 1
American Anthropological Association
http://www.aaanet.org/about_aaa.htm

HIGHWAY 2
Indiana University Anthropology Department
http://www.indiana.edu/~wanthro/theory.htm

example, Chapter 4), including among humans.[21] The only difference between people and other animals is that human societies specify when, where, how, and with whom it is appropriate (just as they do for heterosexual behavior).

A final example relates to the common confusion of *nation* with *state*. The distinction is important: States are politically organized territories, whereas nations are socially organized bodies of people. Rarely do states and nations coincide, nations being split between different states, and states typically being controlled by members of one nation who commonly use their control to gain access to the land, resources, and labor of other nationalities. Rarely is the consent of the other nationals obtained, nor are their interests given much (if any) consideration by those who control the government. As a consequence, oppressed nationals often resort to force to defend their land, resources, and even their very identities, feeling they have no other options. Most of the armed conflicts in the world today are of this sort and not mere outbreaks of tribalism, as commonly asserted. Nor should

they be confused with acts of terrorism carried out by religious or other extremists. For example, the conflict in Chechnya is one between Chechan nationals on the one hand against domination by Russian nationals on the other. The recent attacks on the New York World Trade Center and the Pentagon, by contrast, were carried out by a transnational organization of religious extremists.

In numerous ways, our ignorance about other peoples and their ways is a cause of serious problems. It is as true today as when Edwin Reischauer, a former ambassador, said it some years ago: "Education is not moving rapidly enough in the right directions to produce the knowledge about the outside world and attitudes toward other peoples that may be essential for human survival."[22] What anthropology has to contribute to contemporary life, then, are an understanding of, and way of looking at, the world's peoples, which are nothing less than basic skills for survival in the modern world.

---

[21]Kirkpatrick, R. C. (2000). The evolution of human homosexual behavior. *Current Anthropology, 41,* 384.

[22]Quoted in Haviland, W. A. (1997). Cleansing young minds, or what should we be doing in introductory anthropology? In C. P. Kottak, J. J. White, R. H. Furlow, & P. C. Rice (Eds.), *The teaching of anthropology: Problems, issues, and decisions* (p. 35). Mountain View, CA: Mayfield.

CHAPTER SUMMARY

Throughout human history, people have needed to know who they are, where they came from, and why they behave as they do. Traditionally, myths and legends provided the answers to these questions. Anthropology, as it has emerged over the last 200 years, offers another approach to answering the questions people ask about themselves.

Anthropology is the study of humankind. In employing a scientific approach, anthropologists seek to produce a reasonably objective understanding of both human diversity and those things all humans have in common. The two major branches of anthropology are physical and cultural anthropology. Physical anthropology focuses on humans as biological organisms. Particular emphasis is given by physical anthropologists to tracing the evolutionary development of the human animal and studying biological variation within the species today. Cultural anthropologists study humans in terms of their cultures, the often unconscious standards by which societies operate. Cultural and physical anthropologists share common interests in the interplay between human culture and biology.

Three areas of cultural anthropology are archaeology, anthropological linguistics, and ethnology. Archaeologists study material objects, usually from past cultures, to explain human behavior. Linguists, who study human languages, may deal with the description of a language, with the history of languages, or how they are used in particular social settings. Ethnologists concentrate on cultures of the present or recent past; in doing comparative studies of culture, they focus on a particular aspect of it, such as religious or economic practices, or as ethnographers they may go into the field to observe and describe human behavior as it can be seen, experienced, and discussed with people whose culture is to be understood.

Anthropology is unique among the social and natural sciences in that it is concerned with formulating explanations of human diversity based on a study of all aspects of human biology and behavior in all known societies, past and present, rather than in recent European and North American societies alone. Thus anthropologists have devoted much attention to the study of ancient and contemporary non-Western peoples.

Anthropologists are concerned with the objective and systematic study of humankind. The anthropologist employs the methods of other scientists by developing hypotheses, or assumed explanations, using other data to test these hypotheses, and ultimately arriving at theories—explanations supported by reliable bodies of data. The data used by the cultural anthropologist may be from a single society or from numerous societies, which are then compared.

In anthropology, the humanities and sciences come together a genuinely human science. Anthropology's link with the humanities can be seen in its concern with people's beliefs, values, languages, arts, and literature—oral as well as written—but above all in its attempt to convey the experience of living as other people do. As both science and humanity, anthropology has essential skills to offer the modern world, where understanding the other people with whom we share the globe has become a matter of survival.

CLASSIC READINGS

Lett, J. (1987). *The human enterprise: A critical introduction to anthropological theory.* Boulder, CO: Westview.

Part 1 examines the philosophical foundations of anthropological theory, paying special attention to the nature of scientific inquiry and the mechanisms of scientific progress. Part 2 deals with the nature of social science as well as the particular features of anthropology.

Peacock, J. L. (1986). *The anthropological lens: Harsh light, soft focus.* New York: Cambridge University Press.

This lively and innovative book manages to give the reader a good understanding of the diversity of activities undertaken by anthropologists, while identifying the unifying themes that hold the discipline together.

Sanjek, R. (Ed.). (1990). *Fieldnotes: The making of anthropology.* Ithaca, NY: Cornell University Press.

This book goes right to the heart of the ethnographic enterprise. What, how, and why do field-workers write down what they do and how do they deal with it all? How do others assess the credibility of the ethnographer?

Vogt, F. W. (1975). *A history of ethnology.* New York: Holt, Rinehart & Winston.

This history of cultural anthropology attempts to describe and interpret the major intellectual strands, in their cultural and historical contexts, that influenced the development of the field. The author tries for a balanced view of this subject rather than one that would support a particular theoretical position.

CHAPTER 2

METHODS OF STUDYING THE HUMAN PAST

This excavation is of an old Stone Age campsite in France. Vertical strings are markers for a grid by which excavators keep track of exact locations of objects found. Without such meticulous records, the finds tell us nothing about the human past.

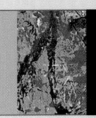

1

WHAT ARE ARCHAEOLOGICAL SITES AND FOSSIL LOCALITIES, AND HOW ARE THEY FOUND?

Archaeological sites are places containing the remains of past human activity. They are revealed by the presence of artifacts as well as soil marks, changes in vegetation, and irregularities of the surface. Fossil localities contain actual remains of organisms that lived in the past. They are revealed by the presence of fossils—any trace or impression of an organism of past geological time that has been preserved in the earth. Although fossils are sometimes found in archaeological sites, not all archaeological sites contain fossils, and localities are often found apart from archaeological sites.

2

HOW ARE SITES AND LOCALITIES INVESTIGATED?

Archaeologists and paleoanthropologists face something of a dilemma. The only way to thoroughly investigate a site or locality is by excavation, which results in its destruction. Thus, every attempt is made to excavate in such a way that the location of everything found, no matter how small, is precisely recorded. Without such records little sense can be made of the data, and the potential of the site or locality to contribute to our knowledge of the past would be lost forever.

3

HOW ARE ARCHAEOLOGICAL OR FOSSIL REMAINS DATED?

Remains can be dated in relative terms by noting their stratigraphic position, by measuring the amount of fluorine contained in fossil bones, or by associating them with different floral or faunal remains. More precise dating is achieved by counting the tree rings in wood from archaeological contexts, by measuring the amount of carbon 14 remaining in organic materials, or by measuring the percentage of potassium that has decayed to argon in volcanic materials. Where problems exist in applying these standard techniques, other specialized methods are available.

popular stereotype of anthropologists is that they are concerned exclusively with the human past. This is not the case, as should now be evident; not even archaeologists and physical anthropologists, those most likely to be engaged in the study of the past, devote all of their time to such pursuits. As explained in Chapter 1, some archaeologists study the refuse of modern peoples, and many physical anthropologists engage in research on such issues as present-day human variation and adaptation. Nevertheless, the study of the human past is an important *part* of anthropology, given its concern with peoples in all places and times. Moreover, knowledge of the human past is essential if we are to understand what it was that made us distinctively human, as well as how the processes of change—both biological and cultural—affect the human species. Indeed, given the radical changes taking place in the world today, one may say that an understanding of the nature of change has never been more important. Although it is not their sole concern, archaeology and physical anthropology are the two branches of anthropology most involved in the study of the human past.

Archaeologists (apart from those engaged in the analysis of modern garbage) study things left behind by people who lived in historic or prehistoric times—tools, trash, traces of shelters, and the like. As the British archaeologist Stuart Piggot put it, "Archaeology is the science of rubbish."[1] Most of us are familiar with some kind of archaeological material: the coin dug out of the earth, the fragment of an ancient jar, the spear point used by some ancient hunter. The finding and cataloguing of such objects is often thought by laypeople to be the chief goal of archaeology. While this was true in the 19th century, the situation changed in the 20th. Today, the aim is to use archaeological remains to reconstruct human societies that can no longer be observed firsthand, in order to understand and explain human behavior. Although it may look as if the archaeologist is digging up things, he or she is really digging up human behavior.

The actual remains of our ancestors, as opposed to the things they lost or discarded, are the concern of physical anthropologists. Those physical anthropologists engaged in the recovery and study of the fossil evidence for human evolution, as opposed to those who study present-day peoples, are generally known as **paleoanthropologists.** Unlike paleontologists, who study all forms of past life, paleoanthropologists confine their attention to humans, near humans, and other ancient primates, the group to which humans belong. Just as the finding and cataloguing of objects was once the chief concern of the archaeologist, so the finding and cataloguing of human and other primate fossils was once the chief concern of the paleoanthropologist. But, again, there has been a major change in the field; although recovery, description, and organization of fossil materials are still important, the emphasis since the 1950s has been on what those fossils can tell us about the processes at work in human biological evolution. It is not so much a case of what you find, but what you find out.

In Chapter 1, we surveyed at some length just what it is that anthropologists do and why they do it. We also looked briefly at the ethnographic methods used by anthropologists to study the cultures of living peoples. Other methods are required, however, when studying peoples of the past—especially those of the prehistoric past, before the existence of written records. The term **prehistoric** is a conventional one that, while not denying the existence of history, recognizes that *written* history is absent. Since the next two parts of this book are about the prehistoric past, in this chapter we shall look at how archaeologists and paleoanthropologists go about their study of the human past.

METHODS OF DATA RECOVERY

Archaeologists, one way or another, work with **artifacts:** any object fashioned or altered by humans—a flint chip, a basket, an axe, a pipe, or such nonportable things as house ruins or walls. An artifact expresses a facet of human culture. Because it is something that someone made, archaeologists like to say that an artifact is a product of human behavior or, in more technical words, that it is a material representation of an abstract ideal.

Just as important as the artifacts themselves is the way they were left in the ground. What people do with the things they have made, how they dispose of them, and how they lose them also reflect important aspects of human behavior. Furthermore, the context in which the artifacts were found tells us which objects were contemporary with which other objects, which are older, and which are younger.

---

[1]Quoted in Fagan, B. M. (1995). The quest for the past. In L. L. Hasten (Ed.), *Annual editions 95/96, Archaeology* (p. 10). Guilford, CT: Dushkin.

Paleoanthropologist.   An anthropologist who studies human evolution from fossil remains.   •   **Prehistoric.**   A conventional term used to refer to the period of time before the appearance of written records. Does not deny the existence of history, merely of *written* history.   •   **Artifact.**   Any object fashioned or altered by humans.

Without this information, the archaeologist is in no position at all even to identify, let alone understand, specific cultures of the past. This importance of context cannot be overstated; without context, the archaeologist in effect knows nothing! Unfortunately, such information is easily lost if the materials have been disturbed, whether by bulldozers or by the activities of relic collectors.

While archaeologists work with artifacts, paleoanthropologists work with human or other primate fossils—the remains of past forms of life. And just as the context of a find is as important to the archaeologist as the find itself, so is the context of a fossil absolutely critical to the paleoanthropologist. Not only does it tell which fossils are earlier or later in time than other fossils, but also by noting the association of human fossils with other nonhuman remains, the paleoanthropologist may go a long way toward reconstructing the environmental setting in which the human lived.

The Nature of Fossils

Broadly defined, a **fossil** is any trace or impression of an organism of past geologic time that has been preserved in the earth's crust. Fossilization typically involves the hard parts of an organism: Bones, teeth, shells, horns, and the woody tissues of plants are the most successfully fossilized materials. Although the soft parts of an organism are rarely fossilized, the casts or impressions of footprints, and even whole bodies, have sometimes been found. Because dead animals quickly attract meat-eating scavengers and bacteria that cause decomposition, they rarely survive long enough to become fossilized. What is required is that they be covered by some protective substance soon after death.

An organism or part of an organism may be preserved in a number of ways. The whole animal may be frozen in ice, like the famous mammoths found in Siberia, safe from the actions of predators, weathering, and bacteria. Or it may be enclosed in a fossil resin such as amber. Specimens of spiders and insects dating back millions of years have been preserved in the Baltic Sea area, which is rich in resin-producing conifers. It may be preserved in the bottoms of lakes and sea basins, where the accumulation of chemicals renders the environment antiseptic. The entire organism may also be mummified or preserved in tar pits, peat, oil, or asphalt bogs, in which the chemical environment prevents the growth of decay-producing bacteria. Such **unaltered fossils,** although not common, are often quite spectacular and may be particularly informative. As an example, consider the recovery in 1994 of the remains of a young girl in Barrow, Alaska.

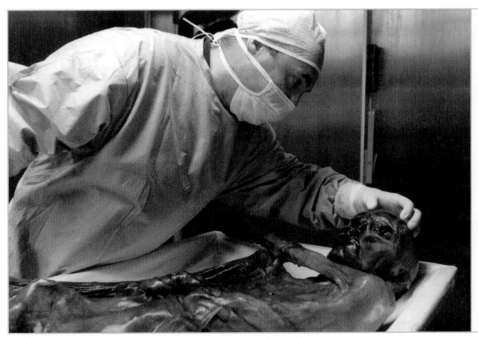

In rare circumstances, human bodies are so well preserved that they could be mistaken for recent corpses. Such is the case of the 5,200-year-old "Ice Man," exposed by the melting of an alpine glacier in northern Italy in 1991.

Fossil.   The preserved remains of plants and animals that lived in the past.   •   **Unaltered fossil.**   Remains of plants and animals that lived in the past and that have not been altered in any significant way.

Original Study

Whispers from the Ice[2]

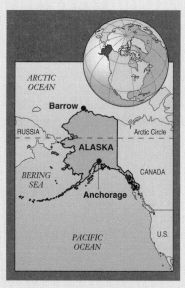

People grew excited when a summer rainstorm softened the bluff known as Ukkuqsi, sloughing off huge chunks of earth containing remains of historic and prehistoric houses, part of the old village that predates the modern community of Barrow. Left protruding from the slope was a human head. Archaeologist Anne Jensen happened to be in Barrow buying strapping tape when the body appeared. Her firm, SJS Archaeological Services, Inc., was closing a field season at nearby Point Franklin, and Jensen offered the team's help in a kind of archaeological triage to remove the body before it eroded completely from the earth. The North Slope Borough hired her and Glenn Sheehan, both associated with Pennsylvania's Bryn Mawr College, to conduct the work. The National Science Foundation, which supported the 3 year Point Franklin project, agreed to fund the autopsy and subsequent analysis of the body and artifacts. The Ukkuqsi excavation quickly became a community event. In remarkably sunny and calm weather, volunteers troweled and picked through the thawing soil, finding trade beads, animal bones, and other items. Teen-age boys worked alongside grandmothers. The smell of sea mammal oil, sweet at first then corrupt, mingled with ancient organic odors of decomposed vegetation. One man searched the beach for artifacts that had eroded from the bluff, discovering such treasures as two feather parkas. Elder Silas Negovanna, originally of Wainwright, visited several times, "more or less out of curiosity to see what they have in mind," he says. George Leavitt, who lives in a house on the bluff, stopped by one day while carrying home groceries and suggested a way to spray water to thaw the soil without washing away valuable artifacts. Tour groups added the excavation to their rounds.

"This community has a great interest in archaeology up here just because it's so recent to their experience," says oral historian Karen Brewster, a tall young woman who interviews elders as part of her work with the North Slope Borough's division of Inupiat History, Language, and Culture. "The site's right in town, and everybody was really fascinated by it."

Slowly, as the workers scraped and shoveled, the earth surrendered its historical hoard: carved wooden bowls, ladles, and such clothing as a mitten made from polar bear hide, birdskin parkas, and mukluks. The items spanned prehistoric times, dated in Barrow to before explorers first arrived in 1826.

The work prompted visiting elders to recall when they or their parents lived in traditional sod houses and relied wholly on the land and sea for sustenance. Some remembered sliding down the hill as children, before the sea gnawed away the slope. Others described the site's use as a lookout for whales or ships. For the archaeologists, having elders stand beside them and identify items and historical context is like hearing the past whispering in their ears. Elders often know from experience, or from stories, the answers to the scientists' questions about how items were used or made. "In this instance, usually the only puzzled people are the archaeologists," jokes archaeologist Sheehan.

A modern town of 4,000, Barrow exists in a cultural continuum, where history is not detached or remote but still pulses through contemporary life. People live, hunt, and fish where their ancestors did, but they can also buy fresh vegetables at the store and jet to other places. Elementary school classes include computer and Inupiaq language studies. Caribou skins, still ruddy with blood, and black brant

[2]Adapted from Simpson, S. (1995, April). Whispers from the ice. *Alaska*, 23–28.

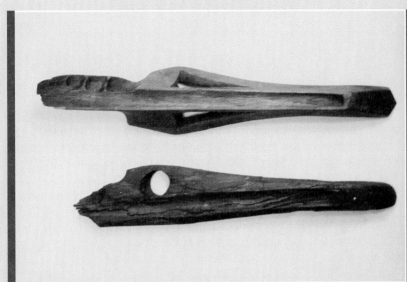
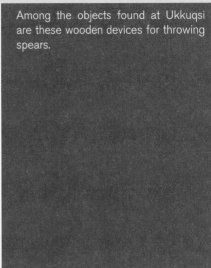

Among the objects found at Ukkuqsi are these wooden devices for throwing spears.

carcasses hang near late-model cars outside homes equipped with television antennas. A man uses power tools to work on his whaling boat. And those who appear from the earth are not just bodies, but relatives. "We're not a people frozen in time," says Jana Harcharek, an Inupiat Eskimo who teaches Inupiaq and nurtures her culture among young people. "There will always be that connection between us [and our ancestors]. They're not a separate entity."

The past drew still closer as the archaeologists neared the body. After several days of digging through thawed soil, they used water supplied by the local fire station's tanker truck to melt through permafrost until they reached the remains, about 3 feet below the surface. A shell of clear ice encased the body, which rested in what appeared to be a former meat cellar. With the low-pressure play of water from the tanker, the archaeologists teased the icy casket from the frozen earth, exposing a tiny foot. Only then did they realize they had uncovered a child. "That was kind of sad, because she was about my daughter's size," says archaeologist Jensen.

The girl was curled up beneath a baleen toboggan and part of a covering that Inupiat elder Bertha Leavitt identified as a kayak skin by its stitching. The child, who appeared to be 5 or 6, remained remarkably intact after her dark passage through time. Her face was cloaked by a covering that puzzled some onlookers. It didn't look like human hair, or even fur, but something with a feathery residue.

Finally they concluded it was a hood from a feather parka made of bird skins. The rest of her body was delineated muscle that had freeze-dried into a dark brick-red color. Her hands rested on her knees, which were drawn up to her chin. Frost particles coated the bends of her arms and legs.

"We decided we needed to go talk to the elders and see what they wanted, to get some kind of feeling as to whether they wanted to bury her right away, or whether they were willing to allow some studies in a respectful manner—studies that would be of some use to residents of the North Slope," Jensen says. Working with community elders is not a radical idea to Jensen or Sheehan, whose previous work in the Arctic has earned them high regard from local officials who appreciate their sensitivity. The researchers feel obligated not only to follow community wishes, but to invite villagers to sites and to share all information through public presentations. In fact, Jensen is reluctant to discuss findings with the press before the townspeople themselves hear it.

"It seems like it's a matter of simple common courtesy," she says. Such consideration can only help researchers, she points out. "If people don't get along with you, they're not going to talk to you, and they're liable to throw you out on your ear." In the past, scientists were not terribly sensitive about such matters, generally regarding human remains—and sometimes living Natives—as artifacts themselves. Once, the girl's body would have

Original Study

been hauled off to the catacombs of some university or museum, and relics would have disappeared into exhibit drawers in what Sheehan describes as "hit-and-run archaeology."

"Grave robbers" is how Inupiat Jana Harcharek refers to early Arctic researchers. "They took human remains and their burial goods. It's pretty gruesome. But, of course, at the time they thought they were doing science a big favor. Thank goodness attitudes have changed."

Today, not only scientists but municipal officials confer with the Barrow Elders Council when local people find skeletons from traditional platform burials out on the tundra, or when bodies appear in the house mounds. The elders appreciate such consultations, says Samuel Simmonds, a tall, dignified man known for his carving. A retired Presbyterian minister, he presided at burial ceremonies of the famous "frozen family" that ancient Inupiats discovered in Barrow 13 years ago. "They were part of us, we know that," he says simply, as if the connection between old bones and bodies and living relatives is self-evident. In the case of the newly discovered body, he says, "We were concerned that it was reburied in a respectful manner. They were nice enough to come over and ask us."

The elders also wanted to restrict media attention and prevent photographs of the body except for a few showing her position at the site. They approved a limited autopsy to help answer questions about the body's sex, age, and state of health. She was placed in an orange plastic body bag in a stainless steel morgue with the temperature turned down to below freezing.

With the help of staff at the Indian Health Service Hospital, Jensen sent the girl's still-frozen body to Anchorage's Providence Hospital. There she assisted with an autopsy performed by Dr. Michael Zimmerman of New York City's Mount Sinai Hospital. Zimmerman, an expert on prehistoric frozen bodies, had autopsied Barrow's frozen family in 1982, and was on his way to work on the prehistoric man recently discovered in the Alps.

The findings suggest the girl's life was very hard. She ultimately died of starvation, but also had emphysema caused by a rare congenital disease—the lack of an enzyme that protects the lungs. She probably was sickly and needed extra care all her brief life. The autopsy also found soot in her lungs from the family's sea mammal oil lamps, and she had osteoporosis, which was caused by a diet exclusively of meat from marine mammals.

The girl's stomach was empty, but her intestinal tract contained dirt and animal fur. That remains a mystery and raises questions about the condition of the rest of the family. "It's not likely that she would be hungry and everyone else well fed," Jensen says.

That the girl appears to have been placed deliberately in the cellar provokes further questions about precontact burial practices, which the researchers hope Barrow elders can help answer. Historic accounts indicate the dead often were wrapped in skins and laid out on the tundra on wooden platforms, rather than buried in the frozen earth. But perhaps the entire family was starving and too weak to remove the dead girl from the house, Jensen speculates. "We probably won't ever be able to say, 'This is the way it was,'" she adds. "For that you need a time machine."

The scientific team reported to the elders that radiocarbon dating places the girl's death in about A.D. 1200. If correct—for dating is technically tricky in the Arctic—the date would set the girl's life about 100 years before her people formed settled whaling villages, Sheehan says.

Following the autopsy and the body's return to Barrow in August, one last request by the elders was honored. The little girl, wrapped in her feather parka, was placed in a casket and buried in a small Christian ceremony next to the grave of the other prehistoric bodies. Hundreds of years after her death, an Inupiat daughter was welcomed back into the midst of her community.

The "rescue" of the little girl's body from the raw forces of time and nature means researchers and the Inupiat people will continue to learn still more about the region's culture. Sheehan and Jensen returned to Barrow in winter 1994 to explain their findings to townspeople. "We expect to learn just as much from them," Sheehan said before the trip. A North Slope

Cultural Center scheduled for completion in 1996 will store and display artifacts from the dig sites.

Laboratory tests and analysis also will contribute information. The archaeologists hope measurements of heavy metals in the girl's body will allow comparisons with modern-day pollution contaminating the sea mammals that Inupiats eat today. The soot damage in her lungs might offer health implications for Third World people who rely on oil lamps, dung fires, and charcoal for heat and light. Genetic tests could illuminate early population movements of Inupiats. The project also serves as a model for good relations between archaeologists and Native people. "The larger overall message from this work is that scientists and communities don't have to be at odds," Sheehan says. "In fact, there are mutual interests that we all have. Scientists have obliga-tions to communities. And when more scientists realize that, and when more communities hold scientists to those standards, then everybody will be happier."

The End

Cases in which an entire organism of any sort, let alone a human, is preserved in a relatively unaltered state are especially rare and comprise possibly less than 1 percent of all fossil finds. Most **fossils** have been **altered** in some way. They generally consist of such things as scattered teeth and fragments of bones found embedded in the earth's crust as part of rock deposits. Thousands, and even millions, of years ago, the organisms died and were deposited in the earth; they may then have been covered by sediments and silt, or sand. These materials gradually hardened, forming a protective shell around the skeleton of the organism. The internal cavities of bones or teeth and other parts of the skeleton are generally filled in with mineral deposits from the sediment immediately surrounding the specimen. Then the external walls of the bone decay and are replaced by calcium carbonate or silica.

Fossilization is most apt to occur among marine animals and other creatures that live near water, because their remains accumulate on shallow sea, river, or lake bottoms, away from waves and tidal action. These concentrations of shells and other parts of organisms are covered and completely enclosed by the soft waterborne sediments that eventually harden into shale and limestone.

Terrestrial animals that do not live near lakes, rivers, or the sea are less likely to be fossilized unless they happened to die in a cave, or their remains were dragged there by some other meat-eating animal. In caves, conditions are often excellent for fossilization, as minerals contained in water dripping from the ceiling may harden over bones left on the cave floor. In northern China, for example, many fossils of *Homo erectus* (discussed in Chapter 8)

Fossils are not always found in the ground. In this picture, paleoanthropologist Donald Johanson searches for fossils in a gully in Ethiopia. The fossils in the foreground were once buried beneath sediments on an ancient lake bottom, but rains in more recent times have eroded the sediments from around them so that they lie exposed on the surface.

Altered fossils. Remains of plants and animals that lived in the past that have been altered, as by the replacement of organic material by calcium carbonate or silica.

and other animals were found in a cave at a place called Zhoukoudian, in deposits consisting of consolidated clays and rock that had fallen from the cave's limestone ceiling. The cave had been frequented by both humans and predatory animals, who left remains of many a meal there.

Unless protected in some way, the bones of a land dweller, having been picked clean and often broken by predators and scavengers, are then scattered and exposed to the deteriorating influence of the elements. The fossil record for many primates, for example, is poor, because organic materials decay rapidly in the tropical forests in which they lived. The records are much more complete in the case of primates that lived on the grassy plains, or savannas, where conditions are far more favorable to the formation of fossils. This is particularly true in places where ash deposited from volcanic eruptions or waterborne sediments along lakes and streams could quickly cover over the skeletons of primates that lived there. At several localities in Ethiopia, Kenya, and Tanzania in East Africa, numerous fossils important for our understanding of human evolution have been found near ancient lakes and streams, often sandwiched between layers of volcanic ash.

SITES AND FOSSIL LOCALITIES

Given that archaeologists and paleontologists work with artifacts and fossils, the question is: Where are they found? Places containing archaeological remains of previous human activity are known as **sites.** There are many kinds of sites, and sometimes it is difficult to define their boundaries, for remains may be strewn over large areas. Some examples are hunting campsites, from which hunters went out to hunt game; kill sites, in which game was killed and butchered; village sites, in which domestic activities took place; and cemeteries, in which the dead, and sometimes their belongings, were buried.

Sometimes human fossil remains are present at archaeological sites. This is the case, for example, at certain early sites in East Africa. Sometimes, though, human remains are found at other localities. For example, in South Africa the fossil remains of early human ancestors have been found in rock fissures, where their remains were dropped by such predators as leopards and eagles. Such places are usually referred to as **fossil localities.**

Stone blocks and notched logs suggest that this site may have been a human habitation prior to the flooding of the Black Sea, ca. 5600 B.C. This site was found along the submerged coast 25 km to the west of Ince Burun on the Sinop peninsula.

Site. In archaeology, a place containing remains of previous human activity. • **Fossil locality.** In paleoanthropology, a place where fossils are found.

Site and Locality Identification

Archaeological sites, particularly very old ones, frequently lie buried underground, and therefore the first task for the archaeologist is actually finding sites to investigate. Most sites are revealed by the presence of artifacts. Chance may play a crucial role in the discovery, as in the previously discussed case of the site at Barrow, Alaska. Usually, however, the archaeologist will have to survey a region in order to plot the sites available for excavation. A survey can be made from the ground, but nowadays more and more use is made of remote sensing techniques, many of them byproducts of space-age technology. Aerial photographs have been used off and on by archaeologists since the 1920s and are widely used today. Among other things, they were used for the discovery and interpretation of the huge geometric and zoomorphic markings on the coastal desert of Peru. More recently, use of high-resolution aerial photographs, including satellite imagery, resulted in the astonishing discovery of over 500 miles of prehistoric roadways connecting sites in the four-corners region (where Arizona, New Mexico, Colorado, and Utah meet) with other sites in ways that archaeolo-

gists had never suspected. This led to a new understanding of prehistoric Pueblo Indian economic, social, and political organization. Evidently, large centers like Pueblo Bonito were able to exercise political control over a number of satellite communities, mobilize labor for large public works, and see to the regular redistribution of goods over substantial distances.

On the ground, sites can be spotted by **soil marks,** or stains, that often show up on the surface of recently plowed fields. From soil marks, many Bronze Age burial mounds were discovered in northern Hertfordshire and southwestern Cambridgeshire, England. The mounds hardly rose out of the ground, yet each was circled at its core by chalky soil marks. Sometimes the very presence of certain chalky rock is significant. A search for Stone Age cave sites in Europe would be simplified with the aid of a geological map showing where limestone—a mineral necessary in the formation of caves—is to be found.

Some sites may be spotted by the kind of vegetation they grow. For example, the topsoil of ancient storage and refuse pits is often richer in organic matter than that of the surrounding areas, and so it grows a distinct vegetation.

Some archaeological features are best seen from the air, such as this figure of a hummingbird made in prehistoric times on the Nazca Desert of Peru.

Soil marks. Stains that show up on the surface of recently plowed fields that reveal an archaeological site.

Revealed by unusually low water levels are these remains of a 1,700-year-old fish weir, for trapping fish, in Maine. Until their discovery, submersion beneath the water preserved the lower portions of wooden stakes.

At Tikal, an ancient Maya site in Guatemala (Chapter 12), breadnut trees usually grow near the remains of ancient houses, so that an archaeologist looking for the remains of houses at Tikal would do well to search where these trees grow. In England, a wooden monument of the Stonehenge type at Darrington, Wiltshire, was discovered from an aerial photograph showing a distinct pattern of vegetation growing where the ancient structure once stood.

Documents, maps, folklore—ethnohistorical data—are also useful to the archaeologist. Heinrich Schliemann, the famous (and controversial) 19th-century German archaeologist, was led to the discovery of Troy after a reading of Homer's *Iliad.* He assumed that the city described by Homer as Ilium was really Troy. Place-names and local lore often are an indication that an archaeological site is to be found in the area. Archaeological surveys in North America depend a great deal upon amateur collectors who are usually familiar with local history.

Sometimes sites in eastern North America are exposed by natural agents, such as soil erosion or droughts. Many prehistoric Indian shell refuse mounds have been exposed by the erosion of river banks. A whole village of stone

huts was exposed at Skara Brae in Britain's Orkney Islands by the action of wind as it blew away sand. And during the long drought of 1853–1854, a well-preserved prehistoric village was exposed when the water level of Lake Zurich, Switzerland, fell dramatically. In 1991, the mummified body of a man who lived 5,200 years ago was found in the Tyrolean Alps, where it had been released by glacial melting.

Often, archaeological remains are accidentally discovered in the course of some other human activity. Plowing sometimes turns up bones, fragments of pots, and other archaeological objects. Stone quarrying at Swanscombe, Kent, in England revealed an important site of the Old Stone Age, with human remains thought to be about 250,000 years old. In 1995, strip mining near the town of Schoningen in Germany led to the discovery of 400,000-year-old spears of *Homo erectus* (see Chapter 8). So frequently do construction projects uncover archaeological remains that in many countries, including the United States, projects that require government approval will not be authorized unless measures are first taken to identify and protect archaeological remains on the construction sites. Archaeological surveys in the United States are now routinely carried out as part of the envi-

Sometimes archaeological sites are marked by dramatic ruins, as shown here. This temple stands at the heart of the ancient Maya city of Tikal. Built by piling up rubble and facing it with limestone blocks held together with mortar, it served as the funerary monument of a king, whose body was placed in a tomb beneath the pyramidal base.

ronmental review process for federally funded or licensed construction projects.

Conspicuous sites, such as the great mounds or "tells" of the Middle East, are easy to spot, for the country is open. But it is difficult to locate ruins, even those that are well above ground, where there is a heavy forest cover. Thus, the discovery of archaeological sites is strongly affected by local geography.

Although archaeological sites may be found just about anywhere, the same is not true for fossil localities. One will find fossils only in geological contexts where conditions are known to have been right for fossilization. Once the paleoanthropologist has identified such regions, specific localities are identified in much the same ways as archaeological sites. Indeed, the discovery of ancient stone tools may lead to the discovery of human fossil remains. For example, it was the presence of very crude stone tools in Olduvai Gorge, East Africa, that prompted Mary and Louis Leakey to search there for the human fossils (discussed in Chapters 6 and 7) they eventually found.

Site and Locality Excavation

Before the archaeologist or paleoanthropologist plans an excavation, he or she must ask the question, "Why am I digging?" Then he or she must consider the amount of time, money, and labor that can be committed to the enterprise. The recovery of archaeological and fossil material long ago ceased to be the province of the enlightened amateur, as it once was when any enterprising collector went out to dig for the sake of digging. A modern excavation is carefully planned and rigorously conducted; it should not only shed light on the human past but should also help us to understand cultural and evolutionary processes in general.

ARCHAEOLOGICAL EXCAVATION

Once a site is located that is likely to contribute to the solution of some important research problem, the next step is to plan and carry out excavation. To begin, the land is cleared, and the places to be excavated are plotted. This is usually done by means of a **grid system.**

Grid system. A system for recording data from an archaeological excavation.

Anthropology Applied

Cultural Resource Management

In June 1979, on a knoll next to a river not far from Lake Champlain, a survey crew working for Peter A. Thomas of the University of Vermont's Consulting Archaeology Program discovered archaeological materials unlike any found before in the region. The following June, Thomas returned to the site with a crew of five in order to excavate a portion of it. What they found were the remains of an 8,000-year-old hunting-and-fishing camp that had been occupied for up to a few months in the spring or fall by perhaps one or two families. From the site they recovered a distinctive tool inventory never recognized before, as well as data related to hunting and fishing subsistence practices, butchery or hide processing, cooking, tool manufacture, and a possible shelter. Because many archaeologists had previously believed the region to be devoid of human occupation 8,000 years ago, recovery of these data was especially important.

What sets this work apart from traditional archaeological research is that it was conducted as part of cultural resource management activities required by state and federal laws to preserve important aspects of the country's prehistoric and historic heritage. In this case, the Vermont Agency of Transportation planned to replace an inadequate highway bridge with a new one. Because the project was partially funded by the U.S. government, steps had to be taken to iden-

tify and protect any significant prehistoric or historic resources that might be adversely affected. To do so, the Vermont Agency of Transportation hired Thomas—first to see if such resources existed in the project area, and then to retrieve data from the endangered portions of the one site that was found. As a result, an important contribution was made to our knowledge of the prehistory of northeastern North America.

Since passage of the Historic Preservation Act of 1966, the National Environmental Policy Act of 1969, and the Archaeological and Historical Preservation Act of 1974, the field of cultural resource management has flourished. Today, most archaeological fieldwork in the United States is carried out as cultural resource management. Consequently, many archaeologists are employed by such agencies as the Army Corps of Engineers, the National Park Service, the U.S. Forest Service, and the U.S. Soil and Conservation Service to assist in the preservation, restoration, and salvage of archaeological resources. Archaeologists are also employed by state historic preservation agencies. Finally, they do a considerable amount of consulting work for engineering firms to help them prepare environmental impact statements. Some of these archaeologists, like Thomas, operate out of universities and colleges, while others are on the staffs of independent consulting firms.

The surface of the site is divided into squares, each square being numbered and marked with stakes. Each object found may then be located precisely in the square from which it came. (Remember, in archaeology, context is everything!) The starting point of a grid system may be a large rock, the edge of a stone wall, or an iron rod sunk into the ground. The starting point is also known as the reference or **datum point.** At a large site covering several square miles, this kind of grid system is not feasible because of the large size of the ruins. In such cases, the

plotting may be done in terms of individual structures, numbered according to the square of a "giant grid" in which they are found (Figure 2.1).

In a gridded site, each square is dug separately with great care. Trowels are used to scrape the soil, and screens are used to sift all the loose soils so that even the smallest artifacts, such as flint chips or beads, are recovered.

A technique employed when looking for very fine objects, such as fish scales or very small bones, is called **flotation.** Flotation consists of immersing soil in water,

---

Datum point.   The starting, or reference, point for a grid system.   •   **Flotation.**   An archeological technique employed to recover very tiny objects by immersion of soil samples in water to separate heavy from light particles.

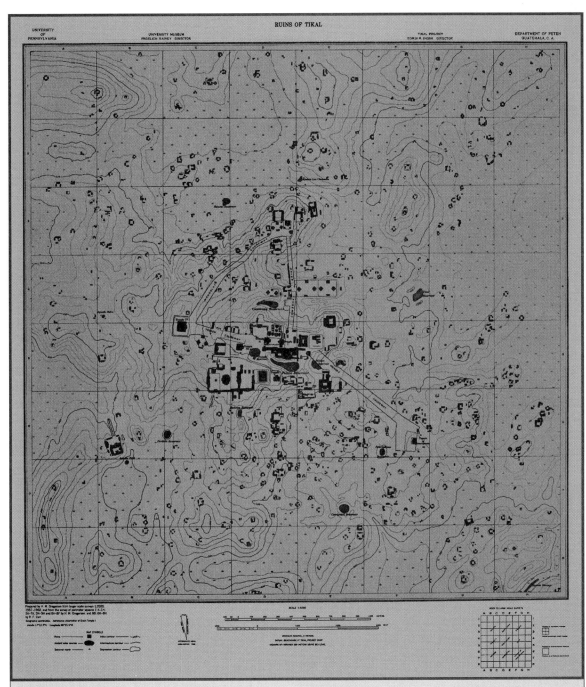

FIGURE 2.1

At large sites covering several square miles, a giant grid is contructed, as shown in this map of the center of the ancient Maya city of Tikal. Each square of the grid is one-quarter of a square kilometer; individual structures are numbered according to the square in which they are found. The temple shown on page 43 can be located near the center of the map, on the east edge of the Great Plaza.

To recover very small objects easily missed in excavation, archaeologists routinely screen the earth they remove.

causing the particles to separate. Some will float, others will sink to the bottom, and the remains can be easily retrieved. If the site is **stratified**—that is, if the remains lie in layers one upon the other—each layer, or stratum, will be dug separately. Each layer, having been laid down during a particular span of time, will contain artifacts deposited at the same time and belonging to the same culture. Culture change can be traced through the order in which artifacts were deposited. But, say archaeologists

This photo shows a section excavated through a building at the ancient Maya site of Tikal and illustrates stratigraphy. Inside the building's base are the remains of walls and floors for earlier buildings. Oldest are the innermost and deepest walls and floors. As time wore on, the Maya periodically demolished upper portions of older buildings, the remains of which were buried beneath new construction.

Frank Hole and Robert F. Heizer, "because of difficulties in analyzing stratigraphy, archaeologists must use the greatest caution in drawing conclusions. Almost all interpretations of time, space, and culture contexts depend on stratigraphy. The refinements of laboratory techniques for analysis are wasted if archaeologists cannot specify the stratigraphic position of their artifacts."[3] If no stratification is present, then the archaeologist digs by arbitrary levels. Each square must be dug so that its edges and profiles are straight; walls between squares are often left standing to serve as visual correlates of the grid system.

EXCAVATION OF FOSSILS

Excavating for fossils is in many ways like archaeological excavation, although there are some differences. The paleoanthropologist must be particularly skilled in the techniques of geology, or else have ready access to geological expertise, because a fossil is of little value unless its temporal place in the sequence of rocks that contain it can be determined. In addition, the paleoanthropologist must be able to identify the fossil-laden rocks, their deposition, and other geological details. In order to provide all the necessary expertise, paleoanthropological expeditions these days generally are made up of teams of experts in various fields in addition to physical anthropology. A great deal of skill and caution is required to remove a

[3]Hole, F., & Heizer, R. F. (1969). *An introduction to prehistoric archeology* (p. 113). New York: Holt, Rinehart & Winston.

Stratified.   Layered; said of archaeological sites where the remains lie in layers, one upon another.

fossil from its burial place without damage. An unusual combination of tools and materials is usually contained in the kit of the paleoanthropologist—pickaxes, enamel coating, burlap for bandages, and plaster of paris.

To remove newly discovered bones, the paleoanthropologist begins uncovering the specimen, using pick and shovel for initial excavation, then small camel-hair brushes and dental picks to remove loose and easily detachable debris surrounding the bones. Once the entire specimen has been uncovered (a process that may take days of back-breaking, patient labor), the bones are covered with shellac and tissue paper to prevent cracking and damage during further excavation and handling.

Both the fossil and the earth immediately surrounding it, or the matrix, are prepared for removal as a single block. The bones and matrix are cut out of the earth (but not removed), and more shellac is applied to the entire block to harden it. The bones are covered with burlap bandages dipped in plaster of paris. Then the entire block is enclosed in plaster and burlap bandages, perhaps splinted with tree branches, and allowed to dry overnight. After it has hardened, the entire block is carefully removed from the earth, ready for packing and transport to a laboratory. Before leaving the discovery area, the investigator makes a thorough sketch map of the terrain and pinpoints the find on geological maps to aid future investigators.

State of Preservation of Archaeological and Fossil Evidence

What is recovered in the course of excavation depends upon the nature of the remains as much as upon the excavator's digging skills. Inorganic materials such as stone and metal are more resistant to decay than organic ones such as wood and bone. Often an archaeologist comes upon an assemblage—a collection of artifacts—made of durable inorganic materials, such as stone tools, and traces of organic ones long since decomposed, such as woodwork (Figure 2.2), textiles, or food.

State of preservation is affected by climate; under favorable climatic conditions, even the most perishable objects may survive over vast periods of time. For example, predynastic Egyptian burials consisting of shallow pits in the sand often yield well-preserved corpses. Because these bodies were buried long before mummification was ever practiced, their preservation can only be the result of rapid desiccation in the very warm, dry climate. The tombs of dynastic Egypt often contain wooden furniture, textiles, flowers, and papyri barely touched by time, seemingly as fresh looking as they were when deposited in the tomb 3,000 years ago—a consequence of the dryness of the atmosphere.

The dryness of certain caves is also a factor in the preservation of fossilized human or animal feces. Human feces are a source of information on prehistoric foods and

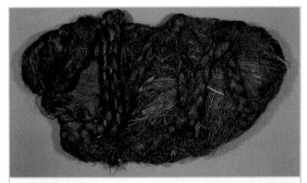

This sandal, made of plant fibers, is over 8,000 years old, making it North America's oldest known footwear. In most soils, objects made of such materials would have long since decayed. This one survived only because of the dry condition of the cave (Arnold Research Cave in Missouri) in which it was found.

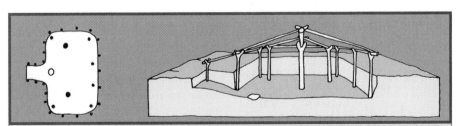

FIGURE 2.2

ALTHOUGH THE WOODEN POSTS OF A HOUSE MAY HAVE LONG SINCE DECAYED, THEIR POSITIONS MAY STILL BE MARKED BY DISCOLORATION OF THE SOIL. THE PLAN SHOWN ON THE LEFT, OF AN ANCIENT POSTHOLE PATTERN AND DEPRESSION AT SNAKETOWN, ARIZONA, PERMITS THE HYPOTHETICAL HOUSE RECONSTRUCTION ON THE RIGHT.

can be analyzed for dietary remains. From such analysis archaeologists can determine not only what the inhabitants ate but also how the food was prepared. Because many sources of food are available only in certain seasons, it is even possible to tell the time of year in which the food was eaten and the excrement deposited.

Certain climates can soon obliterate all evidence of organic remains. Maya ruins found in the very warm and moist tropical rain forests of Mesoamerica are often in a state of collapse—notwithstanding that many are massive structures of stone—as a result of the pressure exerted upon them by the heavy forest vegetation. The rain and humidity soon destroy almost all traces of woodwork, textiles, or basketry. Fortunately, impressions of these artifacts can sometimes be preserved in plaster, and some objects made of wood or plant fibers are depicted in stone carvings and pottery figurines. Thus, even in the face of complete decay of organic substances, something may still be learned about them.

The cultural practices of ancient humans may also account for the preservation of archaeological remains. The ancient Egyptians believed that eternal life could be achieved only if the dead person were buried with his or her worldly possessions. Hence, their tombs are usually filled with a wealth of artifacts. Many skeletal remains of Neandertals (Chapter 9) are known because they practiced burial, perhaps because they, too, believed in some

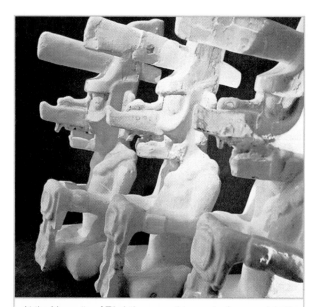

At the Maya site of Tikal, these manikin sceptre figures originally made of wood were recovered from a king's tomb by pouring plaster into a cavity in the soil, left when the original organic material decayed.

sort of afterlife. By contrast, skeletal remains of pre-Neandertal peoples are rare and when found usually consist of mere fragments rather than complete skeletons.

SORTING OUT THE EVIDENCE

It cannot be stressed too strongly that the value of archaeological materials is virtually destroyed if an accurate and detailed record of the excavations is not kept. As one eminent anthropologist has put it:

> The fundamental premise of excavation is that all digging is destructive, even that done by experts. The archaeologist's primary responsibility, therefore, is to record a site for posterity as it is dug because there are no second chances.[4]

Excavation records include a scale map of all the features, the stratification of each excavated square, a description of the exact location and depth of every artifact or bone unearthed, and photographs and scale drawings of the objects. This is the only way archaeological evidence can later be pieced together so as to arrive at a plausible reconstruction of a culture. Although the archaeologist may be interested only in certain kinds of remains, every aspect of the site must be recorded, whether it is relevant to the particular investigation or not, because such evidence may be useful to others and would otherwise be permanently lost. One must remember that archaeological sites are nonrenewable resources, and that their destruction, whether by proper excavation or by looting, is permanent.

After photographs and scale drawings are made, the materials recovered are processed in the laboratory. In the case of fossils, the block in which they have been removed from the field is cut open, and the fossil is separated from the matrix. Like the initial removal from the earth, this is a long, painstaking job involving a great deal of skill and special tools. This task may be done with hammer and chisel, dental drills, rotary grinders, or pneumatic chisels, and, in the case of very small pieces, with awls and tiny needles under a microscope.

Chemicals, such as hydrochloric and hydrofluoric acids, are also used in the separation process to dissolve the surrounding matrix. Some fossils require processing by other methods. For example, precise identification

[4]Fagan, B. M. (1995). *People of the earth* (8th ed., p. 19). New York: HarperCollins.

This ancient Sumerian Tell in Iraq has been so extensively looted that it resembles a moonscape. Such looting destroys irreplaceable evidence.

can be obtained by examining thin, almost transparent strips of some fossils under a microscope. Casts of the insides of skulls (**endocasts**) are made by filling the skull wall with an acid-resistant material, then removing the wall with acid. A skull may be cleaned out and the inside painted with latex. After the latex hardens, it is removed in a single piece, revealing indirect evidence of brain shape and outer appearance. Such endocasts are helpful in determining the size and complexity of ancient brains.

Archaeologists, as a rule of thumb, plan on at least 3 hours of laboratory work for each hour of fieldwork. In the lab, artifacts that have been recovered must first be cleaned and catalogued—often a tedious and time-consuming job—before they are ready for analysis. From the shapes of the artifacts and from the traces of manufacture and wear, archaeologists can usually determine their function. For example, the Russian archaeologist S. A. Semenov devoted many years to the study of prehistoric technology. In the case of a flint tool used as a scraper, he was able to determine, by examining the wear patterns of the tool under a microscope, that the prehistoric individuals who used it began to scrape from right to left and then scraped from left to right, and in

so doing avoided straining the muscles of the hand.[5] From the work of Semenov and others, we now know that most stone tools were made by right-handed individuals, a fact that has implications for brain structure (see also Figure 2.3).

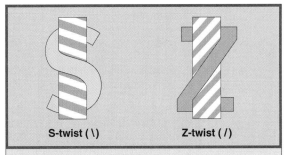

S-twist (\ )   Z-twist (/)

FIGURE 2.3

IN NORTHERN NEW ENGLAND, PREHISTORIC POTTERY WAS OFTEN DECORATED BY IMPRESSING THE DAMP CLAY WITH A CORD-WRAPPED STICK. EXAMINATION OF CORD IMPRESSIONS REVEALS THAT COASTAL PEOPLE TWISTED FIBERS USED TO MAKE CORDAGE TO THE LEFT (Z-TWIST), WHILE THOSE LIVING INLAND DID THE OPPOSITE (S-TWIST). THE NONFUNCTIONAL DIFFERENCES REFLECT MOTOR HABITS SO DEEPLY INGRAINED AS TO SEEM COMPLETELY NATURAL TO THE CORDAGE MAKERS. FROM THIS, WE MAY INFER TWO DISTINCTIVELY DIFFERENT POPULATIONS.

---

[5]Semenov, S. A. (1964). *Prehistoric technology.* New York: Barnes & Noble.

Endocast.   A cast of the inside of a skull; helps determine the size and shape of the brain.

Analysis of vegetable and animal remains provides clues about the environment and the economic activities of the occupants of a site (Figure 2.4). Such analysis may help clarify peoples' relationship to their environment and its influence upon the development of their **technology**— the knowledge they employ to make and use objects. For example, we know that the people responsible for Serpent Mound in Ontario, Canada (a mound having the form of a serpent, consisting of burials and discarded shells), were there only in the spring and early summer, when they came to collect shellfish and perform their annual burial rites; apparently they moved elsewhere at the beginning of summer to pursue other seasonal subsistence activities. Archaeologists have inferred that the mound was unoccupied in winter, because this is the season when deer shed their antlers, yet no deer antlers were found on the site. Nor were duck bones found, and so archaeologists conclude that the mound was also unoccupied in the fall, when ducks stopped on their migratory route southward to feed on the wild rice that grew in the region.

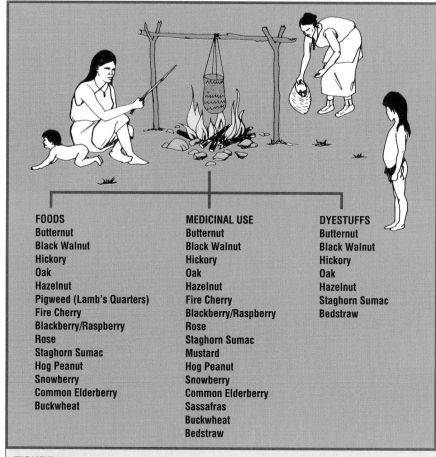

FOODS	MEDICINAL USE	DYESTUFFS
Butternut	Butternut	Butternut
Black Walnut	Black Walnut	Black Walnut
Hickory	Hickory	Hickory
Oak	Oak	Oak
Hazelnut	Hazelnut	Hazelnut
Pigweed (Lamb's Quarters)	Fire Cherry	Staghorn Sumac
Fire Cherry	Blackberry/Raspberry	Bedstraw
Blackberry/Raspberry	Rose	
Rose	Staghorn Sumac	
Staghorn Sumac	Mustard	
Hog Peanut	Hog Peanut	
Snowberry	Snowberry	
Common Elderberry	Common Elderberry	
Buckwheat	Sassafras	
	Buckwheat	
	Bedstraw	

FIGURE 2.4

PLANT REMAINS RECOVERED FROM HEARTHS USED BY PEOPLE BETWEEN 1,000 AND 2,000 YEARS AGO AT AN ARCHAEOLOGICAL SITE IN VERMONT MAY HAVE BEEN UTILIZED AS SHOWN HERE, BASED ON OUR KNOWLEDGE OF HOW THE SAME PLANTS WERE USED BY INDIANS IN THE REGION WHEN FIRST ENCOUNTERED BY EUROPEANS. OCCUPATION OF THE SITE MUST HAVE BEEN IN THE SUMMER AND FALL, THE SEASONS WHEN THESE PLANTS ARE AVAILABLE.

Technology.   The knowledge that people employ to make and use objects.

Analysis of human skeletal material also provides important insights into ancient peoples' diets. Microscopic wear patterns on teeth, for example, may reveal whether abrasive plants were important foods. Similarly, people who eat more plants than meat will have a higher ratio of strontium to calcium in their bones. At the ancient Maya city of Tikal, analysis of human skeletons showed that elite members of society had access to better diets than lower ranking members of society, allowing them to reach their full growth potential with greater regularity. Important insights into life expectancy, mortality, and health status also emerge from the study of human skeletal remains. Unfortunately, such studies have become more difficult to carry out, especially in the United States, as Native American communities demand (and federal law requires) the return of skeletons from archaeological excavations for reburial. Archaeologists find themselves in something of a quandary over this requirement; as scientists, they know the importance of the information that can be gleaned from studies of human skeletons, but as anthropologists, they are bound to respect the feelings of those whose ancestors those skeletons represent. Currently (as illustrated in the Original Study in this chapter), archaeologists are consulting with representatives of Native American communities to work out procedures with which both parties can live.

Dating the Past

With accurate and detailed records of their excavations in hand, archaeologists and paleoanthropologists are able to deal with a question crucial to their research: the question of age. As we have seen, without knowledge of which materials are contemporary, older, or younger, no meaningful analysis is possible. How, then, are objects and events from the past reliably dated? Because archaeologists and paleoanthropologists deal so often with peoples and events in times far removed from our own, the calendar of historic times is of little use to them. Therefore, they must rely on two kinds of dating: relative and "absolute." **Relative dating** consists simply of finding out if an event or object is younger or older than another. **"Absolute"** or (more properly) **chronometric dates** are dates based upon solar years and are reckoned in "years

Some ancient societies devised precise ways of recording dates that archaeologists have been able to correlate with our own calendar. Here is the tomb of an important ruler, Stormy Sky, at the ancient Maya city of Tikal. The glyphs painted on the wall give the date of the burial in the Maya calendar, which is the same as March 18th, A.D. 457, in our calendar.

before the present" (B.P., with "present" defined as A.D. 1950). Many relative and chronometric techniques are available; here, there is space to discuss only the ones most often relied upon (others will be touched on as necessary in succeeding chapters). Ideally, archaeologists try to utilize as many methods as are appropriate, given the materials available to work with and the funds at their disposal. By doing so, they significantly reduce the risk of arriving at erroneous dates.

Relative dating.   In archaeology and paleoanthropology, designating an event, object, or fossil as being older or younger than another. • **"Absolute" or chronometric dates.**   In archaeology and paleoanthropology, dates for archaeological materials based on solar years, centuries, or other units of absolute time.

Methods of Relative Dating

Of the many relative dating techniques available, **stratigraphy** is probably the most reliable. Stratigraphy is based on the simple principle that the oldest layer, or stratum, was deposited first (it is the deepest) whereas the newest layer was deposited last (in undisturbed situations, it lies at the top). Therefore, in an archaeological site the evidence is usually deposited in chronological order. The lowest stratum contains the oldest artifacts and/or fossils, whereas the uppermost stratum contains the most recent ones. Thus, even in the absence of precise dates, one knows the *relative* age of objects in one stratum compared with the ages of those in other strata.

Another method of relative dating is the **fluorine test.** It is based on the fact that the amount of fluorine deposited in bones is proportional to their age. The oldest bones contain the greatest amount of fluorine, and vice versa. The fluorine test is useful in dating bones that cannot be ascribed with certainty to any particular stratum and cannot be dated according to the stratigraphic method. A shortcoming of this method is that the rate of fluorine formation is not constant, but varies from region to region.

Relative dating can also be done on the evidence of botanical and animal remains. A common method, known as **palynology,** involves the study of pollen grains. The kind of pollen found in any geologic stratum depends on the kind of vegetation that existed at the time that stratum was deposited. A site or locality can therefore be dated by determining what kind of pollen was found associated with it. In addition, palynology is also an important technique for reconstructing past environments in which people lived.

Another method, involving faunal analysis, relies on our knowledge of paleontology. Sites containing the bones of extinct animal species are usually older than sites in which the remains of these animals are absent. Very early North American Indian sites have yielded the remains of mastodons and mammoths—animals now extinct—and on this basis the sites can be dated to a time before these animals died out, roughly 10,000 years ago.

Even in the absence of extinct animal remains, faunal assemblages may provide clues to dating. Since the end of the Ice Age, climates have continued to change, in response to natural cycles as well as human activity. The resultant changes in ecology are reflected in the kinds of animal remains to be found. As one learns the sequence of changes, the presence or absence of particular animal species can give at least an approximate age for associated archaeological materials.

Methods of Chronometric Dating

One of the most widely used methods of "absolute" or chronometric dating is **radiocarbon analysis.** It is based on the fact that all living organisms absorb radioactive carbon (known as carbon 14), maintaining equilibrium with the level of this isotope in the atmosphere, and that this absorption ceases at the time of death. It is possible to measure in the laboratory the amount of radioactive carbon left in even a few milligrams of a given organic substance, because radioactive substances break down or decay slowly and at a constant rate over a fixed period of time. Carbon 14 begins to disintegrate, returning to nitrogen 14, emitting radioactive (beta) particles in the process. At death, about 15 beta radiations per minute per gram of material are emitted. The rate of decay is known as "half-life," and the half-life of carbon 14 is 5,730 years. This means that it takes 5,730 years for one-half of the original amount of carbon 14 to decay into nitrogen 14. Beta radiation will be about 7.5 counts per minute per gram. In another 5,730 years, one-half of this amount of carbon 14 will also have decayed. In other words, after 11,460 years, only one-fourth of the original amount of carbon 14 will be present. Thus the age of an organic substance such as charcoal, wood, shell, or bone can be measured by counting the beta rays emitted by the remaining carbon 14. The radiocarbon method can adequately date organic materials up to 70,000 years old and is the standard method of dating such materials. Of course, one has to be sure that the association between organic remains and archaeological materials is valid. For example, charcoal found on a site may have gotten there from a recent

---

Stratigraphy.　　In archaeology and paleoanthropology, the most reliable method of relative dating by means of strata. • **Fluorine test.**　　In archaeology or paleoanthropology, a technique for relative dating based on the fact that the amount of fluorine in bones is proportional to their age. • **Palynology.**　　In archaeology and paleoanthropology, a method of relative dating based on changes in fossil pollen over time. • **Radiocarbon analysis.**　　In archaeology and paleoanthropology, a technique for chronometric dating based on measuring the amount of radioactive carbon (C-14) left in organic materials found in archaeological sites.

forest fire, rather than more ancient activity; or wood used to make something by the people who lived at a site may have been retrieved from some older context.

Because there is always a certain amount of error involved, radiocarbon dates are not as absolute as is sometimes thought. This is why any stated date always has a plus-or-minus (±) factor attached to it. For example, a date of 5,200 ± 120 years ago means that there is a 2 out of 3 chance that the true date falls somewhere within the 240 years between 5,080 and 5,320 radiocarbon years ago. The qualification "radiocarbon years" is necessary, because we have discovered that radiocarbon years are not precisely equivalent to calendar years.

The discovery that radiocarbon years are not precisely equivalent to calendar years was made possible by another method of "absolute" dating, **dendrochronology.** Originally devised for dating Pueblo Indian sites in the North American Southwest, this method is based on the fact that in the right kind of climate, trees add one (and only one) new growth ring to their trunks every year (Figure 2.5). The rings vary in thickness, depending upon the amount of rainfall received in a year, so that climatic fluctuation is registered in the growth ring. By taking a sample of wood, such as a beam from a Pueblo Indian house, and by comparing its pattern of rings with those in the trunk of a tree known to be as old as the artifact, archaeologists can date the archaeological material.

Dendrochronology is applicable only to wooden objects. Furthermore, it can be used only in regions in which trees of great age, such as the giant sequoias and the bristlecone pine, are known to grow. On the other hand, radiocarbon dating of wood from bristlecone pines that have been dated by dendrochronology allows us to correct carbon-14 dates so as to bring them into agreement with calendar dates.

Potassium-argon analysis, another commonly used method of "absolute" dating, is based on a technique similar to that of radiocarbon analysis. Following intense heating, as from a volcanic eruption, radioactive potassium decays at a known rate to form argon, any previously existing argon having been released by the heating. The half-life of radioactive potassium is 1.3 billion years. Deposits that are millions of years old can now be dated by measuring the ratio of potassium to argon in a given rock. Volcanic debris, such as at Olduvai Gorge and other localities in East Africa, is routinely dated by potassium-argon analysis; thus we know when the volcanic eruption occurred. If fossils or artifacts are found sandwiched between layers of volcanic ash, as they are at Olduvai and other sites in East Africa, they can therefore be dated with some precision. But as with radiocarbon dates, there are limits to that precision, and potassium-argon dates are always stated with a plus-or-minus margin of error attached.

Amino acid racemization dating, yet another chronometric technique, is of potential importance

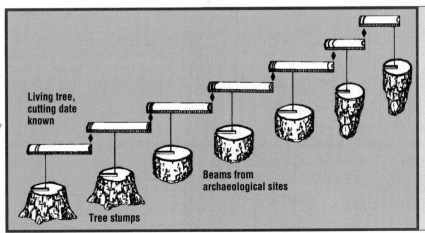

Living tree, cutting date known

Tree stumps

Beams from archaeological sites

FIGURE 2.5

CHRONOMETRIC DATING BASED ON TREE RINGS IS CALLED *DENDROCHRONOLOGY.* STARTING WITH A SAMPLE OF KNOWN AGE, RING PATTERNS TOWARD THE INNER PART ARE MATCHED WITH THOSE FROM THE OUTER PART OF THE OLDER SAMPLE, AND SO ON, BACK IN TIME.

Dendrochronology.   In archaeology, a method of chronometric dating based on the number of rings of growth found in a tree trunk. • **Potassium-argon analysis.**   In archaeology and paleoanthropology, a technique for chronometric dating that measures the ratio of radioactive potassium to argon in volcanic debris associated with human remains. • **Amino acid racemization dating.**   In archaeology and paleoanthropology, a technique for chronometric dating that measures the ratio of right- to left-handed amino acids.

because it bridges a time gap between the effective ranges of the radiocarbon and potassium-argon methods. It is based on the fact that amino acids trapped in organic materials gradually change, or "racemize" after death, from left-handed forms to right-handed forms. Thus, the ratio of left- to right-handed forms should indicate the specimen's age. Unfortunately, in substances like bone, moisture and acids in the soil can leach out the amino acids, thereby introducing a serious source of error. However, ostrich eggshells have proved immune to this problem, the amino acids being so effectively locked up in a tight mineral matrix that they are preserved for thousands of years. Because ostrich eggs were widely used as food, and the shells as containers in Africa and the Middle East, they provide a powerful means of dating sites of the middle part of the Old Stone Age (Paleolithic), between 40,000 and 180,000 years ago.

Radiocarbon, potassium-argon, and amino acid racemization dating are only three of several high-tech dating methods that have been developed in the past few decades. Radiocarbon and potassium-argon, in particular, are the chronometric methods most heavily relied on by archaeologists and paleoanthropologists; nevertheless, other methods are increasingly used as a check on

accuracy and to supplement dates determined by other means. To cite one example, a technique called **electron spin resonance** measures the trapped electron population in bone or shell (the number of trapped electrons indicates the specimen's age). Because electron spin resonance dates derived from an important Middle Paleolithic skull from Qafzeh, Israel (discussed in Chapter 9), agree with those based on amino acid racemization, we can have confidence that the dating is correct. Because other methods of chronometric dating are often complicated, they tend to be expensive; many can be carried out only on specific kinds of materials, and in the case of some, are so new that their reliability is not yet unequivocally established. It is for these reasons that they have not been as widely used as radiocarbon and potassium-argon.

CHANCE AND THE STUDY OF THE PAST

It is important to understand the imperfect nature of the archaeological and fossil records. They are imperfect, first of all, because the chance circumstances of preservation have determined what has and what has not sur-

In this photo, geologist Carl Swisher orients a rock sample for paleomagnetic dating. This method of dating is based on the fact that the earth's magnetic pole has shifted over time. For example, magnetically charged particles in sediments between 1.8 and 1.6 million years old document a reversal, and fossils found in such sediments can be dated accordingly.

Electron spin resonance.   In archaeology and paleoanthropology, a technique for chronometric dating that measures the number of trapped electrons in bone or shell.

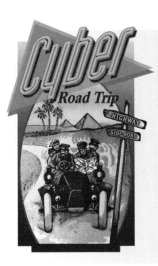

HIGHWAY 1

Visit the award-winning interactive Web site of the University of Pennsylvania's Museum of Archaeology and Anthropology and experience the museum's fabulous collections. You can tour everything from virtual excavations being conducted by Penn faculty in places such as Mesoamerica and Central Asia, to the treasures housed in the Egyptian gallery, to virtual exhibits on the origins and ancient history of wine. www.upenn.edu/museum/

HIGHWAY 2

A trip to this site goes underwater to visit the State of Florida's Underwater Archaeological Preserves. Visit the shipwrecked remains of battleships, steamers, and sailboats. Each shipwreck site contains a location map and a complete site plan as well as ways to become involved in Florida's Underwater Archaeology Program. http://dhr.dos.state.fl.us/bar/uap/

vived the ravages of time. Thus, cultures must be reconstructed on the basis of incomplete and, possibly, unrepresentative samples of artifacts. The problems are further compounded by the large role chance continues to play in the discovery of prehistoric remains. Therefore, one must always be cautious when trying to interpret the human past. No matter how elegant a particular theory may be about what happened in the past, new evidence may at any time force its reexamination and modification, or even rejection, in favor of some better theory.

CHAPTER SUMMARY

Archaeology and physical anthropology, though they do not neglect the present, are the two branches of anthropology most involved in the study of the human past. Archaeologists study material remains to describe and explain human behavior; physical anthropologists called paleoanthropologists study fossil remains to understand and explain the processes at work in human biological evolution. Each specialty contributes to the other's objectives, as well as its own, and the two share many methods of data recovery.

Artifacts are objects fashioned or altered by humans, such as a flint chip, a pottery vessel, or even a house. A fossil is any trace of an organism of past geological time that has been preserved in the earth's crust. Fossilization typically involves the hard parts of an organism and may take place through freezing in ice, preservation in bogs or tar pits, immersion in water, or inclusion in rock deposits. Fossilization is most apt to occur among animals and other organisms that live in or near water because of the likelihood that their corpses will be buried and preserved on sea, lake, and river bottoms. On land, conditions in caves or near active volcanic activity may be conducive to fossilization.

Places containing archaeological remains of previous human occupation are known as sites. Sometimes human fossils are present at archaeological sites, but they may occur by themselves at fossil localities. Sites and localities are generally located by a survey of a region. While fossil localities are revealed by the presence of fossils, archaeological sites are revealed by the presence of artifacts. Irregularities of the ground surface, unusual soil discoloration, and unexpected variations in vegetation type and coloring may also indicate the location of a site. Ethnohistorical data—maps, documents, and folklore—may provide further clues to the location of archaeological sites. Sometimes both fossils and archaeological remains are discovered accidentally, for example, in plowing, quarrying, or in building construction.

Once a site or locality has been selected for excavation, the area is divided and carefully marked with a grid system; the starting point of the dig is called the datum point. Each square within the grid is carefully excavated, and any archaeological or fossil remains are recovered through employment of various tools and screens; for very fine objects, the method of flotation is employed. The location of each artifact when found must be carefully noted. Once excavated, artifacts and fossils undergo further cleaning and preservation in the laboratory with the use of specialized tools and chemicals.

The durability of archaeological evidence depends upon climate and the nature of the artifacts. Inorganic materials are more resistant to decay than organic ones. However, given a very dry climate, even organic materials may be well preserved. Warm, moist climates as well as thick vegetation act to decompose organic material quickly, and even inorganic material may suffer from the effects of humidity and vegetation growth. The durability of archaeological evidence is also dependent upon the social customs of ancient people.

Because excavation in fact destroys a site, the archaeologist must maintain a thorough record in the form of maps, descriptions, scale drawings, and photographs of every aspect of the excavation. All artifacts must be cleaned and classified before being sent to the laboratory for analysis. Often the shape and markings of artifacts can determine their function, and the analysis of vegetable and animal remains may provide information.

There are two kinds of methods for dating archaeological and fossil remains. Relative dating is a method of determining the age of objects relative to one another and includes the method of stratigraphy, based on the position of the artifact or fossil in relation to different layers of soil deposits. The fluorine test is based on the determination of the amount of fluorine deposited in the bones. The analysis of floral remains (including palynology) and faunal deposits is also widely employed. Methods of "absolute," or chronometric, dating include radiocarbon analysis, which measures the amount of carbon 14 that remains in organic objects; potassium-argon analysis, which measures the percentage of radioactive potassium that has decayed to argon in volcanic material; dendrochronology, dating based upon tree rings; and amino acid racemization, based on changes from left- to right-handed amino acids in organic materials, especially eggshells. Other chronometric methods exist, such as electron spin resonance, but are not as widely used, because of limited applicability, difficulty of application, expense, or (as-yet) unproven reliability.

CLASSIC READINGS

Fagan, B. M. (1998). *People of the earth: An introduction to world prehistory* (9th ed.). New York: Longman.

There are a number of good texts that, like this one, try to summarize the findings of archaeologists on a worldwide scale. This book, being one of the more recent ones, is reasonably up to date.

Feder, K. L. (1999). *Frauds, myths, and mysteries* (3rd ed.). Mountain View, CA: Mayfield.

This very readable book is written to enlighten readers about the many pseudo-scientific and even crackpot theories about past cultures that all too often have been presented to the public as "solid" archaeology.

Joukowsky, M. (1980). *A complete field manual of archaeology: Tools and techniques of fieldwork for archaeologists.* Englewood Cliffs, NJ: Prentice-Hall.

This book, encyclopedic in its coverage, explains for the novice and professional alike all of the methods and techniques used by archaeologists in the field. Two concluding chapters discuss fieldwork opportunities and financial aid for archaeological research.

Sharer, R. J., & Ashmore, W. (1993). *Archaeology: Discovering our past* (2nd ed.). Palo Alto, CA: Mayfield.

One of the best presentations of the body of method, technique, and theory that most archaeologists accept as fundamental to their discipline. The authors confine themselves to the operational modes, guiding strategies, and theoretical orientations of anthropological archaeology in a manner well designed to lead the beginner into the discipline.

Shipman, P. (1981). *Life history of a fossil: An introduction to taphonomy and paleoecology.* Cambridge, MA: Harvard University Press.

In order to understand what a fossil has to tell us, one must know how it came to be where the paleoanthropologist found it (taphonomy). In this book, anthropologist-turned-science-writer Pat Shipman explains how animal remains are acted upon and altered from death to fossilization.

Thomas, D. H. (1998). *Archaeology* (3rd ed.). Fort Worth, TX: Harcourt Brace.

Some books tell us how to do archaeology, some tell us what archaeologists have found out, but this one tells us why we do archaeology. It does so in a coherent and thorough way, and Thomas's blend of ideas, quotations, biographies, and case studies makes for interesting reading.

CHAPTER 3

BIOLOGY AND EVOLUTION

Evolution has produced a variety of primates, ranging all the way
from lemurs to humans. Such variety is not the result of progressive
change, but rather the adaptation of organisms to local conditions.
Because these conditions change, essentially at random, so too
do adaptations.

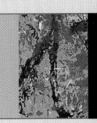

1

WHAT FORCES ARE RESPONSIBLE FOR THE DIVERSITY OF PRIMATES IN THE WORLD TODAY?

Although all primates— lemurs, lorises, tarsiers, monkeys, apes, and humans—share a common ancestry, they have come to differ through the operation of evolutionary forces that have permitted them to adapt to a variety of environments in a variety of ways. Although biologists agree upon the fact of evolution, they are still unraveling the details of how it has proceeded.

2

WHAT IS EVOLUTION?

Biological evolution is descent with modification, as descendant populations come to differ from ancestral ones. Evolution happens as differential reproduction changes the frequency of a population's genetic variants from one generation to another over time.

3

WHAT ARE THE FORCES RESPONSIBLE FOR EVOLUTION?

Evolution works as mutation produces genetic variation, which is acted upon by drift (accidental changes in frequencies of gene variants in a population), gene flow (the introduction of new gene variants from other populations), and natural selection. Natural selection is the adaptive mechanism of evolution, favoring individuals with genetic variants that are adaptive and who produce more offspring than those without.

Humans have long had close contact with other animals. Some—such as dogs, horses, and cows—have lived close to people for so long that little attention is paid to their behavior. We are interested only in how well they do what they were bred for—companionship, racing, milk production, or whatever. Domestic animals are so dependent on humans that they have lost many of the behavioral traits of their wild ancestors. Except to a small child, perhaps, and a dairy farmer, a cow is not a very interesting animal to watch.

By contrast, wild animals, especially exotic ones, have always fascinated people, as the popularity of circuses and zoos attests. In cultures very different from those of the industrialized countries of the world—those of some American Indians, for example—people can have a special relationship with particular animals, believing their fates to be intertwined. Such companion animals may be called upon for assistance to serve as messengers, or the person may be able to transfer his or her state of being into the animal's body.

A curious feature of this interest is the desire of humans to see animals as mirror images of themselves, a phenomenon known as **anthropomorphism.** Stories in which animals talk, wear clothes, and exhibit human virtues and vices go back to antiquity. Many children today learn of Mickey Mouse or Kermit the Frog and Miss Piggy; the animals created by Walt Disney, Jim Henson, and many others have become an integral part of contemporary North American culture. Occasionally one sees on television trained apes dressed like humans eating at a table, pushing a stroller, or riding a tricycle. They are amusing because they look so "human."

Over the ages, people have trained animals to perform tricks, making them mimic human behavior. But in the Western world people never suspected the full extent of the relationship they have with animals. For centuries, Christianity—the dominant religion of the West—preached that humans and animals were quite separate from one another. Nevertheless, the close biological tie between humans and the other **primates**—the group of animals that, besides humans, includes lemurs, lorises, tarsiers, monkeys, and apes—is now better understood. The diversity of primates existing today is the product of

evolution, defined by Darwin in his most famous book as *descent with modification.* Over time the operation of evolutionary forces permitted primates to adapt to environments in a variety of ways. These evolutionary forces are the subject of this chapter.

THE CLASSIFICATION OF LIVING THINGS

Crucial to our understanding of the place of humanity among the animals was the invention by the 18th-century Swedish naturalist Carl von Linné of a system to classify living things. The problem the Linnaean system addressed was simply to create order in the great mass of confusing biological data that had accumulated in the wake of European exploration and exploitation of foreign lands. At the same time, discovering and naming the multitude of creatures was seen as a means of demonstrating the glory of God's creation.

Von Linné—or Linnaeus, as he is generally called—classified living things on the basis of overall similarities into small groups, or species. Modern classification, while retaining the structure of the Linnaean system, has gone beyond this by distinguishing superficial similarities among organisms—called **analogies**—from basic ones—called **homologies.** The latter are possessed by organisms that share a common ancestry; even though homologous structures may serve different functions (the hand of a human and the front paw of a dog, for instance), they arise in similar fashion and pass through similar stages in embryonic development prior to their ultimate differentiation. By contrast, analogous structures look similar and may serve the same purpose (the wings of birds and butterflies, for example), but they are built from different parts, do not pass through similar stages in embryonic development, nor do the organisms share a common ancestry.

On the basis of homologies, as in Linnaeus' original system, groups of like **species** (a species is defined today as a population or group of populations capable of interbreeding that is reproductively isolated from other such populations) are organized into larger, more inclusive groups, called **genera** (the singular term is *genus*). The

---

Anthropomorphism. The ascription of human attributes to nonhuman beings. • **Primates.** The group of mammals that includes lemurs, lorises, tarsiers, monkeys, apes, and humans. • **Evolution.** Descent with modification. • **Analogies.** In biology, structures that are superficially similar; the result of convergent evolution. • **Homologies.** In biology, structures possessed by two different organisms that arise in similar fashion and pass through similar stages during embryonic development. • **Species.** In biology, a population or group of populations that is capable of interbreeding but that is reproductively isolated from other such populations. • **Genera; genus.** In the system of plant and animal classification, a group of like species.

Birds and butterflies exemplify analogy: Both have wings that are used for flight, but the wings are built differently.

characteristics on which Linnaeus based his system were the following:

1. *Body structure:* A Guernsey cow and a Holstein cow are of the same species because they have identical body structure. A cow and a horse do not.

2. *Body function:* Cows and horses bear their young in the same way. Although they are of different species, they are closer than either cows or horses are to chickens, which lay eggs and have no mammary glands.

3. *Sequence of bodily growth:* Both cows and chickens give birth to—or hatch out of the egg—fully formed young. They are therefore more closely related to each other than either one is to the frog, whose tadpoles undergo a series of changes before attaining adult form.

Modern taxonomy (scientific classification) is based on more than body structure, function, and growth. One must also compare chemical reactions of blood, protein structure, and the genetic material itself. Even comparison of parasites is useful, for they tend to show the same degree of relationship as the forms they infest.

Through careful comparison and analysis, Linnaeus and those who have come after him have been able to classify specific animals into a series of larger and more inclusive groups up to the largest and most inclusive of all, the animal kingdom. In Table 3.1 are the main categories of the Linnaean system applied to the classification of the human species, with a few of the more important distinguishing features noted for each category. (Other categories of primates will be dealt with in Chapter 4.)

THE DISCOVERY OF EVOLUTION

As Linnaeus and his contemporaries went about their business of classification, no thought was given to the possibility that species might not be fixed and unchangeable.

An example of homology: Fish have gills but humans do not. Gill structures do develop in the human embryo but then are modified to serve other purposes. From the rudimentary, gill-like structures are built such things as the jaw, bones of the inner ear, thymus, and parathyroid glands.

TABLE 3.1   CLASSIFICATION OF HUMANS

Kingdom	Animalia	Do not make their own food, but depend on intake of living food.
Phylum	Chordata	Have at some stage gill slits as well as **notochord** (a rodlike structure of cartilage) and nerve chord running along the back of the body.
Subphylum*	Vertebrata	Notochord replaced by vertebral column ("backbone") to form internal skeleton along with skull, ribs, and limb bones.
Class	Mammalia	Maintain constant body temperature; young nourished after birth by milk from mother's mammary glands.
Order	Primates	Hands and feet capable of grasping; tendency to erect posture; acute development of vision rather than sense of smell; tendency to large brains.
Superfamily	Hominoidea	Rigid bodies, broad shoulders, and long arms; ability to hang vertically from arms; no tail.
Family	Hominidae	As above but 98% identical at genetic level.
Subfamily	Homininae	Ground-dwelling with bipedal locomotion.
Genus	*Homo*	Large brains; reliance on cultural, as opposed to biological adaption.
Species	*sapiens*	Brains of modern size; relatively small faces.

*Most categories can be expanded or narrowed by adding the prefix "sub" or "super." A family could thus be part of a superfamily, and in turn contain two or more subfamilies.

Rather, species were seen as being just as they had always been since the time of creation. But as the process of classification continued, naturalists became increasingly aware of continuities between different forms of life. At the same time, earth-moving for construction and mining associated with developing industrialism brought to light all sorts of fossils of past life that had to be dealt with. And with industrialization, the idea of progress became ever more prominent in European thought.

In hindsight, it seems inevitable that someone would hit upon the idea of evolution. So it was that, by the start of the 19th century, many naturalists had come to accept the idea that life had evolved, even though they were not clear about how it happened. It remained for Charles Darwin, midway through the century, to discover how evolution worked. Interestingly, he was not alone in his discovery. A Welshman, Alfred Russell Wallace, independently came up with the same idea at the same time. That idea was **natural selection,** and it is based on two observations: All organisms display a range of variation,

As more and more fossils were recovered in the 18th and 19th centuries, it became evident that life forms of past times were not the same as those of the present and that change had occurred.

Natural selection.   The evolutionary process through which factors in the environment exert pressure that favors some individuals over others to produce the next generation. • **Notochord.**   A rodlike structure of cartilage that, in vertebrates, is replaced by the vertebral column.

CHARLES R. DARWIN (1809–1882)

Grandson of Erasmus Darwin (a physician, scientist, poet, and originator of a theory of evolution himself), Charles Darwin began the study of medicine at the University of Edinburgh. Finding himself unfitted for this profession, he then went to Christ's College, Cambridge, to study theology. Upon completion of his studies there, he took the position of naturalist and companion to Captain Fitzroy on the *HMS Beagle,* which was about to embark on an expedition to various poorly mapped parts of the world. The voyage lasted for close to 5 years, taking Darwin along the coasts of South America, over to the Galapagos Islands, across the Pacific to Australia, and then across the Indian and Atlantic oceans back to South America before returning to England. The observations he made on this voyage, his readings of Sir Charles Lyell's *Principles of Geology,* and the arguments he had with the orthodox and dogmatic Fitzroy had a powerful influence on the development of the ideas culminating in Darwin's most famous book, *On the Origin of Species,* which was published in 1859.

Contrary to what many people seem to think, Darwin did not "discover" or "invent" evolution. The general idea of evolution had been put forward by a number of writers, including his grandfather, long before Darwin's time. Nor is evolution a theory, as some people seem to believe, any more than gravity is a theory. To be sure, there are competing theories of gravity—the Newtonian and Einsteinian—that seek to explain its workings, but the evidence in favor of gravity is overwhelming. Similarly, the evidence in favor of evolution is overwhelming, so much so that evolution is now understood in biology as the organizing principle at all levels of life. But, as with gravity, there have been competing theories that seek to explain how evolution works.

Darwin's contribution was one such theory— that of evolution through natural selection. His was the theory that was best able to account both for change within species and for the emergence of new species in purely naturalistic terms. As is usually the case with pioneering ventures, there were weaknesses in Darwin's original theory. Ultimately, however, his basic ideas were vindicated, and modern biology has not only confirmed but (as with all good theories) extended and amplified those ideas. Today, we can say that the evidence in favor of natural selection is about as good as we had for the theory that the earth is spherical, until we were able to put up an astronaut who could see with his own eyes that this indeed is the case.

---

and all have the ability to expand beyond their means of subsistence. It follows that, in their "struggle for existence," organisms with advantageous variations for survival in a particular environment will do better than those without them, thereby reproducing with greater success. Thus, as generation succeeds generation, nature selects the most advantageous variations, and species evolve. So obvious did the idea seem in hindsight that Thomas Huxley, one of the pillars of 19th-century British science, remarked, "How extremely stupid of me not to have thought of that."[1]

If Darwin's idea was so straightforward, why did it arouse such controversy? It wasn't so much that species were no longer seen as changeless entities that were set at the time of divine creation (as Linnaeus and his contemporaries thought); after all, emerging evolutionary ideas recognized that species were not fixed and immutable. But, before Darwin, evolution could still be seen as progressive, leading inexorably and predictably to humans, who stood at the pinnacle. After Darwin, this was no longer possible, as paleontologist Stephen Jay Gould explains in the following Original Study.

---

[1]Quoted in Durant, J. C. (2000, April 23). Everybody into the gene pool. *New York Times Book Review,* p. 11.

Original Study

The Unsettling Nature of Variational Change[2]

The Darwinian principle of natural selection yields temporal change—evolution in the biological definition—by the twofold process of producing copious and undirected variation within a population and then passing along only a biased (selected) portion of this variation to the next generation. In this manner, the variation within a population at any moment can be converted into differences in mean values (average size, average braininess) among successive populations through time. For this fundamental reason, we call such theories of change *variational* as opposed to the more conventional, and more direct, models of *transformational* change imposed by natural laws that mandate a particular trajectory based on inherent (and therefore predictable) properties of substances and environments. (A ball rolling down an inclined plane does not reach the bottom because selection has favored the differential propagation of moving versus stable elements of its totality but because gravity dictates this result when round balls roll down smooth planes.)

To illustrate the peculiar properties of variational theories like Darwin's in an obviously caricatured, but not inaccurate, description: Suppose that a population of elephants inhabits Siberia during a warm interval before the advance of an ice sheet. The elephants vary, at random, and in all directions, in their amount of body hair. As the ice advances and local conditions become colder, elephants with more hair will tend to cope better, by the sheer good fortune of their superior adaptation to changing climates—and they will leave more offpring on average. (This differential reproductive success must be conceived as broadly statistical and not guaranteed in every case: In any generation, the hairiest elephant of all may fall into a crevasse and die.) Because offspring inherit their parents' degree of hairiness, the next generation will contain a higher proportion of more densely clad elephants (who will continue to be favored by natural selection as the climate becomes still colder). This process of increasing hairiness may

continue for many generations, leading to the evolution of woolly mammoths.

This little fable can help us understand how peculiar and how contrary to all traditions of Western thought and explanation the Darwinian theory of evolution, and variational theories of historical change in general, must sound to the common ear. All the odd and fascinating properties of Darwinian evolution—the sensible and explainable but quite unpredictable nature of the outcome (dependent upon complex and contingent changes in local environments), the nonprogressive character of the alteration (adaptive only to these unpredictable local circumstances and not inevitably building a "better" elephant in any cosmic or general sense)—flow from the variational basis of natural selection.

Transformational theories work in a much simpler and more direct manner. If I want to go from A to B, I will have so much less conceptual (and actual) trouble if I can postulate a mechanism that will push me there directly than if I must rely upon the selection of "a few good men" from a random cloud of variation about point A, then constitute a new generation around an average point one step closer to B, then generate a new cloud of random variation about this new point, then select "a few good men" once again from this new array—and then repeat this process over and over until I finally reach B.

When one adds the oddity of variational theories in general to our strong cultural and psychological resistance against their application to our own evolutionary origin (as an unpredictable and not necessary progressive little twig on life's luxuriant tree), then we can better understand why Darwin's revolution surpassed all other scientific discoveries in reformatory power and why so many people still fail to understand, and may even

[2]Gould, S. J. (2000). What does the dreaded "E" word mean, anyway? *Natural History, 109*(1), 34–36.

resist, its truly liberal content. (I must leave the issue of liberation for another time, but once we recognize that the specification of morals and the search for a meaning to our lives cannot be accomplished by scientific study in any case, then Darwin's variational mechanism will no longer seem threatening and may even become liberating in teaching us to look within ourselves for answers to these questions and to abandon a chimerical search for the purpose of our lives, and for the source of our ethical values, in the external workings of nature.)

The End

In order for natural selection to occur, vast time is necessary for gradual changes to accumulate, and it was not until the early 19th century that the idea of vast time took hold as the field of geology developed. It was this that made Darwin and Wallace's formulation possible. Still, there was a problem: No one knew how variation arose in the first place, nor were the mechanisms of heredity understood. This gave Darwin difficulty for the rest of his life, and by the end of his century, Darwin's theory was rejected by many. Ironically, the information he needed was available by 1865, when an obscure monk in what is now the Czech Republic discovered the basic laws of heredity. Even so, it was not until well into the 20th century that genetics and Darwinian theory were reconciled.

HEREDITY

In order to understand how evolution works, one has to have some understanding of the mechanics of heredity, because heritable variation constitutes the raw material for evolution. Our knowledge of the mechanisms of heredity is fairly recent; most of the fruitful research into the molecular level of inheritance has taken place in the past five decades. Although some aspects remain puzzling, the outlines by now are reasonably clear.

The Transmission of Genes

Biologists call the actual units of heredity **genes**, a term that comes from the Greek word for "birth." The presence and activity of genes were originally deduced rather than observed by the Augustine monk, Gregor Mendel, in the 19th century. Working at the time of publication of Darwin's theory of evolution, Mendel sought to answer some of the riddles of heredity by experimenting with garden peas to determine how various traits are passed from one generation to the next. Specifically, he discovered that inheritance was *particulate*, rather than *blending*, as Darwin and many others thought. That is, the units controlling the expression of visible traits retain their separate identities over the generations. This was the basis of Mendel's **law of segregation.** Another of his laws, that of **independent assortment,** was that what we now call genes, controlling different traits, are inherited independently of one another.

In the first half of the 20th century, much was learned about what genes did, but it was not until 1953 that James Watson and Francis Crick discovered that genes are actually portions of molecules of deoxyribonucleic acid, or **DNA.** DNA is a complex molecule with an unusual shape, rather like two strands of a rope twisted around each other. These strands are formed by alternating sugars and phosphates and are connected by four base pairs: adenine, thymine, guanine, and cytosine (usually written as A, T, G, and C). The connections are between complementary bases: A with T and G with C (Figure 3.1). This confers upon genes the unique property of being able to make exact copies of themselves. This happens as a single strand attracts the appropriate bases—A to T, T to A, C to G, and G to C—and forms a new strand. This new strand, by the same process, produces an exact copy of the original. As long as no errors are made in this replication process, new organisms will contain genetic material exactly like that in ancestral organisms.

Genes.   Portions of DNA molecules that direct the synthesis of proteins. DNA molecules have the unique property of being able to produce exact copies of themselves. • **Law of segregation.**   Variants of genes for a particular trait retain their separate identities through the generations. • **Law of independent assortment.** Genes controlling different traits are inherited independently of one another. • **DNA.**   The genetic material, deoxyribonucleic acid; a complex molecule with information to direct the synthesis of proteins. DNA molecules have the unique property of being able to produce exact copies of themselves.

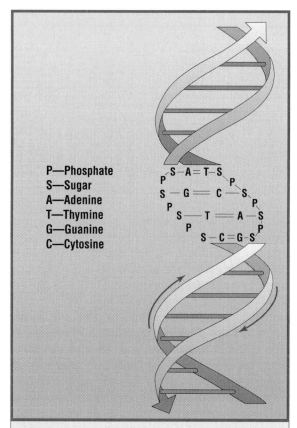

P—Phosphate
S—Sugar
A—Adenine
T—Thymine
G—Guanine
C—Cytosine

FIGURE 3.1

THIS DIAGRAMMATIC REPRESENTATION OF A PORTION OF A DEOXYRIBONUCLEIC ACID (DNA) MOLECULE REPRESENTS THE DOUBLE HELIX STRANDS AND THE CONNECTING NITROGENOUS BASE PAIRS. THE HELIX STRANDS ARE FORMED BY ALTERNATING SUGAR AND PHOSPHATE GROUPS. THE CONNECTION IS PRODUCED BY COMPLEMENTARY BASES—ADENINE WITH THYMINE, CYTOSINE WITH GUANINE—AS SHOWN FOR A SECTION OF THE MOLECULE.

The chemical bases of DNA constitute a recipe for making proteins. As science writer Matt Ridley puts it, "Proteins . . . do almost every chemical, structural, and regulatory thing that is done in the body: they generate energy, fight infection, digest food, form hair, carry oxy-gen, and so on and on."[3] Almost everything in the body is made *of* or *by* proteins.

How is the DNA recipe converted into a protein? Through a somewhat complicated series of intervening steps, each three-base sequence of a gene, called a **codon,** specifies production of a particular amino acid, strings of which build proteins. Because DNA cannot leave the cell's nucleus (Figure 3.2), the directions for a specific protein are first converted into ribonucleic acid or **RNA** in a process called **transcription.** RNA differs from DNA in the structure of its sugar phosphate backbone and in the presence of the base uracil rather than thymine. Next the RNA travels to the **ribosomes,** the cellular structure (see Figure 3.2) where **translation** of the directions found in the codons into proteins occurs. For example, the sequence of CGA specifies the amino acid arginine, GCG alanine, CAG glutamine, and so on. There are 20 amino acids, which are strung together in different amounts and sequences to produce an almost infinite number of different proteins. This is the so-called **genetic code,** and it is the same for every living thing, whether it be a worm or a human being. Some simple living things without nucleated cells, such as the retrovirus that causes AIDS, contain their genetic information only as RNA.

GENES

A gene is a portion of the DNA molecule containing several base pairs that directs the production of a particular protein. Thus, when we speak of the gene for a human blood type in the A-B-O system, we are referring to the portion of a DNA molecule that is 1,062 "letters" long—a medium-sized gene—that specifies production of an **enzyme,** a particular kind of protein that initiates and directs a chemical reaction. This particular enzyme causes molecules involved in immune responses to attach to the surface of red blood cells. Genes, then, are not really separate structures, as had once been imagined, but locations, like dots on a map. These genes provide the recipe for the many proteins that keep us alive and healthy.

---

[3]Ridley, M. (1999). *Genome: The autobiography of a species in 23 chapters* (p. 40). New York: HarperCollins.

Codon.   Three-base sequence of a gene that specifies production of an amino acid.   •   **RNA.**   Ribonucleic acid; similar to DNA but with uracil substituted for the base thymine. Carries instructions from DNA to produce amino acids for protein building.   •   **Transcription.**   Process of conversion of instructions from DNA into RNA.
•   **Ribosomes.**   Structures in the cell where translation occurs.   •   **Translation.**   Process of conversion of RNA instructions into proteins.   •   **Genetic code.**   The sequence of DNA bases that specifies production of a particular amino acid.   •   **Enzyme.**   Proteins that initiate and direct chemical reactions in an organism.

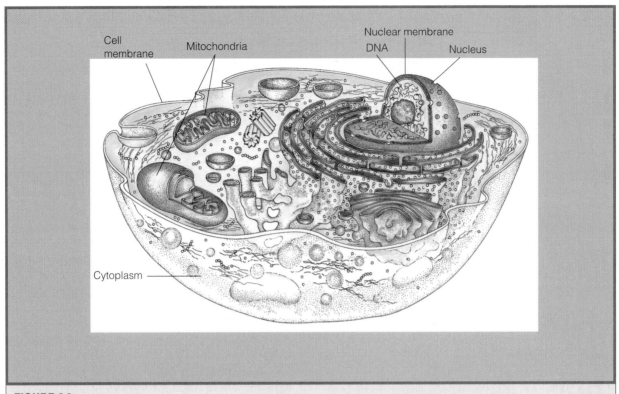

FIGURE 3.2
STRUCTURE OF A GENERALIZED EUKARYOTIC CELL, ILLUSTRATING THE CELL'S THREE-DIMENSIONAL NATURE.

Interestingly, the human **genome**—the complete sequence of human DNA—contains 3 billion chemical bases, with about 30,000 functioning genes. This is a mere three times as many genes as in the lowly fruit fly. How this seemingly modest difference in numbers of genes can produce so much complexity in humans is suggested by the following analogy: A combination lock with two wheels can display almost 100 combinations, but a similar lock with 6 wheels—"only" three times as many—can generate just under 1 million.[4] Those 30,000 human genes account for only 1 to 1.5 percent of the entire genome. As Jerold Lowenstein puts it, our DNA, "like daytime television, is nine-tenths junk."[5] The genes themselves are split by long stretches of this "junk" DNA.

The 1,062 bases of the A-B-O blood group gene, for example, are interrupted by five such longish stretches. In the course of producing proteins, "junk" DNA is metaphorically "snipped out" and left on the "cutting room floor."

Some of this seemingly useless, noncoding DNA was inserted by retroviruses; these are some of the most diverse and widespread infectious entities of vertebrates (they are responsible for many diseases that affect humans, such as immunodeficiencies—including AIDS—hepatitis, anemias, and some neurological disorders).[6] There are several thousand nearly complete viral genomes integrated into our own. Now inert or missing a gene, they account for 1.3 percent of the human genome. Other

---

[4]Solomon, R. (2001, February 20). Genome's riddle. *New York Times,* p. D3.

[5]Lowenstein, J. M. (1992). Genetic surprises. *Discover, 13*(12), 86.

[6]Amábile-Cuevas, C. F., & Chicurel, M. E. (1993). Horizontal gene transfer. *American Scientist, 81,* 338.

Genome.   The complete sequence of DNA for a species.

GREGOR MENDEL   (1822–1884)

Johann Mendel, as he was christened, was raised on a farm in Moravia and attended the local grammar school. Having done well as a student, he became an Augustine monk in order to further his education. As Brother Gregor, he went on to serve as a parish priest but without much success. Since he had previously studied science at the University of Vienna, he thought of becoming a science teacher but failed the examination. So it was that he retreated to the monastery in Bruno, in what is now the Czech Republic. There, he put to work two talents: a flair for mathematics and a passion for gardening.

As with all farmers of his time, Mendel had an intuitive understanding of biological inheritance. He went a step further, though, in that he recognized the need for a more systematic understanding. Thus, at age 34, he began carefully thought-out breeding experiments in the monastery garden,

first with pea plants, then with others.

For 8 years, Mendel worked, planting over 30,000 plants, controlling their pollination, observing the results, and figuring out the mathematics behind it all. This allowed him to predict the outcome of hybridization over successive generations. His findings were published in 1866 in a respected scientific journal found in all the best libraries of Europe. But despite Mendel's straightforward presentation, no one else picked up on the importance of his work until 1900. By then, understanding of cell biology had advanced to the point where rediscovery of Mendel's laws was inevitable, and in that year three European botanists, working independently of one another, rediscovered not only the laws but also Mendel's original paper. With this rediscovery, the science of genetics took off. Still, it would be another 53 years before science understood the true nature of genes, the discreet units of inheritance, the existence of which Mendel had deduced from his experiments.

"junk" DNA consists of decaying hulks of once-useful but now functionless genes; damaged genes that have been "turned off" or stopped being used. All of this litter continues to exist because it is still very good at getting itself replicated. As it does so, mistakes are fairly frequently made, often adding or subtracting repeats of the four bases: A, C, G, and T. This happens with sufficient speed that it is different in every individual, but not so fast that people mostly have the same repeat lengths of their parents. Because there are thousands of series, the result is a unique set of numbers for each person: his or her unique DNA fingerprint.

CHROMOSOMES

Most DNA molecules do not float freely about in our bodies but are organized into structures called **chromosomes** found in the nucleus of each cell. Chromosomes, discovered early in the 20th century, are nothing more than long strands of DNA combined with protein to produce structures that can be seen under a conventional light

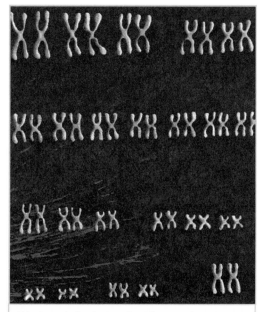

This is a photomicrograph of human chromosomes.

Chromosome.   In the cell nucleus, long strands of DNA combined with a protein that can be seen under the microscope.

The Ethical, Legal, and Social Implications of the Human Genome Project*

The Human Genome Project, an effort to sequence the entire human genetic code, may well be the most massive cooperative scientific undertaking in the history of the natural sciences. The project officially began in 1990 with support from the U.S. Congress. Planners estimated a 15-year time frame and a $3 billion price tag to map the human genetic blueprint. A "working draft" of the human genome has now been completed several years ahead of schedule through a collaboration between government-funded and private researchers.

Though the Human Genome Project will certainly contribute to an understanding of our evolutionary history, the main motivation for this enormous investigation is a hope that detailed genetic knowledge will have revolutionary practical applications for human health. Scientists are currently developing gene therapy models for diseases such as cystic fibrosis and muscular dystrophy that affect tens of thousands of people. Genes that predispose to breast and colon cancer have been identified so that family members can be tested for the presence of these heritable conditions when their loved ones are diagnosed. An increasing number of hereditary conditions can also be diagnosed before birth as new "disease genes" are continually identified. In short, the Human Genome Project is leading to a massive geneticization of our society's health care practices and in turn to the way we think about ourselves. Today, genetics is embedded in our day-to-day lives.

From the Human Genome Project's first conception, scientists were aware that the genetic knowledge they were generating had far-reaching consequences for individuals and society. Therefore, the National Institutes of Health formed a special investigative group to study the ethical, legal, and social implications (ELSI) of the Human Genome Project. The ELSI research program currently has an annual budget of over $12 million and is the largest source of bioethics research. Anthropologists have brought their unique biocultural perspective to the study of the societal effects of knowledge generated from the new genetics.

A primary ELSI research area concerns the study of human genetic variation as the study of the human genome is completed. Initially this DNA sequence will not capture the enormous variation present at the genetic level due to multiple alleles, or alternate forms, that are found for many genes. Anthropologists are contributing to a more complete understanding of this variation through their examination of worldwide genetic diversity so that North Americans are not the only humans represented in the human genome. Ethical issues have been raised by global genetic investigation, such as whether scientists or indigenous people own the patent rights to beneficial genes discovered through such investigations.

A global understanding of genetic diversity raises additional ELSI questions. For instance, how can genetic diversity be examined without falling into the trap of grouping such differences by race? As anthropologists have shown, the concept of race has no validity as a biological concept when applied to humans (see Chapter 13). However, in health care, the field where practical applications of genetic knowledge are most promising, race is often mistakenly considered a biological feature rather than a social feature of an individual. As individual and population variation for specific genes is understood, anthropologists will play an important role in assuring that this information does not lead to the construction of false biological categories. In this way, social determinants of health and disease will not be mistaken for biological difference.

Anthropologists are also uniquely poised to examine how social factors such as race, gender, class, and ethnicity influence the use of clinical genetic services; the understanding and interpretation of genetic information; and the development of public policy about these new genetic technologies. For example, these social factors influence whether an individual will choose to have prenatal genetic testing to assess a fetus' genetic blueprint. Some expectant parents might consider "undesirable" a gene or condition that other parents easily embrace. Cultures and individuals differ as to whether such testing is valuable, ethical, or moral. In a pluralistic society like ours, no simple answer exists to these complex questions. Detailed anthropological study of human beliefs and practices related to the new genetic technology are vital for the development of respectful and fair public policy surrounding this new genetic technology.

---

*Walrath, D. E. (2001). *Anthropology and the ethical, legal, and social implications of the human genome project.* © by author, College of Medicine, University of Vermont, Burlington.

microscope. Each kind of organism has a characteristic number of chromosomes, which are usually found in pairs. For example, the body cells of the fruit fly each contain 4 pairs of chromosomes; those of humans contain 23 pairs; those of some brine shrimp have as many as 160 pairs. The two chromosomes in each pair contain genes for the same traits. The gene for one's A-B-O blood group, for instance, will be found on each chromosome of a particular pair (Chromosome 9 in this instance), but there may be variant forms of these genes. There are three such variants of the A-B-O gene that determine whether one's blood type is A, B, AB, or O. Forms of genes that are located on paired chromosomes and that code for different versions of the same trait are called **alleles.** The difference between the A and B blood alleles is a mere 7 chemical bases out of the total 1,062.

CELL DIVISION

In order to grow and maintain good health, the body cells of an organism must divide and produce new cells. Cell division is initiated when the chromosomes, and hence the genes, replicate, forming a second pair that duplicates the original pair of chromosomes in the nucleus. To do this, the DNA metaphorically "unzips" between the base pairs—adenine from thymine and guanine from cytosine—following which each base on each now-single strand attracts its complementary base, reconstituting the second half of the double helix. Each new pair is surrounded by a membrane and becomes the nucleus that directs the activities of a new cell. This kind of cell division is called **mitosis,** and it produces new cells that have exactly the same number of chromosome pairs, and hence genes, as did the parent cell.

Like most animals, humans reproduce sexually. The reason sex is so popular, from an evolutionary perspective, is that it brings beneficial alleles together, purges the genome of harmful ones, and allows beneficial alleles to spread without being held back by the baggage of disadvantageous variants of other genes. Without sexual reproduction, we would lack genetic diversity, without which we would be more open to attack by various viruses than we already are. Nor would we be able to adapt to changing environments.

When new individuals are produced through sexual reproduction, the process involves the merging of two cells,

one from each parent. If two regular body cells, each containing 23 pairs of chromosomes, were to merge, the result would be a new individual with 46 pairs of chromosomes; such an individual surely could not survive. But this increase in chromosome number does not occur, because the sex cells that join to form a new individual are the product of a different kind of cell division, called **meiosis.**

Although meiosis begins like mitosis, with the replication and doubling of the original genes and chromosomes, it proceeds to divide that number into four new

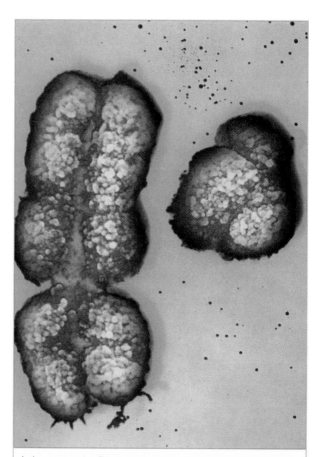

In humans as in all mammals, sex is determined by the male, as everyone inherits an X chromosome (left) from their mother, but has a 50-50 chance of inheriting an X or Y chromosome (right) from their father. Hence, about equal numbers of males as females are born. Compared to the other chromosomes, the Y is tiny and carries little genetic information. The X carries a "normal" complement of genes.

Alleles.   Alternate forms of a single gene.   •   **Mitosis.**   A kind of cell division that produces new cells having exactly the same number of chromosome pairs, and hence genes, as the parent cell.   •   **Meiosis.**   A kind of cell division that produces the sex cells, each of which has half the number of chromosomes, and hence genes, as the parent cell.

cells rather than two (Figure 3.3). Thus each new cell has only half the number of chromosomes with their genes found in the parent cell. Human eggs and sperm, for example, have only 23 single chromosomes (half of a pair), whereas body cells have 23 pairs, or 46 chromosomes.

The process of meiotic division has important implications for genetics. Because paired chromosomes are separated, two different types of new cells will be formed; two of the four new cells will have one-half of a pair of chromosomes, and the other two will have the second half of the original chromosome pair. At the same time, corresponding portions of one chromosome may "cross over" to the other one, somewhat scrambling the genetic material compared to the original chromosomes. Of course, none of this will make any difference if the original pair was **homozygous,** possessing identical alleles

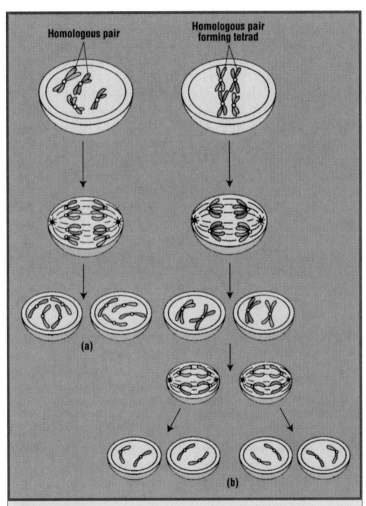

FIGURE 3.3

IN CELL DIVISION BOTH MITOSIS (A) AND MEIOSIS (B) CREATE NEW CELLS. HOWEVER, IN MITOSIS THE NEW CELL HAS THE SAME NUMBER OF CHROMOSOMES AS THE PARENT CELL, WHEREAS IN MEIOSIS THERE ARE HALF OF THE CHROMOSOMES. CHROMOSOMES IN BLUE ORIGINALLY CAME FROM ONE PARENT, THOSE IN PINK FROM THE OTHER.

Homozygous.   Refers to a chromosome pair that bears identical alleles for a single gene.

for a specific gene. For example, if in both chromosomes of the original pair the gene for A-B-O blood type was represented by the allele for Type A blood, then all new cells will have the "A" allele. But if the original pair was **heterozygous,** with the "A" allele on one chromosome and the allele for Type O blood on the other, then half of the new cells will contain only the "O" allele; the offspring have a 50-50 chance of getting either one. It is impossible to predict any single individual's **genotype,** or genetic composition, but (as Mendel originally discovered) statistical probabilities can be established.

What happens when a child inherits the allele for Type O blood from one parent and that for Type A from the other? Will the child have blood of Type A, O, or some mixture of the two? Many of these questions were answered by Mendel's original experiments.

Mendel discovered that certain alleles are able to mask the presence of others; one allele is dominant, whereas the other is recessive. This is his **law of dominance and recessiveness.** Actually, it is the traits that are dominant or recessive, rather than the alleles themselves; geneticists merely speak of dominant and recessive alleles for the sake of convenience. Thus, one might speak of the allele for Type A blood as being dominant to the one for Type O. An individual whose blood type genes are heterozygous, with one "A" and one "O" allele, will have Type A blood. In other words, the heterozygous condition (AO) will show exactly the same physical characteristic, or **phenotype,** as the homozygous (AA), even though the two have a somewhat different genetic composition, or genotype. Only the homozygous recessive genotype (OO) will show the phenotype of Type O blood.

The dominance of one allele does not mean that the recessive one is lost or in some way blended. A Type A heterozygous parent (AO) will produce sex cells containing both "A" and "O" alleles. (This is an example of Mendel's law of segregation, that alleles retain their separate identities.) Recessive alleles can be handed down for generations before they are matched with another recessive in the process of sexual reproduction and show up in the phenotype. The presence of the dominant allele simply renders the recessive allele inactive.

All of the traits Mendel studied in garden peas showed this dominant-recessive relationship, and so for some years it was believed that this was the only relationship possible. Later studies, however, have indicated that patterns of inheritance are not always so simple. In some cases, neither allele is dominant; they are both co-dominant. An example of co-dominance in human heredity can be seen also in the inheritance of blood types. Type A is produced by one allele; Type B by another. A heterozygous individual will have a phenotype of AB, because neither allele can dominate the other.

The inheritance of blood types points out another complexity of heredity. The number of alleles is by no means limited to two; certain traits have three or more allelic forms. Of course, only one allele can appear on each of the pairs of chromosomes, so each individual is limited to two alleles.

Another example of co-dominance is the alleles for normal **hemoglobin** (the protein that carries oxygen in the red blood cells) and the abnormal hemoglobin that is responsible for **sickle-cell anemia** in humans. The abnormality is caused by a change in a single base pair in the DNA of the hemoglobin gene, producing a single amino acid substitution in the protein. Individuals who are homozygous for this particular allele contract sickle-cell anemia, as their red blood cells take on a characteristic sickle shape, causing them to collapse and clump together, blocking the capillaries and so causing tissue damage. With their severe anemia, such individuals commonly die before reaching adulthood. The homozygous dominant condition ($Hb^A Hb^A$; normal hemoglobin is known as hemoglobin A, not to be confused with blood Type A) produces only normal molecules of hemoglobin whereas the heterozygous condition ($Hb^A Hb^S$) produces 50 percent normal and 50 percent abnormal molecules; except under low-oxygen or some other stressful conditions, such individuals suffer no ill effects. We shall return to the sickle-cell condition later, for we now know that under certain conditions the heterozygous condition is actually more advantageous than is the "normal" homozygous condition.

POLYGENETIC INHERITANCE

So far, we have spoken as if the traits of organisms are single-gene traits—that is, the alleles of one particular gene determine one particular trait. Certainly this is the

---

Heterozygous. Refers to a chromosome pair that bears different alleles for a single gene. • **Genotype.** The actual genetic makeup of an organism. • **Law of dominance and recessiveness.** Certain alleles are able to mask the presence of others. • **Phenotype.** The physical appearance of an organism that may or may not reflect a particular genotype because the latter may or may not include recessive alleles. • **Hemoglobin.** The protein that carries oxygen in the red blood cells. • **Sickle-cell anemia.** An inherited form of anemia caused by the red blood cells assuming a sickled shape.

by multiple genes exhibit a continuous range of variation in their phenotype expression.

POPULATION GENETICS

At the level of the individual, the study of genetics shows how traits are transmitted from one generation to the next and enables a prediction about the chances that any given individual will display some phenotypic characteristic. At the level of the group, the study of genetics takes on additional significance, revealing mechanisms that support evolutionary interpretations of the diversity of life.

A key concept in genetics is that of the **population,** or a group of individuals within which breeding takes place. It is within populations that natural selection takes place, as some members produce more than their share of the next generation, while others produce less than their share. Thus, over a period of generations, the population shows a measure of adaptation to its environment as a consequence of this evolution.

The Stability of the Population

In theory, the characteristics of any given population should remain remarkably stable. And indeed, generation after generation, the bullfrogs in my farm pond, for example, look much alike, have the same calls, and exhibit the same behavior when breeding. Another way to look at this remarkable consistency is to say that the **gene pool** of the population—the genetic variants available to that population—seems to remain the same.

The theoretical stability of a population's gene pool is not only easy to observe; it is also easy to understand. As Mendel's experiments with garden peas revealed, and subsequent genetic experiments have confirmed, although some alleles may be dominant to others, the recessive alleles are not just lost or destroyed. Statistically, a heterozygous individual has a 50 percent chance of passing on to the next generation the dominant allele; he or she also has a 50 percent chance of passing on the recessive allele. The recessive allele may again be masked by the presence of a dominant allele in the next generation, but it is there nonetheless and will be passed on again.

Sickle-cell anemia is caused by an abnormal hemoglobin, called hemoglobin S. Those afflicted by the disease are homozygous for the allele S; heterozygotes are not afflicted. Shown here is a sickle cell among normal red blood cells.

case with the A-B-O blood groups and some other things, but in humans, the most obvious traits are usually not ones controlled by a single gene. Skin color, for example, is programmed by the action of many genes, each of which produces a small effect. In such cases, we speak of **polygenetic inheritance,** where two or more genes (as opposed to just two or more alleles) work together to effect one particular phenotypic character. Because so many genes are involved, each of which may have alternative alleles, it is difficult to unravel the genetic underpinnings of a trait like skin color. Theoretically, the observed range of variation in human skin color seems to require the presence of at least three, if not as many as six, separate genes, each of which produces a small additive effect. For this reason, characteristics controlled

Polygenetic inheritance.   When two or more genes work together to effect a single phenotypic character.   •
Population.   In biology, a group of similar individuals that can and do interbreed.   •   **Gene pool.**   The genetic variants available to a population.

Because alleles are not "lost" in the process of reproduction, the frequency with which certain ones occur in the population should remain exactly the same from one generation to the next. The **Hardy-Weinberg principle,** named for the English mathematician and the German physician who worked it out (in 1908) soon after the rediscovery of Mendel's laws, demonstrates algebraically that the percentage of individuals that are homozygous for the dominant allele, homozygous for the recessive allele, and heterozygous will remain the same from one generation to the next provided that certain specified conditions are met: that mating is entirely random; that the population is sufficiently large for statistical averages to express themselves; that no new variants will be introduced into the population's gene pool; and that all individuals are equally successful at surviving and reproducing. In real life, however, these conditions are rarely met, as geographical, physiological, or behavioral factors may favor matings between certain individuals over others; as populations—on islands, for example—may be quite small; as new genetic variants may be introduced through mutation, interspecies gene transfer, or gene flow; and as natural selection may favor the carriers of some alleles over others. Thus, changes in the gene pools of populations, without which there could be no evolution, can and do take place.

EVOLUTIONARY FORCES

Mutation

The ultimate source of change is **mutation** of genes. This happens when copying mistakes are made during cell division. It may involve a change in a single base of a DNA sequence, or at the other extreme, relocation of large segments of DNA. In any event, genes are altered, producing new alleles—ones not inherited from an ancestor, but heritable by descendants. The fact is, every second that you read this page, the DNA in each cell of your body is being damaged.[7] Fortunately, DNA repair enzymes exist that constantly scan DNA for mistakes,

slicing out damaged segments and patching up gaps. Were it not for this repair mechanism, we would have diseases like cancer at a much higher frequency than we do, nor would we get a faithful copy of our parental inheritance (from an evolutionary perspective, the only mutations that count are those in sex cells). Not only would we not live long, but our species would not exist for long. But because the repair mechanism itself is not perfect, not all mistakes are corrected; otherwise, there would be no possibility for evolution to occur.

Geneticists have calculated the rate at which various types of mutant genes appear. In human populations, they run from a low of about 5 mutations per million sex cells formed, in the case of a gene abnormality that leads to the absence of an iris in the eye, to a high of about 100 per million, in the case of a gene involved in a form of muscular dystrophy. (Note that the human male ejaculates hundreds of millions of sperm cells at a single time.) The average is about 30 mutants per million. Because of the repeated replication needed to supply fresh sperm throughout life, the mutation rate throughout the genome is five times higher in men than in women. Although mutations sometimes produce marked abnormalities, the great majority of them produce more subtle effects. Still, they are more often harmful than not.

Research with a variety of organisms indicates that certain factors increase the rate at which mutations occur. These include a number of chemicals, such as some dyes, certain antibiotics, and some chemicals used in the preservation of food. Another important cause of increased mutation rates is irradiation. The ultraviolet rays of sunshine are capable of producing mutations, as are x-rays and other radiation. In at least some organisms, there is even evidence stress can crank up mutation rates, increasing the diversity necessary for selection if successful adaptation is to occur.[8]

In humans, as in all multicelled animals, the very nature of the genetic material itself ensures that mutations will occur. For instance, the fact that genes are split by stretches of "junk" DNA increases the chances that a simple editing mistake in the process of copying DNA will cause significant gene mutations. To cite one exam-

---

[7]Culotta, E., & Koshland, D. E., Jr. (1994). DNA repair works its way to the top. *Science, 266,* 1926.

[8]Chicurel, M. (2001). Can organisms speed their own evolution? *Science, 292,* 1824–1827.

Hardy-Weinberg principle.   Demonstrates algebraically that the percentage of individuals that are homozygous for the dominant allele, homozygous for the recessive allele, and heterozygous should remain constant from one generation to the next, provided that certain specified conditions are met. • **Mutation.**   Chance alteration of a gene that produces a new allele.

One of the most potent mutagenic agents known is tobacco smoke.

ple, the gene for collagen (the main structural protein of the skin, bones, and teeth) is fragmented by no fewer than 50 segments of "junk" DNA. As a consequence, there are 50 chances for error each time the gene is copied. One result of this seemingly inefficient if not dangerous situation is that it becomes possible to shuffle the gene segments themselves like a deck of cards, putting together new proteins with new functions. Although individuals may suffer as a result (the French artist Henri Toulouse-Lautrec's growth abnormality resulted from a mutation of the collagen gene), it does make it possible for an evolving species to adapt more quickly to a new environment. Another source of genetic remodeling from within is the movement of whole DNA sequences from one locality or chromosome to another. This may disrupt the function of other genes or, in the case of so-called jumping genes, carry important functional messages of their own. In humans, about 1 in every 700 mutations is caused by "jumping genes."

One recent finding is that humans have longer strings of repetitive DNA within and between genes than do other primates, so it is not surprising that we have a higher mutation rate. And a consequence of this is an increased incidence of such genetic disorders as Huntington's disease and Fragile X syndrome (a form of mental retardation).[9]

It is important to realize that mutations do not arise out of need for some new adaptation. Indeed, there is no tendency for the frequency of a particular mutation to correlate with the direction in which a population is evolving. They are purely chance events; what happens once they occur depends on whether they happen (by chance) to enhance the survival and reproductive success of the individuals who carry them.

French artist Henri Toulouse-Lautrec, whose growth abnormality resulted from a mutation of the collagen gene.

---

[9]Glausiusz, J. (1995). Micro gets macro. *Discover, 16*(11), 40.

Genetic Drift

Each individual is subject to a number of chance events that determine life or death. For example, an individual squirrel in good health and possessed of a number of advantageous traits may be killed in a forest fire; a genetically well-adapted baby cougar may not live longer than a day if its mother gets caught in an avalanche, whereas the weaker offspring of a mother that does not die may survive. In a large population, such accidents of nature are unimportant; the accidents that preserve individuals with certain alleles will be balanced out by the accidents that destroy them. However, in small populations, such averaging out may not be possible. Because human populations today are so large, we might suppose that human beings are unaffected by chance events. Although it is true that a rock slide that kills 5 campers whose home community has a total population of 100,000 is not statistically significant, a rock slide that kills 5 hunters from a small group of food foragers could significantly alter frequencies of alleles in the local gene pool. The average size of local groups of historically known food foragers (people who hunt, fish, and gather other wild foods for subsistence) varies between about 25 and 50.

Another sort of chance event may occur when an existing population splits up into two or more new ones, especially if one of these new populations is founded by a particularly small number of individuals. What this amounts to is a sampling error; in such cases, it is unlikely that the gene frequencies of the smaller population will duplicate those of the larger one. Even if a population does not split in this way, in a small population, the same sort of sampling error may occur as, by chance, parental alleles may not be passed on to the next generation in the same frequencies. If, for example, a person's genotype for blood type is AO, but he or she has only one offspring, only one of those alleles will be passed on.

The effect of chance events on the gene pool of small populations is called **genetic drift.** Genetic drift plays an important role in causing the sometimes striking characteristics found in isolated island populations. On the isolated island of Tristan de Cuna, for example, over 20 percent of the human population have overt symptoms of asthma, despite living in an environment free of the pollution and other triggers that lead to asthma. Because asthma tends to run in families (regardless of what triggers asthma) and because the underlying biochemical events involved are the same, it is clear that an underlying genetic component exists. Thus, it appears that Tristan

The 1998 Casitas Volcano mudslide in Nicaragua, triggered by the rains of Hurricane Mitch, buried a village, killing over 1,200 people. This is one kind of accident that can produce chance alterations of allele frequency in human gene pools.

de Cuna was populated by descendants of an asthma-susceptible person.[10] Drift is also likely to have been an important factor in human evolution, because until 10,000 years ago all humans were food foragers who probably lived in relatively small, self-contained populations.

Gene Flow

Another factor that brings change to the gene pool of a population is **gene flow,** or the introduction of new alleles from nearby populations. Gene flow occurs when

---

[10]Ridley, M. (1999). *Genome: The autobiography of a species in 23 chapters* (p. 71). New York: HarperCollins.

Genetic drift. Chance fluctuations of allele frequencies in the gene pool of a population. • **Gene flow.** The introduction of alleles from the gene pool of one population into that of another.

In Central America, gene flow between Native Americans (upper left), Spaniards (upper right), and Africans (lower left) has contributed to genetic diversity.

Interspecies Gene Transfer

A recent discovery is that the transfer of genes can occur between unrelated organisms. Unlike gene flow, however, it does not take place by interbreeding but through other means. Hence, like mutation, it is a source of random variation. Such **interspecies gene transfer** is well known between different kinds of bacteria, but seems to take place even among vertebrate animals. In some cases, the agent of transfer can be a retrovirus; how this takes place is depicted in Figure 3.4.

Natural Selection

previously separated groups are once again able to interbreed, as, for example, when a river that once separated two populations of small mammals changes course. Migration of individuals or groups into the territory occupied by others may also lead to gene flow. This genetic change has been observed in several North American rodents that have been forced to leave their territory due to changes in environmental conditions. Gene flow has been an important factor in human evolution, both in terms of early human or near-human groups and in terms of current so-called racial variation. For example, the last 400 years have seen the introduction of alleles into Central and South American populations from both the Spanish colonists and the Africans whom Europeans imported as slaves. The result has been an increase in the range of phenotypic variation.

Although the factors discussed above may produce change in a population, that change would not necessarily make the population better adapted to its biological and social environment. **Adaptation** means both a process, by which organisms achieve a beneficial adjustment to an available environment, and the results of that process, the characteristics of organisms that fit them to the particular set of conditions of the environment in which they are generally found. Genetic drift, for example, often produces strange characteristics that have no survival value; mutant genes may be either helpful or harmful to survival, or simply neutral. So we return to the subject of natural selection, for it is this process that makes evolutionary change adaptive.

Natural selection refers to the evolutionary process through which the environment exerts pressure that

Interspecies gene transfer. Transfer of DNA as when retroviruses insert DNA into the cells of one species from another. • **Adaptation.** A process by which organisms achieve a beneficial adjustment to an available environment; also the results of that process—the characteristics of organisms that fit them to the particular set of conditions of the environment in which they are generally found.

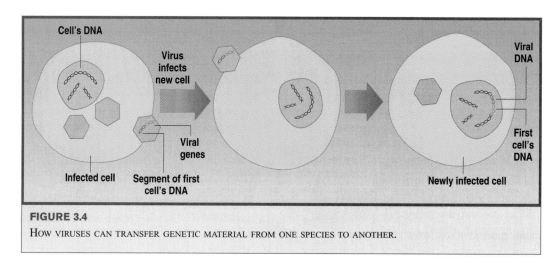

FIGURE 3.4

HOW VIRUSES CAN TRANSFER GENETIC MATERIAL FROM ONE SPECIES TO ANOTHER.

selects some individuals over others to reproduce the next generation of the group. In other words, instead of a completely random selection of individuals whose traits will be passed on to the next generation, there is selection by the forces of nature. In the process, the frequency of genetic variants for harmful or maladaptive traits within the population is reduced while the frequency of genetic variants for adaptive traits is increased.

In popular writing, natural selection is often thought of as "survival of the fittest," a phrase coined by British philosopher Herbert Spencer but never used by Darwin. The phrase implies that the physically weak, being unfit, are eliminated from the population by disease, predation, or starvation. Obviously, the survival of the fittest has some bearing on natural selection; one need hardly point out that the dead do not reproduce. But there are many cases in which individuals survive, and even do quite well, but do not reproduce. They may be incapable of attracting mates, or they may be sterile, or they may produce offspring that do not survive after birth. For example, among the Uganda Kob, a kind of antelope native to eastern Africa, males that are unable to attract females form all-male herds in which they live out their lives. As members of a herd, they are reasonably well protected against predators, and so they may survive to relatively ripe old ages. They do not, however, pass on their genes to succeeding generations.

Change brought about by natural selection in the frequency with which certain genetic variants appear in a population is actually a very slow process. For example, the present frequency of the sickle-cell allele is 0.05 in the entire U.S. population. A 5-percent reduction per generation (about 25 years) would take about 2,000 years to reach a frequency of 0.01, assuming complete selection against those homozygous for the allele. Yet given the great time span involved—life on earth has existed for 3 to 4 billion years—even such small and slow changes will have a significant cumulative impact on both the genotypes and phenotypes of any population.

Natural selection may act to promote change in frequencies of genetic variants, or act to promote stability, rather than change. **Stabilizing selection** occurs in populations that are already well adapted or where change would be disadvantageous. In humans, for instance, there has been no significant change in brain size for the last 200,000 years or so. Stabilizing selection seems to be operating here, as the human birth canal is not adequate for the birth of larger-brained offspring. In cases where change is disadvantageous, natural selection will favor the retention of allele frequencies more or less as they are. The qualification "more or less" is necessary, as "stable" does not mean "static." Still, the evolutionary history of most forms of life is not one of constant change, proceeding as a steady, stately progression over vast periods of time; rather, it is one of prolonged periods of relative stability or gradual change punctuated by shorter periods of more rapid change (or extinction) when altered conditions require new adaptations or when a new mutation

Stabilizing selection.   Natural selection as it acts to promote stability, rather than change, in a population's gene pool.

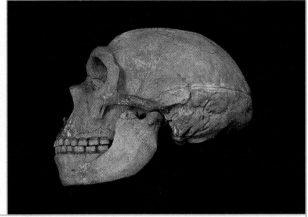

An example of stabilizing selection: The brain of the modern skull on the left is no bigger relative to body mass than that in the ca. 50,000-year-old skull on the right, even though the outer appearance of the skulls has changed.

produces an opportunity to adapt to some other available environment. According to the fossil record, most species survive somewhere between 3 and 5 million years.[11]

Discussions of the action of natural selection typically focus on anatomical or structural changes, such as the evolutionary change in the types of teeth found in primates; ample evidence (fossilized teeth, for example) exists to interpret such changes. By extrapolation, biologists assume that the same mechanisms work on behavioral traits as well. It seems reasonable that individuals in a group of Vervet monkeys capable of warning one another of the presence of predators would have a significant survival advantage over those without this capability. Such situations have constituted an enigma for evolutionary biologists; individuals are typically seen as "survival machines," acting always selfishly in their own interest, but by giving an alarm call, an individual calls attention to itself, thereby becoming an obvious target for the predator. How, then, could the kind of behavior evolve in which individuals place themselves at risk for the good of the group? One biologist's simple solution substitutes money for fitness to illustrate one way in which such cooperative behavior may come about:

> You are given a choice. Either you can receive $10 and keep it all or you can receive $10 million if you give $6 million to your next door neighbor. Which would you do? Guessing that most selfish people would be happy with a net gain of $4 million, I consider the second option to be a form of selfish behavior in which a neighbor gains an incidental benefit. I have termed such selfish behavior benevolent.[12]

Natural selection of beneficial social traits was probably a particularly important influence on human evolution, since in the primates, some degree of cooperative social behavior became important for food-getting, defense, and mate attraction. Indeed, anthropologist Christopher Boehm argues that, "If human nature were merely selfish, vigilant punishment of deviants would be expected, whereas the elaborate prosocial prescriptions that favor altruism would come as a surprise."[13]

ADAPTATION

As a consequence of the process of natural selection, those populations that do not become extinct generally become well adapted to their environments. Anyone who has ever looked carefully at the plants and animals that survive in the deserts of the western United States can cite many instances of adaptation. For example, members of the cactus family have extensive root networks close to the surface of the soil, enabling them to soak up the slightest bit of moisture; they are able to store large

[11]Thomson, K. S. (1997). Natural selection and evolution's smoking gun. *American Scientist, 85,* 516.

[12]Nunney, L. (1998). Are we selfish, are we nice, or are we nice because we are selfish? *Science, 281,* 1619.

[13]Boehm, C. (2000). The evolution of moral communities. *School of American Research, 2000 Annual Report,* 7.

The moths shown in these two pictures are varieties of a single species. Although the mottled brown variant is well-camouflaged on relatively clean tree trunks, it is readily visible on sooty tree trunks and is subject to increased predation. The reverse is true for the black variant, which became especially common when coal fueled British industry.

quantities of water whenever it is available; they are shaped so as to expose the smallest possible surface to the dry air and are generally leafless as adults, thereby preventing water loss through evaporation; and a covering of spines discourages animals from chewing into the juicy flesh of the plant.

Desert animals are also adapted to their environment. The kangaroo rat can survive without drinking water; many reptiles live in burrows where the temperature is lower; most animals are nocturnal or active only in the cool of the night. Many of the stories traditionally offered to explain observable cases of adaptation rely heavily on the purposeful acts of a world creator. The legend of Coyote and Wishpoosh (Chapter 1) is one such example; the belief popular among Europeans early in the 19th century that God created each animal separately to occupy a specific place in a hierarchical ladder of being is another.

The adaptability of organic structures and functions, no matter how much a source of wonder and fascination, nevertheless falls short of perfection. This is so because natural selection can only work with what the existing store of genetic variation provides; it cannot create something entirely new. That exquisite design is not the rule is illustrated by the pains of aching backs, the annoyances of hernias, and problems with hemorrhoids that we humans must endure because the body of a four-footed vertebrate, designed for horizontal posture, has been jury-rigged to be held vertically above the two hind limbs. And surely, truly intelligent design from scratch could have produced an eye without a blind spot. Yet, these defects have been perpetuated by natural selection, because they are outweighed by other aspects of human adaptation that enhance the reproductive success of the species as a whole.

The Case of Sickle-Cell Anemia

Among human beings, a particularly well-studied case of an adaptation paid for by the misery of many individuals brings us back to the case of sickle-cell anemia. This disorder first came to the attention of geneticists when it was observed that most North Americans who suffer from it are of African ancestry. Investigation traced the abnormality to populations that live in a clearly defined belt throughout central Africa (although brought to North America from central Africa, the condition also exists in some non-African populations, as will be noted below).

Geneticists were curious to know why such a deleterious hereditary disability persisted in these populations. According to the theory of natural selection, any alleles that are harmful will tend to disappear from the group, because the individuals who are homozygous for the abnormality generally die—are "selected out"—before they are able to reproduce. Why, then, had this seemingly harmful condition remained in populations from central Africa?

The answer to this mystery began to emerge when it was noticed that the areas in which sickle-cell anemia is prevalent are also areas in which falciparum malaria is common (Figure 3.5). This severe form of malaria causes high fevers that significantly interfere with the reproductive abilities of those who do not actually die from

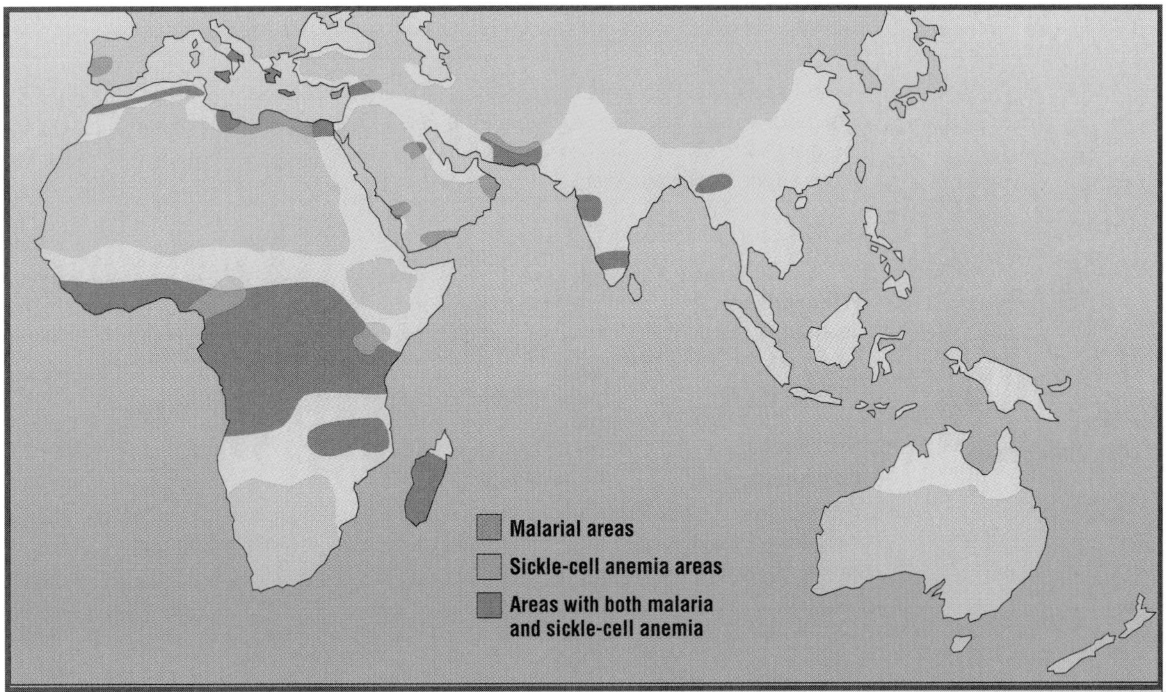

FIGURE 3.5

THE ALLELE THAT, IN HOMOZYGOTES, CAUSES SICKLE-CELL ANEMIA MAKES HETEROZYGOTES RESISTANT TO FALCIPARUM MALARIA. THUS, THE ALLELE IS MOST COMMON IN POPULATIONS NATIVE TO REGIONS WHERE THIS STRAIN OF MALARIA IS COMMON.

the disease. Moreover, it was discovered that the same hemoglobin abnormalities are found in people living in parts of the Arabian Peninsula, Greece, Algeria, and Syria as well as in certain East Indians, all of whom also are native to regions where falciparum malaria is common.

Further research established that the abnormal hemoglobin was associated with an increased ability to survive the effects of the malarial parasite; it seems that the effects of the abnormal hemoglobin in limited amounts were less injurious than the effects of the malarial parasite.

Thus, selection favored heterozygous individuals ($Hb^A Hb^S$). The loss of alleles for abnormal hemoglobin caused by the death of those homozygous for it (from sickle-cell anemia) was balanced out by the loss of alleles for normal hemoglobin, as those homozygous for it experienced reproductive failure.

This example also points out how adaptations tend to be specific; the abnormal hemoglobin was an adaptation to the particular parts of the world in which the malarial parasite flourished. When Africans adapted to that region came to North America, where falciparum malaria is unknown, what had been an adaptive characteristic became an injurious one. Where there is no malaria to attack those with normal hemoglobin, the abnormal hemoglobin becomes comparatively disadvantageous. Although the rates of sickle-cell trait are still relatively high among African Americans—about 9 percent show the sickling trait—this represents a significant decline from the approximately 22 percent who are estimated to have shown the trait when the first slaves were brought from Africa. A further decline over the next several generations is to be expected, as selection pressure continues to work against it.

This example also illustrates the important role culture may play even with respect to biological adaptation. In West Africa, falciparum malaria was not a significant problem until humans abandoned food foraging for farming a few thousand years ago. In order to farm, they had to clear areas of the natural forest cover. In the forest, decaying vegetation on the forest floor had imparted an absorbent quality to the ground so that the heavy rainfall of the region rapidly soaked into the soil. But once stripped of its natural vegetation, the soil lost this quality.

HIGHWAY 1

A trip to this site, designed by students of Connecticut College, follows the route of Charles Darwin's historical voyage on the *HMS Beagle.* Learn about everything from the giant tortoises and finches on the Galapagos Islands to Darwin's thoughts about slavery from his voyage diary.
http://camel2.conncoll.edu/academics/departments/philosophy/courses/beagle/index

HIGHWAY 2

Learn how the genetics revolution is changing the practice of medicine. This site describes the story of the hunt for a cure for the genetic disease cystic fibrosis through gene therapy and also features a great tutorial in genetics.
www.hhmi.org/genetictrail/front/fwd.htm

HIGHWAY 3

The National Institutes of Health maintains this information-packed site that includes all the latest research about the Human Genome Project including its program on the ethical, legal, and social issues.
www.ornl.gov/hgmis/

Furthermore, the forest canopy was no longer there to break the force of the rainfall, and so the impact of the heavy rains tended to compact the soil further. The result was that stagnant puddles commonly formed after rains, and these were perfect for the breeding purposes of the type of mosquito that is the host to the malarial parasite. These mosquitoes then began to flourish and transmit the malarial parasite to humans. Thus, humans unwittingly created the kind of environment that made a hitherto disadvantageous trait, the abnormal hemoglobin associated with sickle-cell anemia, advantageous.

Although it is true that all living organisms have many adaptive characteristics, it is not true that all characteristics are adaptive. All male mammals, for example, possess nipples, even though they serve no useful purpose. To female mammals, however, nipples are essential to reproductive success, which is why males have them. The two sexes are not separate entities, shaped independently by natural selection but are variants upon a single ground plan, elaborated in later embryology. Precursors of mammary glands are built in all mammalian fetuses, enlarging later in the development of females, but remaining small and without function in males.

Nor is it true that current utility is a reliable guide to historical origin. For one thing, nonadaptive characters may be co-opted for later utility following origins as developmental consequences of changing patterns in embryonic

and postnatal growth. The unusually large size of a kiwi's egg, for example, enhances the survivability of kiwi chicks, in that they are particularly large and capable when hatched. Nevertheless, kiwi eggs probably did not evolve such large size because it is adaptive. Kiwis evolved from large, moa-sized ancestors, and in birds, egg size reduces at a slower rate than does body size. Therefore, the out-sized eggs of kiwi birds seem to be no more than a developmental

This x-ray illustrates the unusually large size of a kiwi's egg.

byproduct of a reduction in body size.[14] Similarly, an existing adaptation may come under strong selective pressure for some new purpose, as did insect wings. These did not arise so that insects might fly, but rather as gills that were used to "row," and later skim, across the surface of the water.[15] Later, the larger ones by chance proved useful for purposes of flight. In both these cases, what we see is natural selection operating as "a creative scavenger, taking what is available and putting it to new use."[16]

---

[14]Gould, S. J. (1991). *Bully for brontosaurus* (pp. 109–123). New York: Norton.

[15]Kaiser, J. (1994). A new theory of insect wing origins takes off. *Science, 266,* 363.

[16]Doist, R. (1997). Molecular evolution and scientific inquiry, misperceived. *American Scientist, 85,* 475.

CONCLUSION

As primatologist Frans de Waal notes, "Evolution is a magnificent idea that has won over essentially everyone in the world willing to listen to scientific arguments."[17] We will return to the topic in Chapter 5, as we look at how the primates evolved to produce the many species in the world today. First, however, we will survey the living primates (in Chapter 4) in order to understand the kinds of animals they are, what they have in common, and what distinguishes the various forms.

---

[17]de Waal, F. (2001). Sing the song of evolution. *Natural History, 110*(8), 77.

CHAPTER SUMMARY

In the 18th century, Carl von Linné (Linnaeus) devised a system to classify the great variety of living things then known. On the basis of similarities in body structure, body function, and sequence of bodily growth, he grouped organisms into small groups, or species. Modern taxonomy still uses his basic system but now looks at such characteristics as chemical reactions of blood, protein structure, and the makeup of the genetic material itself. Although Linnaeus regarded species as fixed and unchangeable, this idea was challenged by the finding of fossils, the idea of progress, and the many continuities among different species.

Evolution may be defined as descent with modification, which occurs as genetic variants in the gene pool of a population change in frequency. Genes, the actual units of heredity, are segments of molecules of DNA (deoxyribonucleic acid), and the entire sequence of DNA is known as the genome. DNA is a complex molecule resembling two strands of rope twisted around each other. Connecting the two strands are four chemical bases, adenine always pairing with thymine and guanine with cytosine. The sequence of these bases along the molecules are recipes that direct the production of proteins. These in turn direct the development of such identifiable traits as blood type. Just about everything in the human body is made of or by proteins, and human DNA provides the instructions for the thousands of proteins that keep us alive and healthy. DNA molecules have the unique property of being able to produce exact copies of themselves. As long as no errors are made in the process of replication, new organisms will contain genetic material exactly like that in ancestral organisms.

DNA molecules are located on chromosomes, structures found in the nucleus of each cell. Each kind of organism has a characteristic number of chromosomes, which are usually found in pairs. Humans have 23 pairs. Genes that are located on paired chromosomes and coded for different versions of the same trait are called alleles.

Mitosis, one kind of cell division, begins when the chromosomes (hence the genes) replicate, forming a second pair that duplicates the original pair of chromosomes in the nucleus. It results in new cells with exactly the same number of chromosome pairs as the parent cell. Meiosis, a different kind of cell division, is involved in sexual reproduction. It begins with the replication of original chromosomes, but these are divided into four cells, each containing 23 single chromosomes.

The Augustine monk Gregor Mendel studied the mechanism of inheritance with garden peas. He discovered the particulate nature of heredity and that some alleles are able to mask the presence of others. They are called dominant. The allele not expressed is recessive. The allele for Type A blood in humans, for example, is dominant to the allele for Type O blood. Alleles that are both expressed when present are termed *co-dominant*. An individual with the alleles for Type A and Type B blood has the AB blood type.

Phenotype refers to the physical characteristics of an organism, whereas genotype refers to its genetic composition. Two organisms may have the same phenotype but different genotypes.

A key concept is that of population, or a group of individuals within which most breeding takes place. It is populations, rather than individuals, that evolve. The total number of different alleles of genes available to a population is called its gene pool. The frequency with which certain alleles occur in the same gene pool theoretically remains the same from one generation to another; this is known as the Hardy-Weinberg principle. Nonetheless, change does take place in gene pools as a result of several factors.

The ultimate source of genetic variation is mutation. These are accidents that cause changes in sequences of DNA. Although mutations are inevitable given the nature of cellular chemistry, extrinsic factors—such as heat, certain chemicals, or various kinds of radiation—can increase the mutation rate. Another source of variation is interspecies gene transfer, as retroviruses can introduce DNA from one species into the genome of another.

The effects of chance events (other than mutations and interspecies transfer) on the gene pool of a small population is called genetic drift. Genetic drift may have been an important factor in human evolution because until 10,000 years ago all humans probably lived in relatively small populations. Another factor that brings change to the gene pool of a population is gene flow, or the introduction of new variants of genes from nearby populations. Gene flow occurs when previously separated groups are able to breed again.

Natural selection is the force that makes evolutionary change adaptive. It reduces the frequency of alleles for harmful or maladaptive traits within a population and increases the frequency of alleles for adaptive traits. The term *adaptation* means both the process by which organisms achieve a beneficial adjustment to an available environment and the results of the process—the characteristics of organisms that fit them to the particular set of conditions of the environment in which they are generally found. A well-studied example of adaptation through natural selection in humans is inheritance of the trait for sickling red blood cells. The sickle-cell trait, caused by the inheritance of an abnormal form of hemoglobin, is an adaptation to life in regions in which falciparum malaria is common. In these regions, the sickle-cell trait plays a beneficial role, but in other parts of the world, the sickling trait is no longer advantageous, while the associated sickle-cell anemia remains injurious. Geneticists predict that as malaria is brought under control, within several generations, there will be a decline in the number of individuals who carry the allele responsible for sickle-cell anemia.

CLASSIC READINGS

Berra, T. M. (1990). *Evolution and the myth of creationism.* Stanford, CA.: Stanford University Press.

Written by a zoologist, this book is a basic guide to the facts in the debate over evolution. It is not an attack on religion but a successful effort to assist in understanding the scientific basis for evolution.

Edey, M. A., & Johanson, D. (1989). *Blueprints: Solving the mystery of evolution.* Boston: Little, Brown.

This book is about the evolution of the idea of evolution, told as a scientific detective story. As much about the discoverers of evolution as it is about their discoveries, the book provides insights into the workings of science and gives readers the information they need to ponder the significance of our newfound ability, through genetic engineering, to actually direct the evolution of living things, including ourselves.

Gould, S. J. (1996). *Full house: The spread of excellence from Plato to Darwin.* New York: Harmony.

In this highly readable book, Gould explodes the misconception that evolution is inherently progressive. In the process, he shows how trends should be read as changes in variation within systems.

Ridley, M. (1999). *Genome: The autobiography of a species in 23 chapters.* New York: HarperCollins.

Written just as the mapping of the human genome was about to be announced, this book made *The New York Times* best-seller list. The 23 chapters discuss DNA on each of the 23 human chromosomes. A word of warning, however: The author uncritically accepts some ideas (one example relates to IQ). Still, there's much food for thought here.

Zimmer, C. (2001). *Evolution: The triumph of an idea.* New York: HarperCollins.

This is the companion volume to the seven part television series broadcast by PBS in fall 2001. Covered are a range of topics in modern evolutionary biology in a readable manner. Its drawback is that it pays too much attention to the tension between contemporary biblical literalism and the life sciences.

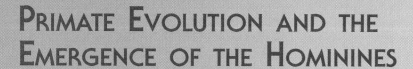

PRIMATE EVOLUTION AND THE EMERGENCE OF THE HOMININES

Chapter 4   Monkeys, Apes, and Humans:
             The Modern Primates

Chapter 5   Macroevolution and the Early Primates

Chapter 6   The Earliest Hominines

INTRODUCTION

In Chapter 1, we saw how the Nez Perce Indians of North America explained their existence in the world. Indeed, all human cultures of which we have record have grappled with such age-old questions as: Where do we come from? What is our place in the overall scheme of things? Each culture has answered these questions in its own way, through bodies of myth and folklore, as did the Nez Perce. It was not until the 20th century that hard scientific evidence was available to apply to these questions. In particular, as physical anthropologists and archaeologists have unearthed the bones and tools of our earliest ancestors, we have begun to glimpse the outline of a fantastic saga in which a tropics-dwelling apelike creature is transformed into a creative being capable of inventing solutions to problems of existence, rather than passively accepting what the environment and its own biology dictate.

This is not to say that humans represent the pinnacle of evolution, for they do not. We are, understandably, fascinated by our own origins, but in the overall scheme of things, we are nothing more than one small twig among many on the evolutionary tree of life. And as we shall see, there was nothing inevitable about our appearance: We are simply one more primate, successful for the moment as others have been in the

past (and some, like baboons and macaques, still are) but with no guarantee that our success will be any more lasting than the successes of others from the past.

This section of the book discusses developments that set the stage for the human transformation. We begin, in Chapter 4, with a review of the modern primates (the zoological order to which humans belong), in order to understand how much we humans are like the other primates. In particular, we can begin to appreciate that many of the physical characteristics we think of as distinctively human are simply our own peculiar versions of characteristics common to other primates. For example, primate brains tend to be large and heavy relative to body size and weight; in humans, this trait is realized to a greater degree than it is in other primates. We can begin to appreciate as well the kind of behavioral versatility of which present-day

members of this order are capable. In the range of modern primate behavior patterns, we find clues to patterns that were characteristic of primates that lived in the past, from which humans descended.

Knowledge of the modern primates sets the stage for a review of the fossil evidence for primate evolution. In Chapter 5, key fossils are interpreted in light of evolutionary theory, our understanding of the biological variation of modern primates, and the behavioral correlates of that variation. This brings us to the apelike creatures of 8 to 16 million years ago, from some of which human ancestors evolved. Our early apelike ancestors seem to have spent more and more time on the ground and probably possessed mental abilities more or less equivalent to those of modern great apes. Because they were small and vulnerable, we think that the greatest measure of reproductive success came to those that

were able to rear up on their hind limbs and scan the savanna, threaten predators with their forelimbs, transport food to a tree or other place where it could be eaten in relative safety, and transport offspring instead of relying on them to hang on by themselves, all the while managing to keep cool in the heat of the day.

With the appearance by 4 million years ago of *Australopithecus*, one of the earliest true hominines, the stage was set for the human transformation. *Australopithecus* may best be thought of as an apelike human; it walked bipedally in a fully human manner, but its mental abilities do not seem to have differed greatly from those of its ancestors of a few million years earlier. This implies essentially apelike behavior patterns, and it is appropriate to complete this section of the book with a chapter on *Australopithecus*. ■

CHAPTER 4

MONKEYS, APES, AND HUMANS: THE MODERN PRIMATES

Monkeys and apes have long fascinated humans, owing to our many shared anatomical and behavioral characteristics. The study of other primates provides us with important clues as to what life may have been like for our own ancestors.

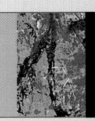

1

WHAT IS THE PLACE OF HUMANITY AMONG THE OTHER ANIMALS?

Humans are classified by biologists as belonging to the primate order, a group that also includes lemurs, lorises, tarsiers, monkeys, and apes. They are so classified on the basis of shared characteristics of anatomy, physiology, protein structure, and even the genetic material itself. Among the primates, humans resemble monkeys, but most closely resemble apes.

2

WHAT ARE THE IMPLICATIONS OF THE SHARED CHARACTERISTICS BETWEEN HUMANS AND THE OTHER PRIMATES?

The similarities on which the modern classification of animals is based are indicative of evolutionary relationships. Therefore, by studying the anatomy, physiology, and molecular structure of the other primates, we can gain a better understanding of what human characteristics we owe to our general primate ancestry and what traits are uniquely ours as humans. Such studies indicate that many of the differences between apes and humans are differences of degree rather than kind.

3

WHY DO ANTHROPOLOGISTS STUDY THE SOCIAL BEHAVIOR OF MONKEYS AND APES?

By studying the behavior of monkeys and apes living today—especially those most closely related to us—we may find essential clues from which to reconstruct the adaptations and behavior patterns involved in the emergence of our earliest ancestors.

All living creatures—be they great or small, fierce or timid, active or inactive—face a fundamental problem in common: that of survival. Simply put, unless they are able to adapt themselves to some available environment, they cannot survive. Adaptation requires the development of behavior patterns that will help an organism utilize the environment to its advantage—to find food and sustenance, avoid hazards, and, if the species is to survive, reproduce its own kind. In turn, organisms need to have the biological equipment that makes possible the development of appropriate patterns of behavior. For the hundreds of millions of years that life has existed on earth, biological adaptation has been the primary means by which the problem of survival has been solved. This is accomplished through natural selection as those organisms of a particular species whose biological equipment is best suited to a particular way of life produce more offspring than those whose equipment is not so adapted. In this way, advantageous characteristics become more common in succeeding generations, while less advantageous ones become less common.

In this chapter, we will look at the biological equipment possessed by the primates, the group of animals to which humans belong. By doing so, we will gain a firmer understanding of those characteristics we share with other primates, as well as those that distinguish us from them and make us distinctively human. We shall also sample the behavior made possible by the biological equipment of primates. The study of that behavior is important in our quest to understand something of the origins of human culture and the origin of humanity itself.

THE PRIMATE ORDER

The primate order (see Table 4.1) is only one of several mammalian orders, such as rodents, carnivores, ungulates (hoofed mammals), and so on. As such, primates share a number of features with other mammals. Generally speaking, mammals are intelligent animals, having more in the way of brains than reptiles or other sorts of vertebrates. In most species, the young are born live, the egg being retained within the womb of the female until the embryo achieves an advanced state of growth. Once born, the young are nourished by their mothers with milk provided from the mammary glands, from which the class Mammalia gets its name. During this period of infant dependency, young mammals are able to learn some of the things that they will need for survival as adults. Overall, these characteristics make for more flexible behavior than found among nonmammal vertebrates.

The traditional (but mistaken) Western notion of an unbridgeable gap between humans and animals is implicitly exemplified by the practice of dressing apes as humans and laughing at their behavior; that is, you can dress 'em up like us, but they sure don't behave like us!

Mammals are also active animals. This is made possible by their relatively constant body temperature, an efficient respiratory system featuring a separation between the nasal and mouth cavities (allowing them to breathe while they eat), a diaphragm to assist in drawing in and letting out breath, and an efficient four-chambered heart that prevents mixing of oxygenated and deoxygenated blood. It is facilitated as well by a skeleton in which the limbs are positioned beneath the body, rather than out at the sides, for ease and economy of movement. The bones of the limbs have joints constructed so as to permit growth in the young while simultaneously providing strong, hard joint surfaces that will stand up to the stresses of sustained activity. In return, they have given up the ability, possessed by reptiles, for bone growth throughout life.

The skeleton of most mammals is simplified, compared to that of most reptiles, in that it has fewer bones. For example, the lower jaw consists of a single bone, rather than several. The teeth, however, are another matter. Instead of the relatively simple, pointed, peglike teeth of reptiles,

TABLE 4.1   THE PRIMATE ORDER

Order	Suborder	Infraorder	Superfamily	Family
			Lemuroidea	
Primates	Strepsirhini	Lemuriformes		Five families of lemurs and lemurlike animals
			Lorisoidea	Three families of lorises
	Haplorhini	Tarsii	Tarsioidea	One family, represented solely by tarsiers
		Platyrrhini	Ceboidea	Three families of New World Monkeys
		Catarrhini	Cercopithecoidea	One family with two subfamilies of Old World monkeys
			Hominoidea	Hylobatidae (small apes)
				Pongidae (Asian great apes)
				Hominidae (African apes, humans, and near humans)

mammals have special teeth for special purposes: incisors for nipping, gnawing, and cutting; canines for ripping, tearing, killing, and fighting; premolars that may either slice and tear or crush and grind (depending on the kind of animal); and molars for crushing and grinding. This enables mammals to eat a wide variety of food—an advantage to them, since they require more food than do reptiles to sustain their high activity. But they pay a price: Reptiles have unlimited tooth replacement, whereas mammals are limited to two sets. The first set serves the immature animal and is replaced by the permanent or adult dentition.

The primate order is divided into two suborders (Table 4.1), of which one is the **Strepsirhini** (from the Greek for "turned nose"). This includes lemurs and lorises (all members of the infraorder **Lemuriformes**). On the whole, strepsirhines are cat-sized or smaller, although there have been some larger forms in the past. Generally, they do not exhibit the characteristics of their order as obviously as do the members of the other suborder, the **Haplorhini** (from the Greek for "simple nose"). The strepsirhines also retain certain features common among nonprimate mammals, such as claws and moist, naked skin on their noses, that have not been retained by the haplorhines.

The haplorhine suborder is divided into three infraorders: the **Tarsii,** or tarsiers; the **Platyrrhini,** or New World monkeys; and the **Catarrhini,** consisting of the superfamilies Cercopithecoidea (Old World monkeys) and Hominoidea. Within the Hominoidea are the families Hylobatidae (small apes, like the gibbon), Pongidae, and Hominidae. Although the traditional classification of primates placed all great apes (bonobo, chimpanzee, gorilla, and orangutan) together in the pongid family, and humans alone as hominids, molecular evidence has demonstrated that this way of grouping apes and humans violates evolutionary relationships. Because the way we classify is supposed to reflect evolutionary genealogies, recent classifications restrict the Pongidae to orangutans, whereas bonobos, chimps, and gorillas are included with humans in the Hominidae, as a reflection of their closer relation to one another than to orangs. Unfortunately, old habits die hard, and it is still common to find scientists using the family names in the outmoded way. But because it misleads, this obsolete practice should be dropped; therefore, in this book we shall use classificatory terminology more reflective of evolutionary genealogy. Only at the level of the subfamily will humans (homininae) be separated from bonobos, chimps, and gorillas, although

Strepsirhini.   A primate suborder that includes the single infraorder Lemuriformes.   •   **Lemuriformes.**   A strepsirhine infraorder that includes lemurs and lorises.   •   **Haplorhini.**   A primate suborder that includes tarsiers, monkeys, apes, and humans.   •   **Tarsii.**   A haplorhine infraorder that includes tarsiers.   •   **Platyrrhini.** A haplorhine infraorder that includes the New World monkeys.   •   **Catarrhini.**   A haplorhine infraorder that includes Old World monkeys, apes, and humans.

Hands that grasp and eyes that see in three dimensions enable primates, like these South American monkeys, to live effectively in the trees.

a case can be made that the separation should be made below even the level of the subfamily.[1]

CHARACTERISTICS

Although the living primates are a varied group of animals, they do have a number of features in common (Table 4.2). We humans, for example, can grasp, throw things, and see stereoscopically because we are primates. Primate features are, however, displayed in varying degree by the different members of this order; in some they are barely detectable, while in others they are greatly elaborated. All are useful in one way or another to **arboreal,** or tree-dwelling, animals, although (as any squirrel knows) they are not essential to life in the trees. For animals preying upon the many insects living on the fruit and flowers of trees and shrubs, however, such primate characteristics as manipulative hands and keen vision would have been enormously adaptive. Probably, it was as arboreal animals relying on visual predation of insects that primates got their start in life.

The Primate Brain

By far the most outstanding characteristic of primate evolution has been the enlargement of the brain among members of the order. Primate brains tend to be large, heavy in proportion to body weight, and very complex. The cerebral hemispheres (the areas of conscious thought) have enlarged dramatically and, in catarrhines, completely cover the cerebellum, which is the part of the brain that coordinates the muscles and maintains body equilibrium.

The reasons for this important change in brain size are many, but it likely began as the earliest primates, along with many other mammals, began to carry out their activities in the daylight hours. Prior to 65 million years ago, mammals seem to have been nocturnal in their habits, but with the extinction of the dinosaurs, inconspicuous, nighttime activity was no longer the key to survival. With the change to diurnal or daytime activity, the sense of vision took on greater importance, and so visual acuity was favored by natural selection. Unlike reptile vision, where the information-processing neurons are in the retina, mammalian vision is processed in the brain, permitting integration with information received by hearing and smelling.

If the evolution of visual acuity led to larger brains, it is likely that the primates' insect predation in an arboreal setting also played a role in enlargement of the brain. This would have required great agility and muscular coordination, favoring development of the brain centers. Thus it is of interest that much of the higher mental faculties are apparently developed in an area alongside the motor centers of the brain.[2]

Another related hypothesis that may help account for primate brain enlargement involves the use of the hand

---

[1]Goodman, M., Bailey, W. J., Hayasaka, K., Stanhope, M. J., Slighton J., & Czelusniak, J. (1994). Molecular evidence on primate phylogeny from DNA sequences. *American Journal of Physical Anthropology, 94,* 7.

[2]Romer, A. S. (1945). *Vertebrate paleontology* (p. 103). Chicago: University of Chicago Press.

Arboreal.   Tree-dwelling.

TABLE 4.2	PRIMATE ANATOMY VARIATION AND SPECIALIZATION			
Suborder, Infraorder, Superfamily	**Skull and Face**	**Dental Pattern and Specializations**	**Locomotor Pattern and Morphology**	**Tail and Other Skeletal Specializations**
Strepsirhini	Complete ring of bone around eye orbit	2-1-3-3 Dental comb for grooming	Hind leg dominance for vertical clinging and leaping	Tail present
Lemuriformes				"Toilet claw" for grooming
Lorisiformes	Upper lip bound down to gum			
Haplorhini	Forward facing orbit fully enclosed in bone Free upper lip Shorter snout			
Tarsiiformes Tarsiers		2-1-3-3	Hind leg dominance	Tail present
Platyrrhini New World Monkeys		2-1-3-3	Quadrupedal	Prehensile tail
Catarrhini Old World Monkeys		2-1-2-3 4-cusped molars	Quadrupedal	Tail present
Apes		2-1-2-3 Y5 molars	Suspensory hanging apparatus	No tail

as a tactile organ to replace the teeth and jaws or snout. The hands assumed some of the grasping, tearing, and dividing functions of the snout, again requiring development of the brain centers for more complete coordination. Thus, while the skull and brain expanded, the teeth and jaws grew smaller. Certain areas of the brain became more elaborate and intricate. One of these areas is the cortex, considered to be the center of an animal's intelligence; it receives impressions from the animal's various sensory receptors, analyzes them, and sends responses back down the motor nerves to the proper receptor.

The enlarged cortex not only served the primates well in the daily struggle for survival but also gave them the basis for more complex cerebration, or thought. Flexibility of thought probably played a decisive role in the evolution of the primates from which human beings emerged.

Primate Sense Organs

Catching insects in the trees, as the early primates did and many still do, demands quickness of movement and the ability to land in the right place without falling. Thus, they had to be adept at judging depth, direction, distance, and the relationships of objects in space—abilities that remain useful to animals that travel through the trees (as most primates still do today), even though they may have given up most insect eating in favor of fruits and leaves. In the haplorhines, these abilities are provided by their binocular **stereoscopic vision,** the ability to see the world in three dimensions—height, width, and depth. It requires two eyes set apart from each other on the same plane, so that each eye views an object from a slightly different angle (binocular vision). In addition, nerve fibers from each eye go to each side of the brain. The result is that

Stereoscopic vision.   Three-dimensional vision.

the object assumes a three-dimensional appearance, indicating spatial relationships. Stereoscopic vision is one of the most important factors in primate evolution, for it evidently led to increased brain size in the visual area and a great complexity at nerve connections.

Visual acuity, however, varies throughout the primate order. Lemuriformes, for example, are the most visually primitive of the primates. With binocular but not stereoscopic vision, their eyes look out from either side of their muzzle or snout with some overlap of visual fields, but their nerve fibers do not cross from each eye to both halves of the brain. Nor do they possess color vision, an advantage for nocturnal animals as it enhances night vision. All other primates possess both color and stereoscopic vision, as well as a unique structure called the **fovea centralis,** or central pit in the retina of each eye. Like a camera lens, this feature enables the animal to focus on a particular object for acutely clear perception, without sacrificing visual contact with the object's surroundings.

The primates' emphasis on visual acuity came at the expense of their sense of smell. One reason is that smell is processed in the snout, and a large protruding snout may interfere with stereoscopic vision. But smell is an expendable sense to tree-dwelling animals in search of insects; they no longer needed to live a "nose-to-the-ground" existence, sniffing close to the ground in search of food. The haplorhines especially have the least-developed sense of smell of all land animals. Strepsirhines still rely on it to a degree, scent marking objects in their territories.

Primate sense of touch also became highly developed as a result of arboreal living. Primates found useful an effective feeling and grasping mechanism to grab their insect prey and to prevent them from falling and tumbling while moving through the trees. The primitive mammals from which primates descended possessed tiny tactile hairs that gave them extremely sensitive tactile capacities. In primates, these hairs were replaced by informative pads on the tips of the animals' fingers and toes.

Primate Dentition

Although they have added other things than insects to their diets, primates have retained less specialized teeth than other mammals. According to primatologist W. E. LeGros Clark,

An arboreal life obviates the necessity for developing highly specialized grinding teeth, since the diet available to most tree-living mammals in the tropics, consisting of leaves, shoots, soft fruits, and insects, can be adequately masticated by molar teeth of relatively simple structure.[3]

In most primates (humans included), on each side of each jaw, in front, are two straight-edged, chisel-like broad teeth called incisors (Figure 4.1). Behind the incisors is a canine, which in many mammals is large, flaring, and fanglike and is used for defense as well as for tearing and shredding food. Among some catarrhines the

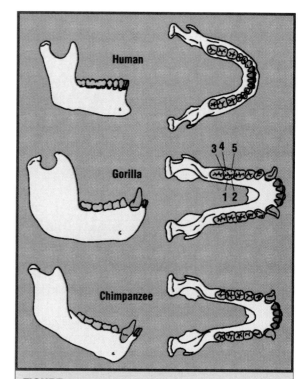

FIGURE 4.1

IN THIS DEPICTION OF THE LOWER JAWS OF A HUMAN, A GORILLA, AND A CHIMPANZEE, INCISORS ARE SHOWN IN BLUE, CANINES IN RED, AND PREMOLARS AND MOLARS IN YELLOW. ON ONE OF THE GORILLA MOLARS, THE CUSPS ARE NUMBERED TO FACILITATE THEIR IDENTIFICATION.

---

[3]LeGros Clark, W. E. (1966). *History of the primates* (5th ed., p. 271). Chicago: University of Chicago Press.

Fovea centralis.   A shallow pit in the retina of the eye that enables an animal to focus on an object while maintaining visual contact with its surroundings.

canine is somewhat reduced in size, especially in females, though it is still large in males. In humans, though, incisors and canines are practically indistinguishable, although the canine has an oversized root, suggestive of larger canines some time back in our ancestry. Behind the canines are the premolars. Last come the molars, usually with four or five cusps, used mostly for crushing or grinding food. This basic dentition contrasts sharply with that of nonprimate mammals.

Comparative anatomy and the fossil record point to the existence of an early primate ancestor that possessed three incisors, one canine, five premolars, and three molars (expressed as the dental formula 3-1-5-3) on each side of the jaw, top and bottom, for a total of 48 teeth. In the early stages of primate evolution, four incisors (one on each side of each jaw) were lost. This change differentiated the primates, with their two incisors on each side of each jaw, from other mammals. The canines of most primates develop into long, daggerlike teeth that enable them to rip open tough husks of fruit and other foods. In a combat situation, male baboons, apes, and other primates flash these formidable teeth at their enemies, intending to scare them off. Only infrequently, when this bluffing action fails, are teeth used to inflict bodily harm.

Other evolutionary changes in primate dentition involve the premolar and molar teeth. Over the millennia, the first and second premolars became smaller and eventually disappeared altogether, while the third and fourth premolars grew larger with the addition of a second pointed projection, or cusp, thus becoming "bicuspid." In humans, all eight premolars are bicuspid, but in apes, the lower first premolar is not. Instead, it is a specialized, single cusped tooth with a sharp edge to act with the upper canine as a shearing mechanism. The molars, meanwhile, evolved from a three-cusp pattern to one with four and even five (in apes and humans) cusps. This kind of molar economically combined the functions of grasping, cutting, and grinding in one tooth.

The evolutionary trend for primate dentition has generally been toward economy, with fewer, smaller, more efficient teeth doing more work. Thus our own 32 teeth (a 2-1-2-3 dental formula shared with the Old World monkeys and apes) are fewer in number than those of some, and more generalized than those of most, primates. Indeed, the absence of third molars in many individuals indicates that the human dentition is undergoing further reduction.

The Primate Skeleton

The skeleton gives an animal its basic shape or silhouette, supports the soft tissues, and helps protect the vital internal organs. In primates (Figure 4.2), for example, the

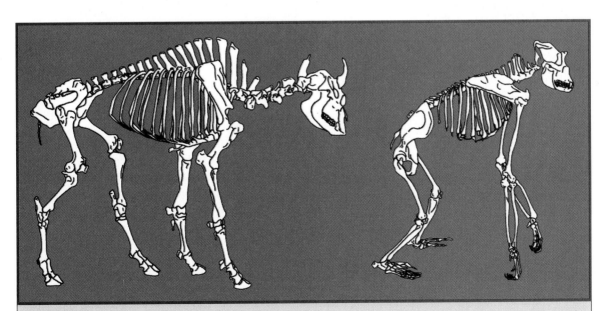

FIGURE 4.2

NOTE WHERE THE SKULLS AND VERTEBRAL COLUMNS ARE JOINED IN THESE SKELETONS OF A BISON (LEFT) AND A GORILLA (RIGHT). IN THE BISON (AS IN MOST MAMMALS) THE SKULL PROJECTS FORWARD FROM THE VERTEBRAL COLUMN, BUT IN THE SEMIERECT GORILLA, THE VERTEBRAL COLUMN IS FURTHER BENEATH THE SKULL. NOTE ALSO THE SPECIALIZED FOOT SKELETON OF THE BISON, COMPARED TO THE GENERALIZED FOOT OF THE GORILLA.

Humans owe their flat facial profile and erect posture to their catarrhine ancestry.

skull protects the brain and the eyes. A number of factors are responsible for the shape of the primate skull as compared with those of most other mammals: changes in dentition, changes in the sensory organs of sight and smell, and increased brain size. The primate brain case, or **cranium,** tends to be high and vaulted. A solid partition exists in most primate species (including humans) between the eye and the temple, affording maximum protection to the eyes from the contraction of the chewing muscles positioned directly next to the eyes.

The **foramen magnum** (the large opening in the skull through which the spinal cord passes and connects to the brain) is an important clue to evolutionary relationships. In most mammals, as in dogs and horses, this opening faces directly backward, with the skull projecting forward from

the vertebral column. In humans, by contrast, the vertebral column joins the skull toward the center of its base, thereby placing the skull in a balanced position as required for habitual upright posture. Other primates, though they frequently cling, sit, or hang with their bodies upright, are not as fully committed to such posture as humans, and so their foramen magnum is not as far forward.

In most primates, the snout or muzzle portion of the skull has grown smaller as the acuity of the sense of smell declined. The smaller snout offers less interference with stereoscopic vision; it also enables the eyes to be placed in the frontal position. As a result, primates have flatter faces than other mammals. Below the primate skull and the neck is the **clavicle,** or collarbone, a holdover from primitive mammal ancestors. Though reduced in quadru-

---

Cranium.   The brain case of the skull.   •   **Foramen magnum.**   A large opening in the skull through which the spinal cord passes and connects to the brain.   •   **Clavicle.**   The collarbone.

Humans are able to grasp and throw things as they do because of characteristics of their hands and shoulders inherited from ape ancestors.

pedal primates like monkeys, in apes and humans it serves as a strut that prevents the arm from collapsing inward when brought across the front of the body. It allows for great maneuverability of the arms, permitting them to swing sideways and outward from the trunk of the body. The clavicle also supports the **scapula** (shoulder blade) and allows for the muscle development that is required for flexible, yet powerful, arm movement, particularly in hominoids, whose shoulders are especially broad. This shoulder and limb structure is associated with considerable acrobatic agility and, in the case of all apes and a few New World monkeys, the ability to **brachiate**—use their arms to swing and hang beneath the branches of trees with the body in a vertical (upright) position.

Primates have retained also the characteristic, found in early mammals, of **pentadactyly.** Pentadactyly, which means possessing five digits, is an ancient characteristic that proved to be of special advantage to tree-dwelling primates. Their grasping feet and hands (Figure 4.3) have

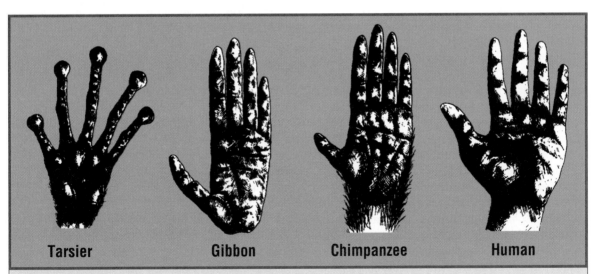

Tarsier Gibbon Chimpanzee Human

FIGURE 4.3
THE HANDS OF PRIMATES ARE SIMILAR. HOWEVER, HUMAN HANDS ARE DISTINGUISHED BY PROMINENT THUMBS THAT CAN BE USED IN OPPOSITION TO THE FINGERS. THE HIGHLY SPECIALIZED HANDS OF THE BRACHIATORS (GIBBONS AND CHIMPANZEES) ARE CHARACTERIZED BY LONG FINGERS AND LESS PROMINENT THUMBS.

Scapula. The shoulder blade. • **Brachiate.** To use the arms to move from branch to branch, with the body hanging suspended beneath the arms. • **Pentadactyly.** Possessing five digits (fingers and toes).

sensitive pads at the tips of their digits, backed up (except in some strepsirhines) by flattened nails. This unique combination of pad and nail provides the animal with an excellent **prehensile** (grasping) device for use when moving from branch to branch. The structural characteristics of the primate foot and hand make grasping possible; the digits are extremely flexible, the big toe is fully opposable to the other digits in all but humans and their immediate ancestors, and the thumb is opposable to the other digits to varying degrees.

Hindsight indicates that the flexible, unspecialized primate hand was to prove a valuable asset for future evolution of this group. Had they not had generalized grasping hands, early hominines (members of the human subfamily) would not have been able to manufacture and utilize tools and thus embark on the new and unique evolutionary pathway that led to the revolutionary ability to adapt through culture.

Reproduction and Care of Young

The breeding of most mammals occurs once or twice a year, but many primate species are able to breed at any time during the course of the year. Generally, the male is ready to engage in sexual activity whenever females are in **estrus,** around the time of ovulation. The female's receptivity is cyclical, corresponding to her period of estrus, which occurs once each month.

This is not to say that females are receptive regularly each month. Rather, the average adult female monkey or ape spends most of her time either pregnant or nursing, at which times she is not sexually receptive. But after her infant is weaned, she will come into estrus for a few days each month, until she becomes pregnant again. Because this can happen at any time, it is advantageous to have males present throughout the year. This is promoted in some species by lack of visual signs of estrus. Thus, sex plays a role in keeping both sexes constantly together, except among some orangutans, among whom adults may only come together when females are in estrus. In most species, however, sex is not the only, or even the most important, cause of males and females remaining together.

Among primates, as among some other mammals, females give birth to few offspring at a time. In the case of lemurs, the primates closest to the ancestral condition, two or three young are produced at each birth. By con-

trast, catarrhines (humans included), usually produce but a single offspring at a time. Natural selection may have favored single births among primate tree dwellers because the primate infant, which has a highly developed grasping ability (the grasping reflex can also be seen in human infants), must be transported about by its mother, and more than one clinging infant would seriously encumber her as she moved about the trees (where twinning is seen, fathers as well as mothers transport offspring). Moreover, a female pregnant with a large litter would be unable to lead a very active life as a tree dweller.

Because primates bear few young at a time, they must devote more time and effort to their care if the species is to survive. This usually means a longer period during which the infant is dependent upon its mother. As a general rule, the more closely related to humans the species is, the smaller, more helpless, and more immature the newborn offspring tend to be. For example, a lemur is dependent upon the mother for only a few months after birth; an ape, for 4 or 5 years; and a human for more than a decade. Prolonged infancy is typically associated with an increase in longevity (Figure 4.4). If the breeding life of primates had not extended, the lengthened infancy could have led to a decrease in numbers of individuals. Something approaching this can be seen in the great apes: A female chimpanzee, for example, does not reach sexual maturity until about the age of 10, and once she produces her first live offspring, there is a period of 5 or 6 (on average 5.6) years before she will bear another. Furthermore, a chimpanzee infant cannot survive if its mother dies before it reaches the age of 4 at the very least. Thus, assuming that none of her offspring die before adulthood, a female chimpanzee must survive for at least 20 or 21 years just to maintain the size of chimpanzee populations at existing levels. In fact, chimpanzee infants and juveniles do die from time to time, and not all females live full reproductive lives. This is one reason why apes are far less abundant in the world today than are monkeys.

The young of catarrhine, and especially hominoid, species are born with relatively underdeveloped nervous systems; moreover, they lack the social knowledge that guides behavior. Thus they depend upon adults not only for protection but also for instruction, as they must learn how to survive. The longer period of dependence in these primates makes possible a longer period of learning, which appears to be a distinct evolutionary advantage.

Prehensile. Having the ability to grasp. • **Estrus.** In primate females, the time of sexual receptivity during which ovulation takes place.

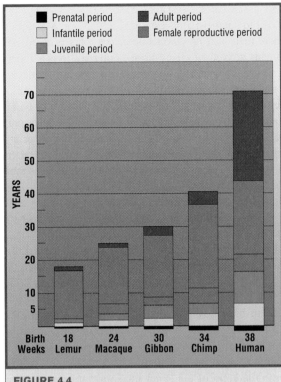

FIGURE 4.4

PRIMATES ARE BORN AT EARLIER STAGES OF DEVELOP-
MENT THAN MANY OTHER ANIMALS. HUMANS ARE BORN
AT A PARTICULARLY EARLY STAGE BECAUSE OF THEIR
LARGER BRAIN; IF BORN LATER, THE BABY'S HEAD WOULD
BE TOO LARGE FOR THE MOTHER'S PELVIS.

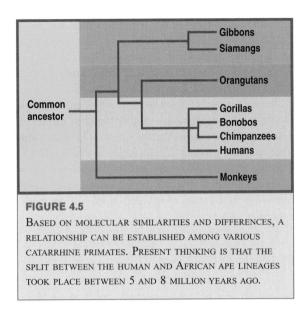

FIGURE 4.5

BASED ON MOLECULAR SIMILARITIES AND DIFFERENCES, A
RELATIONSHIP CAN BE ESTABLISHED AMONG VARIOUS
CATARRHINE PRIMATES. PRESENT THINKING IS THAT THE
SPLIT BETWEEN THE HUMAN AND AFRICAN APE LINEAGES
TOOK PLACE BETWEEN 5 AND 8 MILLION YEARS AGO.

Establishing Evolutionary Relationships

Most of the primate characteristics discussed so far are present at least in a rudimentary sort of way in the strepsirhines, but all are seen to a much greater degree in the haplorhines. The differences between humans and the other haplorhines, especially catarrhines, are rather like those between strepsirhines and haplorhines. In humans many of the characteristic primate traits are developed to a degree not realized by any other species. Among some strepsirhines, some of the distinctive primate traits are missing, whereas others are clearly present, so that the borderline between primate and nonprimate becomes blurred, and the difference is one of degree rather than kind. All of this is fully expectable, given an evolutionary history in which early primates having a rough resemblance to today's strepsirhines developed out of some other mammalian order and eventually gave rise to early haplorhines; from these emerged the catarrhines and, ultimately, hominids.

Similar though our appearance is to other primates, just how close our evolutionary relationship is to them is indicated most dramatically by molecular evidence. There is a striking similarity in blood and protein chemistry among the hominoids especially, indicating close evolutionary relationships. On the basis of tests with blood proteins, it has been shown that the bonobo, chimpanzee, and gorilla are closest to humans; next comes the orangutan; then the smaller apes (gibbons and siamangs); Old World monkeys; New World monkeys; and finally the strepsirhines. Measurements of genetic affinity confirm these findings, providing further evidence of humanity's close kinship to the great apes, especially those of Africa (Figure 4.5). The modern classification of humans, two species of genus *Pan* (bonobos and chimpanzees), and gorillas together in the family hominidae, distinct from the pongidae, reflects the fact that the three genera are more closely related to one another than any is to the orangutan.

At the genetic level, humans, bonobos, and chimpanzees are between 98 and 99 percent identical. The differences are that bonobos and chimps (like gorillas and orangs) have an extra pair of chromosomes; in humans, two medium-sized chromosomes have fused together in Chromosome 2 (the second largest of the human chromosomes). Of the other pairs, 18 are virtually identical between humans and the genus *Pan* whereas the remaining ones have been reshuffled. Overall, the differences are fewer than those between gibbons (with 44 chromosomes) and siamangs (50 chromosomes), which, in captivity, have produced live hybrid offspring. Although some studies of molecular similarities have suggested a closer relationship between *Pan* and humans than either has to gorillas, others disagree, and the safest course at the moment is to regard all three hominid genera as having an equal degree of relationship (the two species of genus *Pan* are, of course, more closely related to each other than either is to gorillas or humans).[4]

To sum up, what becomes apparent when humans are compared to other primates is how many of the characteristics we think of as distinctly human are no such thing; rather, they are variants of typical primate traits. The fact is, we humans look the way we do *because* we are primates, and the differences between us and others of this order—especially the apes—are more differences of degree than kind.

MODERN PRIMATES

The modern primates are mostly restricted to warm areas of the world. As already noted, they are divided into two suborders: Strepsirhini and Haplorhini. Strepsirhines are small Old World animals that do a lot of leaping and clinging; haplorhines include tarsiers, monkeys, apes, and humans.

Strepsirhines

The strepsirhines, the most primitive primates (that is, closest to the ancestral condition), are represented by the single infraorder Lemuriformes, within which are the lemurs and lorises. Although lemurs are restricted to the island of

Madagascar (off the east coast of Africa), lorises range from Africa to southern and eastern Asia. Only on Madagascar, where there was no competition from other primates until humans arrived, are lemuriformes diurnal; lorises by contrast, are all nocturnal. All these animals are small, with none larger than a good-sized dog. In general body outline, they resemble rodents and insectivores, with short pointed snouts, large pointed ears, and big eyes. In the anatomy of the upper lip and snout, lemuriformes resemble nonprimate mammals, in that the upper lip is bound down to the gum and the naked skin on the nose around the nostrils is moist. They also have long tails, with that of a ring-tail lemur somewhat like the tail of a raccoon.

In brain structure, lemuriformes are clearly primates, and they have characteristically primate "hands," although they use them in pairs, rather than one at a time. Their legs are longer than their forelimbs, and when they move on all fours, the forelimbs are in a "palms down" position. They also leap and cling in near vertical positions to branches. Although they retain a claw on their second toe, which they use for scratching and grooming, all other digits are equipped with flattened nails. Also for grooming is a structure unique to lemuriformes: a dental comb made up of the lower incisors and canines, which project forward from the jaw. With their distinctive mix of characteristics, strepsirhine primates appear to occupy a place between the haplorhines and insectivores (the mammalian order that includes moles and shrews).

Haplorhines

The suborder Haplorhini is divided into three infraorders: the Tarsii (tarsiers), Platyrrhini (New World monkeys), and Catarrhini (Old World monkeys, apes, and humans). Most

---

[4]Rogers, J. (1994). Levels of the genealogical hierarchy and the problem of hominid phylogeny. *American Journal of Physical Anthropology, 94,* 81.

Modern strepsirhines represent highly evolved variants of an early primate model.

haplorhines are bigger than the strepsirhines and are strikingly humanlike in appearance. Actually, it is more accurate to say that humans are remarkably like monkeys, but even more like apes, in appearance. The defining traits of the strepsirhines—large cranium, well-developed brain, acute vision, chisel-like incisors, prehensile digits—are especially evident in the haplorhines. Most haplorhines generally move on all four limbs but sit with the body erect, and many stand erect to reach fruit hanging in trees: Some apes even walk occasionally on two feet. Monkeys are often highly arboreal, and New World species have prehensile tails that wrap around a tree branch, freeing the forelimbs to grasp food. A few New World monkeys brachiate; Old World monkeys never do.

All apes may once have been fully arboreal brachiators, but among modern apes, only the gibbon and siamang still are. The larger bonobo, chimpanzee, and gorilla spend most of their time on the ground but sleep in the trees and may also find food there. Orangutans, too, spend time down on the ground, but are more arboreal than the African apes. When on the ground, they move mostly on all fours.

TARSIERS

Tarsiers are the haplorhine primates most like the lemuriformes, and in the past they were usually classified in the same suborder with them. Molecular evidence, however, indicates a closer relationship to the other haplorhines. The head, eyes, and ears of these kitten-sized arboreal creatures are huge in proportion to the body.

Tarsiers are distinctive for their large eyes, adapted for their nocturnal habitat.

They have the remarkable ability to turn their heads 180 degrees, so they can see where they have been as well as where they are going. The digits end in platelike, adhesive discs. Tarsiers are named for the elongated tarsal, or foot bone, that provides leverage for jumps of 6 feet or more. Tarsiers are mainly nocturnal insect eaters. In the structure of the nose and lips, and the part of the brain governing vision, tarsiers resemble monkeys.

NEW WORLD MONKEYS

New World monkeys live in forests and swamps of South and Central America. They are characterized by flat noses with widely separated, outward flaring nostrils, from which comes their name of platyrrhine (platy = flat; rhine = nose) monkeys. All are arboreal, and some have long, prehensile tails by which they hang from trees. These features and a 2-1-3-3 dental formula (three, rather than two, premolars on each side of each jaw) distinguish them from the Old World monkeys, apes, and humans. Platyrrhines walk on all fours with their palms down and scamper along tree branches in search of fruit, which they eat sitting upright. Spider monkeys are accomplished brachiators as well. Although other New World monkeys spend much of their time in the trees, they rarely hang or swing from limb to limb by their arms and have not developed the extremely long forelimbs and broad shoulders characteristic of brachiators.

OLD WORLD MONKEYS

Old World, or catarrhine, monkeys are characterized by noses with closely spaced, downward-pointing nostrils, a 2-1-2-3 dental formula (two, rather than three, premolars on each side of each jaw), and their lack of prehensile tails. They may be either arboreal or terrestrial. The arboreal species include the guereza monkey, the Asiatic langur, and the strange-looking proboscis monkey. Some are equally at home on the ground and in the trees, such as the macaques, of which some 19 species range from Gibraltar (the misnamed "Barbary ape") to Japan.

Several species of baboons are largely terrestrial, living in the savannas, deserts, and highlands of Africa. They have long, fierce faces and move quadrupedally, with all fours in the palms-down position. Like all monkeys, their forelimbs and hindlimbs are of equal length. Their diet consists of leaves, seeds, insects, and lizards, and they live in large, well-organized troops consisting of related females and adult males that have transferred out of other troops. Because baboons have abandoned trees (except for sleeping and refuge) and live in environments like that in which humans may have originated, they are of great interest to primatologists.

SMALL AND GREAT APES

The apes are the closest living relatives we humans have in the animal world. Their general appearance and way of life are related to their semierect posture. In their body chemistry, the position of their internal organs, and even their diseases, they are remarkably close to humans. They are arboreal to varying degrees, but their generally greater size and weight are obstacles to swinging and jumping as freely as monkeys. The exception is the small, lithe gibbon, which can both climb and swing freely through the trees and so spends virtually all of its time in them. At the opposite extreme are gorillas, who climb trees, using their prehensile hands and feet to grip the trunk and branches. Their swinging is limited to leaning outward as they reach for fruit, clasping a limb for support. Most of their time is spent on the ground.

The apes, like humans, have no external tail. Also shared with us are broad shoulders, unlike the narrow ones of monkeys. But, unlike humans, their arms are longer than their legs, indicating that their ancestors specialized for arboreal brachiation in a way that our own did not. In moving on the ground, the African apes "knuckle-walk" on the backs of their hands, resting their weight on the middle joints of the fingers. They stand erect when reaching for fruit, looking over tall grass, or in any activity where they find an erect position advantageous. The semierect position is natural in apes when on the ground because the curvature of their vertebral

Gibbons and orangutans are Southeast Asian apes. Gibbons are brachiators that use their long arms and hands to swing through the trees. Although orangutans sometimes brachiate, their legs move like arms and their feet are like hands; thus, much of their movement is by four-handed climbing.

column places their center of gravity, which is high in their bodies, in front of their hip joint. Thus, they are both "top heavy" and "front heavy." Furthermore, the structure of the ape pelvis is not well suited to support the weight of the torso and limbs easily. Nor do apes have the arrangement of leg muscles that enables humans to stand erect and swing their legs freely before and behind.

Gibbons and siamangs, which are native to Southeast Asia and Malaya, have compact, slim bodies with extraordinarily long arms compared to their short legs, and stand about 3 feet high. Although their usual form of locomotion is brachiation, they can run erect, holding their arms out for balance. Gibbons and siamangs resemble monkeys in size and general appearance more than the other apes.

Orangutans are found in Borneo and Sumatra. They are somewhat taller than gibbons and siamangs and are much heavier, with the bulk characteristic of apes. In the closeness of the eyes and facial prominence, an orangutan looks a little like a chimpanzee, except that its hair is reddish. Orangs walk with their forelimbs in a fists-sideways or a palms-down position. They are, however, somewhat more arboreal than the African apes. Although sociable by nature, the orangs of upland Borneo spend most of their time alone (except in the case of females with young), as they have to forage over a wide area to obtain sufficient food. By contrast, fruits and insects are sufficiently abundant in the swamps of Sumatra to sustain groups of adults and permit coordinated group travel. Thus, gregariousness is a function of habitat productivity.[5]

Gorillas, found in equatorial Africa, are the largest of the apes; an adult male can weigh over 400 pounds. The body is covered with a thick coat of glossy black hair, and mature males have a silvery gray upper back. There is a strikingly human look about the face, and like humans, gorillas focus on things in their field of vision by directing the eyes rather than moving the head. Gorillas are mostly ground dwellers but may sleep in trees in carefully constructed nests. Because of their weight, brachiation is limited to raising and lowering themselves among the tree branches when searching for fruit. They knuckle-walk, using all four limbs with the fingers of the hand flexed, placing the knuckles instead of the palm of the hand on the ground. They will stand erect to reach for fruit, to see something more easily, or to threaten perceived sources of danger with their famous chest-beating displays. Although gorillas are gentle and tolerant, bluffing is an important part of their behavioral repertoire.

Chimpanzees and bonobos are two species of the same genus (*Pan*), bonobos being the least well known and restricted in their distribution to the rain forests of

---

[5]Normile, D. (1998). Habitat seen as playing larger role in shaping behavior. *Science, 279,* 1454.

Chimpanzees and gorillas are African apes.

the Democratic Republic of Congo. The common chimpanzee, by contrast, is widely distributed in the forested portions of sub-Saharan Africa. They are probably the best known of the apes and have long been favorites in zoos and circuses. Although thought of as particularly quick and clever, all four great apes are of equal intelligence, despite some differences in cognitive styles. More arboreal than gorillas, but less so than orangs, chimpanzees and bonobos forage on the ground much of the day, knuckle-walking like gorillas. At sunset, they return to the trees, where they build their nests. Those of chimps are more dispersed than those of bonobos, who prefer to build their nests close to one another.

THE SOCIAL BEHAVIOR OF PRIMATES

The physical resemblance of human beings to the other catarrhines is striking, but the most startling resemblance of all is in their social behavior. Because of their highly developed brains, monkeys and apes behave in ways that are far more complex than most other animals except humans. Only over the past four decades have primatologists made prolonged close-range observations of catarrhines in their natural habitats, and we are discovering much about social organization, learning ability, and communication among our closest relatives in the animal kingdom. In particular, we are finding that a number of behavioral traits that we used to think of as distinctively human are found to one degree or another among other primates, reminding us once again that many of the differences between us and them are differences of degree, rather than kind.

The range of behavior shown by living primates is great—too great to be adequately surveyed in this book. Instead, we shall look primarily at the behavior of those species most closely related to humans: bonobos, chimpanzees, and gorillas.

The Group

Primates are social animals, living and traveling in groups that vary in size from species to species. In most species, females and their offspring constitute the core of the social system. This is true of chimpanzees to a degree. In two Tanzanian communities studied, females often leave their natal group for another, although up to 50 percent do not.[6] In both cases, however, females in ovulation may temporarily leave their group to mate with males of another. But whatever the case, their sons, and often their daughters, remain in their mother's group for life. Among bonobos, females always transfer to another group, in which they establish bonds with females already there. Female bonobos are especially skilled at establishing such bonds with one another, so they are far more sociable than are their chimpanzee counterparts. Among the latter, the stronger bonds are between males, as young ones reaching maturity spend more and more time with the adult males of their group. In the case of gorillas, either sex may or may not leave its natal group for another.

Among chimps, the largest organizational unit is the community, composed of 50 or more individuals. Rarely, however, are all these animals together at a single time. Instead, they are usually found ranging singly or in small subgroups consisting of adult males together, females with their young, or males and females together with their young. In the course of their travels, subgroups may join forces and forage together, but sooner or later these will break up again into smaller units. When they do, members are often exchanged, so that new subunits are different in their composition from the ones that initially came together.

Although relationships among individuals within the community are relatively harmonious, dominance hierarchies exist. Generally, males outrank females, although high-ranking females may dominate low-ranking males. Physical strength and size help determine an animal's rank, but so too does the rank of its mother, its skill at building coalitions with other individuals, and, in the case of the male, its motivation to achieve high status. Highly motivated males, even though they may not be the biggest in their group, may bring considerable intelligence and ingenuity to bear in their quest for high rank. For example, in the community studied by Jane Goodall, a pioneer in the study of primate behavior, one chimp hit upon the idea of incorporating noisy kerosene cans into his charging displays, thereby intimidating all the other males.[7] As a result, he rose from relatively low status to the number one (alpha) position.

On the whole, bonobo females form stronger bonds with one another than do their chimpanzee counterparts. Moreover, the strength of the bond between mother and son is such as to interfere with that between males. Thus, instead of the male dominance characteristic of chimps, one sees female dominance. Not only do bonobo males defer to females in feeding, but alpha females have been observed chasing high-ranking males. Alpha males even yield to low-ranking females, and groups of females form

[6]Moore, J. (1998). Comment. *Current Anthropology, 39,* 412.

[7]Goodall, J. (1986). *The chimpanzees of Gombe: Patterns of behavior* (p. 424). Cambridge, MA: Belknap Press.

JANE GOODALL (b. 1934)

In July 1960 Jane Goodall arrived with her mother at the Gombe Chimpanzee Reserve on the shores of Lake Tanganyika in Tanzania. The first of three women Kenyan anthropologist Louis Leakey sent out to study great apes in the wild (the others were Dian Fossey and Birute Galdikas, who were to study gorillas and orangutans, respectively), her task was to begin a long-term study of chimpanzees. Little did she realize that more than 40 years later she would still be at it.

Though born in London, Jane grew up and was schooled in Bournemouth, England. At the age of 5, she realized that she was born to watch animals, when she entered a chicken coop to find out how eggs were made. Upon her graduation at age 18, she first enrolled in secretarial school and then worked in England before the opportunity came to go to Africa. Having always dreamed of going there to live among animals, when an invitation arrived to visit a friend in Kenya, she jumped at the chance. Quitting her regular job, Goodall worked as a waitress to raise the money for travel and was then on her way. Once in Kenya, she met Louis Leakey, who gave her a job as an assistant secretary. Before long, she was on her

way to Gombe. Within a year, the outside world began to hear the most extraordinary things about this pioneering woman and her work: tales of tool-making apes, cooperative hunts by chimpanzees, and what seemed like exotic chimpanzee rain dances. By the mid-1960s, her work had earned her a Ph.D. from Cambridge University, and Gombe was on its way to becoming one of the most dynamic field stations for the study of animal behavior anywhere in the world.

Although field studies of primates in their natural habitats had been undertaken prior to 1960, they were few in number, and most had produced extremely limited information. It was Goodall's particular blend of patience and determination that showed what could be achieved, and before long her field station became something of a Mecca for aspiring young students interested in primate behavior. The list of those who have worked with her at Gombe, many of them women, reads like a *Who's Who* of eminent scholars in primate behavior.

Although Goodall is still very much involved with her chimpanzees, she spends a good deal of time these days lecturing, writing, and overseeing the work of others. She also is heavily committed to primate conservation, and no one is more dedicated to efforts to halt the illegal trafficking in captive chimps nor a more eloquent champion for humane treatment of captive chimpanzees.

alliances in which they may cooperatively attack males, to the point of inflicting blood-drawing injuries.[8]

The gorilla group is a "family" of 5 to 20 individuals led by a mature, silver-backed male and including younger, black-backed males, females, the young, and sometimes other silverbacks. Subordinate males, however, are usually prevented by the dominant male from mating with the group's females, although he may occasionally allow access to lower ranking ones. Thus, young silverbacks often leave their natal family to start their own families by winning outside females. If the dominant male is weakening with age, however, one of his sons may remain with the group to suc-

ceed to his father's position. Alternatively, an outside male may take over the group. Unlike chimpanzees, gorillas rarely fight over food, territory, or sex, but will fight fiercely to maintain the integrity of the group.

Individual Interaction

One of the most notable primate activities is grooming, the ritual cleaning of another animal's coat to remove parasites, shreds of grass, or other matter. The grooming animal deftly parts the hair of the one being groomed and removes any foreign object, often eating it. Interestingly, different chimp communities have different styles of grooming. In one East African group, for example, the two animals groom each other face to face, with one hand, while the other clasps the

[8]de Waal, F., Kano, T., & Parish, A. R. (1998). Comments. *Current Anthropology, 39,* 408, 410, 413.

Grooming is an important activity among all catarrhine primates, as shown here. Such activity is important for strengthening bonds between individual members of the group.

partner's free hand. In another group 90 miles distant, the hand clasp is unknown. In East Africa, all communities incorporate leaves in their grooming, but in West Africa they do not. However hygienic it may be, it is as well an important gesture of friendliness, submission, appeasement, or closeness. Embracing, touching, and jumping up and down are forms of greeting behavior among chimpanzees. Touching is also a form of reassurance.

Gorillas, though gentle and tolerant, are also aloof and independent, and individual interaction among adults tends to be quite restrained. Friendship or closeness between adults and infants is more evident. Among bonobos, chimpanzees, and gorillas, as among most other primates, the mother-infant bond is the strongest and most long-lasting in the group. It may endure for many years—commonly for the lifetime of the mother. Gorilla infants share their mothers' nests and have been seen sharing nests with mature, childless females. Bonobo, chimpanzee, and gorilla males are attentive to juveniles and may share in parental responsibilities. Bonobo males seem most involved with their young and even carry infants on occasion, including those from different groups. Moreover, a male's interest in a youngster does not elicit the nervous reaction from the mother that it does among chimps. This latter relates to the regular, if infrequent, practice of infanticide on the part of chimpanzee males, a practice never observed among bonobos.

Sexual Behavior

Among the three foregoing species, as with humans, there is no fixed breeding season. Sexual activity between the sexes, however—initiated by either the male or the female—occurs frequently during the period when the female is receptive to impregnation. This is signaled, in the case of chimps, by vivid swelling of the skin around their genitals. Because this swelling continues even after conception up until youngsters are weaned (at about age 4), females continue to attract attention of males. Bonobo females, by contrast, are constantly swollen, concealing their time of ovulation by looking (and behaving) as if they are fertile at all times. Gorillas differ in that they show little interest in sex after conception. To a degree, chimps are promiscuous in their sexual behavior, and 12 to 14 males have been observed to have as many as 50 copulations in one day with a single female. Mostly, females mate with males of their own group and rarely with outsiders. Generally, dominant males try to monopolize females in full estrus, although cooperation from the female is usually required for this to succeed. By making herself scarce, she is able to exercise some choice, showing preference for a male who has previously shared food and groomed her. In the chimpanzee community studied by Jane Goodall, about half the infants were sired by low- or mid-level males. An alpha male, however, is able to monopolize the females to

Swelling of her sexual skin suggests that this female chimpanzee is in estrus and will attract the attention of males.

some extent, and some alphas have been seen to monopolize several estrus females at the same time.

Although mating behavior among bonobos resembles that of chimps, there are differences. For one thing, bonobo females are constantly swollen, making them constantly attractive to males. For another, forced copulation has never been observed among bonobos.[9] But their sexuality goes far beyond male-female mating, and something like three-quarters of their sexual activity has nothing to do with reproduction. Bonobos have been observed having sex in virtually all combinations of ages

and sex.[10] The variety is remarkable, including sporadic oral sex, tongue-kissing, and massage of another's genitals. Male bonobos may mount each other or, standing back to back, one will rub his scrotum against another's. Bonobo males have also been observed "penis fencing," as two males hang from a branch facing each other while rubbing their erect penises together as if crossing swords. Among females genital rubbing is particularly common. The function of most of this sex, both hetero- and homosexual, is to reduce tensions. Whereas chimps often settle disputes by aggressive behavior, bonobos often do so through sex.

In gorilla families, the dominant silverback has exclusive breeding rights with the females, although he may allow a young silverback occasional access to a low-ranking female. In one group studied in Rwanda, in which there was more than one adult male, all but one of 10 juveniles were fathered by a single male.[11] So it is that a young silverback must leave "home" in order to have much of a sex life, usually by luring partners away from other established groups.

Although the vast majority of primate species are not "monogamous" in their mating habits, many smaller species of New World monkeys, a few island-dwelling populations of leaf-eating Old World monkeys, and all of the smaller apes (gibbons and siamangs) do mate for life with a single

---

[9]de Waal, F. (1998). Comment. *Current Anthropology, 39,* 407.

[10]de Waal, F. (2001). *The ape and the sushi master* (pp. 131–132). New York: Basic Books.

[11]Gibbons, A. (2001). Studying humans—and their cousins and parasites. *Science, 292,* 627.

Female bonobos frequently engage in genital rubbing, as here. Such sexual activity is an important means of reducing tension.

individual of the opposite sex. None of these species is closely related to human beings, nor do "monogamous" species ever display the degree of **sexual dimorphism**—anatomical differences between males and females—that is characteristic of our closest primate relatives, or that was characteristic of our own ancient ancestors.

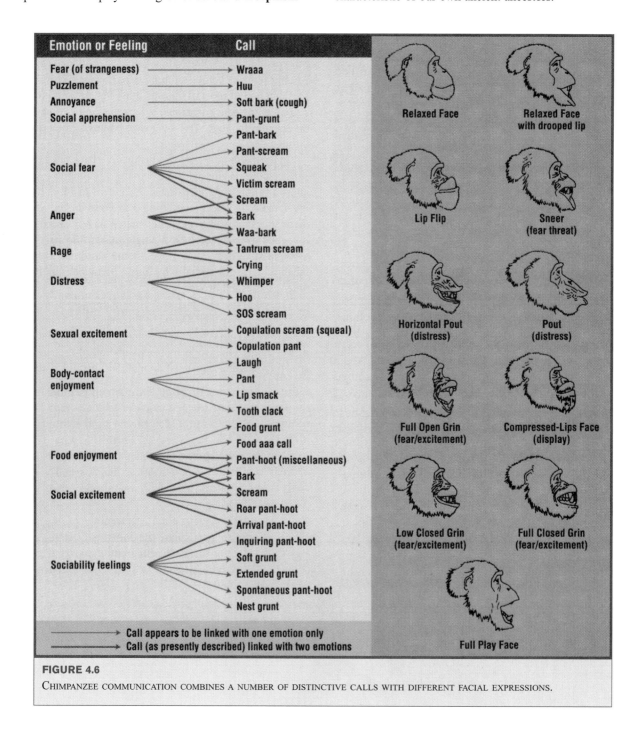

FIGURE 4.6

CHIMPANZEE COMMUNICATION COMBINES A NUMBER OF DISTINCTIVE CALLS WITH DIFFERENT FACIAL EXPRESSIONS.

Sexual dimorphism.   Within a single species, the presence of marked anatomical differences between males and females.

Play

Frequent play activity among primate infants and juveniles is a means of learning about the environment, testing strength (rank in dominance hierarchies is based partially—but only partially—on size and strength), and generally learning how to behave as adults. Chimpanzee infants mimic the food-getting activities of their mothers, "attack" dozing adults, and "harass" adolescents.

Observers have watched young gorillas do somersaults, wrestle, and play tug-of-war, follow the leader, and king of the mountain. One juvenile, becoming annoyed at repeated harassment by an infant, picked it up, climbed a tree, and deposited it on a branch from which it was unable to get down on its own, and its mother had to retrieve it.

Communication

Primates, like many animals, vocalize. They have a great range of calls that are often used together with movements of the face or body to convey a message. Observers have not yet established the meaning of all the sounds, but a good number have been distinguished, such as warning calls, threat calls, defense calls, and gathering calls; the behavioral reactions of other animals hearing the call have also been studied. Among bonobos, chimpanzees, and gorillas, vocalizations are mainly emotional rather than propositional. Much of these species' communication takes place by the use of specific gestures and postures. Indeed, a number of these, such as kissing and embracing, are in virtually universal use today among humans, as well as apes.

Primatologists have classified numerous kinds of chimpanzee vocalization and visual communication (Figure 4.6). Together, these facilitate group protection, coordination of group efforts, and social interaction in general. One form of communication appears to be unique to bonobos: the use of trail markers. When foraging, the community breaks up into smaller groups, rejoining again in the evening to nest together. To keep track of each party's whereabouts, those in the lead will, at the intersections of trails or where downed trees obscure trails, deliberately stomp down the vegetation so as to indicate their direction, or rip off large leaves and place them carefully for the same purpose. Thus, they all know where to come together at the end of the day.[12]

Experiments with captive apes, carried out over several decades, reveal that their communicative abilities exceed what they make use of in the wild. In some of these experiments, bonobos and chimpanzees have been taught to communicate using symbols, as in the case of Kanzi, a bonobo who uses a keyboard. Other chimpanzees, gorillas, and orangutans have been taught American Sign Language. Although this research provoked extreme controversy, it has become evident that all four apes are capable of understanding English quite well and are able to use a primitive grammar. They are able to generate original utterances, distinguish naming something from asking for it, ask questions, develop original ways to tell lies, coordinate their actions, and even spontaneously teach language to others. It is now clear that all of the great ape species can develop language skills to the level of a 2- to 3-year-old child.[13] From such knowledge, we may learn something about the origin of human language.

Home Ranges

Primates usually move about within circumscribed areas, or **home ranges,** which are of varying sizes, depending on the size of the group and on ecological factors such as availability of food. Ranges are often moved seasonally. The distance traveled by a group in a day varies but may include many miles. Some areas of a range, known as *core areas,* are used more often than others; they may contain water, food sources, resting places, and sleeping trees. The ranges of different groups may overlap, as among bonobos, where 65 percent of one territory may overlap with another.[14] By contrast, chimpanzee territories, at least in some regions, are exclusively occupied.

Gorillas do not defend their home ranges against incursions of others of their kind, and in the lowlands of Central Africa, it is not uncommon to find several families feeding in close proximity to one another,[15] although they certainly will defend their group if it is in any way threatened. In encounters with other communities, bonobos will defend their immediate space through vocalizations and

---

[12]Recer, P. (1998, February 16). Apes shown to communicate in the wild. *Burlington Free Press*, p. 12A.

[13]Lestel, D. (1998). How chimpanzees have domesticated humans. *Anthropology Today, 14* (3); Miles, H. L. W. (1993). Language and the orangutan: The "old person" of the forest. In P. Cavalieri & P. Singer (Eds.), *The great ape project* (pp. 45–50). New York: St. Martin's Press.

[14]Parish, A. R. (1998). Comment. *Current Anthropology, 39,* 414.

[15]Parnell, R. (1999). Gorilla exposé. *Natural History, 108*(8), 43.

Home range. The area within which a group of primates usually moves.

Anthropology Applied

Primate Conservation

At present, no fewer than 76 species of primates are recognized as being in danger of extinction. Included among them are all of the great apes, as well as such formerly widespread and adaptable species as rhesus macaques. In the wild, these animals are threatened by habitat destruction in the name of development, by hunting for food and trophies, and by trapping for pets and research. Because monkeys and apes are so closely related to humans, they are regarded as essential for biomedical research in which humans cannot be used. Ironically, using live primates to supply laboratories can be a major factor in their local extinction.

Because of their vulnerability, the conservation of primates has become a matter of urgency. We can take two approaches to the problem, both of which require application of knowledge gained from studies of free-ranging animals. One is to maintain some populations in the wild, either by establishing preserves where animals are already living or by moving populations to places where suitable habitat exists. In either case, constant monitoring and management are necessary to ensure that sufficient space and resources remain available. The other approach is to maintain breeding colonies in captivity, in which case

we must carefully provide the kind of physical and social environment that will encourage psychological and physical well-being, as well as reproductive success. Primates in zoos and laboratories do not successfully reproduce when deprived of such amenities as opportunities for climbing, materials to use for nest building, others to socialize with, and places for privacy.

The value of field studies for effective wild animal management is illustrated by Shirley Strum's relocation in 1984 of three troops of free-ranging baboons in Kenya. The troop she had been studying for 15 years had become a problem, raiding peoples' crops and garbage. Accordingly, it was decided to move this and two other local troops—130 animals in all—to more sparsely inhabited country 150 miles away. Knowing their habits, Strum was able to trap, tranquilize, and transport the animals to their new home; Strum's careful work did not disrupt their social relationships, cause them to abandon their new home, or block the transfer into their troops of new males, with their all-important knowledge of local resources. The success of her effort, which had never been tried with baboons, proves that relocation is a realistic technique for saving endangered primate populations.

---

displays, but rarely through fighting. Usually, they settle down and feed side by side, not infrequently grooming, playing, and engaging in sexual activity between groups as well. Chimpanzees, by contrast, have been observed patrolling their territories to ward off potential trespassers. Moreover, Goodall has recorded the destruction of one chimpanzee community by another that invaded the first one's turf. This sort of lethal intercommunity interaction has never been observed among bonobos. Some have interpreted this apparent territorial behavior as an expression of the supposedly violent nature of chimpanzees, but another interpretation is possible.[16] In Africa today, human encroachment is squeezing chimps into ever smaller pockets of forest. This places considerable stress on animals

whose level of violence tends to increase in the absence of sufficient space. Perhaps the violence that Goodall witnessed was a response to crowding as a consequence of human encroachment. Another factor may be frustration engendered by artificial feeding. Among primates in general, the clearest territoriality appears in arboreal species, rather than in those that are more terrestrial in their habits.

Learning

Observation of monkeys and apes has shown that their learning abilities are remarkably humanlike. Numerous examples of inventive behavior have been observed among Japanese macaques, as well as among apes. One newly discovered example is a technique of food manipulation on the part of captive chimpanzees in the Madrid zoo. It began when a 5-year-old female rubbed apples against a sharp corner of a

---

[16]Power, M. G. (1995). Gombe revisited: Are chimpanzees violent and hierarchical in the "free" state? *General Anthropology, 2*(1), 5–9.

Nut cracking is an important activity among West African chimpanzees. Requiring the use of two objects as tools and complex eye-hand coordination, the task takes years for young chimps to learn from their elders.

concrete wall in order to lick the mashed pieces and juice left on the wall. From this youngster, the practice of "smearing" spread to her peers, and within 5 years, most group members were performing the operation frequently and consistently. The innovation has become standardized and durable, having transcended two generations in the group.[17]

Another dramatic example of learning is afforded by the way chimpanzees in West Africa crack open oil-palm nuts. For this they use tools: an anvil stone with a level surface on which to place the nut and a good-sized hammer stone to crack it. Not any stone will do; it must be of the right shape and weight, and the anvil may require leveling by placing smaller stones beneath one or more edges. Nor does random banging away do the job; the nut has to be hit at the right speed and the right trajectory, or else the nut simply flies off into the forest. Last but not least, the apes must avoid mashing their fingers, rather than the nut. According to fieldworkers, the expertise of the chimps far exceeds that of any human who tries cracking these hardest nuts in the world.

Youngsters learn this process by hanging around adults who are nut cracking, where their mothers share some of the food. This teaches them about the edibility of the nuts, but not how to get at what's edible. This they learn by observing and by "aping" (copying) the adults. At first they play with a nut or stone alone; later they begin to randomly combine objects. They soon learn, however, that placing nuts on anvils and hitting them with a hand or foot gets them nowhere. Only after 3 years of futile efforts do they begin to coordinate all of the multiple actions and objects, but even then it is only after a great deal of practice, by the age of 6 or 7 years, that they become proficient.

In short, after at least 3 years of failure, with no reward to reinforce their effort, they persevere. They do this for over 1,000 days without slacking off. Evidently, it is *social* motivation that keeps them going. At first, they are motivated by a desire to act like the mother; only later does the desire to feed on the tasty nut-meat take over.[18]

Use of Objects as Tools

The nut cracking just discussed is the most complex tool-use task known from the field, involving, as it does, both hands, two tools, and exact coordination. It is not, however, the only case of tool use among apes in the wild. Although gorillas do not make or use tools in any significant way, both chimpanzees and orangutans do. For our purposes, a **tool** may be defined simply as an object used to facilitate some task or activity. Here, a distinction must be made between simple tool use, as when one

---

[17]Fernandez-Carriba, S., & Loeches, A. (2001). Fruit smearing by captive chimpanzees: A newly observed food-processing behavior. *Current Anthropology, 42,* 143–147.

[18]de Waal, F.(2001). *The ape and the sushi master* (pp. 227–229). New York: Basic Books.

Tool. An object used to facilitate some task or activity. Although toolmaking involves intentional modification of the material of which it is made, tool use may involve objects either modified for some particular purpose or completely unmodified.

pounds something with a convenient stone when a hammer is not available, and toolmaking, which involves deliberate modification of some material for its intended use. Thus, otters that use unmodified stones to crack open clams may be tool users, but they are not toolmakers. Not only do chimpanzees modify objects to make them suitable for particular purposes, but chimps to some extent modify them to regular and set patterns. They also pick up, and even prepare, objects for future use at some other location, and they can use objects as tools to solve new and novel problems. Thus, chimps have been observed using stalks of grass, twigs that they have stripped of leaves, and even sticks up to 3 feet long that they have smoothed down to "fish" for termites. They insert the modified stick into a termite nest, wait a few minutes, pull the stick out, and eat the insects clinging to it, all of which requires considerable dexterity. Chimpanzees are equally deliberate in their nest building. They test the vines and branches to make sure they are usable. If they are not, the animal moves to another site.

Other examples of chimpanzee use of objects as tools involve leaves, used as wipes or as sponges, to get water out of a hollow to drink. Large sticks may serve as clubs or as missiles (as may stones) in aggressive or defensive displays. Twigs are used as toothpicks to clean teeth as well as to extract loose baby teeth. They use these dental tools not just on themselves but on other individuals as well.[19]

Interestingly, tool use to fish for termites or to crack open nuts is most often exhibited by females, whereas aimed throwing of rocks and sticks is most often exhibited by males. Such tool-using behavior, which (like nut cracking) young animals learn from their mothers and other adults in their group, may reflect one of the preliminary adaptations that, in the past, led to human cultural behavior.

In the wild, bonobos have not been observed making and using tools to the extent that chimpanzees do. However, the use of large leaves as trail markers may be considered a form of tool use. That these animals do have further capabilities is exemplified by a captive bonobo who has figured out how to make tools of stone that are remarkably like the earliest such tools made by our own ancestors.

Another interesting practice observed among chimps is the use of *Aspilia* leaves for medicinal purposes. When feeling a bit under the weather, they seek out these leaves, hold them in their mouths for a while, then swallow them whole. What this does is to remove parasites from their digestive tract.

Although gorillas (like bonobos and chimps) build nests, they are the only one of the four great apes that have not been observed to make and use other tools in the wild. The reason for this is probably not that gorillas lack the intelligence or skill to do so; rather, their easy diet of leaves and nettles makes tools of no particular use.

Hunting

The hunting, killing, and eating of small to medium-sized mammals, something that is seen only in a few primates, has been observed among bonobos and chimps, but not among gorillas. Although chimpanzee females sometimes hunt, males do so far more frequently. When on the hunt, they may spend up to 2 hours watching, following, and chasing intended prey. Moreover, in contrast to the usual primate practice of each animal finding food for itself, hunting frequently involves teamwork to trap and kill prey. The most sophisticated examples of this occur when hunting baboons; once a potential victim has been partially isolated from its troop, three or more adults will carefully position themselves so as to block off escape routes while another climbs toward the prey for the kill. Once a kill has been made, it is common for most of those present to get a share of the meat, either by grabbing a piece as the chance affords, or by sitting and begging for a piece. Whatever the nutritional value of meat, hunting is not done purely for dietary purposes, but for political and sociosexual reasons as well. The giving of meat helps cement alliances among males, and its sharing may be used also to entice a swollen female to have sex. In fact, males are more apt to hunt if a swollen female is present, and females in estrus are more successful at begging for meat.

Bonobos, too, hunt, but in their case it is usually the females who do so—duikers (a kind of small antelope) being the most frequent prey. The huntresses regularly share the carcasses with other females, but less often with males. Even when the most dominant male throws a tantrum nearby, he may still be denied a share.[20] Not only do females control the spoils of the hunt, they are unusual also in the degree to which they will share fruit. Otherwise, it is interesting to note that, in primates, as among many carnivores, increased cooperation seems to go hand in hand with predation and meat eating.

---

[19]McGrew, W. C. (2000). Dental care in chimps. *Science, 288,* 1747.

[20]Ingmanson, E. J. (1998). Comment. *Current Anthropology, 39,* 409.

THE QUESTION OF CULTURE

The more we learn of the behavior of our nearest primate relatives, the more we become aware of the importance to chimps of learned, socially shared practices and knowledge. This raises the question: Do chimpanzees (and perhaps other apes) have culture? This is a question that is now receiving a good deal of attention, as the following Original Study attests.

The Culture of Chimpanzees[21]

Original Study

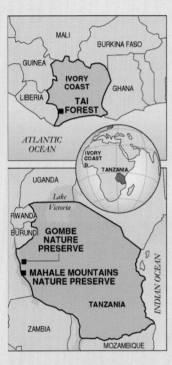

Homo sapiens and *Pan troglodytes* have coexisted for hundreds of millennia and share more than 98 percent of their genetic material, yet only 40 years ago we still knew next to nothing about chimpanzee behavior in the wild. That began to change in the 1960s, when Toshisada Nishida of Kyoto University in Japan and Jane Goodall began their studies of wild chimpanzees at two field sites in Tanzania. (Goodall's research station at Gombe—the first of its kind—is more famous, but Nishida's site at Mahale is the second-oldest chimpanzee research site in the world.)

In these initial studies, as the chimpanzees became accustomed to close observation, the remarkable discoveries began. Researchers witnessed a range of unexpected behaviors, including fashioning and using tools, hunting, meat eating, food sharing, and lethal fights between members of neighboring communities. In the years that followed, other primatologists set up camp elsewhere, and, despite all the financial, political, and logistical problems that can beset African fieldwork, several of these outposts became truly long-term projects. As a result, we live in an unprecedented time, when an intimate and comprehensive scientific record of chimpanzees' lives at last exists not just for one but for several communities spread across Africa.

As early as 1973, Goodall recorded 13 forms of tool use as well as eight social activities that appeared to differ between the Gombe chimpanzees and chimpanzee populations elsewhere. She ventured that some variations had what she termed a "cultural origin." But what exactly did Goodall mean by "culture"? According to the Oxford Encyclopedic English Dictionary, culture is defined as "the customs . . . and achievements of a particular time or people." The diversity of human cultures extends from technological variations to marriage rituals, from culinary habits to myths and legends. Animals do not have myths and legends, of course. But they do have the capacity to pass on behavioral traits from generation to generation—not through their genes but by learning. For biologists, this is the fundamental criterion for a cultural trait: It must be something that can be learned by observing the established skills of others and thus passed on to future generations.

By the 1990s the discovery of new behavioral differences among chimpanzees made it feasible to begin assembling comprehensive charts of cultural variations for these animals. William C. McGrew, in his 1992 book *Chimpanzee Material Cultures*, was able to list 19 different kinds of tool use in distinct communities. One of us (Boesch), along with colleague Michael Tomasello of the Max Planck Institute for Evolutionary Anthropology in Leipzig,

[21]Whitten, A., & Boesch, C. (2001). Cultures of chimpanzees. *Scientific American, 284*(1), 63–67.

Original Study

Germany, identified 25 distinct activities as potential cultural traits in wild chimpanzee populations.

The most recent catalogue of cultural variations results from a unique collaboration of nine chimpanzee experts (including the two of us) who pooled extensive field observations that, taken together, amounted to a total of 151 years of chimp watching. The list cites 39 patterns of chimpanzee behavior that we believe to have a cultural origin, including such activities as using sticks to "fish" for ants, making dry seats from leaves, and a range of social grooming habits. At present, these 39 variants put chimpanzees in a class of their own, with far more elaborate customs than any other animal studied to date. Of course, chimpanzees also remain distinct from humans, for whom cultural variations are simply beyond count. (We must point out, however, that scientists are only beginning to uncover the behavioral complexity that exists among chimpanzees—and so the number 39 no doubt represents a minimum of cultural traits.)

Multicultural Chimpanzees

When describing human customs, anthropologists and sociologists often refer to "American culture" or "Chinese culture"; these terms encompass a wide spectrum of activities—language, forms of dress, eating habits, marriage rituals and so on. Among animals, however, culture has typically been established for a single behavior, such as song dialects among birds. Ornithologists haven't identified variation in courtship patterns or feeding practices, for example, to go alongside the differences in dialect.

Chimpanzees, though, do more than display singular cultural traits: Each community exhibits an entire set of behaviors that differentiates it from other groups. As a result, we can talk about "Gombe culture" or "Taï culture." Indeed, once we observe how a chimpanzee behaves, we can identify where the animal lives. For instance, an individual that cracks nuts, leaf-clips during drumming displays, fishes for ants with one hand using short sticks,

Grooming is an activity seen in all chimpanzee communities, but styles differ between communities. Shown here is the hand clasping style characteristic of one East African community.

and knuckle-knocks to attract females clearly comes from the Taï Forest. A chimp that leaf-grooms and hand-clasps during grooming can come from the Kibale Forest or the Mahale Mountains, but if you notice that he also ant-fishes, there is no doubt anymore: He comes from Mahale.

In addition, chimpanzee cultures go beyond the mere presence or absence of a particular behavior. For example, all chimpanzees dispatch parasites found during grooming a companion. But at Taï they will mash the parasites against their forearms with a finger, at Gombe they squash them onto leaves, and at Budongo they put them on a leaf to inspect before eating or discarding them. Each community has developed a unique approach for accomplishing the same goal. Alternatively, behaviors may look similar yet be used in different contexts: at Mahale, males "clip" leaves noisily with their teeth as a courtship gesture, whereas at Taï chimpanzees incorporate leaf-clipping into drumming displays.

The implications of this new picture of chimpanzee culture are many. The information offers insight into our distinctiveness as a species. When we first published this work in the journal *Nature,* we found some people quite disturbed to realize that the characteristic that had appeared to separate us so starkly from the animal world—our capacity for cultural development—is not such an absolute difference after all.

But this seems a rather misdirected response. The differences between human customs and traditions, enriched and mediated by language as they are, are vast in contrast with what we see in the chimpanzee. The story of chimpanzee cultures sharpens our understanding of our uniqueness, rather than threatening it in any way that need worry us.

Human achievements have made enormous cumulative progress over the generations, a phenomenon Boesch and Tomasello have dubbed the "ratchet effect." The idea of a hammer—once simply a crude stone cobble—has been modified and improved on countless times until now we have electronically controlled robot hammers in our factories. Chimpanzees may show the beginnings of the ratchet effect—some that use stone anvils, for example, have gone a step further, as at Bossou, where they wedge a stone beneath their anvil when it needs leveling on bumpy ground—but such behavior has not become customary and is rudimentary indeed beside human advancements.

The cultural capacity we share with chimpanzees also suggests an ancient ancestry for the mentality that must underlie it. Our cultural nature did not emerge out of the blue but evolved from simpler beginnings. Social learning similar to that of chimpanzees would appear capable of sustaining the earliest stone-tool cultures of human ancestors living two million years ago.

The End

Primate Behavior and Human Evolution

Although not true of all humanity, in many societies there is an unfortunate tendency to erect what paleontologist Stephen Jay Gould refers to as "golden barriers" that set us apart from the rest of the animal kingdom.[22] It is unfortunate, for it blinds us to the fact that there are many continuities between "us" and "them" (animals). We have already seen that the physical differences between humans and apes are largely differences of degree, rather than kind. It now appears that the same is true with respect to behavior. As primatologist Richard Wrangham once put it, "Like humans, [chimpanzees] laugh, make up after a quarrel, support each other in times of trouble, medicate themselves with chemical and physical remedies, stop each other from eating poisonous foods, collaborate in the hunt, help each other over physical obstacles, raid neighboring groups, lose their tempers, get excited by dramatic weather, invent ways to show off, have family traditions and group traditions, make tools, devise plans, deceive, play tricks, grieve, and are cruel and are kind."[23]

This is not to say that we are "just" another ape; obviously, "degree" does make a difference. Nevertheless, the continuities between us and our primate kin are a reflection of a common evolutionary heritage; it is just that our later evolution has taken us in a somewhat different direction. But by looking at the range of practices displayed by contemporary apes and other catarrhines, we may find clues to the practices and capabilities possessed by our own ancestors as their evolutionary path diverged from those of the other hominids.

---

[22]de Waal, F. (2001). *The ape and the sushi master* (p. 235). New York: Basic Books.

[23]Quoted in Mydens, S. (2001, August 12). He's not hairy, he's my brother. *New York Times,* sec. 4, p. 5.

CHAPTER SUMMARY

The modern primates, like most mammals, are intelligent animals that bear their young live and then nourish them with milk from their mothers. Like other mammals, they maintain constant body temperature and have respiratory and circulatory systems that will sustain high activity. Their skeleton and teeth also resemble those of other mammals, although there are differences of detail.

Modern primates are divided into two suborders. The strepsirhines include lemurs and lorises, which resemble small rodents in body outline. The haplorhines include tarsiers, New and Old World monkeys, apes, and humans. To a greater degree among the haplorhines, and a lesser degree among the strepsirhines, primates show a number of characteristics that developed as adaptations to insect predation in the trees. These adaptive characteristics include a generalized set of teeth, suited to insect eating but also a variety of fruits and leaves. These teeth are fewer in number and set in a smaller jaw than in most mammals. Other evolutionary adaptations in the primate line include binocular stereoscopic vision, or depth perception, and an intensified sense of touch. This combination of developments had an effect upon the primate brain, resulting in larger size and greater complexity in later appearing species. There were also changes in the primate skeleton; in particular, a reduction of the snout, an enlargement of the brain case, and numerous adaptations for upright posture and flexibility of limb movement. In addition, changes in reproduction resulted in fewer offspring born to each female and a longer period of infant dependency than among most mammals.

The apes are humans' closest relatives. Apes include gibbons, siamangs, orangutans, gorillas, bonobos, and chimpanzees. In their outward appearance, the great apes seem to resemble each other more than they do humans, but their genetic structure and biochemistry reveal that bonobos, chimpanzees, and gorillas are closer to humans than to orangs and thus must share a more recent common ancestry.

The social life of primates is complex. Primates are social animals, and most species live and travel in groups. Among bonobos and chimpanzees, it is females that may transfer from one group to another, though not all do so; their sons and often their daughters remain with their mothers for life. Among gorillas, either males or females may transfer. In all three species, both males and females are organized into dominance hierarchies. In the case of females, the better food and reduced harassment that are a consequence of high rank enhance their ability to successfully raise offspring.

A characteristic primate activity is grooming, which is a sign of closeness between individuals. Among bonobos, gorillas, and chimpanzees, sexual interaction between adults of opposite sex generally takes place only when a female is in estrus. In bonobos, however, constant swelling of the female's genitals suggests constant estrus, whether or not she is actually fertile. Although dominant males try to monopolize females while they are in estrus, the cooperation of the females is usually required for this to succeed. Among bonobos, sex between both opposite and same-sex indivudials serves as a means of reducing tensions, as in the genital rubbing that frequently takes place between females. Primates have elaborate systems of communication based on vocalizations and gestures. In addition, bonobos employ trail signs to communicate their whereabouts to others. Usually primates move about within home ranges, rather than defended territories.

The diet of most primates is made up of a variety of fruits, leaves, and insects, but bonobos and chimpanzees sometimes hunt, kill, and eat animals as well. Among chimps, most hunting is done by males and may require considerable teamwork. By contrast, it is usually bonobo females that hunt. Once a kill is made, the meat is generally shared with other animals.

Among chimpanzees and other apes, learned behavior is especially important. From adults, juveniles learn to use a variety of tools and substances for various purposes. Innovations made by one individual may be adopted by other animals, standardized, and passed on to succeeding generations. Because practices are learned, socially shared, and often differ from one group to another, we may speak of chimpanzee culture.

HIGHWAY 1
See and hear living primates through this site that features a host of information about primate behavior, biology, and conservation from *Living Links: A Center for the Advanced Study of Ape and Human Evolution.* See classic videos from primate field research such as "Chimpanzee Conflict" and "Chimpanzee Food Sharing."
http://www.emory.edu/living_links/

HIGHWAY 2
The Gorilla Foundation: Conservation Through Communication site demonstrates the amazing lingusitic capacities of Koko the gorilla. Watch her communicate to humans through sign language, and learn how this project is working to protect all of the endangered ape species.
http://www.koko.org/

HIGHWAY 3
A trip to this site explains the action of a conservation group working to protect the endangered primate species being slaughtered for meat and medicine. The project mission states that "the Bushmeat Project has been established to develop and support community-based partnerships that will help the people of equatorial Africa to develop alternatives to unsustainable bushmeat. The programme is a long-term effort to provide economic and social incentive to protect great apes and other endangered wildlife."
http://bushmeat.net/

CLASSIC READINGS

de Waal, F. (1996). *Good natured: The origins of right and wrong in humans and other animals.* Cambridge, MA: Harvard University Press.

Primatologist Frans de Waal, though fully up on field studies of wild primates, has spent much of his career studying bonobos and chimpanzees in captivity. In this book he argues that moral behavior can be found in nonhuman animals, most clearly in apes but also in other primates and even nonprimate species. Written for a general audience, but with a strong scientific foundation, the book communicates its message in a clear and responsible way.

De Waal, F. (2001). *The ape and the sushi master.* New York: Basic Books.

Another by de Waal, one of the best observers of primate behavior in the business. In this book he deals with the question of animal culture in a manner guaranteed to provoke thought. The book is well written and, once begun, almost impossible to put down.

Fossey, D. (1983). *Gorillas in the mist.* Burlington, MA. Houghton Mifflin.

The late Dian Fossey is to gorillas what Jane Goodall is to chimpanzees. Fossey devoted years to the study of gorilla behavior in the field. This book is about the first 13 years of her study; as well as being readable and informative, it is well illustrated.

Goodall, J. (1990). *Through a window.* Boston: Houghton Mifflin.

This fascinating book is a personal account of Goodall's experiences over 35 years of studying wild chimpanzees in Tanzania. A pleasure to read and a fount of information on the behavior of these apes, the book is profusely illustrated as well.

LeGros Clark, W. E. (1966). *History of the primates* (5th ed.). Chicago: University of Chicago Press.

An old classic, this remains a fine introduction to the comparative anatomy of the primates.

Patterson, F., & Linden, E. (1981). *The education of Koko.* New York: Holt, Rinehart & Winston.

Several experiments with captive apes have sought to investigate the full potential of their communicative abilities, and one of the most interesting is that involving Koko the gorilla. This is a particularly readable account of those experiments and their results.

CHAPTER 5

MACROEVOLUTION AND THE EARLY PRIMATES

This is a reconstruction of what one of the earliest catarrhine primates, *Eosimias* of China, may have looked like. Although its bones indicate overall body form, its exterior appearance is pure speculation.

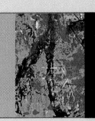

1

HOW DOES EVOLUTION PRODUCE NEW FORMS OF ORGANISMS?

Evolution may proceed in a branching manner, when isolating mechanisms prevent gene flow between separated populations. Then drift and selection may proceed in different ways, leading to the appearance first of divergent subspecies and then of separate species. In the absence of isolation, a species as a whole may evolve in a linear manner through variational change in response to environmental changes. As small changes accumulate from generation to generation, an older species may be transformed into a new one.

2

WHEN DID THE FIRST PRIMATES APPEAR, AND WHAT WERE THEY LIKE?

The earliest primates had developed by 60 million years ago and became widespread in Africa, Eurasia, and North America. The initial adaptation of these small, arboreal insect eaters to life in the trees set the stage for the subsequent appearance of other primate models.

3

WHEN DID THE FIRST MONKEYS AND APES APPEAR, AND WHAT WERE THEY LIKE?

By the late Eocene epoch, about 37 million years ago, small primates ancestral to monkeys and apes were living in Africa and Asia. By about 20 million years ago, they had proliferated and were common in many parts of the Old World. Some forms remained relatively small, while others became quite large, some even larger than present-day gorillas. Small versions of these apelike primates seem to have had the right kind of anatomy, and at least some were exposed to the right kind of selective pressures to transform them into primitive hominines.

Almost a century and a half ago, Charles Darwin shattered the surface calm of the Victorian world with his startling theory that humans are cousins of the living apes and monkeys and are descended from the same prehistoric ancestors. What would have been the public reaction, one wonders, if they had known, as we do, that even earlier ancestors were mouse-sized and smaller creatures that subsisted chiefly on insects and worms? Such primitive creatures date back about 60 million years. These ancient forebears of ours evolved over time into different species as mutations produced variation, which was acted upon by natural selection and genetic drift.

Although many of the primates discussed in this chapter no longer exist, their descendants, which were reviewed in Chapter 4, are to be found living throughout the world. The successful adaptation of the primates is believed to be due largely to their intelligence, a characteristic that provides for adaptive flexibility. Other physical traits, such as stereoscopic vision and a grasping hand, have also been instrumental in the success of the primates.

What is the justification for studying a form of life whose history is, at best, fragmentary and which existed millions of years ago? The study of these prehistoric primates tells us something we can use to interpret the evolution of the entire primate line, including ourselves. It gives us a better understanding of the physical forces that caused these early creatures to evolve into today's primates. Ultimately, the study of these ancient ancestors gives us a fuller knowledge of the processes through which an insect-eating, small-brained animal evolved into a toolmaker and thinker that is recognizably human.

SPECIATION

To understand how the primates evolved, we must first look at how the evolutionary forces discussed in Chapter 3 bring about the emergence of new species from old. As noted in that chapter, the term *species* is usually defined as a population or group of populations that is capable of interbreeding and that is reproductively isolated from other such populations. Thus the bullfrogs in my farm pond are the same species as those in my neighbor's pond, even though the two populations may never actually interbreed; in theory, they are capable of it if they are brought together. This definition is not altogether satisfactory, because isolated populations may be in the process of evolving into different species, and it is hard to tell exactly when they become separate. For example, all dogs belong to the same species, but a male Saint Bernard and a female Chihuahua would surely have trouble with the feat of copulation. On the other hand, Alaskan sled dogs are able to breed with wolves, even though they are of different species. In nature, however, wolves most often mate with their own kind. Although all species definitions are relative rather than absolute, the modern concept of species puts more stress on the question of whether breeding actually takes place in the wild than on the more academic question of whether breeding is technically feasible. After all, gibbons and siamangs, two different species of small apes, sometimes produce live offspring in captivity but do not in the wild.

Biologists define populations within species that are capable of interbreeding but may not regularly do so as **races,** or subspecies. Evolutionary theory suggests that species evolve from races through the accumulation of differences in the gene pools of the separated groups. This can happen, however, only in situations where one race is isolated from others of its species for prolonged periods of time. There is nothing inevitable about races evolving into new species. Because they are by definition genetically open—that is, members of different races are capable of interbreeding—races are impermanent and subject to reamalgamation. This is precisely what happens as long as gene flow remains open.

In the case of humans, as we shall see in Chapter 13, the race concept cannot be applied. For one thing, the human propensity for gene flow makes it impossible to define races with any biological validity. To make matters worse, there has been a deplorable tendency to confuse cultural with biological phenomena under the heading of "race." As applied to humans, races are nothing more than social categories.

Isolating Mechanisms

Certain factors, known as **isolating mechanisms,** separate breeding populations, leading to the appearance first of divergent races and then divergent species. This happens as mutations may appear in one of the isolated populations but not in the other, as genetic drift affects the two populations in different ways and as selective

---

Race.   In biology, a subspecies; a population of a species that differs in allele frequencies from other such populations. Humans cannot be divided into racial categories that have any biological validity.   •   **Isolating mechanisms.**   Factors that separate breeding populations, thereby preventing gene flow, creating divergent subspecies and ultimately (if maintained) divergent species.

Although horses and donkeys (two separate species) can mate and produce live offspring (mules, pictured here), sterility of mules maintains the reproductive isolation of the parental species.

pressures may come to differ slightly in the two places. Because isolation prevents gene flow, changes that affect the gene pool of one population cannot be introduced into the gene pool of the other.

Some isolating mechanisms are geographical—preventing contact, hence gene flow, between members of separated populations. Anatomical structure can also serve as an isolating mechanism, as we saw in the case of the Saint Bernard and the Chihuahua. Other physical isolating factors include early miscarriage of the offspring; weakness or presence of maladaptive traits that cause early death in the offspring; or, as in the case

of horses and donkeys, sterility of the hybrid offspring (mules).

Although physical barriers to reproduction may develop in geographical isolation, as genetic differences accumulate in the gene pools of separate populations, they may also result from accidents as cells undergo meiosis. In the course of such accidents genetic material may be broken off, transposed, or transferred from one chromosome to another. Even a relatively minor mutation, if it involves a gene that regulates the growth and development of an organism, may have a major effect on its adult form. In this way, a kind of instantaneous genetic isolation may occur.

Regulator genes turn other genes on and off, and a mere change in their timing can cause significant evolutionary change. This may have a played a role in differentiating chimps and humans; for example, adult humans retain the flat facial profile of juvenile chimps.

Isolating mechanisms may also be social rather than physical. Speciation due to this mechanism is particularly common among birds. For example, cuckoos (birds that do not build nests of their own but lay their eggs in other birds' nests) attract mates by mimicking the song of the bird species whose nests they usurp; thus cuckoos that are physically capable of mating may have different courtship behavior, which effectively isolates them from others of their kind.

Social isolating mechanisms are thought to have been important factors in human evolution. They continue to play a part in the maintenance of so-called racial barriers. Although there are no physical barriers to mating between any two mature humans of the opposite sex, awareness of social and cultural differences often makes the idea distasteful, perhaps even unthinkable; in India, for example, someone of an upper caste would not think of marrying an "untouchable." This isolation results from the culturally implanted concept of a significant difference between "us" and "them." Yet, as evidenced by the blending of human populations—even hostile ones—that has so often taken place in the world, people are also capable of suspending or even reasoning away social isolating mechanisms that would, in the case of other animals, lead separate populations to evolve into separate species. Such speciation is extremely unlikely in *Homo sapiens*.

Divergence and Convergence

As just described, isolation may cause a single ancestral species to give rise to two or more descendant species. Such **divergent** or **branching evolution** (Figure 5.1) is probably responsible for much of the diversity of life to be observed today. This has happened repeatedly, for example, as the platelike segments of the earth on which the continents ride have shifted position, separating once adjacent land masses (Figure 5.2).

Sorting out evolutionary relationships may be complicated by a phenomenon called **convergence** in which two distant forms develop greater similarities—birds and bats, for example, because their structures serve similar functions. Among the primates, an example is hind-leg dominance in both lemurs and humans. In most primates, the

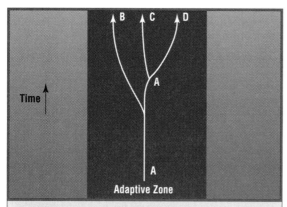

FIGURE 5.1

DIVERGENT EVOLUTION OCCURS AS DIFFERENT POPULATIONS OF AN ANCESTRAL SPECIES BECOME REPRODUCTIVELY ISOLATED. THROUGH DRIFT AND DIFFERENTIAL SELECTION, THE NUMBER OF DESCENDANT SPECIES INCREASES.

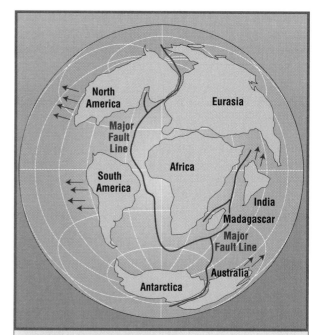

FIGURE 5.2

SEPARATION OF THE EARTH'S CONTINENTS RESULTED FROM MASSIVE SHIFTING IN THE PLATELIKE SEGMENTS OF THE CRUST AS ILLUSTRATED BY THE POSITION OF CONTINENTS AT THE END OF THE CRETACEOUS PERIOD SOME 65 MILLION YEARS AGO, THE TIME OF THE DINOSAUR'S EXTINCTION. THE SEAS, OPENED UP BY CONTINENTAL SEPARATION, CONSTITUTED ISOLATING BARRIERS BETWEEN MAJOR LAND MASSES.

Divergent or branching evolution.   An evolutionary process in which an ancestral population gives rise to two or more descendant populations that differ from one another. • **Convergence.**   A process by which unrelated populations develop similarities to one another.

hind limbs are either shorter or of the same length as the forelimbs. Lemurs and humans are not closely related to each other, but both have longer hind limbs due to aspects of their locomotion. Humans are bipedal while lemurs use their long legs to push off and propel them from tree to tree. Convergent evolution takes place in circumstances where an environment exerts similar pressures on different organisms, so that unrelated species become more like one another. Because the analogies produced by convergent evolution are not always easy to distinguish from the homologies that result from shared ancestry, it is often difficult to reconstruct the evolutionary history of any given species. As a case in point, humans and orangutans both have thick enamel on their molars, but African apes do not. Yet, molecular evidence reveals a closer human relationship to African apes than to orangs. Thus, thick molar enamel may be a case of analogy, rather than homology. Alternatively, thin enamel could have evolved separately in chimps and gorillas, and the presence of this feature in orangutans and humans could be retained from the ancestral condition.

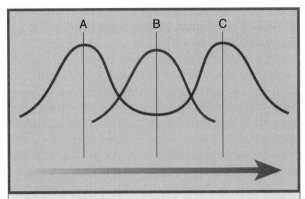

FIGURE 5.3

Linear evolution is a process of variational change that occurs as relatively small changes that (by chance) are advantageous accumulate in a species' gene pool through gene flow, drift, and selection. Over time, this may produce sufficient change to transform an old species into a new one.

Linear Evolution

Another consequence of natural selection may be what appears to be a linear progression from one form to another without any evident branching. Although this may seem like a case of evolution heading in a particular direction, it is not. Rather, it is nothing more than variational change as discussed in the Original Study in Chapter 3. The example given there was of elephants becoming progressively hairier over time in response to climatic cooling. As generation succeeded generation, those elephants best adapted to cold enjoyed the highest reproductive success. The end result was the woolly mammoth. If, as such change proceeds, populations do not become isolated, then the species as a whole appears to evolve in a particular direction. **Linear evolution** may be defined, then, as a sustained directional change in a population's average characteristics (Figure 5.3).

As linear evolution proceeds, more recent populations may appear sufficiently changed from ancestral populations to be called different species. The difficulty arises because, given a reasonably good fossil record, one species will appear to grade into the other without any clear break. Thus, trying to assign a fossil to one species or the other can be an exercise in frustration.

Although linear evolution produces change, it generally does not transform a population into something radically different. Ultimately, stabilizing selection is likely to take over, as available alleles reach their most adaptive frequencies in a species' gene pool. There will be little change thereafter, as long as the adaptation remains viable. Ironically, a species may become extinct if it becomes too well adapted. If the environment changes for some reason, those organisms most highly adapted to the old environment will have the greatest difficulty surviving in a new one. Such changes took place a number of times during the course of vertebrate evolution; one of the most dramatic examples was the sudden extinction of the dinosaurs. In such cases, it is usually the more generalized organisms that survive; later they may give rise to new lines of specialists.

The Nondirectedness of Evolution

In the popular mind, evolution is often seen as leading in a predictable and determined way from one-celled organisms, through various multicelled forms, to humans, who occupy the top rung of a ladder of progress. To be sure, one-celled organisms appeared long before multicellular forms, but the latter could hardly emerge before the basic structure of the cell existed. Furthermore, single-celled organisms were not replaced by multicellular descendants, but remain today, as in the past, the dominant forms

---

Linear evolution. A sustained directional shift in a population's average characteristics.

of life. They exist in greater numbers and diversity than all forms of multicellular life and live in all habitats accessible to *any* form of life.[1]

As for humans, we are indeed recent arrivals in the world (though not as recent as some new strains of bacteria), but our appearance—like that of any kind of organism—was made possible only as a consequence of a whole string of historical accidents. To cite but one example, about 65 million years ago, some sort of extraterrestrial body slammed into earth where the Yucatan Peninsula now exists, disrupting the world's climate to such an extent as to cause the extinction of the dinosaurs (and numerous other species as well). For 100 million years, dinosaurs had ruled most terrestrial environments available for vertebrate animals and would probably have continued to do so were it not for this event. Although mammals appeared at about the same time as reptiles, they existed as small, inconspicuous creatures that an observer from outer space would probably have dismissed as insignificant. But with the demise of the dinosaurs, all sorts of opportunities became available, and mammals began their great expansion into new niches, including the one in which our own ancestors evolved. So it is that an essentially random event—the collision with a comet or asteroid—made possible our own existence. Had it not happened, or had it happened at some other time (before the existence of mammals), we would not be here, and there might not be any consciously intelligent life on earth.[2]

The history of any species is an outcome of many such contingencies. At any point in the chain of events, had any one element been different, the final result would be markedly different. As Stephen Jay Gould puts it, "All evolutionary sequences include . . . a fortuitous series of accidents with respect to future evolutionary success. Human brains and bodies did not evolve along a direct and inevitable ladder, but by a circuitous and tortuous route carved by adaptations evolved for different reasons, and fortunately suited to later needs."[3]

The history of life is not one of progressive advancement in complexity; if anything, it is one of proliferation of enormously varied designs that subsequently have been restricted to a few highly successful forms. Even at that, imperfections remain. As Gould so aptly puts it:

> Our world is not an optimal place, fine tuned by omnipotent forces of selection. It is a quirky mass of imperfections, working well enough (often admirably); a jury-rigged set of adaptations built of curious parts made available by past histories in different contexts.[4]

---

[1]Gould, S. J. (1996). *Full house: The spread of excellence from Plato to Darwin* (pp. 176–195). New York: Harmony Books.

[2]Gould, S. J. (1985). *The flamingo's smile: Reflections in natural history* (p. 409). New York: Norton.

[3]Ibid., p. 410.

[4]Ibid., p. 54.

For more than 260 million years, dinosaurs were the dominant land vertebrates. The later success of mammals was made possible by a chance event: the collision with the earth of an asteroid or comet, the effects of which brought about the dinosaurs' extinction.

EARLY MAMMALS

By 190 million years ago—the end of what geologists call the Triassic period—true mammals were on the scene. We know these and the mammals from the succeeding Jurassic (190–135 million years ago) and Cretaceous (135–65 million years ago) periods from hundreds of finds of mostly teeth and jaw parts. Because these structures are the most durable, they often outlast other parts of an animal's skeleton. Fortunately, investigators often are able to infer a good deal about the total animal on the basis of only a few teeth found lying in the earth. For example, knowledge of the way the teeth fit together indicates much about the operation of the jaws, suggesting the types of muscles needed. This in turn indicates how the skull must have been shaped to provide accommodation for the musculature. The shape of the jaws and details of the teeth also suggest the type of food that they were suited to deal with, indicating the probable diet of the specimen. Thus a mere jawbone reveals a great deal about the animal from which it came.

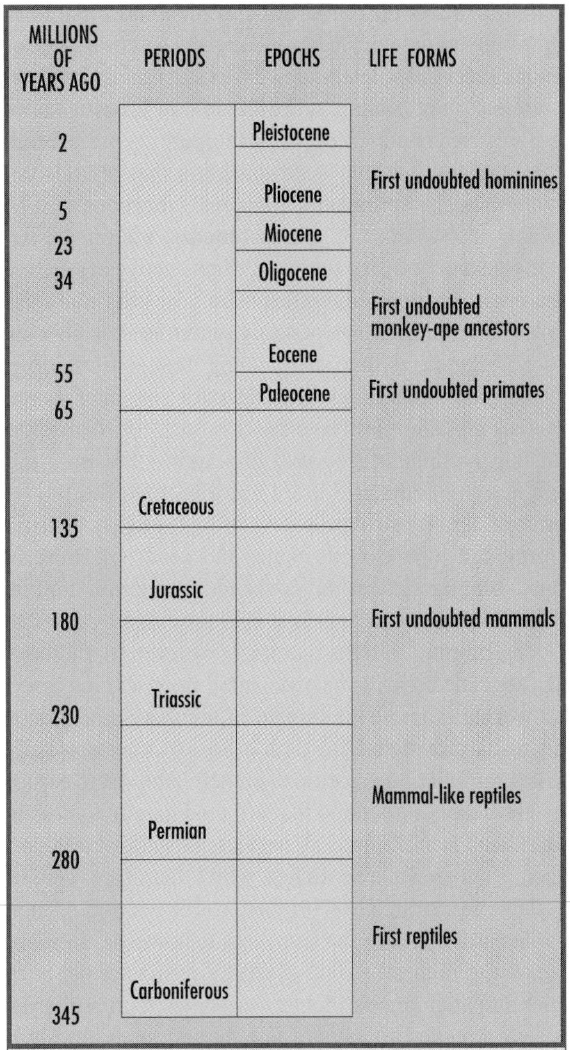

An interesting fact about the evolution of the mammals is that the diverse forms with which we are familiar today, including the primates, are the products of an **adaptive radiation,** the rapid increase in number of related species following a change in their environment. This did not begin until after mammals had been present on the earth for over 100 million years. Actually, the story of mammalian evolution starts as early as 280 to 230 million years ago (Figure 5.4). From deposits of this period, which geologists call the Permian, we have the remains of reptiles with features pointing in a distinctly mammalian direction. These mammal-like reptiles were slimmer than most other reptiles and were flesh eaters. In a series of graded fossils, we can see in them a reduction of bones to a more mammalian number, the shifting of limbs underneath the body, development of a separation between the mouth and nasal cavity, differentiation of the teeth, and so forth.

All of these early mammals were small eaters of flesh—such things as insects, worms, and eggs. They seem to have been nocturnal in their habits, which is probably why the senses of smell and hearing became so developed in mammals. Although things cannot be seen as well in the dark as they can in the light, they can be heard and smelled just as well. Both sound and smell are more complex than sight. If something can be seen it is right there in the animal's line of vision. By contrast, it is possible to smell and hear things around corners and in other hidden places, and

MILLIONS OF YEARS AGO	PERIODS	EPOCHS	LIFE FORMS
2		Pleistocene	
		Pliocene	First undoubted hominines
5		Miocene	
23		Oligocene	
34			First undoubted monkey-ape ancestors
		Eocene	
55		Paleocene	First undoubted primates
65			
135	Cretaceous		
180	Jurassic		First undoubted mammals
230	Triassic		
280	Permian		Mammal-like reptiles
			First reptiles
345	Carboniferous		

FIGURE 5.4

THIS TIMELINE HIGHLIGHTS SOME MAJOR MILESTONES IN THE EVOLUTION OF THOSE MAMMALS FROM WHICH HUMANS ARE DESCENDED.

in addition to figuring out what it is that is smelled or heard and how far away it is, the animal must also figure out where it is. A further complication is the fact that smells linger, and so the animal must figure out if the cause of an odor is still there or, if not, how old the odor is.

As mammals' senses of hearing and smell became keener, they lost the ability (possessed by reptiles) to see in color. But the new, keener senses and the importance of outwitting both prey and predators served to improve

---

Adaptive radiation. Rapid diversification of an evolving population as it adapts to a variety of available niches.

their information-processing capacities and enlarge the part of the brain that handles these—the cerebral cortex— beyond that of reptiles. And to the extent that they become "brainier," they become more flexible in their behavior.

Because mammals were developing as such bright, active creatures, it may seem puzzling that reptiles continued to be the dominant land animals for more than 100 million years. After all, **warm-blooded** mammals, with their constant body temperature, can be active at any time, whereas **cold-blooded** reptiles, who take their body temperature from the surrounding environment, become more sluggish as the surrounding temperature drops. Furthermore, mammals provide care for their young, whereas most reptiles leave theirs to fend for themselves. But the mammals faced two limitations. For one, their high activity demanded more nutrition than did the less constant activity of reptiles. Such high-quality nutrition is provided by the fruits, nuts, and seeds of flowering plants, but these plants did not become common until late in the Cretaceous period. It is also provided by the flesh of other animals, but the mammals were small and therefore dependent particularly on small prey such as insects and worms. These were limited in numbers until flowers and fruits provided them with a host of new **ecological niches,** or functional positions in their habitats, to exploit.

The second limitation that affected mammals was the slight head start enjoyed by reptiles; this allowed them to preempt most available niches, which therefore were not available to mammals. With the mass extinction of many reptiles at the end of the Cretaceous, however, a number of existing niches became available to mammals; at the same time, whole new niches were opened up as the new grasses provided abundant food in arid places, and other flowering plants provided abundant, high-quality food elsewhere. By chance, the mammals had what it took in the way of biological equipment to take advantage of the new opportunities available to them.

RISE OF THE PRIMATES

Considering that primates have tended through the ages to live in environments where the conditions for fossilization are generally poor, we have a surprising number of fossils with which to work. What these fossils

The appearance of angiosperm plants provided not only highly nutritious fruits, seeds, and flowers but also a host of habitats for numerous edible insects and worms—just the sorts of foods required by mammals with their high metabolism.

indicate is that the early primates emerged during a time of great change all over the world. The separation of continents was under way as the result of movement of the great platelike segments of the earth's crust on which they rest. The distribution of fossil primates across the earth makes sense only when one understands that the positions of the continents today differ tremendously from what was found in the past. Although Europe was still joined to North America, South America and India were isolated, while a narrow body of water separated Africa from Eurasia (see Figure 5.2). On the land itself the great dinosaurs had but recently become extinct, and the mammals were undergoing the great adaptive radiation that ultimately led to the development of the diverse forms with which we are familiar today. At the same time, the newly evolved grasses, ivies, shrubs, and other flowering plants were undergoing an enormous proliferation. This diversification, along with a milder climate, favored the spread of dense, lush tropical and subtropical forests over much of the earth, including North and South America and much of Eurasia and Africa. With the spread of these

---

Warm-blooded.   Animals that maintain a relatively constant body temperature. • **Cold-blooded.**   Animals whose body temperature rises or falls according to the temperature of the surrounding environment. • **Ecological niche.**   A species' way of life considered in the context of its environment, including other species found in that environment.

huge belts of forest, the stage was set for the movement of some mammals from niches on the ground into the trees. Forests would provide our early ancestors with the ecological niches in which they would flourish.

The move to an arboreal existence brought for early primates a combination of the problems of earthbound existence with those of flight. In their move into the air, birds developed highly stereotyped behavior; primates, on the other hand, brought with them to the trees the flexible decision-making behavior characteristic of the mammals. The initial forays into the trees must have produced many misjudgments and errors of coordination, leading to falls that injured or killed the individuals poorly adapted to arboreal life. Natural selection favored those that judged depth correctly and gripped the branches strongly. It is quite likely that the early primates that took to the trees were in some measure preadapted, not just with behavioral flexibility but with better vision and more dexterous fingers than their contemporaries.

The relatively small size of the early primates allowed them to make use of the smaller branches of trees; larger, heavier competitors, and most predators, could not follow. The move to the smaller branches also gave them access to an abundant food supply; the primates were able to gather insects, leaves, flowers, and fruits directly rather than waiting for them to fall to the ground.

The strong selection to a new environment led to an acceleration in the rate of change of primate characteristics. Paradoxically, these changes eventually made possible a return to the ground on the part of some primates, including the ancestors of the genus *Homo.*

Paleocene Primates

Both genetics and anatomy suggest that the ancestry of primates lies with the insectivores, a diverse group of small mammals represented today by tree shrews, moles, and hedgehogs. Thus, we would expect to have difficulty distinguishing the earliest primate fossils from ancient insectivores. In fact, the earliest surely known primate fossils, 10 teeth from a site in Morocco, are about 60 million years old. These cheek teeth (molars and premolars) are very similar to the corresponding teeth of the modern mouse lemur, a tiny strepsirhine primate weighing a mere 2 ounces. They are sufficient to show that the primates were going their separate evolutionary way by 60 million years ago, having arisen as part of the great Paleocene adaptive radiation of mammals. Whether they originated in Africa or came from somewhere else is not known; certainly mammals that differed little from early primates were widespread at the time throughout what is now North America and Europe.

The abilities to judge depth correctly and grasp branches strongly are of obvious importance to animals as active in the trees as most primates.

Eocene Primates

The Eocene lasted from about 55 to 34 million years ago and began with an abrupt warming trend. With this, many older forms of mammals became extinct, to be replaced by recognizable progenitors of many of today's forms. Among the latter were numerous forms of lemurlike and tarsierlike primates, of which over 50 genera are known. Fossils of these creatures have been found in Africa, North America, Europe, and Asia, where the warm, wet conditions of the Eocene sustained extensive rain forests.

Most Eocene primates are classified into two families. One family consisted of mostly diurnal (active during daylight) creatures that generally ate fruit and leaves. Although for the most part small, some of these creatures were a bit larger than the smallest of today's monkeys. In many ways they were remarkably similar to modern lemurs and lorises, which likely are their descendants. Smaller in size were members of the other family, which were nocturnal eaters of fruits and insects. Tarsierlike in their anatomy, they are closely related to today's tarsier.

What the members of these early primate families have in common are somewhat enlarged brain cases, slightly reduced snouts, and a somewhat forward position of the eye orbits, which, though not completely walled in, are surrounded by a complete bony ring (Figure 5.5). Their dentition, however, was primitive and unlike that of modern forms in the total number of teeth. In their limb skeleton, they were well adapted to grasping, leaping, and perching. Moreover, nails like those possessed by modern primates, rather than claws, may be seen on some digits.

Other Eocene primates, represented by fossils from China and Egypt's Fayum depression, show unique mixes of lemurlike, tarsierlike, and platyrrhine-catarrhinelike characteristics and probably played a role in the ancestry of later monkeys and apes. The Chinese fossils, which are roughly 45 million years old, represent several species of tiny, insect-eating animals whose locomotion was by a combination of quadrupedalism and leaping. They include the smallest primates ever documented.[5] The Fayum fossils, not as old at 37 million years, are of a small leaf- or insect-eater. Although this creature's front teeth resemble those of the Eocene lemurlike primates, it has the catarrhinelike dental formula of two incisors, a canine, two premolars, and three molars on each side of the jaw, and the eye orbit has a complete wall, the latter being a feature of both catarrhine and platyrrhine primates. The foramen magnum has a somewhat forward position beneath the skull, and the brain was about 3.1 cubic centimeters in size.[6]

Although there is still much to be learned about these Eocene primates, it is clear that they were abundant, diverse, and widespread. Among them were ancestors of today's lemurs, as well as tarsiers and other haplorhines. The tarsierlike forms, with their large eyes, seem to have reverted to nocturnal habits, whereas the ancestors of platyrrhines and catarrhines did not. They shifted to a more herbivorous diet, with greater emphasis on arboreal quadrupedalism, in contrast to the emphasis on leaping seen in lemurlike and in tarsierlike forms.[7]

With the end of the Eocene, substantial changes took place among the primates, as among other mammals. In North America, now well isolated from Europe, primates became extinct, and elsewhere their range seems to have been reduced considerably. A driving force in all this was probably climatic change. Already, through the late Eocene, climates were becoming somewhat cooler and drier, but at the end temperatures took a sudden dive, sufficient to trigger formation of a substantial ice cap over previously forested Antarctica. The result was a marked reduction of the environments to which early primates were adapted. At the same time, some early primate niches may have been more effectively utilized by newly evolved rodent forms. Finally, the precursors of monkeys and apes, up to then overshadowed by lemurlike and

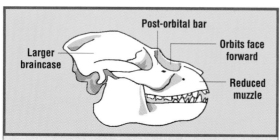

FIGURE 5.5

THE EOCENE GENUS *ADAPIS* IS A LEMURLIKE FORM. LIKE MODERN LEMURS, IT HAS A POSTORBITAL BAR, A BONY RING AROUND THE EYE ORBIT. NOTE THAT THE ORBIT IS OPEN BEHIND THE RING.

[5]Gebo, D. L., Dagosto, D., Beard, K. C., & Tao, Q. (2001). Middle Eocene primate tarsals from China: Implications for haplorhine evolution. *American Journal of Physical Anthropology, 116,* 83–107.

[6]Simons, E. (1995). Skulls and anterior teeth of *Catopithecus* (Primates: Anthropoidea) from the Eocene and anthropoid origins. *Science, 268,* 1,885–1,888.

[7]Kay, R. F., Ross, C., & Williams, B. A. (1997). Anthropoid origins. *Science, 275,* 803–804.

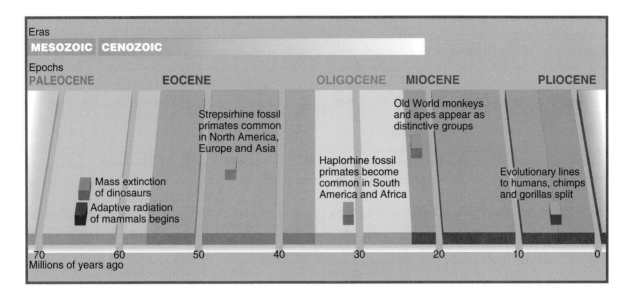

Eras
MESOZOIC CENOZOIC

Epochs
PALEOCENE   EOCENE   OLIGOCENE   MIOCENE   PLIOCENE

Old World monkeys
and apes appear as
distinctive groups

Strepsirhine fossil
primates common
in North America,
Europe and Asia

Haplorhine fossil
primates become
common in South
America and Africa

Mass extinction
of dinosaurs

Evolutionary lines
to humans, chimps
and gorillas split

Adaptive radiation
of mammals begins

70   60   50   40   30   20   10   0
Millions of years ago

tarsierlike forms, may have been able to take over some other niches they formerly occupied.

Oligocene Monkeys and Apes

The Oligocene epoch began about 34 million and ended about 23 million years ago. Primate fossils that have thus far been discovered and definitely placed in the Oligocene are not common, but enough exist to prove that haplorhines were becoming quite prominent and diverse by this time. The scarcity of Oligocene primate fossils stems from the reduced habitat available to them and from the arboreal nature of primates then living, which restricted them to damp forest environments where conditions are exceedingly poor for fossil formation.

Fortunately, Egypt's Fayum depression has yielded sufficient fossils (more than 1,000) to reveal that by 33 million years ago, haplorhine primates existed in considerable diversity. Moreover, the cast of characters is growing, as new fossils continue to be found in the Fayum, as well as in newly discovered localities in Algeria and

Egypt's Fayum depression in the desert west of Cairo. Here, winds and flash floods have uncovered sediments more than 22 million years old, exposing the remains of a tropical rain forest that was home to a variety of primates that combine monkeylike and apelike features.

Oman. At present, we have evidence of at least 60 genera included in two families. All show a combination of monkeylike and apelike features, and their origins probably lie in the group of Eocene primates in which traits of platyrrhines and catarrhines are first evident. But in the Oligocene the tables have been turned; now lemurlike and tarsierlike forms have become far less prominent than forms that combine monkeylike and apelike features. Only on the island of Madagascar (off the coast of East Africa), which was devoid of haplorhines until humans arrived, did lemurs thrive. In their isolation, they underwent a further adaptive radiation.

Included among the smaller Oligocene haplorhine species may be the ancestors of true monkeys. In their dental formula and limb bones, these primates (about the size of a modern squirrel monkey) resemble platyrrhine monkeys. Some of them could easily have gotten to South America, which at the time was not attached to any other land mass, by means of floating masses of vegetation of the sort that originate even today in the great rivers of West and Central Africa. In the Oligocene, the distance between the two continents was far less than it is today; favorable winds and currents could easily have carried "floating islands" of vegetation across within the 13 days that platyrrhine ancestors could have survived, given an existing adaptation to seasonal variation in availability of fresh water.[8]

The earliest surely known true catarrhine monkey fossil comes from the Miocene epoch, but its ancestry may lie among the same primates that gave rise to the platyrrhines. This fossil's molars look as if they evolved from a similar form, and loss of one premolar on each side of the jaw would result in the typical catarrhine formula.

Given our obsession with our own ancestry, one particular genus of Oligocene catarrhine is worth a closer look. This is *Aegyptopithecus* ("Egyptian ape"). It is one of a number of genera with a specifically apelike dentition: Its lower molars have the five cusps of an ape, and the upper canine and lower first premolar exhibit the sort of shearing mechanism found in monkeys and apes. Its skull possesses eye sockets that are in a forward position and completely protected by a bony wall, as is typical of modern monkeys and apes. Evidently *Aegyptopithecus,* and probably its Fayum contemporaries as well, possessed vision superior to the lemurlike and tarsierlike primates of the Eocene. In fact, the inside of the skull of *Aegyptopithecus* reveals that its brain had a larger visual cortex and smaller olfactory lobes than do modern lemurs or tarsiers. Although the brain of *Aegyptopithecus* was smaller relative to body size than that of more recent catarrhines, this primate seems to have had a larger brain than any lemur or tarsier, past or present.

Aegyptopithecus, besides being the best-known Oligocene primate, is also of interest to us because its teeth suggest that it belongs in the ancestry of those Miocene forms that gave rise to both humans and today's African apes. Although no bigger than a modern house cat, *Aegyptopithecus* was nonetheless one of the larger Oligocene primates. Possessed of a monkeylike skull and body, with limb proportions not unlike those seen in some modern platyrrhine monkeys, and fingers and toes capable of powerful grasping, it evidently moved about in a quadrupedal monkeylike manner.[9] Differences between males and females include larger body size, more formidable canine teeth, and deeper mandibles (lower jaws) in the males. In modern catarrhines, species with these traits generally live in groups that include several adult females with one or more adult males.

Miocene Apes

The beginning of the Miocene epoch, which succeeded the Oligocene about 23 million years ago, saw a proliferation of apes in the forests that covered many parts of

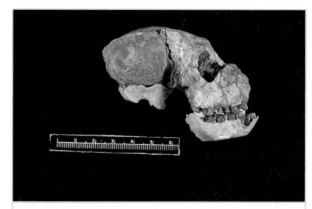

This *Aegyptopithecus* skull dates to the Oligocene epoch. The enclosed eye sockets and dentition mark it as a catarrhine primate, probably ancestral to *Proconsul.*

---

[8]Houle, A. (1999). The origin of platyrrhines: An evaluation of the Antarctic scenario and the floating island model. *American Journal of Physical Anthropology, 109,* 554–556.

[9]Ankel-Simons, F., Fleagle, J. G., & Chatrath, P. S. (1998). Femoral anatomy of *Aegyptopithecus zeuxis,* an early Oligocene anthropoid. *American Journal of Physical Anthropology, 106,* 421–422.

the Old World. Thus began a kind of golden age of ape-like forms. East Africa is an area particularly rich in the fossils of apes from the early through the middle part of the Miocene. One of the earliest of these apes, *Proconsul* (Consul was the name of a chimpanzee prominent on the London vaudeville circuit), is one of the best known, owing to preservation of almost all elements of its skeleton. Four recognized species of *Proconsul* varied considerably in size, the smallest being no larger than a modern female baboon while the largest was the size of a female gorilla. That they were apes is clearly shown by their dentition, particularly the five-cusped lower molars. Moreover, their skull, compared to that of Oligocene proto-apes like *Aegyptopithecus,* shows a reduced snout and a fuller, more rounded brain case. Cranial capacity for one species is estimated at about 167 cubic centimeters, about 1.5 times larger than that typical of a mammal of comparable body size and relatively larger than in modern monkeys. Still, some features are reminiscent of monkeys, particularly the forward thrust and narrowness of the face.

Although its overall configuration is not quite like any living monkey or ape, the elbow, hip, knee, and foot anatomy of *Proconsul* is similar to what one sees in living apes, and like them, it had no tail (Figure 5.6). The wrist and pelvis, however, are monkeylike, and the lumbar vertebrae and leg bones show features that are intermediate between those of a gibbon and a monkey. Overall, the vertebral column was longer and more flexible and the torso narrower than in apes, but the hind limb was less monkeylike, being more mobile as are ape hind limbs. The consensus is that *Proconsul* represents

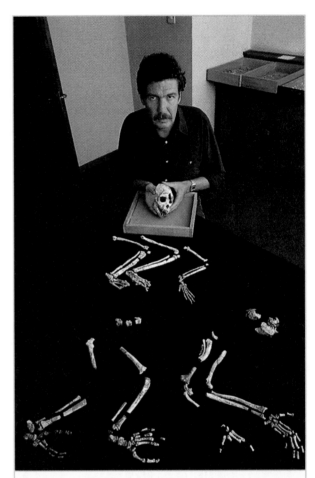

Paleoanthropologist Alan Walker displays bones of *Proconsul,* an unspecialized tree-dwelling, fruit-eating hominoid of the early Miocene.

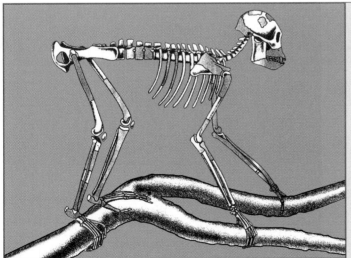

FIGURE 5.6

RECONSTRUCTED SKELETON OF *PROCONSUL.* NOTE APELIKE ABSENCE OF TAIL, BUT MONKEYLIKE LIMB AND BODY PROPORTIONS. *PROCONSUL,* HOWEVER, WAS CAPABLE OF GREATER ROTATION OF FORELIMBS THAN MONKEYS.

an unspecialized tree-dwelling, fruit-eating **hominoid** (the catarrhine superfamily to which modern apes and humans belong).

Some of *Proconsul*'s contemporaries were even more apelike. At least one species had a shoulder joint allowing suspension of the body when hanging by the arms. Its leg bones suggest strong climbing ability, and vertebrae are indicative of a stiff, apelike body. Otherwise, details of the teeth, face, and body are comparable to *Proconsul*.[10] Like *Proconsul*, this species is easily derivable from an animal like *Aegyptopithecus* and was almost certainly ancestral to hominoids of the middle Miocene. Like their probable ancestor as well as their descendants, *Proconsul* and other early Miocene apes were sexually dimorphic, the males being the larger sex with more formidable canine teeth.

Hominoids of the middle and late Miocene (from roughly 16 million to 5 million years ago) were a varied lot that ranged over a remarkably wide geographical area: Their fossils have been found in Europe, Asia, and Africa (by this time, Africa had collided with the Eurasian land mass, allowing faunal interchange). Such abundance and wide distribution indicates that these primates were very successful animals. With teeth and jaws very much like those of *Proconsul*, they seem to have been somewhat more apelike than monkeylike in their overall appearance; like some of *Proconsul*'s contemporaries, they had relatively rigid bodies as well as limb bones well adapted for suspension and climbing. Some species surely were ancestral to later large-bodied apes, including the **hominids**—the primate family in which the African apes and humans are placed. According to David Pilbeam, who has made the study of Miocene hominoids his lifework, "Any . . . would make excellent ancestors for the living hominoids: human bipeds, chimpanzee and gorilla knucklewalkers, Orangutan contortionists."[11] Figure 5.7 shows some important similarities and differences among hominoids. Over the years, these forms have been known by a confusing assortment of generic and specific names, not all of which have turned out to be justified, as the following Original Study explains.

---

[10]Gebo, D. L., MacLatchy, L., Kityo, R., Deino, A., Kingston, J., & Pilbeam, D. (1997). A hominoid genus from the early Miocene of Uganda. *Science, 276,* 401–404.

[11]Pilbeam, D. (1986). *Human origins* (p. 6). David Skamp Distinguished Lecture in Anthropology, Indiana University.

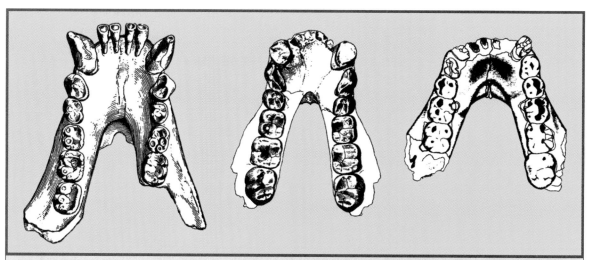

FIGURE 5.7

THE LOWER JAWS OF TWO MIOCENE APES (A) AND (B) AND EARLY *AUSTRALOPITHECUS* (C), A HOMININE WHO LIVED 4 MILLION YEARS AGO. RELATIVE TO THE CHEEK TEETH, ALL HAVE COMPARATIVELY SMALL TEETH AT THE FRONT OF THE JAW. THERE IS GENERAL SIMILARITY BETWEEN A AND B, AS WELL AS BETWEEN B AND C. THE MAJOR DIFFERENCE BETWEEN B AND C IS THAT THE ROWS OF CHEEK TEETH ARE FARTHER APART IN THE HOMININE.

Hominoid. A catarrhine primate superfamily that includes apes and humans. • **Hominid.** Hominoid family to which humans alone used to be assigned; now includes African apes and humans, with the latter assigned to the subfamily *Homininae*.

Will the Real Human Ancestor Please Stand Up?[12]

Original Study

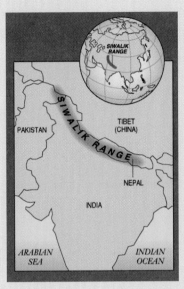

Today, humans are the only "ape" to have a global distribution. We inhabit every continent, including areas as inhospitable as the icy Antarctic or the scorching Sahara. Our closest living relatives, the other members of the superfamily *Hominoidea*, don't come close to occupying as much real estate. Instead these apes live in very circumscribed areas of the Old World tropical rain forest. Chimps, bonobos, and gorillas can be found only in portions of Central Africa. Orangutans are limited to the treetops on the islands of Sumatra and Borneo. Gibbons and siamangs swing through the branches only of the Southeast Asian forests.

This was not always the case. In the distant past, long before any human ancestor walked upon two legs, apes could be found throughout much of the Old World. True apes first appeared in the fossil record during the Miocene epoch, 5 to 23 million years ago. It was also during this time period that the African and Eurasian land masses made direct contact. For most of the preceding 100 million years, the Tethys Sea was a continuous body of water that more or less joined what are now the Mediterranean and Black Seas to the Indian Ocean. The Tethys Sea was a formidable barrier to migration. Once Africa and Eurasia were joined together

through what is now the Middle East, Old World primate species that got their start in Africa could expand their ranges into Eurasia. Miocene ape fossil remains have been found everywhere from the caves of China, to the forests of France, to eastern Africa where the earliest fossil remains of bipeds have been found.

So varied and ubiquitous were the fossil apes of this period that the Miocene has even been labeled by some as the "golden age of the hominoids." The word *hominoid* comes from the Latin roots *Homo* and *Homin* (meaning "human being") and the suffix *oïdes* ("resembling"). As a group, the hominoids get their name from their resemblance to humans. The likeness between humans and the other apes bespeaks an important evolutionary relationship. One of the Miocene apes is the direct ancestor of the human lineage. Exactly which one is a question still to be resolved.

Looking at some of the history of the "contenders" for direct human ancestor among the Miocene apes illustrates how reconstructing evolutionary relationships draws on much more than bones alone. Fossil finds are always interpreted against the backdrop of scientific discoveries in a variety of fields as well as prevailing beliefs and biases. Interpretations are also affected by whether fossilization and discovery are likely to occur in any given region. Fortunately the self-correcting nature of scientific investigation allows evolutionary lineages to be redrawn in light of all new discoveries.

The first Miocene ape fossil remains were found in Africa in the 1930s and 1940s by A. T. Hopwood and the renowned paleoanthropologist Louis Leakey. These fossils turned up on one of the many islands in Lake Victoria, the 27,000-square-mile lake that separates Kenya, Tanzania, and Uganda. Impressed with the chimplike appearance of these fossil remains, Hopwood suggested that the new species be named *Proconsul* after a chimpanzee

[12]Walrath, D. E. (2001). *Will the real human ancestor please stand up?* © by author, College of Medicine, University of Vermont.

Original Study

who was performing on the London stage at the time. *Pro* is the Latin root for "before" and Consul was the stage name of the acting chimp. Dated to the early Miocene 17 to 21 million years ago, *Proconsul* has some of the classic hominoid features, namely no tail and the characteristic pattern of Y5 grooves in the lower molar teeth. However, the adaptations of the upper body seen in later apes (including humans) for hanging suspended below tree branches in search of ripe fruits were absent. In other words, *Proconsul* has some apelike features as well as some features of more generalized four-footed Old World monkeys. This mixture of ape and monkey features makes *Proconsul* a contender for a "missing link" between monkeys and apes but not as a connection between Miocene apes and bipeds. We know that the ape who stood was fully apelike in all the ways that humans are apes. Our broad shoulders and mobile upper limb joints are fully adapted for hanging from branches. A dentist would recognize the cusp pattern of human molars in the mouth of any hominoid.

At least seven groups besides *Proconsul* have been found in East Africa in the early to middle Miocene. But between 14 and 5 million years ago this fossil record thins out. It is not that all the apes suddenly moved from Africa to Eurasia, but rather that the geologic conditions for preservation of bones as fossils made it less likely that any of the African remains would survive. Tropical forests inhabited by chimps and gorillas today are just about the worst conditions for the preservation of bones. In order to become a fossil, bones must be quickly incorporated into the earth before any rotting or decomposition occurs. In tropical forests the heat, humidity, and the general abundance of life make this unlikely. The bones' organic matrix is consumed by other creatures before it can be fossilized.

Nevertheless, the scarcity of African fossil evidence for this time period fits well with prevailing notions about human origins. Two factors were at work to take the focus away from Africa. First, at this time no investigators thought that humans were any more closely related to the African apes

than they were to the other intelligent great ape—the Asian orangutan. Chimps, bonobos, gorillas, and orangutans were thought to be more closely related to each other than any of them were to humans. Moreover, the construction of evolutionary relationships still relied upon visual similarities between species much as it did when Linnaeus developed the taxonomic scheme that grouped humans with other primates. Chimps, bonobos, gorillas, and orangutans all possess the same basic body plan adapted to hanging by their arms from branches or knuckle-walking on the ground. Humans and their ancestors had an altogether different form of locomotion: walking upright on two legs. On an anatomical basis, it seemed as though the first Miocene ape to stand up and become a hominine could have come from any part of the vast Old World range of the Miocene apes.

The second factor at work to pull attention away from African origins was more subtle and embedded not in the bones from the earth but in the subconscious of the scientists of the day. It was hard for these scientists to imagine that humans originated entirely in Africa. Indeed, it took many years for the first bipedal hominine fossils discovered in South Africa in the 1920s to be accepted by the scientific community as a key part of the human line (see Chapter 6). Instead, human origins were imagined to involve a close link between those who invented the first tools and the people responsible for Western civilization. In this regard, a contender for a Miocene ape ancestor from southern Asia, near the ruins of the great Indus Valley civilization, may have been more palatable to anthropologists in the middle of the 20th century.

During the 1960s, it appeared as though this Miocene human ancestor lived in the Siwalkis, the foothills of the majestic Himalayan mountain range along the northern borders of India and Pakistan. The Himalayas are some of the youngest mountains of the world. They began forming during the Miocene when the Indian subcontinent collided with the rest of Eurasia and have been growing taller ever since.

In honor of the Hindu religion practiced in the region where the fossils were found, the contender was given the name *Ramapithecus*, after the Indian deity Rama and the Greek word for ape, *pithekos*. Rama is the avatar, or incarnation, of the Hindu god Vishnu, the preserver. He is meant to portray what a perfect human can be. He is benevolent, protects the weak, and embodies all noble human characteristics. Features like the relative delicacy and curvature of the jaw and palate as well as thick tooth enamel led paleoanthropologists David Pilbeam and Elwyn Simons to suggest that this was the first hominoid to become a hominine. They suggested that *Ramapithecus* was a bipedal tool-user—the earliest human ancestor. With these qualities, *Ramapithecus* was perfectly named.

Other Miocene apes were also present in the foothills of the Himalayas. *Sivapithecus* was named after the Hindu deity Siva, the god of destruction and regeneration. In the Hindu religion Siva is depicted as an asocial hermit who, when provoked, reduces his enemies to smoldering ashes in fits of rage. Though never an aspiring human ancestor, *Sivapithecus* also has the humanlike characteristic of thick molar tooth enamel (unlike the African apes). *Sivapithecus* also had large projecting canine teeth more suitable to a destroyer than to a human ancestor. The *Sivapithecus* and *Ramapithecus* fossils were dated to between 7 and 12 million years ago.

Fossils are not the only discoveries that have changed our understanding of human evolutionary history. By the 1970s, biochemical and genetic evidence was beginning to be used to establish evolutionary relationships. A Berkeley biochemist named Vince Sarich brought molecular techniques to evolutionary studies and developed the revolutionary concept of a "molecular clock." Such clocks help detect when the branching of related species from a common ancestor took place in the distant past.

Sarich used a molecular technique that had been around since the beginning of the 20th century: comparison of the blood proteins of living groups. He worked on serum albumin, a protein from the fluid portion of the blood that (like the albumin that forms egg whites) can be precipitated out of solution. One of the forces that will cause such precipitation is contact of this protein with antibodies directed against it, as in the immune response of the body when fighting an infection. The technique relies on the notion that the stronger the biochemical reaction between the protein and the antibody, the closer the evolutionary relationship, because the antibodies and proteins of closely related species will resemble one another more than the antibodies and proteins of distant species.

Sarich made immunological comparisons between a variety of species and suggested that he could establish a molecular clock by calculating a rate of change over time. By assuming a constant rate of change in the protein structure of each species over time, Sarich used these results to predict times of divergence between related groups. Each molecular clock needs to be set, or calibrated, by a known event such as the divergence between strepsirhine and haplorhine primates or Old World monkeys and apes. These dates are established directly by well-dated fossil specimens.

Using this technique, Sarich proposed a sequence of divergence for the living hominoids that showed that human, chimp, and gorilla lines split roughly 5 million years ago. He boldly stated that it was impossible to have a direct human ancestor before 7 million years ago "no matter what it looked like". In other words, anything that old would also have to be ancestral to chimps and gorillas. Because *Ramapithecus*, even with its humanlike jaws, was dated to between 7 and 12 million years ago, it could no longer be considered a human ancestor.

As recently as 1965, the renowned paleoanthropologist F. Clark Howell had described *Ramapithecus* as the earliest "manlike" primate, endorsing its direct place on the human line. However, the molecular evidence of the next decade did not strengthen this claim that, "the impressive thing about *Ramapithecus* is that each new piece of additional evidence about it has tended to strengthen rather than weaken the claim being made for it" as a human ancestor. Instead, the molecular data initiated an entirely new interpretation of the fossil evidence.

In the meantime, David Pilbeam and Elwyn Simons continued fossil hunting in the Himalayan foothills. Further specimens began to show that *Ramapithecus* was actually a smaller, perhaps

Original Study

female version of *Sivapithecus*. Eventually all the specimens referred to as *Ramapithecus* were "sunk" or absorbed into the *Sivapithecus* group so that today *Ramapithecus* no longer exists as a valid name for a Miocene ape. Instead of two distinct groups, one of which went on to evolve into humans, they are considered males and females of the sexually dimorphic species *Sivapithecus*. A spectacularly complete specimen found in the Potwar Plateau by David Pilbeam showed that *Sivapithecus* was undoubtedly the ancestor of living orangutans. This conclusion matched well with the molecular evidence that the separate line to orangutans originated 10–12 million years ago.

All of these changes might make paleoanthropologists seem fickle, but they are not. They are participants in an unusual kind of science. Paleoanthropology, like all paleontology, is a science of discovery. What is seen or discovered determines what interpretations can be made. As new discoveries come to light, interpretations inevitably change, making for better understanding of our evolutionary history. Today, discoveries can occur in the laboratory as easily as on the site of an excavation. Molecular studies provided a new line of evidence that can be seen in much the same way that fossils provide new data as they are unearthed. A discovery in the laboratory, like Sarich's molecular clocks, can drastically change the interpretation of the fossil evidence.

What we discover is also shaped by what we believe, since beliefs shape the search process itself. In the past, it seemed right to look for our Miocene ancestor in the foothills of the Himalayas. Today, though we still have very little fossil evidence from Africa between 5 and 14 million years ago, the molecular studies allow us to "see" that the human line got its start in Africa when chimps, gorillas, and hominines diverged.

As the human lineage developed since the Miocene, our closest living relatives—the chimpanzees and gorillas—followed their own separate evolutionary trajectories. Today they inhabit the tropical forested pockets of Central Africa leaving little trace of their evolutionary history behind. Hominines took a different course and have left behind a rich fossil record in eastern and southern Africa beginning about 5 million years ago. Several million years after the ability to walk on two feet appeared, hominines began to spread throughout the Old World. Today, humans inhabit every continent. The details of our evolutionary history will continue to be redrawn in light of new evidence that appears from the bones, the molecules, or some area yet to be discovered. Though we have not found the fossil remains of the common ancestor of chimps, gorillas, and hominines, we know from the molecules that Africa is the place where the first ape stood up.

The End

For many years, potential hominid ancestors were known exclusively from the remains of teeth and jaws. Relative to the size of the cheek teeth (premolars and molars), their incisor teeth are comparable in size to those of other large hominoids of the time, although they are placed a bit more vertically in the mouth. The canines are substantially larger in males than in females, but even in males they are significantly smaller relative to the cheek teeth than the canines of the other hominoids. Still, they do project beyond adjacent teeth so that, when closed, the jaws interlock. Furthermore, the shearing function of the upper canine with the first lower premolar is retained. The molars, which show the same five-cusp pattern as the other hominoids, have noticeably thicker enamel and low, rounded cusps. The tooth row tends to be slightly V-shaped, whereas that of the other hominoids is more like a U, with the rows of cheek teeth parallel to one another (see Figure 5.7). The palate, or roof of the mouth, is high and arched. Finally, the lower facial region is narrow, short, and deep. Overall, the dental apparatus was built for powerful chewing, especially on the back teeth.

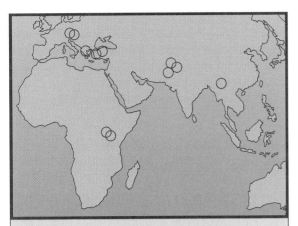

FIGURE 5.8

FOSSILS OF HOMINOIDS HAVE BEEN FOUND IN EAST AFRICA, EUROPE, AND ASIA THAT COULD BE ANCESTRAL TO LARGE APES AND HUMANS.

This *Sivapithecus* skull is remarkably similar to skulls of modern orangutans, so much so that an ancestor-descendant relationship is probable. The last common ancestor of chimpanzees, gorillas, and humans may not have differed greatly from *Sivapithecus*.

In the past three decades, our dependence on teeth and jaws for our knowledge of these hominoids has lessened as a number of their skull and limb bone fragments have been found in China, Greece, Hungary, Pakistan, and Turkey (Figure 5.8). In the best-known genus (*Sivapithecus*), the face is remarkably orangutanlike in its profile and a number of other details. The mandible, however, is only broadly rather than specifically similar to that of an orang, nor are the upper arm bones quite the same.

MIOCENE APES AND HUMAN ORIGINS

As long as several late Miocene apes were known only from fossils of teeth and jaws, it was easy to postulate some sort of relationship between them and ourselves. This was because a number of features—the position of the incisors, the reduced canines, the thick enamel of the molars, and the shape of the tooth row—seemed to point in a somewhat human direction. Some fossils (notably one from East Africa called *Kenyapithecus*) even show a shallow concavity above the position of the canine tooth, a feature not found in any recent ape but often found in humans. Indeed, some anthropologists went so far as to see such creatures as the earliest representatives of a human, as opposed to any ape lineage. This view was challenged when molecular evidence indicated a more recent split between apes and humans. The discovery of the orangutanlike skulls and apelike limb bones of *Sivapithecus* added fuel to the fire, leading many anthropologists to conclude that this and similar forms could have nothing to do with human origins. Rather, orangutans were seen as the sole modern survivors of an ancient group from which the line leading to the hominids (African apes and humans) had branched off, as molecular evidence suggested, some 18 to 12 million years ago.

Eventually, opinion shifted back to a middle position. Although a link between Miocene *Sivapithecus* and modern orangutans seems undeniable, this does not rule out the possibility of a link between other related late Miocene hominoids on the one hand and hominids on the other.[13] For example, some late Miocene species from

---

[13]Ciochon, R. L., & Fleagle, J. G. (1987). *Ramapithecus* and human origins. In R. L. Ciochon & J. G. Fleagle (Eds.), *Primate evolution and human origins* (p. 208). Hawthorne, NY: Aldine de Gruyter.

Although not identical, the modern ape most like *Sivapithecus* is the orangutan. Chimpanzees and gorillas, like humans, have come to differ more from the ancestral condition than have these Asian apes.

lion years ago. We know from the fossils that forms like *Sivapithecus* were still on the scene at that time (indeed, a form larger than a modern gorilla survived in Asia until about 300,000 years ago) and also that our own human ancestors were going their separate evolutionary way by at least 4.4 million, if not 6 million, years ago.

Hominoid Adaptations and Late Miocene Climatic Change

Molar teeth like those of some late Miocene apes that feature low crown relief, thick enamel, and surfaces poorly developed for cutting, are found in a number of modern primates.[14] Some of these species are terrestrial and some are arboreal, but all have one thing in common: They eat very hard nuts, fruits with very tough rinds, and some seeds. This provides them with a rich source of easily digested nutrients that are not accessible to species with thin molar enamel incapable of standing up to the stresses of tough rind removal or nut cracking. Thus these Miocene apes probably ate food similar to that eaten by these latter-day nut crackers.

Analysis of other materials from deposits in which these fossils have been found suggests utilization of a broad range of habitats, ranging from tropical rain forests to drier bush country. Of particular interest to us, from the standpoint of human origins, are those populations that lived in mosaic environments, where there was forested as well as some open country, where food could be obtained through foraging on the ground as well as in the trees of the forests. As it happened, a climatic shift was under way, associated with the geological events involved in the formation of East Africa's rift valleys. This caused a gradual but persistent breaking up of forested areas, with a consequent expansion of open grassland.[15] Under such circumstances, it seems likely that those populations of late Miocene hominoids living at the edge of forests were obliged to supplement food from the trees more and more with other foods readily available on

Africa seem closer in dental proportions and other features of their teeth to early **hominines** than do related Asian fossils.

That the ancestry of humans may ultimately be among late Miocene apes of Africa that show some resemblance to *Sivapithecus,* then, is consistent with dental evidence. It is consistent as well with estimates, based on molecular similarities and differences among humans, bonobos, chimpanzees, and gorillas, that they could not have separated from a common ancestral stock more than 8 mil-

[14]Kay, R. F. (1981). The nut-crackers—A new theory of the adaptations of the Ramapithecinae. *American Journal of Physical Anthropology, 55,* 141–151.

[15]Conroy, G. C. (1997). *Reconstructing human origins: A modern synthesis* (pp. 84–86). New York: Norton.

Hominine.   Member of the *Homininae,* the subfamily of hominids to which humans belong.

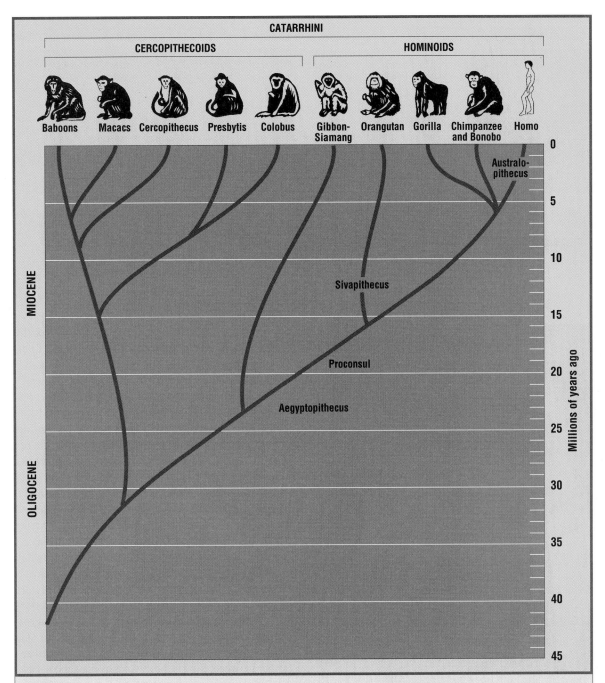

FIGURE 5.9

ALTHOUGH DEBATE CONTINUES OVER DETAILS, THIS CHART REPRESENTS A REASONABLE RECONSTRUCTION OF EVOLUTIONARY RELATIONSHIPS AMONG THE CATARRHINE PRIMATES. (NOT SHOWN ARE EXTINCT EVOLUTIONARY LINES.)

Cyber Road Trip

HIGHWAY 1

Find out about plate tectonics and continental drift from this nifty site created by NASA. Use interactive maps to understand how these phenomena shape our world and beyond.
http://kids.earth.nasa.gov/archive/pangaea/

HIGHWAY 2

This comprehensive primate evolution site provides a complete taxonomic listing of fossil primates as well as an excellent glossary of terms related to primate evolution.
http://members.tripod.com/cacajao/evolution.html

HIGHWAY 3

A trip to the Wisconsin Regional Primate Research Center's Primate Info Net opens the door to information about living and fossil primates as well as the people who study them. The site's search engine is a tremendous resource.
www.primate.wisc.edu/pin/

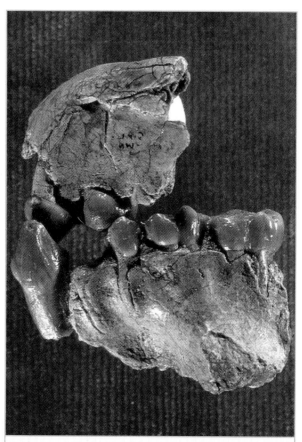

Kenyapithecus from East Africa is a Miocene ape that has relatively small canine teeth and a facial profile suitable for an ancestor of African apes and humans.

the ground in more open country. Consistent with this theory, late Miocene ape fossils are typically found in association with greater numbers of the remains of animals adapted to grasslands than are earlier ones.

Those Miocene apes that already had large, thickly enameled molars were capable of dealing with the tough and abrasive foods available on the ground when necessary. What they lacked, however, were canine teeth of sufficient size to have served as effective weapons of defense. By contrast, most modern monkeys and apes that spend much time down on the ground rely heavily for defense on the massive, fanglike canines possessed by the males. Because catlike predators were even more numerous on the ground than now, these Miocene apes, especially the smaller ones (which probably weighed no more than about 40 pounds[16]), would seem to have been especially vulnerable primates. Probably the forest fringe was more than just a source of foods different from those on the ground; its trees would have provided refuge when danger threatened. Yet, with continued expansion of open country, trees for refuge would have become fewer and farther between. Slowly, however, physical and behavioral changes must have improved these primates' chances for survival out in the open on the ground. For reasons discussed in the next chapter, bipedal locomotion was a key element in this new adaptation.

---

[16]Pilbeam, D. R. (1987). Rethinking human origins. In Ciochon & Fleagle, p. 217.

Ground-dwelling primates, like this male baboon, depend heavily on their massive canine teeth for protection from other animals. Some Miocene apes, by contrast, lacked such massive weapons of defense.

EARLY APES AND HUMAN EVOLUTION

Although some late Miocene apes display a number of features from which hominine characteristics may be derived, and some may occasionally have walked bipedally, they were much too apelike to be considered hominines. No matter how often some of them may have resorted to bipedalism, they had not yet developed the anatomical specializations for this mode of locomotion that are seen in the earliest known hominines. They were optional rather than obligatory bipeds. Nevertheless, existing anatomical and molecular evidence allows the hypothesis that apes and humans separated from a common evolutionary line sometime near the end of the Miocene, and some fossils, particularly the smaller hominoids, do possess traits seen in humans. Moreover, the Miocene apes possessed a limb structure less specialized for brachiation than modern apes; this structure could well have provided the basis for the development of human as well as ape limb types.

Clearly not all late Miocene apes evolved into hominines. Those that did might, in a sense, be regarded as losers, in that they were squeezed out of the most favorable forested habitat. It was just their good luck that their physical characteristics enabled them to make a go of it under changed conditions. Most contemporary hominoids, by contrast, remained in the forests and woodlands where they continued to develop as arboreal apes, although ultimately some of them, too, took up a more terrestrial life. These are the bonobos, chimpanzees, and gorillas, who have changed far more from the ancestral hominoid condition than have the still arboreal orangutans.

EARLY PRIMATE EVOLUTION: AN OVERVIEW

Looking back over the first several million years of primate evolution, what we see is an initial diversification of strepsirhine and some haplorhine forms as they adapt to life in the trees. Despite their initial success, however, the strepsirhines tended to lose out to competition from rodents and the haplorhines. The exceptions were those forms that made it to Madagascar, or that adapted to nocturnal niches. Meanwhile, haplorhines diversified into a large variety of monkeylike apes, from which developed true monkeys, true apes, and (later) humans. Like the strepsirhines before them, the apes did well at first but eventually took a back seat in the forests to monkeys. This happened at least in part because monkeys, with shorter reproductive cycles, can out-reproduce apes. At the same time, forests continued to shrink, with some apes eventually adopting more terrestrial lifestyles. But unfortunately for them, by the time they did this, ground-dwelling niches for primates were already occupied by baboons and humans.

CHAPTER SUMMARY

Over time, evolutionary forces act to produce new species from old ones. A species is a population or a group of populations that is capable of interbreeding. The concept of species is relative rather than absolute; whether breeding actually takes place in the wild or not is more important than the academic question of whether it is technically feasible. Biologists define populations within species that are capable of interbreeding but do so to a limited extent as subspecies or races. Although species are reasonably discreet and stable units in nature, races are impermanent and subject to reamalgamation. Among humans, it is not possible to define races with any biological validity.

Isolating mechanisms serve to separate breeding populations, creating first divergent races and then (if isolation continues) divergent species. Isolating mechanisms can be geographical; physical, as in the differing anatomical structures of the Saint Bernard and Chihuahua; or social, such as in the caste system of India.

As evolution proceeds it may be divergent (branching) or linear. The latter occurs as selection over time favors some variants over others, causing a change in a population's average characteristics. Convergence occurs when two unrelated species come to resemble each other owing to functional similarities.

Evolution is not a ladder of progress leading in a predictable and determined way to ever more complex forms. Rather, it has produced, through a series of accidents, a diversity of enormously varied designs that subsequently have been restricted to a lesser number of still less-than-perfect forms.

The primates arose as part of a great adaptive radiation, a branching of mammalian forms that began more than 100 million years after the appearance of the first mammals. The reason for this late diversification was that most ecological niches that mammals have since occupied were either preempted by the reptiles or were nonexistent until the flowering plants became widespread beginning about 65 million years ago.

The first primates were arboreal insect eaters, and the characteristics of all primates developed as adaptations to this initial way of life. Although some primates no longer inhabit the trees, it is certain that those adaptations that evolved in response to life in the trees were (by chance) preadaptive to the niche now occupied by the hominines.

The earliest primates had developed by 60 million years ago in the Paleocene epoch and were small arboreal creatures. A diversity of lemurlike and tarsierlike forms were common in the Eocene across what is now North America and Eurasia. By the late Eocene, perhaps 45 million years ago, small primates combining lemurlike and tarsierlike features with those seen in monkeys and apes were on the scene. In the Miocene epoch, apes proliferated and spread over many parts of the Old World. Among them were apparent ancestors of the large apes and humans. These appeared by 16 million years ago and were widespread even as recently as 8 million years ago. Details of dentition suggest that hominines, as well as the African apes, arose from these earlier apes. At least some populations of these primates lived in parts of Africa where the right kind of selective pressures existed to transform a creature just like it into a primitive hominine. Other populations remained in the forests, developing into today's bonobo, chimpanzee, and gorilla.

CLASSIC READINGS

Ciochon, R. L., & Fleagle, J. (Eds.). (1987). *Primate evolution and human origins.* Hawthorne, NY: Aldine de Gruyter.

Articles in Part IV of this book summarize recent knowledge of early catarrhine evolution, while those in Part V examine Miocene apes and their possible significance respecting human origins. Editors' introductions to each section provide the necessary overall perspective on the issues discussed in the articles.

Conroy, G. C. (1997). *Reconstructing human origins: A modern synthesis.* New York: Norton.

Though it says little about earlier primates, this book has an excellent, up-to-date chapter (3) on the Miocene hominoids. *Proconsul* and the other apes are discussed in the context of climate changes in Africa and elsewhere in the Old World.

Jones, S., Martin, R., & Pilbeam, D. (Eds.). (1992). *The Cambridge encyclopedia of human evolution.* New York: Cambridge University Press.

This useful reference work has good sections on primate evolution, molecular studies, and the geological context for primate evolution.

CHAPTER 6

THE EARLIEST HOMININES

Ethiopian paleoanthropologist Haile Selassie sifting sediments in which he found the remains of a hominine that lived between 5.6 and 5.8 million years ago. Although early hominines walked bipedally, their behavior was otherwise more apelike than human.

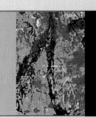

1

WHEN AND WHERE DID THE FIRST HOMININES APPEAR, AND WHAT WERE THEY LIKE?

The earliest indisputable hominine, *Australopithecus,* appeared in Africa by 4 million years ago, although there are earlier candidates that date as early as 6 million years ago. *Australopithecus,* remarkably human from the waist down, had become fully adapted for moving about on the ground on its hind legs in the distinctive human manner. But from the waist up, *Australopithecus* was still essentially apelike, with a brain suggesting intellectual abilities roughly comparable to those of a modern-day African ape.

2

WHAT IS THE RELATION BETWEEN THE VARIOUS FORMS OF *AUSTRALOPITHECUS?*

The earliest forms of *Australopithecus* preserve a number of features indicative of a more apelike ancestor. By 2.5 million years ago, this form gave rise to one whose chewing apparatus had become larger and more massive while its brain size remained relatively stable. For a while, this late form coexisted with a less radically altered version of the earlier form.

3

WHY HAD *AUSTRALOPITHECUS* BECOME A BIPEDAL WALKER?

Early hominines venturing out in the open on the ground would have been vulnerable in two ways: to damaging buildup of heat in the brain from direct exposure to the sun and to the many predators that prowled on the ground. Bipedal locomotion solves the heat problem by reducing the exposure of the body to direct solar radiation and positioning the body for most effective heat loss through convection. It also enabled *Australopithecus* to scan the savanna for danger, carry food to places where it could be consumed in safety, transport offspring, and grab hold of objects with which to threaten predators.

For a long time, the fossil evidence of the early stages of human evolution was both sparse and tenuous. Not until 1924 did the first important fossil come to light, from a site in South Africa. This unusual fossil, consisting of a partial cranium and natural brain cast, was brought to the attention of Professor Raymond Dart of the University of Witwatersrand in Johannesburg, and it was unlike any creature he had ever seen before in South Africa. Recognizing in this unusual fossil an intriguing mixture of simian and human characteristics, anatomist Dart named his discovery *Australopithecus africanus,* or southern ape of Africa. Based on the position of the foramen magnum, the large hole in the skull where the spinal cord enters, Dart claimed that *Australopithecus* was probably a biped.

In the scientific world, Dart's find was not greeted with enthusiasm. The problem was that fossils had already been found at Piltdown, England, that seemed to show that early humans had large-sized brains but retained apelike jaws. But according to Dart, his fossil had an ape-sized brain with humanlike jaws. Not until the 1950s was the Piltdown discovery shown to be a deliberate hoax, by which time other **Australopithecus** fos-

sils had come to light from various South African sites. Overall, these finds confirmed the correctness of Dart's original claim.

With the advent of World War II, the search for early hominine fossils came to a halt. Although the search was resumed after the war, it was not until the 1960s that the real rush of paleoanthropologists into the field got under way. Numerous international expeditions—including over 100 researchers from Belgium, Great Britain, Canada, France, Israel, Kenya, the Netherlands, South Africa, and the United States—swarmed over parts of East and South Africa, where they unearthed unprecedented amounts of fossil material. The process continues today, and with so many fossils, coming fast and furiously, our ideas of early human evolution have had to be constantly revised. Nevertheless, there is widespread agreement over the broad outline, even though debate, often heated, continues over details. What is clear is that the course of human evolution has not been a simple, steady "advance" in the direction of modern humanity. Rather, it proceeded in fits and starts, sometimes producing divergent lines of hominines. In this chapter we will discuss some of these, beginning with the best-known fossils of *Australopithecus.* We will then see how they relate to earlier forms.

Raymond Dart, who described the first fossil of *Australopithecus* and correctly diagnosed its bipedal mode of locomotion.

AUSTRALOPITHECUS

Since Dart's original find, hundreds of other fossils of *Australopithecus* have been found, first in South Africa and later in Tanzania, Malawi, Kenya, Ethiopia, and Chad (Figure 6.1). As they were discovered, many were given a number of different specific and generic names, but now usually all are considered to belong to the single genus *Australopithecus.* Most anthropologists recognize at least four species of the genus, if not as many as seven (Table 6.1 and Figure 6.2). For our purposes, we may discuss them in terms of two broad categories: **gracile** and **robust** *Australopithecus.* The latter are notable for having jaws that are massive (robust) relative to the size of the brain case. The gracile forms are slightly smaller on average and lack such robust jaws.

Australopithecus. The first well-known hominine; lived between 4.2 and 1 million years ago. Characterized by bipedal locomotion when on the ground, but with an apelike brain; includes at least five species: *afarensis, africanus, anamensis, boisei,* and *robustus.* • **Gracile Australopithecines.** Smaller, more lightly built members of the genus *Australopithecus.* • **Robust Australopithecines.** Slightly larger and more robust than gracile members of genus *Australopithecus,* with larger, more powerful jaws.

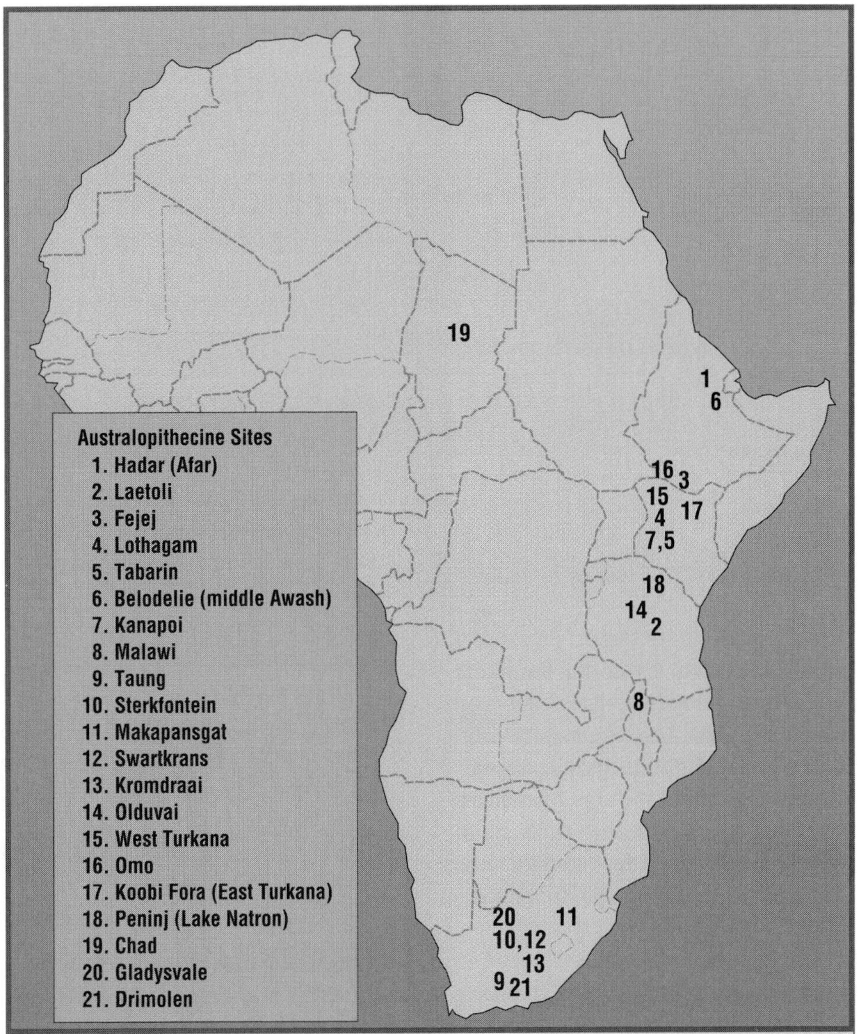

Australopithecine Sites
1. Hadar (Afar)
2. Laetoli
3. Fejej
4. Lothagam
5. Tabarin
6. Belodelie (middle Awash)
7. Kanapoi
8. Malawi
9. Taung
10. Sterkfontein
11. Makapansgat
12. Swartkrans
13. Kromdraai
14. Olduvai
15. West Turkana
16. Omo
17. Koobi Fora (East Turkana)
18. Peninj (Lake Natron)
19. Chad
20. Gladysvale
21. Drimolen

FIGURE 6.1

Australopithecine fossils have been found in South Africa, Malawi, Tanzania, Kenya, Ethiopia, and Chad.

Gracile Australopithecines

Included in this group are numerous fossils found beginning in the 1930s at Sterkfontein and Makapansgat in South Africa, in addition to Dart's original find from Taung (Figure 6.1). One unusually complete skeleton discovered in 1994 has been dated by paleomagnetism to about 3.5 million years ago. The other South African remains are difficult to date but seem to fit between 3 and 2.3 million years ago. Specimens from Ethiopia's Afar region, first discovered in 1970, are securely dated by potassium argon to between 3.9 and 2.9 million years ago. These include the famous "Lucy," represented by bones from almost all parts of a single skeleton, and "the First Family," a collection of bones from at least 13 individuals of both sexes, ranging in age from infancy to adulthood, who died together as a result of some single calamity. Also securely dated is material, close to 4 million years old, from Laetoli, in Tanzania, that is usually assigned to the same species as the Afar fossils. Thus, although there is overlap, the East African fossils seem for the most part to be earlier than those of South Africa.

Other pieces of gracile Australopithecines have been found at other East African sites that generally are

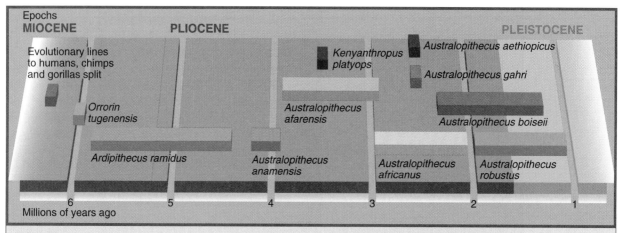

FIGURE 6.2

THE EARLIEST HOMININE FOSSILS AND THE SCIENTIFIC NAMES BY WHICH THEY HAVE BEEN KNOWN, ARRANGED ACCORDING TO WHEN THEY LIVED. *A. AETHIOPICUS, A. BOISEI,* AND *A. ROBUSTUS* ARE ALL ROBUST AUSTRALOPITHECINES; *A. AFARENSIS, A. AFRICANUS,* AND *A. ANAMENSIS* ARE GRACILE AUSTRALOPITHECINES. WHETHER ALL THE DIFFERENT SPECIES NAMES ARE WARRANTED IS HOTLY DEBATED.

2 million or more years old. The oldest so far found are some jaw and limb bones from Kenya that date to between 4.2 and 3.9 million years ago (see *Australopithecus anamensis* in Table 6.1 and Figure 6.2). All gracile species were erect, bipedal hominines about the size of modern pygmies (Figure 6.3), though far more powerfully built. Their stature ranged between 3.5 and 5 feet, and they are estimated to have weighed between 29 and 45 kilograms.[1]

TABLE 6.1	SPECIES OF *AUSTRALOPITHECUS**
Gracile Species	**Location**
A. afarensis	Ethiopia and Tanzania
A. africanus	South Africa
A. anamensis	Kenya
Robust Species	
A. aethiopicus	Kenya
A. boisei	Kenya
A. gahri	Ethiopia
A. robustus	South Africa

*Not all paleoanthropologists recognize as many as seven species; *A. aethiopicus,* for example, could be an early variety of *A. boisei.*

[1]McHenry, H. M. (1992). Body size and proportions in early hominids. *American Journal of Physical Anthropology, 87,* 407.

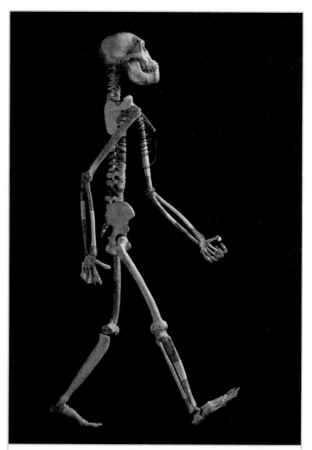

Sufficient parts of the skeleton of "Lucy" an Australopithecine that lived between 3.3 and 2.6 million years ago, survived to permit this reconstruction. Her hip and leg bones reveal that she walked about in a distinctively human manner.

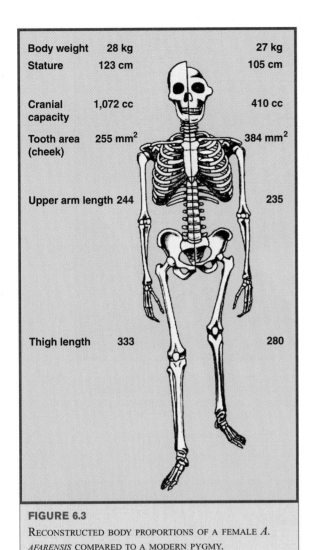

Body weight	28 kg	27 kg
Stature	123 cm	105 cm
Cranial capacity	1,072 cc	410 cc
Tooth area (cheek)	255 mm^2	384 mm^2
Upper arm length	244	235
Thigh length	333	280

FIGURE 6.3

RECONSTRUCTED BODY PROPORTIONS OF A FEMALE *A. AFARENSIS* COMPARED TO A MODERN PYGMY.

chewed food in a hominine fashion, even though they were probably capable of 2 to 4 times the crushing force of modern human beings. Heavy wear indicates that the food chewed was high in tough plant fibers. There is usually no gap between the canines and the teeth next to them on the upper jaw, as there would be in apes. Further, the large mandible is very similar to that of the later hominine, *Homo erectus* (Chapter 8).

As one might expect, there are differences between the later South African fossils and the earlier ones from East Africa. The teeth of the Ethiopian specimens, but especially those from Laetoli, show numerous features reminiscent of some late Miocene apes that the later ones do not (see Figure 5.7). Generally, the incisors and canines are a bit larger in the earlier ones, there is sometimes a gap between upper lateral incisors and canines, the canines tend to project noticeably, the first lower premolars are less like molars and show more shearing wear, and the dental arch is less rounded. One jaw from Laetoli even shows a partial interlock of upper canines with lower canines and premolars. The oldest jaws of all, from Kenya (*A. anamensis*), are even more apelike with a shallow palate, large canines, and nearly parallel rows of cheek teeth.

In addition to differences between earlier and later gracile Australopithecines, there were also differences between the sexes. For one thing, males were about $1^1/_2$ times the size of females. In this respect, they were somewhat like the Miocene apes, with sexual dimorphism greater than one sees in a modern chimpanzee but less than one sees in gorillas and orangs. Male canines, too, are significantly larger than those of females (Figure 6.6). There is as well a clear evolutionary trend for the first lower premolar of males to become more molarlike, through development of a second cusp. Those of females, by contrast, do not. By analogy with modern orangutans, such differences might be expected if male and female foraging patterns were not quite the same—for example, if females got more of their food from the trees, while males consumed large amounts of lower-quality food to be found on or near the ground. Consistent with this pattern, some features of the skeleton are somewhat better suited to climbing in females than in males.[2]

Although the brain is small and apelike and the general conformation of the skull seems nonhuman (even the semicircular canal, a part of the ear crucial to maintenance of balance, is apelike), the foramen magnum of these Australopithecines is placed forward and is downwardlooking, as it is in later bipedal hominines

Their physical appearance was unusual by our standards: They may be described as looking like an ape from the waist up and like a human from the waist down (Figure 6.4). Their cranium was relatively low, the forehead sloped backward, and the brow ridge that helps give apes such massive-looking foreheads was also present. The lower half of the face was chinless and accented by jaws that were quite large, relative to the size of the skull.

Much has been written about Australopithecine teeth. Speaking generally, the gracile forms possessed small incisors, short canines in line with adjacent teeth, and a rounded dental arch. The molars and premolars are larger in size but similar in form to modern human teeth (Figure 6.5). The molars are unevenly worn; the upper cheek teeth are worn from the inside, and the lower cheek teeth are worn from the outside. This indicates that both species

---

[2]Simons, E. L. (1989). Human origins. *Science, 245,* 1,346.

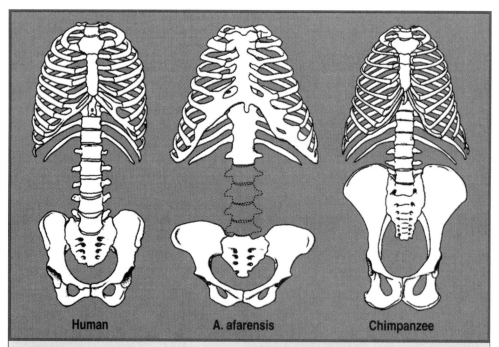

FIGURE 6.4

Trunk skeletons of modern human, gracile *Australopithecus*, and chimpanzee, compared. In its pelvis, the Australopithecine resembles the modern human, but its rib cage shows the pyramidal configuration of the ape.

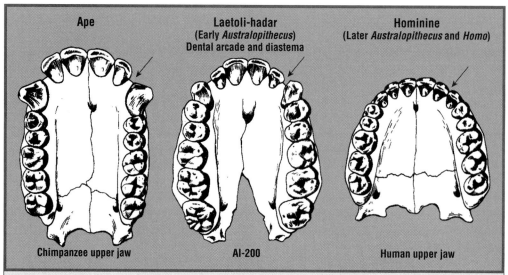

FIGURE 6.5

The upper jaws of an ape, *Australopithecus*, and modern human show important differences in the dental arch and the spacing between the canines and adjoining teeth. Only in the earliest Australopithecines can a diastema (a large gap between the teeth) be seen.

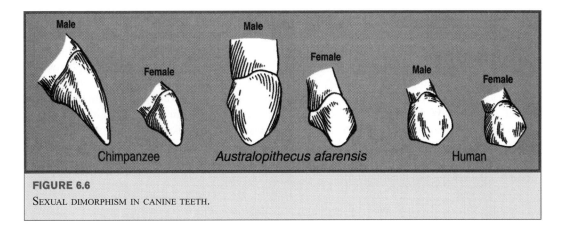

FIGURE 6.6

SEXUAL DIMORPHISM IN CANINE TEETH.

of the **genus *Homo*.** Cranial capacity, commonly used as an index of brain size, varied from 310 to 485 cubic centimeters in East African and 428 to 510 cubic centimeters in South African representatives,[3] roughly the size of a large chimpanzee brain. Although 3 times larger than the brain of any Miocene ape, it was only about a third the size of a modern human brain. Intelligence, however, is not indicated by absolute brain size alone but is roughly indicated by the ratio of brain to body size. Unfortunately, with such a wide range of adult weights it is not clear whether brain size was larger than a modern ape's relative to body size. Although some researchers think they see evidence for some expansion of the brain, others vigorously disagree. Moreover, the outside appearance of the brain, as revealed by casts of the insides of skulls, is more apelike than human, suggesting that cerebral reorganization toward a human condition had not yet occurred.[4] Consistent is the fact that the system for drainage of the blood from the cranium of the earlier Australopithecines is significantly different from that of the genus *Homo*. At the moment, the weight of the evidence favors mental capabilities for all gracile Australopithecines as being comparable to those of modern great apes.

The fossil remains of gracile *Australopithecus* have provided anthropology with two indisputable facts. First, as early as 4 million years ago, this hominine was bipedal, walking erect. This is indicated first of all by the curvature of the spine, which is like that of humans rather than of apes. This served to place the center of gravity over, rather than in front of, the hip joint. In addition, a forearm bone from "Lucy," which is shorter than that of an ape, suggests that the upper limb was lighter and the center of gravity lower in the body than in apes. Still, the arms of Lucy and her kind are long compared to their

Shown here is the skull of a gracile *Australopithecine* from Ethiopia.

---

[3]Grine, F. E. (1993). Australopithecine taxonomy and phylogeny: Historical background and recent interpretation. In R. L. Ciochon & J. G. Fleagle (Eds.), *The human evolution source book* (pp. 201–202). Englewood Cliffs, NJ: Prentice-Hall.

[4]Falk, D. (1989). Apelike endocast of "ape-man" Taung. *American Journal of Physical Anthropology, 80*, 339.

Genus *Homo*.   Hominine genus characterized by expansion of brain, reduction of jaws, and reliance on cultural adaptation; includes at least three species: *habilis, erectus,* and *sapiens*.

relatively short legs. While these make for a shorter stride length than in *Homo,* they were well suited to vertical climbing. Moreover, the somewhat elevated position of the shoulder joint was more adapted to arboreal performance; fingers and toes show more curvature; and a partial foot skeleton between 3.5 and 3 million years old from Sterkfontein, South Africa (Figure 6.7), shows a long, flexible toe still useful for grabbing onto tree limbs.[5] The combination of traits indicate that the tree-climbing abilities of the gracile Australopithecines exceeded those of more recent hominines and that they spent time in trees as well as on the ground.

Bipedal locomotion is also indicated by a number of leg and hip remains (Figure 6.8). There is general agreement that even the relatively short legs are nonetheless much more human than apelike. In fact, a trait-by-trait comparison of individual bones shows that *Australopithecus* frequently falls within the range of modern *Homo,* even though the overall configuration is not exactly the same. But the most dramatic confirmation of *Australopithecus'* walking ability comes from Laetoli, where, nearly 4 million years ago, three individuals walked across newly fallen volcanic ash. Because it was damp, the ash took the impressions of their feet, and these were sealed beneath subsequent ash falls until discovered by Dr. Paul Abell in 1978. The shape of the footprints, the linear distance between the heels where they struck, and the amount of "toe off" are all quite human.

The second indisputable fact provided by gracile *Australopithecus* is that hominines acquired their erect bipedal position long before they acquired their highly enlarged brain. Not only is the latter more apelike than human in its size and structure, but also it is probable that *Australopithecus* did not have prolonged maturation as do modern humans; instead they grew up rapidly as do

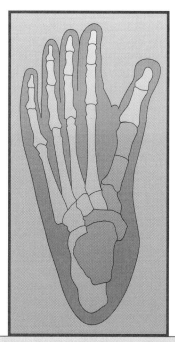

FIGURE 6.7

D<small>RAWING OF THE FOOT BONES OF A</small> 3- <small>TO</small> 3.5-<small>MILLION-YEAR-OLD</small> *A<small>USTRALOPITHECUS</small>* <small>FROM</small> S<small>TERKFONTEIN</small>, S<small>OUTH</small> A<small>FRICA, AS THEY WOULD HAVE BEEN IN THE COMPLETE FOOT.</small> N<small>OTE HOW LONG AND FLEXIBLE THE FIRST TOE (AT RIGHT) IS.</small>

These footprints from Laetoli, Tanzania, confirm that *Australopithecus* walked bipedally. They were made by three individuals, one of whom was careful to walk directly in the footsteps of one in front.

[5]Oliwenstein, L. (1995). New footsteps into walking debate. *Science, 269,* 476.

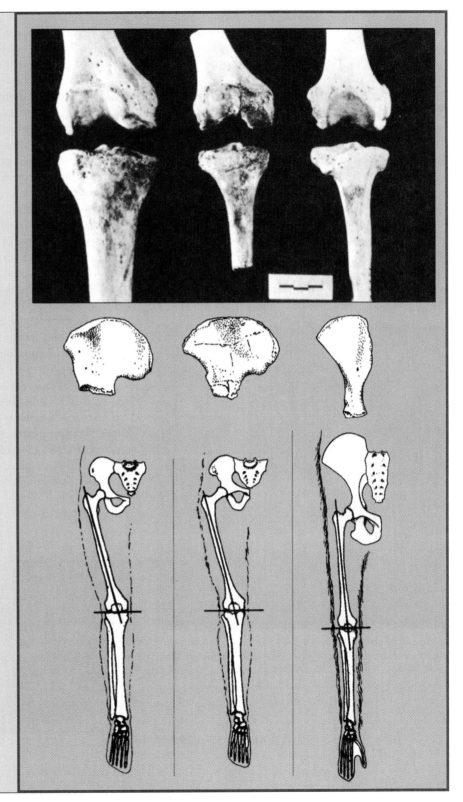

FIGURE 6.8

EXAMINATION OF THE UPPER HIP BONES AND LOWER LIMBS OF (FROM LEFT) *HOMO SAPIENS*, *AUSTRALOPITHECUS*, AND AN APE CAN BE USED TO DETERMINE MEANS OF LOCOMOTION. THE SIMILARITIES OF THE HUMAN AND AUSTRALOPITHECINE BONES ARE STRIKING AND ARE INDICATIVE OF BIPEDAL LOCOMOTION. (THE RECONSTRUCTION OF THE AUSTRALOPITHECINE LIMB IS BASED ON THE KNEE JOINT SHOWN IN THE PHOTOGRAPH.)

apes.[6] Thus, no matter how important bipedal locomotion may have been in setting the stage for the later expansion and elaboration of the human brain, it cannot by itself account for those developments.

Robust Australopithecines

The remains of robust Australopithecines were first found at Kromdraai and Swartkrans in South Africa by Robert Broom and John Robinson in 1948 in deposits that, unfortunately, cannot be securely dated. Current thinking puts them anywhere from 1.8 to 1.0 million years ago. Usually referred to as the species *A. robustus* (see Table 6.1 and Figure 6.2), it shared practically all of the traits listed for the species of gracile *Australopithecus* just discussed, especially the South African ones. Although of similar size, the bones of *robustus'* body were thick for their size, with prominent markings where their muscles attached. The skull of the robust form was thicker and larger than that of the graciles, with a slightly larger cranial capacity (around 530 cubic centimeters). Its skull also possessed a simianlike **sagittal crest** (more evident in males than in females) running from front to back along the top. This feature provides sufficient area on a relatively small braincase for attachment of the huge temporal muscles required to operate powerful jaws, such as robust *Australopithecus* possessed and gorillas have today; hence what we have here is an example of convergent evolution in gorillas and hominines.

The first robust Australopithecine to be found in East Africa was discovered by Mary Leakey in the summer of 1959, the centennial year of the publication of Darwin's *On the Origin of Species*. She found it in Olduvai Gorge, a fossil-rich area near Ngorongoro Crater, on the Serengeti Plain of Tanzania, East Africa. Olduvai is a huge gash in the earth, about 25 miles long and 300 feet deep, which cuts through Pleistocene and recent geological strata revealing close to 2 million years of the earth's history.

Mary Leakey's discovery was reconstructed by her husband, Louis, who gave it the name "*Zinjanthropus boisei*." At first, he thought this hominine seemed more humanlike than *Australopithecus* and extremely close to modern humans in evolutionary development. Further study, however, revealed that *Zinjanthropus,* the remains of which consisted of a skull and a few limb bones, was

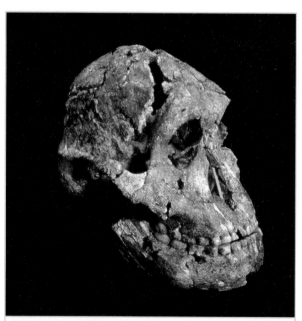

Sexual dimorphism was marked in the robust Australopithecines from South Africa. Although male skulls show a sagittal crest, female skulls like the one shown here do not.

Olduvai Gorge, Tanzania

---

[6]Tardieu, C. (1998). Short adolescence in early hominids: Infantile and adolescent growth of the human femur. *American Journal of Physical Anthropology, 107,* 173–174.

Sagittal crest. A crest running from front to back on the top of the skull in the midline.

LOUIS S. B. LEAKEY (1903–1972)
MARY LEAKEY (1913–1996)

Few figures in the history of paleoanthropology discovered so many key fossils, received so much public acclaim, or stirred up as much controversy as Louis Leakey and his second wife, Mary Leakey. Born in Kenya of missionary parents, Louis received his early education from an English governess and subsequently was sent to England for a university education. He returned to Kenya in the 1920s to begin his career there.

It was in 1931 that Louis and his research assistant from England, Mary Nicol (whom he married in 1936), began working in their spare time at Olduvai Gorge in Tanzania, searching patiently and persistently for remains of early hominines. It seemed a good place to look, for there were numerous animal fossils, as well as crude stone tools lying scattered on the ground and eroding out of the walls of the gorge. Their patience and persistence were not rewarded until 1959, when Mary found the first hominine fossil. A year later, another skull was found, and Olduvai was on its way to being recognized as one of the most important sources of hominine fossils in all of Africa. While Louis reconstructed, described, and interpreted the fossil material, Mary made the definitive study of the Oldowan tools.

The Leakeys' important discoveries were not limited to those at Olduvai. In the early 1930s, they found the first fossils of Miocene apes in Africa at Rusinga Island in Lake Victoria. Also in the 1930s, Louis found a number of skulls at Kanjera, Kenya, that show a mixture of modern and more primitive features. In 1961, at Fort Ternan, Kenya, the Leakeys found the remains of a late Miocene ape with features that seemed appropriate for a hominine ancestor. After Louis' death, a member of an expedition led by Mary Leakey found the first footprints of *Australopithecus* at Laetoli, Tanzania.

In addition to their own work, Louis Leakey promoted a good deal of important work on the part of others. He made it possible for Jane Goodall to begin her landmark field studies of chimpanzees; later on, he was instrumental in setting up similar studies among gorillas (by Dian Fossey) and orangutans (by Birute Galdikas). Last but not least, the Leakey tradition has been continued by son Richard and his wife, Maeve.

Louis Leakey had a flamboyant personality and a way of making interpretations of fossil materials that frequently did not stand up well to careful scrutiny, but this did not stop him from publicly presenting his views as if they were the gospel truth. It was this aspect of the Leakeys' work that generated controversy. Nonetheless, the Leakeys accomplished and promoted more work that resulted in the accumulation of knowledge about human origins than anyone before them. Anthropology clearly owes them a great deal.

---

an East African representative of *Australopithecus.* Although similar in many ways to *A. robustus,* most commonly it is referred to as *Australopithecus boisei* (see Table 6.1 and Figure 6.2). Potassium-argon dating places this early hominine at about 1.75 million years old. Since the time of Mary Leakey's original find, numerous other fossils of this robust species have been found at Olduvai, as well as north and east of Lake Turkana in Ethiopia and Kenya. Although one (often referred to as the "Black Skull," sometimes as *A. aethiopicus*) is known to be as much as 2.5 million years old, some date to as recently as 1.3 million years ago.

The size of the teeth and certain cranial features of these East African fossils are reminiscent of the robust Australopithecines from South Africa. Molars and premolars are enormous, as are the mandible and palate. Even so, the anterior teeth (canines and incisors) are often crowded, owing to the room needed for the cheek teeth.

The heavy skull, more massive even than its robust South African relative's, has a sagittal crest and prominent brow ridges; cranial capacity ranges from about 500 to 530 cubic centimeters. Body size, too, is somewhat larger; whereas the robust South Africans are estimated to have weighed between 32 and 40 kilograms, the East Africans probably weighed from 34 to 49 kilograms.

Because the earliest robust skull from East Africa (2.5 million years), the so-called Black Skull from Kenya (*A. aethiopicus* in Table 6.1 and Figure 6.2), retains a number of primitive features shared with East African graciles, it is probable that it evolved from gracile ancestors, giving rise to the later robust East Africans. Whether the South African robusts represent a southern offshoot of the East African lineage or convergent evolution from a South African ancestor is so far not settled; arguments can be presented for both interpretations. In either case, what happened was that the later Australopithecines developed molars and premolars that are both absolutely and relatively larger than those of earlier gracile ones (though some tendency in this direction can be seen in the South African graciles). Larger teeth require more bone to support them, hence the prominent jaws of the robust Australopithecines. Finally, the larger jaws and the chewing of more food require more jaw musculature that attaches to the skull. The marked crests seen on skulls of the late Australopithecines provide for the attachment of such a musculature on a skull that has increased very little in size. In effect, robust Australopithecines had evolved into highly efficient chewing machines. Clearly, their immense cheek teeth and powerful chewing muscles bespeak the kind of heavy chewing a diet restricted to uncooked plant foods requires. Many anthropologists believe that, by becoming a specialized consumer of plant foods, the late Australopithecines avoided competing for the same niche with early *Homo,* with which they were contemporaries (see Figure 6.2). In the course of evolution, the **law of competitive exclusion** dictates that when two closely related species compete for the same niche, one will out-compete the other, bringing about the loser's extinction. That early *Homo* and late *Australopithecus* did not compete for the same niche is suggested by their coexistence for something like 1.5 million years.

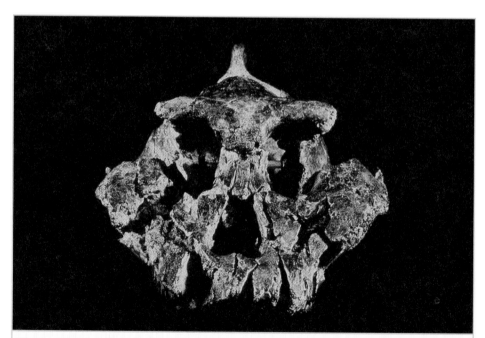

The so-called Black Skull, found at West Turkana, Kenya, is the earliest known robust *Australopithecus.* At 2.5 million years old, it appears ancestral to later robust Australopithecines from East Africa.

Law of competitive exclusion. When two closely related species compete for the same niche, one will out-compete the other, bringing about the latter's extinction.

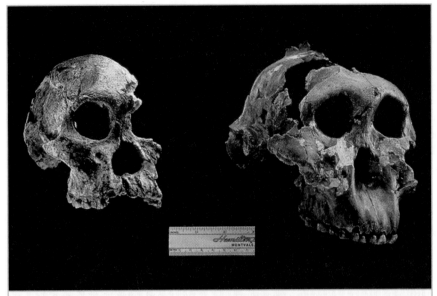

This photo contrasts gracile (left) and robust (right) Australopithecine skulls. Both were probably male; the gracile skull is from South Africa, the robust from East Africa.

AUSTRALOPITHECINE PREDECESSORS

Although the Australopithecines are now fairly well known, the same cannot be said about their immediate predecessors. As already noted, the earliest fossils of *Australopithecus* displayed a number of traits suggestive of an ancestry among the late Miocene apes. In addition to the features of the teeth, hands, and feet already noted, the earliest *Australopithecus* skulls are thick-boned and have a forward thrust to the face, large flaring cheek bones, and heavy cresting. But what about fossils that date between late Miocene apes on the one hand and early *Australopithecus* on the other?

Up until the 1990s, fossils from the crucial period of about 6 to 4 million years ago were so few and fragmentary that they provided scant information. Then in 1994, pieces of several individuals were discovered in 4.4 million-year-old deposits along Ethiopia's Awash River. Subsequent finds in the same region date between 5.8 and 5.2 million years. They are thought to represent early and later varieties of a single species, ***Ardipithecus ramidus*** (the name is fitting for an ultimate human ancestor as, in the local Afar language, *Ardi* means "floor" and *ramid* means "root"). Unfortunately, the task of freeing the actual fossils from their matrix has proved time-consuming and is not yet complete; hence a full description of this important material is not yet available.

Preliminary indications are that *Ardipithecus,* which was about the size of a modern chimpanzee, was more apelike than any Australopithecine. Although the large

These teeth and jaw fragment are from *Ardipithecus,* a hominine that lived between 5.8 and 4.4 million years ago in Ethiopia.

Ardipithecus ramidus.   Probable early hominine; lived about 5.8 to 4.4 million years ago.

canines and lower first premolar resemble those of apes, chewing did not sharpen the upper canines as happens in apes. The thin-enameled molars are larger than in apes, and the diet included a greater variety of fibrous foods than typical of chimpanzees. Although the relative proportions of *Ardipithecus'* arms and legs appear chimplike, the foramen magnum is in the forward position consistent with bipedal locomotion. Consistent, too, is an upper arm bone that is not built to sustain the weight of a quadruped. Moreover, a toe bone is more like that of a human than an ape; unfortunately, it was not found in association with the other material. Still, it is likely that *Ardipithecus* walked bipedally when on the ground. But because it lived in a more forested environment than later hominines, it undoubtedly spent significant time in the trees.

Even earlier than *Ardipithecus* is the 6-million-year-old "Millennium Man," so called because its discovery was announced at the turn of the millennium (Figure 6.2). Its discoverers have dubbed it **Orrorin tugenensis** (*orrorin* means "original man" in the local dialect). Found in Kenya,[7] the remains include 13 pieces of lower jaw,

teeth, and broken thigh bones. Because the head of the thigh bone is relatively large (though not as large as in modern humans), *Orrorin* may have walked bipedally, though this is by no means certain (the crucial knee joint, which would give this away, is missing). The molars, like those of *Australopithecus,* are thickly enameled but much smaller. At the moment, specialists are unsure what to make of this creature; some see it as the earliest human ancestor, whereas others doubt that it was even a hominine. It could even be on the line to chimps, or to an extinct side branch.

To further complicate matters, Maeve Leakey, daughter-in-law of Louis and Mary Leakey, announced the discovery in 1998 and 1999 of an almost complete cranium, parts of two upper jaws, and assorted teeth from a site in northern Kenya.[8] Contemporary with early East African *Australopithecus* (Figure 6.2), she sees this as a different species named **Kenyanthropus platyops** ("flat-faced man of Kenya"). Unlike contemporary *Australopithecus, Kenyanthropus* is said to have a small braincase and small molars set in a large, flat face. But

[7]Balter, M. (2001). Scientists spar over claims of earliest human ancestor. *Science, 291,* 1,460–1,461.

[8]Balter, M. (2001). Fossil tangles roots of human family tree. *Science, 291,* 2,289–2,291.

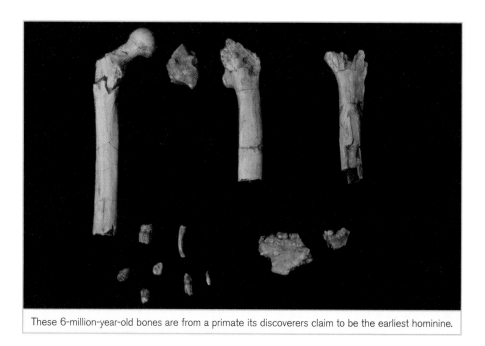

These 6-million-year-old bones are from a primate its discoverers claim to be the earliest hominine.

Orrorin tugenensis.   Possible hominine; lived 6 million years ago.   •   **Kenyanthropus platyops.**   Hominine contemporary with early Australopithecines; not certainly a separate species.

This 3- to 4-million-year-old skull could be an Australopithecine or a separate species its discoverer calls *Kenyanthropus platyops*.

ago, the East African robust species, at least, shows relatively little change.[9] Evidently, the pattern in early hominine evolution has been relatively short periods of marked change with diversification, separated by prolonged periods of relative stasis of surviving species.

ENVIRONMENT, DIET, AND AUSTRALOPITHECINE ORIGINS

Having described the fossil material, we may now consider *how* evolution transformed an early ape into *Australopithecus.* Because a major driving force in evolution is climatic change, we must take into account the effects of such changes in the late Miocene epoch that were profound enough to cause the temporary drying up of the Mediterranean Sea. On the land, tropical forests underwent reduction or, more commonly, broke up into mosaics where patches of forest were interspersed with savanna or other types of open country. The forebears of the hominine line lived in places where there was access to both trees and open country. With the breaking up of forests, these early ancestors of ours found themselves spending more and more time on the ground and had to adapt to this new, more open environment.

The most obvious problem facing these hominine ancestors in their new situation, other than getting from one patch of trees to another, was food getting. As the forest thinned or shrank, the traditional ape-type foods found in trees became less available to them, especially in seasons of reduced rainfall. Therefore, it became more and more necessary to forage on the ground for foods such as seeds, grasses, and roots. Associated with this change in diet is a change in their dentition; male canines (used by other primates as defensive weapons), not large to begin with, became as small as those of females (Figure 6.9), leaving both sexes relatively defenseless when down on the ground and easy targets for numerous carnivorous predators. That predators were a problem is revealed by the South African fossils, most of which are from individuals that were dropped into rock fissures by leopards or, in the case of Dart's original find, by an eagle.

Many investigators have argued that the hands of early hominines took over the weapon functions of the reduced canines, enabling them to threaten predators by using wooden objects as clubs and throwing stones. This set the

again, there is controversy; Leakey sees her fossil as ancestral to the genus *Homo,* whereas others are not convinced it falls outside the range of variation for early gracile *Australopithecus.*

So what are we to make of these fossils? Until we have better samples, we will not know for sure. What seems likely on present evidence is that hominines evolved from late Miocene apes, becoming distinct by 5 million years ago. This move into a new primate niche probably saw the emergence of more than one bipedal model, but just how many is not known. Whether *Ardipithecus* or any other candidates for "human ancestor" discussed here really were ancestral to later humans, or side branches that went extinct, remains to be seen. The thin enamel of *Ardipithecus'* molars might suggest the latter. But out of this early hominine branching emerged *Australopithecus.*

Undoubtedly this evolution took place in fits and starts, rather than at a steady pace. For example, fragments of an *Australopithecus* skull 3.9 million years old are virtually identical to the corresponding parts of one 3 million years old. Evidently, once a viable bipedal adaptation was achieved, stabilizing selection took over, and there was little change for at least a million years. But 2.5 million years ago, change was again in the works, resulting in the branching out of new forms, including one or two robust species. But again, from about 2.3 million years until it became extinct around 1 million years

_____

[9]Wood, B., Wood, C., & Konigsberg, L. (1994). *Paranthropus boisei:* An example of evolutionary stasis? *American Journal of Physical Anthropology, 95,* 134.

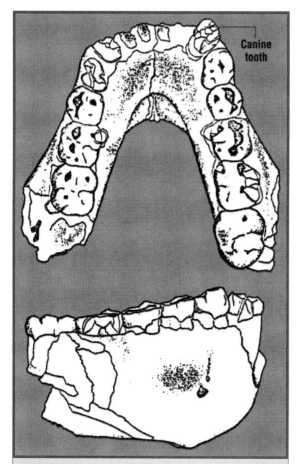

FIGURE 6.9

THIS LOWER JAW FROM LAETOLI, TANZANIA, IS BETWEEN 3.6 AND 3.8 MILLION YEARS OLD AND BELONGED TO *AUSTRALOPITHECUS*. ALTHOUGH ITS CANINE TOOTH PROJECTS A BIT BEYOND THE OTHER TEETH, IT IS A FAR CRY FROM THE PROJECTION SEEN IN MOST OTHER PRIMATES.

This bonobo figured out by himself how to make stone tools similar to those made by our ancestors 2.5 million years ago.

stage for the much later manufacture of more efficient weapons from bone, wood, and stone. Although the hands of the later Australopithecines were suitable for tool-making, there is no evidence that any of them actually made stone tools. To illustrate the problem: Experiments with captive bonobos have shown that they are capable of making crude chipped stone tools, but they have never been known to do so under natural conditions. Thus, to be able to do something is not necessarily equivalent to doing it. In fact, the earliest known stone tools are at least 1.5 million years younger than the oldest undoubted fossils of *Australopithecus,* nor has anyone been able to establish a clear association between stone tools and later *Australopithecus* (as opposed to *Homo*). Considering the

number of sites and fossils known (several hundred), this appears to be significant. However, *Australopithecus* certainly had no less intelligence and dexterity than do modern great apes, all of whom make use of tools when it is to their advantage to do so. Orangutans, bonobos, and chimpanzees have all been observed in the wild making and using simple tools such those described in Chapter 4. Gorillas seem not to do so in the wild only because they developed a diet of leaves and nettles that made tools pointless. Most likely, the ability to make and use simple tools is something that goes back to the last common ancestor of the Asian and African apes, before the appearance of hominines.

It is reasonable to suppose, then, that Australopithecines were tool users, though not toolmakers. Unfortunately, few tools that they used are likely to have survived for a million and more years, and any that did

Just as chimpanzees use wooden probes to fish for termites, so do orangutans use probes to extract termites, ants, or honey. Such tool use likely goes back to a time preceding the split between Asian and African hominoids, long before the appearance of hominines.

would be hard to recognize as such. Although we cannot be certain about this, in addition to clubs and missiles for defense, stout sticks may have been used to dig edible roots, and convenient stones may have been used (as some chimpanzees do) to crack open nuts. In fact, some animal bones from Australopithecine sites in South Africa show microscopic wear patterns suggesting their use to dig edible roots from the ground. We may also allow the possibility that, like chimpanzees, females may more often have used tools to get and process food than males, but the latter may more often have used tools as "weapons."[10]

Humans Stand on Their Own Two Feet

From an apelike carriage, the early hominines developed a fully erect posture; they became bipedal. Their late Miocene forebears seem to have been primates that combined quadrupedal climbing with at least some brachiation and, on the ground, were capable of assuming an upright stance, at least on occasion (optional, versus

obligatory, bipedalism). On the basis of the few scrappy fossils that we have for the period of 2 or so million years between the last known African apes of the late Miocene and the first known *Australopithecus,* we may assume that those hominine ancestors that did exist during the period were evolving into fully erect bipeds.

We cannot understand the emergence of bipedalism as a means of locomotion without realizing its very serious drawbacks. For example, it makes an animal more visible to predators, exposes its soft underbelly, or gut, and interferes with the ability to change direction instantly while running. Nor does it make for particularly fast running; quadrupedal chimpanzees and baboons, for example, are 30 to 34 percent faster than we bipeds. For 100-meter distances, our best athletes today may attain speeds of 34–37 kilometers per hour, but the larger African carnivores can attain speeds up to 60–70 kilometers per hour. Other drawbacks include the frequent lower back problems, hernias, hemorrhoids, and other circulatory problems to which humans are prone by virtue of their bipedal specialization. Nor can we overlook the consequences of a serious leg or foot injury; a quadruped can do amazingly well on three legs, but a biped with only one functional leg is seriously hindered—an easy meal for some carnivore. Each of these drawbacks would have placed our early hominine ancestors at risk from

[10]Goodall, J. (1986). *The chimpanzees of Gombe: Patterns of behavior* (pp. 552, 564). Cambridge, MA: Belknap Press.

predators. And so, we must ask, what made bipedal loco-motion worth paying such a high price? It is hard to imagine bipedalism becoming a viable adaptation in the absence of strong selective pressure in its favor.

One once-popular suggestion is that bipedal locomotion allowed males to gather food on the savanna and transport it back to females, who were restricted from doing so by the dependence of their offspring.[11] This explanation is unlikely, however, because female apes, not to mention women among food-foraging peoples, routinely combine infant care with foraging for food. Indeed, among food foragers, it is the women who commonly supply the bulk of the food eaten by both sexes. Moreover, the pair bonding (one male attached to one female) presumed by this model is not characteristic of terrestrial primates, nor of those displaying the degree of sexual dimorphism that was characteristic of *Australopithecus.* Nor is it really characteristic of *Homo sapiens;* in a substantial majority of recent human societies, including those in which people forage for their food, some form of polygamy—marriage to two or more people at the same time—is not only permitted, but preferred. And even in the supposedly monogamous United States, it is relatively common for an individual to marry two or more others (the only requirement is that he or she not be married to them at one and the same time).

Another suggestion, that bipedal locomotion arose as an adaptation for nonterritorial scavenging of meat,[12] is also unlikely. Although it is true that a biped is able to travel long distances without tiring, and that a daily supply of dead animal carcasses would have been available to hominines only if they were capable of ranging over vast areas, there is no evidence that hominines did much in the way of scavenging prior to about 2.5 million years ago. Furthermore, the heavy wear seen on Australopithecine teeth is indicative of a diet high in tough, fibrous plant foods. Thus, scavenging was likely an unforeseen byproduct of bipedal locomotion, rather than a cause of it.

Yet more recent is the suggestion that our ancestors stood up as a way to cope with heat stress out in the open.

---

[11]Lovejoy, C. O. (1981). The origin of man. *Science, 211,* 341–350.

[12]Lewin, R. (1987). Four legs good, two legs bad. *Science, 235,* 969–971.

Original Study

The Naked and the Bipedal[13]

Human beings are a peculiar species. Among other things, we're the only mostly hairless, consistently bipedal primate. Ever since Darwin, evolutionary biologists have wondered how we acquired these unique traits. Not long ago most would have argued that our upright stance evolved as part of a feedback loop that helped free our hands to use tools. But by the early 1980s a series of discoveries in Africa—including fossilized footprints and early hominine bones—made it clear that bipedalism preceded tool use by at least 2 million years. Lately a new theory has been gaining ground: It holds that our forebears reared up on two legs to escape the heat of the African savanna.

"The African savanna is one of the most thermally stressing habitats on the planet as far as large mammals are concerned," says Pete Wheeler, a physiologist at Liverpool John Moores University in England. For several years now Wheeler has been studying just how stressful such an environment would have been for the first primates to venture out of the shade of the forest. Among the apes, our ancestors are the only ones that managed the switch; no other ape today lives on the savanna full-time.

Most savanna animals, says Wheeler, cope with the heat by simply letting their body temperature rise during the day, rather than waste scarce water by sweating. (Some antelope allow their body temperature to climb above 110 degrees.) These animals have evolved elaborate ways of protecting the brain's delicate neural circuitry from overheating.

---

[13]Adapted from Folger, T. (1993). The naked and the bipedal. *Discover, 14*(11), 34–35.

Antelope, for instance, allow venous blood to cool in their large muzzles (the cooling results from water evaporation in the mucous lining), then run that cool blood by the arteries that supply the brain, thereby cooling it, too.

"But the interesting thing about humans and other primates," says Wheeler, "is that we lack the mechanisms other savanna animals have. The only way an ape wanting to colonize the savanna could protect its brain is by actually keeping the whole body cool. [See Figure 6.10.] We can't uncouple brain temperature from the rest of the body, the way an antelope does, so we've got to prevent any damaging elevations in body temperature. And of course the problem is even more acute for an ape, because in general, the larger and more complex the brain, the more easily it is damaged. So there were incredible selective pressures on early hominines favoring adaptations that would reduce thermal stress—pressures that may have favored bipedalism."

Just how would bipedalism have protected the brain from heat? And why did our ancestors become bipedal rather than evolve some other way to keep cool? Before moving out onto the savanna, says Wheeler, our forebears were preadapted to evolve into bipeds. Swinging from branch to branch in the trees, they had already evolved a body plan that could, under the right environmental pressures, be altered to accommodate an upright stance. Such a posture, says Wheeler, greatly reduces the amount of the body's surface area that is directly exposed to the intense midday sun. It thereby reduces the amount of heat the body absorbs.

Although this observation is not new, Wheeler has done the first careful measurements and calculations of the advantages such a stance would have offered the early hominines. His measurements were rather simple. He took a 1-foot-tall scale model of a hominine similar to Lucy—the 3-million-year-old, chimp-size Australopithecine that is known from the structure of her pelvis and legs to have been at least a part-time biped. Wheeler mounted a camera on an overhead track and moved it in a semicircular arc above the model, mimicking the daily path of the sun. Every 5 degrees along that path—the equivalent of 20 minutes on a summer day—Wheeler stopped the camera and snapped a photograph of the model. He repeated this process with the model in a variety of postures, both quadrupedal and bipedal. To determine how much of the hominine's surface area would have been exposed to the sun's rays, Wheeler simply measured how much of the model's surface area was visible in the sun's-eye-view photos. He found that a quadrupedal stance would have exposed the hominine to about 60 percent more solar radiation than a bipedal one.

Not only does a biped expose less of its body to the sun, it also exposes more of its body to the cooler breezes a few feet above ground. The bottom line, says Wheeler, is that "on a typical savanna day, a knuckle-walking chimp-size hominine would

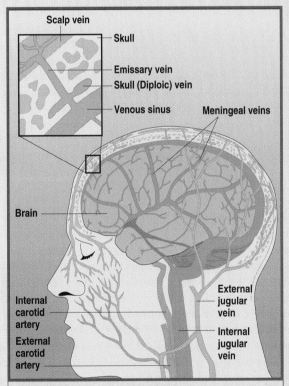

FIGURE 6.10

HOW THE BRAIN IS COOLED IN MODERN HUMANS: BLOOD FROM THE FACE AND SCALP, INSTEAD OF RETURNING DIRECTLY TO THE HEART, MAY BE SHUNTED INSTEAD INTO THE BRAINCASE, AND THEN TO THE HEART. ALREADY COOLED AT THE SURFACE OF THE SKIN, IT IS ABLE TO CARRY AWAY HEAT FROM THE BRAIN.

→ →

Original Study

require something in the region of five pints of water a day. Whereas simply by standing upright you cut that to something like three pints. In addition to that, you can also remain out in the open away from shade for longer, and at higher temperatures. So for an animal that was foraging for scattered resources in these habitats, bipedalism is really an excellent mode of locomotion."

Wheeler suspects that bipedalism also made possible two other uniquely human traits: our naked skin and large brains. "Our work suggests that you can't get a naked skin until you've become bipedal," he says.

"The problem has always been explaining why we don't see naked antelope or cheetahs. The answer appears to be that in those conditions in which animals are exposed to high radiation loads, the body hair acts as a shield. We always think of body hair as keeping heat in, but it also keeps heat out. If you take the fleece off a sheep and stand the animal out in the desert in the outback of Australia, the sheep will end up gaining more heat than you're helping it to dis-

sipate. However, if you do that to a bipedal ape, because the exposure to solar radiation is so much less, it helps the ape lose more heat. Bipedalism, by reducing exposure to the sun, is tipping the balance and turning hair loss, which in quadrupeds would be a disadvantage, into an asset."

We bipeds maximize our heat loss, says Wheeler, by retaining a heat shield only on our most exposed surface—the top of our skull—and by exposing the rest of our body to cooling breezes. And bipedalism and naked skin together, he says, probably allowed us to evolve our oversize brains.

"The brain is one of the most metabolically active tissues in the body," he explains. "In the case of humans it accounts for something like 20 percent of total energy consumption. So you've got an organ producing a lot of heat that you've got to dump. Once we'd become bipedal and naked and achieved this ability to dump heat, that may have allowed the expansion of the brain that took place later in human evolution. It didn't cause it, but you can't have a large brain unless you can cool it."

The End

An objection to the above scenario might be that when bipedalism developed, savanna was not as extensive in Africa as it is today (Figure 6.11). In both East and South Africa, environments included both closed and open bush and woodlands. Moreover, fossil flora and fauna found with *Ardipithecus* are typical of a moist, closed, wooded habitat. Yet this may not tell us much, as we cannot rule out the possibility that *Ardipithecus* represents a side branch of hominine evolution that moved back into the forest from more open country. Alternatively, even today, similar floral and faunal elements can be found in the otherwise rather desolate region where *Ardipithecus* once lived,[14] and between 5 and 4 million years ago, the environments of eastern and southern Africa can best be described as a mosaic of both open and closed country. Although climbing ability would still have been useful to hominine ances-

tors, inevitably they would have had to spend significant amounts of time out in the open, away from trees.

Persuasive though the "stand up to keep cool" hypothesis may be, we should not overlook other life-or-death considerations. The fact is that the causes of bipedalism are likely to have been multiple. Although we may reject as culture-bound the idea of male "breadwinners" provisioning "stay-at-home moms," it is true that bipedal locomotion does make transport of bulky foods possible. A fully erect biped on the ground—whether male or female—has the ability to gather such foods for transport back to a tree or other place of safety for consumption; the animal does not have to remain out in the open, exposed and vulnerable, to do all of its eating. But food may not have been the only thing transported. As we saw in Chapter 4, primate infants must be able to cling to their mothers in order to be transported; because the mother is using her forelimbs in locomotion, to either walk or swing by, she can't very well carry her infant. Chimpanzee infants, for example, must cling for themselves to

---

[14]Conroy, G. C. (1997). *Reconstructing human origins: A modern synthesis* (p. 152). New York: Norton.

HIGHWAY 1
Learn about the most famous hoax in the history of science through a trip to this site about Piltdown Man. Learn who was thought to be behind this hoax and how it interfered with the acceptance of Australopithecines as human ancestors when they were discovered.
www.talkorigins.org/faqs/piltdown.html

HIGHWAY 2
Visit this site to use the interactive evolutionary tree and figure out the relationships among the ancestral hominine groups.
www.pbs.org/wgbh/aso/tryit/evolution/#

HIGHWAY 3
Visit the Institute of Human Origins Web site and discover more about Lucy and other fossil hominines, as well as the people who discovered them. Also visit the institute's educational site *www.becominghuman.org/*.
www.asu.edu/clas/iho/

HIGHWAY 4
A trip to National Geographic's Committee for Research and Exploration site follows the trail of paleoanthropologist Lee Berger as he searches for human origins in Botswana.
www.nationalgeographic.com/research/index.html

their mother, and even at the age of 4, they make long journeys on their mothers' backs. Injuries caused by falling from the mother are a significant cause of infant mortality. Thus, mothers able to carry their infants would have made a significant contribution to the survivorship of their offspring, and the ancestors of *Australopithecus* would have been capable of doing just this.

Besides making food transport possible, bipedalism could have facilitated the food quest in other ways. With their hands free and body upright, the animals could reach otherwise unobtainable food on thorn trees too flimsy and too spiny to climb. Furthermore, with both hands free, they could gather other small foods twice as fast. And in times of scarcity, their ability to travel far without tiring would help get them between widely distributed sources of food. Because the head is positioned higher than in a quadrupedal stance, sources of food and water are easier to spot from afar, thereby facilitating their location.

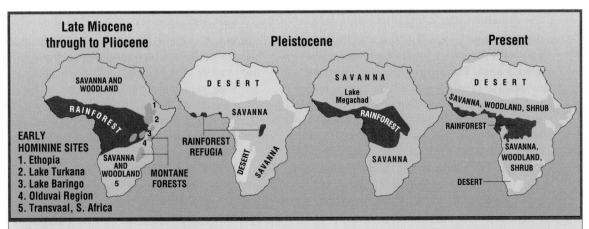

FIGURE 6.11

SINCE THE LATE MIOCENE, THE VEGETATION ZONES OF AFRICA HAVE CHANGED CONSIDERABLY.

Because apes do not normally walk bipedally, they cannot easily hold on to their infants when moving about. By holding on to their infants while walking bipedally, our own ancestors probably reduced the risk of fatal falls for their infants.

Still other advantages of bipedalism would have enhanced survivability. With their heads well up above the ground, bipeds are more likely to spot predators before they get too close for safety. Finally, if hominines did get caught away from a safe place of refuge by a predator, manipulative and dexterous hands freed from locomotion provided them with a means of protecting themselves by brandishing and throwing objects at their attackers. But, as the fate of the South African specimens attests, even this strategy was not foolproof.

CHAPTER SUMMARY

The course of hominine evolution, revealed by fossil finds, has not been a simple, steady advance in the direction of modern humans. One early hominine that appeared by 4 million years ago was *Australopithecus,* a genus that anthropologists divide into at least four and as many as seven species. All walked erect; the early gracile species were about the size of a modern human pygmy. They chewed food like humans, but their general appearance was that of an apelike human. The size and outward appearance of their brain suggest a degree of intelligence probably not greatly different from that of a modern bonobo, chimpanzee, or gorilla. Like most great apes, gracile Australopithecines may have made some use of objects as tools.

Robust Australopithecines shared practically all of the traits listed for the gracile species but were more highly specialized for the consumption of plant foods. The earliest Australopithecines exhibit traits reminiscent of some of the late Miocene apes of Africa. Fossils that fit time-wise between these apes and *Australopithecus* suggest the latter arose as part of an early diversification of bipeds.

During the late Miocene and Pliocene, the climate became markedly cooler and drier; many areas that had once been heavily forested became a mosaic of woodland and more open country. The ancestors of hominines likely found themselves spending more and more time on the ground; they had to adapt to this altered, more open environment, and food getting became a problem. As their diet changed, so did their dentition. On the whole, teeth became smaller, and many of the defensive functions once performed by the teeth seem to have been taken over by the hands.

Some of the Miocene apes are believed to have been part-time brachiators who may at times have walked erect. *Australopithecus* was a fully bipedal hominine with erect posture, and its immediate predecessors, such as *Ardipithecus,* may have also been.

Some disadvantages of bipedalism as a means of locomotion, besides anatomical and circulatory weaknesses, are that it makes an animal more visible to predators, exposes its "soft underbelly," slows the animal down, interferes with its ability to change direction instantly while walking or running, and leaves nothing to fall back on when one leg is injured. Its advantages are that it provides hominines with a means of keeping their brains from overheating, of protecting themselves and holding objects while running, of traveling long distances without tiring, and of seeing farther.

CLASSIC READINGS

Ciochon, R. L., & Fleagle, J. G. (Eds.). (1993). *The human evolution source book.* Englewood Cliffs, NJ: Prentice-Hall.

In the first four parts of this book, the editors have assembled articles to present data and survey different theories on the evolution and diversification of the earliest hominines. A short editors' introduction to each section places the various articles in context.

Conroy, G. C. (1997). *Reconstructing human origins: A modern synthesis.* New York: Norton.

This text devotes two chapters to *Australopithecus* that are reasonably up-to-date and are comprehensive in their description of the various fossils, discussion of environmental considerations, and coverage of competing interpretations of the material.

Johanson, D., & Edey, M. (1981). *Lucy: The beginnings of humankind.* New York: Simon & Schuster.

This book tells the story of the discovery of Lucy and the other fossils of *Australopithecus afarensis,* and how they have enhanced our understanding of the early stages of human evolution. It reads like a first-rate detective story, while giving an excellent description of Australopithecines and an accurate account of how paleoanthropologists analyze their fossils.

Evolution of the Genus *Homo* and the Development of Early Human Culture

Chapter 7   *Homo habilis* and Cultural Origins

Chapter 8   *Homo erectus* and the Emergence of Hunting and Gathering

Chapter 9   Archaic *Homo sapiens* and the Middle Paleolithic

Chapter 10   *Homo sapiens* and the Upper Paleolithic

INTRODUCTION

By 2.5 million years ago, long after the line of human evolution had branched off from that of apes, a new kind of evolutionary process was set in motion. Early hominines began to increase their manipulation of the

physical world, inventing new solutions to the problems of human existence. With the passage of time, they came to intensify their reliance on cultural, rather than biological, adaptation as a more rapid and effective way of adjusting to environmental pressures. Even less than apes did they have to depend on physical attributes to survive. Moreover, as culture became more efficient at solving the problems of existence, human populations began to spread geographically, inhabiting new and even harsh environments, all of which is illustrated by human habitations of the cold regions of the world. Instead of being dependent on the evolution of humans capable of growing heavy coats of fur, as do other mammals that live in such regions, humans devised forms of

ual basis for vegetables and fruits, supplemented by eggs, grubs, lizards, and similar sources of animal protein, early *Homo* invented stone tools with which they could butcher the carcasses of larger animals than even chimpanzees can deal with. Thus, they were able to increase significantly the amount of meat in their diet. This made possible a degree of economic specialization; males scavenged for meat, and females gathered a wide variety of other wild foods. It also made possible new patterns of social interaction: Females and males began sharing the results of their food-getting activities on a regular basis.

Over the next nearly 2.5 million years—a period known as the Paleolithic, or Old Stone Age—the evolving genus *Homo* relied increasingly on expanded mental abilities for survival, as we shall see in Chapters 8, 9, and 10. In the process, hunting came to replace scavenging as the main means by which meat was procured, and other improvements of this food-foraging way of life took place. As a consequence, the human species, essentially a tropical one, was able to free itself from its tropical habitat and, through invention, adapt itself to colder climates. By 200,000 years ago, humans had acquired essentially modern brains. Shortly thereafter, they achieved the ability to survive under true Arctic conditions. To invent ways of surviving under such forbidding and difficult conditions ranks as no less an achievement than sending the first man to the moon. ■

clothing and shelter that, coupled with the use of fire, enabled them to overcome the cold. Moreover, once this kind of cold adaptation was accomplished, it could readily be changed when circumstances required it. The fact is that cultural equipment and techniques can change rapidly, whereas biological change can be accomplished only over many generations.

The next four chapters discuss how evolving hominines developed the ability to invent their own solutions to the problems of existence and how this ingenuity gained primacy over biological change as the human mechanism for adapting to the environment. We begin, in Chapter 7, with the appearance of the genus *Homo*. Although the earliest members of this genus had far smaller brains than ours, they were significantly larger than those of *Australopithecus*. Their appearance is associated with a new way of surviving: Instead of foraging, as do most primates, on a more or less individ-

HOMO HABILIS AND CULTURAL ORIGINS

Though first found at Olduvai Gorge in Tanzania, some of the best finds of *Homo habilis* have come from Koobi Fora in Kenya (above). *Homo habilis,* the earliest maker of stone tools, was a scavenger of dead carcasses for meat and the first hominine to show evidence of significant increase in brain size beyond what is seen in apes.

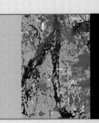

1

WHEN, WHERE, AND HOW DID HUMAN CULTURE DEVELOP?

Human culture appears to have developed in Africa, beyond what one sees in modern apes, as some populations of early hominines began making stone tools with which they could butcher animals for their meat. Actually, the earliest stone tools and evidence of significant meat eating date to about 2.6 million years ago, just prior to the appearance of the genus *Homo.*

2

WHEN DID REORGANIZATION AND EXPANSION OF THE HUMAN BRAIN BEGIN?

Reorganization and expansion of the human brain did not begin until at least 1.5 million years after the development of bipedal locomotion. It began in conjunction with scavenging and the making of stone tools. This marks the appearance of the genus *Homo,* an evolutionary offshoot of *Australopithecus.* The two forms coexisted for a million years or so, during the course of which *Australopithecus* relied on a vegetarian diet while developing a massive chewing apparatus. In contrast, *Homo* ate more meat and became brainier.

3

WHY DID THE EATING OF MORE MEAT LEAD TO IMPROVED BRAINS?

The making of stone tools—needed to skin, butcher, and crack open the bones of animals for marrow—put a premium on improved eye-hand coordination and precision grip, both of which selected for more complex brains. Increased meat eating, too, led to changes in the subsistence activities of both females and males. These changes required both sexes to do more in the way of thinking and planning, which again selected for larger, more complex brains.

In 1931 when Louis and Mary Leakey began work at Olduvai Gorge, they did so because of the presence of crude stone tools in deposits dating back to very early in the Pleistocene epoch, which began almost 2 million years ago. When they found the bones of the robust *Australopithecus boisei* in 1959, in association with some of these tools, they thought they had found the remains of one of the toolmakers. They later changed their minds, however, and suggested that these tools were not produced by *A. boisei,* nor were the bones of the birds, reptiles, antelopes, and pigs found with the remains of *A. boisei* the remains of the latter's dinner. Instead, *A. boisei* may have been a victim of a rather different contemporary who created the tools, ate the animals, and possibly had the unfortunate *A. boisei* for dessert. That contemporary was called by the Leakeys **Homo habilis** ("handy man").

Of course we don't really know that the Leakey's *boisei* met its end in this way, but we do know that cut marks from a stone tool are present on a 2.4-million-year-old hominine from South Africa.[1] This was done, presumably, to remove the mandible, but for what purpose we do not know. Although it might have involved cannibalism, other possibilities include curation or just plain mutilation. In any event, it does lend credibility to the idea of *boisei* on occasion being dismembered by *H. habilis.*

EARLY REPRESENTATIVES OF THE GENUS *HOMO*

The Leakeys discovered the remains of this second hominine in 1960, only a few months after their earlier discovery, just a few feet below it. The remains, which were those of more than one individual, consisted of a few cranial bones, a lower jaw, a clavicle, some finger bones (Figure 7.1), and the nearly complete left foot of an adult (Figure 7.2). These fossils date from about 1.8 million years ago and represent a hominine with a cranial capacity in the 650 to 690 cubic centimeter range, a skull that lacks noticeable bony crests, and almost modern-looking hands and feet. Subsequent work at Olduvai has unearthed not only more skull fragments but other parts of the skeleton of *Homo habilis* as well. These indicated that, aside from their more

modern-looking heads, hands, and feet, the skeleton of this hominine from the neck down does not differ greatly from that of the gracile Australopithecines. Overall size was about the same, as was the degree of sexual dimorphism (Figure 7.3), and they were equally adept at climbing trees.[2] Moreover, dental evidence suggests that, as with *A. afarensis* and *africanus,* the period of infancy and childhood in *H. habilis* was not prolonged, as it is in modern humans, but was more in line with apes.[3]

Since the late 1960s, fossils of the genus *Homo* that are essentially contemporaneous with those from Olduvai have been found elsewhere in Africa—in South Africa, in Kenya near Lake Baringo as well as east of Lake Turkana at Koobi Fora, and in Ethiopia just north of Lake Turkana. One of the best of these, known as KNM ER 1470, was discovered by the Leakeys' son Richard. (The letters *KNM* stand for Kenya National Museum; the *ER,* for East Rudolf, the former name for Lake Turkana.) The deposits in which it was found are about 1.9 million years old; these deposits, like those at Olduvai, also contain crude stone tools. The KNM ER 1470 skull is more modern in appearance than any *Australopithecus* skull and has a cranial capacity of 752 cubic centimeters. Furthermore, the inside of the skull shows a pattern in the left cerebral hemisphere that, in living people, is associated with a speech area.[4] This shape is in keeping with indications of brain asymmetry more like that of humans than apes, as is evident from wear patterns on tools used by early *Homo* that reveal that these hominines were predominately right-handed. In humans, the speech organs and the right hand are controlled by adjacent areas in the left cerebral hemisphere. Although this doesn't prove that early *Homo* had a spoken language, it does show that its brain was not only larger than that of *Australopithecus* but was reorganized along more human lines.

Although the 1470 skull and other early *Homo* fossils from localities other than Olduvai are frequently assigned to the same species, *H. habilis,* there are those who argue that a second distinct species (*H. Rudolfensis*) may be present. A rigorous evaluation of the arguments in favor of the two species hypothesis, however, by an independent investigator, failed to sustain them. The conclusion, then, is that "the data, at this point, are actually quite consistent

---

[1]White, T. D., & Toth, N. (2000). Cutmarks on a Plio-Pleistocene hominid from Sterkfontein, South Africa. *American Journal of Physical Anthropology, 111,* 579–584.

[2]Wood, B., & Collard, M. (1999). The human genus. *Science, 284,* 68.

[3]Ibid., p. 69.

[4]Ambrose, S. H. (2001). Paleolithic technology and human evolution. *Science, 291,* 1,750.

Homo habilis.   Earliest representative of the genus *Homo;* lived between 2.4 and 1.6 million years ago. Characterized by expansion and reorganization of the brain, compared to *Australopithecus.*

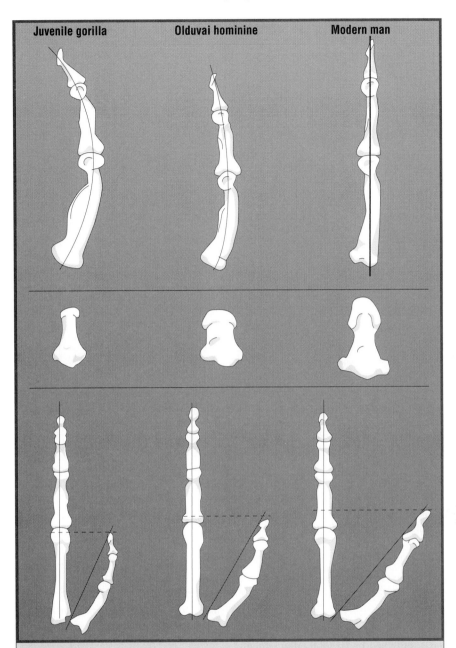

FIGURE 7.1

A COMPARISON OF HAND BONES OF A JUVENILE GORILLA, *HOMO HABILIS* FROM OLDUVAI, AND A MODERN HUMAN HIGHLIGHTS IMPORTANT DIFFERENCES IN THE STRUCTURE OF FIN-GERS AND THUMBS. IN THE TOP ROW ARE FINGERS AND IN THE SECOND ROW ARE TERMINAL THUMB BONES. ALTHOUGH TERMINAL FINGER BONES ARE MORE HUMAN, LOWER FINGER BONES ARE MORE CURVED AND POWERFUL. THE BOTTOM ROW COMPARES THUMB LENGTH AND ANGLE RELATIVE TO THE INDEX FINGER.

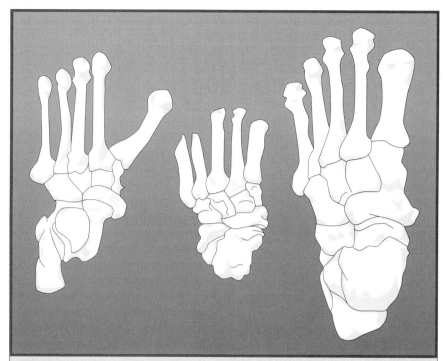

FIGURE 7.2

A partial foot skeleton of *Homo habilis* (center) is compared with the same bones of a chimpanzee (left) and modern human (right). Note how *habilis'* bone at the base of the great toe is in line with the others, as in modern humans, making for effective walking but poor grasping.

in showing that the *H. habilis* sample is neither too great in degree nor too different in pattern of variation to warrant rejection of the single species hypothesis."[5]

Relations Between *Homo habilis* and *Australopithecus*

A consideration of brain size relative to body size clearly indicates that *Homo habilis* had undergone enlargement of the brain far in excess of values predicted on the basis of body size alone. This means that there was a marked increase in information-processing capacity over that of the Australopithecines. Because larger brains generate more heat, it is not surprising to find that *habilis'* brain was provided with a heat exchanger of a sort not seen in *Australopithecus*, save to a very rudimentary degree in the late gracile forms.[6] This heat-exchange system con-

sists of small openings in the braincase through which veins pass allowing cooled blood from the face and scalp to be shunted to the brain, from which the blood can then carry off excess heat (see Figure 6.10). In this way, damage to the brain from excessive heat is prevented.

Although these hominines had teeth that are large by modern standards—or even by those of a half-million years ago—they are smaller in relation to the size of the skull than those of any Australopithecine. Because major brain-size increase and tooth-size reduction are important trends in the evolution of the genus *Homo*, but not of *Australopithecus*, it looks as if ER 1470 and similar hominines were becoming somewhat more human. Consistent with this are the indications that the brain of KNM ER 1470 was less apelike and more human in structure. It is probably no accident that the earliest fossils to exhibit these features appear by 2.4 million years ago (the age of the Baringo fossil), soon after the earliest evidence (to be discussed shortly) for stone tool-making and increased consumption of meat.

[5]Miller, J. M. A. (2000). Craniofacial variation in *Homo habilis:* An analysis of the evidence for multiple species. *American Journal of Physical Anthropology, 112,* 122.

[6]Falk, D. (1993). A good brain is hard to cool. *Natural History, 102*(8), 65.

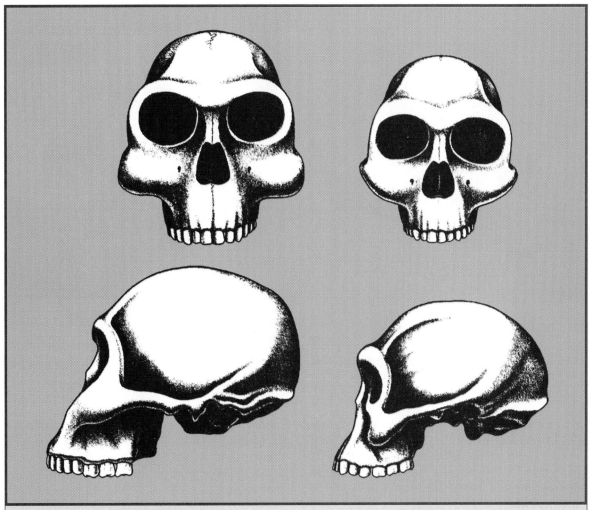

FIGURE 7.3

As these two skulls from Koobi Fora demonstrate, that of female *H. habilis* (right) was markedly smaller than that of the male (left).

As noted earlier, the Australopithecine diet seems to have consisted largely of plant foods, although the gracile species may have consumed limited amounts of animal protein as well. The later robust Australopithecines from East and South Africa evolved into more specialized "grinding machines" as their jaws became markedly larger (Figure 7.4), while their brain size did not. Nor is there firm evidence that they made stone tools. Thus, in the period between 2.5 and 1 million years ago, two kinds of hominines were headed in very different evolutionary directions.

If none of the robust species of *Australopithecus* belong in the direct line of human ancestry, what of earlier species of *Australopithecus*? From the standpoint of anatomy alone, it has long been recognized that either gracile species con-stitutes suitable ancestors for the genus *Homo,* and it now seems clear that the body of *Homo habilis* had changed little from that of either species. Precisely which of the two gave rise to *H. habilis* is vigorously debated. The arguments have become more complex with the discovery of *Kenyanthropus* (Chapter 6), which Maeve Leakey argues excludes all Australopithecines from the ancestry of *Homo.* At the moment, hers is a minority view. Most see the early East African graciles as sufficiently generalized to have given rise to both *Homo* and the robust *Australopithecus,* noting that the earliest skull to show the latter, the so-called Black Skull, nonetheless shows some holdovers from the earlier East Africans. This skull's age, 2.5 million years, is too old for any but the very earliest South African gracile

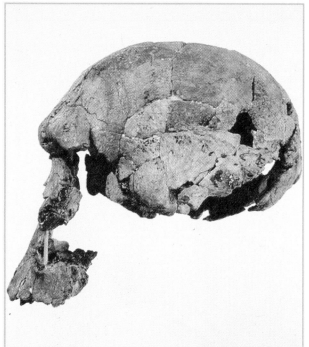 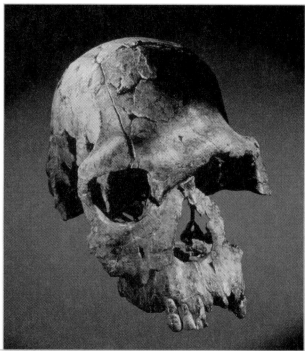

The ER 1470 skull (left): One of the most complete skulls of *Homo habilis* is close to 2 million years old and is probably a male; it contrasts with the ER 1813 skull (right), probably a female.

to have figured in its ancestry. Because the earliest *Homo habilis* skull is nearly as old, the same must be true for it. Evidently, at least a three-way split was under way by 2.5 million years ago, with the third line represented by late South African gracile *Australopithecus* (Figure 7.5). This persisted until about 2 million years ago (or later, if South African robusts are descended independently from graciles, rather than from East African robusts), by which time the other two lineages had become widespread in nonforested parts of Africa.

LOWER PALEOLITHIC TOOLS

The earliest tools known to have been made by hominines have been found in the vicinity of Lake Turkana in Kenya and southern Ethiopia, Olduvai Gorge in Tanzania, and Hadar in Ethiopia. Their appearance marks the beginning of the **Lower Paleolithic,** the first part of the Old Stone Age.

The makers of these early tools were highly skilled, consistently producing many well-formed flakes with few

misdirected blows.[7] The object was to obtain large, sharp-edged flakes from available raw materials with the least effort. At Olduvai and Lake Turkana, these tools are close to 2 million years old; the Ethiopian tools are older at 2.6 million years.

Olduvai Gorge

What is now Olduvai Gorge was once a lake. Almost 2 million years ago, its shores were inhabited not only by numerous wild animals but also by groups of hominines, including robust Australopithecines and *Homo habilis* as well as the later *Homo erectus* (Chapter 8). The gorge, therefore, is a rich source of Paleolithic remains as well as a key site providing evidence of human evolutionary change. Among the finds are assemblages of stone tools that are about 2 million years old. These were found little

---

[7]Ambrose, p. 1,749.

Lower Paleolithic. The first part of the Old Stone Age; its beginning is marked by the appearance 2.6 million years ago of Oldowan tools.

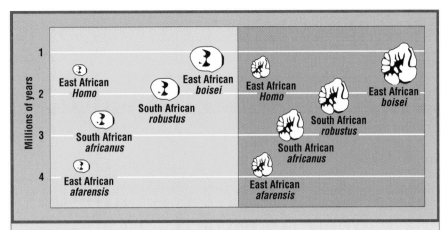

FIGURE 7.4

PREMOLARS (LEFT) AND MOLARS (RIGHT) OF *AUSTRALOPITHECUS* AND *HOMO HABILIS* COMPARED. THOUGH THERE IS LITTLE DIFFERENCE IN ABSOLUTE SIZE BETWEEN THE TEETH OF EARLY *AUSTRALOPITHECUS* (*AFARENSIS*) AND THOSE OF *HABILIS*, THOSE OF *AFARENSIS* ARE LARGER RELATIVE TO THE SIZE OF THE SKULL. MOREOVER, THE TEETH BECOME EVEN LARGER IN LATER SPECIES OF *AUSTRALOPITHECUS*.

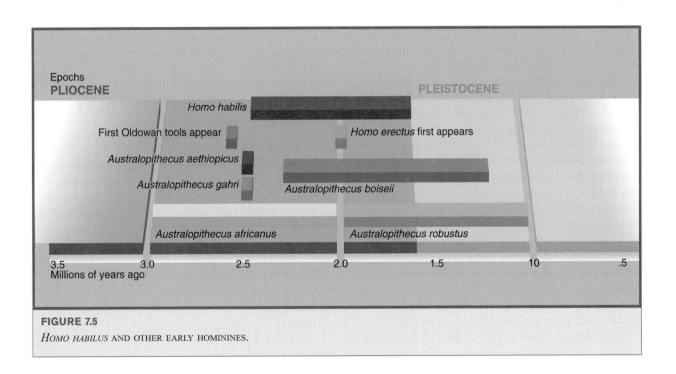

FIGURE 7.5

HOMO HABILUS AND OTHER EARLY HOMININES.

disturbed from when they were left, together with the bones of now-extinct animals that provided food. At one spot, in the lowest level of the gorge, the bones of an elephant lay in close association with more than 200 stone tools. Apparently, the animal was butchered here; there are no indications of any other activity. At another spot, on an occupation surface 1.8 million years old, basalt stones were found grouped in small heaps forming a circle. The interior of the circle was practically empty, while numerous tools and food debris littered the ground outside, right up to the edge of the circle. This was once interpreted as evidence for some sort of shelter, seeing the stone piles as supports for the framework of a protective fence of thorn branches, or perhaps a hut with a covering of animal skins or grass. Subsequence analysis suggests that the stones were "stockpiled" ahead of time, to be made into tools as needed, or to be hurled as missiles to hold off carnivorous animals while the hominines extracted meat, marrow, hide, and sinew from pieces of animal carcass.

Oldowan Tools

The oldest tools found at Olduvai Gorge belong to the **Oldowan tool tradition,** which is characterized by flakes struck from a stone (often a large, water-worn pebble) either by using another stone as a hammer (a hammerstone) or by striking the pebble against a large rock (anvil) to remove the flakes. This system of manufacture is called the **percussion method** (Figure 7.6). The finished flakes had two sharp edges, effective for cutting and scraping. Microscopic wear patterns show that these flakes were used for cutting meat, reeds, sedges, and grasses, and for cutting and scraping wood. The leftover cores, from which the flakes were struck, were also useful for bashing open bones for marrow and perhaps also defending the user.

Crude as they were, Oldowan tools mark an important technological advance for early hominines; previously, they depended on found objects requiring little or no modification, such as bones, sticks, or conveniently shaped stones. Oldowan tools made possible new additions to the diet, because, without such tools, hominines could eat few animals (only those that could be skinned by tooth or nail); therefore, their diet was limited in terms of animal proteins. The advent of Oldowan tools meant more than merely saving labor and time: They made possible the addition of meat to the diet on a frequent, rather than occasional, basis.

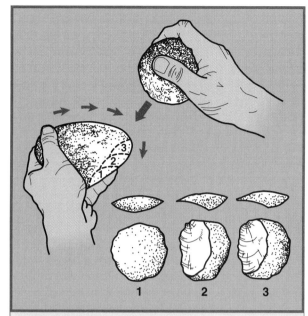

FIGURE 7.6

BY 2.6 MILLION YEARS AGO, HOMININES IN AFRICA HAD INVENTED THE PERCUSSION METHOD OF STONE TOOL MANUFACTURE. THIS DRAWING ILLUSTRATES HOW OLDOWAN TOOLMAKERS DETACHED FLAKES FROM A CORE USING THIS TECHNIQUE. A TECHNOLOGICAL BREAKTHROUGH, THE PRODUCTION OF STONE TOOLS BY PERCUSSION MADE POSSIBLE THE BUTCHERING OF MEAT FROM SCAVENGED CARCASSES.

Much popular literature has been written about this penchant for meat, often with numerous colorful references to "killer apes." Such references are misleading, not only because hominines are not apes but also because killing has been greatly overemphasized. Meat can be obtained, after all, by scavenging or by stealing it from other predators. What is significant is that a dentition such as that possessed by *Australopithecus* and *Homo habilis* is poorly suited for meat eating. What is needed if substantial amounts of meat are to be eaten, without teeth like those possessed by carnivorous animals (or chimpanzees), are sharp tools for butchering.

The initial use of tools was probably the result of adaptation to an environment that we know was changing between 3 and 2 million years ago from forests to grasslands (see Figure 6.11). The physical changes that adapted hominines for spending increasing amounts of

---

Oldowan tool tradition. The earliest identifiable stone tools. • **Percussion method.** A technique of stone tool manufacture performed by striking the raw material with a hammerstone or by striking raw material against a stone anvil to remove flakes.

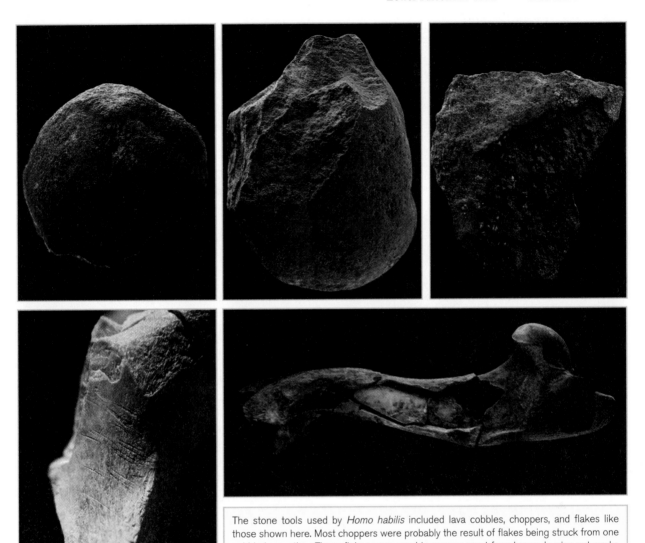

The stone tools used by *Homo habilis* included lava cobbles, choppers, and flakes like those shown here. Most choppers were probably the result of flakes being struck from one cobble by another. These flakes were used to remove meat from bones, leaving cut marks (lower left). The cobbles and choppers were used to break open bones (lower right) to get at the marrow.

time on the new grassy terrain encouraged toolmaking. It has been observed that monkeys and apes, for example, often use objects, such as sticks and stones, in their threat displays. The change to a nearly upright bipedal posture, coupled with existing flexibility at the shoulder, arms, and hands, allowed hominines to do so as well, helping them to compete successfully with the large predatory carnivores that shared their environment.

What else do these assemblages of Oldowan tools and broken animal bones have to tell us about the life of early *Homo*? First, they tell us that both *Homo habilis* and large carnivorous animals were active at these locations, for in addition to marks on the bones made by slicing, scraping, and chopping with stone tools, there are tooth marks from gnawing. Some of the gnawing marks over-

lie the butcher marks, indicating that enough flesh remained on the bones after the hominines were done with them to attract the other carnivores. In other cases, though, the butcher marks overlie the tooth marks of carnivores, indicating that the animals got there first. This is what we would expect if *H. habilis* were scavenging the kills of other animals, rather than doing its own killing. Consistent with this picture is that whole carcasses are not represented; evidently, only parts were transported away from the original location where they were obtained, again what we would expect if they were "stolen" from the kill of some other animal. The stone tools, too, were made of raw material procured at distances of up to 10 kilometers from where they were used to process the parts of carcasses. Finally, the incredible density of bones at some of the sites

Homo habilis filled the same niche on the ground that these vultures fill in the air: a nonterritorial scavenger.

and patterns of weathering indicate that, although *H. habilis* didn't linger longer than necessary at any one time (and for good reason—the carnivores attracted by the meat could have made short work of *habilis* as well), the sites were repeatedly used over periods guessed to be on the order of 5 to 15 years.

All of this is quite unlike the behavior of historically known food-foraging peoples, who bring whole carcasses back to camp, where they are completely processed; neither meat nor marrow is left (as they were at Oldowan sites), and the bones themselves are broken up not just to get at the marrow (as at Oldowan sites) but to fabricate tools and other objects of bone (unlike at Oldowan sites). Nor do historically known food foragers normally camp in the midst of so much garbage. The picture that emerges of our Oldowan forebears, then, is of scavengers, getting

Becoming scavengers put *Homo habilis* in competition with formidable adversaries like hyenas.

their meat from the Lower Paleolithic equivalent of modern-day road kills, taking the spoils of their scavenging to particular places where tools, and the raw materials for making them (often procured from faraway sources), had been stockpiled in advance for the purpose of butchering. At these sites, the remains were quickly processed, so that those doing the butchering could clear out before their lives were endangered by carnivores attracted by the meat. Thus, the Oldowan sites were not campsites or "home bases" at all. Quite likely, *H. habilis* continued to sleep in trees or rocky cliffs, as do other small-bodied terrestrial or semiterrestrial primates, in order to be safe from predators. However, the advanced preparation for meat processing implied by the caching of stone tools, and the raw materials for making tools, attests to considerable foresight and ability to plan ahead.

Tools, Meat, and Brains

As we have seen, by 1.5 million years or so after early hominines became fully bipedal, the size and structure of the brain were beginning to change. Until about 2.5 million years ago, early hominines lived on foods that could be picked or gathered: plants, fruits, invertebrate animals such as ants and termites, and perhaps even an occasional piece of meat scavenged from kills made by other animals. After 2.5 million years ago, meat became more important in their diet, and they began to scavenge for it on a more regular basis.

Because early hominines lacked size and strength to drive off predators, or to compete directly with other scavengers attracted to kills, they must have had to rely on their wit and cunning for success. One may imagine them lurking in the vicinity of a kill, sizing up the situation as the predator ate its fill while hyenas and other scavengers gathered, and devising strategies to outwit them all so as to seize a piece of the carcass. A hominine depending on stereotyped instinctual behavior in such a situation would have been at a competitive disadvantage. One that could anticipate problems, devise distractions, bluff competitors into temporary retreat, and recognize, the instant it came, its opportunity to rush in and grab what it could of the carcass stood a much better chance of surviving, reproducing, and proliferating.

One means by which early hominines gained access to a reasonably steady supply of carcasses while at the same time minimizing the risks involved is suggested by recent field studies of leopards. How this could have worked and the arguments in favor of it are the subject of the following Original Study.

Cat in the Human Cradle[8]

Original Study

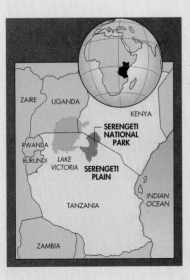

Recent evidence, such as marks on some of the Olduvai bones, indicates that animals the size of wildebeests or larger were killed, eaten, and abandoned by large predators such as lions, hyenas, and saber-toothed cats; hominines may have merely scavenged the leftovers. Several specialists now agree that early hominines obtained at least marrow mainly in this way. The picture with regard to the remains of smaller animals, such as gazelle-sized antelopes, is less certain. Paleoanthropologists Henry Bunn and Ellen Kroll believe that the cut-marked upper limb bones of small, medium-sized, and large animals found at Olduvai Gorge demonstrate that hominines were butchering the meaty limbs with cutting tools. Since modern-day lions and hyenas rapidly and completely consume small prey, leaving little or nothing for potential scavengers, Bunn and Kroll conclude that hominines must have acquired the smaller animals by hunting. But

---

[8]Adapted from Cavallo, J. A. (1990). Cat in the human cradle. *Natural History*, 54–56, 58–60.

Original Study

another scholar, Kay Behrensmeyer, suggests that a small group of hominines could have obtained these bones, not by hunting, but by driving off timid predators, such as cheetahs or jackals, from their kills.

Since carnivores play a key role in all these scenarios, three years ago I began thinking about studying their behavior and ecology. About the same time, a colleague directed me to a paper on the tree-climbing abilities of early hominines. The authors (anatomists Randall L. Susman, Jack T. Stern, and William L. Jungers) analyzed the limb bones of *Homo habilis* specimens from Olduvai Gorge, as well as those of the early hominine *Australopithecus afarensis* (better known as Lucy). They concluded that early hominines were probably not as efficient as we are at walking on two feet, but they were better than we are at climbing trees and suspending themselves from branches. At the very least, given their apparent lack of fire, early hominines must have used trees as refuges from large predators and as sleeping sites.

One evening, as I watched a documentary film by Hugh Miles about a female leopard and her cubs in Kenya's Masai Mara Reserve, carnivore behavior and early hominine tree climbing suddenly connected for me. In the film, a pack of hyenas attempt to scavenge an antelope that the mother leopard

has killed. At the sight of the hyenas, the leopard grabs the prey in her jaws and carries it up a small tree. This striking behavior sparked my curiosity and sent me to the library the next morning to find out more about leopards.

I learned that the leopard differs from other large African carnivores in a variety of ways. Although it occasionally kills large animals, such as adult wildebeests and topi or young giraffes, the leopard preys primarily on smaller antelopes, such as Thomson's gazelles, impala, and Grant's gazelles, and on the young of both large and small species. Unable to defend its kills on the ground from scavenging by lions and spotted hyenas, both of which often forage in groups, the usually solitary leopard stores each kill in a tree, returning to feed but otherwise frequently abandoning it for varying lengths of time.

Although the leopard may not consume its entire prey immediately, the tree-stored kills are relatively safe from theft. (Even lions, which can climb trees, usually take little notice of this resource.) As a result, a kill can persist in a tree for several days. Also, leopard kills appear to be more predictably located than those of lions and hyenas because leopards tend to maintain a small territorial range for several years and occasionally

This leopard has carried part of a Thomson's gazelle up into a tree to prevent other scavengers from consuming what is left. Such tree-stored carcasses may have been the principal source of meat for *Homo habilis*.

reuse feeding trees. Finally, leopard kills are usually found in the woodlands near lakes and rivers, the habitat apparently preferred by early hominines. Such circumstances, I reasoned, might have once provided an ideal feeding opportunity for tree-climbing hominines, particularly *Homo habilis*. By scavenging from the leopard's temporarily abandoned larder, early hominines could have obtained the fleshy and marrow-rich bones of small- to medium-sized prey animals in relative safety.

Fossil evidence shows that ancestors of present-day leopards were contemporaneous with early hominines and shared the same habitats. The antiquity of tree-caching behavior is harder to prove, but it is supported by paleoanthropologist C. K. Brain's excavations of ancient caves in southern Africa's Sterkfontein Valley. In the vertical, shaftlike caves, Brain found the fossil remains of hominines, baboons, and antelopes, and of leopards and other large carnivores. The size of the prey animals and the selection of body parts, as well as puncture marks on some of the cranial bones of hominines and baboons, suggested that many of these fossils were the remains of leopard meals. Brain guessed that they had fallen into the caves from leopard-feeding trees growing out of the mouths of the caves.

Given its similarities to the ancient environments represented at the early archeological sites— extensive grasslands with wooded lakes, rivers, and streams—the Serengeti National Park in northern Tanzania seemed an ideal living laboratory in which to test my hypothesis. I traveled there in July 1987, accompanied by Robert J. Blumenschine, who had conducted an earlier study there on scavenging opportunities provided by lions and hyenas. Along the Wandamu River, a tributary of the Seronera, we were fortunate to find an adult female leopard and her 13-month-old (nearly full-grown) male cub that tolerated our Land-Rover. We spent a total of about 50 hours, during the day and at night, observing these leopards at three fresh, tree-stored kills of Thomson's gazelles. The leopards frequently left the carcasses unguarded between feedings. On one occasion, a complete young Thomson's gazelle, killed the previous evening, was abandoned for 9 daylight hours (we found the leopards resting approximately 2 miles away). Without directly confronting these predators, therefore, a creature able to climb trees could have easily carried off the same amount of flesh and marrow as it could obtain from hunting.

While Brain's work in South Africa implicates leopards as predators of early hominines, including the genus *Homo*, some hominines may have also benefited from living near these carnivores. Tree-stored leopard kills could have provided an important resource to early scavenging hominines and the sharp, broken limb bones from the partly eaten prey could have been used to peel back the hide, expose the flesh of the carcasses, and remove large muscle bundles. This activity may even have given early hominines the initial impetus to make and use tools in the extraction of animal nutrients.

Some paleoanthropologists have argued that scavenging was an unlikely subsistence strategy for early hominines, since large predators require expansive home ranges, and kills by these carnivores are rare in any particular area. They also contend that very little is left over from such kills after the predator is finished and that hominine competition with large carnivores for these leftovers would be a dangerous activity. My 1988 observations suggest something quite different. During approximately 2 months in the dry season, I documented 16 kills of small and medium antelopes made by my adult male and female leopards within an approximately 4-by-8-mile area. The majority of these kills, still retaining abundant flesh and marrow, were temporarily abandoned by the leopard for 3 to $8\frac{1}{2}$ hours during a single day.

The tree-stored leopard kills consisted mainly of adult and juvenile Thomson's gazelles. Compared with kills of similar-sized prey made on the ground by Serengeti lions and hyenas, as recorded by Blumenschine, the tree-stored leopard kills lasted longer, offering large quantities of flesh and marrow for 2 or more days. In part this was because they were not subject to many scavengers. The leopard kills were also more predictably located on the landscape than those of lions in the same area. In modern leopard populations, a male maintains a relatively large territory that overlaps with the usually smaller territories of several females. This pattern often means that several tree-stored kills are available simultaneously during a given period of time within a relatively small area.

An obvious question is how leopards would have responded to repeated theft of their tree-stored kills

Original Study

by early hominines. Would they, perhaps, have abandoned portions of their ranges if such thefts occurred with sufficient regularity? Although I haven't yet tested this, I don't think they would have. According to my observations and those of other researchers, leopards are usually more successful at hunting larger prey, such as gazelles and impala, at night. This gives them the opportunity to consume part of such kills before the arrival of any daytime scavengers. They thus should be able to obtain enough nourishment to warrant remaining in a territory, despite some such losses.

Like modern baboons and chimpanzees, early hominines may have killed some small animals, such as newborn antelopes. But they could have acquired all sizes of animal carcasses without hunting if the prey killed by leopards is taken into account. The wide assortment of animal bones at sites like Olduvai Gorge, which have been attributed to ground-based hunting and scavenging, could instead be attributed to scavenging only, both in trees and on the ground. Leopard kills would then have provided much of the flesh consumed by early hominines, while carcasses abandoned on the ground by other large predators would have yielded primarily bone marrow. Additional flesh may have come from the remains of large kills made by saber-toothed cats or from the carcasses of animals that drowned when herds migrated across ancient lakes.

While we can't observe the behavior of our early ancestors, the present-day interactions between leopards and some other primate species can be instructive. Baboons, for example, often fall victim to leopards while they sleep at night in trees or caves. During the day, however, baboons regularly attack, displace, and according to one account, even kill leopards. In western Tanzania, a park ranger reported that during the day, a group of baboons saw a leopard in a tree with the carcass of an impala. Barking out alarm calls, the adult and adolescent male baboons chased the leopard for about $3/10$ of a mile. The females and young baboons stayed with the carcass and began to eat, until the males returned and took possession of the kill.

Similarly, although chimpanzees in western Tanzania are the occasional prey of leopards, there is a report that one day some chimpanzees scavenged what was apparently a tree-stored leopard kill. On a more dramatic occasion, also during the day, a group of chimpanzees was observed noisily surrounding a leopard lair from which an adult leopard was heard growling. A male chimpanzee entered the lair and emerged with a leopard cub, which it and the others killed without reprisal from the adult leopard. This type of shifting day-night, predatory-parasitic relationship may once have existed between leopards and our early hominine ancestors.

The End

Although difficult to prove, several lines of evidence combine to suggest it was probably the early hominine males, rather than females, who did most of the scavenging. What predisposed them for such a division of labor may have been the foraging habits of the earlier Australopithecines. As already noted (in Chapter 6), dental and skeletal differences between males and females raise the possibility that males may have fed on the ground and lower levels of trees more heavily than females, who had a higher proportion of fruit in their diet.[9] Something like this pattern is seen today among orangutans, where it is a response to highly dispersed resources. As a consequence, males consume larger amounts of low-quality food such as bark than do females. A major difference, of course, is that orangutan males still forage in the forest, whereas male *Australopithecus* foraged in a mosaic woodland, bushland, and grassland environment. In such a situation, the latter may have been forced to try out supplementary sources of food on the ground, especially if existing sources became scarcer, as they likely did; in the crucial period between 3 and 2 million years ago climates became markedly cold and dry.[10] Already bipedal,

[9]Leonard, W. R., & Hegman, M. (1987). Evolution of P3 morphology in *Australopithecus afarensis*. *American Journal of Physical Anthropology, 73,* 60.

[10]Behrensmeyer, A. K., Todd, N. E., Potts, R., & McBrinn, G. E. (1997). Late Pliocene faunal turnover in the Turkana basin, Kenya and Ethiopia. *Science, 278,* 1,589–1,594.

ADRIENNE ZIHLMAN (b. 1940)

Up until the 1970s, the study of human evolution, from its very beginnings, was permeated by a deep-seated bias reflecting the privileged status enjoyed by men in Western society. Beyond the obvious labeling of fossils as particular types of "men," irrespective of the sex of the individual represented, it took the form of portraying males as the active players in human evolution. Thus, it was males who were seen as providers and innovators, using their wits to become ever more effective providers of food and protection for passive females. The latter were seen as spending their time getting pregnant and caring for offspring, while the men were getting ahead by becoming ever smarter. Central to such thinking was the idea of "man the hunter," constantly honing his wits through the pursuit and killing of animals. Thus, hunting by men was seen as the pivotal humanizing activity in evolution.

We now know, of course, that such ideas are culture-bound, reflecting the hopes and expectations of late-19th- and early-20th-century European and European American culture. This recognition came in the 1970s and was a direct consequence of the entry of a number of highly capable women into the profession of paleoanthropology. Up until the 1960s, there were few women in any field of physical anthropology, but with the expansion of graduate programs and changing attitudes toward the role of women in society, increasing numbers of them went on to earn a PhD. One of these was Adrienne Zihlman, who earned her doctorate at the University of California at Berkeley in 1967. Subsequently, she authored a number of important papers critical of "man the hunter" scenarios. She was not the first to do so; as early as 1971, Sally Linton had published a preliminary paper on "Woman the Gatherer," but it was Zihlman from 1976 on who especially elaborated on the importance of female activities for human evolution. Others have joined in the effort, including Zihlman's companion in graduate school and later colleague, Nancy Tanner, who collaborated with Zihlman on some of her papers and has produced important works of her own.

The work of Zihlman and her coworkers was crucial in forcing a reexamination of existing "man the hunter" scenarios, out of which came recognition of the importance of scavenging in early human evolution as well as the importance of female gathering and other activities. Although there is still plenty to learn about human evolution, thanks to these women we now know that it wasn't a case of women being "uplifted" as a consequence of their association with progressively evolving men. Rather, the two sexes evolved together with each making its own important contribution to the process.

Australopithecines were capable of covering, in an energetically efficient way, the considerable distances (on the order of 32 square miles, based on the Original Study) necessary to ensure a steady supply of meat.

Another consideration is that, without contraceptive devices and formulas that could be bottle-fed to infants, females in their prime, when not pregnant, must have had infants to nurse. Although this would not have restricted their local mobility, any more than it does a female ape or monkey or a woman among historically known food-foraging peoples, it would have been less easy for them than for males to range over the substantial distances required to search out carcasses. Also essential for the successful scavenger would have been the capacity for the massive bursts of energy needed to elude the many carnivores active on the savanna. Although anatomical and physiological differences between the sexes in humans today are relatively insignificant compared to *H. habilis,* as a general rule, men can still run faster than women (even though some women can certainly run faster than some men). Finally, even for the smartest and swiftest individuals, scavenging would still have been a risky business. To place early *Homo* females at risk would have been to place their offspring, actual and potential, at risk as well. Males, on the other hand, would have been relatively expendable, for, to put the matter bluntly, a very few males are capable of impregnating a large number of females. In evolutionary terms, the population that places its males at risk is less likely to jeopardize its chances for reproductive success than is the one that places its females at risk.

Early hominine females, as well as males, had to sharpen their wits in order to gain access to some of the meat scavenged. For the most part, females continued to gather the same kinds of foods that their ancestors had been eating all along. But instead of consuming all this food themselves as they gathered it (as other primates do), they provided some to the males who, in turn, provided the females with meat. To do this, they had to plan ahead so as to know where food would be found in sufficient quantities, devise means by which it could be transported to some agreed-upon location for division at the proper time, while at the same time preventing its loss through spoilage or to such animals as rats and mice. At the least, this may have required fabrication of carrying devices such as net bags and use of trail signs of the sort (described in Chapter 4) used by modern bonobos. Thus, female gathering played just as important a role in the development of larger, more complex brains as did male scavenging.

Evolving hominines' increased interest in meat is a point of major importance. Out on the savanna, it is hard for a primate with a digestive system like that of humans to satisfy its amino acid requirements from available plant resources. Moreover, failure to do so has serious consequences: growth depression, malnutrition, and ultimately death. The most readily accessible plant sources would have been the proteins available in leaves and legumes (nitrogen-fixing plants, familiar modern examples being beans and peas), but these are hard for primates like us to digest unless they are cooked. The problem is that leaves and legumes contain substances that cause the proteins to pass right through the gut without being absorbed.[11]

Chimpanzees have a similar problem when out on the savanna. In such a setting, they spend about 37 percent of their time on a yearly basis going after insects like ants and termites, while at the same time increasing their predation of eggs and vertebrate animals. Such animal foods not only are easily digestible, but they provide high-quality proteins that contain all the essential amino acids in just the right percentages. No one plant food does this by itself; only if the right combination is consumed can plants provide what meat does by itself in the way of amino acids. Moreover, there is abundant meat to be had

One means by which bonobos indicate to others where they are headed is to deliberately trample down the vegetation. *H. habilis* may have made use of similar trail signs.

on the savanna. All things considered, then, we should not be surprised if our own ancestors solved their protein problem in somewhat the same way that chimps on the savanna do today.

Increased meat consumption on the part of early hominines did more than merely ensure an adequate intake of essential amino acids, important though this was. Animals that live on plant foods must eat large quantities of vegetation, and obtaining such foods consumes much of their time. Meat eaters, by contrast, have no need to eat so much, or so often. Consequently, meat-eating hominines may have had more leisure time available to explore and manipulate their environment; like lions and

---

[11]Stahl, A. B. (1984) Hominid dietary selection before fire. *Current Anthropology, 25,* 151–168.

Meat-eating animals, like these lions, do not have to spend as much time eating as do those that rely on plant foods alone. Consequently, they have more time available for play and exploration.

leopards, they would have time to spend lying around and playing. Such activity, coupled with the other factors already mentioned, may have been a stimulus to hominine brain development.

The importance of increased consumption of meat for early hominine brain development is suggested by the size of their brains: The cranial capacity of the largely plant-eating *Australopithecus* ranged from 310 to 530 cubic centimeters; that of the most primitive known meat eater, *Homo habilis* from East Africa, ranged from 580 to 752 cc; whereas *Homo erectus,* who eventually hunted as well as scavenged for meat, possessed a cranial capacity of 775 to 1,225 cc.

THE EARLIEST SIGNS OF CULTURE: TOOLS

The use of specially made tools of stone appears to have arisen out of a need for implements to butcher and prepare meat, because hominine teeth were inadequate for the task. Even chimpanzees, whose canine teeth are far larger and sharper, frequently have trouble tearing

through the skin of other animals.[12] Besides overcoming this problem, the manufacture of stone tools must have played a role in the evolution of the human brain, first by putting a premium on manual dexterity and fine manipulation over mere power in the use of the hands. This in turn put a premium on improved organization of the nervous system. Second, the transformation of a lump of stone into a "chopper," "knife," or "scraper" is a far cry from what a chimpanzee does when it transforms a stick into a termite probe. Although the probe is not unlike the stick, the stone tool is (with the exception of hammerstones) quite unlike the lump of stone. Thus, the toolmaker must have in mind an abstract idea of the tool to be made, as well as a specific set of steps that will accomplish the transformation from raw material to finished product. Furthermore, only certain kinds of stone have the flaking properties that will allow the transformation to take place. The toolmaker must know about these, as well as where such stone can be found.

---

[12]Goodall, J. (1986) *The chimpanzees of Gombe: Patterns of behavior* (p. 372). Cambridge, MA: Belknap Press.

Chimpanzees' hunting and consumption of meat is made possible by their large, sharp canines. *Homo habilis,* by contrast, lacked such teeth.

A power grip (left) utilizes more of the hand, whereas the precision grip (right) relies on the fingers for control.

HIGHWAY 1
This Web site provides a comprehensive source of information about human evolutionary history and takes the evolution–creationism controversy head on. Search the site for excellent description of each of the fossil hominine species discovered.
www.talkorigins.org/faqs/homs/

HIGHWAY 2
The Leakey Foundation Web site is true to its mission to increase scientific knowledge and public understanding of human origins and evolution. The site provides an interactive timeline of key discoveries in paleoanthropology and documents the groundbreaking research conducted by the Leakey family and the investigators they have supported for over three decades.
www.leakeyfoundation.org/

HIGHWAY 3
This handsome Web site is packed with information about human evolution including each new discovery, a comprehensive glossary, and a perspective feature where new voices and ideas in the field can be heard.
www.archaeologyinfo.com/

COOPERATION AND SHARING

With an apelike brain and a diet like that of monkeys and apes when out in open country, *Australopithecus* probably behaved much like other hominoids. Like apes, adults probably foraged for their own food, which was not regularly shared with other adults. Among modern apes, however, there are two notable exceptions to this behavior. Among bonobos, females sometimes share meat and even fruits with one another and sometimes with males. Adult chimpanzees, by contrast, rarely share plant food with one another, but males almost always share meat, frequently with females. Increased consumption of meat on the part of *Homo habilis* may have promoted even more sharing among adults. Moreover, a regular supply of meat would have required that substantial amounts of time and energy be devoted to the search for carcasses, and food gathered by females and shared with males could have provided the latter with both.

Sharing and cooperation between the sexes need not necessarily have been between mated males and females, but may just as well have been between brothers and sisters and mothers and sons. On the other hand, the capacity to engage in sexual activity at any time the female deemed appropriate may have promoted sharing and cooperation between a male and one or more sex partners. Among most catarrhine primates, males attempt to monopolize females when the latter are at the height of sexual receptivity. Moreover, male chimpanzees frequently use the sharing of meat to entice females to have sex, and females in estrus are more successful at begging for meat from males. Males, too, are more apt to hunt if a sexually receptive female is present.[13] The willingness of human females to engage in sex at any time it suits them is shared with our nearest relatives (chimps and especially bonobos) and so probably is retained from our common ancestry. Hence, we can safely ascribe such behavior to the earliest hominines. Sharing with sex partners (who may have been multiple) therefore seems likely.

Although chimpanzees can and do hunt singly, they frequently cooperate in the task. In the case of *Homo habilis*, cooperation would seem to have been even more crucial to success in scavenging. It is hard to imagine a creature lacking the formidable canines of a chimpanzee competing on an individual basis with carnivores far more powerful than itself.

In summary, then, it seems reasonable to assume that *Homo habilis* engaged in more sharing and cooperative behavior than one sees among present-day chimpanzees. How much more is certainly not known, and certainly fell far short of what has been observed among any historically known food-foraging peoples. After all, *Homo habilis* was not just a different sort of hominine from *Australopithecus;* it was different from *Homo sapiens* as well.

---

[13]Moore, J. (1998). Comment. *Current Anthropology, 39,* 413.

LANGUAGE ORIGINS

The evident importance of cooperation, planning, and foresight in the life of *H. habilis* raises the issue of this species' ability to communicate. Modern apes communicate through a combination of calls and gestures, and humans, though we rely on spoken language, also use this gesture-call system. Like the apes, we have inherited this from ancient ancestors that predate the evolutionary split between hominids and pongids. After three decades of experiments by several different researchers with captive apes, there is a growing consensus that all great apes share an ability to develop language skills at least to the level of a 2- to 3-year-old.[14] Of course, they do not do so in the wild, even though the potential is there (just as bonobos do not make chipped stone tools in the wild, even though experiments show they are capable of it). Nor do they display these language skills through speech, but rather through use of gestures. Again, because this linguistic potential is shared, it must be one that the earliest hominines possessed as well. In view of these considerations, the previously noted features of the brain of *H. habilis* that in modern humans are associated with language take on added interest.

Moreover, the speech area is adjacent to and probably derived from that involved in precise hand control. This brings us back to the fact that the manufacture of Oldowan tools requires manual skills that go beyond those of chimpanzees, or even Kanzi: the bonobo.[15] And, as previously noted, the Oldowan toolmakers, like modern humans, were overwhelmingly right-handed; in making tools, they gripped the core in the left hand, striking flakes off with the right. Chimpanzees, by contrast, show no overall preference for right-handedness at the population level.[16] Handedness (whether right or left) is associated with lateralization of brain functions, that is, the two hemispheres specialize for different functions; rather than duplicating each other. Lateralization, in turn, is associated with language. Thus, toolmaking may have set the stage for language development. Putting this all together, we must at least allow the possibility that *H. habilis* had developed gestural language, though it may have been rudimentary. With the hands freed from locomotion to do other things, they were certainly more available for communication than are the hands of apes.

---

[14]Miles, H. L. W. (1993). Language and the orangutan: The old person of the forest. In P. Singer (Ed.), *The great ape project* (p. 46). New York: St. Martin's.

[15]Ambrose, p. 1,749.

[16]Ibid., p. 1,750

CHAPTER SUMMARY

Since 1960 a number of fossils have been found in East Africa at Olduvai Gorge, Lake Baringo, and east of Lake Turkana, and in South Africa at Sterkfontein and Swartkrans, which have been attributed to *Homo habilis,* the earliest representative of this genus. Among them is the well-known KNM ER 1470 skull, which is more modern in appearance than any *Australopithecus* skull. From the neck down, however, the skeleton of *Homo habilis* differs little from that of *Australopithecus*. Because it does show a significant increase in brain size and some reorganization of its structure, *Homo habilis'* mental abilities must have exceeded those of *Australopithecus*. By 2.4 million years ago, the evolution of *Homo* was proceeding in a direction different from that of *Australopithecus*.

The same geological strata that have produced *Homo habilis* have also produced the earliest known stone tools. These Lower Paleolithic artifacts from Olduvai Gorge, Lake Turkana, and sites in Ethiopia are simple in form but required considerable skill and knowledge for their manufacture.

Finds made at Olduvai Gorge have provided important evidence of human evolutionary development. The oldest Lower Paleolithic tools found at Olduvai are in the Oldowan tool tradition, which is characterized by all-purpose generalized flakes and chopping tools. Used to make them was the percussion method of manufacture. The simple but effective Oldowan choppers and flakes made possible the addition of meat to the diet on a regular basis because one could now butcher meat, skin any animal, and break open bones for marrow. Many Oldowan archaeological sites appear to be temporary places where meat was processed, rather than campsites.

Some changes in the brain structure of *Homo habilis* seem to have been associated with the changed diet. Increased consumption of meat, beginning about 2.5 million years ago, made new demands on their coordination and behavior. Successful procurement of meat through scavenging depended on *H. habilis'* ability to outthink far more powerful predators and scavengers. Obtaining animal food presented problems that very often had to be solved on the spot; a small scavenger depending on stereotyped instinctual behavior alone would have been at a competitive disadvantage in such a situation. Moreover, eaters of high-protein foods, such as meats, do not have to eat as often as vegetarians do. Consequently, meat-eating hominines may have had more leisure time available to explore and experiment with their environment.

Toolmaking and use also favored the development of a more complex brain. To make stone tools, one must have in mind at the beginning a clear vision of the tool to be made, one must know the precise set of steps necessary to transform the raw material into the tool, and one must be able to recognize the kind of stone that can be successfully worked. Complex eye-hand coordination is also required.

A prime factor in the success of early hominines may have been the development of some cooperation in the procurement of foods. Although the males probably supplied much of the meat, the females continued to gather the sorts of food eaten by other primates; however, instead of consuming what they gathered as they gathered it, they shared a portion with the males in exchange for meat. This required foresight and planning on the part of females, which played as important a role as male scavenging in favoring the development of larger, more complex brains. Food sharing with a sexual division of labor is characteristic of modern food foragers, and some hint of it can be seen among chimpanzees and bonobos, among whom meat is frequently shared.

The cooperation, planning, and foresight inferred for *Homo habilis* suggest the existence of some sort of rudimentary language, as do some features of this species' brain. Experiments with captive apes favor some sort of gestural language.

CLASSIC READINGS

Campbell, B. G., & Loy, J. D. (1995). *Humankind emerging* (7th ed.). New York: HarperCollins.

This well-written and lavishly illustrated text has excellent coverage of the earliest hominines.

Ciochon, R. L., & Fleagle, J. G. (Eds.). (1993). *The human evolution source book.* Englewood Cliffs, NJ: Prentice-Hall.

This collection of articles by specialists provides a more detailed look at the different theories on early hominine evolution.

Johanson, D., & Shreeve, J. (1989). *Lucy's child: The discovery of a human ancestor.* New York: Avon.

This sequel to *Lucy* is written in the same engaging style. Although it covers some of the same ground with respect to *Australopithecus,* its focus is on *Homo habilis.* Besides giving a good description of this earliest member of the genus *Homo,* it presents one of the best discussions of the issues concerning when (and why) *Homo* appeared.

CHAPTER 8

HOMO ERECTUS AND THE EMERGENCE OF HUNTING AND GATHERING

More "human" than *Homo habilis*, though less so than *Homo sapiens*, *Homo erectus* emerged about 1.8 million years ago, by which time the genus *Homo* was spreading to parts of Asia. Shown here is one of the most famous *Homo erectus* sites, at Zhoukoudian, China. Discovered in the 1920s, it is now included on UNESCO's World Heritage List.

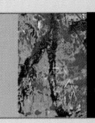

1

WHO WAS *HOMO ERECTUS*?

Homo erectus was the direct descendant of early members of the genus *Homo* as evidenced by findings in various parts of Africa. Populations of *Homo erectus* were widespread between about 1.8 million and 400,000 years ago, from Africa and Europe in the West, to Southeast Asia and China in the East.

2

WHAT WERE THE CULTURAL CAPABILITIES OF *HOMO ERECTUS*?

Having a larger brain than its ancestors, *Homo erectus* became increasingly able to adapt to different situations through the medium of culture. This is reflected by better-made tools, a greater variety of tool types, regional diversification of tool kits, use of fire, and improved organizational skills.

3

WHAT WERE THE CONSEQUENCES OF *HOMO ERECTUS'* IMPROVED ABILITIES TO ADAPT THROUGH CULTURE?

As culture became more important as the vehicle through which this species secured its survival, life became somewhat more secure than it had been. The result was increased reproductive success, allowing populations to grow, with "spillover" into previously uninhabited regions. This expansion in turn contributed to the further evolution of culture, as populations of *Homo erectus* had to find solutions to new problems of existence in newly inhabited regions.

In 1891, the Dutch army surgeon Eugene Dubois, intent upon finding the fossils of a "missing link" between humans and apes, set out for Indonesia (then the Dutch East Indies), which he considered to have provided a suitable environment for such a creature. At Trinil, on the island of Java, Dubois found what he was searching for: the fossil remains of a primitive kind of hominine, consisting of a skull cap, a few teeth, and a thighbone. Its features seemed to Dubois part ape, part human. Indeed Dubois at first thought the remains did not even belong to the same individual. The flat skull, for example, with its low forehead and enormous brow ridges, appeared to be like that of an ape; but it possessed a cranial capacity much larger than an ape's, even though small by modern human standards. The femur, or thighbone, was clearly human in shape and proportions and indicated the creature was a biped. Although Dubois called his find *Pithecanthropus erectus,* or "erect ape man," it has since been assigned to the species *Homo erectus.*

HOMO ERECTUS FOSSILS

Until 1.8 million years ago, hominines were not to be found living anywhere but in Africa. It was on this continent that hominines, and later the genus *Homo,* originated. It was also in Africa that the first stone tools were invented. But by the time of *Homo erectus,* hominines had spread far beyond the confines of their original homeland. Fossils of this species are now known from a number of localities not just in Africa, but in China, Europe, Georgia, and India, as well as Java (Figure 8.1). Although remains of this species have been found in many different places in three continents, the remains show very little significant physical variation. Evidence suggests, however, that populations of *H. erectus* in different regions of Africa, Asia, and Europe do show some differences from one another on a subspecific level.

Homo erectus from Java

For a long time, the scientific community was reluctant to accept Dubois' claim that his Javanese fossils were of human lineage. It was not until the 1930s, particularly when other fossils of *H. erectus* were discovered by G. H. R. von Königswald at Sangiran, Java, in the Early Pleistocene Djetis beds, that scientists almost without exception agreed that both discoveries were the remains of an entirely new kind of early hominine. Von Königswald found a small skull that fluorine analysis and (later) potassium-argon dating indicated be older than Dubois' approximately 500,000-

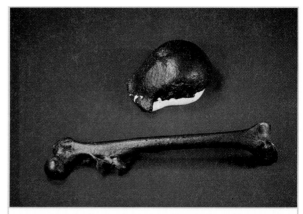

These casts of the skull cap and thighbone of *Homo erectus* were made from the original bones found by Eugene Dubois at Trinil, Java.

to 700,000-year-old Trinil specimen. Since 1960, additional fossils have been found in Java, and we now have remains of something like 40 individuals. A long continuity of *H. erectus* populations in Southeast Asia is indicated, from perhaps as many as 1.8 million to about 500,000 years ago. Interestingly, the teeth and jaws of some of the earliest Javanese fossils are in many ways quite similar to those of *Homo habilis.*[1]

---

[1]Tobias, P. V., & von Königswald, G. H. R. (1964). A comparison between the Olduvi hominines and those of Java and some implications for hominid phylogeny. *Nature, 204,* 515–518.

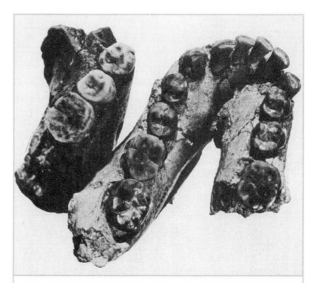

The fragment of the early *Homo erectus* jaw from Java on the left is nearly identical to the jaw of *Homo habilis* from Olduvai Gorge on the right.

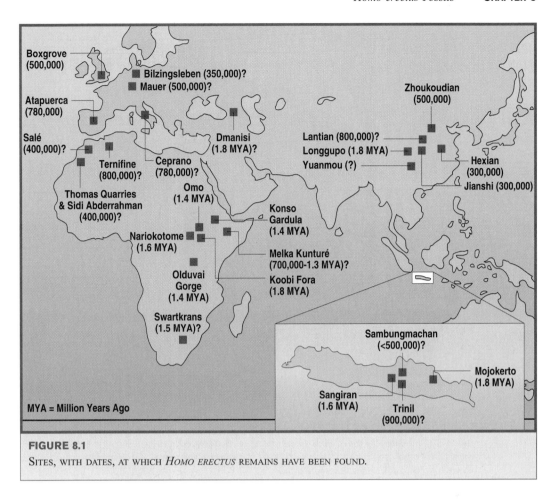

FIGURE 8.1

SITES, WITH DATES, AT WHICH *HOMO ERECTUS* REMAINS HAVE BEEN FOUND.

Homo erectus from China

A second population of *H. erectus* was found in the mid-1920s by Davidson Black, a Canadian anatomist then teaching at Peking Union Medical College. After purchasing in a Peking drugstore a few teeth for sale to local inhabitants for their supposed medicinal properties, Black set out for the nearby countryside to discover the owner of the teeth and perhaps a species of early hominine. At a place called Dragon Bone Hill in Zhoukoudian, 30 miles from Beijing, on the day before closing camp at the end of his first year of excavation, he found one molar tooth. Subsequently, a skull encased in limestone was found by W. C. Pei, Black's associate; and between 1929 and 1934, the year of his death, Black labored along with Pei in the fossil-rich deposits of Zhoukoudian, uncovering fragment after fragment of the hominine Black had named, on the basis of that first molar tooth, *Sinanthropus pekinensis,* or "Chinese man of Peking," now recognized as an East Asian representative of *H. erectus.*

After his death, Black's work was continued by Franz Weidenreich, a Jewish refugee from Nazi Germany. By 1938, the remains of more than 40 individuals, more than half of them women and children, had been dug out of the limestone. Most were represented by teeth, jawbones, and incomplete skulls. World War II brought a halt to the digging, and the original Zhoukoudian specimens were lost during the Japanese invasion of China. Fortunately, Weidenreich had made superb casts of most of the fossils and sent them to the United States. After the war, other specimens of *H. erectus* were discovered in China, at Zhoukoudian and at a number of other localities (Figure 8.1). The oldest skull is about 700,000 to 800,000 years old and comes from Lantian in Shensi Province. Even older is a fragment of a lower jaw from a cave in south-central China (Lunggupo) that is as old as the oldest Javanese fossils. Like some of their Javanese contemporaries, this Chinese fossil is reminiscent of African *H. habilis.* By contrast with these ancient remains, the original Zhoukoudian fossils appear to date between 600,000 and 300,000 years ago.

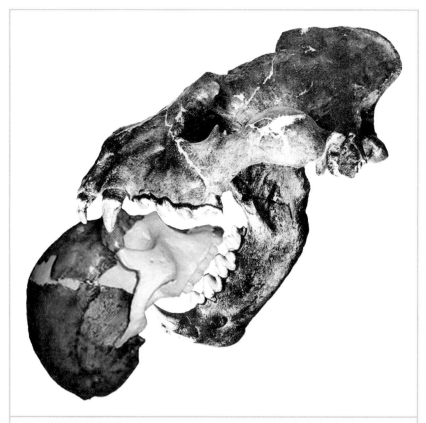

The fossils of *Homo erectus* from the cave at Dragon Bone Hill are the remains of individuals who were consumed in the cave by the now-extinct giant hyena. This composite shows how the giant hyena attacked the face.

Although the two populations overlap in time, the Chinese fossils are, on the whole, not quite as old as those from Java. Not surprisingly, Chinese *H. erectus* is a bit less "primitive" looking. Its average cranial capacity is about 1,000 cubic centimeters, compared to 900 cc for Javanese *H. erectus* (see Figure 8.2). The smaller teeth, short jaw, and lack of diastema in the lower dentition—a gap in the teeth to accommodate a large upper canine when the jaws are closed—of the Chinese are further evidence of their more modern status.

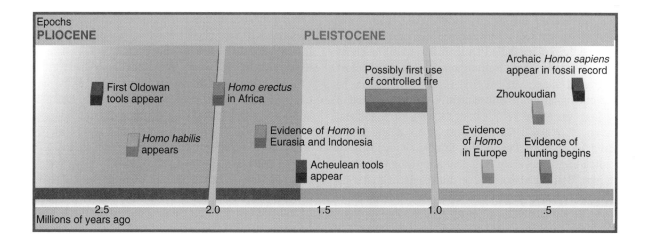

Epochs
PLIOCENE   PLEISTOCENE

Archaic *Homo sapiens* appear in fossil record

Possibly first use of controlled fire

First Oldowan tools appear

Homo erectus in Africa

Zhoukoudian

Homo habilis appears

Evidence of *Homo* in Eurasia and Indonesia

Evidence of *Homo* in Europe

Evidence of hunting begins

Acheulean tools appear

2.5   2.0   1.5   1.0   .5
Millions of years ago

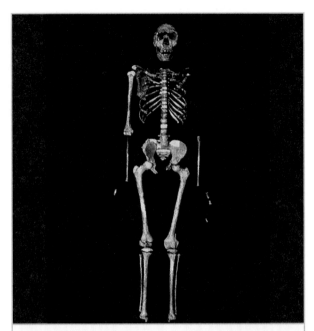

One of the oldest and certainly the most complete *Homo erectus* fossil is the Strapping Youth from Lake Turkana. The remains are those of a boy who died in his early teens.

Homo erectus from Africa

Although our samples of *H. erectus* from Asia remain among the best, several important specimens are now known from Africa. Fossils assigned to this species were discovered there as long ago as 1933, but the better-known finds have been made since 1960, at Olduvai and at Lake Turkana. Among them is the most complete *H. erectus* skeleton ever found, that of a boy who died 1.6 million years ago at about the age of 12. Another partial skeleton, that of an adult, had diseased bones, possibly the result of a massive overdose of vitamin A. This excess could have come from eating the livers of carnivorous animals, for they accumulate vitamin A in their livers at levels that are poisonous to human beings. Another possibility might have been heavy consumption of bee brood and other immature insects, producing the same result.

Generally speaking, African *H. erectus* skulls are similar to those from Asia; one difference is that their bones aren't quite as thick; another is that some Africans had smaller brow ridges. It may be, too, that individuals living in China were shorter and stockier, on the whole, than those living in Africa. Although some anthropologists

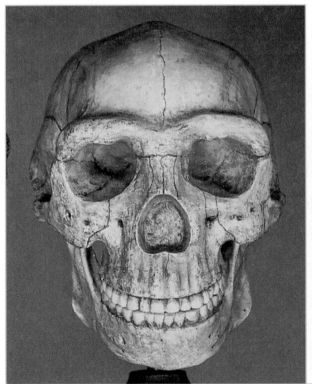

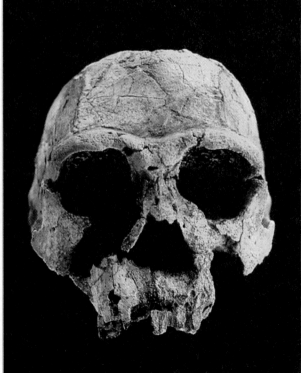

This photo of a reconstructed late *H. erectus* skull from Zhoukoudian, China, may be compared with the earlier African *erectus* skull shown at right.

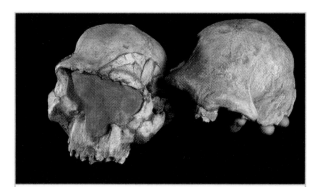

These two skulls of *Homo erectus* from Dmanisi, Georgia, are probably from a male and female. They are about 1.8 million years old and similar to contemporary fossils from Africa.

have argued that the African fossils represent a separate species (*H. ergaster*) and would restrict *H. erectus* to Asia, neither detailed anatomical comparisons nor measurements support such a separation.[2] Such differences as exist are minor and approximate the variation seen in *H. sapiens*. Consistent with this is the fact that a mandible almost 1.8 million years old from Dmanisi, Georgia—a region that lies between Africa on the one hand and Indonesia on the other—shows a mix of characters seen in African and Asian *erectus* populations.[3] Overall, it seems the Africans reveal no more significant physical variations from their Asian counterparts than are seen if modern human populations from East and West are compared. As in Asia, the most recent African fossils are less primitive in appearance, and the oldest fossils (up to 1.8 million years old) display features reminiscent of the earlier *Homo habilis*. Indeed, one of the problems is distinguishing early *H. erectus* from late *H. habilis*—precisely what one would expect if the one evolved from the other.

Homo erectus from Europe

Although Europe has been inhabited since at least 780,000 years ago, few fossils attributable to *H. erectus* have so far been found there. A robust shinbone from Boxgrove, England, and a large lower jaw from Mauer, Germany, are close to half a million years old. The jaw certainly came

from a skull wide at the base, as is that of *H. erectus*. Older yet are fragments of four individuals from Atapuerca Hill in north-central Spain and a skull from Ceprano in southern Italy. As might be expected, these remains are similar to contemporary *erectus* material from North Africa. This finding, and the fact that the earliest evidence of hominines in Europe comes from Spain and Italy, suggests that they arrived there by crossing from North Africa.[4] At the time, a mere 6 or 7 kilometers separated Gibraltar from Morocco (compared to 13 kilometers today), and islands dotted the straits from Tunisia to Sicily. Still there was no land connection, requiring that open water be crossed, but evidence from Indonesia (discussed later in this chapter) demonstrates that *H. erectus* was capable of doing this by 800,000 years ago. And all of this evidence, in turn, undermines arguments made by some European researchers that the early Europeans represent a separate species from *H. erectus* (Table 8.1). Such

TABLE 8.1	NAMES SOMETIMES USED FOR *HOMO ERECTUS* FOSSILS FROM EUROPE
Name	**Explanation**
Homo antecessor	Coined for the earliest fossils from Spain; *antecessor* is Latin for "explorer" or "pioneer."
Homo heidelbergensis	Originally coined for the Mauer jaw (Mauer is not far from Heidelberg), this name is now used by some as a designation for all European fossils from about 500,000 years ago until the appearance of the Neandertals (Chapter 9).

Because multiple species coexisted in the early period of hominine evolution, some paleoanthropologists believe the same must have been true in later hominine evolution. Acting on this belief, they refer to the European fossils by different species names than contemporaries in Africa and Asia, which they refer to as *H. ergaster* and *H. erectus*, respectively. Such a belief, however, remains to be proved. Because all these fossils share a suite of characteristics as well as a common niche, and gene flow between populations seems likely, a reasonable interpretation is that they constitute a single species with regional variation.

[2]Rightmire, G. P. (1998). Evidence from facial morphology for similarity of Asian and African representatives of *Homo erectus*. *American Journal of Physical Anthropology, 106,* 61.

[3]Rosas, A., & Bermdez de Castro, J. M. (1998). On the taxonomic affinities of the Dmanisi mandible (Georgia). *American Journal of Physical Anthropology, 107,* 159.

[4]Balter, M. (2001). In search of the first Europeans. *Science, 291,* 1,724.

This skull, from Ceprano, Italy, is one of the oldest fossils of *H. erectus* from Europe. It is close to 800,000 years old.

speciation would require isolation of Europeans from other populations, but if ancient humans could cross between North Africa and southern Europe at least once, if not twice, they could do it any number of times and thus maintain at least a modicum of gene flow between populations.

Other European fossils are not as old as the Mauer and Boxgrove remains and display a mosaic of features characteristic of both *H. erectus* and subsequent archaic *H. sapiens.* Here, as in Africa and Asia, a distinction between late *erectus* and early *sapiens* is difficult to make.

Physical Characteristics of *Homo erectus*

Apart from its skull, the skeleton of *H. erectus* differs only subtly from that of modern humans. Although its bodily proportions are like ours, it was more heavily muscled, its rib cage was conical rather than barrel-shaped, and its hips were narrower. Stature seems to have been in the modern range, as the youth from Lake Turkana was about 5 feet 3 inches tall. Long legs and short toes made for effective long-distance walking. Compared to *Homo habilis, H. erectus* was notably larger but displayed significantly less sexual dimorphism.

Cranial capacity in *H. erectus* ranged from 700 to 1,225 cubic centimeters (average about 1,000 cc), which compares with 752 cc for the nearly 2-million-year-old KNM ER 1470 skull from East Africa and 1,000 to 2,000 cc (average 1,300 cc) for modern human skulls (Figure 8.2). The cranium itself had a low vault, and the head was long and narrow. When viewed from behind, its width was greater than its height, with its greatest width at the base. The skulls of modern humans when similarly viewed are higher than they are wide, with the widest dimension in the region above the ears. The shape of the inside of *H. erectus'* braincase showed near-modern development of the brain, especially in the speech area. Although some anthropologists argue that the vocal apparatus was not adequate for speech, others argue that asymmetries of the brain suggest the same pattern of right-handedness with left cerebral dominance that, in modern peoples, is correlated with the capacity for language.[5]

Massive ridges over the eyes gave this early hominine a somewhat simian, beetle-browed appearance. *H. erectus* also possessed a sloping forehead and a receding chin. Powerful jaws with large teeth, a protruding mouth, and huge neck muscles added to the generally rugged appearance. Nevertheless, the face, teeth, and jaws of this hominine are smaller than those of *Homo habilis.*

---

[5]Holloway, R. L. (1981). The Indonesian *Homo erectus* brain endocasts revisited. *American Journal of Physical Anthropology, 55,* 521.

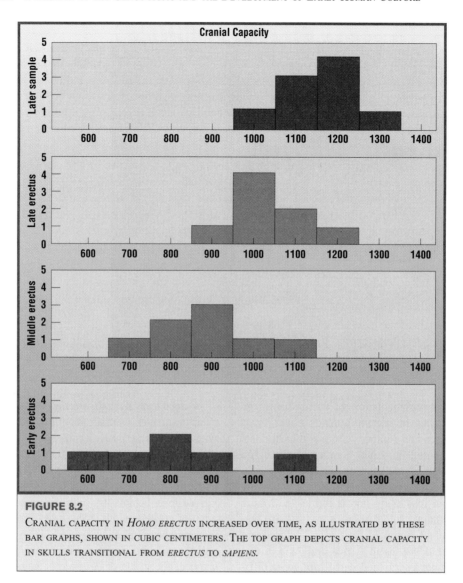

FIGURE 8.2

CRANIAL CAPACITY IN *HOMO ERECTUS* INCREASED OVER TIME, AS ILLUSTRATED BY THESE BAR GRAPHS, SHOWN IN CUBIC CENTIMETERS. THE TOP GRAPH DEPICTS CRANIAL CAPACITY IN SKULLS TRANSITIONAL FROM *ERECTUS* TO *SAPIENS*.

Relationship Between *Homo erectus* and *Homo habilis*

The smaller teeth and larger brains of *H. erectus* seem to mark continuation of a trend first seen in *Homo habilis*. What is new is the increased body size, reduced sexual dimorphism, and more "human" body form of *erectus*. Nonetheless, there is some resemblance to *habilis,* for example, in the conical shape of the rib cage, the long neck and low neck angle of the thighbone, the long low vault and marked constriction of the skull behind the eyes, and smaller brain size in the earliest *erectus* fossils. Indeed, as already noted, it is very difficult to distinguish

between the earliest *erectus* and the latest *habilis* fossils (Figure 8.3). Presumably the one form evolved from the other, evidently fairly abruptly, in the period between 1.8 and 1.6 million years ago.

THE CULTURE OF *HOMO ERECTUS*

As one might expect given its larger brain, *H. erectus* outstripped its predecessors in cultural ability. In Africa, Europe, and Asia, there was refinement of the stone toolmaking technology begun by the makers of earlier flake and chopper tools. At some point, fire began to be used

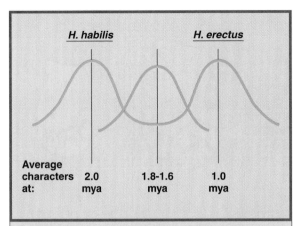

FIGURE 8.3

To understand the evolution of any species, the full range of variation must be considered, not merely typical representatives. The fact that fossils seemingly attributed to *H. habilis* and *H. erectus* coexisted between 1.8 and 1.6 million years ago (mya) need not mean coexistence of two separate species. If one evolved from the other, we would expect that at some point, the full range of variation included some individuals that still resembled *habilis*, whereas others were increasingly taking on the appearance of *erectus*.

Homo erectus made a variety of Acheulean handaxes.

for protection, warmth, and cooking, though precisely when is still a matter for debate. Finally, there is indirect evidence that the organizational and planning abilities of *H. erectus,* or at least the later ones, were improved over those of their predecessors.

The Acheulean Tool Tradition

Associated with the remains of *Homo erectus* in Africa, Europe, and Southwest Asia are tools of the **Acheulean tradition.** The signature piece of this tradition is the handaxe: a teardrop-shaped tool pointed at one end with a sharp cutting edge all around. In East Africa, the earliest handaxes are about 1.6 million years old; those found in Europe are no older than about 500,000 years. At the same time that handaxes appeared, archaeological sites in Europe became dramatically more common than earlier ones, suggesting an influx of people bringing with them

Acheulean technology (and implying continued gene flow into Europe). Since the spread of the genus *Homo* from Africa took place before the invention of the handaxe, it is not surprising to find that different forms of tools were developed in East Asia.

That the Acheulean grew out of the Oldowan tradition is indicated by an examination of the evidence discovered at Olduvai. In Bed I, the lowest level, chopper tools were found along with remains of *Homo habilis.* In lower Bed II, the first crude handaxes were found intermingled with chopper tools. Acheulean handaxes having a more finished look about them appear in middle Bed II, together with *H. erectus* remains.

Early Acheulean tools represent a significant step beyond the generalized cutting, chopping, and scraping tools of the Oldowan tradition. The shapes of Oldowan tools were largely controlled by the original form, size, and mechanical properties of raw materials. The shapes of handaxes and some other Acheulean tools, by contrast, are more standardized, apparently reflecting arbitrary preconceived designs imposed upon a diverse range of primary forms.[6] Overall, sharper points and more regular cutting edges were produced, and more cutting edge was available from the same amount of stone.

---

[6]Ambrose, S. H. (2001). Paleolithic technology and human evolution. *Science, 291,* 1,750.

Acheulean tradition.   The toolmaking tradition of *Homo erectus* in Africa, Europe, and Southwest Asia in which handaxes were developed from the earlier Oldowan chopper.

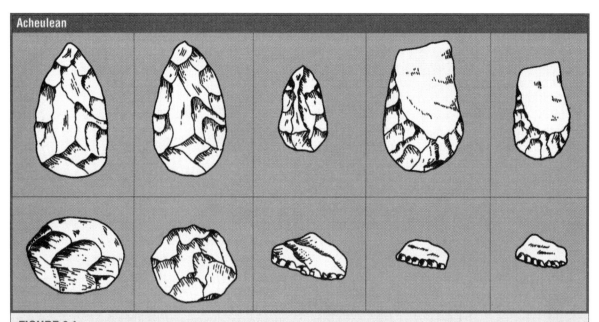

FIGURE 8.4

TEN PERCENT OF THE SHAPED TOOLS IN A TYPICAL ACHEULEAN ASSEMBLAGE ARE THE FORMS DRAWN HERE.

During this part of the ***Paleolithic,*** or Old Stone Age, tool kits began to diversify (Figure 8.4). Besides handaxes, *H. erectus* used tools that functioned as cleavers (these were handaxes with a straight, sharp edge where the point would otherwise be), picks and knives (variants of the handaxe form), and flake tools (generally smaller tools made by hitting a flint core with a hammerstone, thus knocking off flakes with sharp edges).

Many flake tools were byproducts of handaxe and cleaver manufacture. Their sharp edges made them useful as is, but many were retouched to make points, scrapers, borers, and other sorts of tools. Diversification of tool kits is also indicated by the smaller numbers of handaxes in northern and eastern Europe, where people relied more on simple flaked choppers, a wide variety of unstandardized flakes, and supplementary tools of bone, antler,

HIGHWAY 1

Take a trip to the Sierra de Atapuerca and learn about the earliest hominines of Europe. See virtual fossils, learn about the research team, their excavation techniques, and the place of these recently discovered specimens in human evolutionary history.
www.ucm.es/info/paleo/ata/english/main.html

HIGHWAY 2

The Peking Man World Heritage Site at Zhoukoudian presents the history, fossils, and artifacts from this site known by locals as Dragon Bone Hill. Review the evidence for the use of fire and hunting and gathering by *Homo erectus*.
www.unesco.org/ext/field/beijing/whc/pkm-site.htm

Paleolithic.   The Old Stone Age, characterized by manufacture and use of chipped stone tools.

The 803,000-year-old stone tool on the right is from the Bose Basin in southern China. Though not identical to Acheulean tools such as the handaxe on the left, the Bose Basin tools represent a comparable technology.

and wood. In eastern Asia, by contrast, people developed a variety of choppers, scrapers, points, and burins (chisel-like tools) different from those in the West. Besides direct percussion, anvil (striking the raw material against a stationary stone) and bipolar percussion (holding the raw material against an anvil, but striking it at the same time with a hammerstone) were used to make them. Although tens of thousands of stone tools have been found with *H. erectus* remains at Zhoukoudian, stone implements are not at all common in Southeast Asia. Here, favored materials likely were bamboo and other local woods, from which excellent knives, scrapers, and so on can be made.

Homo erectus and the Use of Bamboo[7]

Original Study

Bamboo provides, I believe, the solution to a puzzle first raised in 1943, when the late archaeologist Hallam Movius of Harvard began to publish his observations on Paleolithic (Old Stone Age) cultures of the Far East. In 1937 and 1938 Movius had investigated a number of archeological localities in India, Southeast Asia, and China. Although most of the archeological "cultures" that he recognized are no longer accepted by modern workers, he made another, more lasting contribution. This was the identification of the "Movius line" (which his colleague Carleton Coon named in his honor): a geographical boundary, extending through northern India, that separates two long-lasting Paleolithic cultures. West

---

[7]Adapted from Pope, G. C. (1989). Bamboo and human evolution. *Natural History, 10,* 50–54.

Original Study

of the line are found collections of tools with a high percentage of symmetrical and consistently proportioned handaxes (these are called Acheulean tools, after the French site of Saint Acheul). More or less similar tool kits also occur in Mongolia and Siberia, but with few exceptions (which are generally relatively late in time), not in eastern China or Southeast Asia, where more tools known as choppers and chopping tools prevail [Figure 8.5].

My own research on the Movius line and related questions evolved almost by accident. During the

course of my work in Southeast Asia, I excavated many sites, studied a variety of fossil faunal collections, and reviewed the scientific literature dealing with Asia. As part of this research I compared fossil mammals from Asia with those recovered from other parts of the world. In the beginning, my purpose was biostratigraphic—to use the animals to estimate the most likely dates of various sites used by early hominines. On the basis of the associated fauna, for example, I estimate that Kao Pah Nam [a site in Thailand] may be as old as 700,000

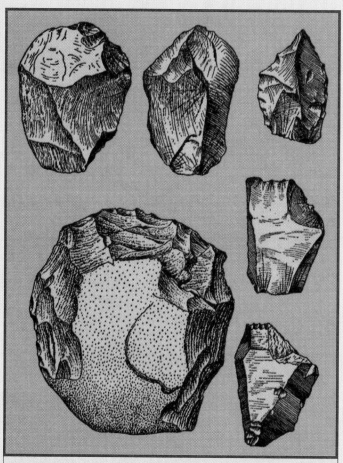

FIGURE 8.5

Choppers and flakes like these were used by *Homo erectus* at Zhoukoudian, China.

years. After years of looking at fossil collections and faunal lists, I realized that something was very strange about the collections from Southeast Asia: There were no fossil horses of Pleistocene age or for a considerable time before that. The only exceptions were a few horse fossils from one place in southern China, the Yuanmou Basin which was and is a special small grassland habitat in a low, dry valley within the Shan-Yunnan Massif.

To mammalian biostratigraphers this is unusual, since members of the horse family are so common in both the Old and New World that they are a primary means of dating various fossil localities. Fossil horses have been reported from western Burma, but the last one probably lived there some 20 million years ago. Not a single fossil horse turns up later than that in Southeast Asia, although they are known from India to the west and China to the north and every other part of Europe and Asia.

I then began to wonder what other normally common animals might be missing. The answer soon became apparent: camels—even though they too were once widespread throughout the world—and members and relatives of the giraffe family. Pleistocene Southeast Asia was shaping up as a kind of "black hole" for certain fossil mammals! These animals—horses, camels, and giraffids—all dwell in open country. Their absence on the Southeast Asian mainland and islands (all once connected, along with the now inundated Sunda Shelf) is indicative of a forested environment. The mammals that are present—orangutans, tapirs, and gibbons—confirm this conclusion.

The significance of this is that most reconstructions of our evolutionary past have emphasized the influence of savanna grassland habitats, so important in Africa, the cradle of hominine evolution. Many anthropologists theorize that shrinking forests and spreading grasslands encouraged our primarily tree-dwelling ancestors to adapt to ground-dwelling conditions, giving rise to the unique bipedal gait that is the hallmark of hominines. Bipedalism, in turn, freed the hands for tool use and ultimately led to the evolution of a large-brained, cultural animal. Tropical Asia, instead, apparently was where early hominines had to readapt to tropical forest.

In studying the record, I noticed that the forested zone—the zone that lacked open-dwelling mammals—coincided generally with the distribution of the chopper-chopping tools. The latter appeared to be the products of a forest adaptation that, for one reason or another, deemphasized the utilization of standardized stone tools. At least this held for Southeast Asia; what at first I could not explain was the existence of similar tools in northern China, where fossil horses, camels, and giraffids were present. Finally, I came upon the arresting fact that the distribution of naturally occurring bamboo coincided almost directly with the distribution of chopper-chopping tools. The only exceptions that may possibly be of real antiquity—certain handaxe collections from Kehe and Dingcun, in China, and Chonggok-Ni, in Korea—fall on the northernmost periphery of the distribution of bamboo and probably can be attributed to fluctuation of the boundary.

Today there are, by various estimates, some 1,000 to 1,200 species of bamboo. This giant grass is distributed worldwide, but more than 60 percent of the species are from Asia. Only 16 percent occur in Africa, and those on the Indian subcontinent—to an unknown extent the product of human importation and cultivation—are discontinuous in distribution and low in diversity. By far, the greatest diversity occurs in East and Southeast Asia.

Based on these observations, I hypothesized that the early Asians relied on bamboo for much of their technology. At first I envisioned bamboo simply as a kind of icon representing all nonlithic technology. I now think bamboo specifically must have been an extremely important resource. This was not, in my opinion, because appropriate rock was scarce but because bamboo tools would have been efficient, durable, and highly portable.

There are few useful tools that cannot be constructed from bamboo. Cooking and storage containers, knives, spears, heavy and light projectile points, elaborate traps, rope, fasteners, clothing, and even entire villages can be manufactured from bamboo. In addition to the stalks, which are a source of raw material for the manufacture of a variety of artifacts, the seeds and shoots of many species can be eaten. In historical times, bamboo has been to Asian civilization what the olive tree was to the

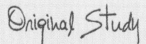

Original Study

Greeks. In the great cities of the Far East, bamboo is still the preferred choice for the scaffolding used in the construction of skyscrapers. This incomparable resource is also highly renewable. One can actually hear some varieties growing, at more than 1 foot per day.

Some may question how bamboo tools would have been sufficient for killing and processing large and medium-size animals. Lethal projectile and stabbing implements can in fact be fashioned from bamboo, but their importance may be exaggerated. Large game accounts for a relatively small proportion of the diet of many modern hunters and gatherers. Furthermore, animals are frequently trapped, collected, killed, and then thrown on a fire

and cooked whole prior to using bare hands to dismember the roasted carcass. There are many ethnographic examples among forest peoples of this practice.

The only implements that cannot be manufactured from bamboo are axes or choppers suitable for the working of hard woods. More than a few archaeologists have suggested that the stone choppers and resultant "waste" flakes of Asia were created with the objective of using them to manufacture and maintain nonlithic tools. Bamboo can be easily worked with stone flakes resulting from the manufacture of choppers (many choppers may have been a throwaway component in the manufacture of flakes).

The End

The greater variety and sophistication of tools found in the Acheulean and contemporary traditions is indicative of *H. erectus'* increased ability to deal with the environment. The greater the range of tools used, the greater the range of natural resources capable of being exploited in less time, with less effort, and with a higher degree of efficiency. For example, handaxes may have been used to kill game and dig up roots; cleavers to butcher; scrapers to process hides for bedding and clothes; and flake tools to cut meat and shape wooden objects. As argued in the Original Study, the differences between tool kits from the Far East and West are likely indicative of adaptation to specific regions. The same may be indicated by the differences between the tool kits of northern and eastern Europe on the one hand, and southern and western Europe on the other. One suggested explanation for this is that certain resources were scarcer in the latter region, which was more heavily forested than the former, and that this scarcity was a spur to increasing the efficiency of technology.[8]

The improved technological efficiency of *H. erectus* is also evident in the selection of raw materials. Although Oldowan toolmakers frequently used coarse-grained stone such as basalt, their Acheulean counterparts generally used such stone only for their heavier implements, preferring flint or other stones with a high silica content for the smaller ones. During later Acheulean times, two techniques were developed that produced thinner, more elegant axes with straighter edges and more regular forms. The **baton method** of percussion manufacture involved using a bone or antler punch to strike the edge of the flint core. This method produced shallow flake scars, rather than the crushed edge that the hammerstone method produced on the earlier Acheulean handaxes. In later Acheulean times, the striking-platform method was also used to create sharper, thinner axes; the toolmakers would often strike off flakes to create a flat surface near the edge. These flat surfaces, or striking platforms, were set up along the edge of the tool perpendicular to its sides, so that the toolmaker could remove long, thin flakes stretching from the edge across each side of the tool.

[8]Gamble, C. (1986). *The paleolithic settlement of Europe* (p. 310). Cambridge, England: Cambridge University Press.

Baton method. The technique of stone tool manufacture performed by striking the raw material with a bone or antler "baton" to remove flakes.

Large cutting tools, like this one (both sides are shown) from the Bose Basin of south China, were made and used in substantial numbers for only a brief period around 803,000 years ago. At the time, a large meteorite struck the region, igniting fires that caused widespread deforestation. The tools appear to be an adaptation to this event; once the vegetation recovered, early humans may have reverted to the use of bamboo for tools.

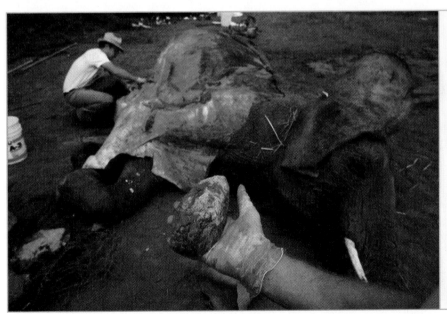

Experimentation on an elephant that died of natural causes demonstrates the effectiveness of Acheulean tools. Simple flint flakes easily slice through the thick hide, while handaxes sever large muscles. With such tools, two men working together can each butcher 100 pounds of meat in an hour.

Use of Fire

Another sign of *H. erectus'* developing technology is evidence of fires and cooking. Compelling evidence comes from the 700,000-year-old Kao Poh Nam rock shelter in Thailand, where a roughly circular arrangement of fire-cracked basalt cobbles was found in association with artifacts and animal bones. Because such rocks are not native to the rock shelter and are quite heavy, they probably had to have been carried in by hominines. The reason more readily available limestone rocks were not used for hearths is that, when burned, they produce a quicklime, which causes itchy and burning skin rashes.[9] The bones associated with the hearth (which was located near the rock shelter entrance, away from the deeper recesses favored by denning animals) show clear evidence of cut marks from butchering, as well as burning.

Homo erectus may have been using fire even earlier, based on evidence from Swartkrans, in South Africa. Here, in deposits estimated to date between 1.3 and 1 million years ago, bones have been found that had been heated to temperatures far in excess of what one would expect as the result of natural fires. Natural grass fires in the region will not heat bones above 212 degrees Fahrenheit, whereas coals in campfires reach temperatures from 900° to 1200° F. Consequently, bones thrown into such fires reach temperatures higher than 212° F. Furthermore, the burned bones do not occur in deeper deposits, even though natural grass fires would have been no less common. South African paleoanthropologists Andrew Sillen and C. K. Brain suggest that the purpose of the Swartkrans fires was protection from predators, as the bones were heated to such high temperatures that any meat on them would have been inedible.[10] Thus, fire may not have been "tamed" initially for cooking or to keep people warm; such uses may have come later.

---

[9]Pope, G. C. (1989). Bamboo and human evolution. *Natural History, 10,* 56.

[10]Sillen, A., & Brain, C. K. (1990). Old flame. *Natural History, 4,* 10.

Archaeologists excavate a hearth at a rock shelter in Kao Poh Nam, Thailand. This hearth testifies to human use of fire 700,000 years ago.

Whatever the reason for *Homo erectus'* original use of fire, it proved invaluable to populations that spread out of the tropics into regions with cooler climates. Not only did it provide warmth, but it may have assisted in the quest for food. In places like Europe and China, food would have been hard to come by in the long, cold winters, as edible plants were unavailable and the large herds of animals, whose mobility exceeded the potential of humans to maintain contact, dispersed and migrated. One solution could have been to search out the frozen carcasses of animals that had died naturally in the late fall and winter, using long wooden probes to locate them beneath the snow, wooden scoops to dig them out, and fire to thaw them so that they could be butchered and eaten.[11] Furthermore, such fire-assisted scavenging would have made available meat and hides of woolly mammoths, woolly rhinoceroses, and bison, which were probably beyond the ability of *H. erectus* to kill, at least until late in the species' career.

Perhaps it was the use of fire to thaw carcasses that led to the idea of cooking food, thereby altering the forces of natural selection, which previously favored individuals with heavy jaws and large, sharp teeth (food is tougher and needs more chewing when it is uncooked), thus favoring further reduction in tooth size along with supportive facial architecture. And it is a fact that, between early and late *H. erectus,* chewing-related structures undergo reduction at a rate markedly above the fossil vertebrate average.[12] Cooking did more than soften food, though. Cooking detoxifies a number of otherwise poisonous plants; alters digestion-inhibiting substances so that important vitamins, minerals, and proteins can be absorbed while in the gut, rather than just passing through it unused; and makes complex carbohydrates like starch—high-energy foods—digestible. With cooking, the nutritional resources available to humans were substantially increased and made more secure. The partial predigestion of food by cooking also may have caused a reduction in the size of the digestive tract. Despite its overall similarity of form to those of apes, the digestive tract of modern humans is substantially smaller. The advantage of this gut reduction is that it draws less energy to operate, thereby competing less with the high energy requirements of a larger brain. (Although a mere 2 percent of body weight, the brain accounts for about 20 to 25 percent of energy consumed at resting metabolism in modern human adults.[13])

Like tools, then, fire gave people more control over their environment. Possibly, *H. erectus* in Southeast Asia used fire, as have more recent populations living there, to keep areas in the forest clear for foot traffic. Certainly, the resistance to burning characteristic of many hardwood trees in this forest today indicates that fire has for a long time been important in their evolution. Fire may also have been used by *H. erectus,* as it was by subsequent hominines, not just for protection from animals out in the open but to frighten away cave-dwelling predators so that the fire-users might live in the caves themselves; and fire could then be used to provide warmth and light in these otherwise cold and dark habitations. Even more, it modified the natural succession of day and night, perhaps encouraging *H. erectus* to stay up after dark to review the day's events and plan the next day's activities. That *H. erectus* was capable of at least some planning is implied by the existence of populations in temperate climates, where the ability to anticipate the needs of the winter season by preparing in advance to protect against the cold would have been crucial to survival.[14]

OTHER ASPECTS OF *HOMO ERECTUS'* CULTURE

There is no evidence that populations of *H. erectus* lived anywhere outside the Old World tropics prior to a million years ago. Presumably, control of fire was a key element in permitting them to move into cooler regions like Europe and China. In cold winters, however, a fire is of little use without adequate shelter, and *H. erectus'* increased sophistication in the construction of shelters is suggested by three circular foundations of bone and stone 9 to 13 feet across at a 350,000-year-old site in Bilzingsleben, Germany. These could mark the bases of shelters of poles and grass similar to those used in recent times by people like the Bushmen of southern Africa. In the middle of one foundation was found a long elephant tusk, possibly used as a center post. Adjacent to these possible huts were hearths.

Keeping warm by the hearth is one thing, but keeping warm away from the hearth when procuring food or other necessities is another. Studies of modern humans

---

[11]Gamble, p. 387.

[12]Wolpoff, M. H. (1993). Evolution in *Homo erectus:* The question of stasis. In R. L. Ciochon & J. G. Fleagle (Eds.), *The human evolution source book* (p. 396). Englewood Cliffs, NJ: Prentice-Hall.

[13]Leigh, S. R., & Park, P. B. (1998). Evolution of human growth prolongation. *American Journal of Physical Anthropology, 107,* 347.

[14]Goodenough, W. H. (1990). Evolution of the human capacity for beliefs. *American Anthropologist, 92,* 601.

At some point, *H. erectus* ceased relying on scavenging as a source of meat, in favor of hunting live animals. One of those animals was the elephant hunted at Ambrona, Spain, where the tusk remains.

indicate that they can remain reasonably comfortable down to 50 degrees Fahrenheit with a minimum of clothing as long as they are active; below that temperature, the extremities cool to the point of pain;[15] thus the dispersal of early humans into regions where winter temperatures regularly went below 50° F, as they must have in China and Europe, was probably not possible without more in the way of clothing than hominines had hitherto worn. Unfortunately, clothing, like many other aspects of behavior, does not fossilize, so we have no direct evidence as to the kind of clothing worn by *H. erectus*. We only know that it must have been more sophisticated than before.

That *H. erectus* developed the ability to organize in order to hunt live animals is suggested by remains such as those from the 400,000-year-old sites of Ambrona and Torralba, in Spain. At the latter site, in what was an ancient swamp, were found the remains of several elephants, horses, red deer, wild oxen, and rhinoceroses. Their skeletons were dismembered, rather than in proper anatomical order, a fact that cannot be explained as a result of any natural geological process. Therefore, it is clear that these animals did not accidently get mired in a swamp where they simply died and decayed.[16] In fact,

the bones are closely associated with a variety of stone tools—a few thousand of them. Furthermore, there is very little evidence of carnivore activity, and none at all for the really big carnivores. Clearly, hominines were involved—not just in butchering the animals but evidently in killing them as well. It appears that the animals were actually driven into the swamp so that they could be easily dispatched. The remains of charcoal and carbon, widely but thinly scattered in the vicinity, raises the possibility that grass fires were used to drive the animals into the swamp. In any event, what we have here is evidence for more than opportunistic scavenging; not only was *H. erectus* able to hunt, but considerable organizational and communicative skills are implied as well.

Additional evidence for hunting 400,000 years ago was discovered accidently in 1995 in the course of strip mining at Schöningen in northern Germany. Here were found five well-made and finely balanced spears made entirely of wood, the longest one measuring more than 7 feet in length. These are sophisticated weapons made by hunters who clearly knew what they were doing; no novices were they! The effectiveness of their weapons is attested by the butchered bones of more than a dozen horses nearby.

There is no reason to suppose that *H. erectus* became an accomplished hunter all at once. Presumably, the most ancient members of this species, like *Homo habilis* before them, got the bulk of their meat through scavenging. As their cultural capabilities increased, however, they could have devised ways of doing their own killing, rather than waiting for animals to die or be killed by other predators.

---

[15]Whiting, J. W. M., Sodergem, J. A., & Stigler, S. M. (1982). Winter temperature as a constraint to the migration of preindustrial peoples. *American Anthropologist, 84,* 289.

[16]Freeman, L. G. (1992). *Ambrona and Torralba: New evidence and interpretation.* Paper presented at the 91st Annual Meeting, American Anthropological Association, San Francisco.

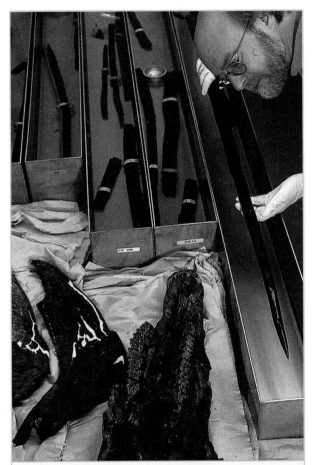

Shown here are wooden spears made by *Homo erectus* 400,000 years ago. Found in a bog in northern Germany, they are anything but crude, testifying to the sophisticated toolmaking and hunting skills developed by then.

At Bilzingsleben, Germany, archaeologists have uncovered an arrangement of stones and bones suggesting pavement of an area, perhaps for group rituals.

As they became more proficient predators over time, they would have been able to count on a more reliable supply of meat.

Yet other evidence of *H. erectus'* capabilities comes from the island of Flores, in Indonesia. This island lies east of a deepwater strait that has acted as a barrier to the passage of animals to and from Southeast Asia. To get to Flores, even at times of lowered sea levels, required crossing open water: at minimum 25 kilometers from Bali to Sumbawa, with a further 19 kilometers to Flores. That early humans did just this is indicated by the presence of 800,000-year-old stone tools.[17] Precisely how they navigated across the deep, fast-moving water is not known, but at the least it required some sort of substantial raft.

Evidence for a developing symbolic life is suggested by the increased standardization and refinement of Acheulean handaxes over time. Moreover, at several sites in Europe deliberately marked objects of stone, bone, and ivory have been found in Acheulean contexts (see p. 212). These include several objects from Bilzingsleben, Germany, among them an elephant bone with a series of regular lines that appear to have been deliberately engraved. Though a far cry from the later Paleolithic cave art of France and Spain, these are among the earliest Paleolithic artifacts that have no obvious utility or model in the natural world. Such apparently symbolic artifacts became more common in later phases of the Paleolithic, as more modern forms of the genus *Homo* appeared on the scene. Similarly, the world's oldest known rock carvings are associated with Acheulean tools in a cave in India.[18] Alexander Marshack argues that the use of such

---

[17]Gibbons, A. (1998). Ancient island tools suggest *Homo erectus* was a seafarer. *Science, 279,* 1,635.

This 300,000-year-old ox rib from a site in France is one of several from the Lower Paleolithic that exhibit engraved designs.

symbolic images requires some sort of spoken language, not only to assign meaning to the images but to maintain the tradition they seem to represent.[19] That such a symbolic tradition did exist is suggested by similar motifs on later Paleolithic artifacts. It is also in late Acheulean contexts on three continents that we have our earliest evidence for the use of red ochre, a pigment that more modern forms of *Homo* employed to color symbolic as well as utilitarian artifacts, to stain the bodies of the dead, to paint the bodies of the living, and (ultimately) to make notations and paint pictures.

THE QUESTION OF LANGUAGE

We do not, of course, know anything definitive about *H. erectus'* linguistic abilities, but the evidence for a developing symbolic life, as well as the need to plan for

seasonal changes and to coordinate hunting activities (and cross bodies of open water?), implies improving linguistic competence. In fact, the vocal tract and brain of *erectus* are intermediate between those of *H. sapiens* on the one hand and earlier *Australopithecus* on the other. Another clue is the size of the **hypoglossal canal,** the opening in the skull through which the nerve that controls tongue movements, so important for spoken language, passes from the skull (Figure 8.6). In modern humans this is twice the size that it is in any ape. It is in the skulls of late *H. erectus,* about 500,000 years ago, that we first see this characteristic in fossil remains.[20] Possibly, a changeover from gestural to spoken language was a driving force in these evolutionary changes. It also may have played a role in reduction of tooth and jaw size, thereby facilitating the ability to articulate speech sounds.

Certainly, the advantages of a spoken language over a gestural one seem to be obvious; not only does one *not* have to stop whatever one is doing with one's hands to "talk" (useful to a species increasingly dependent on tool use), but it is possible to talk in the dark, past opaque

[18]Bednarik, R. G. (1995). Concept-mediated marking in the lower Paleolithic. *Current Anthropology, 36,* 610–611.

[19]Marshack, A. (1976). Some implications of the paleolithic symbolic evidence for the origin of language. *Current Anthropology, 17,* 280.

[20]Cartmill, M. (1998). The gift of gab. *Discover 19*(11), 64.

Hypoglossal canal. The opening in the skull through which the tongue-controlling hypoglossal nerve passes.

objects, or among people whose gaze is concentrated on something else (potential prey, for example).

With *H. erectus,* then, we find a clearer manifestation of the interplay among cultural, physical, and environmental factors than ever before. However slowly, social organization, technology, and communication developed in tandem with an increase in brain size and complexity. In fact, the cranial capacity of late *H. erectus* is 31 percent greater than the mean for early *erectus,* a rate of increase more rapid than the average fossil vertebrate rate.[21] As a consequence of these, *H. erectus'* resource base was enlarged significantly; the supply of meat could be increased by hunting as well as by scavenging, and the supply of plant foods was increased as cooking allowed the consumption of vegetables that otherwise are toxic or indigestible. This, along with an increased ability to modify the environment in advantageous ways—for example, by using fire to provide warmth—undoubtedly contributed to a population increase and territorial expansion. In humans, as in other mammals, any kind of adaptation that enhances reproductive success causes population growth. This growth causes fringe populations to spill over into neighboring regions previously uninhabited by the species.

Thus, *Homo erectus* was able to move into areas that had never been inhabited by hominines before; first into the warm, southern regions of Asia, and ultimately into the cooler regions of China and Europe.

---

[21]Wolpoff, pp. 392, 396.

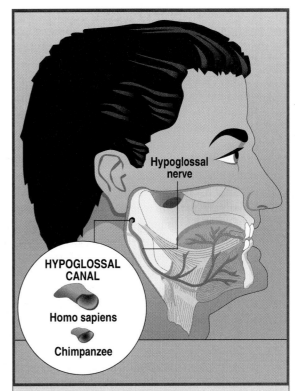

FIGURE 8.6

THE SIZE OF THE HYPOGLOSSAL CANAL IS MUCH LARGER IN HUMANS THAN IN CHIMPANZEES. THE NERVE THAT PASSES THROUGH THIS CANAL CONTROLS TONGUE MOVEMENT, AND COMPLEX TONGUE MOVEMENTS ARE INVOLVED IN SPOKEN LANGUAGE. ALL HOMININES AFTER ABOUT 500,000 YEARS AGO HAVE THIS ENLARGED HYPOGLOSSAL CANAL.

CHAPTER SUMMARY

The remains of *Homo erectus* have been found at several sites in Africa, Europe, China, and Java. The earliest is 1.6 million years old, and the species endured until about 400,000 years ago, by which time fossils exhibit a mosaic of features characteristic of both *H. erectus* and *H. sapiens*. *Erectus* appears to have evolved, rather abruptly, from *Homo habilis*. From the neck down, the body of *H. erectus* was essentially modern in appearance, and much larger than in earlier hominines. The brain, although small by modern standards, was larger than that of *H. habilis*. The skull was generally low, with maximum breadth near its base, and massive brow ridges. Powerful teeth and jaws added to a generally rugged appearance.

With *H. erectus* we find a greater interaction among cultural, physical, and environmental factors than ever before. Social organization and improved technology developed along with an increase in brain size. The Oldowan chopper evolved into the Acheulean handaxe. These tools, the earliest of which are about 1.4 million years old, are teardrop-shaped, with a pointed end and sharp cutting edges. They were remarkably standardized in form over large areas. During Acheulean times, tool cultures began to diversify. Along with handaxes, tool kits included cleavers, picks, scrapers, and flakes. Further signs of *H. erectus'* developing technology was the selection of different stone for different tools and the use of fires to provide protection, warmth, and light; thawing frozen carcasses; and cooking. Cooking is a significant cultural adaptation because it took the place of certain physical adaptations such as large, heavy jaws and teeth, because cooked food is easier to chew. Because it detoxifies various substances in plants, cooking also increased the food resources available and allowed reduction in the size of the digestive tract. Reduced jaw and tooth size may also correlate with a change from a gestural to spoken language. The complex tongue movements associated with speech are also indicated by features of the skull, and aspects of *H. erectus'* behavior imply improved communicative skills.

During later Acheulean times, *H. erectus* used the baton and striking-platform methods to make thinner axes with straighter, sharper cutting edges. From Germany comes evidence of the building of huts and the making of nonutilitarian artifacts; from Spain comes evidence of cooperative efforts to kill large amounts of game.

H. erectus' improved organizational, technological, and communicative abilities led to more effective hunting and a greater ability to modify the environment in advantageous ways. As a result, the populations of these early hominines increased and they expanded into new geographic areas.

CLASSIC READINGS

Campbell, B. G., & Loy, J. D. (1995). *Humankind emerging* (7th ed.). New York: HarperCollins.

This well-illustrated book has three good chapters on *Homo erectus* and their way of life.

Ciochon, R. L., & Fleagle, J. G. (Eds.). (1993). *The human evolution source book.* Englewood Cliffs, NJ: Prentice-Hall.

Part V of this book reproduces eight articles that deal with a variety of topics on the history of recovery, diversity, tempo, and mode of evolution and culture of *H. erectus.* An introduction by the editors puts the articles in context.

Gamble, C. (1986). *The Paleolithic settlement of Europe.* Cambridge, England: Cambridge University Press.

Although it does not deal exclusively with *Homo erectus,* this work does discuss material from Europe associated with this species. In doing so, it takes a critical stance as to conventional interpretations and offers novel explanations of *H. erectus'* behavior based on a better understanding of the process of archaeological site formation.

Rightmire, G. P. (1990). *The evolution of Homo erectus: Comparative anatomical studies of an extinct human species.* Cambridge, England: Cambridge University Press.

This is the standard work on our current understanding of *Homo erectus.*

White, E., & Brown, D., et al., and the editors of Time-Life. (1973). *The first men.* New York: Time-Life.

This magnificently illustrated volume in the Time-Life *Emergence of Man* series deals with *Homo erectus.* Its drawbacks are that it is not up-to-date, and it portrays early *H. erectus* as too much of a big game hunter; nevertheless, it remains a good introduction to many of the classic fossils, sites, and tools associated with this hominine.

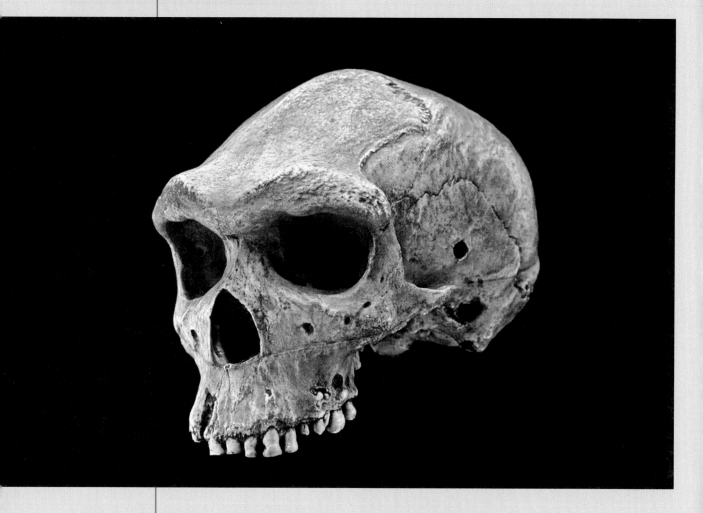

CHAPTER 9

ARCHAIC *HOMO SAPIENS* AND THE MIDDLE PALEOLITHIC

This skull from Kabwe, in Zambia, is an example of archaic *Homo sapiens* from Africa. Like its contemporaries elsewhere in Africa, China, Europe, and Southeast Asia, it has a modern-sized brain in a skull that retains on the outside features of its *Homo erectus* ancestry.

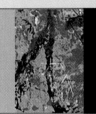

1

WHO WAS "ARCHAIC" HOMO SAPIENS?

"Archaic" *Homo sapiens* is the name used for members of this species with essentially modern-sized brains in skulls that still retained a number of ancestral features. Descended from *Homo erectus,* the transition took place between about 400,000 and 200,000 years ago. Best known of archaic *sapiens* are the Neandertals, who lived in Europe and western Asia between about 200,000 and 35,000 years ago. Other populations somewhat like them lived in Africa, China, and Southeast Asia.

2

WHAT WAS THE CULTURE OF ARCHAIC HOMO SAPIENS LIKE?

By 200,000 years ago, the human brain had reached its modern size, and by then human culture everywhere had become rich and varied. People not only made a wide variety of tools for special purposes, but they also made objects for purely symbolic purposes, engaged in ceremonial activities, and cared for the old and disabled.

3

WHAT BECAME OF THE NEANDERTALS?

Although there is some debate, the most likely explanation is that their contemporaries, and at least some of the Neandertals themselves, evolved into anatomically modern versions of *Homo sapiens*. This seems to have happened as different features of modern anatomy arose in different regional populations and were carried to others through gene flow. Thus, human populations on all three continents of the Old World seem to have contributed to the making of modern humans.

The anthropologist attempting to piece together the innumerable parts of the puzzle of human evolution must be as good a detective as a scholar, for the available evidence is often scant, enigmatic, or full of misleading clues. The quest for the origin of modern humans from more ancient representatives of the genus *Homo* has elements of a detective story, for it contains a number of mysteries concerning the emergence of humanity, none of which has been completely resolved to this day. The mysteries involve the appearance of the first fully sapient humans, the identity of the Neandertals, and the relationship of both to more modern forms.

THE APPEARANCE OF *HOMO SAPIENS*

At various sites in Europe and Africa, a number of hominine fossils—primarily skulls, jaws, and jaw fragments—have been found that seem to date roughly between 400,000 and 200,000 years ago. Most consist of parts of one or a very few individuals, the one exception consisting of a large number of bones and teeth from the Sierra de Atapuerca in northern Spain. Here, sometime between 325,000 and 205,000 years ago,[1] the remains of at least 32 individuals of both sexes, juveniles as well as adults, were deliberately dumped (after defleshing their skulls)

by their contemporaries into a deep cave shaft known today as Sima de los Huesos ("Pit of the Bones"). This makes it the best population sample from this time period anywhere in the world. As expected of any population, this one displays a significant degree of variation; cranial capacity ranges, for example, from 1,125 to 1,390 cubic centimeters, overlapping the upper end of the range for *H. erectus* and the lower end of the range for *H. sapiens*. Overall, the bones display a mix of features, some typical of *erectus,* others of *sapiens,* including some incipient Neandertal characteristics. Of interest is the fact that, varied as it is, the sample shows no more sexual dimorphism than displayed by modern humans.[2]

Other remains from Africa and Europe dating between 400,000 and 200,000 years ago have sometimes been classified as *H. sapiens*—for example, skulls from Ndutu in Tanzania, Swanscombe in England, and Steinheim in Germany—and sometimes as *H. erectus,* as in the case of skulls from several African sites as well as Arago, France; Bilzingsleben, Germany; and Petralona, Greece. Yet all have cranial capacities that fit within the range exhibited by the Sima de los Huesos skulls, and all display the same mosaic of *erectus* and *sapiens* features. Compared to us, for instance, the Swanscombe and Steinheim skulls are large and robust, with their maximum breadth lower on the

[1]Parés, J. M., Perez-Gonzalez, A., Weil, A. B., & Arsuaga, J. L. (2000). On the age of hominid fossils at the Sima de los Huesos, Sierra de Atapuerca, Spain: Paleomagnetic evidence. *American Journal of Physical Anthropology,* 111, 451–461.

[2]Lorenzo, C., Carretero, J. M., Arsuaga, J. L., Gracia, A., & Martinez, I. (1998). Intrapopulational body size variation and cranial capacity variation in middle Pleistocene humans: The Sima de los Huesos sample (Sierra de Atapuerca, Spain). *American Journal of Physical Anthropology, 106,* 30.

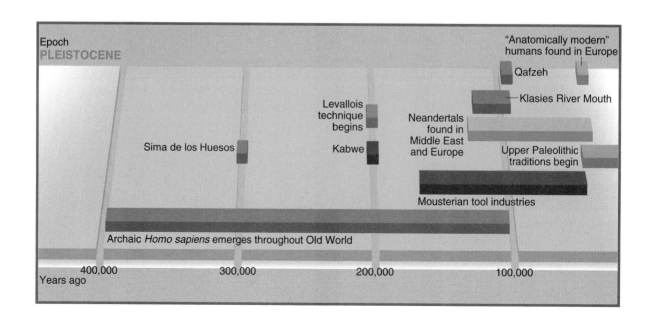

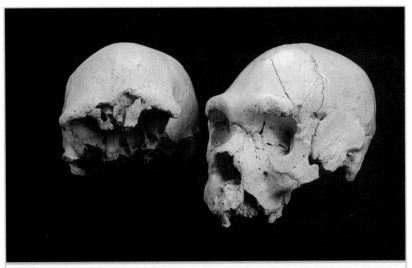

These two skulls are from the 300,000-year-old site of Sima de los Huesos in Spain and represent the transition from *H. erectus* to archaic *H. sapiens* in Europe.

skull, and they had more prominent brow ridges, larger faces, and bigger teeth. Similarly, the face of the Petralona skull resembles European Neandertals, but its back looks like *H. erectus.* Conversely, a skull from Salé in Morocco, which had a rather small brain for *H. sapiens* (930–960 cc), looks surprisingly modern from the back. Finally, various jaws from Morocco and France seem to combine features of *H. erectus* with those of the European Neandertals.

A similar situation exists in East Asia, where skulls from several sites in China exhibit the same sort of mix of *erectus* and *sapiens* characteristics. To call some of these early humans late *H. erectus* or early *H. sapiens* serves no useful purpose and merely obscures their apparently transitional status. Despite their retention of a number of features of *H. erectus,* their brain size shows a clear increase over that of even late representatives of that species (see Figure 8.2).

This skull from Ethiopia is one of several from Africa indicative of a transition from *Homo erectus* to *Homo sapiens.*

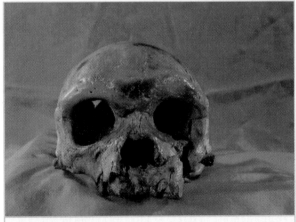

This skull from Dali, China, is representative of archaic *H. sapiens* in East Asia.

Levalloisian Technique

With the appearance of hominines transitional between *H. erectus* and *H. sapiens,* the pace of culture change began to accelerate. Although handaxes and other Acheulean tools were still made, a new method of flake manufacture was invented. This is the **Levalloisian technique,** and flake tools produced by this technique have been found widely in Africa, Europe, the Middle East, and even China. In the latter region, the technique could represent a case of independent invention, because eastern Asia is somewhat distinct culturally from the West. Or, it could represent the spread of ideas from one part of the inhabited world to another. In the Levalloisian technique, the core was shaped by removal of small flakes over its surface, following which a striking platform was set up by a crosswise blow at one end of the core of stone (Figure 9.1). Then the platform was struck, removing three or four long flakes, whose size and shape had been predetermined by the preceding preparation. What was left, besides small waste flakes, was a nodule that looked like a tortoise shell. This method produced a longer edge for the same amount of flint than the previous ones. The edges were sharper and could be produced in less time.

At about the same time, another technological breakthrough took place. This was the invention of hafting—the affixing of small stone bifaces and flakes in handles of wood—to make improved spears and knives. Unlike the older handheld tools made simply by reduction (flaking of stone or working of wood), these new composite tools involved three components: assembly of a handle or shaft, a stone insert, and binding materials. The acquisition and modification of each component involved planned sequences of actions that could be performed at different times and places.

With this new technology, regional stylistic and technological variants are clearly evident, suggesting emergence of more distinct cultural traditions and culture areas. At the same time, proportions of raw materials procured from faraway sources increases; whereas sources of stone for Acheulean tools were rarely more than 20 km away, Levalloisian tools are found up to 300 km from the sources of their stone.[3]

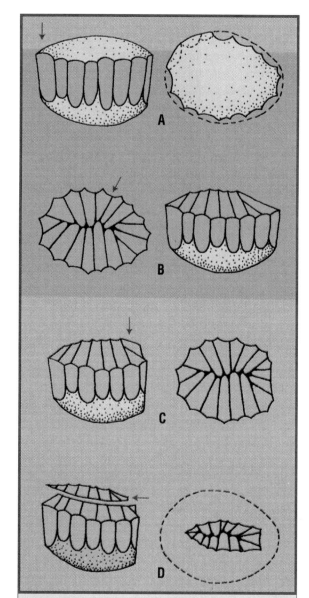

FIGURE 9.1

These drawings show top and side views of the steps in the Levalloisian technique. Drawing A shows the preparatory flaking of the stone core; B, the same of the top surface; C, the striking platform; and D, the final step of detaching a flake of a size and shape predetermined by the preceding steps.

---

[3]Ambrose, S. H. (2001). Paleolithic technology and human evolution. *Science, 291,* 1,752.

Levalloisian technique. Toolmaking technique by which three or four long triangular flakes were detached from a specially prepared core. Developed by humans transitional from *Homo erectus* to *Homo sapiens.*

Another development, in Africa, was the increasing use of yellow and red pigments of iron oxide, becoming especially common by 130,000 years ago.[4] This may signal a rise in ritual activity, as may the deliberate deposition of the human remains in the Sima de los Heusos, already noted. One possibility is that this involved ritual activity that presaged burial of the dead, a practice that became common after 100,000 years ago. Alternatively, the presence of other animal bones in the same pit with humans raises the possibility that all were eaten by the people who then simply dumped the bones.

Archaic *Homo sapiens*

Of all the remains of archaic *H. sapiens,* none have received more attention that those from Europe. The first publicized discovery came in 1856, 3 years before publication of Darwin's *On the Origin of Species.* In that year, the skeletal remains of a man were found in the Neander Valley—Neandertal in German—near Dusseldorf, Germany. Although the discovery was of considerable interest, the experts were generally at a loss as to what to make of it. Examination of the fossil skull, a few ribs, and some limb bones revealed that the individual was a human being, but it did not look "normal." Some people believed the bones were those of a sickly and deformed contemporary. Others thought the skeleton belonged to a soldier who had succumbed to "water on the brain" during the Napoleonic Wars. One prominent anatomist thought the remains were those of an idiot suffering from malnutrition, whose violent temper had gotten him into many scrapes, flattening his forehead and making his brow ridges bumpy.

The idea that **Neandertals,** as remains like this came to be called, were somehow deformed or aberrant was given impetus by an analysis of a skeleton found in 1908 near La Chapelle-Aux-Saints in France. The analysis mistakenly concluded that the specimen's brain was apelike and that it walked like an ape. Although a team of North American investigators subsequently proved that this French Neandertal specimen was that of an elderly

H. sapiens who had suffered from malnutrition, severe arthritis, and other deformities, the apelike image has persisted. To many nonanthropologists, Neandertal has become the quintessential "caveman," portrayed by imaginative cartoonists as a slant-headed, stooped, dim-witted individual clad in animal skins and carrying a big club as he plods across the prehistoric landscape, perhaps dragging behind him an unwilling female or a dead leopard. The stereotype has been perpetuated in many a work of fiction, one of the more recent being John Darnton's *Neanderthal,* published in 1997. So it is that many people still think of Neandertals as brutish and incapable of spoken language, abstract or innovative thinking, or even thinking ahead.

Despite this popular stereotype, evidence was forthcoming that Neandertals were nowhere near as brutish and apelike as originally portrayed, and some scholars began to see them as no more than "less finished" versions of the anatomically modern populations that held exclusive sway in Europe and the Middle East after 30,000 years ago. For example, C. Loring Brace of the University of Michigan observes that such "classic" Neandertal features as a sloping forehead, a bunlike back of the skull, and a distinctively small, inward-sloping mastoid process (behind the ear) are commonly present in medieval skulls from Denmark and Norway.[5] Nevertheless, Neandertals are somewhat distinctive, when compared to more recent populations. Although they held modern-sized brains (average cranial capacity 1,400 cc, versus 1,300 cc for modern *H. sapiens*), Neandertal skulls are notable in the projection of their noses and teeth and the swollen appearance of the midfacial region. This is due at least in part to the large size of their front teeth, which were heavily used for tasks other than chewing. In many individuals, front teeth were worn down to the stubs of their roots by 35 to 40 years of age. The large noses, for their part, probably were necessary to warm frigid air to prevent damage to the lungs and brain, and to moisten and clean the dry, dusty air of the glacial climate. The eye sockets were also positioned well forward, with prominent brow ridges above them. At the back of the skull, a bunlike bony mass provided for

---

[4]Barham, L. S. (1998). Possible early pigment use in south-central Africa. *Current Anthropology, 39,* 703–710.

[5]Ferrie, H. (1997). An interview with C. Loring Brace. *Current Anthropology, 38,* 861.

Neandertals.   Representatives of "archaic" *Homo sapiens* in Europe and western Asia, living from about 130,000 years ago to about 35,000 years ago.

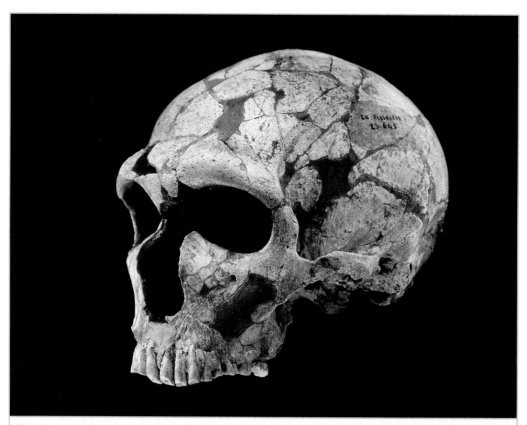

This Neandertal, from a site in France, shows the marked bony ridge above the eyes, receding forehead, and heavy wear on the front teeth that are common in these Europeans.

attachment of powerful neck muscles, needed to counteract the weight of a heavy face.

Both sexes were extraordinarily muscular, with extremely robust and dense limb bones. Relative to body mass, the limbs were relatively short (as they are in modern humans native to especially cold climates). Details of the shoulder blades indicate the importance of overarm and downward thrusting movements; their arms were exceptionally powerful, and pronounced attachments on their hand bones attest to a remarkably strong grip. It has been suggested that a healthy Neandertal could lift an average NFL linebacker over his head and throw him through the goalposts.[6] Their massive foot and leg bones (their shin bones, for example, were twice as strong as those of any recent human population) suggests a high level of endurance; evidently, Neandertals spent long hours walking and scrambling about. Because brain size is related to overall body mass as well as intelligence, the large average size of the Neandertal brain (compared to that of modern humans) is accounted for by their heavy, robust bodies.

The Neandertal pelvis, too, shows differences from that of anatomically modern humans, but these do not support suggestions that obstetric requirements were different for Neandertals than they are for modern humans. Dimensions of the pelvic outlet are fully consistent with those of a modern woman of the same size.[7] Differences in pelvic shape are easily accounted for as a consequence of posture-related biomechanics and deviation in modern humans from a shape characteristic of earlier hominines.

[6]Shreeve, J. (1995). *The Neandertal enigma: Solving the mystery of modern human origins* (p. 5). New York: William Morrow.

[7]Wolpoff, M. H. (1999). Review of Neandertals and modern humans in western Asia. *American Journal of Physical Anthropology, 109,* 418.

As this face-off between paleoanthropologist Milford Wolpoff and his reconstruction of a Neandertal shows, the latter did not differ all that much from modern humans of European descent.

African, Chinese, and Javanese Populations

Because Neandertal fossils are so numerous, have been known for so long, and are relatively well dated (30,000 to 130,000 years ago), they have received much more attention than have other populations of archaic *H. sapiens.* Nevertheless, outside Europe and western Asia, a number of skulls have been found in Africa, China, and Java that date to roughly the same time period.

Among them are 11 skulls that were found in the 1930s at Ngandong, Java. Though their dating was not precisely known, they were generally considered to be Southeast Asian equivalents of the Neandertals with modern-sized brains (from 1,013 to 1,252 ccs), while on the exterior they retained features of earlier Javanese *H. erectus.* With time, opinion on their dating changed, with scholars regarding them as considerably earlier than the Neandertals. This opinion focused attention on their resemblance to *erectus,* so that when their dating was recently revised (to sometime between 53,000 and 27,000 years ago) some concluded that this proved a late survival of *erectus* in Asia, contemporary with *H. sapiens*

In China, the Maba skull is the one most like the Neandertals. Its round eye orbits are without precedent in the Far East and suggest gene flow from Western populations.

elsewhere. But the skulls remain what they always were: representatives of archaic *sapiens,* with modern brains in otherwise ancient-looking skulls.

Shown on the left is one of the skulls of archaic *H. sapiens* from Ngandong, Java. On the right is an anatomically modern human skull from lake Mungo in Australia. A similarity between the two is obvious and suggests continuity of populations in Southeast Asia.

African and Asian contemporaries of the Neandertals differ from the Neandertals primarily in their lack of midfacial projection and massive muscle attachments on the back of the skull. Thus, the Neandertals represent an extreme form of archaic *sapiens*. Elsewhere, the archaics look like robust versions of the early modern populations that lived in the same regions or, if one looks backward, somewhat less primitive versions of the *H. erectus* populations that preceded them. All had fully modern-sized brains in skulls that still retained some older features on the outside.

THE CULTURE OF ARCHAIC *HOMO SAPIENS*

As the first hominines to possess brains of modern size, archaic *H. sapiens* had, as we would expect, greater cultural capabilities than their near ancestors. Such a brain made possible technological innovations as well as conceptual thought of considerable sophistication and, almost surely, communication by speech. In short, Neandertals and others like them were a fully sapient species of human being, relatively successful in surviving and thriving even in environments that would seem to us impossibly cold and hostile.

Middle Paleolithic

The improved toolmaking capabilities of archaic *H. sapiens* are represented by various **Middle Paleolithic** traditions, of which the best known are the Mousterian and Mousterianlike traditions of Europe, western Asia, and North Africa. These date between about 166,000 and 40,000 years ago. Comparable traditions are found as far east as China and Japan, where they arose independently from local predecessors. All these traditions represent a technological advance over what had preceded them. For example, the 16 inches of working edge that an Acheulean flint worker could get from a 2-pound core compares with the 6 feet the Mousterian could get from the same core.

THE MOUSTERIAN TRADITION

The **Mousterian tradition** is named after the Neandertal site of Le Moustier, France. The presence of Acheulean handaxes at Mousterian sites is one indication that this culture was ultimately rooted in the older Acheulean

Middle Paleolithic. The middle part of the Old Stone Age characterized by the emergence of archaic *H. sapiens* and the development of the Mousterian tradition of toolmaking. • **Mousterian tradition.** Toolmaking tradition of the Neandertals and their contemporaries of Europe, western Asia, and northern Africa, featuring flake tools that are lighter and smaller than earlier Levalloisian flake tools.

tradition. Neandertals and their contemporaries developed Levalloisian techniques to make Mousterian flake tools that are lighter and smaller than those of the Levalloisian. Whereas Levalloisian toolmakers obtained only two or three flakes from one core, Mousterian toolmakers obtained many more smaller flakes, which were then skillfully retouched and sharpened for special purposes.

The Mousterian tool kits contained a much greater variety of tool types than the previous traditions: handaxes, flakes, scrapers, borers, gravers, notched flakes for sawing and shredding wood, and many types of points that could be attached to wooden shafts to form thrusting spears. Many other tools also were hafted in handles of wood or bone, and some populations were experimenting with bitumen as a glue. With this new and varied tool kit, humans intensified their utilization of food resources and increased the availability and quality of clothing and shelter. For the first time, people could cope with the nearly arctic conditions that became prevalent in Europe as the glaciers began to expand about 70,000 years ago.

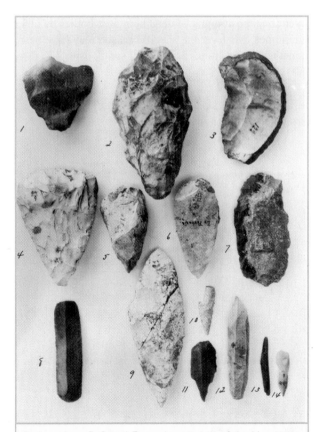

Tools such as 5, 6, and 7 are characteristic of the Mousterian tradition (1–4 are earlier, 8–14 later).

People likely came to live in cold climates as a result of a slow but steady population increase during the Paleolithic era. As this caused populations to gradually expand into previously uninhabited colder regions, humans developed a series of cold-climate adaptations that increased their cultural variability. Under near arctic conditions, vegetable foods are only rarely or seasonally available, and meat is the staff of life. In particular, animal fats, rather than carbohydrates, become the chief source of energy due to their slower rate of metabolism. Abundant animal fat in the diets of cold-climate meat eaters provides them with the extra energy needed for full-time hunting, as well as needed body heat. Insufficient fat in the diet produces lower resistance to disease, lassitude, and a loss of the will to work.

That meat was important to the makers of Mousterian tools is indicated by an abundance of associated animal bones, often showing clear cut marks. Frequently, the remains consist almost entirely of very large game—wild cattle (including bison), wild horses, and even mammoths and woolly rhinoceroses. At several sites there is striking evidence that particular species were singled out for the hunt. For example, at one site in the French Pyrenees, well over 90 percent of the faunal assemblage (representing at least 108 animals) consists of large members of the cattle family. These bones accumulated at the foot of a steep riverside escarpment, over which the animals were evidently stampeded. Similar mass hunting techniques are documented at other Mousterian sites: At La Quina in western France, a dense accumulation of cattle, horse, and reindeer bones (many with clear cut marks from butchering) occurred at the base of a steep cliff; at another site in the Channel Islands, dense deposits of mammoth and woolly rhinoceros bones indicate use of a deep coastal ravine for cliff-fall hunting. Clearly, the Neandertals were not mere unstructured or opportunistic hunters but engaged in a great deal of deliberate hunting of very large and potentially dangerous game.[8] This required careful planning, forethought, and logistical organization.

The importance of hunting to Mousterian peoples may also be reflected in their hunting implements, which are more standardized with respect to size and shape than are their domestic and maintenance implements (for maintaining necessary equipment). The complexity of the tool kit needed for survival in a cold climate may have played a role in lessening the mobility of the users of all these

---

[8]Mellars, P. (1989). Major issues in the emergence of modern humans. *Current Anthropology, 30,* 356–357.

possessions. That they were less mobile is suggested by the greater depth of deposits at Mousterian sites compared with those from the earlier ("Lower") Paleolithic. Similarly, evidence for long sequences of production, resharpening and discarding of tools, and large-scale butchering and cooking of game, along with evidence of efforts to improve accommodations in some caves and rock shelters through pebble paving, construction of simple walls, and the digging of postholes and artificial pits, all suggest that Mousterian sites were more than mere stopovers in peoples' constant quest for food. The large number of Mousterian sites uncovered in Europe and western Asia, as well as clear differences between them, is closely related to Neandertal's improved hunting techniques, based on superior technology in weapon and toolmaking and more efficient social organization than before. These, in turn, were closely related to Neandertal's fully modern brain size.

Neandertal society had developed, evidence shows, even to the point of being able to care for physically disabled members of the group. For the first time, the remains of "oldsters"—individuals well past their prime—are well represented in the fossil record. Furthermore virtually every elderly Neandertal skeleton that is reasonably complete shows evidence of trauma having been treated, with extensive healing of wounds and little or no infection.[9] Particularly dramatic examples include the remains of a blind man with a withered arm discovered in Shanidar Cave in Iraq, an individual found at Krapina in Croatia whose hand may have been surgically amputated, and a man badly crippled by arthritis unearthed at La Chapelle. The earliest example comes from a 200,000-year-old site in France, where a toothless man was able to survive probably because others in his group processed his food so he could swallow it. Whether or not this evidence indicates true compassion on the part of these early people is not known; what is certain is that culture had become more than barely adequate to ensure survival.

The Symbolic Life of Neandertals

Although earlier reports of evidence for some sort of "cave bear cult" have turned out to be far-fetched, indications of a symbolic life do exist. At several sites, there is clear evidence for deliberate burial of the dead. This is one reason for the relative abundance of reasonably complete Neandertal skeletons. To dig a grave large enough to receive an adult body without access to shovels suggests how important a social activity this was. Moreover, intentional positioning of dead hominine bodies by other hominines, whatever the specific reason may have been, nonetheless constitutes evidence of symbolism.[10] To date,

[9]Conroy, G. C. (1997). *Reconstructing human origins: A modern synthesis* (p. 427). New York: Norton.

[10]Schepartz, L. A. (1993). Language and modern human origins. *Yearbook of Physical Anthropology, 36,* 113.

This Neandertal skeleton from Shanidar Cave is of a man with a badly withered arm.

Forensic Archaeology

Anthropology Applied

Although the fields of Paleolithic and forensic archaeology might appear to have little in common, the two do share techniques of data recovery. The difference is that in one case what is recovered is evidence to be used in legal proceedings involving cases of murder, human rights abuses, and the like; in the other, the evidence is used to reconstruct ancient human behavior.

Forensic archaeologists commonly work closely with forensic anthropologists (Chapter 1). The relation between them is rather like that between a forensic pathologist, who examines a corpse to establish time and manner of death, and a crime scene investigator who searches the site for clues. While the forensic anthropologist deals with the human remains—often only bones and teeth—the forensic archaeologist controls the site, recording the position of all relevant finds and recovering any clues associated with the remains. In Rwanda, for example, a team assembled in 1995 to investigate a mass atrocity for the United Nations included archaeologists from the U.S. National Park Service's Midwest Archaeological Center. They performed the standard archaeological procedures of mapping the site, determining its boundaries, photographing and recording all surface finds, and excavating, photographing, and recording buried skeletons and associated materials in mass graves.[*]

In another example, Karen Burns of the University of Georgia was part of a team sent to northern Iraq after the Gulf War to investigate alleged atrocities. On a military base where there had been many executions, she excavated the remains of a man's body found lying on its side facing Mecca, conforming to Islamic practice. Although there was no intact clothing, two threads of polyester used to sew clothing were found along the sides of both legs. Although the threads survived, the clothing, because it was made of natural fiber, had decayed. "Those two threads at each side of the leg just shouted that his family didn't bury him," says Burns.[†] Proper though his position was, no Islamic family would bury their own in a garment sewn with polyester thread; proper ritual would require a simple shroud.

[*]Connor, M. (1996). The archaeology of contemporary mass graves. *SAA Bulletin, 14*(4), 6 & 31.

[†]Cornwell, T. (1995, November 10). Skeleton staff. *Times Higher Education*, p. 20.

at least 17 sites in Europe, South Africa, and Southwest Asia include Middle Paleolithic burials. To cite but two examples, at Kebara Cave in Israel, sometime between 64,000 and 59,000 years ago, a Neandertal male aged between 25 and 35 years was placed in a pit on his back, with his arms folded over his chest and abdomen. Some time later, after complete decay of attaching ligaments, the grave was reopened and the skull removed (a practice that, interestingly, is sometimes seen in burials in the same region roughly 50,000 years later). Another example is from Shanidar Cave in Iraq, where evidence was found of a burial accompanied by funeral ceremonies. In the back of the cave a Neandertal was buried in a pit. Pollen analysis of the soil around the skeleton indicated that flowers had been placed below the body and in a wreath about the head. Because the key pollen types were from insect-pollinated flowers, few if any of the pollen

grains could have found their way into the pit via air currents. The flowers in question consist solely of varieties valued in historic times for their medicinal properties.

Other evidence for symbolic behavior in Mousterian culture comes from the use of two different naturally occurring pigments: manganese dioxide and red ocher. Finds of these in human trash reveal clear evidence of scraping to produce powder, as well as crayonlike facets from use. Thus, Mousterian peoples were clearly using these for applying color to things. An example is the carved and shaped section of a mammoth tooth, illustrated on page 228, that was worked by Mousterian peoples about 50,000 years ago. One of a number of carved and engraved objects that may have been made for purely symbolic purposes, it is similar to a number of plaques of bone and ivory made by later Paleolithic peoples, and it is also similar to the *churingas* made of wood by

This carved symbolic plaque or *churinga* made from a section of a mammoth molar was excavated at the Mousterian site of Tata, Hungary. The edge is rounded and polished from long handling. The plaque has been symbolically smeared with red ocher. The reverse face of the plaque (right) shows the beveling and shaping of the tooth.

historic Australian aborigines for ritual purposes. The Mousterian object, which was once smeared with red ocher, has a highly polished face as if from long handling. Microscopic examination reveals that it was never provided with a working edge for any utilitarian purpose. As Alexander Marshack observes, "A number of researchers have indicated that the Neandertals did in fact have conceptual models and maps as well as problem-solving capacities comparable to, if not equal to, those found among anatomically modern humans."[11]

Evidence for symbolic activity on the part of Neandertals raises the possibility of the presence and use of musical instruments. One such may be a bone flute from a Mousterian site in Slovenia. The object consists of a hollow bone with perforations, and it has sparked controversy. Some see it as nothing more than a cave bear bone that was chewed on by carnivores—hence the perforations. Its discoverer, on the other hand, sees it as a flute. Unfortunately, the object is fragmentary; surviving are five holes, four on one side and one on the opposite side. The regular spacing of the four holes, the fact that

they fit perfectly the fingers of a human hand, and the location of the fifth hole at the base of the opposite side, at the natural location of the thumb, all lend credence to the flute hypothesis. Furthermore, signs of gnawing by animals is superimposed on traces of human activity.[12] Thus, the object cannot be rejected as a flute. Were it found in a later Paleolithic context, it would probably be accepted without argument; only because it was clearly made by a Neandertal, who some are reluctant to accept as fully human, has it been called into question.

Neandertals and Spoken Language

Among modern humans, the sharing of thoughts and ideas, as well as the transmission of culture from one generation to the next, is dependent upon a spoken language. Because the Neandertals had modern-sized brains and a tool kit comparable to that being used in historic times by Australian aborigines, it might be supposed that they had some form of spoken language. And as pointed out

[11]Marshack, A. (1989). Evolution of the human capacity: The symbolic evidence. *Yearbook of Physical Anthropology, 32,* 22.

[12]Otte, M. (2000). On the suggested bone flute from Slovenia. *Current Anthropology, 41,* 271.

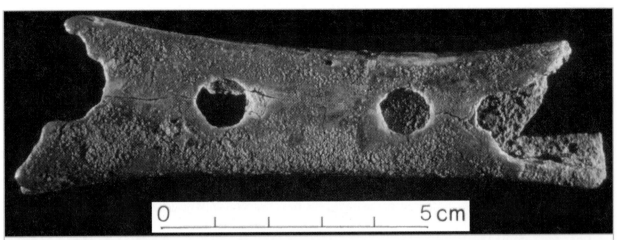

The first musical instrument? There is a strong possibility that this object, found in trash left by Neandertals, is all that remains of a flute made of bone.

by anthropologist Stanley Ambrose, the composite tools of Mousterian and contemporary peoples involved assembly of components in different configurations to produce functionally different tools. He likens this hierarchical assembly of parts into tools to grammatical language, "because hierarchical assemblies of sounds produce meaningful phrases and sentences, and changing word order changes meaning."[13] Furthermore, "a composite tool may be analogous to a sentence, but explaining how to make one is the equivalent of a recipe or a short story."[14] Talking Neandertals make a good deal of sense, too, in view of the evidence for the manufacture of objects of symbolic significance. Objects such as the mammoth tooth *churinga* already described would seem to have required some form of linguistic explanation.

Despite such considerations, some have argued that the Neandertals lacked the physical features necessary for spoken language. For example, the larynx was asserted to be higher in the throat than it is in modern humans, a reconstruction we now know to be faulty. In the skeleton from the Kebara Cave burial, for instance, the shape and position of the hyoid bone (the "wish bone," associated with the larynx) show that the vocal tract was quite adequate for speech. This is especially noteworthy, for humans pay a high price for the way their vocal tract is positioned. With the lowered position of our larynx, it is far easier for us to choke to death than it is for other mammals. (Before the Heimlich maneuver, choking on

food was the sixth leading cause of accidental death in the United States.)[15] The only advantage worth such a price seems to be the ability to speak.

With respect to the brain, paleoneurologists, working from endocranial casts, are agreed that Neandertals had the neural development necessary for spoken language. Indeed, they argue that the changes associated with speech began even before the appearance of archaic *Homo sapiens*.[16] Consistent is the size of the hypoglossal canal, which in Neandertals is like that of modern humans and unlike that of apes.[17] As discussed in the last chapter, this feature is apparent in hominine fossils that are at least 400,000 years old and indicates an ability to make the tongue movements necessary for articulate speech. Consistent, too, is an expanded thoracic vertebral canal (the thorax is the upper part of the body), a feature Neandertals share with modern humans but not early *Homo erectus* (or any other primate). This feature suggests the increased breath control required for speech.[18] This control enables production of long phrases or single expirations of breath, punctuated with quick inhalations at meaningful linguistic breaks.

Another argument—that a relatively flat base in Neandertal skulls would have prevented speech—has no

[13]Ambrose, P. 1,751.

[14]Ibid.

[15]Shreeve, p. 273.

[16]Schepartz, p. 98.

[17]Cartmill, M. (1998). The gift of gab. *Discover, 19* (11), 62.

[18]MacLarnon, A. M. & Hewitt, G. P. (1999). The evolution of human speech: The role of enhanced breathing control. *American Journal of Physical Anthropology, 109,* 341–363.

HIGHWAY 1

Play "Name that Skull" and learn to identify fossil hominines and other primate species from their skulls. This site has three graded levels of play.
www.geocities.com/athens/acropolis/5579/knowyourskull.html

HIGHWAY 2

A trip to the site "Neandertals: A Cyber Perspective" provides comprehensive evidence about the Neandertals. Learn about their discovery, lifeways, tool kits, and ritual practices.
http://sapphire.indstate.edu/~ramanank/index.html

HIGHWAY 3

Visit this site to learn more about the Neandertal question including features about making a documentary television program on this controversial subject.
www.pbs.org/wgbh/nova/neanderthals/

merit, as some modern adults show as much flattening, yet have no trouble talking. Clearly, when the evidence is considered in its totality, there seems no compelling reason to deny Neandertals the ability to speak.

ARCHAIC *HOMO SAPIENS* AND MODERN HUMAN ORIGINS

One of the hot debates in paleoanthropology today is over the question: Did populations of archaic *H. sapiens* in most, if not all, parts of the Old World connected by gene flow, evolve together into anatomically modern humans (the multiregional hypothesis)? Or, was there a single, geographic place of origin, from which a new species, anatomically modern *H. sapiens,* spread to replace existing populations of the archaic species everywhere else (the "Eve" or "Out of Africa" hypothesis)? Based on the fossil evidence from Africa and some parts of Asia, a good case can be made for the former, as opposed to the latter, hypothesis.

The Multiregional Hypothesis

As several anthropologists have noted, African, Chinese, and Southeast Asian fossils of archaic *H. sapiens* imply local population continuity from *Homo erectus,* through archaic, to modern *Homo sapiens,*[19] lending strong support to the interpretation that there was genetic continuity in these regions. For example, in China hominine fossils consistently have small forward-facing cheeks and flatter faces than their contemporaries elsewhere, as is still true today. In Southeast Asia and Australia, by contrast, skulls are consistently robust, with huge cheeks and forward projection of the jaws.

Although the idea of continuity from the earliest European fossils through the Neandertals is widely accepted, the idea that Neandertals were involved in the ancestry of modern Europeans has been resisted by many. No earlier than 36,500 years ago[20] a new technology, known as the **Aurignacian tradition,** spread into Europe from Southwest Asia, where its appearance marks the start of the **Upper Paleolithic** period. In both regions, human skeletons associated with Aurignacian tools are usually modern in their features (but a notable exception is the central European site of Vindija, where Neandertals are associated with an Aurignacian split-bone point).[21]

---

[19]Wolpoff, M. H., & Caspari, R. (1997). *Race and human evolution.* New York: Simon & Schuster.

[20]Zilhão, J. (2000). Fate of the Neandertals. *Archaeology, 53*(4), 30.

[21]Karavani, I., & Smith, F. H. (2000). More on the Neanderthal problem: The Vindija case. *Current Anthropology, 41,* 839.

Aurignacian tradition. Toolmaking tradition in Europe and western Asia at the beginning of the Upper Paleolithic. • **Upper Paleolithic.** The last part of the Old Stone Age, characterized by the emergence of more modern-looking hominines and an emphasis on the blade technique of toolmaking.

FRANZ WEIDENREICH (1873–1948)

Franz Weidenreich was born and educated in Germany, where he later held professorships in anatomy, first at Strassburg and then at Heidelberg. Although his early work was primarily in hematology (the study of blood), his scientific work shifted to the study of bones and related tissues, and in 1926 he published his first study of a human fossil, an archaic *Homo sapiens* cranium from Ehringsdorf. Two years later, he was appointed professor of anthropology at the University of Frankfurt.

In 1935, he was sent by the Rockefeller Foundation to take up the study of fossils of *Homo erectus* from Zhoukoudian, China, following the death of their discoverer, Davidson Black. When the Japanese invasion of China forced Weidenreich to leave, he took with him to the United States several painstakingly prepared casts, as well as detailed notes on the actual fossils. From these he was able to prepare a major monograph that set new standards for paleoanthropological reports. For this alone, anthropology owes him a great debt, for the fossils themselves were among the casualties of World War II.

Unlike many physical anthropologists of his time or ours, Weidenreich had an extensive firsthand knowledge of extant human fossils from several parts of the Old World: Europe (where he had worked before going to China), China, and Southeast Asia (he collaborated in the 1930s study of *Homo erectus* and later fossils from Java). What struck him about the fossils in each of these regions was the evident continuity from the earliest to the latest specimens. From this observation, he developed his polycentric theory of human evolution, which received its first clear statement in a 1943 publication. In it, he argued the thesis that human populations of common ancestry thereafter evolved in the same direction in four different geographical regions (Africa was the fourth). Although some have (mis)understood this as the completely separate but parallel evolution of four lineages, Weidenreich was quite clear about the continued operation of gene flow in the process. As the number of human fossils has increased, and our knowledge of evolutionary processes has grown, Weidenreich's ideas have been taken up by others and developed into the modern multiregional theory of human evolution.

Nevertheless, fossils described as Neandertals are known from sites in western Europe that date to 35,000 to 33,000 years ago, in which case coexistence between the modern and archaic forms of *sapiens* would seem to be indicated. Given the anatomical differences between the two, some form of population replacement, rather than simple evolution from one to the other, may have occurred.

An alternate explanation is possible, however. If we think in terms of varied populations—as we should[22]—instead of ideal types, we find that features reminiscent of modern humans can be discerned in some of the latest Neandertals. A specimen from Saint Césaire in France, for example, has a higher forehead and chin. A number of other Neandertals, too, show incipient chin development as well as reduced facial protrusion and thinning of the brow ridges. Conversely, the earliest anatomically modern human skulls from Europe often exhibit features reminiscent of Neandertals (see Chapter 10). Accordingly, we might view the population of this region between 40,000 and 30,000 years ago as a varied one, with some individuals retaining a stronger Neandertal heritage than others, in whom modern characteristics are more prominent (Figure 9.2).

Nothing in the physical or mental makeup of Neandertals would have prevented them from leading a typical Upper Paleolithic way of life, as in fact the latest Neandertals of western, central, and eastern Europe did.[23] Out of the earlier Mousterian, they created their own Upper Paleolithic cultures (Figure 9.3). In some respects, they outdid their Aurignacian contemporaries, as in the

---

[22]Gould, S. J. (1996). *Full house: The spread of excellence from Plato to Darwin* (pp. 72–73). New York: Harmony Books.

[23]Mellars, p. 378.

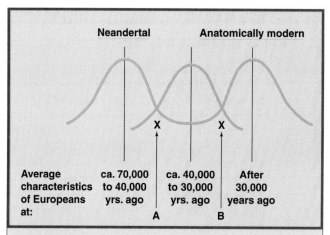

FIGURE 9.2

GRAPHICALLY PORTRAYED HERE IS A SHIFT IN AVERAGE CHARAC-
TERISTICS OF AN OTHERWISE VARIED POPULATION OVER TIME FROM
NEANDERTAL TO MORE MODERN FEATURES. BETWEEN 40,000 AND
30,000 YEARS AGO, WE WOULD EXPECT TO FIND INDIVIDUALS WITH
CHARACTERISTICS SUCH AS THOSE OF THE SAINT CÉSAIRE
"NEANDERTAL" (A) AND THE ALMOST (BUT NOT QUITE) MODERN
CRO-MAGNON (B; THIS FOSSIL IS DISCUSSED IN CHAPTER 10).

use of red ocher, a substance less frequently used by the Aurignacians than by their late Neandertal neighbors.[24] This cannot be a case of borrowing ideas and techniques from Aurignacians, as these developments clearly predate the Aurignacian.[25]

Another often cited case of coexistence of the two forms is in Southwest Asia. Although Neandertal skeletons are clearly present at sites such as Kebara and Shanidar caves, skeletons from some older sites have been described as anatomically modern. At Qafzeh in Israel, for example, 90,000-year-old skeletons are said to show none of the Neandertal hallmarks; although their faces and bodies are large and heavily built by today's standards, they are nonetheless claimed to be within the range of living peoples. Yet, a statistical study comparing a number of measurements among Qafzeh, Upper Paleolithic, and Neandertal skulls found those from Qafzeh to fall in between the Aurignacian and Neandertal norms, though slightly closer to the Neandertals.[26] Nor is the dentition

functionally distinguishable when Qafzeh and Neandertal are compared.[27]

At the nearby site of Skuhl, a skeleton similar to those from Qafzeh was part of a population whose continuous range of variation included individuals with markedly Neandertal characteristics. Furthermore, the idea of two distinctly different but coexisting populations receives no support from cultural remains, inasmuch as the people living at Skuhl and Qafzeh were making and using the same Mousterian tools as those at Kebara and Shanidar. Thus, there are no indications of groups with different cultural traditions coexisting in the same region. For that matter, the actual behaviors represented by Middle Paleolithic and early Upper Paleolithic cultures were not significantly different. For example, the Upper Paleolithic people who used Kebara Cave continued to live in exactly the same way as their Neandertal predecessors: They procured the same foods, processed them in the same way, used similar hearths, and disposed of their trash in the same way. The only evident difference is that the Neandertals did not bank their fires for warmth with small stones or cobbles as did their Upper Paleolithic successors.[28]

[24]Bednarik, R. G. (1995). Concept-mediated marking in the lower Paleolithic. *Current Anthropology, 36,* 606.

[25]Zilhão, p. 40.

[26]Corruccini, R. S. (1992). Metrical reconsideration of the Skhul IV and IX and Border Cave I crania in the context of modern human origins. *American Journal of Physical Anthropology, 87,* 433–445.

[27]Brace, C. L. (2000). *Evolution in an anthropological view* (p. 206). Walnut Creek, CA: Altamira.

[28]Corruccini, p. 436.

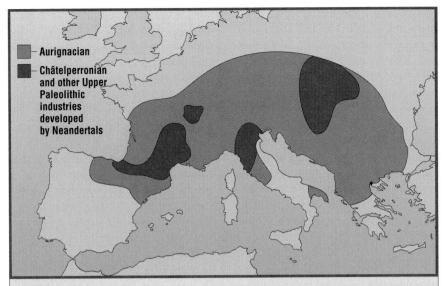

FIGURE 9.3

BETWEEN 36,500 AND 30,000 YEARS AGO, UPPER PALEOLITHIC INDUSTRIES DEVELOPED FROM THE MOUSTERIAN BY EUROPEAN NEANDERTALS COEXISTED WITH THE AURIGNACIAN INDUSTRY, USUALLY ASSOCIATED WITH ANATOMICALLY MODERN HUMANS.

Legend:
- Aurignacian
- Châtelperronian and other Upper Paleolithic industries developed by Neandertals

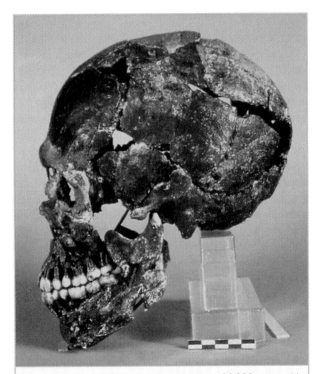

This *H. sapiens* skull from Qafzeh, Israel, is 90,000 years old. Though it looks more modern than a Neandertal, measurements taken on the skull fall slightly closer to those of the Neandertals than they do to those of more modern-looking Upper Paleolithic people.

The "Eve" or "Out of Africa" Hypothesis

This alternative to the multiregional hypothesis states that anatomically modern humans are descended from one specific population of *H. sapiens*, replacing not just the Neandertals, but other populations of archaic *H. sapiens* as our ancestors spread out of their original homeland. This idea came not from fossils but from a relatively new technique that uses mitochondrial DNA to reconstruct family trees. Unlike nuclear DNA (in the cell nucleus), mitochondrial DNA is located elsewhere in the cell, in compartments that produce the energy needed to keep cells alive. Because sperm does not contribute mitochondrial DNA to the fertilized egg, it is inherited only from one's mother and is not "rescrambled" with each succeeding generation. Therefore, it should be altered only by mutation. By comparing the mitochondrial DNA of living individuals from diverse geographical populations, anthropologists and molecular biologists seek to determine when and where modern *H. sapiens* originated. As widely reported in the popular press (including a cover story in *Newsweek*), preliminary results suggested that the mitochondrial DNA of all living humans could be traced back to a "Mitochondrial Eve" who lived in Africa (though some argued for Asia) some 200,000 years ago. If so, all other populations of archaic *H. sapiens,* as well as non-African *H. erectus,* would have to be ruled out of the ancestry of modern humans.

Most scholars today accept that fossils from Africa, scrappy though they are, exhibit the transition from *H. erectus* through archaic to anatomically modern *sapiens* on that continent. This by itself, however, offers no confirmation of the "Out of Africa" hypothesis. After all, proponents of the multiregional model also argue that the transition took place here, as in other parts of the Old World. If, however, anatomically modern fossils could be shown to be significantly older in Africa than elsewhere, this would bolster the argument for an African homeland for modern humanity. To date, the strongest candidates for such fossils consist of a skull from Border Cave and fragments of jaws of at least 10 people from a cave at the Klasies River mouth. Both sites are in South Africa. Unfortunately, the Border Cave skull is not adequately dated, nor is it as similar to modern African skulls as is often claimed.[29] The Klasies River material is well dated to between 120,000 and 90,000 years ago but is too fragmentary (the bones were cut and burned anciently, suggesting cannibalism) to permit categorical statements as to its modernity. Although one mandible displays what looks like a well-developed chin, this could be a result of

loss of the front teeth, something that leads to resorption of supporting bone. This does not affect the bottom of the jaw, however, leaving it to protrude and appear more chinlike than it may have been.[30] Apart from this, chins are not entirely unknown in archaic *sapiens* (for example, some European Neandertals, as already discussed). Certainly, the Klasies remains are not inconsistent with the sort of wide variation just discussed for Southwest Asia.

It is true that the people of Klasies River were culturally precocious. For one thing, they are the first people we know of to augment resources of the land with those from the sea; their gathering of shellfish led to the buildup of middens (refuse heaps) comparable to those left by later Upper Paleolithic peoples. Their technology was also advanced in the common production of blades—long parallel-sided flakes of a sort not commonly made in Europe until some 36,500 years ago. By 70,000 years ago, the people at Klasies River were blunting the backs of blades, much as later Europeans did, for hafting in composite tools. Some take these signs of cultural advancement as indicative of anatomically modern status. The fallacy of such argument, however, is revealed by the evidence from Europe and Southwest Asia that the cognitive abilities of archaic and modern *H. sapiens* were the same.

The fossil evidence presents other problems for the "Out of Africa" hypothesis as well. For one thing, we would expect an early replacement of archaic *sapiens* in Southwest Asia as more anatomically modern humans moved up out of Africa but, as we have already seen, we have no clear evidence for such a replacement. The same is true for East Asia, where evidence for continuity from regional *H. erectus*, through archaic, to anatomical *H. sapiens* populations is even better than it is in Africa. Consistent with this, the archaeological record of East Asia, though distinctly different from Europe, Africa, and western Asia, shows the same kind of continuity as do the fossils.[31] There is no sign of invasion by people possessing a superior, or even different, technology, as an "Out of Africa" scenario would require.

Given the problems in reconciling the "Out of Africa" hypothesis with the archaeological and fossil records, one may ask: What about the DNA analysis that gave birth to the hypothesis? Here, things are not as certain as proponents of "Out of Africa" maintain.

[29]Bar-Yosef, O., Vandermeesch, B., Arensburg, B., Belfer-Cohen, A., Goldberg, P., Laville, H., Meignen, L., Rak, Y., Speth, J. D., Tchernov, E., Tillier, A. M., & Weiner, S. (1992). The excavations in Kebara Cave, Mt. Carmel. *Current Anthropology, 33,* 534.

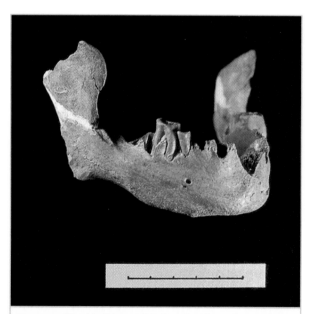

Because of its chin, this mandible from the Klasies River in South Africa has often been called "modern." Yet a number of archaic *sapiens* skulls, including several Neandertals, have this feature.

[30]Wolpoff & Caspari, p. 331.

[31]Pope, G. C. (1992). Craniofacial evidence for the origin of modern humans in China. *Yearbook of Physical Anthropology, 35,* 291.

Even older than the blades from the Klasies River mouth are these, from a site in Kenya. Struck from preshaped cores, they are greater than 280,000 years old, predating any known or possible fossils of anatomically modern humans.

African Origin or Ancient Population Size Differences?[32]

Original Study

The Eve theory depends on genetic evidence indicating an African origin for modern humanity, because . . . the fossil evidence is quite equivocal on this issue. But there is no particular reason to suggest Africa was the place of origin for the current mtDNA [mitochondrial DNA] lineages. The original studies suggesting an African origin were invalid because the computer program used in the analysis was not applied correctly. Then the greater genetic variability in Africans was taken to mean humans evolved there longer: The variation was thought to reflect more mutations and therefore a

longer time span for their accumulation. Templeton [a geneticist] has argued that no statistical analysis shows that the genetic variation of Africans actually is greater than that of other populations; but even if it is, there is another, more compelling explanation.

Ancient population sizes expanded first and are larger in Africa than in other regions, which would have the same effect, creating more African variation. Consider what happens in an expanding population. Average family size is greater than two, and all variations have a good chance of being passed on; at least, if they are not selected against, they will probably not get lost by accident. But if a population is decreasing, drift can play a very active

---
[32]Wolpoff & Caspari, pp. 305–307.

Original Study

role since average family size is less than two. The role of drift is greatly amplified for mtDNA, because for transmission of this molecule the number of female offspring is important. Decreasing populations stand an excellent chance of losing mtDNA lineages.

Now, consider a small but stable population, neither increasing nor decreasing. Here, existing variations may each occur in only one individual. If it is a woman, and she has no female offspring, which can happen one-fourth of the time in a stable population, her unique variation is lost, her mtDNA lineage terminated. But in a large stable population with the same amount of genetic variability, it is likely each mtDNA variant is shared by many individuals. The odds are the same against one woman having no female offspring, but it is very unlikely all the women with a certain mtDNA variant will lack female offspring. It is much harder for mtDNA lines to end by accident in large populations.

These comparisons show that prehistoric population demography, how large or small populations were in the past and how much they fluctuated, can affect mtDNA evolution. Small, fluctuating populations will lose many mtDNA lines. The last common ancestor for the remaining mtDNA variations will be more recent because there is less remaining variation. Large or increasing populations will retain more variation. For them, the roots will be deeper and the last common ancestor will be farther in the past since more variations are retained.

Thus, ancient population size can dictate how long genetic lineages have existed, and therefore when they arose. Because ancient population size differences are an alternate explanation that unlinks the origin of genetic lineages from the origin of a population, it seems as though genetic analysis cannot help solve the problem of whether today's variation reflects African origin or ancient population size differences.

However, genetic analysis can indicate ancient population expansions. Henry Harpending and colleagues studied the probability distributions of pairwise mtDNA comparisons within populations for evidence of past population structure and size expansions. They conclude: "Our results show human populations are derived from separate ancestral populations that were relatively isolated from each other before 50,000 years ago." These studies clearly reveal there have been a series of recent, very significant, population expansions. Some of these are without question associated with the development and spread of agricultural revolutions. But others are earlier.

This means population size history by itself can explain the pattern of mtDNA variation. If, as we believe and as the archaeological record seems to show,

- there were more people living in Africa for most of human prehistory, and
- human populations outside of Africa were smaller and fluctuated more because of the changing ice-age environments,

we would expect just what we do see—African mtDNA has deeper roots, while in other places the coalescent time is more recent. But this explanation does not mean the populations living out of Africa have a more recent origin, or that they originated in Africa. MtDNA history, in other words, is not population history.

John Relethford and Henry Harpending examined the consequences of the possibility that greater African population size, and not greater time depth for modern humans in Africa, may account for their greater variation.

Our results support our earlier contention that regional differences in population size can explain the genetic evidence pertaining to modern human origins. Our work thus far has involved examination of the classic genetic markers and craniometrics, but it also has implications for mitochondrial DNA. The greater mtDNA diversity in sub-Saharan African populations could also be a reflection of a larger long-term African population.

Moreover, they write, a unique African ancestry implies there was a bottleneck for the human species, as moderns would be able to trace their ancestry to only a small portion of humanity, as it existed then.

While this seems at first glance a reasonable notion, it soon becomes apparent that the actual effect of such a [bottleneck] event depends on both the magnitude

and duration of a shift in population size. Rogers and Jorde show that given reasonable parameters for our species, the bottleneck would have to be more severe and long-lasting than considered plausible. We have to think of a population of 50 females for 6,000 years, for example.

The End

Other assumptions made by DNA analysts are problematic. For example, it is assumed that rates of mutation are steady, when in fact they can be notoriously uneven. Another assumption is that mtDNA is not subject to selection, when in fact variants have been implicated in epilepsy and a disease of the eye.[33] A third is that DNA is seen as traveling exclusively *from* Africa, when it is known that, over the past 10,000 years, there has been plenty of movement the other way. In fact, one study of DNA carried on the Y chromosome (and inherited exclusively in the male line) suggests that some DNA seen on the Y chromosome of some Africans was introduced from Asia, where it originated some 200,000 years ago.[34]

Since 1997, studies of mitochondrial DNA have not been limited to living people. In that year, mtDNA was extracted from the original German Neandertal, and two others have since been studied. Because the mtDNA of each of these differs substantially from modern Europeans, many have concluded that there can be no Neandertal ancestry in living humans and that Neandertals must constitute a separate species that went extinct. But as John Relethford (a specialist in anthropological genetics) points out, these conclusions

are premature.[35] For one thing, the average differences are not as great as those seen among living subspecies of the single species of chimpanzee. For another, the differences between populations separated in time by tens of thousands of years tells us nothing about differences between populations contemporaneous with each other. More meaningful would be comparison of the DNA from a late Neandertal with an early Aurignacian European. Finally, if we are to reject Neandertals in the ancestry of modern Europeans because their DNA cannot be detected in their supposed ancestors, then we must also reject any connection between a 40,000- to 62,000-year-old skeleton from Australia (that everyone agrees is anatomically modern) and more recent native Australians. In this case, an mtDNA sequence present in an ancient human seems to have become extinct, in which case we must allow the same possibility for the Neandertals.[36]

In short, it is definitely premature to read out of the modern human ancestry all populations of archaic *sapiens* save those of Africa. Not even the Neandertals can be excluded. We shall return to this problem in the next chapter, but at the moment, the evidence seems to favor a multiregional emergence of anatomically modern humans. Still, the debate is by no means resolved.

---

[33]Shreeve, p. 121.

[34]Gibbons, A. (1997). Ideas on human origins evolve at anthropology gathering. *Science, 276,* 535–536.

[35]Relethford, J. H. (2001). Absence of regional affinities of Neandertal DNA with living humans does not reject multiregional evolution. *American Journal of Physical Anthropology, 115,* 95–98.

[36]Gibbons, A. (2001). The riddle of coexistence. *Science, 291,* 1,726

CHAPTER SUMMARY

At various sites in Europe, Africa, and East Asia, a number of fossils have been found that date between about 400,000 and 200,000 years ago and that show a mixture of traits of both *H. erectus* and *H. sapiens*. They are indicative of evolution from the older into the younger species. Their culture was enriched by development of a new technique of tool manufacture known as the Levalloisian.

By 200,000 years ago, populations of archaic *H. sapiens* lived in all parts of the inhabited world. In Europe and western Asia, archaic *H. sapiens* is represented by the Neandertals, some of whom, in Europe and western Asia, are said to have survived until at least 35,000 years ago. Alternatively, they may be members of varied populations in which some individuals show modern characteristics more strongly than others.

The brains of archaic *H. sapiens* were no different in size and organization than our own, although their skulls retained some ancestral characteristics. With a larger brain, they were able to utilize culture as a means of adaptation to a far greater extent than any of their predecessors; they were capable of complex technology and sophisticated conceptual thought.

The cultures of archaic *H. sapiens* are known as Middle Paleolithic, and the best known is the Mousterian of Europe, northern Africa, and western Asia. Mousterian tools included handaxes, flakes, scrapers, borers, wood shavers, and spears. These flake tools were lighter and smaller than those of the Levalloisian. Mousterian tools increased the availability and quality of food, shelter, and clothing. Archaeological evidence indicates that Mousterian peoples buried their dead, cared for the disabled, and made a variety of objects for purely symbolic purposes.

All populations of archaic *H. sapiens* are easily derivable from earlier populations of *H. erectus* from the same regions, and all could be ancestral to more modern populations in the same regions. Gene flow between populations would have prevented branching. An alternative hypothesis is that the transition from archaic to anatomically modern *H. sapiens* took place in one specific population, probably in Africa. From here, people spread to other regions, replacing older populations as they did so.

CLASSIC READINGS

Shreeve, J. (1995). *The Neandertal enigma: Solving the mystery of modern human origins.* New York: William Morrow.

Shreeve is a science writer who has written extensively about human evolution. This book is engagingly written and covers most of the major issues in the Neandertal-Modern debate.

Stringer, C. B., & McKie, R. (1996). *African exodus: The origins of modern humanity.* London: Jonathan Cape.

Chris Stringer of the British Museum is a leading champion of the "Out of Africa" hypothesis, and in this book one will find a vigorous presentation of his arguments.

Trinkaus, E., & Shipman, P. (1992). *The Neandertals: Changing the image of mankind.* New York: Alfred A. Knopf.

The senior author of this book is a long-time specialist on the Neandertals. Eminently readable, the book chronicles the changing interpretations of these fossils since the first recognized find in 1856. For a good look at what is known about the Neandertals, there is no better place to go than this.

Wolpoff, M., & Caspari, R. (1997). *Race and human evolution.* New York: Simon & Schuster.

One of the problems in evaluating the multiregional and "Out of Africa" hypotheses is that many writers misrepresent the former. That is no problem in this book, written by the leading champion of multiregionalism and his wife. The hypothesis is presented and defended in a straightforward and thorough way so that anyone can understand it.

CHAPTER 10

HOMO SAPIENS AND THE UPPER PALEOLITHIC

In the Upper Paleolithic period, evidence of human creativity becomes both widespread and dramatic, as this 32,000-year-old painting from the recently discovered (in 1994) Chauvet Cave in France shows. Equally old, and in some cases older, art is known from Africa and Australia.

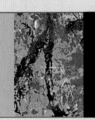

1

WHEN DID ANATOMICALLY MODERN FORMS OF *HOMO SAPIENS* APPEAR?

The answer to this question depends on what is meant by "anatomically modern." Because all humans today are members of a single species, all are equally modern. Although populations of archaic *H. sapiens* such as the Neandertals are commonly seen as not anatomically modern, to exclude them requires exclusion of some modern populations—an obvious impossibility. Still, it is generally agreed that by 30,000 years ago, in the Upper Paleolithic period, populations in all parts of the inhabited world show some resemblance to more recent human populations.

2

WHAT WAS THE CULTURE OF UPPER PALEOLITHIC PEOPLES LIKE?

Upper Paleolithic cultures generally include a greater diversity of tools. Techniques of toolmaking became widespread, including the manufacture of blades, pressure flaking, and use of burins to fashion implements of bone and antler. In Europe, large game hunting was improved by invention of the spear-thrower, while net hunting allowed effective procurement of small game. In Africa the bow and arrow were invented. There was as well an explosion of creativity, represented by impressive works of art from Africa, Australia, and Europe.

3

WHAT WERE THE CONSEQUENCES OF THE NEW UPPER PALEOLITHIC TECHNOLOGIES?

First Upper Paleolithic and then Mesolithic technologies improved peoples' abilities to adapt through the medium of culture. This resulted in increased regionalism, as people refined their adaptations to local conditions, and further population growth promoted expansion into new regions, most dramatically Australia and the Americas. Biological consequences included final reduction of the human face to modern proportions, and the new hunting technologies led to reduction of body mass.

The remains of a Stone Age people who looked much like us were first discovered in 1868 at Les Eyzies in France, in a rock shelter together with tools of the Upper (late) Paleolithic. Consisting of eight skeletons, they are commonly referred to as **Cro-Magnons,** after the rock shelter in which they were found. The name was extended to 13 other specimens unearthed between 1872 and 1902 in the caves of the Côte d'Azur near the Italian Riviera, and since then, to other Upper Paleolithic skeletons discovered in other parts of Europe.

Because Cro-Magnons were found with Upper Paleolithic tools and seemed responsible for the production of impressive works of art, they were seen as particularly clever, when compared with the Neandertals. The idea that the latter were basically dim-witted fit comfortably with the prevailing stereotype of their brutish appearance, and their Mousterian tools were interpreted as evidence of cultural inferiority. Hence the idea was born of an anatomically modern people with a superior culture sweeping into Europe and replacing a primitive, local population.

UPPER PALEOLITHIC PEOPLES: THE FIRST MODERN HUMANS

Much as Neandertals were stereotyped as particularly brutish, the Cro-Magnons of Europe were stereotyped as having a somewhat godlike appearance, epitomizing modern European ideals of beauty. This image found its way into popular culture, as in a best-selling novel of the 1970s, *The Clan of the Cave Bear.* In this book, the heroine is portrayed as a tall, slender, blonde-haired, blue-eyed beauty. But as Upper Paleolithic remains (from various parts of Africa and Asia as well as Europe) have become better understood, it has become clear that the differences from earlier populations have been greatly exaggerated. In the case of Europeans, for example, there is some resemblance between Cro-Magnons and later populations: in braincase shape, high broad forehead, narrow nasal openings, and common presence of chins. But Cro-Magnon faces were shorter and broader than those of modern Europeans, their brow ridges were a bit more prominent, and their teeth and jaws were as large as those of Neandertals. Some (a skull from the original Cro-Magnon site, for instance) even display the distinctive "occipital bun" of the Neandertals on the back of the

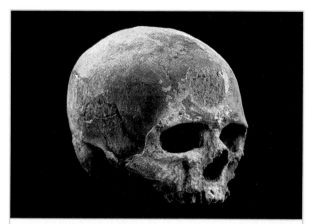

Though the original Cro-Magnon skull shows some resemblance to modern European skulls, it is not identical.

skull.[1] Nor were they particularly tall, as their height of 5 feet 7 or 8 inches does not fall outside the Neandertal range.

Although the Cro-Magnons and Upper Paleolithic people from Africa and Asia are now routinely referred to as anatomically modern, it is surprisingly hard to be precise about what we mean by this. We think of people with brains the size of modern people, but this had already been achieved by archaic *H. sapiens,* among whom brain size actually peaked at 10 percent larger than ours. The reduction to today's size correlates with a reduction in brawn, as bodies have become less massive overall. Modern faces and jaws are, by and large, less massive as well, but there are exceptions. For example, anthropologists Milford Wolpoff and Rachel Caspari have pointed out that any definition of modernity that excludes Neandertals also excludes substantial numbers of recent and living native Australians, although they are, quite obviously, a modern people. The fact is, no multidimensional diagnosis of modern humans can be both exclusive of archaic populations and inclusive of all contemporary humans.[2]

The appearance of modern-sized brains in archaic *H. sapiens* no doubt was a consequence of increased reliance

[1]Brace, C. L. (1997). Cro-Magnons "Я" us? *Anthropology Newsletter, 38*(8), 1.

[2]Wolpoff, M., & Caspari, R. (1997). *Race and human evolution* (pp. 344–345, 393). New York: Simon & Schuster.

Cro-Magnons.   Europeans of the Upper Paleolithic after about 36,000 years ago.

on cultural adaptation. Ultimately, this emphasis on cultural adaptation led to the development of more complex tool kits. Among Upper Paleolithic peoples, as specialized tools increasingly took over the cutting, softening, and clamping functions once performed by the front teeth, there followed a reduction in the size of the teeth and, eventually, the jaws. The cooking of food (which began with *H. erectus)* had already favored some reduction in size of the teeth and muscles involved in chewing; consequently, the jaws diminished in size, and robust sites for muscle attachment disappeared along with features like brow ridges that buttress the skull from the stresses and strains imposed by the action of massive jaw muscles.

Technological improvements also reduced the intensity of selective pressures that had previously favored especially massive, robust bodies. With new emphasis on elongate tools having greater mechanical advantages, more effective techniques of hafting, a switch from thrusting to throwing spears, and development of net hunting, there was a marked reduction in overall muscularity. Moreover, the skeletons of Upper Paleolithic peoples show far less evidence of trauma than do those of archaic

H. sapiens, whose bones almost always show evidence of injury.

UPPER PALEOLITHIC TOOLS

The Upper Paleolithic was a time of great technological innovation. Typical were blades, flint flakes at least twice as long as they are wide. Although Middle Paleolithic toolmakers, especially in Africa, already made blades (some are illustrated in Chapter 9), they did not do so to the extent that their Upper Paleolithic successors did. What made this possible were new techniques of core preparation that allowed more intensive production of highly standardized blades. The toolmaker formed a cylindrical core, struck the blade off near the edge of the core, and repeated this procedure, going around the core in one direction until finishing near its center (Figure 10.1). The procedure is analogous to peeling long leaves off an artichoke. With this **blade technique,** an Upper Paleolithic flint knapper could get 75 feet of working edge from a 2-pound core; a Mousterian knapper could get only 6 feet from the same-sized core.

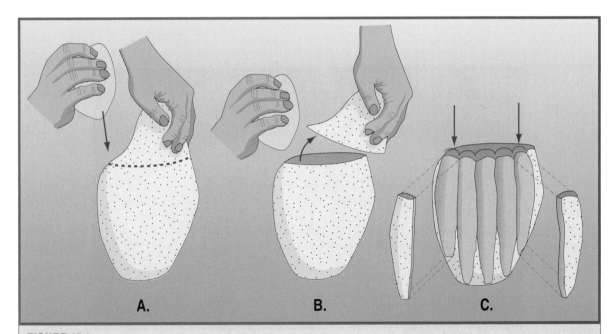

FIGURE 10.1

DURING THE UPPER PALEOLITHIC, A NEW TECHNIQUE WAS USED TO MANUFACTURE BLADES. THE STONE IS FLAKED TO CREATE A STRIKING PLATFORM; LONG, ALMOST PARALLEL-SIDED FLAKES THEN ARE STRUCK AROUND THE SIDES, PROVIDING SHARP-EDGED BLADES.

Blade technique.   A technique of stone tool manufacture by which long, parallel-sided flakes are struck off the edges of a specially prepared core.

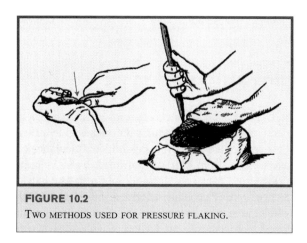

FIGURE 10.2
TWO METHODS USED FOR PRESSURE FLAKING.

are examples of this technique. The longest of these blades is 13 inches in length but only about a quarter of an inch thick. Through pressure flaking, blades could be worked with great precision into a variety of final forms; and worn tools could be effectively resharpened over and over until they were too small for further use.

Another common Upper Paleolithic tool was the **burin,** although it too was invented earlier, in the Middle Paleolithic. These implements, with their chisel-like edges, facilitated the working of bone, horn, antler, and ivory into such useful things as fishhooks, harpoons, and eyed needles, all of which made life easier for *H. sapiens,* especially in northern regions. The spear-thrower, too, appeared at this time. Spear-throwers are wooden devices, one end of which is gripped in the hunter's hand, while the other end has a hole or hook, in or against which the end of the spear is placed (Figure 10.3). It is held so as to effectively extend the length of the hunter's arm, thereby increasing the velocity of the spear when thrown. Using a spear-thrower greatly added to the efficiency of the spear as a hunting tool. With handheld spears, hunters had to get close to their quarry to make the kill, and because many of the animals they hunted were quite large and fierce, this was a dangerous business. The need to approach closely, and the improbability of an instant kill,

Other efficient techniques of tool manufacture also came into common use at this time. One such method was **pressure flaking,** in which a bone, antler, or wooden tool was used to press rather than strike off small flakes as the final step in stone tool manufacture (Figure 10.2). The advantage of this technique was that the toolmaker had greater control over the final shape of the tool than is possible with percussion flaking alone. The so-called Solutrean laurel leaf blades found in Spain and France

Shown here is one of the Solutrean laurel leaf bifaces from Europe. Such fine flint work requires a high degree of skill.

Pressure flaking. A technique of stone tool manufacture in which a bone, antler, or wooden tool is used to press, rather than strike off, small flakes from a piece of flint or similar stone. • **Burins.** Stone tools with chisel-like edges used for working bone and antler.

exposed the spear hunter to considerable risk. But with the spear-thrower, the effective killing distance was increased; experiments demonstrate that the effective killing distance of a spear when used with a spear-thrower is between 18 and 27 meters (as opposed to 0.6 or 0.9 meters without).[3]

Another important innovation, net hunting, appeared some time between 29,000 and 22,000 years ago.[4] Knotted nets, made from the fibers of wild plants such as hemp or nettle, left their impression on the clay floors of huts when people walked on them. These impressions were baked in when the huts later burned, which is how we know that nets existed. Their use accounts for the high number of hare, fox, and other small mammal and bird bones at archaeological sites. Like historically known net hunters, everyone—men, women, and chil-

dren—probably participated, frightening animals with loud noises to drive them to where hunters were stationed with their nets. In this way, large amounts of meat could be amassed in ways that did not put a premium on speed or strength.

A further improvement of hunting techniques came with the invention of the bow and arrow, which appeared first in Africa, but not until the end of the Upper Paleolithic in Europe. The greatest advantage of the bow is that it increases the distance between hunter and prey; beyond 18 to 27 meters, the accuracy and penetration of a spear thrown with a spear-thrower is quite poor, whereas even a poor bow will shoot an arrow farther, with greater accuracy and penetrating power. A good bow is effective even at 91 meters. Thus, hunters were able to maintain an even safer distance between themselves and dangerous prey, dramatically decreasing their chances of being seriously injured by an animal fighting for its life.

These changes in hunting weaponry and techniques likely were responsible for the less robust bodies of Upper Paleolithic people. Spear hunting, particularly where large, fierce animals are the prey as they often were in Europe, demands strength, power, and overall robusticity

---

[3]Frayer, D. W. (1981). Body size, weapon use, and natural selection in the European Upper Paleolithic and Mesolithic. *American Anthropologist, 83,* 58.

[4]Pringle, H. (1997). Ice Age communities may be earliest known net hunters. *Science, 277,* 1,203.

Anthropology Applied

Stone Tools for Modern Surgeons

When anthropologist Irven DeVore of Harvard University was to have some minor melanomas removed from his face, he did not leave it up to the surgeon to supply his own scalpels. Instead, he had graduate student John Shea make a scalpel. Making a blade of obsidian (a naturally-occurring volcanic "glass") by the same techniques used by Upper Paleolithic people to make blades, he then hafted this in a wooden handle, using melted pine resin as glue and then lashing it with sinew. After the procedure, the surgeon reported that the obsidian scalpel was superior to metal ones.[*]

DeVore was not the first to undergo surgery in which stone scalpels were used. In 1975, Don Crabtree, then at Idaho State University, prepared the scalpels that his surgeon would use in Crabtree's heart surgery. In 1980, Payson Sheets at the University of Colorado prepared obsidian scalpels that were used successfully in eye surgery. And in 1986, David Pokotylo of the Museum of Anthropology at

the University of British Columbia underwent reconstructive surgery on his hand with blades he himself had made (the hafting was done by his museum colleague, Len McFarlane).

The reason for these uses of scalpels modeled on ancient stone tools is that the anthropologists realized that obsidian is superior in almost every way to materials normally used to make scalpels: It is 210 to 1,050 times sharper than surgical steel, 100 to 500 times sharper than a razor blade, and 3 times sharper than a diamond blade (which not only costs much more, but cannot be made with more than 3 mm of cutting edge). Obsidian blades are easier to cut with and do less damage in the process (under a microscope, incisions made with the sharpest steel blades show torn ragged edges and are littered with bits of displaced flesh).[†] As a consequence, the surgeon has better control over what she or he is doing and the incisions heal faster with less scarring and pain. Because of the supe-

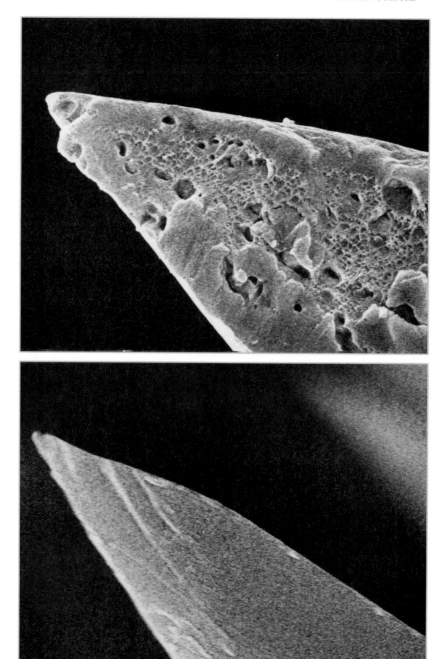

These microphotographs of an obsidian blade (bottom photo) and a modern steel scalpel (top photo) illustrate the superiority of the obsidian.

riority of obsidian scalpels, Sheets went so far as to form a corporation in partnership with Boulder, Colorado, eye surgeon Dr. Firmon Hardenbergh. Together, they developed a means of producing cores of uniform size from molten glass, as well as a machine to detach blades from the cores.

[*]Shreeve, J. (1995). *The Neandertal enigma: Solving the mystery of modern human origins* (p. 134). New York: William Morrow.

[†]Sheets, P. D. (1987). Dawn of a New Stone Age in eye surgery. In R. J. Sharer & W. Ashmore (Eds.), *Archaeology: Discovering our past* (p. 231). Palo Alto, CA: Mayfield.

FIGURE 10.3

SHOWN HERE IS THE WAY AN UPPER PALEOLITHIC HUNTER WOULD THROW A SPEAR USING A SPEAR-THROWER, AS WELL AS A STONE POINT SUITABLE FOR THE SPEAR. THE HUNTER'S CLOTHING AND HAIR STYLE ARE PURE SPECULATION.

on the part of the hunter. Without them, the hunter is poorly equipped to withstand the rigors of close-quarter killing. A high nutritional price must be paid, however, for large, powerful, and robust bodies. Therefore, as speed and strength become less important for success, selection for them slacked off, and people tended to become weaker and less robust. As a consequence, nutritional requirements were reduced.

Upper Paleolithic peoples not only had better tools but also a greater diversity of types than earlier peoples (Figures 10.4 and 10.5). The highly developed Upper Paleolithic kit included tools for use during different seasons, and regional variation in tool kits was greater than ever before. Thus, it is really impossible to speak of an Upper Paleolithic culture, even in a relatively small peripheral region like Europe; instead, one must make note of the many different traditions that made it possible for people to adapt ever more specifically to the various environments in which they were living. Just how proficient (and even wasteful) people had become at securing a livelihood is indicated by boneyards containing thousands of skeletons. At Solutré in France, for example, Upper Paleolithic hunters killed 10,000 horses; at Predmost in Czechoslovakia, they were responsible for

the deaths of 1,000 mammoths. The favored big game of European hunters, however, was reindeer, which they killed in even greater numbers.

UPPER PALEOLITHIC ART

Although the creativity of Upper Paleolithic peoples is evident in the tools and weapons they made, it is nowhere more evident than in their outburst of artistic expression. Some have argued that this was made possible by a newly evolved biological ability to manipulate symbols and make images, but in view of the modern-sized brains of archaic *sapiens* and increasingly compelling evidence that even the Neandertals were capable of speech, such an idea is hard to maintain. Like agriculture, which came later (see Chapter 11), the artistic explosion may have been no more than a consequence of innovations made by a people who had the capacity to make them for tens of thousands of years already.

In fact, just as many of the distinctive tools that were commonly used in Upper Paleolithic times first appear in the Middle Paleolithic, so too do objects of art. In Southwest Asia, a crude figurine of volcanic tuff is some 250,000 years

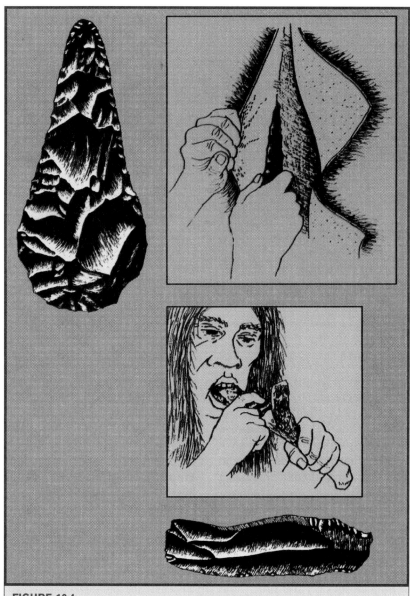

FIGURE 10.4

TWO UPPER PALEOLITHIC STONE TOOLS, AND HOW THEY MIGHT HAVE BEEN USED TO SKIN AN ANIMAL AND CUT MEAT WHILE EATING.

old.[5] Although it is unusual, the fact that it exists at all indicates that people had the ability to carve all sorts of things from wood, a substance easier to work than volcanic tuff but rarely preserved for long periods of time. Furthermore, ocher "crayons" from Middle Paleolithic contexts in various parts of the world must have been used to decorate or mark something. In southern Africa, for example, regular use of yellow and red ocher goes back 130,000 years, with some evidence as old as 200,000 years.[6] Perhaps pigments were used on people's bodies, as well as objects, as the 50,000-year-old mammoth-tooth *churinga,* discussed and illustrated in Chapter 9, might suggest.

[5]Appenzeller, T. (1998). Art: Evolution or revolution? *Science, 282,* 1,452.

[6]Barham, L. S. (1998). Possible early pigment use in south-central Africa. *Current Anthropology, 39,* 709.

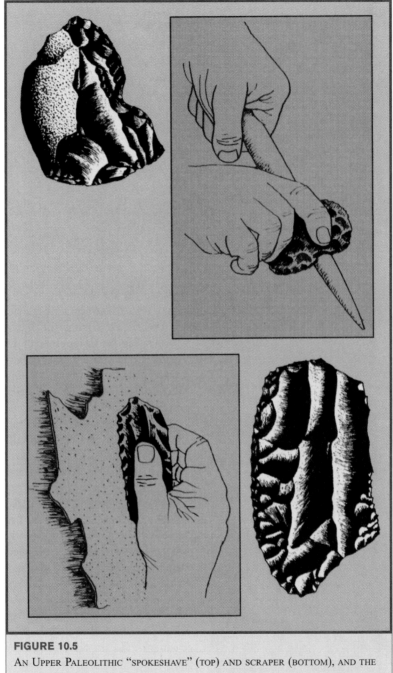

FIGURE 10.5

AN UPPER PALEOLITHIC "SPOKESHAVE" (TOP) AND SCRAPER (BOTTOM), AND THE WAYS THEY WERE USED.

That there was music in the lives of Upper Paleolithic peoples is indicated by the presence of bone flutes and whistles in sites, some up to 30,000 years old. But again, such instruments may have their origin in Middle Paleolithic prototypes, such as the probable "Neandertal flute" discussed in Chapter 9. Although we cannot be sure just where and when it happened, some genius discovered that bows could be used not just for killing, but to make music as well. Because the bow and arrow is an Upper Paleolithic invention, the musical bow likely is as well. We do know that the musical bow is the oldest of all stringed instruments, and its invention ultimately made

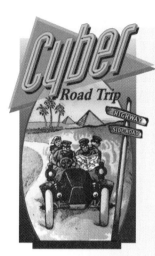

HIGHWAY 1

A trip to this site is a visual treat. It features cave rock art from Australia to Africa, some of which dates back to the Paleolithic.
www.bradshawfoundation.com/index.html

HIGHWAY 2

In order to protect the magnificent cave art at Lascaux Cave, only six people per day can go inside. To share this national treasure more widely, the French government has built an entire replica of the site as well as this Web site for a virtual tour.
www.culture.fr/culture/arcnat/lascaux/en/

Crude though it may be, this piece of tuff, carved some 250,000 years ago, looks like a woman if viewed from the right angle. It was found in 1980 on the Golan Heights in the Middle East.

possible the development of all of the stringed instruments with which we are familiar today.

The earliest evidence of figurative pictures goes back 32,000 years in Europe and is probably equally old in Africa. Both engravings and paintings are known from many rock shelters and outcrops in southern Africa, where they continued to be made by Bushman peoples up until about 100 years ago. Scenes feature both humans and animals, depicted with extraordinary skill, often in association with geometric and other abstract motifs.

Because this rock art tradition continued unbroken into historic times, it has been possible to discover what this art means. There is a close connection between the art and shamanism, and many scenes depict visions seen in states of trance. Distortions in the art, usually of human figures, represent sensations felt by individuals in a state of trance, whereas the geometric designs depict illusions that originate in the central nervous system in altered states of consciousness. These **entoptic phenomena** are luminous grids, dots, zigzags, and other designs that seem to shimmer, pulsate, rotate, and expand, and are seen as one enters a state of trance (sufferers of migraines experience similar hallucinations). The animals depicted in this art, often with startling realism, are not the ones most often eaten. Rather, they are powerful beasts like the eland, and this power is important to shamans—individuals skilled at manipulating supernatural powers and spirits for human benefit—who try to harness it for their rain-making and other rituals.

Rock art in Australia goes back at least 45,000 years, with the earliest examples consisting entirely of entoptic

Entoptic phenomena. Bright pulsating forms that are generated by the central nervous system and seen in states of trance.

In South Africa, rock art, like these engravings and paintings from Namibia, depict things seen by dancers while in states of trance.

motifs. But the Upper Paleolithic art that is most famous—largely because most students of prehistoric art are themselves of European background—is that of Europe. The earliest of this art took the form of sculpture and engravings often portraying such animals as reindeer, horses, bears, and ibexes, but there are also numerous portrayals of voluptuous women with exaggerated sexual and reproductive characteristics. Many appear to be pregnant, and some are shown in birthing postures. These so-called Venus figures have been found at sites from southwestern France to as far east as Siberia. Made of stone, ivory, antler, or baked clay, they differ little in style from place to place, testifying to the sharing of ideas over vast distances. Although some have interpreted the Venuses as objects associated with a fertility cult, others suggest that they may have been exchanged to cement alliances among groups.

Most spectacular are the paintings on the walls of 200 or so caves in southern France and northern Spain, the oldest of which date from about 32,000 years ago. Most common are visually accurate portrayals of Ice Age mammals, including bison, bulls, horses, mammoths, and stags, often painted one on top of another. Although well repre-

sented in other media, humans are not commonly portrayed in cave paintings, nor are scenes or depictions of events at all common. Instead, the animals are often abstracted from nature and rendered two-dimensionally without regard to the conformations of the surfaces they are on—no small achievement for these early artists. Sometimes, though, the artists did make use of bulges and other features of the rock to impart a more three-dimensional feeling. Frequently, the paintings are in hard-to-get-at places while suitable surfaces in more accessible places remain untouched. In some caves, the lamps by which the artists worked have been found; these are spoon-shaped objects of sandstone in which animal fat was burned. Experimentation has shown that such lamps would have provided adequate illumination over several hours.

The techniques used by Upper Paleolithic people to create their cave paintings were unraveled a decade ago through the experimental work of Michel Lorblanchet. Interestingly, they turn out to be the same ones used by native rock painters in Australia. Lorblanchet's experiments are described in the following Original Study by science writer Roger Lewin.

Upper Paleolithic art was quite varied: a carved antler spear-thrower ornamented by two headless ibexes (from Enlene Cave, France); a female Venus figurine of yellow steatite (from a cave at Liguria, Italy); and one of the sandstone lamps by which artists worked in caves (from Lascaux Cave, France).

Original Study

Paleolithic Paint Job[7]

Lorblanchet's recent bid to re-create one of the most important Ice Age images in Europe was an affair of the heart as much as the head. "I tried to abandon my skin of a modern citizen, tried to experience the feeling of the artist, to enter the dialogue between the rock and the man," he explains. Every day for a week in the fall of 1990 he drove the 20 miles from his home in the medieval village of Cajarc into the hills above the river Lot. There, in a small, practically inaccessible cave, he transformed himself into an Upper Paleolithic painter.

And not just any Upper Paleolithic painter, but the one who 18,400 years ago crafted the dotted horses inside the famous cave of Pech Merle.

You can still see the original horses in Pech Merle's vast underground geologic splendor. You enter through a narrow passageway and soon find yourself gazing across a grand cavern to where the painting seems to hang in the gloom. "Outside, the

[7]Lewin, R. (1993). Paleolithic paint job. *Discover, 14*(7), 67–69.

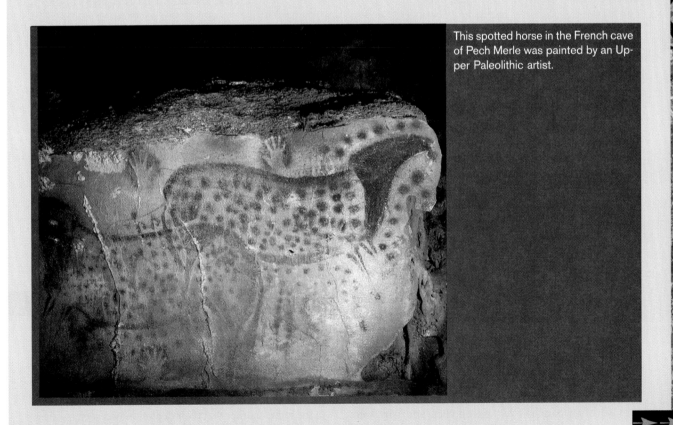

landscape is very different from the one the Upper Paleolithic people saw," says Lorblanchet. "But in here, the landscape is the same as it was more than 18,000 years ago. You see what the Upper Paleolithic people experienced." No matter where you look in this cavern, the eye is drawn back to the panel of horses.

The two horses face away from each other, rumps slightly overlapping, their outlines sketched in black. The animal on the right seems to come alive as it merges with a crook in the edge of the panel, the perfect natural shape for a horse's head. But the impression of naturalism quickly fades as the eye falls on the painting's dark dots. There are more than 200 of them, deliberately distributed within and below the bodies and arcing around the right-hand horse's head and mane. More cryptic still are a smattering of red dots and half-circles and the floating outline of a fish. The surrealism is completed by six disembodied human hands stenciled above and below the animals.

Lorblanchet began thinking about re-creating the horses after a research trip to Australia over a decade ago. Not only is Australia a treasure trove of rock art, but its aboriginal people are still creating it. "In Queensland I learned how people painted by spitting pigment onto the rock," he recalls. "They spat paint and used their hand, a piece of cloth, or a feather as a screen to create different lines and other effects. Elsewhere in Australia people used chewed twigs as paintbrushes, but in Queensland the spitting technique worked best." The rock surfaces there were too uneven for extensive brushwork, he adds—just as they are in Quercy.

When Lorblanchet returned home he looked at the Quercy paintings with a new eye. Sure enough,

This spotted horse in the French cave of Pech Merle was painted by an Upper Paleolithic artist.

Original Study

he began seeing the telltale signs of spit-painting—lines with edges that were sharply demarcated on one side and fuzzy on the other, as if they had been airbrushed—instead of the brushstrokes he and others had assumed were there. Could you produce lines that were crisp on both edges with the same technique, he wondered, and perhaps dots too? Archeologists had long recognized that hand stencils, which are common in prehistoric art, were produced by spitting paint around a hand held to the wall. But no one had thought that entire animal images could be created this way. Before he could test his ideas, however, Lorblanchet had to find a suitable rock face—the original horses were painted on a roughly vertical panel 13 feet across and 6 feet high. With the help of a speleologist, he eventually found a rock face in a remote cave high in the hills and set to work.

Following the aboriginal practices he had witnessed, Lorblanchet first made a light outline sketch of the horses with a charred stick. Then he prepared black pigment for the painting. "My intention had been to use manganese dioxide, as the Pech Merle painter did," says Lorblanchet, referring to one of the minerals ground up for paint by the early artists. "But I was advised that manganese is somewhat toxic, so I used wood charcoal instead." (Charcoal was used as pigment by Paleolithic painters in other caves, so Lorblanchet felt he could justify his concession to safety.) To turn the charcoal into paint, Lorblanchet ground it with a limestone block, put the powder in his mouth, and diluted it to the right consistency with saliva and water. For red pigment he used ocher from the local iron-rich clay.

He started with the dark mane of the right hand horse. "I spat a series of dots and fused them together to represent tufts of hair," he says, unself-consciously reproducing the spitting action as he talks. "Then I painted the horse's back by blowing the pigment below my hand held so"—he holds his hand flat against the rock with his thumb tucked in to form a straight line—"and used it like a stencil to produce a sharp upper edge and a diffused lower edge. You get an illusion of the animal's rounded flank this way."

He experimented as he went. "You see the angular rump?" he says, pointing to the original painting. "I reproduced that by holding my hand perpendicular to the rock, with my palm slightly bent, and I spat along the edge formed by my hand and the rock." He found he could produce sharp lines, such as those in the tail and in the upper hind leg, by spitting into the gap between parallel hands. The belly demanded more ingenuity; he spat paint into a V-shape formed by his two splayed hands, rubbed it into a curved swath to shape the belly's outline, then finger-painted short protruding lines to suggest the animals' shaggy hair. Neatly outlined dots, he found, could not be made by blowing a thin jet of charcoal onto the wall. He had to spit pigment through a hole made in an animal skin. "I spent seven hours a day for a week," he says. "Puff . . . puff . . . puff. . . . It was exhausting, particularly because there was carbon monoxide in the cave. But you experience something special, painting like that. You feel you are breathing the image onto the rock—projecting your spirit from the deepest part of your body onto the rock surface."

Was that what the Paleolithic painter felt when creating this image? "Yes, I know it doesn't sound very scientific," Lorblanchet says of his highly personal style of investigation, "but the intellectual games of the structuralists haven't got us very far, have they? Studying rock art shouldn't be an intellectual game. It is about understanding humanity. That's why I believe the experimental approach is valid in this case."

The End

Hypotheses to account for the early European cave art are difficult because they so often depend on conjectural and subjective interpretations. Some have argued that it is art for art's sake; but if that is so, why were animals so often painted over one another, and why were they so often placed in inaccessible places? The latter might suggest that they were for ceremonial purposes and that the caves served as religious sanctuaries. One suggestion is that the animals were drawn to ensure success in the hunt, another that their depiction was seen as a way to promote fertility and increase the size of the herds on which humans depended. In Altimira Cave in northern Spain, for example, the art shows a pervasive concern for the sexual reproduction of the bison.[8] In cave art generally, though, the animals painted bear little relationship to those most frequently hunted. Furthermore, there are few depictions of animals being hunted or killed, nor are there depictions of animals copulating or with exaggerated sexual parts as there are in the Venus figures. Another suggestion is that rites by which youngsters were initiated into adulthood took place in the painted galleries. In support of this idea, footprints, most of which are small, have been found in the clay floors of several caves, and in one, they even circle a modeled clay bison. The animals painted, so this argument goes, may have had to do with knowledge being transmitted from the elders to the youths. Furthermore, the transmission of information might be implied by countless so-called signs, apparently abstract designs that accompany much Upper Paleolithic art. Some have interpreted these as tallies of animals killed, a reckoning of time according to a lunar calendar, or both.

---

[8]Halverson, J. (1989). Review of the book *Altimira revisited and other essays on early art. American Antiquity, 54,* 883.

These abstract designs, including such ones as the spots on the Pech Merle horses, suggest yet another possibility. For the most part, these are just like the entoptic designs seen by subjects in experiments dealing with altered states of consciousness, and which are so consistently present in the rock art of southern Africa. Furthermore, the rock art of southern Africa shows the same painting of new images over older ones, as well as the same sort of fixation on large, powerful animals instead of the ones most often eaten. Thus, the cave art of Europe may well represent the same depictions of trance experiences, painted after the fact. Consistent with this interpretation, the caves themselves are conducive to the sort of sensory distortion that can induce trance.

Artistic expression, whatever its purpose may have been, was not confined to rock surfaces and portable objects alone. Upper Paleolithic peoples also ornamented their bodies with necklaces of perforated animal teeth, shells, beads of bone, stone, and ivory; rings; bracelets; and anklets. Clothing, too, was adorned with beads. This should alert us to the probability that quite a lot of art was executed in perishable materials—wood carving, paintings on bark or animal skins, and the like. Thus, the rarity or absence of Upper Paleolithic art in

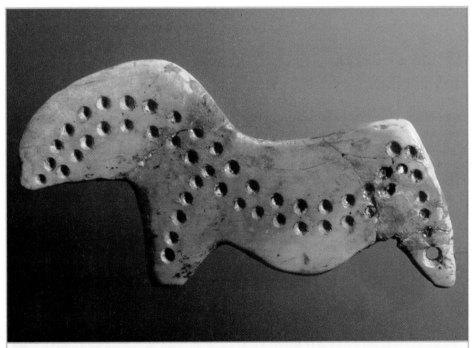

Dots are a common entoptic form, and in art depicting visions seen in trance, lines of dots are not uncommon, as on this 24,000-year-old ivory pendant from Sungir, Russia.

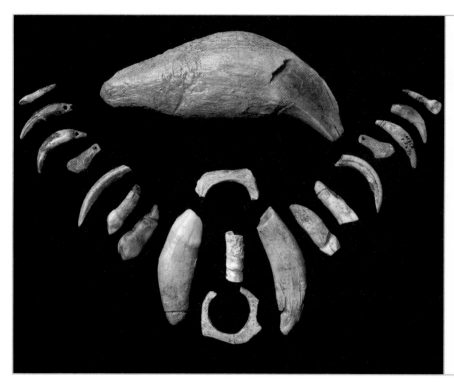

Pendants and beads for personal adornment became common in the Upper Paleolithic. In Europe, most were made by Cro-Magnons, but some—like those shown here—were made by Neandertals. The earliest undisputed items of personal adornment are some 40,000-year-old beads from Africa made from ostrich egg shell.

some parts of the inhabited world may be more apparent than real, as people elsewhere worked with materials unlikely to survive so long in the archaeological record.

OTHER ASPECTS OF UPPER PALEOLITHIC CULTURE

Upper Paleolithic peoples lived not only in caves and rock shelters, but also in structures built out in the open. In Ukraine, for example, the remains have been found of sizable settlements, in which huts were built on frameworks of intricately stacked mammoth bones. Where the ground was frozen, cobblestones were heated and placed in the earth to sink in, thereby providing sturdy, dry floors. Their hearths, no longer shallow depressions or flat surfaces that radiated back little heat, were instead stone-lined pits that conserved heat for extended periods and made for more efficient cooking. For the outdoors, they had the same sort of tailored clothing worn in historic times by the natives of Siberia, Alaska, and Canada. And they engaged in long-distance trade, as indicated, for example, by the presence of seashells and Baltic amber at sites several hundred kilometers from the sources of

these materials. Although Middle Paleolithic peoples also made use of rare and distant materials, they did not do so with the regularity seen in the Upper Paleolithic.

THE SPREAD OF UPPER PALEOLITHIC PEOPLES

Such was the effectiveness of their cultures that Upper Paleolithic peoples were able to expand into regions previously uninhabited by their archaic forebears. Colonization of Siberia began about 42,000 years ago, although it took something like 10,000 years before they reached the northeastern part of that region. Much earlier, by 60,000 years ago, people managed to get to Australia and New Guinea. To do this, they had to use some kind of watercraft to make the difficult crossing of at least 90 kilometers of water that separated Australia and New Guinea (then a single landmass) from the Asian continent throughout Paleolithic times. Once in Australia, these people created some of the world's earliest sophisticated rock art, some 10,000 to 15,000 years earlier than the more famous European cave paintings. Other evidence for sophisticated ritual activity in early Australia is provided by the burial of a man at least 40,000 and

Reconstruction of an Upper Paleolithic hut with walls of interlocked mammoth mandibles.

possibly 60,000 years ago.[9] His fingers were intertwined around his penis and red ochre had been scattered over the body. It may be that this pigment had more than sym-

bolic value; for example, its iron salts have antiseptic and deodorizing properties, and there are recorded instances in which red ochre is associated with prolonging life and is used medicinally to treat particular conditions or infections. One historically known native Australian society is reported to use ochre to heal wounds, scars, and burns, and a person with internal pain is covered with the substance and placed in the sun to promote sweating. What

[9]Rice, P. (2000). Paleoanthropology 2000—part 1. *General Anthropology, 7*(1), 11; Zimmer, C. (1999). New date for the dawn of dream time. *Science, 284,* 1,243.

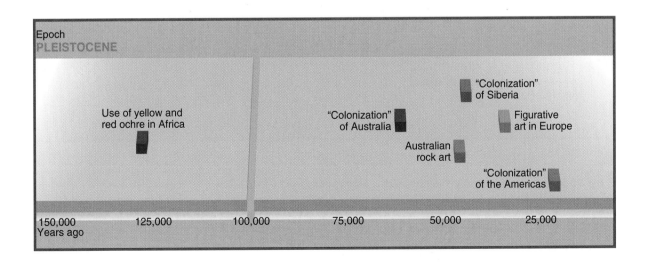

is especially interesting in view of the impressive accomplishments of native Australians is that the tools used by these people are remarkably similar to those of the Eurasian Middle Paleolithic. Clearly, simplicity of tool kits does not bespeak absence of sophisticated intellectual capabilities.

Just when people arrived in the Americas has been a matter of lively debate, but securely dated remains from Monte Verde, a site in south-central Chile, place people there by 12,500 years ago, if not earlier. Assuming the first populations spread from Siberia to Alaska, linguist Johanna Nichols suggests that the first people to arrive in North America did so by 20,000 years ago. She bases this estimate on the time it took various languages to spread from their homelands—Celtic languages in Europe, Eskimo languages in the Arctic, and Athabaskan languages from interior western Canada to New Mexico and Arizona (Navajo). Her conclusion is that it would have taken at least 7,000 years for people to reach south-central Chile.[10]

The conventional wisdom has long been that the first people spread into North America over dry land that connected Siberia to Alaska. This so-called land bridge was a consequence of the buildup of great continental glaciers. As these ice masses grew, there was a worldwide lowering of sea levels, causing an emergence of land in places like the Bering Straits where seas today are shallow. Thus, Alaska became, in effect, an eastward extension of Siberia (Figure 10.6).

Although ancient Siberians may indeed have spread eastward, it is now clear that their way south was blocked by massive glaciers until 13,000 years ago at the earliest.[11] By then, people were already living further south. Thus the question of how people first came to the Americas has been reopened. One possibility is that, like the first Australians, the first Americans may have come by boat, perhaps traveling between islands or ice-free pockets of coastline, from as far away as the Japanese islands and down North America's northwest coast. Hints of such voyages are provided by a handful of North

---

[10]The first Americans, ca. 20,000 B.C. (1998). *Discover, 19*(6), 24.

[11]Marshall, E. (2001). Preclovis sites fight for acceptance. *Science, 291,* 1,732.

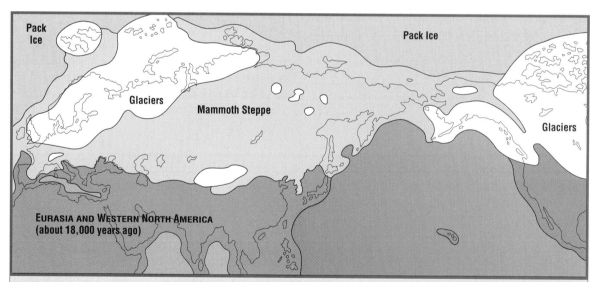

FIGURE 10.6

AS THIS MAP SHOWS, THE LAND CONNECTING SIBERIA AND ALASKA AT THE HEIGHT OF THE LAST GLACIATION WAS NOT SO MUCH A BRIDGE FOR PEOPLE TO CROSS INTO NORTH AMERICA AS IT WAS A PERIPHERAL PORTION OF A REGION INTO WHICH HUMAN POPULATIONS IN THE UPPER PALEOLITHIC SPREAD. OTHER POPULATIONS LIKELY MOVED BY BOAT ALONG THE COAST, ARRIVING IN NORTH AMERICA SOUTH OF THE ICE. ONCE THE ICE BARRIER BETWEEN LOWER NORTH AMERICA AND ALASKA RECEDED, OPPORTUNITIES FOR GENE FLOW BETWEEN NATIVE AMERICANS AND EAST ASIANS WOULD HAVE INCREASED.

Fluted points, such as these, tipped the spears of Paleoindian hunters in North America about 12,000 years ago.

American skeletons that bear a closer resemblance to the aboriginal Ainu people of Japan and their forebears than they do to other Asians or modern Native Americans. Unfortunately, because sea levels were lower than they are today, coastal sites used by early voyagers would now be under water.

The picture currently emerging, then, is of people, who did not look like modern American Indians, arriving by boat, spreading southward and eastward over time. There is no reason to suppose that contact back and forth between North America and Siberia ever stopped. In all probability, it became more common as the glaciers melted away. As a consequence, through gene flow as well as later arrivals of people from the East, those living in the Americas came to have the broad faces, prominent cheekbones, and round cranial vaults that characterize American Indians today.

Although the earliest technologies in the Americas remain poorly known, they gave rise in North America, about 12,000 years ago, to the distinctive fluted spear points of **Paleoindian** hunters of big game, such as mammoths, caribou, and now extinct forms of bison. Fluted points are finely made, with large channel flakes removed from one or both surfaces. This thinned section was inserted into the notched end of a spear shaft for a sturdy

Paleoindians, like their Upper Paleolithic contemporaries in Eurasia, were such accomplished hunters that they, too, could kill more animals than could possibly be used at one time. These bones are the remains of some 200 bison that Paleoindian hunters stampeded over a cliff 8,500 years ago.

Paleoindian.   The earliest inhabitants of North America.

haft. Fluted points are found from the Atlantic seaboard to the Pacific coast, and from Alaska down into Panama. So efficient were the hunters who made these points that they may have hastened the extinction of the mammoth and other large Pleistocene mammals. By driving large numbers of animals over cliffs, they killed many more than they could possibly use, thus wasting huge amounts of meat.

WHERE DID UPPER PALEOLITHIC PEOPLE COME FROM?

As noted in Chapter 9, scholars still debate whether the transition from archaic to anatomically modern *H. sapiens* took place in one specific population or was the result of several populations living in Africa, Asia, and even Europe between 100,000 and 40,000 years ago evolving together. At the moment, though, the odds seem to favor

the latter hypothesis. Even in Europe, where the argument for replacement of archaic by modern *sapiens* has been most strongly made, the most recent Neandertals display modern features, whereas the most ancient moderns show what appear to be Neandertal holdovers. For example, the Saint Césaire skull has the high forehead and chin of moderns. Similarly, a late Neandertal from Vindija, northern Croatia, shows a thinning of brow ridges toward their outer margins. Conversely, early Upper Paleolithic skulls from Brno, Mladec, and Predmosti, in the Czech Republic, retain heavy brow ridges and Neandertal-like muscle attachments on their backs.[12] As noted early in this chapter, some of the skulls from the Cro-Magnon rock shelter look Neandertal-like from the back. Of course, these features could all be the result of interbreeding between two populations that overlapped in time, rather than simple evolution from one into the other. Or, they could represent a single varied population whose average characters were shifting in a more "modern" direction. In either case, they do not fit with the idea of the complete extinction of the older population.

Looking at the larger picture, what we see in all regions of the Old World, since the time of *H. erectus,* is more and more emphasis placed on cultural, as opposed to biological, adaptation. To handle environmental stress, reliance was placed increasingly on the development of appropriate tools, clothes, shelter, use of fire, and so forth, as opposed to alteration of the human organism itself. This was true whether human populations lived in hot or cold, wet or dry, forest or grassland areas. Because culture is learned and not carried by genes, it is ultimately based on what might loosely be called "brain power" or, more formally, **cognitive capacity.** Although this includes intelligence in the IQ sense, it is broader than that, for it also includes such aptitudes as educability, concept formation, self-awareness, self-evaluation, reliability of performance under stress, attention span, sensitivity in discrimination, and creativity.

The major thrust in the evolution of the genus *Homo,* then, has been toward improved cognitive capacity through the evolution of the brain regardless of the environmental and climatic differences among the regions in

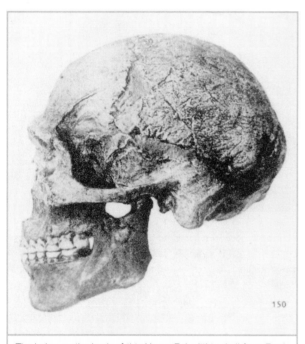

150

The bulge on the back of this Upper Paleolithic skull from Predmosti in the Czech Republic, along with its still prominent brow ridges, is reminiscent of the earlier Neandertals.

[12]Bednarik, R. G. (1995). Concept-mediated marking in the Lower Paleolithic. *Current Anthropology, 36,* 627; Minugh-Purvis, N. (1992). The inhabitants of Ice Age Europe. *Expedition, 34*(3), 33–34.

Cognitive capacity.   A broad concept including intelligence, educability, concept formation, self-awareness, self-evaluation, attention span, sensitivity in discrimination, and creativity.

In 1998, this skeleton of a 4-year-old child was found in a Portuguese rock shelter, where it had been ritually buried. It displays a mix of Neandertal and Cro-Magnon traits, but its 25,000-year-old date makes it too recent to be the product of a chance encounter between two populations (by then, Neandertals were long gone). Instead, it bespeaks earlier extensive interbreeding, or else is one more example of an Upper Paleolithic European showing evidence of Neandertal ancestry. In either case, the idea of Neandertals and Cro-Magnons as separate species is effectively ruled out.

which populations of the genus lived. Hence, there has been a certain similarity of selective pressures in all regions. At the same time, gene flow among populations would have spread whatever genes happen to relate to cognitive capacity. In an evolving species, in the absence of isolating mechanisms, genes having survival value anywhere tend to spread from one population to another. As a case in point, wolves, like humans, have a wide distribution, ranging all the way from the Atlantic coast of Europe eastward across Eurasia and North America to Greenland. Yet, wolves constitute a single species—*Canis lupus*—and never in its 5- to 7-million-year evolutionary history has more than a single species coexisted.[13] That wolves never split into multiple species relates to the size of territories occupied by successful packs, and exchange of mates between packs. Both promoted gene flow across the species' entire range.

It is impossible to know just how much gene flow took place among ancient human populations, but that some took place is consistent with the sudden appearance of novel traits in one region later than their appearance somewhere else. For example, Upper Paleolithic remains from North Africa exhibit the kind of mid-facial flatness previously seen only in East Asian fossils; similarly, various Cro-Magnon fossils from Europe show the short upper jaws, horizontally oriented cheek bones, and rectangular eye orbits previously seen in East Asians. Conversely, the round orbits, large frontal sinuses, and thin cranial bones seen in some archaic *sapiens* skulls from China represent the first appearance there of traits that have greater antiquity in the West.[14] What appears to be happening, then, is that genetic variants from the East are being introduced into Western gene pools and vice versa. Support for this comes from studies of the

[13]Brace, C. L. (2000). *Evolution in an anthropological view* (p. 341). Walnut Creek, CA: Altamira.

[14]Pope, G. C. (1992). Craniofacial evidence for the origin of modern humans in China. *Yearbook of Physical Anthropology, 35,* 287–288.

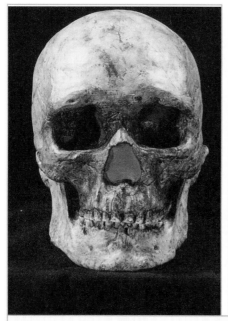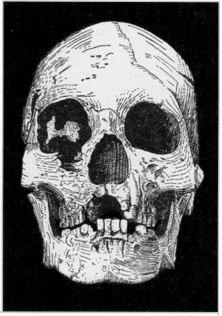

These Upper Paleolithic skulls from China (left) and Africa (right) are easily derivable from earlier archaic *sapiens* skulls in the same region.

Y chromosome in humans (found only in males). These studies indicate that some DNA carried by this chromosome originated in Asia at least 200,000 years ago and spread from there to Africa.[15] Not only is such gene flow consistent with the remarkable tendency historically known humans have to "swap genes" between populations, even in the face of cultural barriers to gene flow, it is also consistent with the tendency of other primates to produce hybrids when two subspecies (and sometimes even species) come into contact.[16] Moreover, without such gene flow, multiregional evolution inevitably would have resulted in the appearance of multiple species of modern humans, something that clearly has *not* happened. In fact, the low level of genetic differentiation among modern humans can be explained easily as a consequence of high levels of gene flow.[17]

MAJOR PALEOLITHIC TRENDS

Certain trends stand out from the information anthropologists have gathered about the Old Stone Age, in most parts of the world. One was toward increasingly more sophisticated, varied, and specialized tool kits. Tools became progressively lighter and smaller, resulting in the conservation of raw materials and a better ratio between length of cutting edge and weight of stone. Tools became specialized according to region and function. Instead of crude all-purpose tools, more effective particularized devices were made to deal more effectively with the differing conditions of savanna, forest, and shore.

This more efficient tool technology enabled human populations to grow and spill over into more diverse environments; it also was responsible for the loss of heavy physical features, favoring instead decreased size and weight of face and teeth, the development of larger and more complex brains, and ultimately a reduction in body size and robusticity. This dependence on intelligence rather than bulk provided the key for humans' increased reliance on cultural rather than physical adaptation. As the brain became modernized, conceptual thought developed, as evidenced by symbolic artifacts and signs of ritual activity.

[15]Gibbons, A. (1997). Ideas on human origins evolve at anthropology gathering. *Science, 276,* 535–536.

[16]Simons, E. L. (1989). Human origins. *Science, 245,* 1,349.

[17]Relethford, J. H., & Harpending, H. C. (1994). Craniometric variation, genetic theory, and modern human origins. *American Journal of Physical Anthropology, 95,* 265.

By the Upper Paleolithic, the amount of sexual dimorphism, too, was greatly reduced, as size differences between men and women were relatively slight compared to what they were in *Australopithecus, Homo habilis,* or (to a lesser extent) *Homo erectus.* This has important implications for gender relations. As noted in earlier chapters, among primates marked sexual dimorphism is associated with male dominance over females. Lack of sexual dimorphism, by contrast, correlates with a lack of such dominance. In evolving humans, it appears that a loss of male dominance went hand in hand with the ever-increasing importance of cooperative relationships. (Paradoxically, humans reinvented male dominance in the context of civilization, a relatively recent development that is the subject of Chapter 12.)

Through Paleolithic times, at least in the colder parts of the world, there appeared a trend toward the importance of and proficiency in hunting. Humans' intelligence enabled them to develop tools that exceeded other animals' physical equipment, as well as the improved social organization and cooperation so important for survival and population growth. As discussed in the next chapter, this trend was reversed during the Mesolithic, when hunting lost its preeminence, and the gathering of wild plants and seafood became increasingly important.

As human populations grew and spread, regionalism also became more marked. Tool assemblages developed in different ways at different times in different areas. General differences appeared between north and south, east and west. Although there are some indications of cultural contact and intercommunication, such as the development of long-distance trade in the Upper Paleolithic, regionalism was a dominant characteristic of Paleolithic times. The persistence of regionalism was probably due to two factors: a perceived need to distinguish symbolically one's own people from others and the need to adapt to differing environments. Paleolithic peoples eventually spread over all the continents of the world, including Australia and the Americas, and as they did so, changes in climate and environment called for new kinds of adaptations. Thus Paleolithic tool kits had to be altered to meet the requirements of many varying locations. In forest environments, people needed tools for working wood; on the open savanna and plains, they came to use the bow and arrow to hunt the game they could not stalk closely; the people in settlements that grew up around lakes and along rivers and coasts developed harpoons and hooks; in the subarctic regions they needed tools to work the heavy skins of seals and caribou. The fact that culture is first and foremost an adaptive mechanism meant that it was of necessity a regional thing.

CHAPTER SUMMARY

The Cro-Magnons and the other Upper Paleolithic peoples of the world, in addition to a full-sized brain, possessed a physical appearance somewhat similar to our own. The modernization of the face of Upper Paleolithic peoples is a result of a reduction in the size of the teeth and the muscles involved in chewing and relates to the fact that teeth were no longer being used as tools. Similarly, bodies became somewhat less massive and robust as improved technology reduced the need for brute strength.

Upper Paleolithic cultures evolved out of the Middle Paleolithic cultures of Africa, Asia, and Europe. The typical Upper Paleolithic tool was the blade. The blade technique of toolmaking was less wasteful of flint than Middle Paleolithic methods. Other efficient Upper Paleolithic toolmaking techniques were pressure flaking of stone and using chisel-like tools called burins to fashion bone, antler horn, and ivory into tools. The cultural adaptation of Upper Paleolithic peoples became specific; they developed different tools in different regions. Northern Upper Paleolithic cultures supported themselves by the hunting of large herd animals and catching smaller animals in nets. Hunting with the bow and arrow developed in Africa, spreading later to Europe and other regions. Upper Paleolithic cultures are the earliest in which artistic expression is common.

The emphasis in evolution of the genus *Homo* in all parts of the world was toward increasing cognitive capacity through development of the brain. This took place regardless of environmental or climatic conditions under which the genus lived. In addition, evolution of the genus *Homo* undoubtedly involved gene flow among populations. Lack of much genetic differentiation among human populations today bespeaks high levels of gene flow among populations in the past.

Three trends are evident in the Paleolithic period. First was a trend toward more sophisticated, varied, and specialized tool kits. This trend enabled people to increase their population and spread to new environments. It also had an impact on human anatomy, favoring decreased size and weight of face and teeth, the development of larger, more complex brains, and ultimately a reduction in body size, mass, and degree of sexual dimorphism. Second was a trend toward the importance of and proficiency in hunting. Third was a trend toward regionalism, as people's technology and life habits increasingly reflected their association with a particular environment.

CLASSIC READINGS

Campbell, B. G., & Loy, J. D. (1995). *Humankind emerging* (7th ed.). New York: HarperCollins.

Adapted in part from Time-Life's *Emergence of Man* and *Life Nature Library,* this is a richly illustrated, up-to-date account of the Paleolithic. In it, Campbell integrates paleontological and archaeological data with ethnographic data on modern food foragers to present a rich picture of evolving Paleolithic ways of life.

Pfeiffer, J. E. (1985). *The creative explosion.* Ithaca, NY: Cornell University Press.

A fascinating and readable discussion of the origins of art and religion. Its main drawback is its focus on European art.

Prideaux, T., et al. (1973). *Cro-Magnon man.* New York: Time-Life.

This beautifully illustrated volume in the Time-Life *Emergence of Man* series, though dated, is worth looking at for the illustrations. It also shows that, although our ideas about human evolution have changed over the past 30 years, some old biases still persist.

Wolpoff, M., & Caspari, R. (1997). *Race and human evolution.* New York: Simon & Schuster.

This book is a detailed but readable presentation of the multiregional hypothesis of modern human origins. Among its strengths is a discussion of the problem of defining what "anatomically modern" means.

HUMAN BIOLOGICAL AND CULTURAL EVOLUTION SINCE THE OLD STONE AGE

Chapter 11   Cultivation and Domestication

Chapter 12   The Rise of Cities and Civilization

Chapter 13   Modern Human Diversity

INTRODUCTION

Up until the Middle Paleolithic, the story of the evolution of the genus *Homo* is one of a close interrelation between developing culture and developing humanity. The critical importance of culture as the human adaptive mechanism seems to have imposed selective pressures favoring a bigger, more elaborate brain, with greater cognitive power.

This in turn made possible improved cultural adaptation. Indeed, it seems fair to say that modern humans look the way they do today because cultural adaptation came to play such a vital role in the survival of our ancient ancestors.

By 200,000 years ago, the human brain had become as big as it would get, and there has been no subsequent increase in size. Human culture, by contrast, continued to change at an even faster pace than before. Hence, there was a kind of "disconnect" between culture and biology; as humans became modern in form, macroevolution came to a halt, even though microevolution continues to this day.

By 36,000 years ago, humans everywhere had developed cultures comparable to those of historically known food-foraging peoples. Although these cultures served humans well through tens of thousands of years of the Upper

Paleolithic, far-reaching changes began to take place in some parts of the world as early as 11,000 years ago. This second major cultural revolution consisted of the emergence of food production, the subject of Chapter 11. Eventually, most of the world's peoples became food producers, even though food foraging remained a satisfactory way of life for some.

At the present time, fewer than a quarter of a million people—less than 0.00005 percent of a world population of over 6 billion—remain food foragers. Just as the emergence of food foraging was followed by modifications and improvements leading to regional variants of this pattern, so the advent of food production opened the way for new cultural variants based upon it. Chapter 12 discusses the result: further cultural diversity, out of which developed civilization, the basis of modern life.

Despite the increasing effectiveness of culture as the primary mechanism by which humans adapt to diverse environments, and the lack of macroevolutionary change since the emergence of the modern human species, microevolutionary change has continued. In the course of their movement into other parts of the world, humans had already developed a certain amount of biological variation from one population to another. On top of this, populations of food producers were exposed to selective pressures of a different sort than those affecting food foragers, thereby inducing further changes in human gene pools. Such changes continue to affect humans today, even though we remain the same species now as at the end of the Paleolithic. Chapter 13 discusses how the variation to be seen in *Homo sapiens* today came into existence as the result of forces altering the frequencies of alleles in human gene pools and why such variation probably has nothing to do with intelligence. The chapter concludes with a look at forces apparently active today to produce further changes in those same gene pools.

CHAPTER 11

CULTIVATION AND DOMESTICATION

Beginning about 11,000 years ago, some of the world's people embarked on a new way of life based on food production. Though farming has changed dramatically in the millennia since then, all of the crops we rely on today originated with those earliest farmers.

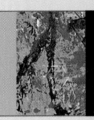

1

When and Where Did the Change from Food Foraging to Food Production Begin?

Independent centers of early plant and animal domestication exist in Africa, China, Mesoamerica, North and South America, as well as Southwest and Southeast Asia. From these places, food production spread to most other parts of the world. It began at more or less the same time in these different places—perhaps a bit earlier in Southwest Asia, but a bit later in Southeast Asia.

2

Why Did the Change Take Place?

Because food production by and large requires more work than hunting and gathering, it is not necessarily a more secure means of subsistence; and because it requires people to eat more of the foods that food foragers eat only when they have no other choice, it can be assumed that people probably did not become food producers through choice. Of various theories that have been proposed, the most likely is that food production came about as a consequence of a chance convergence of separate natural events and cultural developments.

3

What Were the Consequences of the Change to Food Production?

Although food production generally provides less leisure time than food foraging, it does permit some reallocation of the workload. Some people can produce enough food to support others who undertake other tasks, and so a number of technological developments, such as weaving and pottery making, generally accompany food production. In addition, it facilitates a sedentary way of life in villages, with more substantial housing. Finally, the new modes of work and resource allocation require new ways of organizing people, generally into lineages, clans, and common-interest associations.

Throughout the Paleolithic, people depended exclusively on wild sources of food for their survival. In cold northern regions, they came to rely on the hunting of large animals such as the mammoth, bison, and horse, but especially reindeer, as well as smaller animals such as hares, foxes, and birds. Elsewhere, they hunted, fished, or gathered whatever nature provided. There is no evidence in Paleolithic remains to indicate that livestock was kept or plants cultivated. Paleolithic people followed wild herds and gathered wild plant foods, relying on their wits and muscles to acquire what nature provided. Whenever favored sources of food became scarce, as sometimes happened, people adjusted by increasing the variety of food eaten and incorporating less favored food into their diets.

About 12,000 years ago, the subsistence practices of some people began to change in ways that were to transform radically their way of life, although no one involved had any way of knowing it at the time. Not until these changes were well advanced could people realize that their mode of subsistence differed from that of other cultures—that they had become farmers, rather than food foragers.[1] This change in the means of obtaining food had important implications for human development, for it meant that by taking matters into their own hands, people could lead a more sedentary existence. Moreover, by reorganizing the workload, some of them could be freed from the food quest to devote their energies to other sorts of tasks. With good reason, the **Neolithic period,** when this change took place, has been called a revolutionary one in human history. This period, and the changes that took place within it, are the subjects of this chapter.

THE MESOLITHIC ROOTS OF FARMING AND PASTORALISM

By 12,000 years ago, glacial conditions in the world were moderating, causing changes in human habitats. Throughout the world, sea levels were on the rise, ultimately flooding many areas that had been above sea level during periods of glaciation, such as the Bering Straits,

parts of the North Sea, and an extensive area that had joined the eastern islands of Indonesia to Southeast Asia. In northern regions, milder climates brought about marked changes as, in some regions, tundras were replaced by hardwood forests. In the process, the herd animals upon which northern Paleolithic peoples had depended for much of their food, clothing, and shelter disappeared from many areas. Some, like the reindeer and musk ox, moved to colder climates; others, like the mammoths, died out completely. Thus, the northerners especially were forced to adapt to new conditions. In the new forests, animals were more solitary in their habits and so not as easy to hunt as they had been, and large, cooperative hunts were less productive than before. However, plant food was more abundant, and there were new and abundant sources of fish and other food around lake shores, bays, and rivers. Hence, human populations developed new and ingenious ways to catch and kill a variety of smaller birds and animals, while at the same time they devoted more energy to fishing and the collection of a broad spectrum of wild plant foods. This new way of life marks the end of the Paleolithic and the start of the **Mesolithic,** or Middle Stone Age.

Mesolithic Tools and Weapons

New technologies were developed for the changed post-glacial environment. Ground stone tools, shaped and sharpened by grinding the tool against sandstone (often using sand as an additional abrasive), made effective axes and adzes. Such implements, though they do take longer to make, are less prone to breakage under heavy-duty usage than are those made of chipped stone. Thus, they were helpful in clearing forest areas and in the woodwork needed for the creation of dugout canoes and skin-covered boats. Although some kind of water craft had been developed early enough to get humans to the island of Flores (and probably Italy and Spain) by 800,000 years ago, sophisticated boats become prominent only in Mesolithic sites, indicating that human foraging for food frequently took place on the water as well as the land. Thus, it was possible to make use of deep-water resources as well as those of coastal areas.

The characteristic Mesolithic tool was the **microlith,** a small but hard, sharp blade. Although a microlithic

---

[1]Rindos, D. (1984). *The origins of agriculture: An evolutionary perspective* (p. 99). Orlando: Academic Press.

Neolithic period.   The New Stone Age; began about 11,000 years ago in Southwest Asia.   •   **Mesolithic.** The Middle Stone Age of Europe and Southwest Asia; began about 12,000 years ago.   •   **Microlith.**   A small blade of flint or similar stone, several of which were hafted together in wooden handles to make tools; widespread in the Mesolithic.

Two examples of ground stone tools used for heavy woodworking: an axe and a gouge. The groove on the axe was for hafting in a wooden handle. Gouges like this one were used to make dugout canoes.

tradition existed in Central Africa by about 40,000 years ago,[2] such tools did not become common elsewhere until the Mesolithic. Microliths could be mass produced because they were small, easy to make, and could be fashioned from materials other than flint. Also, they could be attached to arrow shafts by using melted resin as a binder. Thus, the bow and arrow with the microlith arrowhead became the deadliest and most common weapon of the Mesolithic.

The reliance of Mesolithic peoples on microliths provided them with an important advantage over their Upper Paleolithic forebears: The small size of the microlith enabled them to devise a wider array of composite tools made out of stone and wood or bone (Figure 11.1). Thus, they could make sickles, harpoons, arrows, and daggers by fitting microliths into slots in wood or bone handles.

Later experimentation with these forms led to more sophisticated tools and weapons.

It appears that the Mesolithic was a more sedentary period for humans than earlier eras. Dwellings from this period seem more substantial, an indication of permanency. Indeed, this is a logical development. Most hunting cultures, and especially those depending on herd animals, are nomadic: To be successful, one must follow the game. This is not necessary for people who subsist on a diet of seafood and plants, as the location of shore and vegetation remains relatively constant.

Cultural Diversity in the Mesolithic

In the warmer parts of the world, the collection of wild plant foods had been more of an equal partner with hunting in subsistence activities in the Upper Paleolithic than had been the case in the colder north. Hence, in areas like Southwest Asia, the Mesolithic represents less of a

---

[2]Bednarik, R.G. (1995). Concept-mediated marking in the Lower Paleolithic. *Current Anthropology 36,* 606.

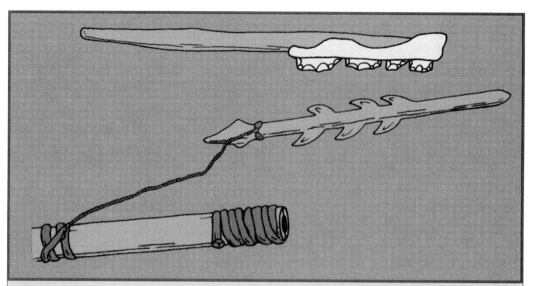

FIGURE 11.1

THIS DRAWING SHOWS A MESOLITHIC COMPOSITE TOOL CONSISTING OF MICROLITHS SET INTO A WOODEN HANDLE. ALSO SHOWN IS A BONE HARPOON HEAD WITH THE END OF ITS WOODEN SHAFT. HARPOONS ACTUALLY CAME INTO USE BEFORE THE MESOLITHIC.

changed way of life than was true in Europe. Here, the important **Natufian culture** flourished.

The Natufians were a people who lived between 12,500 and 10,200 years ago at the eastern end of the Mediterranean Sea in caves, rock shelters, and small villages with stone- and mud-walled houses. Nearby, their dead were buried in communal cemeteries, usually in shallow pits without grave goods or decorations. A small shrine is known from one of their villages, a 10,500-year-old settlement at Jericho. Basin-shaped depressions in the rocks found outside homes at Natufian sites are thought to have been storage pits. Plastered storage pits beneath the floors of the houses were also found, indicating that the Natufians were the earliest Mesolithic people known to have stored plant foods. Certain tools found among Natufian remains bear evidence that they were used to cut grain. These Mesolithic sickles, for that is what they were, consisted of small stone blades set in straight handles of wood or bone.

In the Americas, cultures comparable to Mesolithic cultures of the Old World developed, but here they are referred to as **Archaic cultures.** Outside of the Arctic, microlithic tools are not prominent in them, as they are in parts of the Old World, but ground stone tools such as axes, adzes, gouges, plummets, and spear-thrower weights are common. Archaic cultures were widespread in the Americas; one of the more dramatic was the **Maritime Archaic,** which began to develop about 7,000 years ago around the Gulf of St. Lawrence. These people developed an elaborate assortment of bone and ground slate tools with which they hunted a wide variety of sea mammals, including whales; fish, including swordfish; and sea birds. To get some of these, they regularly paddled their dugout canoes far offshore. To appreciate the skills this required, one need only recognize the difficulty of landing a 500-pound swordfish, as these are extremely aggressive fish. They are known historically to have driven their swords through the hulls of substantial wooden vessels. The Maritime Archaic people also developed the first elaborate burial cult in North America, involving the use of red ochre ("red paint") and the placement of finely made grave goods with the deceased.

Natufian culture.   A Mesolithic culture of Israel, Lebanon, and western Syria, between about 12,500 and 10,200 years ago. • **Archaic cultures.**   Term used to refer to Mesolithic cultures in the Americas. • **Maritime Archaic culture.**   An Archaic culture of northeastern North America, centered on the Gulf of St. Lawrence, that emphasized the utilization of marine resources.

At Nulliak, Labrador, Maritime Archaic people lived in large, long houses with stone foundations. The alignments of stones seen in this photo are all that remain of one such house.

Varied though Mesolithic and Archaic cultures were, this new way of life generally offered more secure supplies of food and therefore an increased margin of survival. In some parts of the world, people started living in larger and more sedentary groups and cooperating with others outside the sphere of family or hunting band. They became settled village dwellers, and some of these settlements were shortly to expand into the first farming villages, towns, and (ultimately) cities.

THE NEOLITHIC REVOLUTION

The Neolithic, or New Stone Age, was characterized by the transition from foraging for food to dependence upon domesticated plants and animals. It was by no means a smooth or rapid transition; in fact, the switch to food production spread over many centuries—even millennia— and was a direct outgrowth of the preceding Mesolithic. Where to draw the line between the two periods is not always clear.

The term *New Stone Age* is derived from the polished stone tools that are characteristic of this period. But more important than the presence of these tools is the transition from a hunting, gathering, and fishing economy to one based on food production, representing a major change in the subsistence practices of early peoples. One of the first regions to undergo this transition, and certainly the most intensively studied, was Southwest Asia. The remains of domesticated plants and animals are known from parts of Israel, Jordan, Syria, Turkey, Iraq, and Iran, all before 8,000 years ago.

Domestication: What Is It?

Domestication is an evolutionary process whereby humans modify, either intentionally or unintentionally, the genetic makeup of a population of plants or animals, sometimes to the extent that members of the population are unable to survive and/or reproduce without human assistance. As such, it constitutes a special case of a kind

Domestication. An evolutionary process whereby humans modify, either intentionally or unintentionally, the genetic makeup of a population of plants or animals, sometimes to the extent that members of the population are unable to survive and/or reproduce without human assistance.

of relationship between different species frequently seen in the natural world, as in the case of one species that has come to depend for its protection and reproductive success on some other that feeds upon it. A particularly dramatic example is offered by species of New World ants that grow fungi in their nests, providing the ants with most of their nutrition. Like human farmers, the ants add manure to stimulate fungal growth and eliminate competing weeds both mechanically and through use of antibiotic herbicides. They propagate their crops vegetatively, as do humans for some of their crops (bananas, for example), and even share crops, as when one ant species borrows from another's nest or when several nests become disturbed and mixed. Finally, like human farming, ant farming did not develop just once, but at least five different times.[3]

Looked at from the perspective of the fungi, the benefit gained is protection and ensured reproductive success. Turning from fungi to plants, we find that there are numerous species that rely on some type of animal—in some cases birds, in others mammals, and in yet others insects—for protection and dispersal of their seeds. The important thing is that both parties benefit from the arrangement; reliance on animals for seed dispersal ensures that the latter will be carried further afield than would otherwise be possible, thereby cutting down on competition for sun and nutrients between young and old plants and reducing the likelihood that any diseases or parasites harbored by one will be transmitted to the others. Added vigor is apt to come to plants that are freed from the need to provide themselves with built-in defensive mechanisms such as thorns, toxins, or chemical compounds that make them taste bad. This enhanced vigor may be translated into larger and more tasty edible parts to attract the animals that feed upon them, thereby cementing the relationship between the protected and protector.

Evidence of Early Plant Domestication

The characteristics of plants under human domestication that set them apart from their wild ancestors and have made them attractive to those who eat them include increased size, at least of edible parts; reduction or loss of natural means of seed dispersal; reduction or loss of protective devices such as husks or distasteful chemical compounds; loss of delayed seed germination (important to wild plants for survival in times of drought or other adverse conditions of temporary duration); and development of simultaneous ripening of the seed or fruit. Many of these characteristics can be seen in plant remains from archaeological sites; thus, paleobotanists can often tell the fossil of a wild plant species from a domesticated one, for example, by studying the seed of cereal grasses, such as barley, wheat, and maize (corn). Wild cereals have a very fragile stem, whereas domesticated ones have a tough stem. Under natural conditions, plants with fragile stems scatter their seed for themselves, whereas those with tough stems do not.

Worker ants have made a path as they go out to cut pieces of leaf that they bring back to their nest to make the soil in which they plant their fungus gardens.

---

[3]Diamond, J. (1998). Ants, crops, and history. *Science, 281,* 1,974–1,975.

Wild wheat kernels from a site in Syria (left) are compared with those of a domestic variety grown in Greece 2,000 to 3,000 years later (right). Increased size of edible parts is a common feature of domestication.

The structural change from a soft to a tough stem in early domesticated plants involves a genetic change, undoubtedly the result of what Darwin referred to as **unconscious selection:** the preservation of valued individuals and the destruction of less valued ones, with no thought as to long-range consequences.[4] When the grain stalks were harvested, their soft stem would shatter at the touch of sickle or flail, and many of their seeds would be lost. Inevitably, most of the seeds that people harvested would have been taken from the tough plants. Early domesticators probably also tended to select seed from plants having few husks or none at all—eventually breeding them out—because husking prior to pounding the grains into meal or flour was much too time-consuming. Size of plants is another good indicator of the presence of domestication. For example, the large ear of corn (maize) we know today is a far cry from the tiny ears (about an inch long) characteristic of early maize. In fact, the ear of corn may have arisen as a simple gene mutation transformed male tassel spikes of the wild grass teosinte into small and primitive versions of the female corn ear.[5] Small and primitive though these were (an

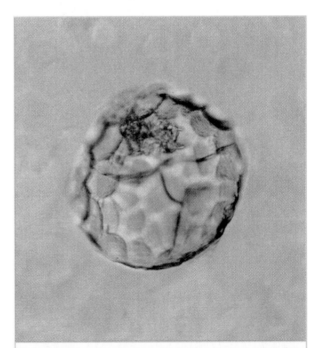

Shown here is a magnification of a phytolith of squash. Phytoliths are microscopic silica bodies formed as plants take up silica from groundwater. As the silica gradually fills plant cells, it assumes their distinctive size and shape. They are important for archaeologists, as they survive in humid climates where organic remains rapidly decay.

[4]Rindos, p. 86.

[5]Gould, S. J. (1991). *The flamingo's smile: Reflections in natural history* (p. 368). New York: Norton.

Unconscious selection.   The preservation of valued variants of a plant or animal species and the destruction of less valued ones, with no thought as to the long-range consequences.

Evidence of Early Animal Domestication

Domestication also produced changes in the skeletal structure of some animals. For example, the horns of wild goats and sheep differ from those of their domesticated counterparts (domesticated female sheep have none). Another structural change that occurred in domestication involves the size of the animal or its parts. For example, certain teeth of domesticated pigs are smaller than those of wild ones.

A study of age and sex ratios of butchered animals at a site may indicate whether or not animal domestication was practiced. Investigators have assumed that if the age and/or sex ratios at the site differ from those in wild herds, the imbalances are due to conscious selection. For example, at 10,000-year-old sites in the Zagros Mountains of Iran and Iraq, there was a sharp rise in the numbers of young male goats killed. Evidently, people were slaughtering the young males for food and saving the females for breeding. Although such herd management does not prove that the goats were fully domesticated, it does indicate a first step in the domestication process.[6]

In Peru, the prominence of bones of newborn llamas at archaeological sites (up to 72 percent at some), dating to around 6,300 years ago, is probably indicative of at least incipient domestication. Such high mortality rates for newborn animals are uncommon in wild herds but are common where animals are penned up. Under confined conditions, the inevitable buildup of mud and filth harbors bacteria that cause diarrhea and enterotoxemia, both of which are fatal to newborn animals.

Beginnings of Domestication

Over the past 30 years, a good deal of information has accumulated about the beginnings of domestication, primarily in Southwest Asia as well as Central and South America. We still do not have all the answers about how and why it took place. Nonetheless, some observations of general validity can be made that help us to understand how the switch to food production may have taken place.

The first of these observations is that the switch to food production was not the result of such discoveries

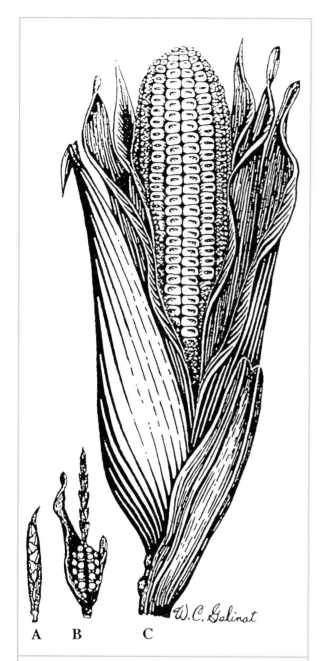

A **B** **C**

Teosinte (A), compared to the 5,500-year-old maize (B) and modern maize (C). The wild grass from which maize originated, teosinte is far less productive than maize and doesn't taste very good. Like most plants that were domesticated, it was not a first- or even second-choice food for foraging people.

entire ear contained less nourishment than a single kernel of modern maize), they were radically different in structure from the ears of teosinte.

---

[6]Zeder, M. A., & Hesse, B. (2000). The initial domestication of goats *(Capra hircus)* in the Zagros Mountains 10,000 years ago. *Science, 287,* 2,254–2,257.

that seeds, if planted, grow into plants. Food foragers are far from ignorant about the forces of nature and are perfectly aware of the role of seeds in plant growth, that plants grow better under certain conditions than others, and so forth. Physiologist Jared Diamond calls such peoples "walking encyclopedias of natural history with individual names for as many as a thousand or more plant and animal species, and with detailed knowledge of those species' biological characteristics, distribution and potential uses."[7] What's more, they frequently apply their knowledge so as to manage actively the resources on which they depend. For example, Indians living in the northern part of Canada's Alberta Province put to use a sophisticated knowledge of the effects of fire to create local environments of their own design. Similarly, Indians in California used fire to perpetuate oak woodland savanna, to promote hunting and the collection of acorns. And in northern Australia, runoff channels of creeks were deliberately altered so as to flood extensive tracts of land, converting them into fields of wild grain. People do not remain food foragers through ignorance, but through choice.

A second observation is that a switch from food foraging to food production does not free people from hard work. The available ethnographic data indicate just the opposite—that farmers, by and large, work far longer hours than do most food foragers. Furthermore, it is clear that early farming required people not only to work longer hours but also to eat more "third-choice" food. Typically, food foragers divide potentially edible food resources into first-, second-, and third-choice categories; third-choice foods are eaten only by necessity, when there is no other option. And in Southwest Asia and Mexico, at least, the plants that were brought under domestication were clearly third-choice plants.

A final observation is that food production is not necessarily a more secure means of subsistence than food foraging. Seed crops in particular—of the sort domesticated in Southwest Asia, Mexico, and Peru—are highly productive but very unstable on account of low species diversity. Without constant human attention, their productivity suffers.

From all of this, it is little wonder that food foragers do not necessarily regard farming and animal husbandry as superior to hunting, gathering, and fishing. Thus, there are some people in the world who have remained food foragers down into the 1990s, although it has become

increasingly difficult for them as food-producing peoples have deprived them of more and more of the land base necessary for their way of life. But as long as existing practices worked well, there was no need to abandon them. After all, their traditional way of life gave them all the food they needed and an eminently satisfactory way of living in small, intimate groups. Free from tedious routine, their lives were often more exciting than those of farmers. Food could be hunted, gathered, or fished for as needed, but in most environments they could relax when they had enough to eat. Why raise crops through backbreaking work when the whole family could camp under a tree bearing tasty and nutritious nuts? Farming brings with it a whole new system of human relationships that offers no easily understood advantages and disturbs an age-old balance between humans and nature as well as the people who live together.

WHY HUMANS BECAME FOOD PRODUCERS

In view of what has been said so far, we may well ask: Why did any human group abandon food foraging in favor of food production?

Several theories have been proposed to account for this change in human subsistence practices. One older theory, championed by V. Gordon Childe, is the desiccation, or oasis, theory based on climatic determinism. Its proponents advanced the idea that the glacial cover over Europe and Asia caused a southern shift in rain patterns from Europe to northern Africa and Southwest Asia. When the glaciers retreated northward, so did the rain patterns. As a result, northern Africa and Southwest Asia became dryer, and people were forced to congregate at oases for water. Because of the scarcity of wild animals in such an environment, people were driven by necessity to collect the wild grasses and seeds growing around the oases. Eventually they had to cultivate the grasses to provide enough food for the community. According to this theory, animal domestication began because the oases attracted hungry animals, such as wild goats, sheep, and also cattle, which came to graze on the stubble of the grain fields. People, finding these animals too thin to kill for food, began to fatten them up.

In spite of its initial popularity, evidence in support of the oasis theory was not immediately forthcoming. Moreover, as systematic fieldwork into the origins of domestication began in the late 1940s, other theories

---

[7]Diamond, J. (1997). *Guns, germs and steel* (p. 143). New York: Norton.

V. GORDON CHILDE (1892–1957)

This distinguished Australian, once the private secretary to the premier of New South Wales, became one of the most eminent British archaeologists of his time. His knowledge of the archaeological sequences of Europe and the Middle East was unsurpassed, enabling him to write two of the most popular and influential descriptions of prehistory ever written: *Man Makes Himself* in 1936 and *What Happened in History.* In these, he described two great "revolutions" that added measurably to the capacity of humans to survive: the Neolithic and urban revolutions. The first of these transformed food foragers into farmers and brought with it a drastic reordering of society; populations increased, a cooperative group spirit arose, trade began on a large scale, and new religions arose to ensure the success of crops. This set the stage for the urban revolution, which transformed society from one of egalitarianism with a simple age-sex division of labor into one of social classes and organized political bodies. The result of these ideas was to generate a whole new interest in the evolution of human culture in general.

gained favor. One of the pioneers in this work was Robert Braidwood of the University of Chicago, who proposed what is sometimes called the "hilly flanks" theory. Contrary to Childe, Braidwood argued that plants and animals were domesticated by people living in the hill country surrounding the Fertile Crescent (Figure 11.2). They had reached the point in their evolutionary development where they were beginning to "settle in"—that is, become more sedentary—a situation that allowed them to become intimately familiar with the plants and animals around their settlements. Given the human capacity and enthusiasm for experimentation, it was inevitable that they would have experimented with grasses and animals, bringing them under domestication. Problems with this theory include the ethnocentric notion that nonsedentary food foragers are not intimately familiar with the plants and animals on which they rely for survival and its projection onto all human cultures of the great value Western culture places on experimentation and innovation for its own sake. In short, the theory was culture-bound, strongly reflecting the notions of progress in which people in the Western world had such faith in the period following World War II.

Yet another theory that became popular in the 1960s is one in which population growth played a key role. In Southwest Asia, so this theory goes, people adapted to the cool, dry conditions of the last glacial period by developing a mixed pattern of resource utilization: They hunted such animals as were available, harvested wild cereal grasses, gathered nuts, and collected a wide variety of birds, turtles, snails, crabs, and mussels. They did so well that their populations grew, requiring the development of new ways of providing sufficient food. The result, especially in marginal situations where wild foods were least abundant, was to improve productivity through the domestication of plants and animals.

Just as there are problems with Braidwood's theory, so are there problems with this one. The most serious is that it requires an intentional decision on the part of the people involved to become producers of domestic crops, whereas, as we have already seen, domestication (as illustrated by ant farmers) does not require intentional design. Furthermore, prior to domestication, people could have had no way of knowing that plants and animals could be so radically transformed as to permit a food-producing way of life (even today, the long-term outcome of plant breeding cannot be predicted). Finally, even if people had wanted to become producers of their own food, there is no way such a decision could have had an immediate and perceptible effect; in fact, a complete switch to food production took more than a thousand years to accomplish. Although this may seem a relatively short period of time compared to the 200,000 or 300,000 years since the appearance of *H. sapiens,* it was still too long to have made any difference to people faced with immediate food shortages. Under such conditions, the usual response among food foragers is to make use of a wider variety of foods than before, which acts as a brake on domestication by diverting attention from potential domesticates, while alleviating the immediate problem.

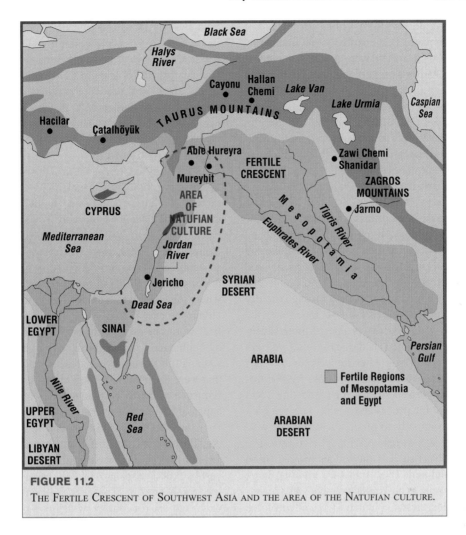

FIGURE 11.2

THE FERTILE CRESCENT OF SOUTHWEST ASIA AND THE AREA OF THE NATUFIAN CULTURE.

Another theory—in accord with the evidence as we now know it but also more in accord with the role played by chance both in evolution (Chapters 3 and 5) and in cultural innovation—takes us back to some of the ideas of Childe, who, as it turns out, guessed what the environmental circumstances were, even though he didn't fully understand the process. We now know that the earliest plant domestication took place in the lands just east of the Mediterranean Sea (Figure 11.2). As early as 13,000 years ago people living at a site (Abu Hureyra) east of Aleppo, Syria, were growing domestic rye, although they otherwise continued to rely heavily on wild plants and animals for food. Not until 3 millennia later did they become full-fledged farmers.[8] By 10,300 years ago, however, others in the region were also domesticating plants.

Evidently, the process was a consequence of a chance convergence of independent natural events and cultural developments.[9] The process is exemplified by the Natufians, whose culture we looked at earlier in this chapter. These people lived at a time of dramatically changing climates in the region. With the end of the last glaciation, climates not only became significantly warmer, but markedly seasonal as well. Between 12,000 and 6,000 years ago, the region experienced the most extreme seasonality in its history, with summer aridity significantly longer and more pronounced than today. As a consequence of increased evaporation, many shallow lakes dried up, leaving just three in the Jordan River

[8]Pringle, H. (1998). The slow birth of agriculture. *Science, 282,* 1,449.

[9]McCorriston, J., & Hole, F. (1991). The ecology of seasonal stress and the origins of agriculture in the Near East. *American Anthropologist, 93,* 46–69.

Valley. At the same time, the region's plant cover changed dramatically. Those plants best adapted to environmental instability and seasonal aridity were annuals, including wild cereal grains and legumes (plants that fix nitrogen in the soil, including peas, lentils, chickpeas, and bitter vetch). Such plants can evolve very quickly under unstable conditions, because they complete their life cycle in a single year. Moreover, they store their reproductive abilities for the next wet season in abundant seeds, which can remain dormant for prolonged periods.

The Natufians, who lived where these conditions were especially severe, adapted by modifying their subsistence practices in two ways: They probably regularly fired the landscape to promote browsing by red deer and grazing by gazelles, the main focus of their hunting activities; and they placed greater emphasis on the collection of wild seeds from the increasingly abundant annual plants that could be effectively stored to see people through the dry season. The importance of stored foods, coupled with the scarcity of reliable water sources, promoted more sedentary living patterns, reflected in the substantial villages of late Natufian times. The greater importance of seeds in Natufian subsistence was made possible by the fact that they already possessed sickles for harvesting grain and grinding stones for processing seeds. The grinding stones were used originally to process a variety of wild foods, whereas the sickles may originally have served to procure nonfood plants such as the sedges or reeds used to make baskets and mats (Natufian sites yielding large numbers of sickles tend to be located near coastal marshes and swamps).[10] Thus, these implements were not invented to enable people to become farmers, even though they turned out to be useful for that purpose.

The use of sickles to harvest grain turned out to have important consequences, again unexpected, for the Natufians. In the course of harvesting, it was inevitable that many easily dispersed seeds would be "lost" at the harvest site, whereas those from plants that did not readily scatter their seeds would mostly be carried back to where people processed and stored them.[11] Genetic mutations against easy dispersal would inevitably arise in the wild stocks, but they would be at a competitive disadvantage compared to variants that could readily disperse their seeds. However, the rate of this and other mutations potentially useful to human consumers might have been unknowingly increased by the periodic burning of vegetation carried out to promote the deer and gazelle herds, for heat is known to be an effective mutagenic agent, and fire can drastically and quickly change gene frequencies. In any event, with seeds for nondispersing variants being carried back to settlements, it was inevitable that some lost seeds would germinate and grow there on dump heaps and other disturbed sites (latrines, areas cleared of trees, or burned over).

As it turns out, many of the plants that became domesticated were colonizers, which do particularly well in disturbed habitats. Moreover, with people becoming increasingly sedentary, disturbed habitats became more extensive as resources in proximity to settlements were depleted over time; thus variants of plants particularly susceptible to human manipulation had more and more opportunity to flourish where people were living and where they would inevitably attract attention. Under such circumstances, it was inevitable that people sooner or later would begin to actively promote their growth, even by deliberately sowing them, especially as people otherwise had to travel farther afield to procure the resources that were depleted near their villages. An inevitable consequence of increased human manipulation would be the appearance of other mutant strains of particular benefit. For example, barley, which in its wild state can be tremendously productive but difficult to harvest and process, had developed the tougher stems that make it easier to harvest by 9,000 years ago; by 8,000 years ago "naked" barley, which is easier to process, was common, and by 7,500 years ago six-row barley, which is more productive than the original two-row, was widespread. Sooner or later, people realized that they could play a more active role in the process by deliberately trying to breed more useful strains. With this, domestication may be said to have shifted from a process that was unintentional to one that was intentional.

The development of animal domestication in Southwest Asia seems to have proceeded along somewhat similar lines but in the hilly country of southeastern Turkey, northern Iraq, and the Zagros Mountains of Iran (Figure 11.2). In the latter two regions were to be found large herds of wild sheep and goats, as well as much environmental diversity. From the low, alluvial plains of the valley of the Tigris and Euphrates rivers, for example, travel to the north or east takes one into the high country through three other zones: first steppe, then oak and pistachio woodlands, and, finally, high plateau country with grass, scrub, or desert vegetation. Valleys that run at right angles to the mountain ranges afford relatively easy access between these zones. Today, a number of

---

[10]Olszewski, D. I. (1991). Comment. *Current Anthropology, 32,* 43.

[11]Blumer, M. A., & Byrne, R. (1991). The ecological genetics and domestication and the origins of agriculture. *Current Anthropology, 32,* 30.

Today, deliberate attempts to create new varieties of plants take place in many a greenhouse, experiment station, or lab. But when first begun, the creation of domestic plants was not deliberate; rather, it was the unforeseen outcome of traditional food-foraging activities.

pastoral peoples in the region practice a pattern of **transhumance,** in which they graze their herds of sheep and goats on the low steppe in the winter and move to high pastures on the plateaus in the summer.

Moving 12,000 years backward in time to the Mesolithic, we find that the region was inhabited by peoples whose subsistence pattern, like that of the Natufians, was one of food foraging. Different plants were found in different ecological zones, and, because of the difference in altitude, plant foods matured at different times in different zones. The animals hunted for meat and hides by these people included several species, among them bear, fox, boar, and wolf. Most notable, though, were the hoofed animals: deer, gazelles, wild goats, and wild sheep. Their bones are far more common in human refuse piles than those of other animals. This is significant, for most of these animals are naturally transhumant in the region, moving back and forth from low winter pastures to high summer pastures. People followed these animals in their seasonal migrations, making use along the way of other wild foods in the zones through which they passed: dates in the lowlands; acorns, almonds, and pistachios higher

up; apples and pears higher still; wild grains maturing at different times in different zones; woodland animals in the forested zone between summer and winter grazing lands. All in all, it was a rich, varied fare.

There was in hunting, then, a concentration on hoofed animals, including wild sheep and goats, which provided meat and hides. At first, animals of all ages and sexes were hunted. But, beginning about 11,000 years ago, the percentage of immature sheep eaten, for example, increased to about 50 percent of the total. At the same time, the percentage of females among animals eaten decreased. Apparently, people were learning that they could increase yields by sparing the females for breeding, while feasting on ram lambs. This marks the beginning of human management of sheep. As this management of flocks became more and more efficient, sheep were increasingly shielded from the effects of natural selection. Eventually, they were introduced into areas outside their natural habitat. So we find sheep and goats being kept by farmers at ancient Jericho, in the Jordan River Valley, 8,000 years ago (by which time farming, too, had spread widely, into Turkey to the north and into

Transhumance.   Among pastoralists, the grazing of sheep and goats in low steppe lands in the winter and then moving to high pastures on the plateaus in the summer.

Although sheep and goats were first valued for their meat, hides, and sinew, the changes wrought by domestication made them useful for other purposes as well. This impression, from a 4,500-year-old seal, shows a goat being milked.

the Zagros Mountains in the east). As a consequence of this human intervention, variants that usually were not successful in the wild were able to survive and reproduce. Although variants that were perceived as being of immediate advantage would have attracted peoples' attention, they did not arise out of need, but independently of it at random, as mutations do. In such a way did those features characteristic of domestic sheep—such as greater fat and meat production, excess wool (Figure 11.3), and

so on—begin to develop. By 9,000 years ago, the bones of domestic sheep had become distinguishable from those of wild sheep.

At about the same time that these events were happening, similar developments were taking place in southeastern Turkey, where pigs were the focus of attention.[12]

_____

[12]Pringle, p. 1,448.

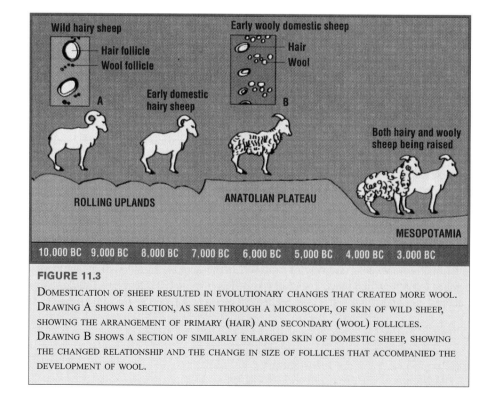

FIGURE 11.3

Domestication of sheep resulted in evolutionary changes that created more wool. Drawing A shows a section, as seen through a microscope, of skin of wild sheep, showing the arrangement of primary (hair) and secondary (wool) follicles. Drawing B shows a section of similarly enlarged skin of domestic sheep, showing the changed relationship and the change in size of follicles that accompanied the development of wool.

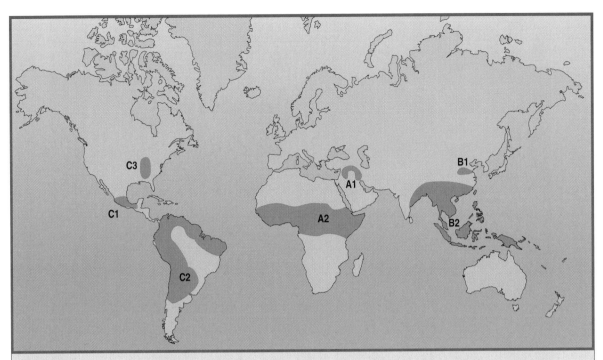

FIGURE 11.4

EARLY PLANT AND ANIMAL DOMESTICATION TOOK PLACE IN SUCH WIDELY SCATTERED AREAS AS SOUTHWEST ASIA (A1), CENTRAL AFRICA (A2), CHINA (B1), SOUTHEAST ASIA (B2), MESOAMERICA (C1), SOUTH AMERICA (C2), AND NORTH AMERICA (C3).

Here, an increase in pig bones in human trash, coupled with a heavy bias in favor of very young animals, is indicative of a taste for suckling pigs and the beginning of stock management by 10,500 years ago.

To sum up, the domesticators of plants and animals sought only to maximize the food sources available to them. They were not aware of the revolutionary consequences their actions were to have. But as the process continued, the productivity of the domestic species increased relative to wild species. Thus they became increasingly more important to subsistence, resulting in further intensification of interest in, and management of, the domesticates. Inevitably, the result would be further increases in productivity.

OTHER CENTERS OF DOMESTICATION

In addition to Southwest Asia, the domestication of plants and, in some cases, animals took place independently in Southeast Asia, parts of the Americas (southern Mexico,

Peru, the tropical forests of South America, and eastern North America), northern China, and Africa (Figure 11.4). In China, domestication of rice was underway along the middle Yangtze River by about 11,000 years ago.[13] It was not until 4,000 years later, however, that domestic rice dominated wild rice to become the dietary staple.

In Southeast Asia the oldest domestic plant so far identified is rice, in pottery dated to some time between 8,800 and 5,000 years ago. What was distinctive in this region, however, was domestication of root crops, most notably yams and taro. Root crop farming, or **vegeculture,** typically involves the growing of many different species together in a single field. Because this approximates the complexity of the natural vegetation, vegeculture tends to be more stable than seed crop cultivation. Propagation (as in the case of the fungi-farming ants discussed earlier) is by vegetative means—the planting of cuttings—rather than the planting of seeds.

---

[13]Ibid., p. 1,449.

Vegeculture.   The cultivation of domesticated root crops, such as yams and taro.

At this archaeological site in Diatonghuan Cave, China, archaeologists recover evidence of the transition from wild to domestic rice.

In the Americas, the domestication of plants began about as early as it did in these other regions. One species of domestic squash may have been grown as early as 10,000 years ago in the coastal forests of Ecuador at the same time another species was being grown in an arid region of highland Mexico.[14] Evidently, these developments were independent of one another. Other crops were eventually added later; the earliest occurrence of maize, for example, is from a site on the Gulf Coast of the Mexican state of Tobasco dated 7,700 years ago.[15] Because genetic evidence puts its place of origin somewhere in the highlands of western Mexico, it must have appeared somewhat earlier there. Ultimately, Native Americans domesticated over 300 food crops, including two of the four most important ones in the world today: potatoes and maize (the other two are wheat and rice). In fact, 60 percent of the crops grown in the world today were invented by American Indians, who not only remain the developers of the world's largest array of nutritious foods but are also the primary contributors to the world's varied cuisines.[16] After all, where would Italian cuisine be without tomatoes? Thai cooking without peanuts? Northern European cooking without potatoes? Or Chinese cooking without sweet potatoes (the daily food of peasants, but also used to make noodles rivaling in popularity those made of wheat)? Small wonder American Indians have been called the world's greatest farmers.[17]

Archaeological evidence for the beginning of farming in Mexico comes from the highland valleys of Oaxaca, Puebla, and Tamaulipas. In the Tehuacan Valley of Puebla, for example, crops such as maize, beans, and squash very gradually came to make up a greater percentage of the food eaten (Figure 11.5). Like the hill country of Southwest Asia, the Tehuacan Valley is environmentally diverse, and the people living there had a cyclical pattern of hunting and gathering that made use

[14]Ibid., p. 1,447.

[15]Piperno, D. R. (2001). On maize and the sunflower. *Science, 292,* 2,260.

[16]Weatherford, J. (1988). *Indian givers: How the Indians of the Americas transformed the world* (pp. 71, 115). New York: Fawcett Columbine.

[17]Ibid., p. 95.

Domestic plants were useful for purposes other than food. Although cotton was independently invented three times—in the Old World, Mesoamerica, and Peru—95 percent of the cotton grown in the world today is the Mesoamerican species, owing to its superiority.

CULTIGENS		PERCENTAGE			BC
		Hunting	Horti-culture	Wild plant use	
Squash Chili Amaranth Avocado	Cotton Maize Beans Gourd Sapote	29%		31%	1000 1500 2000
Squash Chili Amaranth Avocado	Maize Beans Gourd Sapote	25%		50%	2500 3000
Squash Chili Amaranth Avocado	Maize Beans Gourd Sapote	34%		52%	3500 4000 4500
Squash Chili Amaranth Avocado		54%		40%	5000 5500 6000 6500

FIGURE 11.5

SUBSISTENCE TRENDS IN TEHUACAN VALLEY SHOW THAT HERE, AS ELSEWHERE, DEPENDENCE ON HORTICULTURE CAME ABOUT GRADUALLY, OVER A PROLONGED PERIOD OF TIME.

of the resources of different environmental zones. In the course of their seasonal movements, people carried the wild precursors of future domesticates out of their native habitat, exposing them to different selective pressures. Under such circumstances, potentially useful (to humans) variants that did not do well in the native habitat would, by chance, do well in novel settings, again (as in Southwest Asia) attracting human attention.

The change to food production also took place in South America, including the highlands of Peru—again, an environmentally diverse region. Although a number of crops first grown in Mexico eventually came to be grown here, there was greater emphasis on root crops, the best known being potatoes (of which about 3,000 varieties were grown, versus the mere 250 grown today in North America), sweet potatoes, and manioc (originally developed in the tropics). South Americans domesticated guinea pigs, llamas, alpacas, and ducks, whereas the Mexicans never did much with domestic livestock. They limited themselves to dogs, turkeys, and bees.

Although the Native Americans living north of Mexico ultimately adopted several crops, such as maize and beans, from their southern neighbors, this occurred after they developed some of their own indigenous domesticates. These included local varieties of squash and sunflower (today, grown widely in Russia as a reliable source of edible oil). Other native crops such as lambs-quarter and sumpweed reverted to the wild as preferred foods appeared from Mexico.

Considering all of the separate innovations of domestic plants, it is interesting to note that in all cases people developed the same categories of foods. Everywhere,

Archaeology for and by Native Americans

In the Americas, the practice of archaeology is closely tied to Native Americans because it is their ancestors who were responsible for the record those archaeologists seek to investigate. Yet, relationships between native people and archaeologists have not always been easy. Part of the problem has to do with power relationships: Archaeologists have been members of a dominant society with a long record of appropriating native lands and resources while denying native people political and even human rights. To have nonnative scholars appropriate their cultural heritage, while collecting their sacred objects and even the bodies of their ancestors, was the last straw. This is not to say that all archaeologists were insensitive to native concerns, but all too often the aims of the discipline and the interests of those whose past was being studied were at odds.

As a consequence, some native people today want nothing to do with archaeology and those who practice it. Others, however, recognize that archaeology can serve their own interests. Today, there are more than 43 tribes or native communities in 23 states that conduct their own archaeological research. At the same time, nonnative archaeologists have become more sensitive to native concerns and have been actively working to reconcile those interests with those of science. The result is that opportunities have been opened for fruitful collaboration. Today, a number of archaeologists are actually employed by native organizations, and programs have been set up to train native people themselves in archaeology.

One archaeologist who has worked for native organizations, including the Hopi tribe and the Pueblo of Zuni in Arizona and New Mexico, is T. J. Ferguson.* He points out that there are many reasons that American Indians need archaeology. A major one is that archeologists are needed to implement the National Historic Preservation Act and other federal legislation governing archaeological research. Many natives, too, are genuinely interested in uncovering their own history, using archaeological evidence to litigate land and water claims, attaining intellectual parity with non-Indian researchers, facilitating development on Indian lands, retaining financial benefits from mandated archaeology, and maintaining tribes' political sovereignty by controlling the management and protection of their own cultural resources and burials. There are benefits for the archaeologist as well. Ferguson has found working for native people to be personally rewarding, as it has resulted in modification of scientific values he learned in graduate school. This has not, however, prevented him from making important contributions to the profession. Moreover, it generates new and fruitful research questions to pursue.

*Ferguson, T. J. (1996, November). *Archaeology for and by Native Americans.* Paper presented at the 95th Annual Meeting of the American Anthropological Association, San Francisco.

---

starchy grains (or root crops) are accompanied by one or more legumes—wheat and barley with peas, chickpeas, bitter vetch, and lentils in Southwest Asia—maize with various kinds of beans in Mexico, for example. The starchy grains are the core of the diet and are eaten at every meal in the form of bread, some sort of food wrapper (like a tortilla), or a gruel or thickening agent in a stew along with one or more legumes. Being rather bland, these sources of carbohydrates and proteins are invariably combined with flavor-giving substances that help the food go down. In Mexico, for example, the flavor enhancer par excellence is the chili pepper; in other cuisines it may be a bit of meat, a dairy product, mushrooms, or whatever. Anthropologist Sidney Mintz refers to this as the core-fringe-legume pattern (CFLP), noting that only recently has it been upset by the worldwide spread of processed sugars and high-fat foods.[18]

[18]Mintz, S. (1996). A taste of history. In W. A. Haviland & R. J. Gordon (Eds.), *Talking about people* (2nd ed., pp. 81–82). Mountain View, CA: Mayfield.

In Mexico, chili peppers enhanced the flavor of foods and aided digestion. (They help break down cellulose in diets heavy in plant foods.) They had other uses as well: This illustration from a 16th-century Aztec manuscript shows a woman threatening her child with punishment by being exposed to smoke from chili peppers. Chili smoke was also used as a kind of chemical weapon in warfare.

THE SPREAD OF FOOD PRODUCTION

Although population growth and the need to feed more people cannot explain the origin of the food-producing way of life, it does have a lot to do with its subsequent spread. As already noted, domestication inevitably leads to higher yields, and higher yields make it possible to feed more people. In addition, unlike most food foragers, farmers have available a variety of foods that are soft enough to be fed to infants. Hence, farmers do not need to nurse their children so intensively nor for so many years. In humans, prolonged nursing, as long as it involves frequent stimulation of the nipple by the infant, has a dampening effect on ovulation. As a result, women in food-foraging societies are less likely to become fertile as soon after childbirth as they are in food-producing societies. Coupled with this, having too many children to care for at once interferes with the foraging activities of women in hunting, gathering, and fishing societies. Among farmers, however, numerous children are frequently seen as assets, to help out with the many household chores. Small wonder, then, that increased dependence on farming is associated with increased fertility across human populations.[19]

Paradoxically, although domestication increases productivity, so does it increase instability. This is so because those varieties with the highest yields become the focus of human attention, while other varieties are less valued and ultimately ignored. As a result, farmers become dependent on a rather narrow range of resources, compared to the wide range utilized by food foragers. Modern agriculturists, for example, rely on a mere dozen species for about 80 percent of the world's annual tonnage of all crops.[20] By contrast, the Bushmen of Africa's Kalahari Desert regard more than 100 species as edible. This dependence upon fewer varieties means that when a crop fails, for whatever reason, farmers have less to fall back on than do food foragers. Furthermore, the likelihood of failure is increased by the common farming practice of planting crops together in one locality, so that a disease contracted by one plant can easily spread to others. Moreover, by relying on seeds from the most productive plants of a species to establish next year's crop, farmers favor genetic uniformity over diversity. The result is that if some virus, bacterium, or fungus is able to destroy one plant, it will likely destroy them all. This is what happened in the famous Irish potato famine of 1845–1846, which sent waves of Irish immigrants to the United States.

[19]Sellen, D. W., & Mace, R. (1997). Fertility and mode of subsistence: A phylogenetic analysis. *Current Anthropology, 38,* 886.

[20]Diamond, p. 132.

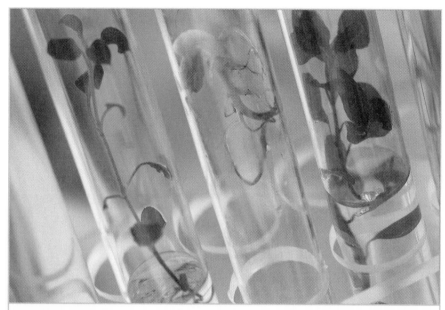

To the extent that genetic engineering strives to produce crops with uniform characteristics, genetic homogeneity will make them vulnerable to plant diseases and predators.

The Irish potato famine illustrates how the combination of increased productivity and vulnerability may contribute to the geographic spread of farming. Time and time again in the past, population growth followed by crop failures has triggered movements of people from one place to another, where they have reestablished the subsistence practices with which they were familiar. Thus, once farming came into existence, it was more or less guaranteed that it would spread to neighboring regions (Figure 11.6). From Southwest Asia, for instance, it spread to southeastern Europe by 8,000 years ago, reaching Central Europe and the Netherlands by 4,000 years ago, and England between 4,000 and 3,000 years ago. Those who brought crops to Europe brought other things as well, including new alleles for human gene pools. As a consequence, those modern Europeans who most resemble their Upper Paleolithic predecessors are to be found around the northern fringes of the region.[21] Early

---

[21]Brace, C. L. (1997). Cro-Magnons "Я" us? *Anthropology Newsletter, 38*(8), 2.

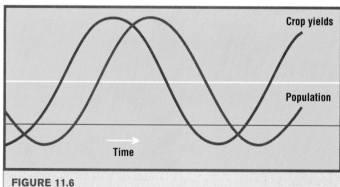

FIGURE 11.6

POPULATION GROWTH HAS A TENDENCY TO FOLLOW INCREASES IN FARMING YIELDS. INEVITABLY, THIS RESULTS IN TOO LARGE A POPULATION TO BE FED WHEN CROPS FAIL, AS THEY PERIODICALLY DO. THE RESULT IS AN OUTWARD MIGRATION OF PEOPLE TO OTHER REGIONS.

farmers likely introduced languages ancestral to most of today's European languages as well, leaving Basque (spoken today on the Atlantic coast where France and Spain meet) as the sole survivor of languages once spoken by earlier Mesolithic people.

From Southwest Asia, farming also spread westward in North Africa and eastward to India. Here, crops domesticated in the west met those spreading from Southeast Asia, some of which spread farther west. Facilitating this east-west exchange was the fact that localities shared the same seasonal variations in day length and more or less the same diseases, temperature, and rainfall.

In sub-Saharan Africa, a similar spread occurred and accounts for the modern distribution of speakers of Bantu languages. Crops including sorghum (so valuable today it is grown in hot, dry areas on all continents), pearl millet, watermelon, black-eyed peas, African yams, oil palms, and kola nuts (source of modern cola drinks) were first domesticated in West Africa but began spreading east by 5,000 years ago.

Between 3,000 and 2,000 years ago Bantu speakers with their crops reached the east coast, and a few centuries later, reached the Great Fish River, 500 miles east of Capetown. Being well adapted to summer rains, African crops spread no farther, for the Cape has a Mediterranean climate with winter rains.

In some instances, farming appears to have been adopted by food foragers from food-producing neighbors. By way of illustration, a crisis developed on the coast of Peru some 4,500 years ago as continental uplift caused lowering of the water table and destruction of marine habitats at a time of growing population; the result was an increasing shortage of the wild food resources on which people depended. Their response was to begin growing along the edges of rivers many of the domestic plants that their highland neighbors to the east had begun to cultivate a few thousand years earlier. Here, then, farming appears to have been a subsistence practice of last resort, which a food-foraging people took up only because they had no real choice.

CULTURE OF NEOLITHIC SETTLEMENTS

A number of Neolithic settlements have been excavated, particularly in Southwest Asia. The structures, artifacts, and food debris found at these sites have revealed much about the daily activities of their former inhabitants as they pursued the business of making a living.

Earliest Full-Fledged Farming Settlements

The earliest known sites containing domesticated plants and animals found in Southwest Asia date mostly between 10,300 and 9,000 years ago. These sites occur in a region extending from the Jordan Valley northward across the Taurus Mountains into Turkey, eastward across the flanks of the Taurus Mountains into northeastern Iran, and southward into Iraq and Iran along the hilly flanks of the Zagros Mountains. The sites contain evidence of domesticated barley, wheat, peas, chickpeas, bitter vetch, lentils, flax, goats, sheep, dogs, and pigs.

These sites are generally the remains of small village farming communities—small clusters of houses built of mud, each with its own storage pit and clay oven. Their occupants continued to use stone tools of Mesolithic type, plus a few new types of use in farming. Probably the people born into these communities spent their lives in them in a common effort to make their crops grow and their animals prosper. At the same time, they participated in long-distance trade networks. Obsidian found at Jarmo, Iraq, for instance, was imported from 300 miles away.

In coastal Peru, the earliest domesticates were the nonedible bottle gourd (like the one shown here) and cotton. They were used to make nets and floats to catch fish, which was an important source of food.

Stands of wild wheat are still to be found in parts of the Middle East.

Jericho: An Early Farming Community

At the Neolithic settlement that later grew to become the biblical city of Jericho, excavation has revealed the remains of a sizable farming community occupied as early as 10,350 years ago. Located in the Jordan River Valley, what made the site attractive was the presence of a bounteous spring and the rich soils of an Ice Age lake that had dried up some 3,000 years earlier. Here, crops could be grown almost continuously, because the fertility of the soil was regularly renewed by flood-borne deposits originating in the Judean Highlands, to the west. To protect their settlement against these floods and associated mudflows, the people of Jericho built massive walls of stone around it.[22] Within these walls, an estimated 400 to 900 people lived in houses of mud brick with plastered floors arranged around courtyards. In addition to these houses, a stone tower that would have taken 100 people 104 days to build was located inside one corner of the wall, near the spring. A staircase inside it probably led to a mud brick building on top. Nearby were mud brick storage facilities as well as peculiar structures of possible ceremonial significance. A village cemetery also reflects the sedentary life of these early people; nomadic groups, with few exceptions, rarely buried their dead in a single central location.

---

[22]Bar-Yosef, O. (1986) The walls of Jericho: An alternative interpretation. *Current Anthropology, 27,* 160.

Evidence of domestic plants and animals is scant at Jericho. However, indirect evidence in the form of harvesting tools and milling equipment has been uncovered at the site, and wheat, barley, and other domestic plants are known from sites of similar age in the region. We do know that the people of Jericho were keeping sheep and goats by 8,000 years ago, although some hunting still went on. Some of the meat from wild animals may have been supplied by food-foraging peoples whose campsites have been found everywhere in the desert of the Arabian peninsula. Close contacts between these people and the farmers of Jericho and other villages are indicated by common features in art, ritual, use of prestige goods, and burial practices. Other evidence of trade consists of obsidian and turquoise from Sinai as well as marine shells from the coast, all discovered inside the walls of Jericho.

Neolithic Technology

Early harvesting tools were made of wood or bone into which serrated flints were inserted. Later tools continued to be made by chipping and flaking stone, but during the Neolithic period, stone that was too hard to be chipped was ground and polished for tools (Figure 11.7). People developed scythes, forks, hoes, and plows to replace their simple digging sticks. Pestles and mortars were used for preparation of grain. Plows were later redesigned when, after 8,000 years ago, domesticated cattle became available for use as draft animals.

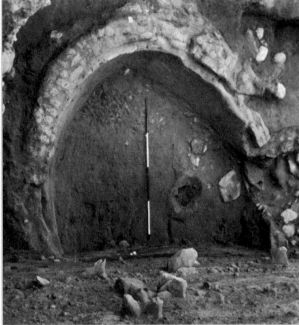

Neolithic farming communities, such as Jericho in the Jordan River Valley, were made possible by the result of the domestication of plants and animals. Jericho was surrounded by a stone wall as protection against floods. The wall included a tower (left). People lived in substantial houses (right).

Pottery

In addition to the domestication of plants and animals, one of the characteristics of the Neolithic period is the extensive manufacture and use of pottery. In food-foraging societies, most people are involved in the food quest. In food-producing societies, even though people have to work as long—if not longer—at subsistence activities than food foragers, the whole community need not be involved in the food quest. Hard work on the part of those producing the food may support other members of the society who devote their energies to other craft specialties. One such craft is pottery making, and different forms of pottery were created for transporting and storing food, artifacts, and other material possessions. Because pottery vessels are impervious to damage by insects, rodents, and dampness, they could be used for storing small grain, seeds, and other materials. Moreover, food can be boiled in pottery vessels directly over the fire rather than by such ancient techniques as dropping stones heated directly in the fire into the food being cooked. Pottery is also used for pipes, ladles, lamps, and other objects, and some cultures used large vessels for disposal

of the dead. Significantly, pottery containers remain important for much of humanity today.

Widespread use of pottery, which is manufactured of clay and fired, is a good, though not foolproof, indication of a sedentary community. It is found in abundance in all but a few of the earliest Neolithic settlements. At ancient Jericho, for example, the earliest Neolithic people lacked pottery. Its fragility and weight make it impractical for use by nomads and hunters, who use baskets and hide containers. Nevertheless, there are some modern nomads who make and use pottery, just as there are farmers who lack it. In fact, food foragers in Japan were making pottery by 13,000 years ago, long before it was being made in Southwest Asia.

The manufacture of pottery is a difficult art and requires a high degree of technological sophistication. To make a useful vessel requires knowledge of clay, how to remove impurities from it, how to shape it into desired forms without it slumping, and how to dry it without cracking. Proper firing is tricky as well; it must be heated sufficiently that the clay will harden and resist future disintegration from moisture, but care must be taken to prevent the object from cracking or even exploding as it heats and later cools down.

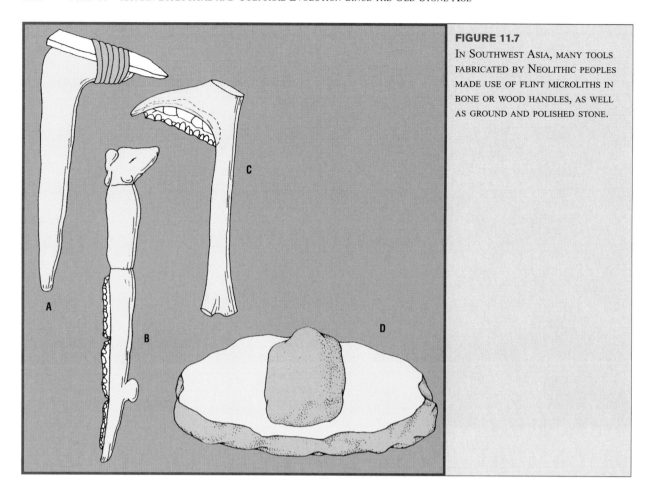

FIGURE 11.7
IN SOUTHWEST ASIA, MANY TOOLS FABRICATED BY NEOLITHIC PEOPLES MADE USE OF FLINT MICROLITHS IN BONE OR WOOD HANDLES, AS WELL AS GROUND AND POLISHED STONE.

Coloration of the pot, too, is affected by the way it is fired; the presence of oxygen produces a reddish color, whereas absence of oxygen produces a darker color.

Pottery is decorated in various ways. For example, designs can be engraved on the vessel before firing, or special rims, legs, bases, and other details may be made separately and fastened to the finished pot. Painting is the most common form of pottery decoration, and there are literally thousands of painted designs found among the pottery remains of ancient cultures.

Housing

Food production and the new sedentary lifestyle engendered another technological development—house building. Permanent housing is of limited interest to most food foragers who frequently are on the move. Cave shelters, pits dug in the earth, and simple lean-tos made of hides and tree limbs serve their purpose of keeping the weather out. In the Neolithic, however, dwellings became more complex in design and more diverse in type. Some, like Swiss lake dwellings, were constructed of wood, housed several families per building, had doors, and contained beds, tables, and other furniture. In other places, more elaborate shelters were made of stone, sun-dried brick, or branches plastered together with mud or clay.

Although permanent housing frequently goes along with food production, there is evidence that one can have substantial houses without food production. For example, on the northwestern coast of North America, people lived in substantial houses made of heavy planks hewn from cedar logs. Yet their food consisted entirely of wild plants and animals, especially fish.

Clothing

During the Neolithic, for the first time in human history, clothing was made of woven textiles. The raw materials and technology necessary for the production of clothing came from several sources: flax and cotton from farm-

This pottery vessel from Turkey was made around 7,600 years ago. Pigs were under domestication as early as 10,500 to 11,000 years ago in southeastern Turkey.

ing, wool from domesticated sheep, silk from silk worms, and the spindle for spinning and the loom for weaving from the inventive human mind.

Social Structure

Evidence of all the economic and technological developments listed thus far has enabled archaeologists to draw certain inferences concerning the organization of Neolithic society. The general absence of elaborate buildings in all but a few settlements may suggest that neither religion nor government was yet a formally established institution able to wield real social power. Although there is evidence of ceremonial activity, little evidence of a centrally organized and directed religious life has been found. Burials, for example, show a marked absence of patterning; variation seems to have been common. Because early Neolithic graves were rarely constructed of or covered by stone slabs and rarely included elaborate grave goods, it is believed differences in social status were not great. Evidently, no person had attained the kind of exalted status that would have required an elaborate funeral. The smallness of most villages suggests that the inhabitants knew one another very well, so that most of their relationships were probably highly personal ones, charged with emotional significance.

The general picture that emerges is one of a relatively egalitarian society with minimal division of labor and probably little development of new and more specialized social roles. Villages seem to have been made up of several households, each providing for most of its own needs. The organizational needs of society beyond the household level were probably met by kinship groups and common-interest associations.

NEOLITHIC CULTURE IN THE NEW WORLD

Outside Mesoamerica (southern Mexico and northern Central America) and Peru, hunting, fishing, and the gathering of wild plant foods remained important elements in the economy of Neolithic peoples in the New World. Apparently, most American Indians never made a complete change from a food-foraging to a food-producing mode of life, even though maize and other domestic

Sometimes Neolithic villagers got together to carry out impressive communal works. Shown here is Stonehenge, the famous ceremonial and astronomical center in England, which dates back to about 2500 B.C. Its construction relates to the new attitudes toward the earth and forces of nature associated with food production.

crops came to be cultivated just about everywhere that climate permitted. Farming developed independently of Europe and Asia, with different crops and different technologies.

The Neolithic developed even more slowly in the New World than in the Old. For example, Neolithic agricultural villages were common in Southwest Asia between 9,000 and 8,000 years ago, but similar villages did not appear in the New World until about 4,500 years ago, in Mesoamerica and Peru. Moreover, pottery, which arose in the Old World shortly after plant and animal domestication, did not develop in the New World until about 4,500 years ago. Neither the potter's wheel nor the loom and spindle were used by early Neolithic people in the New World. Both pottery and textiles were manufactured by hand; evidence of the loom and spindle does not appear in the New World until 3,000 years ago. None of these absences indicate any backwardness on the part of New World peoples, who, as we have already seen, were highly sophisticated farmers and plant breeders. Rather,

the effectiveness of existing practices was such that they continued to be satisfactory.

THE NEOLITHIC AND HUMAN BIOLOGY

Although we tend to think of the invention of food production in terms of its cultural impact, it obviously had a biological impact as well. From studies of human skeletons from Neolithic burials, physical anthropologists have found evidence for a somewhat lessened mechanical stress on peoples' bodies and teeth. Although there are exceptions, the teeth of Neolithic peoples show less wear, their bones are less robust, and osteoarthritis (the result of stressed joint surfaces) is not as marked as in the skeletons of Paleolithic and Mesolithic peoples. On the other hand, there is clear evidence for a marked deterioration in health and mortality. Anthropologist Anna Roosevelt sums up our knowledge of this in the following Original Study.

Original Study

History of Mortality and Physiological Stress[23]

Although there is a relative lack of evidence for the Paleolithic stage, enough skeletons have been studied that it seems clear that seasonal and periodic physiological stress regularly affected most prehistoric hunting-gathering populations, as evidenced by the presence of enamel hypoplasias [horizontal linear defects in tooth enamel] and Harris lines [horizontal lines near the ends of long bones]. What also seems clear is that severe and chronic stress, with high frequency of hypoplasias, infectious disease lesions, pathologies related to iron-deficiency anemia, and high mortality rates, is not characteristic of these early populations. There is no evidence of frequent, severe malnutrition, and so the diet must have been adequate in calories and other nutrients most of the time. During the Mesolithic, the proportion of starch in the diet rose, to judge from the increased occurrence of certain dental diseases, but not enough to create an impoverished diet. At this time, diets seem to have been made up of a rather large number of foods, so that the failure of one food source would not be catastrophic. There is a possible slight tendency

for Paleolithic people to be healthier and taller than Mesolithic people, but there is no apparent trend toward increasing physiological stress during the Mesolithic. Thus, it seems that both hunter-gatherers and incipient agriculturalists regularly underwent population pressure, but only to a moderate degree.

During the periods when effective agriculture first comes into use, there seems to be a temporary upturn in health and survival rates in a few regions: Europe, North America, and the eastern Mediterranean. At this stage, wild foods are still consumed periodically and a variety of plants are cultivated, suggesting the availability of adequate amounts of different nutrients. Based on the increasing frequency of tooth disease related to high carbohydrate consumption, it seems that cultivated plants probably increased the storable calo-

---

[23]Roosevelt, A. C. (1984). Population, health, and the evolution of subsistence: Conclusions from the conference. In M. N. Cohen & G. J. Armelagos (Eds.), *Paleopathology at the origins of agriculture* (pp. 572–574). Orlando: Academic Press.

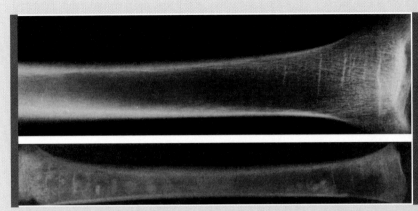

Harris lines near the ends of these youthful thigh bones, found in a prehistoric farming community in Arizona, are indicative of recovery after growth arrest, caused by famine or disease.

rie supply, removing for a time any seasonal or periodic problems in food supply. In most regions, however, the development of agriculture seems not to have had this effect, and there seems to have been a slight increase in physiological stress.

Stress, however, does not seem to have become common and widespread until after the development of high degrees of sedentism, population density, and reliance on intensive agriculture. At this stage in all regions the incidence of physiological stress increases greatly, and average mortality rates increase appreciably. Most of these agricultural populations have high frequencies of porotic hyperostosis and cribra orbitalia [bone deformities indicative of chronic iron-deficiency anemia], and

Enamel hypoplasias such as those shown on these teeth are indicative of arrested growth caused by disease or famine. The teeth are from an adult who lived in an ancient farming community in Arizona.

there is a substantial increase in the number and severity of enamel hypoplasias and pathologies associated with infectious disease. Stature in many populations appears to have been considerably lower than would be expected if genetically determined height maxima had been reached, which suggests that the growth arrests documented by pathologies were causing stunting. Accompanying these indicators of poor health and nourishment, there is a universal drop in the occurrence of Harris lines, suggesting a poor rate of full recovery from the stress. Incidence of carbohydrate-related tooth disease increases, apparently because subsistence by this time is characterized by a heavy emphasis on a few starchy food crops. Populations seem to have grown beyond the point at which wild food resources could be a meaningful dietary supplement, and even domestic animal resources were commonly reserved for farm labor and transport rather than for diet supplementation.

It seems that a large proportion of most sedentary prehistoric populations under intensive agriculture underwent chronic and life-threatening malnutrition and disease, especially during infancy and childhood. The causes of the nutritional stress are likely to have been the poverty of the staple crops in most nutrients except calories, periodic famines caused by the instability of the agricultural system, and chronic lack of food due to both population growth and economic expropriation by elites. The increases in infectious disease probably reflect both a poorer diet and increased interpersonal contact in crowded settlements, and it is, in turn, likely to have aggravated nutritional problems.

The End

For the most part, the crops on which Neolithic peoples came to depend were selected for their higher productivity and storability rather than their nutritional value. Moreover, as already noted, their nutritional shortcomings would have been exacerbated by their susceptibility to periodic failure, particularly as populations grew in size. Thus, the worsened health and mortality of Neolithic peoples is not surprising. Some have gone so far as to assert that the switch from food foraging to food production was the worst mistake that humans ever made!

Another key contributor to the increased incidence of disease and mortality was probably the new mode of life in Neolithic communities. Sedentary life in fixed villages brings with it sanitation problems as garbage and human waste accumulate. These are not a problem for small groups of people who move about from one campsite to another. Moreover, airborne diseases are more easily transmitted where people are gathered into villages. Another factor, too, was the close association between humans and their domestic animals, a situation conducive to the transmission of some animal diseases to humans. A host of life-threatening diseases, including smallpox, chicken pox, and in fact all of the infectious diseases of childhood that were not overcome by medical science until the latter half of the 20th century, were transmitted to humans through their close association with domestic animals (Table 11.1).

Another example of the biological impact of food production on human biology is that of the abnormal hemoglobin responsible for sickle-cell anemia, discussed in Chapter 3. Other abnormal hemoglobins are associated with the spread of farming from Southwest Asia westward around the Mediterranean as well as eastward to India, and also with the spread of farming in Southeast Asia. In all these regions, changes in human gene pools took place as a biological response to malaria, which had become a problem as a result of farming practices.

Higher mortality rates in Neolithic villages were offset by increased fertility, for population growth accelerated dramatically at precisely the moment that health and mortality worsened. The factors responsible for this increased natality have already been discussed in this chapter.

THE NEOLITHIC AND THE IDEA OF PROGRESS

One of the more deeply held biases of Western culture is that human history is basically a record of steady progress over time. The transition from food foraging to food production is generally viewed as a great step upward on a

Crops bred for higher productivity and storability, rather than nutritional value, contributed to the poor health of Neolithic people. Even today, plants are still bred for nonnutritional characteristics: long shelf life, appearance, and the like. This is true, too, of genetically engineered crops, which are altered to survive massive applications of herbicides and pesticides and to not produce viable seed (the latter solidifies corporate control of the food system). One may only wonder what the long-term consequences of such practices will be.

TABLE 11.1	DISEASES ACQUIRED FROM DOMESTICATED ANIMALS
Human Disease	**Animal with Most Closely Related Pathogen**
Measles	Cattle (rinderpest)
Tuberculosis	Cattle
Smallpox	Cattle (cowpox) or other livestock with related pox viruses
Influenza	Pigs, ducks
Pertussis ("whooping cough")	Pigs, dogs

Some of the diseases that humans have acquired from domestic animals. Close contact with animals provides a situation in which variants of animal pathogens may establish themselves in humans.

SOURCE: Diamond, J. (1997). *Guns, germs, and steel* (p. 207). New York: Norton.

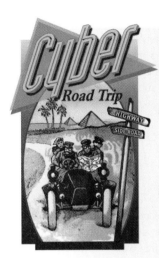

HIGHWAY 1
This site spans time and space as it considers the global origins of agriculture and civilization as well as the ability of countries to feed their populations in the future.
www.mc.maricopa.edu/anthro/lost_tribes/hg_ag/

HIGHWAY 2
Visit this site to see the ruins and get a sense of what the ancient city of Jericho is like today.
www.visit-palestine.com/jericho/je-main.htm

supposed ladder of progress. To be sure, farming allowed people to increase the size of their populations, to live together in substantial sedentary communities, and to reorganize the workload in ways that permitted craft specialization. If one chooses to regard this as progress, that is fine—progress is, after all, whatever it is defined as, and different cultures define it differently.

Whatever the benefits of food production, however, a substantial price was paid. As anthropologists Mark Cohen and George Armelagos put it,

Taken as a whole, indicators fairly clearly suggest an overall decline in the quality—and probably in the length—of human life associated with the adoption of agriculture. This decline was offset in some regions, but not in others, by a decline in physical demands on the body. The studies support recent ethnographic statements and theoretical arguments about the relatively good health and nutrition of hunter-gatherers. They also suggest that hunter-gatherers were relatively well buffered against episodic stress. These data call in question simplistic popular ideas about human progress. They also call in question models of human population growth that are based on assumed progressive increases in life expectancy. The data suggest that the well documented expansion of early farming populations was accomplished in spite of general diminution of both

child and adult life expectancy rather than being fueled by increased survivorship.[24]

Rather than imposing ethnocentric notions of progress on the archaeological record, it is best to view the advent of food production as but one more factor contributing to the diversification of cultures, something that had begun in the Paleolithic. Although some societies continued to practice hunting, gathering, and fishing, others became **horticultural**—small communities of gardeners working with simple hand tools and using neither irrigation nor the plow. Horticulturists typically cultivate a variety of crops in small gardens they have cleared by hand. Some horticultural societies, however, developed **intensive agriculture.** Technologically more complex than the horticulturalists, intensive agriculturalists employ such techniques as irrigation, fertilizers, and the wooden or metal plow pulled by two harnessed draft animals, such as oxen or water buffalo, to produce food on larger plots of land. The distinction between horticulturalist and intensive agriculturalist is not always an easy one to make. For example, the Hopi Indians of the North American Southwest traditionally employed irrigation in their farming while at the same time using simple hand tools.

Some societies became specialized **pastoralists** in environments that were too dry, too grassy, too steep, or too

---

[24]Cohen, M. N., & Armelagos, G. J. (1984). Paleopathology at the origins of agriculture: Editors' summation. In *Paleopathology at the origins of agriculture* (p. 594). Orlando: Academic Press.

Horticulture. Cultivation of crops carried out with hand tools such as digging sticks or hoes. • **Intensive agriculture.** Intensive farming of large plots of land, employing fertilizers, plows, and/or extensive irrigation. • **Pastoralists.** People who rely on herds of domestic animals for their subsistence.

cold for effective horticulture or intensive agriculture. For example, the Russian steppes, with their heavy grass cover, were not suitable to farming without a plow, but they were ideal for herding. Thus, a number of peoples living in the arid grasslands and deserts that stretch from northwestern Africa into Central Asia kept large herds of domestic animals, relying on their neighbors for plant foods. A comparable development took place in the high, intermountain basins of Peru and Bolivia. Finally, some societies went on to develop civilizations—the subject of the next chapter.

CHAPTER SUMMARY

The end of the glacial period saw great physical changes in human habitats. Sea levels rose, vegetation changed, and herd animals disappeared from many areas. The European Mesolithic period marked a shift from big game hunting to the hunting of smaller game and gathering a broad spectrum of plants and aquatic resources. Increased reliance on seafood and plants made the Mesolithic a more sedentary period for people. Ground stone tools, including axes and adzes, responded to postglacial needs for new technologies. Many Mesolithic tools in the Old World were made with microliths—small, hard, sharp blades of flint or similar stone that could be mass produced and hafted with others to produce implements like sickles.

The change to food production, which (in Southwest Asia) was becoming widespread by 10,300 years ago, took place as people were becoming more sedentary and allowed reorganization of the workload, so that some people could pursue other tasks. From the end of the Mesolithic, human groups became larger and more permanent as people turned to animal breeding and crop growing.

A domesticated plant or animal is one that has become genetically modified as an intended or unintended consequence of human manipulation. Analysis of plant and animal remains at a site will usually indicate whether or not its occupants were food producers. Wild cereal grasses, for example, usually have fragile stems, whereas cultivated ones have tough stems. Domesticated plants can also be identified because their edible parts are usually larger than those of their wild counterparts. Domestication produces skeletal changes in some animals. The horns of wild goats and sheep, for example, differ from those of domesticated ones. Age and sex imbalances in herd animals may also indicate manipulation by human domesticators.

Several theories have been proposed to account for the changes in the subsistence patterns of early humans. One theory, the "oasis" or "desiccation" theory, is based on climatic determination. Domestication began because the oasis attracted hungry animals, which were domesticated instead of killed by early humans. Although once popular, this theory fell out of favor as systematic studies of the origins of domestication were begun in the late 1940s. One alternative idea was that domestication began in the hilly flanks of the Fertile Crescent because culture was ready for it. This somewhat culture-bound idea was replaced by theories, popular in the 1960s, that saw domestication as a response to population growth. However, this would require a deliberate decision on the part of people who could have had no prior knowledge of the long-range consequences of domestication. The most probable theory is that domestication came about as a consequence of a chance convergence of separate natural events and cultural developments. This happened independently even if at more or less similar times in Southwest and Southeast Asia, highland Mexico and Peru, South America's Amazon forest, eastern North America, China, and Africa. In all cases, however, people developed food complexes based on starchy grains and/or roots, that were consumed with protein-containing legumes plus some other flavor enhancers.

Two major consequences of domestication are that crops become more productive but also more vulnerable. This combination periodically causes population to outstrip food supplies, whereupon people are apt to move into new regions. In this way, farming has often spread from one region to another, as into Europe from Southwest Asia. Sometimes, food foragers will adopt the cultivation of crops from neighboring peoples, in response to a shortage of wild foods, as happened in ancient coastal Peru.

Among the earliest known sites containing domesticated plants and animals, about 10,300 to 9,000 years old, are those of Southwest Asia. These sites were mostly small villages of mud huts with individual storage pits and clay ovens. There is evidence not only of cultivation and domestication but also of trade. At ancient Jericho, remains of tools, houses, and clothing indicate the oasis was occupied by Neolithic people as early as 10,350 years ago. At its height, Neolithic Jericho had a population of 400 to 900 people. Comparable villages developed independently in Mexico and Peru by about 4,500 years ago.

During the Neolithic, stone that was too hard to be chipped was ground and polished for tools. People developed scythes, forks, hoes, and plows to replace simple digging sticks. The Neolithic was also characterized by the extensive manufacture and use of pottery. The widespread use of pottery is a good indicator of a sedentary community; it is found in all but a few of the earliest Neolithic settlements. The manufacture of pottery requires a knowledge of clay and the techniques of firing or baking. Other technological developments that accompanied food production and the sedentary life were the building of permanent houses and the weaving of textiles.

Archaeologists have been able to draw some inferences concerning the social structure of Neolithic society. No evidence has been found indicating that religion or government was yet a centrally organized institution. Society was probably relatively egalitarian, with minimal division of labor and little development of specialized social roles.

The development of food production had biological, as well as cultural, consequences. New diets, living arrangements, and farming practices led to increased incidence of disease and higher mortality rates. Increased fertility of women, however, more than offset mortality.

CLASSIC READINGS

Childe, V. G. (1951). *Man makes himself.* New York: New American Library.

In this classic, originally published in 1936, Childe presented his concept of the "Neolithic Revolution." He places special emphasis on the technological inventions that helped transform humans from food gatherers to food producers.

Coe, S. D. (1994). *America's first cuisines.* Austin: University of Texas Press.

Writing in an accessible style, Coe discusses some of the more important crops grown by Native Americans and explores their early history and domestication. Following this she describes how these foods were prepared, served, and preserved by the Aztec, Maya, and Incas.

Diamond, J. (1997). *Guns, germs, and steel.* New York: Norton.

This book, which won a Pulitzer Prize and became a best-seller, tries to answer the question: Why are wealth and power distributed as they are in the world today? For him, the answer requires an understanding of events associated with the origin and spread of food production. Although Diamond is a bit of an environmental determinist and falls into various ethnocentric traps, there is a great deal of solid information on the domestication and spread of crops and the biological consequences for humans. It is a lively book that can be read with pleasure.

MacNeish, R. S. (1992). *The origins of agriculture and settled life.* Norman: University of Oklahoma Press.

MacNeish was a pioneer in the study of the start of food production in the New World. In this book, he reviews the evidence from around the world in order to develop general laws about the development of agriculture and evolution of settled life.

Rindos, D. (1984). *The origins of agriculture: An evolutionary perspective.* Orlando: Academic Press.

This is one of the most important books on agricultural origins to appear in recent times. After identifying the weaknesses of existing theories, Rindos presents his own evolutionary theory of agricultural origins.

Zohary, D., & Hopf, M. (1993). *Domestication of plants in the Old World* (2nd ed.). Oxford: Clarenden Press.

This book deals with the origin and spread of domestic plants in western Asia, Europe, and the Nile Valley. Included is a species-by-species discussion of the various crops, an inventory of remains from archaeological sites, and a conclusion summarizing present knowledge.

THE RISE OF CITIES AND CIVILIZATION

One of the hallmarks of a city is a well-defined nucleus. Shown here is the
nucleus of Tikal, an ancient Maya city in Central America. In the foreground
are the palaces where the city's rulers lived and carried out their administrative
tasks. Beyond are the temples erected over the tombs of past kings.

1

WHEN AND WHERE DID THE WORLD'S FIRST CITIES FIRST DEVELOP?

Cities—urban settlements with well-defined nuclei, populations that are large, dense, and diversified both economically and socially—are characteristic of civilizations that developed initially between 6,000 and 4,500 years ago in China, the Indus and Nile valleys, Mesopotamia, Mesoamerica, and Peru. The world's oldest cities were those of Mesopotamia, but one of the world's largest was located in Mesoamerica.

2

WHAT CHANGES IN CULTURE ACCOMPANIED THE RISE OF CITIES?

Four basic culture changes mark the transition from Neolithic village life to that in civilized urban centers. These are agricultural innovation, as new farming methods were developed; diversification of labor, as more people were freed from food production to pursue a variety of full-time craft specialties; the emergence of centralized governments to deal with the new problems of urban life; and the emergence of social classes as people were ranked according to the work they did or the position of the families into which they were born.

3

WHY DID CIVILIZATIONS DEVELOP IN THE FIRST PLACE?

A number of theories have been proposed to explain why civilizations develop. For example, some civilizations may have developed as populations grew, causing competition for space and scarce resources, which favored the development of centralized authority to control resources and organize warfare. Some civilizations, though, appear to have developed as a result of certain beliefs and values that brought people together. In some cases, too, the actions of powerful individuals to promote their own interests may have played a role. Thus, it may be that civilizations arose in different places for somewhat different reasons.

A walk down a street of a busy North American city brings us in contact with numerous activities that are essential to the well-being of North American society. The sidewalks are crowded with people going to and from offices and stores. The traffic of cars, taxis, and trucks is heavy, sometimes almost at a standstill. In a brief two-block stretch, there may be a department store; shops selling clothing, appliances, or books; a restaurant; a newsstand; a gasoline station; and a movie theater. Perhaps there will also be a museum, a police station, a school, a hospital, or a church. That is quite a number of services and specialized skills to find in such a small area.

Each of these services or places of business is dependent on others. A butcher shop, for instance, depends on slaughterhouses and beef ranches. A clothing store depends on designers, farmers who produce cotton and wool, and workers who manufacture synthetic fibers. Restaurants depend on refrigerated trucking and vegetable and dairy farmers. Hospitals depend on a great variety of other institutions to meet their more complex needs. All institutions, finally, depend on the public utilities—the telephone, gas, water, and electric companies. Although interdependence is not immediately apparent to the passerby, it is an important aspect of modern cities.

The interdependence of goods and services in a big city is what makes so many products readily available to people. For example, refrigerated air transport makes it possible to buy fresh Maine lobsters on the West Coast. This same interdependence, however, has undesirable effects if one service stops functioning, for example, because of strikes, bad weather, or acts of violence such as the attack on New York's World Trade Center. Thus, every so often, major North American cities have had to do without services as vital as newspapers, subways, schools, and trash removal. The question is not so much "Why does this happen?" but rather "Why doesn't it happen more often, and why does the city continue to function as well as it does when one of its services stops?" The answer is that services are not only interdependent, but they are also adaptable. When one breaks down, others take over its functions. During a long newspaper strike in New York City in the 1960s, for example, several new magazines were launched, and television expanded its coverage of news and events. Currently, we are adapting to changes in air travel in response to heightened terrorist activity.

On the surface, city life seems so orderly that we take it for granted; but a moment's reflection reminds us that the intricate fabric of city life did not always exist, and the goods that are widely accessible to us were once simply not available.

WHAT CIVILIZATION MEANS

This complicated system of goods and services available in such a small space is a mark of civilization itself. The history of civilization is intimately bound up with the history of cities. This does not mean that civilization is to be equated with modern industrial cities or with present-day European or North American society. People as diverse as the ancient preindustrial Aztecs of Mexico and the industrial North Americans of today are included in the term *civilization,* but each represents a very different kind. It was with the development of the earliest preindustrial cities, however, that civilization first developed (Figure 12.1). In fact, the word comes from the Latin *civis,* which refers to one who is an inhabitant of a city, and *civitas,* which refers to the community in which one dwells. The word *civilization* contains the idea of "citification," or "the coming-to-be of cities."

Civilization is one of those words that is used in different ways by different people. In everyday usage, it carries the notion of refinement and progress, two ethnocentric concepts that mean whatever a culture holds them to mean. In anthropology, by contrast, the term has a very precise meaning that avoids such culture-bound notions. As used by anthropologists, **civilization** refers to societies in which large numbers of people live in cities, are socially stratified, and are governed by centrally organized political systems called states. We shall elaborate on all of these points in the course of this chapter.

The world's first cities sprang up in some parts of the world as Neolithic villages of the sort discussed in Chapter 11 grew into towns, some of which in turn grew into cities. This happened first in Mesopotamia (in modern-day Iraq), then in Egypt and the Indus Valley, between 6,000 and 4,500 years ago. The inhabitants of Sumer, in southern Mesopotamia, developed the world's first civilization about 5,500 years ago. In China, civilization was under way by 5,000 years ago. Independent of these developments in the Old World, the first cities appeared in Peru around 4,000 years ago and in Mesoamerica about 2,000 years ago.

Civilization. In anthropology a type of society marked by the presence of cities, social classes, and the state.

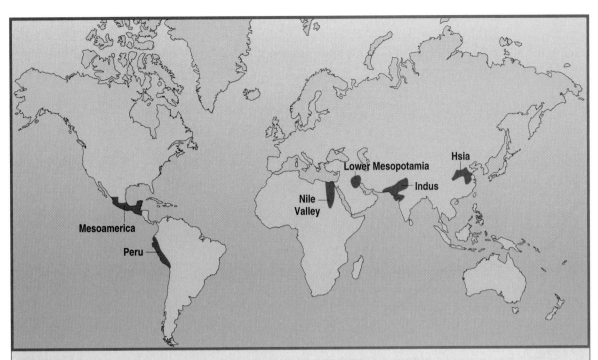

FIGURE 12.1

THE MAJOR EARLY CIVILIZATIONS SPRANG FROM NEOLITHIC VILLAGES IN VARIOUS PARTS OF THE WORLD. THOSE OF NORTH AND SOUTH AMERICA DEVELOPED WHOLLY INDEPENDENTLY OF THOSE IN AFRICA AND ASIA; CHINESE CIVILIZATION SEEMS TO HAVE DEVELOPED INDEPENDENTLY OF SOUTHWEST ASIA (INCLUDING THE NILE AND INDUS) CIVILIZATIONS.

What characterized these first cities? Why are they called the birthplaces of civilization? The first characteristic of cities—and of civilization—is their large size and population. But is this all that a city is? Consider the case of Çatalhöyük, a 9,500-year-old settlement in south-central Turkey (see Figure 11.2).[1] Home to 5,000 or more people, its houses were so tightly packed together in an area of roughly 12 hectares that there were no streets. To get into one's own house, one dropped through a hole in the roof, after having traversed the roofs of neighboring houses. For subsistence, people grew crops and tended livestock, but because the village was located in the middle of a swamp, these activities were carried out at locations at least 12 kilometers away. But there is no evidence

for intensification of agriculture; furthermore, people's diets included significant amounts of food from wild plants and animals.

The reason for Çatalhöyük's location in the middle of a swamp may have been to take advantage of lime-rich clay that people used to plaster their walls, floors, and ovens. The walls were covered with all sorts of paintings, often of small men confronting outsize beasts, as well as reliefs of leopards, bulls, and female breasts. But there was little division of labor, nor is there any evidence of centralized authority. The houses are all pretty much alike, and there is no known public architecture. It is as if a

---

[1] Material on Çatalhöyük is drawn from Balter, M. (1998). Why settle down? The mystery of communities. *Science, 282,* 1,442–1,444; Balter, M. (1999). A long season puts Çatalhöyük in context. *Science, 286,* 890–891; Balter, M. (2001). Did plaster hold Neolithic society together? *Science, 294,* 2,278–2,281; Kunzig, R. (1999). A tale of two obsessed archaeologists, one ancient city and nagging doubts about whether science can ever hope to reveal the past. *Discover, 20*(5), 84–92.

Çatalhöyük in Turkey was a compact village, as suggested by this photo, but it was not a true city.

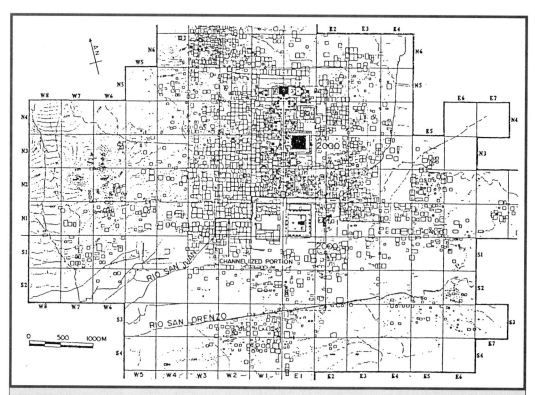

FIGURE 12.2

THE FOUNDERS OF TEOTIHUACAN IMPOSED AN AUDACIOUS PLAN ON SEVERAL SQUARE KILOMETERS OF LANDSCAPE IN CENTRAL MEXICO. AT THE CENTER IS THE AVENUE OF THE DEAD, RUNNING FROM THE TEMPLE OF THE MOON (NEAR TOP), PAST THE TEMPLE OF THE SUN AND, SOUTH OF THE RIO SAN JUAN, THE PALACE COMPOUND. NOTE THE GRIDDED LAYOUT OF SURROUNDING APARTMENT COMPOUNDS, AND THE CHANNELIZED RIO SAN JUAN.

number of what otherwise would be separate Neolithic villages were all crammed together in one place.

One may compare Çatalhöyük with Teotihuacan, America's first great experience in urbanism (Figure 12.2). Located in central Mexico, in the first 400 years after its founding 2,200 years ago, its population grew rapidly, until it reached perhaps 80,000 people. Slower growth thereafter brought this figure to around 100,000, all packed within an area of about 20 km². As revealed by regional surveys, one reason for the early rapid growth was that the population of the entire 5,000 km² Basin of Mexico (where modern Mexico City is located today) was removed and relocated to Teotihuacan. Furthermore, the layout of the city was planned from the very start. At its center is what is known as the Street of the Dead, a grand north-south axis along which are located the huge Sun and Moon pyramids as well as a royal palace compound (associated with the planet Venus) and other monumental construction. The Sun pyramid was built above a cave, seen as a portal to the underworld, home of deities associated with death. The street itself was deliberately oriented to an astronomical alignment east of true north. Surrounding this core were thousands of apartment compounds, separated from one another by narrow streets laid out in a grid, maintaining the east-of-north orientation throughout the city. Key linear dimensions of construction and distance between compounds seem to have translated calendrical numbers into a unified spatial pattern. So rigid was this layout that the Rio San Juan, where it runs through the city, was channelized to conform with the grid. Finally, there is clear evidence for both social and economic diversity. Some six levels of society can be recognized by variation in size and quality of apartment rooms. Those at and near the top of the social scale lived on or near the Street of the Dead. Exotic goods and raw materials were imported from afar to be worked by Teotihuacano artisans, and at least two enclaves housed people with foreign affiliations, one to Oaxaca, the other ("merchant's barrio") to the Gulf and Maya lowlands. Also resident in the city were farmers, whose labor in fields (some of them irrigated) supplied the food on which the city dwellers relied.[2]

---

[2]Cowgill, G. L. (1997). State and society at Teotihuacan, Mexico. *Annual Review of Anthropology, 26,* 129–161.

This photo looks south down Teotihuacan's principal avenue, the Street of the Dead, an urban axis unequaled in its scale until construction of such modern-day avenues as the Champs Elysées in Paris.

As this comparison shows, early cities were far more than expanded Neolithic villages. The changes that took place in the transition from village to city were so great that the emergence of urban living is considered by some to be one of the great revolutions in human culture. The following case study gives us a glimpse of another of the world's ancient cities, how it was studied by archaeologists, and how it may have grown from a smaller farming community.

TIKAL: A CASE STUDY

The ancient city of Tikal, one of the largest lowland Maya centers in existence, is situated in Central America about 200 miles by air north of Guatemala City. Tikal was built on a broad limestone terrace in a rain forest. Here the Maya settled in the 1st millennium B.C., and their civilization flourished until about A.D. 869 (dates were recorded by the Maya in their own calendar, which can be precisely correlated with our own).

At its height, Tikal covered about 120.5 km^2, and its nucleus, or "epicenter," was the Great Plaza, a large, paved area surrounded by about 300 major structures and thousands of houses (see the photo that opens this chapter). Starting from a small, dispersed population, the population of Tikal swelled to large proportions. By A.D. 550, the density of Tikal was on the order of 600 to 700 persons per square kilometer, 6 times that of the surrounding regions.

From 1956 through the 1960s, Tikal and the surrounding region were intensively explored under the joint auspices of the University of Pennsylvania Museum and the Guatemalan government. Until 1959, the Tikal Project had investigated only major temple and palace structures found in the vicinity of the Great Plaza, at the site's epicenter. It became evident, however, that in order to gain a balanced view of Tikal's development and composition, considerable attention would have to be devoted to hundreds of small mounds, thought to be the remains of dwellings, which surround the larger buildings. Just as one cannot get a realistic view of Washington, DC, by looking at its monumental public buildings alone, so one cannot obtain a realistic view of Tikal without examining the full range of ruins in the area.

It became evident that a long-range program of excavation of small structures, most of which were probably houses, was necessary at Tikal. Such a program would provide some basis for an estimate of the city's population size and density—information critical for testing the conventional assumption that the Maya could not have sustained large concentrations of population because their subsistence practices were not adequate. Extensive excavation would also provide a sound basis for a reconstruction of the everyday life of the Maya, a people up till then known almost entirely through a study of ceremonial remains. Moreover, the excavation might shed light on the social organization of the Maya. For example, differences in house construction and in the quality and quantity of associated remains might suggest social class differences; or features of house distribution might reflect the existence of extended families or other types of kin groups. The excavation of both large and small structures could reveal the variations in architecture and associated artifacts and burials; such variations might reflect the social structure of the total population of Tikal.[3]

Surveying the Site

By the time the first excavations of small structures were undertaken, 6 km^2 surrounding the Great Plaza had already been extensively surveyed by mapping crews (see Figure 2.1). For this mapping, aerial photography was worthless because the tree canopy in this area is often 100 feet above the ground and obscures all but the tallest temples; many of the small ruins are practically invisible even to observers on the ground. The only effective way to explore the region is on foot. Once a ruin is found, it is not easy to mark its exact location. Even after 4 years of careful mapping, the limits of the site still had not been revealed. Ancient Tikal was far larger than the 6 km^2 surveyed till then. More time and money were required to continue surveying the area in order to define the city's boundaries. To simplify this problem, straight survey trails oriented toward the four cardinal directions, with the Great Plaza as the center point, were cut through the forest, measured, and staked by government surveyors. The distribution of ruins was plotted, using the trails as reference points, and the overall size of Tikal was calculated.[4]

The area selected for the first small-structure excavation was surveyed in 1957 while it was still covered by forest. A map was drafted, and 2 years later the first excavations were undertaken.[5] Six structures, two plazas, and

---

[3]Haviland, W. A. (2002). Settlement, society and demography at Tikal. In J. Sabloff (Ed.), *Tikal.* Santa Fe: School of American Research (in press).

[4]Puleston, D. E. (1983). *The settlement survey of Tikal.* Philadelphia: University Museum.

[5]Haviland, W. A., et al. (1985). *Excavations in small residential groups of Tikal: Groups 4F-1 and 4F-2.* Philadelphia: University Museum.

At Tikal, only the tallest temples are visible above the forest canopy. The two farthest temples are at either end of the Great Plaza, the civic and ceremonial heart of the city. (Those familiar with the original *Star Wars* movie will recognize this view.)

a platform were investigated. The original plan was to strip each of the structures to bedrock in order to obtain every bit of information possible. Three obstacles prevented this procedure, however. First was the discovery of new structures not visible before excavation; second, the structures turned out to be far more complex architecturally than anyone had expected; and, finally, the enormous quantity of artifacts found then had to be washed and catalogued, a time-consuming process. Consequently, not every structure was completely excavated, and some remained uninvestigated.

Evidence from the Excavation

Following this initial work, over 100 additional small structures were excavated in different parts of the site in order to ensure that a representative sample was investigated. Numerous test pits were sunk in various other small structure groups to supplement the information gained from more extensive excavations.

Excavation at Tikal revealed evidence of trade in nonperishable items. Granite, quartzite, hematite, pyrite, jade, slate, and obsidian all were imported, either as raw materials or finished products. Marine materials came from Caribbean and Pacific coastal areas. Tikal itself is located on a source of abundant flint, which may have been exported in the form of raw material and finished objects. The site also happens to be located between two river systems to the east and west, and so may have been on a major overland trade route between the two. There is indirect evidence that trade went on in perishable goods such as textiles, feathers, salt, and cacao. We can safely conclude that there were full-time traders among the Tikal Maya.

In the realm of technology, specialized woodworking, pottery, obsidian, and shell workshops have been found. The skillful stone carving displayed on stone monuments suggests that this was done by occupational specialists. The same is true of the fine artwork exhibited on ceramic

This painting from Cacaxtla in southern Mexico shows a deity with the typical backpack of a Maya merchant.

vessels. Those who painted these had to envision what their work would look like after their pale, relatively colorless slips had been fired. The complex Maya calendar required astronomers, and in order to control the large population, estimated to have been at least 50,000 people, there must have been some form of bureaucratic organization. We do know that the government was headed by a hereditary ruling dynasty, and that it had sufficient power to organize the construction and continuing maintenance of a massive system of defensive ditches and embankments on the northern and southern edges of the city (the longest of these ran for a distance of perhaps 19, if not 28 km). Although we do not have direct evidence, there are clues to the existence of textile workers, dental workers, makers of bark cloth "paper," scribes, masons, and other occupational specialists.

Carved monuments like this were commissioned by Tikal's rulers to commemorate important events in their reigns. Portrayed on this one is a king who ruled between A.D. 768 and A.D. 790 or a bit later. Such skilled stone carving could only have been accomplished by a specialist. (For a translation of the inscription on the monument's left side, see Figure 12.4.)

The religion of the Tikal Maya probably developed initially as a means to cope with the uncertainties of agriculture. When people are faced with problems unsolvable by technological or organizational means, they resort to manipulation of magic and the supernatural. Soils at Tikal are thin, and there is no water except that which can be collected in ponds. Rain is abundant in season, but its onset tends to be unreliable. Once the wet season arrives, there may be dry spells of varying duration that can seriously affect crop productivity. Or there may be too much rain, so that crops rot in the fields. Other risks include storm damage, locust plagues, and incursions of wild animals. To this day, the native inhabitants of the region display great concern about these very real risks involved in agriculture over which they have no direct control.

The Maya priesthood devoted much of its time to calendrical matters; the priests tried not only to placate the deities in times of drought but also to propitiate them in times of plenty. They determined the most auspicious time to plant crops and were concerned with other agricultural matters. The dependence of the population in and around Tikal upon their priesthood to manipulate supernatural beings and forces in their behalf, in order that their crops would not fail, tended to keep them in or near the city, although a slash-and-burn method of agriculture, which was probably the prevailing method early in Tikal's history, requires the constant shifting of plots and consequently tended to disperse the population over large areas.

As the population increased, land for agriculture became scarcer, and the Maya were forced to find new methods of food production that could sustain the dense population concentrated at Tikal. To slash-and-burn agriculture as their main form of subsistence, they added the planting and tending of fruit trees and other crops that could be grown around their houses in soils enriched by human waste (unlike houses at Teotihuacan, those at Tikal were not built close to one another). Along with increased reliance on household gardening went the construction of artificially raised fields in areas that were flooded each rainy season. In these fields, crops could be intensively cultivated year after year, as long as they were carefully maintained. Measures also were taken to maximize catchment of water for the dry season, by converting low areas into reservoirs and constructing channels to carry runoff from plazas and other architecture into these reservoirs. As these changes were taking place, a class of artisans, craftspeople, and other occupational specialists emerged to serve the needs first of religion, then of an elite consisting of the priesthood and a ruling dynasty. The arts flourished, and numerous temples, public buildings, and houses were built.

Economic Development and Tropical Forests

Prime targets for development in the world today, in the eyes of governments and private corporations alike, are vast tracts of tropical forests. On a global basis, forests are being rapidly cleared for lumber and fuel, as well as to make way for farms, ranches, mines, and other forms of economic development. The world's largest uninterrupted tracts are the forests of the Amazon and Orinoco watersheds of South America, which are being destroyed at about the rate of 4 percent a year. Just what the rate is for the world as a whole no one is quite sure, but it is clearly accelerating. And already there are signs of trouble, as extensive tracts of once-lush growth have been converted to semi-desert. Essential nutrients are lost, either through erosion (which increases by several orders of magnitude under deforestation) or by leaching too deeply, as soils are exposed to the direct force of the heavy tropical rains.

The problem is that developers, until recently, have lacked reliable models by which the long-term impact of their actions might be assessed. Such a model now exists, thanks to the efforts of archaeologists unraveling the mystery of how the ancient Maya, in a tropical rainforest setting, carried out large-scale urban construction and sustained huge numbers of people successfully for 2 millennia. The key to the Maya success was their implementation of sophisticated practices to reduce regionwide

processes of nutrient loss, deterioration of soil structure, destabilization of water flows, soil erosion, and loss of productive components of their environment.[*] These included construction of terraces, canals, and raised fields, the fertility of which was maintained through mulching with water plants and the addition of organic wastes. Coupled with all this, crops were planted in such a way as to produce complex patterns of foliage distribution, canopy heights, and nutrient demands. Far different from "modern" monocrop agriculture, this reduced the impact on the soils of intensive farming, while making maximum use of nutrients and enhancing their cycling in the system.

In Mexico, where population growth has threatened the country's ability to provide sufficient food for its people, archaeologists and agriculturalists are already cooperating to apply our knowledge of ancient Maya techniques to the problems of modern food production in the tropics. Application of these techniques in other tropical forested countries, like Brazil, could do much to alleviate food shortages.

---

[*]Rice, D. S., & Rice, P. M. (1984). Lessons from the Maya. *Latin American Research Review, 19*(3), 24–28.

For several hundred years, Tikal was able to sustain its ever-growing population. Then the pressure for food and land reached a critical point, and population growth was halted. At the same time, warfare with other cities was becoming increasingly destructive. All of this is marked archaeologically by abandonment of houses on prime land in rural areas, by the advent of nutritional problems as evidenced by the bones from burials, and by the construction of the previously mentioned defensive ditches and embankments. In other words, a period of readjustment set in, which must have been directed by an already strong central authority. Activities then continued as before, but without further population growth for another 250 years or so.

CITIES AND CULTURAL CHANGE

If someone who grew up in a small village of Maine, Wyoming, or Mississippi were to move to Chicago, Detroit, or Los Angeles, that person would experience a number of marked changes in his or her way of life. The same sorts of changes in daily life would have been felt 5,000 years ago by a Neolithic village dweller upon moving into one of the world's first cities in Mesopotamia. Of course, the differences would be less extreme today. In the 20th century, every North American village, however small, is part of civilization; back when cities first developed, *they* were civilization, and the villages for the

HIGHWAY 1

Take a trip to the ancient Maya ruins of Tikal, and experience life in this large city over 2,000 years ago through this 360-degree virtual tour of the site. Learn about the cultural practices of this great ancient civilization through the artifacts and ruins.
www.destination360.com/tikal.htm

HIGHWAY 2

Visit the Teotihuacan home page to learn about this incredible pre-Aztec city. Stroll down the Avenue of the Dead and visit the pyramids of the Sun and the Moon.
http://archaeology.la.asu.edu/teo/

most part represented a continuation of Neolithic life. Four basic culture changes mark the transition from Neolithic village life to life in the first urban centers.

Agricultural Innovation

The first culture change characteristic of life in cities—hence, of civilization itself—occurred in farming methods. The ancient Sumerians, for example, built an extensive system of dikes, canals, and reservoirs to irrigate their farmlands. With such a system, they could control water resources at will; water could be held and then run off into the fields as necessary. Irrigation was an important factor affecting an increase of crop yields. Because farming could now be carried on independently of the seasons, more crops could be harvested in one year. On the other hand, this intensification of agriculture did not necessarily mean that people ate better than before. Under centralized governments, intensification was generally carried out with less regard for human health than when such governments did not exist.[6]

The ancient Maya who lived at Tikal developed systems of tree cultivation and constructed raised fields in seasonally flooded swamplands to supplement their earlier slash-and-burn farming. The resultant increase in crop yields provided for a higher population density.

Increased crop yields, resulting from agricultural innovations such as those of the ancient Maya and Sumerians, were undoubtedly a factor contributing to the high population densities of all civilized societies.

This clay tablet map of farmland outside of the Mesopotamian city of Nippur dates to 1300 B.C. Shown are irrigation canals separating the various fields, each of which is identified with the name of the owner.

---

[6]Roosevelt, A. C. (1984). Population, health, and the evolution of subsistence: Conclusions from the conference. In M. N. Cohen & G. J. Armelagos (Eds.), *Paleopathology at the origins of agriculture* (p. 568). Orlando: Academic Press.

Diversification of Labor

The second culture change characteristic of civilization is diversification of labor. In a Neolithic village that possessed neither irrigation nor plow farming, the members of every family were primarily concerned with the raising of crops. The high crop yields made possible by new farming methods and the increased population meant that a sizable number of people were available to pursue nonagricultural activities on a full-time basis. In the early cities, some people still farmed (as at Tikal and Teotihuacan), but a substantial number of the inhabitants were skilled workers or craftspeople.

Ancient public records indicate there was a considerable variety of such skilled workers. For example, an early Mesopotamian document from the city of Lagash lists the artisans, craftspeople, and others paid from crop surpluses stored in the temple granaries. Among them were coppersmiths, silversmiths, sculptors, merchants, potters, tanners, engravers, butchers, carpenters, spinners, barbers, cabinetmakers, bakers, clerks, and brewers. At the ancient Maya city of Tikal we have evidence for traders, potters, woodworkers, obsidian workers, painters, scribes, and sculptors, and perhaps textile workers, dental workers, shell workers, and paper makers.

With specialization came the expertise that led to the invention of new and novel ways of making and doing things. In the Old World, civilization ushered in what archaeologists

One technique of agricultural intensification used by the Maya reclaimed swampland by constructing raised fields surrounded by canals. Traces of these raised fields can still be seen, as shown here in Belize, at Pulltrous swamp.

often refer to as the **Bronze Age,** a period marked by the production of tools and ornaments of this metal. Metals were in great demand for the manufacture of farmers' and artisans' tools, as well as for weapons. Copper and tin—the raw

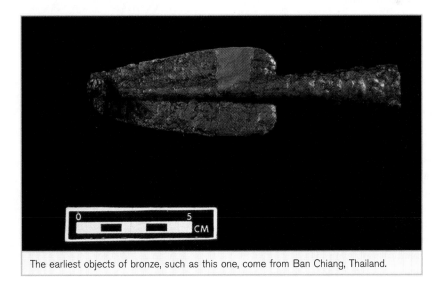

The earliest objects of bronze, such as this one, come from Ban Chiang, Thailand.

Bronze Age. In the Old World, the period marked by the production of tools and ornaments of bronze; began about 3000 B.C. in China and Southwest Asia and about 500 years earlier in Southeast Asia.

Bronze tools and weapons were more durable than their stone counterparts, which were more easily broken. The bronze sword (above) comes from Mycaenae, Greece, dating to about 1200 B.C. The ear pendant from Greece of about the same age is a fine example of the artistry that became possible with the introduction of bronze.

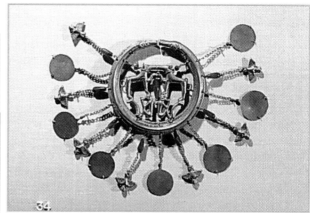

materials from which bronze is made—and eventually iron were smelted, separating them from their ores, then purified, and cast to make plows, swords, axes, and shields. In wars over border disputes or to extend a state's territory, stone knives, spears, and slings could not stand up against bronze spears, arrowheads, swords, or armor.

The native civilizations of the Americas also used metals—in South America, for tools as well as ceremonial and ornamental objects, but in Mesoamerica, mostly for ceremonial and ornamental objects. Why people like the Aztecs and Maya continued to rely on stone for their everyday tools has puzzled those who assume that metal is inherently superior. The answer, however, is simple: The ready availability of obsidian (a glass formed by volcanic activity), its extreme sharpness (many times sharper than the finest steel), and the ease with which it could be worked made it perfectly suited to their needs. With obsidian, these people fabricated tools with the sharpest cutting edges ever made.

In order to procure the raw materials needed for their technologies, extensive trade systems were developed by the early civilizations. The city of Teotihuacan, for example, controlled most of the obsidian trade in central Mexico. Trade agreements were maintained with distant peoples, not only to secure basic raw materials but to provide luxury items as well.

Boats gave greater access to trade centers; they could easily carry back to cities large loads of imports at less cost than if they had been brought back overland. A one-way trip from Egypt to the northern city of Byblos in Phoenicia (now Lebanon) took only four to eight days by rowboat. With a sailboat, it took even less.

Egyptian pharaohs sent expeditions to the Sinai Peninsula for copper; to Nubia for gold; to Arabia for spices and perfumes; to Asia for lapis lazuli (a blue semi-precious stone) and other jewels; to Lebanon for cedar, wine, and funerary oils; and to central Africa for ivory, ebony, ostrich feathers, leopard skins, cattle, and slaves.

With technological innovation, along with increased contact with foreign peoples through trade, came new knowledge. It was within the early civilizations that sciences such as geometry and astronomy were first developed. Geometry was used by the Egyptians for such purposes as measuring the area of a field or staking off an accurate right angle at the corner of a building.

Aztec spears tipped and edged with obsidian blades are shown in this 16th-century drawing of a battle with the Aztecs' Spanish conquerors. Though superior to steel for piercing, cutting, and slashing, the brittleness of obsidian placed the Aztecs at a disadvantage when faced with Spanish swords.

Paper making, invented in China 2,000 years ago, is an example of technological innovation by which farming societies evolved into civilizations.

Astronomy grew out of the need to know when to plant and harvest crops or to hold religious observances and to find exact bearings on voyages. Astronomy and mathematics were used to devise calendars. The Maya calculated that the solar year was 365 days (actually, it is $365^{1}/_{4}$ days), accurately predicted the appearances over time of the planet Venus as morning and evening "star," predicted eclipses, and tracked other astronomical events. As one scholar comments, "Maya science, in its representation of numbers, and its empirical base, is in many respects superior to the science of their European contemporaries."[7]

Central Government

The third culture change characteristic of civilization is the emergence of a governing elite, a strong central authority required to deal with the many problems arising within the new cities because of their size and complexity. The new governing elite saw to it that different interest groups, such as farmers, craft specialists, or money lenders, provided the services that were expected of them and did not infringe on one another's rights (to the extend that they had rights). It ensured that the city was safe from its enemies by constructing fortifications (such as those at Tikal)

and raising an army. It levied taxes and appointed tax collectors so that construction workers, the army, and other public expenses could be paid. It saw to it that merchants, carpenters, or farmers who made legal claims received justice (however "justice" was defined). It guaranteed safety for the lives and property of ordinary people and assured that any harm done one person by another would be justly handled. In addition, surplus food had to be stored for times of scarcity, and public works such as extensive irrigation systems or fortifications had to be supervised by competent, disinterested individuals. The mechanisms of government served all these functions.

EVIDENCE OF CENTRALIZED AUTHORITY

Evidence of centralized authority in ancient civilizations comes from such sources as law codes, temple records, and royal chronicles. Excavation of the city structures themselves provides further evidence. For example, archaeologists believe that the cities of Mohenjo-Daro and Harappa in the Indus Valley, which flourished between 4,800 and 3,700 years ago, were governed by a centralized authority because they show definite signs of city planning. Both cities stretch out over a 3 mile distance; their main streets are laid out in a rectangular grid pattern; and both contain citywide drainage systems. Similar evidence for centralized planning comes from Teotihuacan where, in addition, the sudden relocation of people from the Basin of Mexico also attests to strong, centralized control.

---

[7]Frake, C. O. (1992). Lessons of the Mayan sky: A perspective from medieval Europe. In A. F. Aveni (Ed.), *The sky in Mayan literature* (p. 287). New York: Oxford University Press.

Construction of large-scale public works such as the Great Wall of China reflects the power of a centralized government to mobilize and supervise the labor necessary to carry out such monumental undertakings.

Monumental buildings and temples, palaces, and large sculptures are usually found in civilizations. The Maya city of Tikal contained over 300 major structures, including temples, ball courts, and "palaces" (residences of the aristocracy). The Pyramid of the Sun in the pre-Aztec city of Teotihuacan is 700 feet long and more than 200 feet high. Its interior is filled by more than 1 million cubic yards of sun-dried bricks. The tomb of the Egyptian pharaoh Khufu, known as the Great Pyramid, is 755 feet long and 481 feet high. It contains about 2,300,000 stone blocks, each with an average weight of 2.5 tons. The Greek historian Herodotus reports that it took 100,000 men 20 years to build this tomb. Such gigantic structures could be built only because the considerable labor force, engineering skills, and raw materials necessary for their construction could be harnessed by a powerful central authority.

Another indicator of the existence of centralized authority is writing, or some form of recorded information (Figure 12.3). With writing, central authorities could disseminate information and store, systematize, and deploy memory for political, religious, and economic purposes. In Mesopotamia, early governments found it useful to keep records of state affairs, such as accounts of their food surplus, tribute records, and other business receipts. The earliest documents appear to be just such records—lists of vegetables and animals bought and sold, tax lists, and storehouse inventories. Being able to record information was an extremely important invention, because govern-ments could keep records of their assets instead of simply relying upon the memory of administrators.

Before 5,500 years ago, records consisted initially of "tokens," ceramic pieces with different shapes indicative of different commercial objects. Thus, a cone shape could represent a measure of grain, or a cylinder an animal. As the system developed, tokens represented different animals, processed foods such as oil, trussed ducks or bread, and manufactured or imported goods such as textiles and metal.[8] Ultimately, these tokens were replaced by clay tablets with impressed marks representing objects.

In the Mesopotamia city of Uruk, by 5,100 years ago, a new writing technique emerged, which used a reed stylus to make wedge-shaped markings on a tablet of damp clay. Originally, each marking stood for a word. Because most words in this language were monosyllabic, the markings came, in time, to stand for syllables. There were about 600 signs, half of them ideograms, the others functioning either as ideograms or as syllables.

In the New World, systems of writing came into use among various Mesoamerican peoples, but the most sophisticated was that of the Maya. Their hieroglyphic system had less to do with keeping track of state belongings than with "dynastic bombast." Maya lords glorified themselves by recording their dynastic genealogies, important

[8]Lawler, A. (2001). Writing gets a rewrite. *Science, 292,* 2,419.

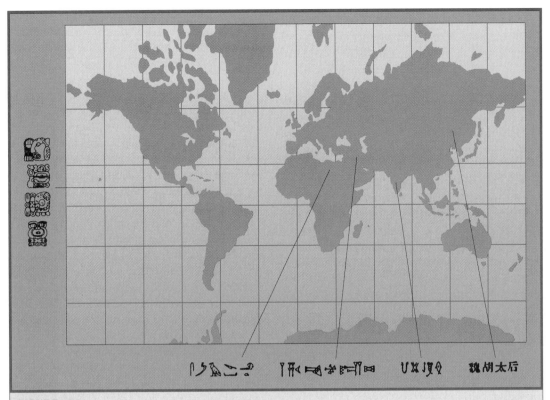

FIGURE 12.3

THE IMPERMANENCE OF SPOKEN WORDS CONTRASTS WITH THE RELATIVE PERMANENCE OF WRITTEN RECORDS. IN ALL OF HUMAN HISTORY, WRITING HAS BEEN INDEPENDENTLY INVENTED NO MORE THAN 5 TIMES.

conquests, and royal marriages; by using grandiose titles to refer to themselves; and by associating their actions with important astrological events (Figure 12.4). Often, the latter involved complicated mathematical calculations. So important was the written word in reinforcing the power and authority of Maya kings that scribes were high-ranking members of royal courts. So closely tied to kings were they that, when a king was defeated in warfare, his scribes were captured, tortured, and then sacrificed. The torture was highly symbolic, involving finger mutilation that destroyed their ability to produce politically persuasive texts for any rival of the victor.

THE EARLIEST GOVERNMENTS

The government of the earliest cities was typically headed by a king and his special advisors. In addition, there were sometimes councils of lesser advisors. Formal laws were enacted, and courts sat in judgment over the claims of rival litigants or the criminal charges brought by the government against an individual.

Of the many ancient kings known, one stands out as truly remarkable for the efficient government organization and highly developed legal system that characterized his reign. This is Hammurabi, the Babylonian king who lived sometime between 1950 and 1700 B.C. He promulgated a set of laws for his kingdom, known as the Code of Hammurabi, which is notable for its thorough detail and standardization. It prescribes the correct form for legal procedures and determines penalties for perjury, false accusation, and injustice done by judges. It contains laws applying to property rights, loans and debts, family rights, and damages paid for malpractice by a physician. There are fixed rates to be charged in various trades and branches of commerce. The poor, women, children, and slaves are protected against injustice. The code was publicly displayed on huge stone slabs so that no one accused could plead ignorance. Even the poorest citizen was supposed to know his or her rights.

Some civilizations flourished under a ruler with extraordinary governing abilities, such as Hammurabi. Other civilizations possessed a widespread governing bureaucracy that was very efficient at every level. Teotihuacan was probably of this sort, but the government of the Inca civilization is better known.

The Inca empire of Peru reached its zenith 500 years ago, just before the arrival of the Spanish. In the mid-1400s A.D., the Inca kingdom probably did not extend more than 20 miles beyond the modern-day city of Cuzco, which was then its center. Within a 30-year period, in the late 1400s, the Inca kingdom enlarged a thousand times its original size. By A.D. 1525, it stretched 2,500 miles from north to south and 500 miles from east to west, making it at the time the greatest empire on the face of the earth. Its population numbered in the millions, composed of people of various ethnic groups. In the achievements of its governmental and political system, Inca civilization surpassed every other civilization of the New World and most of those of the Old World. At the head of the government was the emperor, regarded as semi-divine, followed by the royal family, the aristocracy, imperial administrators, the lower nobility, and the masses of artisans, craftspeople, and farmers.

The empire was divided into four administrative regions, further subdivided into provinces, and so on down to villages and families. Planting, irrigation, and harvesting were closely supervised by government agricultural and tax officials. Teams of professional relay runners could carry messages up to 250 miles in a single day over a network of roads and bridges that remains impressive even today. The Inca are unusual in that they had no writing that we know about; public records and historical chronicles were kept in the form of an ingenious system of colored beads, knots, and ropes.

Social Stratification

The rise of large, economically diversified populations presided over by centralized governing authorities brought with it the fourth culture change characteristic of civilization: social stratification, or the emergence of social classes. Thus, we note that symbols of special status and privilege appeared in the ancient cities of Mesopotamia,

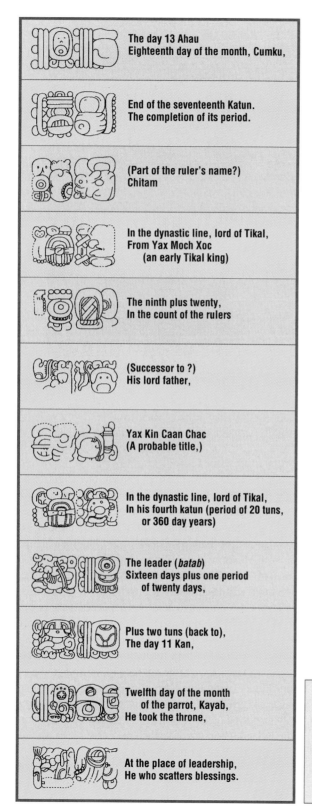

The day 13 Ahau
Eighteenth day of the month, Cumku,

End of the seventeenth Katun.
The completion of its period.

(Part of the ruler's name?)
Chitam

In the dynastic line, lord of Tikal,
From Yax Moch Xoc
(an early Tikal king)

The ninth plus twenty,
In the count of the rulers

(Successor to ?)
His lord father,

Yax Kin Caan Chac
(A probable title,)

In the dynastic line, lord of Tikal,
In his fourth katun (period of 20 tuns,
or 360 day years)

The leader (*batab*)
Sixteen days plus one period
of twenty days,

Plus two tuns (back to),
The day 11 Kan,

Twelfth day of the month
of the parrot, Kayab,
He took the throne,

At the place of leadership,
He who scatters blessings.

FIGURE 12.4

The translation of the text on the monument shown on p. 308 gives some indication of the importance of dynastic genealogy to Maya rulers. The "scattering" mentioned may refer to bloodletting as part of the ceremonies associated with the end of one 20-year period, or Katun, and the beginning of the next.

and people were ranked according to the kind of work they did or the family into which they were born.

People who stood at or near the head of government were the earliest holders of high status. Although economic specialists of one sort or another—metal workers, tanners, traders, or the like—generally outranked farmers, such specialization did not necessarily bring with it high status. Rather, people engaged in economic activity were either of the lower class or outcasts.[9] The exception was those merchants who were in a position to buy their way into some kind of higher class. With time, the possession of wealth and the influence it could buy became in itself a requisite for high status.

EVIDENCE OF SOCIAL STRATIFICATION

How do archaeologists know that there were different social classes in ancient civilizations? One way they are revealed is by burial customs. Graves excavated at early Neolithic sites are mostly simple pits dug in the ground, containing few, if any, grave goods. Grave goods consist of things such

as utensils, figurines, and personal possessions, which are placed in the grave in order that the dead person might use them in the afterlife. The lack of much variation between burials in terms of the wealth implied by grave goods in Neolithic sites indicates an essentially classless society. Graves excavated in civilizations, by contrast, vary widely in size, mode of burial, and the number and variety of grave goods. This indicates a stratified society—one divided into social classes. The graves of important persons contain not only a great variety of artifacts made from precious materials, but sometimes, as in some early Egyptian burials, even the remains of servants evidently killed to serve their master in the afterlife. The skeletons from the burials may also give evidence of stratification. At Tikal, skeletons from elaborate tombs indicate that the subjects of these tombs had longer life expectancy, ate better food, and enjoyed better health than the bulk of that city's population. In stratified societies, the elite usually live longer, eat better, and enjoy an easier life than other members of society.

As an example of what upper-class burials may look like, and what more they can tell us about the customs of the people placed in them, we may look at a spectacular tomb from one of the civilizations that preceded that of the Incas in Peru.

---

[9]Sjoberg, G. (1960). *The preindustrial city* (p. 325). New York: Free Press.

Finding the Tomb of a Moche Priestess[10]

Original Study

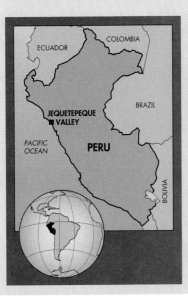

The Moche kingdom flourished on the north coast of Peru between A.D. 100 and 800. Although the Moche had no writing system, they left a vivid artistic record of their beliefs and activities on beautifully modeled and painted ceramic vessels. Because of the realism and detail of these depic-

tions, we are able to reconstruct various aspects of Moche society such as religious ceremonies and mythology, as well as activities like hunting, weaving, and combat rarely preserved in the archaeological record.

During the past 20 years we have developed a major photographic archive of Moche art at the University of California, Los Angeles, which serves as an important resource for the study of their culture. Our goal has been to reconstruct aspects of Moche culture by combining systematic studies of their art with archaeological fieldwork in Peru. Our

---

[10]Donnan, C. B., & Castillo, L. J. (1992). Finding the tomb of a Moche priestess. *Archaeology, 45*(6), 38–42.

Original Study

analyses of sites, including residential compounds, palaces, temples, and cemeteries, and the artifacts associated with them have allowed us to document archaeologically some of the complex scenes illustrated in Moche art, and to understand aspects of their culture that are not portrayed in the art.

During the past 10 years our research has focused on the Jequetepeque Valley, located in the northern portion of the territory occupied by the Moche. In this region we have undertaken several lines of research, concentrating our efforts on the relationship between Moche ceremonial activities and socio-economic organization. In June 1991, UCLA began excavations at San José de Moro, a major ceremonial center in the lower Jequetepeque Valley. It was clear from its various ceramic styles that the site had a long history of occupation and thus would be ideal for answering questions about the cultural sequence of the region. Moreover, the quantity and variation in monumental construction at the site strongly suggested that it had served as a major ceremonial center through most of its occupation and thus could provide us with good insights about the nature of Moche ceremonial activity.

During our first field season we excavated three complex late-Moche tombs—each consisting of a room-sized burial chamber made of mud bricks. The tomb chambers had originally been roofed with large wooden beams. The principal occupant of each tomb was lying face up in an extended position, with the remains of complete llamas, humans, or both, at their feet. In two of the tombs the principal occupants were flanked by other individuals. Hundreds of ceramic vessels and metal objects, including ceremonial knives, lance points, sandals, cups, masks, and jewelry, had been placed in the tombs as offerings.

The most elaborate of the three tombs was that of a high-status adult female. It is the richest Moche female burial ever scientifically excavated and clearly demonstrates that in Moche society extraordinary wealth and power were not the exclusive domain of males. The tomb chamber was approximately 7-$\frac{1}{2}$ by 14 feet. The walls, which were made of mud brick, had niches—six on each side and four at the head of the tomb—in which ceramic vessels and parts of llamas had been placed. Additional ceramic vessels had been stacked on the floor of the tomb chamber.

Some of the artifacts associated with this burial provide clear evidence that the Moche were involved in long-distance trade and that their elite

A silver-copper alloy mask (left) was found near the priestess' skull. Her body (right) was covered with hammered metal arms and legs.

The Moche Sacrifice Ceremony

The Sacrifice Ceremony, an event at which prisoners of war are sacrificed and their blood ritually consumed, is a common iconographic theme in Moche art. One of the better-known representations of this ceremony appears on a stirrup spout bottle. The scene, center, shows four principal figures and attendants. Below them are bound captives having their throats slashed. During recent excavations at San José de Moro and at Sipán, the remains of several people who participated in this ceremony have been identified. Figure C, a priestess, was discovered at San José de Moro, while Figure A, a warrior-priest, and Figure B, a bird-warrior, were excavated at Sipán.

A goblet, recovered during the excavation of the priestess's tomb at San José de Moro, is decorated with a scene of anthropomorphic war clubs and shields drinking the blood of captives from tall goblets. A similar goblet is being passed between Figure A and Figure B in the drawing below.

Silver-copper alloy tassels worn by the principal occupant of the tomb allowed her to be identified as the priestess depicted in the Sacrifice Ceremony. The tassels are identical to those worn by Figure C in both the drawing and the Pañamarca mural, bottom.

The Pañamarca mural, right, painted on an adobe wall at a Moche ceremonial center in the Nepeña Valley, shows Figure C accompanied by several attendants bearing goblets. Pictured too are three bound captives with their throats slashed and a ceramic basin containing cups. A similar basin, below, was found in the priestess's tomb.

Original Study

expended a great deal of effort to obtain precious materials. Included among the offerings were three imported ceramic vessels—a plate of Cajamarca style, which must have been brought to San José de Moro from the highland area located more than 70 miles to the east, and two exotic ceramic bottles of Nieveria style, a type of pottery that was made in the area of Lima, more than 350 miles to the south. Two other kinds of materials associated with the tomb provide further evidence of long-distance trade. Over the woman's chest and hands were *Spondylus princeps* shells that had been brought from Ecuador to the north, and around her neck were cylindrical beads of lapis lazuli that had been brought from Chile to the south.

The most remarkable aspect of this woman's tomb, however, was that the objects buried with her allow us to identify her as a specific priestess who is depicted in Moche art. This priestess was first identified in the Moche Archive at UCLA in 1975, at which time she was given the name "Figure C." Five years later, Anne Marie Hocquenghem and Patricia Lyon convincingly demonstrated that this individual was female. She was one of the principal participants in the "Sacrifice Ceremony," an event depicted in Moche art where prisoners of war were sacrificed and their blood ritually consumed in tall ceremonial goblets.

Figure C is always depicted with her hair in wrapped braids that hang across her chest, and wearing a long dresslike garment. Also characteristic of Figure C is her headdress, which is unique in having two prominent tassels. The tomb of the woman at San José de Moro contained an identical headdress with two huge tassels made of a silver copper alloy.

In one corner of the tomb was a large blackware ceramic basin containing cups and a tall goblet. An identical blackware basin with cups in it is shown associated with Figure C in a famous mural at the site of Pañamarca, a ceremonial center located in the Nepeña Valley. Furthermore, the tall goblet contained in the ceramic basin was of the type used in the Sacrifice Ceremony. It is decorated with a scene of anthropomorphized clubs and shields

drinking blood from similar goblets. The tall goblet is a prominent feature in all depictions of the Sacrifice Ceremony, and it is often seen being presented by Figure C. Finding the tall goblet in her grave thus supports her identification as Figure C.

The tomb of Figure C at San José de Moro has profound implications for Moche studies. Excavations by Walter Alva at Sipán, located in a valley to the north of San José de Moro, have revealed the tombs of two other participants, Figure A and Figure B, in the Sacrifice Ceremony. The richest of these tombs is that of the Lord of Sipán, Figure A. He was buried with his characteristic crescent-shaped headdress, crescent-shaped nose ornament, large circular ear ornaments, and warrior's back-flap, and was holding a rattle like that shown in representations of Figure A. The occupant of another tomb appears to be Figure B, a bird-warrior who is frequently shown as companion to Figure A. He was found wearing a headdress adorned with an owl. Although no grave of Figure C has yet been excavated at Sipán, it seems likely that someone who performed this role was also buried at that site.

How do the tombs at Sipán relate to the tomb of Figure C at San José de Moro? First, it should be noted that the two tombs at Sipán date to approximately A.D. 300, and those at San José de Moro at least 250 years later—sometime after A.D. 550. Clearly, the Sacrifice Ceremony had a long duration in Moche culture, with individuals consistently dressing in traditional garments and headdresses to perform the roles of specific members of the priesthood.

The Sacrifice Ceremony was also widespread geographically. The Pañamarca mural, which clearly depicts this ceremony, was found in the Nepeña Valley, in the southern part of the Moche kingdom. San José de Moro is more than 150 miles to the north of Pañamarca, and Sipán is another 40 miles further north. Moreover, in the 1960s rich tombs containing artifacts with Sacrifice Ceremony iconography were looted from the site of Loma Negra in the Piura Valley, more than 300 miles north of Pañamarca.

The four sites where evidence of the Sacrifice Ceremony has been found have certain characteristics in common. Each is located on an elevated area that rises naturally above the intensively cultivated valley floor and is near, but not immediately adjacent to, a river. Each was a major ceremonial complex, with multiple pyramids that for centuries served as staging areas for religious activities. Perhaps each of the other river valleys that made up the Moche kingdom also had a central ceremonial precinct where the Sacrifice Ceremony was enacted.

The fact that the Sacrifice Ceremony was so widespread in both time and space strongly implies that it was part of a state religion, with a priesthood in each part of the kingdom comprised of individuals who dressed in prescribed ritual attire. When members of the priesthood died, they were buried at the temple where the Sacrifice Ceremony took place, wearing their ceremonial paraphernalia and accompanied by the objects they had used to perform the ritual. Subsequently, other men and women were chosen to replace them, to dress like them, and to perform the same ceremonial role.

The careful excavation of the tomb of Figure C at San José de Moro has provided important new insights into the nature of Moche religious practices. As our excavations continue at this remarkable site, we expect to find additional archaeological evidence that will refine and improve upon these insights.

The End

In addition to burials, there are three other ways by which archaeologists may recognize the stratified nature of ancient civilizations:

1. The Size of Dwellings   In early Neolithic sites, dwellings tended to be uniformly small in size. Even at Çatalhöyük, there was little difference in size between houses. In the oldest excavated cities, however, some dwellings were notably larger than others, well spaced, and located together in one district, whereas dwellings in other parts of the city were much smaller, sometimes little more than hovels. In the city of Eshnunna in Mesopotamia, archaeologists excavated houses that occupied an area of 200 meters situated on main thoroughfares and huts of but 50 meters located along narrow back alleys. The rooms in the larger houses often contained impressive artwork, such as friezes or murals. At Tikal, and other Maya cities, the elite lived in large, multi-roomed, masonry houses, mostly in the city's center, whereas lower-class people lived in small, peripherally scattered houses of one or two rooms, built partly or wholly of pole and thatch materials.

2. Written Documents   Preserved records of business transactions, royal chronicles, or law codes of a civilization reveal much about the social status of its inhabitants. Babylonian and Assyrian texts reveal three main social classes—aristocrats, commoners, and slaves. The members of each class had different rights and privileges. This stratification was clearly reflected by the law. If an aristocrat put out another's eye, then that person's eye was to be put out too; hence, the saying "an eye for an eye." If the aristocrat broke another's bone, then the first aristocrat's bone was to be broken in return. If the aristocrat put out the eye or broke the bone of a commoner, however, the punishment was to pay a mina of silver.[11]

Even in the absence of written information, people may record much about their society in other ways. As the Original Study demonstrates, the Moche recorded much information about their society in their art. The stratified nature of this ancient society is clearly revealed by the scenes painted on ceramic vessels.

3. Correspondence   European documents describing the aboriginal cultures of the New World as seen by early European explorers and adventurers also offer evidence of social stratification. Letters written by the Spanish conquistadors about the Aztec empire indicate that they found a social order divided into three main classes: nobles, commoners, and serfs. The nobles operated outside the lineage system on the basis of land and serfs allotted them by the ruler from conquered peoples. The commoners were divided into lineages, on which they were dependent for land. Within each of these, individual status depended on the degree of descent from the founder; those more closely related to the lineage founder had higher status than those whose kinship was more distant. The third class in Aztec society consisted of serfs bound to the land and porters employed as carriers by

[11]Moseati, S. (1962). *The face of the ancient orient* (p. 90). New York: Doubleday.

This "palace," which housed members of Tikal's ruling dynasty, may be compared with the lower-class house in the photo below.

merchants. Lowest of this class were the slaves. Some had voluntarily sold themselves into bondage; others were captives taken in war.

Informative though accounts of other civilizations by Europeans may be, they are not without their problems. For example, the explorers, missionaries, and others did not always understand what they saw; moreover, they had their own interests (or those of their sponsors) to look out for, and were not above falsifying information to further those interests. These points are of major importance, given the tendency of Western peoples, with their tradition of literacy, to assume that written documents are reli-

able. In fact, they are not always reliable, and must be checked for accuracy against other sources of information. The same is true of ancient documents written by other people about themselves, for they, too, had their particular agendas. Ancient Maya inscriptions, for example, were often propagandistic in their intent, which was to impress people with particular rulers' importance.

THE MAKING OF CIVILIZATION

From Mesopotamia to China to the South American Andes, we witness the enduring achievements of the human intellect: magnificent palaces built high above ground; sculptures so perfect as to be unrivaled by those of contemporary artists; engineering projects so vast and daring as to awaken in us a sense of wonder. Looking back to the beginnings of written history, we can see a point at which humans transform themselves into "civilized" beings; they begin to live in cities and to expand the scope of their achievements at a rapid pace. How is it, then, that humans at a certain moment in history became consummate builders, harnessing mighty rivers so that they could irrigate crops, developing a system whereby their thoughts could be preserved in writing? The fascinating subject of the development of civilization has occupied the minds of philosophers and anthropologists alike for a long time. We do not yet have the answers, but a number of theories have been proposed.

Lower-class residents of Tikal lived in the same sort of houses in which most Maya live today.

Theories of Civilization's Emergence

Each of the theories sees the appearance of centralized government as the point at which there is no longer any question whether or not a civilization exists. So, the question they pose is: What brought about the appearance of a centralized government? Or, stated another way: What caused the transition from a small, egalitarian farming village to a large urban center in which population density, social inequality, and diversity of labor required a centralized government?

IRRIGATION SYSTEMS

One popular theory concerning the emergence of civilization was given its most forceful statement by Karl Wittfogel[12], and variants of this theory are still held by some anthropologists. Simply put, the irrigation or **hydraulic theory,** holds that Neolithic farmers in ancient Mesopotamia and Egypt, and later in the Americas, noticed that the river valleys that were periodically flooded contained better soils than those that were not; but they also noted that violent floods destroyed their planted fields and turned them into swamps. So the farmers built dikes and reservoirs to collect the floodwater and save it until it was needed. Then they released it into canals and ran it over the fields. At first, these dikes and canals, built by small groups of neighboring farmers, were very simple. The success of this measure led to larger, more complex irrigation systems, which eventually necessitated the emergence of a group of "specialists"—people whose sole responsibility was managing the irrigation system. The centralized effort to control the irrigation process blossomed into the first governing body and elite social class, and civilization was born.

There are several objections to this theory. One of them is that some of the earliest large-scale irrigation systems we know about anywhere in the world developed in highland New Guinea, where strong centralized governments never emerged. Conversely, actual field studies of ancient Mesopotamian irrigation systems reveal that by

4,000 years ago, by which time many cities had already flourished, irrigation was still carried out on a small scale, consisting of small canals and diversions of natural waterways. If there were state-managed irrigation, it is argued, such a system would have been far more extensive than excavations show it really was. Moreover, documents indicate that irrigation was regulated by officials of local temples and not by centralized government. The oldest irrigation system in the Americas is at Caral, in the coastal desert of Peru. By 4,600 years ago, a shallow channel had been cut to a river, where a simple headgate controlled the flow. The system was far simpler than later irrigation works in Peru, and one can argue here, as elsewhere in South America and Mesoamerica, that large-scale irrigation works were a consequence of civilization's development, rather than a cause.

TRADE NETWORKS

Some anthropologists argue that trade was a decisive factor in the development of civilizations. In regions of ecological diversity, so the argument goes, trade mechanisms are necessary to procure scarce resources. In Mexico, for example, maize was grown just about everywhere; but chilis were grown in the highlands, cotton and beans were planted at intermediate elevations, certain animals were found only in the river valleys, and salt was obtained along the coasts.

This theory holds that some form of centralized authority was necessary in order to organize trade for the procurement of these and other commodities. Once procured, some system was necessary in order to redistribute commodities throughout the population. Redistribution, like procurement, must have required a centralized authority, promoting the growth of a centralized government.

Although trade may have played an important role in the development of some civilizations, it did not invariably do so. For example, the native peoples of northeastern North America traded widely with one another for at least 6,000 years without developing civilizations comparable to those of Mexico or Peru. In the course of this trade, copper from deposits around Lake Superior wound up in such faraway places as New England, as did chert from Labrador and marine shells from the Gulf of Mexico. Wampum, made on the shores of Long Island

---

[12]Wittfogel, K. A. (1957). *Oriental despotism, a comparative study of total power.* New Haven, CT: Yale University Press.

Hydraulic theory.   The theory that sees civilization's emergence as the result of the construction of elaborate irrigation systems, the functioning of which required full-time managers whose control blossomed into the first governing body and elite social class.

Sound, was carried westward, and obsidian from the Yellowstone region has been found in mounds in Ohio.[13]

ENVIRONMENTAL AND SOCIAL CIRCUMSCRIPTION

In a series of papers, Robert Carneiro[14] has advanced the theory that civilization develops where populations are hemmed in by such things as mountains, seas, or other human populations. As such populations grow, they have no space in which to expand, and so they begin to compete for increasingly scarce resources. Internally, this results in the development of social stratification, in which an elite controls important resources to which lower classes have limited access. Externally, this leads to warfare and conquest, which, to be successful, require elaborate organization under a centralized authority.

RELIGION

The three theories just summarized exemplify ecological approaches to explaining the development of civilization. Such theories emphasize the interrelation between people and what they do on the one hand and the environment in which they live on the other. Theories of the emergence of civilization have commonly taken some such approach. Although few anthropologists would deny the importance of the human-environment interrelationship, a growing number of them are dissatisfied with theories that do not take into account the beliefs and values that regulate the interaction between people and their environment.[15]

An example of a theory that does take into account the role of beliefs is one that seeks to explain the emergence of Maya civilization in Mesoamerica.[16] This theory holds that Maya civilization was the result of a process of urbanization that occurred at places like Tikal. In the case study on Tikal earlier in this chapter, it is suggested that Maya religion probably developed initially as a means of coping with the uncertainties of agriculture. In its early days, Tikal seems to have been an important religious center. Because of its religious importance, people sought to settle there, with the result that its population grew in size and density. A similar process may be seen at Çatalhöyük. As noted early in this chapter, this village was located so as to be near sources of lime-rich clay. This material was required to plaster the walls of houses, the medium for paintings and other art of apparently ritual significance. This seems to have been of such importance as to take precedence over convenient proximity to agricultural fields. Perhaps the inconvenience of having to travel so far to get to one's fields was a reason that Çatalhöyük never developed into a true city.

At Tikal, by contrast, the process went further. Because the concentration of a growing population was incompatible with the prevailing slash-and-burn agriculture, which tends to promote dispersed settlement, new subsistence techniques—such as raised fields—were developed. By chance, these were sufficiently productive to permit further population growth, and, by 1,500 years ago, Tikal had become an urban settlement of at least 50,000 people. By then, craft specialization had developed, at first in the service of religion but soon in the service of an emerging social elite as well. This social elite was concerned at first with calendrical ritual, but through the control of ritual it developed into the centralized governing elite that could control a population growing larger and more diversified in its interests.

Developing craft specialization itself served as another factor to pull people into Tikal, where their products were in demand. It also required further development of trade networks, if only to provide exotic raw materials. More long-distance trade contacts, of course, brought more contact with outside ideas, including some from as far afield as Teotihuacan. In other words, what we seem to have is a complex system with several factors—religious, economic, and political—acting to reinforce one another, with religion playing a central role in getting the system started in the first place.

A criticism that may be leveled at all of the above theories is that they fail to recognize the capacity of aggressive, charismatic leaders to shape the course of human history. Accordingly, anthropologists Joyce Marcus and Kent Flannery have developed what they call **action theory**.[17] This recognizes the systemic nature of

---

[13]Haviland, W. A., & Power, M. W. (1994). *The original Vermonters* (2nd ed., Chap. 3 & 4). Hanover, NH: University Press of New England.

[14]Carneiro, R. L. (1970). A theory of the origin of the state. *Science, 169,* 733–738.

[15]Adams, R. M. (2001). Scale and complexity in archaic states. *Latin American Antiquity, 11,* 188.

[16]Haviland, W. A. (1975). The ancient Maya and the evolution of urban society. *University of Colorado Museum of Anthropology, Miscellaneous Series,* no. 37.

[17]Marcus, J., & Flannery, K. V. (1996). *Zapotec civilization: How urban society evolved in Mexico's Oaxaca Valley.* New York: Thames & Hudson.

Action theory. The theory that self-serving actions by forceful leaders play a role in civilization's emergence.

At Çatalhöyük as at Tikal, religion seems to have been the initial impetus for nucleation. Here we see a reproduction of some wall paintings from Çatalhöyük. The site was located near the source of the material used for the wall plaster.

society and the impact of the environment in shaping social and cultural behavior but recognizes as well that forceful leaders in any society strive to advance their material or political positions through self-serving actions. In so doing, they may create change. Applying this to the Maya, for example, local leaders, who once relied on personal charisma for the economic and political support needed to sustain them in their positions, may have seized upon religion to solidify their grip on power. They did this by developing an ideology endowing them and their descendants with supernatural ancestry. Only they were seen as having the kind of access to the gods on which their followers depended. In this case, the nature of the existing system presented a situation in which certain individuals could monopolize power and emerge as divine kings, using their power to subjugate any rivals.

As the above example makes clear, the context in which a forceful leader operates is critical. In the case of the Maya, it was the combination of existing cultural and ecological factors that opened the way for emergence of political dynasties. Thus, explanations of civilization's emergence are likely to involve multiple causes, rather than just one. Furthermore, we may also have the cultural equivalent of what biologists call *convergence*, where somewhat similar forms come about in quite different ways. Consequently, a theory that accounts for the rise of civilization in one place may not account for its rise in another.

This mosaic death mask of greenstone, pyrite, and shell was worn by a king of the Maya city of Tikal who died about A.D. 527. Obviously the product of skilled craft work, such specialization developed first to serve the needs of religion, but soon served the needs of an emerging elite as well.

CIVILIZATION AND ITS DISCONTENTS

Living in the context of civilization ourselves, we are inclined to view its development as a great step upward on some sort of ladder of progress. Whatever benefits civilization has brought, though, the cultural changes it represents produced new sorts of problems. Among them is the problem of waste disposal. Actually, waste disposal probably began to be a problem in settled, farming communities even before the emergence of civilization. But as villages grew into towns and towns grew into cities, the problem became far more serious, as the buildup of garbage and sewage created optimum environments for

Unlike most ancient cities, Mohenjo-Daro, a 4,000-year-old metropolis in the Indus River Valley, had an extensive system of drains. Lack of adequate drains in cities contributed to poor public health.

such diseases as bubonic plague and typhoid. The latter is an intestinal disease caused by a *Salmonella* bacterium. In northern Europeans, mutation of a gene on Chromosome 7 that deletes 3 DNA bases (out of the gene's total of 250,000) makes carriers of this allele virtually immune to typhoid and other bacterial diarrheas.[18] Because of the mortality imposed by these diseases, selection favored spread of the allele among northern Europeans. But as with sickle-cell anemia, protection comes at a price. That price is cystic fibrosis, a usually fatal disease of the lungs and intestines contracted by those who are homozygous for the altered gene.

Quite apart from sanitation problems and their attendant diseases, the rise of towns and cities brought with it a problem of acute, infectious diseases. In a small population, such diseases as chicken pox, influenza, measles, mumps, pertussis, polio, rubella, and smallpox will kill or immunize so high a proportion of the population that the virus cannot continue to propagate. Measles, for example, is likely to die out in any human population with fewer than half a million people.[19] Hence, such diseases, when introduced into small communities, spread immediately to the whole population and then die out. Their continued existence depends upon the presence of large population aggregates, such as towns and cities provide.

Another disease that became a serious problem in towns and cities (and is becoming so again in the 21st century) is tuberculosis. And here again it has triggered a genetic response not unlike what we have seen in response to malaria (sickle cell and other abnormal hemoglobins) and bacterial diarrheas (the cystic fibrosis gene). Among the Ashkenazi Jews of eastern Europe, a genetic variant that causes Tay-Sachs disease in homozygotes became comparatively common. Crammed into urban ghettos over several centuries, the Ashkenazim were especially exposed to tuberculosis, but those individuals heterozygous for the Tay-Sachs allele were protected from this disease.[20]

In essence, early cities tended to be disease-ridden places, with relatively high death rates. At Teotihuacan, for instance, very high infant and child mortality rates set a limit to the city's growth. Not until relatively recent times did public health measures reduce the risk of

---

[18]Ridley, M. (1999). *Genome, the autobiography of a species in 23 chapters* (p. 142). New York: HarperCollins.

[19]Diamond, J. (1997). *Guns, germs and steel* (p. 203). New York: Norton.

[20]Ridley, p. 191.

living in cities, and had it not been for a constant influx of rural peoples, they would have been hard pressed to maintain their population size, let alone increase it. Europe's urban population, for example, did not become self-sustaining until early in the 20th century.[21] One might wonder, then, what would have led people to go live in such unhealthy places? The answer is, they were attracted by the same sorts of things that lure people to cities today: They are vibrant, exciting places that also provide people with opportunities not available in rural communities. Of course, their experience in the cities did not always live up to advance expectations, any more than is true today.

In addition to health problems, early cities faced social problems strikingly similar to those found in modern North America. Dense population, class systems, and a strong centralized government created internal stress. The slaves and the poor saw that the wealthy had all the things that they themselves lacked. It was not just a question of luxury items; the poor did not have enough food nor space in which to live with comfort and dignity.

Evidence of warfare in early civilizations is common. Cities were fortified; documents list many battles, raids, and wars between groups; cylinder seals, paintings, and sculpture depict battle scenes, victorious kings, and captured prisoners of war. Increasing population and the accompanying scarcity of good farming land often led to boundary disputes and quarrels over land between civilized states or between so-called tribal peoples and a state. Open warfare often developed. People tended to crowd into walled cities for protection and to be near irrigation systems.

The class system also caused internal stress. As time went on, the rich became richer and the poor poorer. In early civilizations one's place in society was relatively fixed. Wealth was based on free labor from slaves. For this reason there was little or no impetus for social reform. Records from the Mesopotamian city of Lagash indicate that social unrest due to exploitation of the poor by the rich grew during this period. Members of the upper class received tracts of farmland some 20 times larger than those granted the lower class. An upper-class reformer, Urukaginal saw the danger and introduced changes to

Signs of warfare are common in ancient civilizations. China's first emperor wanted his army to remain with him—in the form of 7,000 life-sized terra-cotta figures of warriors.

protect the poor from exploitation by the wealthy, thus preserving the stability of the city.

Given the problems associated with civilization, it is perhaps not surprising that a recurring phenomenon is their collapse. Nonetheless, the rise of cities and civilization laid the basis for modern life. It is discouraging to note that many of the problems associated with the first civilizations are still with us. Waste disposal, pollution-related health problems, crowding, social inequities, and warfare continue to be serious problems. Through the study of past civilizations, we now stand a chance of understanding why such problems persist. Such an understanding will be required if the problems are ever to be overcome. It would be nice if the next cultural revolution saw the human species transcending these problems. If this comes about, anthropology, through its comparative study of civilizations, will have played a key role.

---

[21]Diamond, p. 205.

CHAPTER SUMMARY

The world's first cities grew out of Neolithic villages between 6,000 and 4,500 years ago, first in Mesopotamia, then in Egypt and the Indus Valley. In China, the process was under way by 5,000 years ago. Somewhat later, and completely independently, similar changes took place in Mesoamerica and Peru. Four basic culture changes mark the transition from Neolithic village life to life in civilized urban centers. The first culture change is agricultural innovation as new farming methods were developed. For example, the ancient Sumerians built an irrigation system that enabled them to control their water resources and thus increase crop yields.

The second culture change is diversification of labor. With the growth of large populations in cities, some people could provide sufficient food for others to devote themselves fully to specialization as artisans and craftspeople. With specialization came the development of new technologies, leading to the beginnings of extensive trade systems. An outgrowth of technological innovation and increased contact with foreign people through trade was new knowledge; within the early civilizations sciences such as geometry and astronomy were first developed.

The third culture change that characterized urban life is the emergence of central government with authority to deal with the complex problems associated with cities. Evidence of a central governing authority comes from such sources as law codes, temple records, and royal chronicles. With the invention of writing, governments could keep records of their transactions and/or boast of their own power and glory. Further evidence of centralized government comes from monumental public structures and signs of centralized planning.

Typically, the first cities were headed by a king and his special advisors. The reign of the Babylonian King Hammurabi, sometime between 1950 and 1700 B.C., is well known for its efficient government organization and the standardization of its legal system. In the New World the Inca empire in Peru reached its culmination 500 years ago. With a population of several million people, the Inca state, headed by an emperor, possessed a widespread governing bureaucracy that functioned with great efficiency at every level.

The fourth culture change characteristic of civilization is social stratification, or the emergence of social classes. In the early cities of Mesopotamia, symbols of status and privilege appeared for the first time, and individuals were ranked according to the work they did or the position of their families. Archaeologists have been able to verify the existence of social classes in ancient civilizations in four ways: by studying burial customs, as well as skeletons, through grave excavations; by noting the size of dwellings in excavated cities; by examining preserved records in writing and art; and by studying the correspondence of Europeans who described the great civilizations that they destroyed in the New World.

A number of theories have been proposed to explain why civilizations developed. The hydraulic theory holds that the effort to build and control an irrigation system required a degree of social organization that eventually led to civilization. There are several objections to this theory, however. One might argue simply that sophisticated irrigation systems were a result of the development of civilization rather than a cause. Another theory suggests that in the multicrop economies of both the Old and New Worlds, some kind of system was needed to distribute the various food products throughout the population. Such a procedure would have required a centralized authority, leading to the emergence of a centralized government. A third theory holds that civilization develops where populations are circumscribed by environmental barriers or other societies. As such populations grow, competition for space and scarce resources leads to the development of centralized authority to control resources and organize warfare.

These theories all emphasize the interrelation of people and what they do on the one hand and the environment in which they live on the other. A theory that lays greater stress on the beliefs and values that regulate the interaction between people and their environment seeks to explain the emergence of Maya civilization in terms of the role religion may have played in keeping the Maya in and about cities like Tikal. Finally, action theory focuses attention on the actions of forceful leaders, whose efforts to promote their own interests may play a role in social change. Probably, several factors acted together, rather than singly, to bring about civilization's rise.

Sanitation problems in early cities, coupled with large numbers of people living in close proximity, created environments in which infectious diseases were rampant. Early urban centers also faced social problems strikingly similar to our own. Dense pop-ulation, class systems, and a strong centralized government created internal stress. Warfare was common; cities were fortified, and armies served to protect the state. Nevertheless, a recurrent phenomenon in all civilizations has been their ultimate collapse.

CLASSIC READINGS

Diamond, J. (1997). *Guns, germs and steel.* New York: Norton.

Also recommended in the last chapter, this book has an excellent discussion of the relation among diseases, social complexity, and social change.

Marcus, J., & Flannery, K. V. (1996). *Zapote civilization: How urban society evolved in Mexico's Oaxaca Valley.* New York: Thames & Hudson.

With its lavish illustrations, this looks like a book for coffee table adornment, but it is in fact a thoughtful and serious work on the rise of a pristine civilization. In it, the authors present their action theory.

Meltzer, D., Fowler, D., & Sabloff, J. (Eds.). (1986). *American archaeology: Past and future.* Washington, DC: Smithsonian Institution Press.

This collection of articles contains one by Henry Wright, "The Evolution of Civilization," an excellent comparative consideration of the subject.

Pfeiffer, J. E. (1977). *The emergence of society.* New York: McGraw-Hill.

This is a comprehensive survey of the origins of food production and the world's first cities. In order to write the book, the author traveled to archaeological sites throughout the world and consulted with numerous investigators. The book is notable for its readability.

Redman, C. E. (1978). *The rise of civilization: From early farmers to urban society in the ancient Near East.* San Francisco: Freeman.

One of the best-documented examples of the rise of urban societies is that of Greater Mesopotamia in the Middle East. This clearly written textbook focuses on that development, presenting the data, discussing interpretations of those data, as well as problems.

Sabloff, J. A. (1997). *The cities of ancient Mexico* (Rev. ed.). New York: Thames & Hudson.

This well-written and lavishly illustrated book describes the major cities of the Olmecs, Zapotecs, Maya, Teotihuacanos, Toltecs, and Aztecs. Following the descriptions, Sabloff discusses the question of origins, the problems of archaeological reconstruction, and the basis on which he provides vignettes of life in the ancient cities. The book concludes with a gazetteer of 50 sites in Mesoamerica.

Sabloff, J. A., & Lamberg-Karlovsky, C. C. (Eds.). (1974). *The rise and fall of civilizations, modern archaeological approaches to ancient cultures.* Menlo Park, CA: Cummings.

The emphasis in this collection of articles is theoretical or methodological rather than purely descriptive. Special emphasis is on Mesopotamia and Mesoamerica, but papers are included on Peru, Egypt, the Indus Valley, China, and Europe.

CHAPTER 13

MODERN HUMAN DIVERSITY

One of the notable characteristics of the human species today is its great variability. Human diversity has long fascinated people, but unfortunately, it also has led to discrimination and even bloodshed.

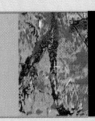

1

WHAT ARE THE CAUSES OF PHYSICAL VARIABILITY IN MODERN ANIMALS?

In a species like *Homo sapiens,* there are various alleles for any given physical characteristic. When such a species is divided into geographically dispersed populations, forces such as drift and natural selection cause the store of genetic variability to be unevenly expressed. For example, alleles for dark skin are found in high frequency in human populations native to regions of heavy ultraviolet radiation, whereas alleles for light skin have a high incidence in populations native to regions of reduced ultraviolet radiation.

2

IS THE CONCEPT OF RACE USEFUL FOR STUDYING HUMAN PHYSICAL VARIATION?

No. Because races are arbitrarily defined, it is impossible to agree on any specific classification. The problem is compounded by the tendency for "racial" characteristics to occur in gradations from one population to another without sharp breaks. Furthermore, because genes are assorted independently of one another, one characteristic may be distributed in a north-south gradient while another may occur in an east-west gradient. For these and other reasons, most anthropologists have actively worked to get rid of race as a biological category.

3

ARE THERE DIFFERENCES IN INTELLIGENCE FROM ONE POPULATION TO ANOTHER?

No, although some populations receive lower average scores on IQ tests than others. Even so, many individuals in "lower-scoring" populations score higher than some in the "higher-scoring" populations. There is no agreement on what intelligence really is, but there is agreement that intelligence involves several different talents and abilities. Certainly, there are genes affecting these, but like other genes, they may be independently assorted, and their expression is affected significantly by environmental factors.

W hat a piece of work is man," said Hamlet. "How noble in reason, how infinite in faculties, in form and moving how express and admirable, in action how like an angel, in apprehension how like a god: the beauty of the world, the paragon of animals! And yet to me what is this quintessence of dust?"

What people are to one another is the province of anthropology: Physical anthropology reveals what we are; cultural anthropology reveals what we think we are. Our dreams of ourselves are as varied as our languages and our physical bodies. We are the same, but we differ. We speak English or French, our hair is curly or straight, our skin is lightly to heavily pigmented, and in height we range from short to tall. Human genetic variation generally is distributed in such a continuous range, with varying clusters of frequency. The significance we give our variations, the way we perceive them—in fact, whether we perceive them at all—is determined by our culture. For example, in many Polynesian countries, where skin color is not a determinant of social status, people really pay little attention to this physical characteristic; in the United States and South Africa, it is one of the first things people do notice.

VARIATION AND EVOLUTION

Many behavioral traits—reading, for instance—are learned or acquired by living in a society; other characteristics, such as blue eyes, are passed on physically by heredity. Environment affects both. A person growing up surrounded by books learns to read. If the culture insists that brown-eyed people watch TV and blue-eyed people read, the brown-eyed people may end up making videotapes while the blue-eyed people are writing books. These skills or tastes are acquired characteristics. Changes in such things within one population but not another are capable of making the two distinct in learned behavioral characteristics within relatively few generations.

PHYSICAL VARIABILITY

The physical characteristics of both populations and individuals, as we saw in Chapter 3, are a product of the interaction between genes and environments. Thus, one's genes predispose one to a particular skin color, for example, but the skin color one actually has is strongly affected by environmental factors such as the amount of solar radiation. In this case, phenotypic expression is strongly influenced by environment; in some others, such as one's A-B-O blood type, phenotypic expression closely reflects genotype.

For most characteristics, there are within the gene pool of *Homo sapiens* variant forms of genes, known as alleles. In the color of an eye, the shape of a hand, the texture of skin, many variations can occur. This kind of variability, found in many animal species, signifies a rich potential for new combinations of characteristics in future generations. Such a species is called **polymorphic** (meaning "many shapes"). Our blood types, determined by the alleles for Types A, B, and O blood, are an example of polymorphism, which in this case may appear in any of four distinct phenotypic forms. A polymorphic species faced with changing environmental conditions has within its gene pool the possibility of producing individuals with traits appropriate to its altered life. Many may not achieve reproductive success, but those whose physical characteristics enable them to do well in the new environment will usually reproduce, so that their genes will become more common in subsequent generations. Thus, humankind, being polymorphic, has been able to occupy a variety of environments.

A major expansion into new environments was under way by the time *Homo erectus* appeared on the scene (Chapter 8). Populations of this species were living in Africa, Southeast Asia, Europe, and China. Each of these places constitutes a different **faunal region,** which is to say that each possesses its own distinctive assemblage of animal life, not precisely like that of other regions. This differentiation of animal life is the result of selective pressures that, through the Pleistocene, differed from one region to another. For example, the conditions of life were quite different in China, which lies in the temperate zone, than they were in tropical Southeast Asia. Coupled with differing selective pressures were geographic features that restricted or prevented gene flow between populations of different faunal regions.

When a polymorphic species is divided into geographically dispersed populations, it usually is **polytypic** (many types); that is, the store of genetic variability is unevenly expressed. Genetic variants will be expressed

---

Polymorphic.   A species with alternative forms (alleles) of particular genes.   •   **Faunal region.**   A geographic region with its own distinctive assemblage of animal life, not precisely like that of other regions.   •   **Polytypic.** The expression of genetic variants in different frequencies in different populations of a species.

in different frequencies in different populations. For example, in the Old World, populations of *H. sapiens* living in the tropics have a higher frequency of alleles for dark skin color than do those living in more northerly regions. In blood type, *H. sapiens* is polymorphic, with four distinct groups (A, B, O, or AB). In the distribution of these types, the species is again polytypic. The frequency of the O allele is highest in American Indians, especially among some populations native to South America; the highest frequencies of the allele for Type A blood tend to be found among certain European populations (although the highest frequency of all is found among the Blackfoot and Blood Indians of North America); the highest frequencies of the B allele are found in some Asian populations (Figure 13.1). We would expect the earlier species, *H. erectus,* with populations in the four faunal regions of the Old World, to have been polytypic. This appears to have been the case, for the fos-

sils from each of the four regions show some differences from those in the others. African *Homo erectus,* for example, had the tall linear body build often seen in some modern African populations, whereas Chinese *erectus,* like the modern Chinese, seems to have been shorter of stature. It seems, then, that the human species has been polytypic since at least the time of *H. erectus.*

THE MEANING OF RACE

Early anthropologists tried to explore the polytypic nature of the human species by systematically classifying *H. sapiens* into subspecies, or **races,** based on geographic location and phenotypic (physical) features such as skin color, body size, head shape, and hair texture. Such classifications were continually being challenged by the presence of individuals who did not fit the categories, such

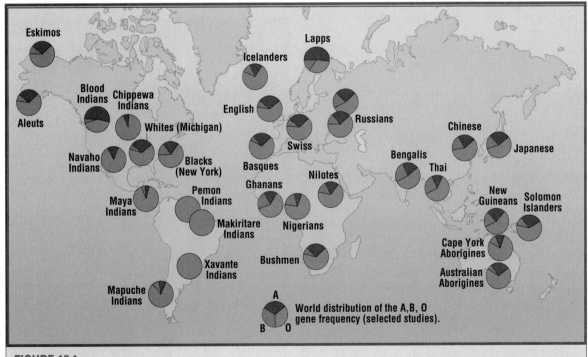

FIGURE 13.1

FREQUENCIES OF THE THREE ALLELES FOR THE A, B, AND O BLOOD GROUPS FOR SELECTED POPULATIONS AROUND THE WORLD DEMONSTRATE THE POLYTYPIC NATURE OF *H. SAPIENS.*

Race.   In biology, a population of a species that differs in the frequency of the variants of some gene or genes from other populations of the same species.

as light-skinned Africans or dark-skinned "Caucasoids"; to get around the problem, it was assumed that these individuals were hybrids or the product of racial mixtures. Lack of concordance among traits—for example, the fact that long prominent noses are not only common among Europeans but have a high frequency in various East African populations as well—was usually explained away in a similar manner. The fact is, generalized references to human types such as "Asiatic" or "Mongoloid," "European" or "Caucasoid," and "African" or "Negroid" were at best mere statistical abstractions about populations in which certain physical features appeared in higher frequencies than in other populations; no example of "pure" racial types could be found. These categories turned out to be neither definitive nor particularly helpful. The visible traits were found to occur not in abrupt shifts from population to population but in a continuum that changed gradually, with few sharp breaks. To compound the problem, one trait might change gradually over a north-south gradient, whereas another might show a similar change from east to west. Human skin color, for instance, becomes progressively darker as one moves from northern Europe to central Africa, whereas blood Type B becomes progressively more common as one moves from western to eastern Europe.

Finally, there were many variations within each group, and those within groups were often greater than those between groups. In Africa, the skin color of someone from the Kalahari Desert might more closely resemble that of a person of East Indian extraction than the darkly pigmented Nilotic Sudanese who was supposed to be of the same race.

The Negroid was characterized as having dark skin, thick lips, a broad nose, and tightly curled hair; the Mongoloid, straight hair, a flat face, a flat nose, and spread nostrils; and the Caucasoid, pale skin, a narrow nose, and varied eye color and hair form. The classification then expanded to take in American Indians,

Among the tallest people in the world are the Tutsi (left), whereas among the smallest are the Efe (right). Both are from central Africa and illustrate the wide range of variation seen in a (supposedly) single racial category.

ASHLEY MONTAGU (1905–1999)

Born Israel Ehrenberg to a working-class immigrant Jewish family living in London's East End, Ashley Montagu (a name he adopted in the 1920s) went on to become a pioneering critic of the race concept and one of the best-known anthropologists of his time. An avid reader as a child, in 1922 he attended University College of London, where he studied anthropology and psychology. Among his professors were founders of the eugenics movement—a proposal to improve humanity by identifying those with supposedly undesirable hereditary characteristics and removing them from the breeding population. It was also at this time that he changed his name in response to the strong ethnic and class prejudice he experienced.

Also, in the 1920s, Montagu studied under the founders of British social anthropology at the London School of Economics. In 1927, however, he left for the United States, where he considered the society to be more congenial to social justice. At Columbia University, he studied under Franz Boas and other pioneers of North American anthropology, earning his doctorate in 1937 with a dissertation on knowledge of paternity among Australian aborigines.

Having felt the sting early on of ethnic and class prejudice himself, it is not surprising that Montagu became a strong critic of eugenics and other racist doctrines. As early as 1926, he focused on the mistake of viewing races as typological, bounded categories. This put him at odds with many of his old professors and colleagues but, as he put it, he learned early on "not to let the shadows of great men block out the light."* All his life, Montagu fought racism in his writing, in academic and public lectures, and in the courts.

Ashley Montagu wrote over 60 books and hundreds of articles, including a series in *Ladies Home Journal.* These ranged over subjects from primate anatomy to the importance of nurturance in human development, and even the history of human swearing. Of all his works, none is more important than his book *Man's Most Dangerous Myth: The Fallacy of Race.* Published in 1942, it took the lead in exposing, on purely scientific grounds, the fallacy of human races as biological entities. The book has since gone through six editions, the last in 1999. Although Montagu's once controversial ideas have since become mainstream, the book remains the most comprehensive treatment of its subject.

*Sperling, S. (2000). Ashley Montagu (1905–1999). *American Anthropologist, 102,* 584.

Australians, and Polynesians, but even the expanded system failed to account for dramatic differences in appearance among individuals, or even populations, in each racial category; for example, Europeans, Arabs, and East Indians were all lumped together as Caucasoids.

In an attempt to encompass such variations, schemes of racial classification proliferated. In 1926, J. Deniker classified 29 races according to texture of hair, presumably improving upon Roland B. Dixon's 1923 classification based on three indexes of body measures. Hair texture and body build were the characteristics used for another set of racial categories proposed in 1930. By 1947, Earnest Hooton had proposed three new composite races resulting from the interbreeding of "primary" races. Despite these classificatory attempts on the part of Western anthropologists, no definitive grouping of distinct, discontinuous biological groups was found for modern humanity.

While many anthropologists struggled with the problem of defining human races, others began to question the whole exercise. Most notable was Ashley Montagu, whose effective criticism of race as a valid biological concept began to influence people's thinking on the subject.

Also influential was a book, published in 1950, called *Races* by Carleton Coon, Stanley Garn, and Joseph Birdsell. Unlike Ashley Montagu, they did not reject the race concept, and like their predecessors, they too tried to classify modern humans into a number of racial groups, 30 in their case. They did, however, reject a trait-list approach. Instead, they recognized races as populations that owed certain common characteristics to environmental, primarily climatic, adaptation, which continued to change in response to evolutionary forces such as gene flow and altered selective pressures. Although this book certainly had its weaknesses—its continued assumption that races existed, for one—it did represent a significant departure from previous attempts at racial classification and was influential in paving the way for a sounder understanding of human variation.

RACE AS A BIOLOGICAL CONCEPT

To understand why the racial approach to human variation has been so unproductive, we must first understand the race concept in strictly biological terms. In biology, a race is defined as a population of a species that differs in the frequency of different variants of some gene or genes from other populations of the same species. Simple and straightforward though such a definition may seem, there are three very important things to note about it. First, it is arbitrary; there is no agreement on how many genetic differences it takes to make a race. For some who are interested in the topic, different frequencies in the variants of one gene are sufficient; for others, differences in frequencies involving several genes are necessary. Ultimately, it proved impossible to reach agreement on the number of genes and precisely which ones are the most important for defining races.

The arbitrariness of racial classification is well illustrated by the following Original Study.

Original Study

Race Without Color[1]

Science often violates simple common sense. Our eyes tell us that the Earth is flat, that the sun revolves around the Earth, and that we humans are not animals. But we now ignore that evidence of our senses. We have learned that our planet is in fact round and revolves around the sun, and that humans are slightly modified chimpanzees. The reality of human races is another commonsense "truth" destined to follow the flat Earth into oblivion.

What Could Be More Objective?

The commonsense view of races goes somewhat as follows. All native Swedes differ from all native Nigerians in appearance: There is no Swede whom you would mistake for a Nigerian, and vice versa. Swedes have lighter skin than Nigerians do. They also generally have blond or light brown hair, while Nigerians have very dark hair. Nigerians usually have more tightly coiled hair than Swedes do, dark eyes as opposed to eyes that are blue or gray, and fuller lips and broader noses.

In addition, other Europeans look much more like Swedes than like Nigerians, while other peoples of sub-Saharan Africa—except perhaps the Khoisan peoples of southern Africa—look much more like Nigerians than like Swedes. Yes, skin color does get darker in Europe toward the Mediterranean, but it is still lighter than the skin of sub-Saharan Africans. In Europe, very dark or curly hair becomes more common outside Scandinavia, but European hair is still not as tightly coiled as in Africa. Since it's easy then to distinguish almost any native European from any native sub-Saharan African, we recognize Europeans and sub-Saharan Africans as distinct races, which we name for their skin colors: whites and blacks, respectively.

As it turns out, this seemingly unassailable reasoning is not objective. There are many different, equally valid procedures for defining races, and those different procedures yield very different classifications. One such procedure would group Italians and Greeks with most African blacks. It would classify Xhosas—the South African 'black' group to which President Nelson Mandela belongs—with Swedes rather than Nigerians. Another equally valid procedure would place Swedes with Fulani (a Nigerian "black" group) and not with Italians, who would again be grouped with most other African blacks. Still another procedure would keep Swedes and Italians separate from all

---

[1]Diamond, J. (1994). Race without color. *Discover, 15*(11), 83–88.

African blacks but would throw the Swedes and Italians into the same race as New Guineans and American Indians. Faced with such differing classifications, many anthropologists today conclude that one cannot recognize any human races at all.

If we were just arguing about races of nonhuman animals, essentially the same uncertainties of classification would arise. But the debates would remain polite and would never attract attention outside the halls of academia. Classification of humans is different "only" in that it shapes our views of other peoples, fosters our subconscious differentiation between "us" and "them," and is invoked to justify political and socioeconomic discrimination. On this basis, many anthropologists therefore argue that even if one could classify humans into races, one should not.

To understand how such uncertainties in classification arise, let's steer clear of humans for a moment and instead focus on warblers and lions, about which we can easily remain dispassionate. Biologists begin by classifying living creatures into species. A species is a group of populations whose individual members would, if given the opportunity, interbreed with individuals of other populations of that group. But they would not interbreed with individuals of other species that are similarly defined. Thus all human populations, no matter how different they look, belong to the same species because they do interbreed and have interbred whenever they have encountered each other. Gorillas and humans, however, belong to two different species because—to the best of our knowledge—they have never interbred despite their coexisting in close proximity for millions of years.

We know that different populations classified together in the human species are visibly different. The same proves true for most other animal and plant species as well, whenever biologists look carefully. For example, consider one of the most familiar species of bird in North America, the yellow-rumped warbler. Breeding males of eastern and western North America can be distinguished at a glance by their throat color: white in the east, yellow in the west. Hence they are classified into two different races, or subspecies (alternative words with identical meanings), termed the myrtle and Audubon races, respectively. The white-throated eastern birds differ from the yellow-throated west-

ern birds in other characteristics as well, such as in voice and habitat preference. But where the two races meet, in western Canada, white-throated birds do indeed interbreed with yellow-throated birds. That's why we consider myrtle warblers and Audubon warblers as races of the same species rather than different species.

Racial classification of these birds is easy. Throat color, voice, and habitat preference all vary geographically in yellow-rumped warblers, but the variation of those three traits is "concordant"—that is, voice differences or habitat differences lead to the same racial classification as differences in throat color because the same populations that differ in throat color also differ in voice and habitat.

Racial classification of many other species, though, presents problems of concordance. For instance, a Pacific island bird species called the golden whistler varies from one island to the next. Some populations consist of big birds, some of small birds; some have black-winged males, others green-winged males; some have yellow-breasted females, others gray-breasted females; many other characteristics vary as well. But, unfortunately for humans like me who study these birds, those characteristics don't vary concordantly. Islands with green-winged males can have either yellow-breasted or gray-breasted females, and green-winged males are big on some islands but small on other islands. As a result, if you classified golden whistlers into races based on single traits, you would get entirely different classifications depending on which trait you chose.

Classification of these birds also presents problems of "hierarchy." Some of the golden whistler races recognized by ornithologists are wildly different from all the other races, but some are very similar to one another. They can therefore be grouped into a hierarchy of distinctness. You start by establishing the most distinct population as a race separate from all other populations. You then separate the most distinct of the remaining populations. You continue by grouping similar populations, and separating distinct populations or groups of populations as races or groups of races. The problem is that the extent to which you continue the racial classification is arbitrary, and it's a decision about which taxonomists disagree passionately. Some taxonomists, the "splitters," like to recognize

Original Study

many different races, partly for the egotistical motive of getting credit for having named a race. Other taxonomists, the "lumpers," prefer to recognize few races. Which type of taxonomist you are is a matter of personal preference.

How does that variability of traits by which we classify races come about in the first place? Some traits vary because of natural selection: That is, one form of the trait is advantageous for survival in one area, another form in a different area. For example, northern hares and weasels develop white fur in the winter, but southern ones retain brown fur year-round. The white winter fur is selected in the north for camouflage against the snow, while any animal unfortunate enough to turn white in the snowless southern states would stand out from afar against the brown ground and would be picked off by predators.

Other traits vary geographically because of sexual selection, meaning that those traits serve as arbitrary signals by which individuals of one sex attract mates of the opposite sex while intimidating rivals. Adult male lions, for instance, have a mane, but lionesses and young males don't. The adult male's mane signals to lionesses that he is sexually mature, and signals to young male rivals that he is a dangerous and experienced adversary. The length and color of a lion's mane vary among populations, being shorter and blacker in Indian lions than in African lions. Indian lions and lionesses evidently find short black manes sexy or intimidating; African lions don't.

Finally, some geographically variable traits have no known effect on survival and are invisible to rivals and to prospective sex partners. They merely reflect mutations that happened to arise and spread in one area. They could equally well have arisen and spread elsewhere—they just didn't.

Nothing that I've said about geographic variation in animals is likely to get me branded a racist. We don't attribute higher IQ or social status to black-winged whistlers than to green-winged whistlers. But now let's consider geographic variation in humans. We'll start with invisible traits, about which it's easy to remain dispassionate.

Many geographically variable human traits evolved by natural selection to adapt humans to particular climates or environments—just as the winter color of a hare or weasel did. Good examples are the mutations that people in tropical parts of the Old World evolved to help them survive malaria, the leading infectious disease of the Old World tropics. One such mutation is the sickle-cell gene, so-called because the red blood cells of people with that mutation tend to assume a sickle shape. People bearing the gene are more resistant to malaria than people without it. Not surprisingly, the gene is absent from northern Europe, where malaria is nonexistent, but it's common in tropical Africa, where malaria is widespread. Up to 40 percent of Africans in such areas carry the sickle-cell gene. It's also common in the malaria-ridden Arabian Peninsula and southern India, and rare or absent in the southernmost parts of South Africa, among the Xhosas, who live mostly beyond the tropical geographic range of malaria.

The geographic range of human malaria is much wider than the range of the sickle-cell gene. As it happens, other antimalarial genes take over the protective function of the sickle-cell gene in malarial Southeast Asia and New Guinea and in Italy, Greece, and other warm parts of the Mediterranean basin. Thus human races, if defined by antimalarial genes, would be very different from human races as traditionally defined by traits such as skin color. As classified by antimalarial genes (or their absence), Swedes are grouped with Xhosas but not with Italians or Greeks. Most other peoples usually viewed as African blacks are grouped with Arabia's "whites" and are kept separate from the "black" Xhosas.

Antimalarial genes exemplify the many features of our body chemistry that vary geographically under the influence of natural selection. Another such feature is the enzyme lactase, which enables us to digest the milk sugar lactose. Infant humans, like infants of almost all other mammal species, possess lactase and drink milk. Until about 6,000 years ago most humans, like all other mammal species, lost the lactase enzyme on reaching the age of weaning. The obvious reason is that it was unnecessary—no human or other mammal drank milk as an adult. Beginning around 4000 B.C., however, fresh milk obtained from domestic mammals became a major food for adults of a few human populations. Natural selection caused individuals in these populations to retain lactase into adulthood. Among such peoples are northern and central Europeans, Arabians, northern Indians, and several milk-drinking black African peoples, such as the Fulani of West Africa. Adult lactase is much less common in southern European populations and in most other African black populations, as well as in all populations of east Asians, aboriginal Australians, and American Indians.

Once again races defined by body chemistry don't match races defined by skin color. Swedes belong with Fulani in the "lactase-positive race," while most African "blacks," Japanese, and American Indians belong in the "lactase-negative race."

Not all the effects of natural selection are as invisible as lactase and sickle cells. Environmental pressures have also produced more noticeable differences among peoples, particularly in body shapes. Among the tallest and most long-limbed peoples in the world are the Nilotic peoples, such as the Dinkas, who live in the hot, dry areas of East Africa. At the opposite extreme in body shape are the Inuit, or Eskimo, who have compact bodies and relatively short arms and legs. The reasons have to do with heat loss. The greater the surface area of a warm body, the more body heat that's lost, since heat loss is directly proportional to surface area. For people of a given weight, a long-limbed, tall shape maximizes surface area, while a compact, short-limbed shape minimizes it. Dinkas and Inuit have opposite problems of heat balance: The former usually need desperately to get rid of body heat, while the latter need desperately to conserve it. Thus natural selection molded their body shapes oppositely, based on their contrasting climates.

Other visible traits that vary geographically among humans evolved by means of sexual selec-

tion. We all know that we find some individuals of the opposite sex more attractive than other individuals. We also know that in sizing up sex appeal, we pay more attention to certain parts of a prospective sex partner's body than to other parts. Men tend to be inordinately interested in women's breasts and much less concerned with women's toenails. Women, in turn, tend to be turned on by the shape of a man's buttocks or the details of a man's beard and body hair, if any, but not by the size of his feet.

But all those determinants of sex appeal vary geographically. Khoisan and Andaman Island women tend to have much larger buttocks than most other women. Nipple color and breast shape and size also vary geographically among women. European men are rather hairy by world standards, while Southeast Asian men tend to have very sparse beards and body hair.

What's the function of these traits that differ so markedly between men and women? They certainly don't aid survival: It's not the case that orange nipples help Khoisan women escape lions, while darker nipples help European women survive cold winters. Instead, these varying traits play a crucial role in sexual selection. Women with very large buttocks are a turn-on, or at least acceptable, to Khoisan and Andaman men but look freakish to many men from other parts of the world. Bearded and hairy men readily find mates in Europe but fare worse in Southeast Asia. The geographic variation of these traits, however, is as arbitrary as the geographic variation in the color of a lion's mane.

There is a third possible explanation for the function of geographically variable human traits, besides survival or sexual selection—namely, no function at all. A good example is provided by fingerprints, whose complex pattern of arches, loops, and whorls is determined genetically. Fingerprints also vary geographically: For example, Europeans' fingerprints tend to have many loops, while aboriginal Australians' fingerprints tend to have many whorls.

Fingerprints' patterns of loops, whorls, and arches are genetically determined. Grouping people on this basis would place most Europeans, sub-Saharan Africans, and East Asians together as "loops," Australian aborigines and the people of Mongolia together as "whorls," and central Europeans and the Bushmen of southern Africa together as "arches."

Original Study

If we classify human populations by their fingerprints, most Europeans and black Africans would sort out together in one race, Jews and some Indonesians in another, and aboriginal Australians in still another. But those geographic variations in fingerprint patterns possess no known function whatsoever. They play no role in survival: Whorls aren't especially suitable for grabbing kangaroos, nor do loops help bar mitzvah candidates hold on to the pointer for the Torah. They also play no role in sexual selection: While you've undoubtedly noticed whether your mate is bearded or has brown nipples, you surely haven't the faintest idea whether his or her fingerprints have more loops than whorls. Instead it's purely a matter of chance that whorls became common in aboriginal Australians, and loops among Jews. Our rhesus factor blood groups and numerous other human traits fall into the same category of genetic characteristics whose geographic variation serves no function.

The End

After arbitrariness, the second thing to note about the biological definition of race is that it does not mean that any one race has exclusive possession of any particular variant of any gene or genes. In human terms, the frequency of the allele for blood group O may be high in one population and low in another, but it is present in both. Races are genetically "open," meaning that gene flow takes place between them. Because they are genetically open, they are apt to be impermanent and subject to reamalgamation. Thus, one can easily see the fallacy of any attempt to identify pure races; if gene flow cannot take place between two populations, either directly or indirectly through intermediate populations, then they are not races but separate species.

The third thing to note about the biological definition of race is that individuals of one race will not necessarily be distinguishable from those of another. In fact, as we have just noted with respect to humans, the differences among individuals within a population are generally greater than the differences among populations. As

The "openness" of races to gene flow is illustrated by this picture of an Asian and African American couple with their children.

the science writer James Shreeve puts it, "most of what separates me genetically from a typical African or Eskimo also separates me from another average American of European ancestry."[2] This follows from the genetic "openness" of races; no one race has an exclusive claim to any particular gene or allele.

THE CONCEPT OF HUMAN RACES

As a device for understanding polytypic variation in humans, the biological race concept has serious drawbacks. One is that the category is arbitrary to begin with, which makes agreement on any given classification difficult, if not impossible. For example, if one researcher emphasizes skin color while another emphasizes blood group differences, they will not classify people in the same way. Perhaps if the human species were divided into a number of relatively discrete breeding populations, this wouldn't be such a problem, but even this is open to debate. What has happened, though, is that human populations have grown in the course of human evolution, and with this growth have come increased opportunities for contact and gene flow between populations. Since the advent of food production, the process has accelerated as higher birthrates and periodic food shortages (discussed in Chapter 11) have prompted the movement of farmers from their homelands to other places. In East Asia, for example, the development of farming, followed by the invention of bronze and a host of other technologies in China resulted in expansion of northern Chinese populations and displacement of southern Chinese peoples into Southeast Asia. This expansion effectively "swamped" the original populations of this region, except in a few out-of-the-way places like the Andaman Islands.[3] As a consequence of such movements, differences between human populations today are probably less clear-cut than back in the days of *H. erectus,* or even archaic *H. sapiens.*

Things are complicated even moreso because humans are complicated genetically. Thus, the genetic underpinnings of the phenotypic traits upon which traditional racial classifications are usually based are poorly understood. Compounding the problem, "race" exists as a cultural, as well as a biological, category. In various different ways, cultures define religious, linguistic, and ethnic groups as races, thereby confusing linguistic and cultural traits with physical traits. For example, in many Central and South American countries, people are commonly classified as "Indian," "Mestizo" (mixed), or "Ladino" (of Spanish descent). But despite the biological connotations of these terms, the criteria used for assigning individuals to these categories consist of things such as whether they wear shoes, sandals, or go barefoot; speak Spanish or some Indian language; live in a thatched hut or a European-style house; and so forth. Thus, an Indian—by speaking Spanish, wearing Western-style clothes, and living in a house in a

[2]Shreeve, J. (1994) Terms of estrangement. *Discover, 15*(11), 60.

[3]Diamond, J. (1996). Empire of uniformity. *Discover, 17*(3), 83–84.

The Andaman Islanders (left) are a remnant of the original inhabitants of Southeast Asia; the Vietnamese (right) are descendants of people from southern China who spread into the region after the invention of agriculture. In the process there was mixing of gene pools.

non-Indian neighborhood—ceases to be an Indian, no matter how many "Indian genes" he or she may possess.

This sort of confusion of nonbiological characteristics with what are spoken of as biological categories is by no means limited to Central and South American societies. To one degree or another, such confusion is found in most Western societies, including those of Europe and North America. Take, for example, the racial categories used by the U.S. Census Bureau: White, Black, American Indian, Asian, and Pacific Islander are large catchall categories that include diverse people. *Asian,* for example, includes such different people as Chinese and East Indians (to which Indians, at least, take exception), whereas *Eskimo* (a term these people, the Inuit, find offensive) and *Aleut* are far more restrictive. *Hispanic* is another problematic category, as it includes people who, in their countries of origin, might be classified as Indian, Mestizo, or Ladino. Addition of slots for native Hawaiians, Middle Easterners, and people who consider themselves multiracial does nothing to improve the situation. To compound the confusion, inclusion in one or another of these categories is usually based on self-identification. In short, what we are dealing with here are not biological categories at all, but rather social constructs.

To make matters even worse, this confusion of social with biological factors is frequently combined with attitudes that are then taken as excuses to exclude whole categories of people from certain roles or positions in society. In the United States, for example, the idea of race originated in the 18th century to refer to the diverse peoples—European settlers, conquered Indians, and Africans imported as slaves—that were brought together in colonial North America. This racial worldview assigned some groups to perpetual low status on the basis of their supposedly biological inferiority, whereas access to privilege, power, and wealth was reserved for favored groups of European descent.[4]

Different ways in which this discrimination plays out may be illustrated with two quite different examples. An old stereotype is that Blacks are born with rhythm, which somehow is thought to give them a natural affinity for jazz, soul music, rap, and related forms of musical expression. A corollary of this myth is that African Americans are unsuited "by nature" for symphonic music. Hence, until recently, one did not find an African American at the head of any major symphony orchestra in the United States, even though African American conductors such as James de Priest, Paul Freeman, and Dean Dixon made distinguished careers for themselves in Canada and Europe.

A particularly evil consequence of the racial worldview occurred when the Nazis declared the superiority of the "Aryan race" (which is really a linguistic grouping and not a race at all), and the inferiority of the Gypsy and Jewish "races" (really ethno-religious categories), and then used this distinction as an excuse to exclude Gypsies and Jews from life altogether. In all, 11 million people (Jews, Gypsies, Africans, homosexuals, and other supposedly inferior people) were deliberately put to death.

Tragically, such programs of extermination of one group by another continue to occur in many parts of the

---

[4]American Anthropological Association. (1998). Statement on "race." Available: *www.ameranthassn.org.*

Far from being a thing of the past, genocide continues to occur in the world today, as this picture taken in 1998 in the Yugoslav province of Kosovo vividly illustrates.

world today, including parts of South America, Africa, Europe, and Asia. Holocausts are by no means things of the past, nor are Gypsies and Jews their only victims. The well-meant vow "never again" contrasts with the reality of "frequently again."

Considering all the problems, confusion, and evil consequences, it is small wonder that there has been a lot of debate not just about how many human races there may be, but about what race is and is not. Often forgotten is the fact that a race, even if it can be defined biologically, is the result of the operation of evolutionary processes. Because it is these processes rather than racial categories themselves in which we are really interested, most anthropologists have abandoned the race concept as being of no particular utility in understanding human biological variation. Instead, they have found it more productive to study the distribution and significance of specific, genetically based characteristics, or else the characteristics of small breeding populations that are, after all, the smallest units in which evolutionary change occurs.

Some Physical Variables

Not only have attempts to classify people into races proved futile and counterproductive, it has also become apparent that the amount of genetic variation in humans is relatively low, compared to that of other primate species. Nonetheless, human biological variation is a fact of life, and physical anthropologists have learned a great deal about it. Much of it is related to climatic adaptation. For example, a correlation has been noted between body build and climate. Generally, people native to regions with cold climates tend to have greater body bulk (not to be equated with fat) relative to their extremities (arms and legs) than do people native to regions with hot climates, who tend to be long and slender. Interestingly, these differences show up as early as the time of *Homo erectus,* as already noted. Anthropologists generally argue that such differences of body build represent a climatic adaptation; certain body builds are better suited to particular living conditions than others. A person with larger body bulk and shorter extremities may suffer more from summer heat than someone whose extremities are long and whose body is slender. But they will conserve needed body heat under cold conditions. The reason is that a bulky body tends to conserve more heat than a less bulky one, because it has less surface relative to volume. People living in hot, open country, by contrast, benefit from a body build that can get rid of excess heat quickly so as to keep from overheating; for this, long extremities and a slender body, which increase surface area relative to volume, are advantageous.

Studies of body build and climatic adaptation are complicated by the intervening effects on physique of diet, because dietary differences will cause variation in body build. Another complicating factor is clothing. Thus, much of the way people adapt to cold is cultural, rather than biological. For example, Inuit peoples (the proper name for "Eskimos") live in a region where it is cold much of the year. To cope with this, they long ago developed efficient clothing to keep the body warm. Because of this, the Inuit are provided with what amount to artificial tropical environments inside their clothing. In spite of such considerations, it remains true that in

African Americans are disproportionately represented among professional basketball players in part because of the prevalence of tall, linear body shapes among them. This does not mean, however, that "Whites can't jump" or that the anatomy of Blacks necessarily makes them better basketball players. In fact, one reason there are so many African American basketball players has nothing to do with biology but is due rather to socioeconomic opportunities available to them in a society that still discriminates on the basis of skin color.

northerly regions of the world, bulky body builds predominate, whereas the reverse is true in the tropics.

Anthropologists have also studied such body features as nose and eye shape and hair textures in relation to climate. A wide flaring nose, for example, is common in populations living in tropical forests; here the air is warm and damp, and so the warming and humidifying functions of the nose are secondary. Longer, more prominent noses, common among cold dwellers, are helpful in humidifying and warming cold air before it reaches the lungs. They are also useful in cleaning and humidifying dry, dusty air in hot climates, which is why long prominent noses are not restricted to places like Europe. Coon, Garn, and Birdsell

The epicanthic eye fold is common among people native to East Asia. Still, a comparison of this individual with those shown on p. 341 shows the absurdity of lumping all Asians in a single category.

once proposed that the "Mongoloid face," common in populations native to East and Central Asia, as well as arctic North America, exhibits features adapted to life in very cold environments. The **epicanthic eye fold,** which minimizes eye exposure to the cold, a flat facial profile, and extensive fatty deposits may help to protect the face against frostbite. Although experimental studies have failed to sustain the frostbite hypothesis, it is true that a flat facial profile generally goes with a round head. A significant percentage of body heat may be lost from the head; however, a round head, having less surface area relative to volume, loses less heat than a longer, more elliptical head. As one would predict from this, long-headed populations are generally found in hotter climates; round-headed ones are more common in cold climates.

Skin Color: A Case Study in Adaptation

In the United States, race is most commonly equated with skin color. Perhaps this is not surprising, because it is a highly visible trait. Skin color is subject to great variation, and there are at least four main factors associated with it: transparency or thickness of the skin, a copper-colored pigment called carotene, reflected color from the blood vessels (responsible for the rosy color of lightly pigmented people), and the amount of **melanin** found in a given area of skin. Exposure to sunlight increases the amount of melanin, a dark pigment, causing the skin to darken. Melanin is known to protect skin against damaging ultraviolet solar radiation;[5] consequently, darkly pigmented peoples are less susceptible to skin cancers and sunburn than are those whose skin has less melanin. They also seem to be less susceptible to photo-destruction of certain vitamins. Because the highest concentration of dark-skinned people tends to be found in the tropical regions of the world, it appears that natural selection has favored heavily pigmented skin as a protection against the strong solar radiation of equatorial latitudes, where ultraviolet radiation is most intense. Because skin cancers generally do not develop until later in life, they are unlikely to have interfered with the reproductive success of lightly pigmented

---

[5]Neer, R. M. (1975). The evolutionary significance of vitamin D, skin pigment, and ultraviolet light. *American Journal of Physical Anthropology, 43,* 409–416.

Epicanthic eye fold. A fold of skin at the inner corner of the eye that covers the true corner of the eye; common in Asiatic populations. • **Melanin.** The chemical responsible for dark skin pigmentation, which helps protect against damage from ultraviolet radiation.

individuals in the tropics, and so are unlikely to have been the agent of selection. On the other hand, severe sunburn, which is especially dangerous to infants, causes the body to overheat and interferes with its ability to sweat, by which it might rid itself of excess heat. Furthermore, it makes one susceptible to other kinds of infection. In addition to all this, decomposition of folate, an essential vitamin sensitive to heavy doses of ultraviolet radiation, can cause anemia, spontaneous abortion, and infertility.[6]

Although dark skin pigmentation has enjoyed a selective advantage in the tropics, the opposite is true in northern latitudes, where skins have generally been lightly pigmented. This lack of heavy amounts of melanin enables

the weak ultraviolet radiation of northern latitudes to penetrate the skin and stimulate formation of vitamin D, necessary for calcium regulation. Dark pigmentation interferes with this process. Without access to external sources of vitamin D, once provided by cod liver oil but now more often provided in vitamin D-fortified milk, individuals incapable of synthesizing enough of this vitamin in their own bodies were selected against, for they contracted rickets, a disease that seriously deforms children's bones. At its worst, rickets prevents children from reaching reproductive age; at the least, it interferes with a woman's ability to give birth if she does reach reproductive age (Figure 13.2).

Given what we know about the adaptive significance of human skin color, and the fact that, until 800,000 years ago, hominines were exclusively creatures of the tropics, it is likely that lightly pigmented skins are a recent development in human history. Darkly pigmented skins likely are quite ancient. Consistent with this, the enzyme tyrosinase, which converts the amino acid tyrosine into the compound that forms melanin, is present in lightly pigmented peoples in sufficient quantity to make them very "black." The reason it does not is that they have genes that inactivate or inhibit it.[7] Human skin is more

[6]Branda, R. F., & Eatoil, J. W. (1978). Skin color and photolysis: An evolutionary hypothesis. *Science, 201,* 625–626.

[7]Wills, C. (1994). The skin we're in. *Discover, 15*(11), 79.

These photos of people from Spain, Scandinavia, Senegal, and Indonesia illustrate the range of variation in human skin color. Generally, the closer to the equator populations live, the darker the skin color.

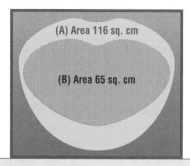

FIGURE 13.2

THE OUTLINE OF A NORMAL PELVIC INLET (A) COMPARED WITH THAT OF A WOMAN WITH RICKETS (B), WHICH WOULD INTERFERE WITH HER CAPACITY TO GIVE BIRTH. RICKETS IS CAUSED BY A DEFICIENCY OF VITAMIN D. IN THE ABSENCE OF ARTIFICIAL SOURCES OF THIS VITAMIN AMONG PEOPLE LIVING IN NORTHERN LATITUDES, LIGHTLY PIGMENTED PEOPLE ARE LEAST LIKELY TO CONTRACT RICKETS.

Although Tasmania is as far south of the equator as Europe is north of it, native Tasmanians were more darkly pigmented. Although the ancestors of both Europeans and Tasmanians lived in tropical regions, populations did not arrive in Tasmania until a good deal later than they reached Europe. Consequently, Tasmanians have not been subject to selection for light pigmentation for as long as have Europeans.

liberally endowed with sweat glands than is the skin of other mammals; in combination with our lack of heavy body hair, this makes for effective elimination of excess body heat in a hot climate. This would have been especially advantageous to early hominines on the savanna, who could have avoided confrontations with carnivorous animals by carrying out most of their activities in the heat of the day. For the most part, carnivores rest during this period, being active from dusk until early morning. Without much hair to cover early hominine bodies, selection would have favored dark skins; hence all humans appear to have had a "Black" ancestry, no matter how "White" some of them may be today.

One should not conclude that, because it is newer, lightly pigmented skin is better, or more highly evolved, than heavily pigmented skin. The latter is clearly more highly evolved to the conditions of life in the tropics, although with protective clothing, hats, and sunscreen lotions, lightly pigmented peoples can survive there. Conversely, the availability of supplementary sources of vitamin D allows heavily pigmented peoples to do quite well away from the tropics. In both cases, culture has rendered skin color differences largely irrelevant.

An interesting question is how long it took for light pigmentation to develop in populations living outside the tropics. We now know that the first people to reach Australia did so about 60,000 years ago. They came there from tropical Southeast Asia and, as we would expect, had darkly pigmented skin. In Australia, those populations that spread south of the tropics (where, as in northern latitudes, ultraviolet radiation is less intense) underwent some reduction of pigmentation. But for all that, their skin color is still far

darker than that of Europeans or East Asians (remember that most of today's Southeast Asian population spread there from southern China following the invention of farming—hence their relatively light pigmentation). The obvious conclusion is that 60,000 years is not enough to produce advanced depigmentation and that Europeans and East Asians lived outside the tropics for a far longer period.[8]

The inheritance of skin color is not well understood, except that several genes (rather than variants of a single gene), each with several alleles, must be involved. Nevertheless, its geographical distribution, with few

---

[8]Ferrie, H. (1997). An interview with C. Loring Brace. *Current Anthropology, 38,* 864.

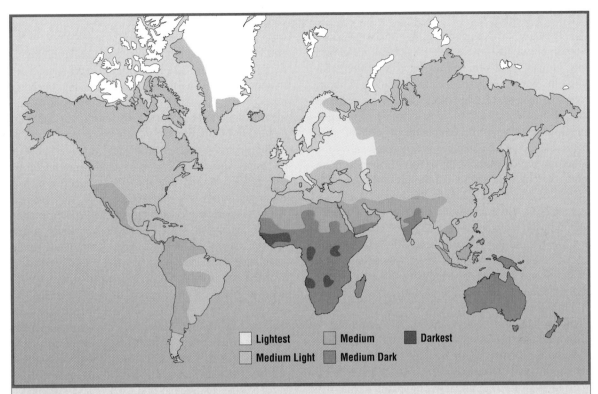

FIGURE 13.3

THIS MAP ILLUSTRATES THE DISTRIBUTION OF DARK AND LIGHT HUMAN SKIN PIGMENTATION BEFORE A.D. 1492. MEDIUM-LIGHT SKIN COLOR IN SOUTHEAST ASIA REFLECTS THE SPREAD INTO THAT REGION OF PEOPLE FROM SOUTHERN CHINA, WHEREAS THE MEDIUM DARKNESS OF PEOPLE NATIVE TO SOUTHERN AUSTRALIA IS A CONSEQUENCE OF THEIR TROPICAL SOUTHEAST ASIAN ANCESTRY. LACK OF A DARK SKIN PIGMENTATION AMONG TROPICAL POPULATIONS OF NATIVE AMERICANS REFLECTS THEIR ANCESTRY IN NORTHEAST ASIA A MERE 20,000 YEARS AGO.

exceptions, tends to be continuous, like that of other human traits (Figure 13.3). The exceptions have to do with the movement of certain populations from their original homelands to other regions or the practice of selective mating, or both. For example, there have been repeated invasions of the Indian subcontinent by peoples from the north, who were then incorporated into the Hindu caste system. Still today, the higher the caste, the lighter its skin color. This skin color gradient is maintained by strict in-group marriage rules. In the United States, statistical studies have shown that there has been a similar trend among African Americans, with African American women of higher status choosing to marry lighter-skinned males, reflecting the culture's emphasis on the supposed superiority of people with light skin. It is quite possible that the Black Pride movement, which places positive value on features common among those of West African descent—such as dark skins, tightly curled hair, and broad, flat noses—is leading to a reversal of this cultural selection factor.

THE SOCIAL SIGNIFICANCE OF RACE: RACISM

Scientific facts, unfortunately, have been slow to change what people think about race. **Racism** can be viewed solely as a social problem, although at times it has been used by politicians as a purportedly scientific tool. It is an emotional phenomenon best explained in terms of collective psychology. Racial conflict results from long-suppressed resentments and hostilities. The racist responds to social stereotypes, not to known scientific facts.

Racism. A doctrine of racial superiority by which one group asserts its superiority over another.

Race and Behavior

The assumption that there are behavioral differences among human races remains an issue to which many people in contemporary society tenaciously cling. Throughout history, certain "races" have been attributed certain characteristics that assume a variety of names— national character, spirit, temperament—all of them vague and standing for a number of concepts totally unrelated to any biological concept of race. Common myths involve the "coldness" of Scandinavians or the "martial" character of Germanics or the "indolent" nature of Africans. These generalizations serve to characterize a people unjustly; German citizens do not necessarily advocate genocide, nor do Africans necessarily hate to work. The term *race* has a precise biological meaning, but in popular usage, as we have already seen, the term often acquires a meaning unrelated to that given by scientists, often with disastrous results.

To date, no innate behavioral characteristic can be attributed to any group of people that the nonscientist would most probably term a "race" that cannot be explained in terms of cultural practices. If the Chinese happen to exhibit exceptional visuo-spatial skills, it is probably because the business of learning to read Chinese characters requires a visuo-spatial kind of learning that is not needed to master Western alphabets.[9] If African Americans are not as well represented in managerial positions as their fellow citizens, it is because for a long time they were allowed neither the necessary training nor the opportunity (nor is the problem fully rectified today). The list could go on, and all such differences or characteristics can be explained in terms of culture.

Similarly, high crime rates among certain groups can be explained with reference to culture rather than biology. Individuals alienated and demoralized by poverty, injustice, and inequality of opportunity tend to display what the dominant members of society regard as antisocial behavior more frequently than those who are culturally well-integrated. For example, American Indians, when they have been equipped and allowed to compete on an equal footing with other North Americans, have not suffered from the high rate of alcoholism and criminal behavior exhibited by Indians living under conditions of poverty, whether on or off reservations.

Race and Intelligence

A question frequently asked by those unfamiliar with the deficiencies of the race concept is whether some races are inherently more intelligent than others. Intelligence tests carried on in the United States by European American investigators among people of European and African descent have often shown that European Americans attain higher scores. During World War I, a series of IQ tests known as Alpha and Beta were regularly given to draftees. The results showed that the average score attained by European Americans was higher than that obtained by African Americans. Even though many African Americans scored higher than some European Americans, and some African Americans scored higher than most European Americans (African Americans from northern states, for instance, score better on average than southern Whites), many people took this as proof of the intellectual superiority of "White people." But all the tests really showed was that, on the average, European Americans outperformed African Americans in certain social situations. The tests did not measure "intelligence" per se, but the ability, conditioned by culture, of certain individuals to respond to certain socially conditioned problems. These tests had been conceived by European Americans for comparable middle-class European Americans. Although people of color coming from similar backgrounds generally did well (Chinese and Japanese Americans, for example, generally outperform Whites), African Americans as well as people of color coming from other backgrounds to meet the challenge of these tests were clearly at a disadvantage. It would be unrealistic to expect individuals unfamiliar with European American middle-class values and linguistic behavior to respond to a problem based on a familiarity with these.

Many large-scale intelligence tests continue to be administered in the United States. Notable among these are several series that attempt to hold environmental factors constant. Where this is done, African and European Americans tend to score equally well.[10] Nor is this surprising; because genes assort themselves independently of one another, there is no reason to suppose that whatever alleles may be associated with intelligence are likely to be concordant with the ones for skin pigmentation. Intelligence tests, however, have increasingly become the subject of controversy. There are many psychologists as well as anthropologists who are convinced that their use is overdone. Intelligence tests, they say, are of limited use, because they

---

[9]Chan, J. W. C., & Vernon, P. E. (1988). Individual differences among the peoples of China. In J. W. Berry (Ed.), *Human abilities in cultural context* (pp. 340–357). Cambridge, England: Cambridge University Press.

[10]Sanday, P. R. (1975). On the causes of IQ differences between groups and implications for social policy. In M. F. A. Montagu (Ed.), *Race and IQ* (pp. 232–238). New York: Oxford.

are applicable only to particular cultural circumstances. Only when these circumstances are carefully met can any meaningful generalizations be derived from the use of tests.

Notwithstanding the foregoing, there continue to be some who insist that there are significant differences in intelligence among human populations. Recent proponents of this view are the psychologist Richard Herrnstein and Charles Murray, a social scientist who is a fellow of the American Enterprise Institute, a conservative think tank. Their argument, in a lengthy (and highly publicized) book entitled *The Bell Curve,* is that a well-documented 15-point difference in IQ exists between African and European Americans, with the latter scoring higher, though not quite as high as Asian Americans. Furthermore, they assert that these differences are mostly determined by genetic factors and are therefore immutable.

Herrnstein and Murray's book has been justly criticized on many grounds, including violation of basic rules of statistics and their practice of utilizing studies, no matter how flawed, that appear to support their thesis while ignoring or barely mentioning those that contradict it. But does this mean that they are wrong? On purely theoretical grounds, could we not suppose that, just as we see a spectrum of inherited variations in physical traits—skin color, hair texture, height, or whatever—might not there be similar variation in innate intellectual potential of different populations? It is likely that just as there are genes affecting the development of such things as blue eyes, curly hair, or heavily pigmented skin, there are others affecting the development of intelligence. Of course, even if genes affecting intelligence do exist, we would still need to ask why their distribution should be any more concordant with those for skin color than with ones that determine whether one has A, B, or O blood, normal or abnormal (antimalarial) hemoglobin, sufficient lactase to digest raw milk, or whatever.

A number of studies have appeared to indicate an appreciable degree of hereditary control of intelligence. First, there is a general tendency for those pairs of individuals who are most genetically similar (identical twins) to be most similar in intelligence, even when reared in different environments. Furthermore, the scores on IQ tests of biological parents and their children are correlated and tend to be similar, whereas foster parents and their foster children show less of this tendency. There are, however, enormous problems in attempting to separate genetic components from environmental contributors.[11] As biologists Richard Lewontin and Steven Rose with psychologist Leon Kamin observe, twin studies are plagued by a host of problems: inadequate sample sizes, biased subjective judgments, failure to make sure that "separated twins" really were raised separately, unrepresentative samples of adoptees to serve as controls, untested assumptions about similarity of environments. In fact, children reared by the same mother resemble her in IQ to the same degree, whether or not they share her genes.[12] Clearly, we do not know what the heritability of intelligence really is.[13]

Whatever the degree of heritability may be, it is clear that the effects of environment are important for intelligence. This should not surprise us, as even traits of high heritability are strongly influenced by environmental

---

[11]Andrews, L. B., & Nelkin, D. (1996). The bell curve: A statement. *Science, 271,* 13.

[12]Lewontin, R. C., Rose, S., & Kamin, L. J. (1984). *Not in our genes* (pp. 100, 113, 116). New York: Pantheon.

[13]Ibid., pp. 9, 121.

These photos show how important the environment is in the expression of genetic traits. The same strain of corn that flourishes in one set of circumstances may do quite poorly in another.

factors. Height in humans, for example, is genetically determined while being dependent both upon nutrition and health status (severe illness in childhood arrests growth, and renewed growth never makes up for this loss). With respect to intelligence, in the early 1900s, new immigrants to the United States, many of whom were Jews, scored lower on IQ tests than U.S.-born Whites. Today, the descendants of those Jewish immigrants score 10 points higher on average than Whites. In fact, as in most industrial countries, IQ scores of all groups in the United States have risen some 15 points in the last 40 years, some faster than others. The gap between African and European Americans, for example, is narrower today than in the past. Nor is this surprising, for there are studies showing impressive IQ scores for African American children from poor backgrounds who have been adopted into affluent and intellectual homes. It is now known that disadvantaged children adopted into affluent and stable families can boost their IQs by 20 points. It is also well known that IQ scores rise with the amount of schooling the test-takers have. More such cases could be cited, but these suffice to make the point: The assertion that IQ is fixed and immutable is clearly false. Just as millions of people routinely overcome deficiencies of vision that are far more heritable than *anyone* claims intelligence to be, so may enriched education increase intelligence.

Intelligence: What Is It?

A question that must now be asked is: What do we mean by the term *intelligence*? To some, the answer is: that which is measured by IQ tests. Unfortunately, there is no general agreement as to what abilities or talents actually make up what we call intelligence, even though there are some psychologists who insist that it is a single quantifiable thing. Many more psychologists have come to believe intelligence to be the product of the interaction of different sorts of cognitive abilities: verbal, mathematical-logical, spatial, linguistic, musical, bodily kinesthetic, social, and personal.[14] Each may be thought of as a particular kind of intelligence, unrelated to the others. This being so, they must be independently inherited (to the degree they are inherited), just as height, blood type, skin color, and so forth are independently inherited. Thus, the various abilities that constitute intelligence may be independently distributed as are, for example, the previously discussed skin color and blood type (compare Figures 13.3 and 13.4).

The next question is: If we are not exactly sure what IQ tests are measuring, how can we be sure of the valid-

[14]Jacoby, R., & Glauberman, N. (Eds.). (1995). *The Bell Curve debate* (pp. 7, 55–56, 59). New York: Random House.

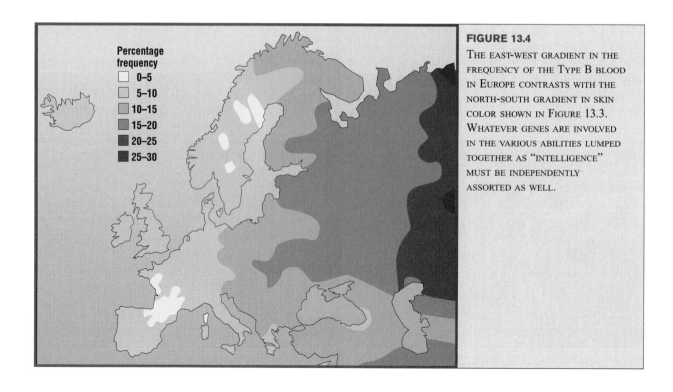

Percentage frequency
- 0–5
- 5–10
- 10–15
- 15–20
- 20–25
- 25–30

FIGURE 13.4

THE EAST-WEST GRADIENT IN THE FREQUENCY OF THE TYPE B BLOOD IN EUROPE CONTRASTS WITH THE NORTH-SOUTH GRADIENT IN SKIN COLOR SHOWN IN FIGURE 13.3. WHATEVER GENES ARE INVOLVED IN THE VARIOUS ABILITIES LUMPED TOGETHER AS "INTELLIGENCE" MUST BE INDEPENDENTLY ASSORTED AS WELL.

On one IQ test designed to be fair to both Black and White American students, they are asked to identify either of two famous scientists, Albert Einstein or George Washington Carver. Unfortunately, Carver is mostly a White person's Black hero, so a White is more likely to identify either than is a Black (see Mark Cohen, 1995, "Anthropology and Race: The Bell Curve Phenomenon," *General Anthropology* 2(1), p. 3).

ity of such tests—that is, can we be sure an IQ test measures what it is supposed to measure? The answer, of course, is that we cannot be sure. But, even at best, an IQ test measures performance (something that one does) rather than genetic disposition (something that lies within the individual). Reflected in one's performance are one's past experiences and present motivational state, as well as one's innate ability. In sum, it is fair to say that an IQ test is not a reliable measure of innate intelligence.

Attempts to prove the existence of significant differences in intelligence among human populations have been going on as long as people have been talking about race. But in spite of all, the hypothesis remains unproved. Nor is it ever likely to be proved, in view of what we saw in Chapter 10 as the major thrust in the evolution of the genus *Homo*. Over the past 2.5 million years, in all populations of this genus, the emphasis has been on cultural adaptation—actively inventing solutions to the problems of existence, rather than passively relying on biological adaptation. Thus, we would expect a comparable degree of intelligence in all present-day human populations. But even if this were not the case, it would mean only that dull and bright people are to be found in all human populations, though in different frequencies. Remember: Within-group variation is greater than between-group variation. Thus, geniuses can and do appear in any population, regardless of what that population's average intelligence may be. The fact of the matter is that the only way to be sure that individual human beings develop their innate abilities and skills, whatever they may be, to the fullest is to make sure they have access to the necessary resources and the opportunity to do so. This certainly cannot be accomplished if whole populations are assumed at the outset to be inferior.

This photo of African, Asian, Native American, and other winners of the Nobel Peace Prize was taken in 1998. It illustrates the point that individuals of exceptional ability can and do appear in any human population.

CONTINUING HUMAN BIOLOGICAL EVOLUTION

In the course of their evolution, humans in all parts of the world came to rely on cultural rather than biological adaptation for their survival. Nevertheless, as they spread beyond their tropical homeland into other parts of the world, they did develop considerable physical variation from one population to another. The forces responsible for this include genetic drift—especially at the margins of their range where small populations were easily isolated for varying amounts of time—and biological adaptation to differing climates.

Although much of this physical variation can still be seen in human populations today, the increasing effectiveness of cultural adaptation has often reduced its importance. For instance, the consumption of cod liver oil or vitamin D-fortified milk has canceled out the selective advantage of lightly pigmented skins in northern peoples. At the same time, culture has also imposed its own selective pressures, as we have seen in preceding chapters. Just as the invention of the spear-thrower was followed by a reduction in overall muscularity, or just as the transition to food production was followed by worsened health and mortality, so cultural practices today are affecting the human organism in important, often surprising, ways.

The probability of alterations in human biological makeup induced by culture raises a number of important questions. By trying to eliminate genetic variants for balanced polymorphic traits, such as the sickle-cell trait discussed in Chapter 3, are we also removing alleles that have survival value? Are we weakening the gene pool by allowing people with hereditary diseases and defects to reproduce? Are we reducing chances for genetic variation by trying to control population size?

We do not have answers to all of these questions. If we are able to wipe out sickle-cell anemia, we also may be able to wipe out malaria; thus, we would have eliminated the condition that made the sickle-cell trait advantageous. On the other hand, antimalarial campaigns have had no more than limited success, as the disease afflicts some 270 million people around the world. In 1997, 1.5 million to 2.7 million deaths were caused by malaria, making it the fifth largest infectious killer in the world. Moreover, as a consequence of global warming, the disease could spread (with a number of others) into more northerly regions. Although it is not certain, it is at least possible that over the next century, an average temperature increase of $3°C$ could result in 50 million to 80 million new malaria cases per year.[15] Nor is it strictly true that medical science is weakening the gene pool by letting those with disorders for which there may be a genetic predisposition, such as diabetes, reproduce. In the present environment, where medication is easily available, such people are as fit as anyone else. However, if such people are denied access to the needed medication, their biological fitness is lost and they die out. In fact, one's financial status affects one's access to medication, and so, however unintentional it may be, one's biological

---

[15]Stone, R. (1995). If the mercury soars, so may health hazards. *Science, 267*, 958.

fitness in North American society may be decided by one's financial status.

Examples of culture enabling individuals to reproduce even though they suffer from genetic disorders are familiar. Perhaps less familiar are the cases in which medical technology selects against some individuals by removing them from the reproducing population. One example can be seen in South Africa. About 1 percent of South Africans of Dutch descent have a gene that, in its dominant form, causes porphyria, a disorder that renders the skin of its victims sensitive to light and causes skin abrasions. If these Afrikaners remain in a rural environment, they suffer only minor skin abrasions as a result of their condition. However, the allele renders them very sensitive to modern medical treatment, such as they might receive in a large urban center like Johannesburg. If they are treated for some problem unrelated to porphyria, with barbiturates or similar drugs, they suffer acute attacks and very often die. In a relatively quiet rural environment where medical services are less readily accessible, the Afrikaners with this peculiar condition are able to live normal lives; it is only in an urban context, where they are more likely to receive medical attention, that they suffer physical impairment or loss of life.

Another example of culture acting as an agent of biological selection has to do with lactose tolerance: the ability to assimilate **lactose,** the primary constituent of fresh milk. This ability depends on the presence of a particular enzyme, **lactase,** in the small intestine. Failure to retain lactase into adulthood, although controlled by recessive alleles, is characteristic of mammals in general, as well as most human populations—especially Asian, native Australian, Native American, and many (but not all) African populations. Hence, only 10 to 30 percent of Americans of African descent and 0 to 30 percent of adult Asians retain lactase into adulthood and so are lactose tolerant.[16] By contrast, lactase retention and lactose tolerance are normal for over 80 percent of adults of northern European descent. Eastern Europeans, Arabs, and some East Africans are closer to northern Europeans in lactase retention than they are to Asians and other Africans. Generally speaking, a high retention of lactase is found in populations with a long tradition of fresh milk as an important dietary item. In such populations, selection has in the past favored those individuals with the dominant allele that confers the ability to assimilate lactose, selecting out those without this allele.

In developing countries, milk supplements are used in the treatment of acute protein-calorie malnutrition. Tube-fed diets of milk are used in connection with other medical procedures. Quite apart from medical practices, powdered milk has long been a staple of economic aid to other countries. Such practices in fact discriminate against the members of populations in which lactase is not commonly retained into adulthood. At the least, those individuals who are not lactose tolerant will be unable to

---

[16]Harrison, G. G. (1975). Primary adult lactase deficiency: A problem in anthropological genetics. *American Anthropologist, 77,* 815–819.

The routine use of antibiotics to prevent disease and reduce the amount of feed needed to fatten animals has produced lethal strains of bacteria (previously harmless to humans) that resist antibiotic treatment. One example is the emergence of enterococci as a threat to public health. These bacteria usually dwell peacefully in the human gut, but new strains have emerged that poison organs and cause the immune system to go haywire. Because of the bacteria's resistence to antibiotics, thousands of people die each year.

Lactose.   The primary constituent of fresh milk.   •   **Lactase.**   An enzyme in the small intestine that enables humans to assimilate lactose.

utilize the nutritive value of milk; frequently they will suffer diarrhea, abdominal cramping, and even bone degeneration, with serious results. In fact, the shipping of powdered milk to victims of South American earthquakes in the 1960s caused many deaths among them.

Among Europeans, the evolution of lactose tolerance is linked with evolution of a nonthrifty genotype.[17] Until about 6,000 years ago all humans were characterized by a **thrifty genotype.** This permitted efficient storage of fat to draw on in times of food shortage, and in times of scarcity conserved glucose (a simple sugar) for use in brain and red blood cells (as opposed to other tissues such as muscle), as well as nitrogen (vital for growth and health) through the body's diminished exertion. Regular access to lactose, a source of glucose, led to selection for the nonthrifty genotype as protection against adult-onset diabetes, or at least its onset relatively late in life (at a nonreproductive age). By contrast, populations that are lactose intolerant retain the thrifty genotype. As a consequence, when they are introduced to Western-style diets, characterized by abundance, particularly of foods high in sugar content, the incidence of diabetes skyrockets.

In recent years, there has been considerable concern about human activities that damage the earth's ozone layer. A major contributor to the ozone layer's deterioration has been the use of chlorofluorocarbons in aerosol sprays, refrigeration and air conditioning, and the manufacture of Styrofoam. Because the ozone layer screens out some of the sun's ultraviolet rays, its continued deterioration will expose humans to increased ultraviolet radiation. As we saw earlier in this chapter, some ultraviolet radiation is necessary for the production of vitamin D, but excessive amounts lead, among other things, to an increased incidence of skin cancers. Hence a rising incidence of skin cancers is not surprising, as the ozone layer continues to deteriorate.

Although a ban on the use of chlorofluorocarbons in aerosol sprays was imposed some years ago, the destruction of the ozone layer continued about twice as fast as scientists had predicted it would, even without the ban. Subsequently, an international treaty further limiting the use of chlorofluorocarbons was negotiated, but this ban has merely slowed, rather than halted, further deterioration. In fact, the ozone hole over Antarctica in October 1994 was the severest ever recorded in 35 years. Most

immediately affected by the consequent increase in ultraviolet radiation are the world's lightly pigmented peoples, but ultimately, all will be affected.

Ozone depletion is merely one of a host of problems confronted by humans today that ultimately have an impact on human gene pools. In view of the consequences for human biology of such seemingly benign innovations as dairying or (as discussed in Chapter 11) farming, we may wonder about many recent practices—for example, the effects of increased exposure to radiation from increased use of x-rays and CT scans, nuclear accidents, increased production of radioactive wastes, and the like. To be sure, we are constantly reassured by various experts that we are protected by adequate safety regulations, but one is not reassured by discoveries, such as the one announced by the National Academy of Sciences in 1989, that what were accepted as safe levels of radiation were in fact too high; or the earlier discovery that the supposedly safe treatment of sinus disorders in the 1940s by massive doses of x-ray radiation produced a bumper crop of thyroid cancers in the late 1960s. But it is not just increased exposure to radiation that we confront but increased exposure to other known mutagenic agents, including a wide variety of chemicals, such as pesticides. Despite repeated assurances about their safety, there have been tens of thousands of cases of poisonings in the United States alone (probably more in so-called underdeveloped countries, where controls are even less effective than in the United States and where substances banned in the United States are routinely used), and thousands of cases of cancer related to the manufacture and use of pesticides. All this on top of the several million birds killed each year (many of which would otherwise have been happily gobbling down bugs and other pests), serious fish kills, honey bee kills (bees are needed for the efficient pollination of many crops), and the like. In all, pesticides alone (never mind other agricultural chemicals) are responsible for an estimated $8 *billion* worth of environmental and public health damage in the United States each year.[18]

Aside from pesticides, there are other dangerous substances, like the hormone-disrupting chemicals. In 1938, a synthetic estrogen known as DES was developed and subsequently prescribed for a variety of ailments ranging from acne to prostate cancer. Moreover, tons of it are routinely added to animal feeds. It was not until 1971, however, that the first indication that DES causes vaginal

---

[17]Allen, J. S., & Cheer, S. M. (1996). The non-thrifty genotype. *Current Anthropology, 37,* 831–842.

[18]Pimentel, D. (1991). Response. *Science, 252,* 358.

Thrifty genotype. Human genotype that permits efficient storage of fat to draw on in times of food shortage and conservation of glucose and nitrogen.

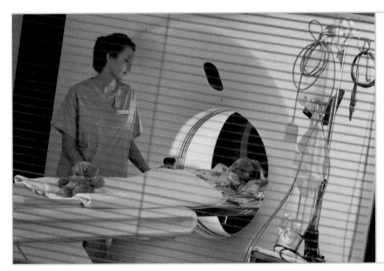

In 2001, the leading radiology journal in the United States published studies showing that children in this country receiving CT scans of the head and abdomen absorb 2 to 6 times the radiation needed to produce clear images. As a consequence, about 1,500 of them will die later of radiation-induced cancers.

cancer in young women came to light. Subsequent research has shown that DES causes problems with the male reproductive system and causes deformities of the female reproductive tract. DES mimics the natural hormone, binding with appropriate receptors in and on cells and thereby turns on biological activity associated with the hormone. As one group of scientists observes,

> The synthetic hormone has two troublesome traits. First, it triggers certain parts of the reproductive system more effectively than does estradiol, one of the body's own estrogens. . . . Even more important, it manages to circumvent a mechanism that protects the fetus from the developmentally disruptive effects of excessive estrogen exposure. Normally, special maternal and fetal blood proteins soak up almost all excess circulating estrogen. But they do not recognize DES. As a consequence, DES in the fetal blood supply remains biologically active.[19]

DES is not alone in its effects: At least 51 chemicals—many of them in common use—are now known to disrupt hormones, and even this could be the tip of the iceberg. Some of these chemicals mimic hormones in the manner of DES, whereas others interfere with other parts of the endocrine system, such as thyroid and testosterone metabolism. Included are such supposedly benign and inert substances as plastics widely used in laboratories and chemicals added to polystyrene and polyvinyl chloride (PVCs) to make them more stable and less break-

able. These plastics are widely used in plumbing, food processing, and food packaging. Hormone disrupting chemicals are also found in many detergents and personal care products, contraceptive creams, the giant jugs used to bottle drinking water, and plastic linings in cans (about 85 percent of food cans in the United States are so lined).

In the spring of 2000 Dursban, the most widely used pesticide, was phased out of use in the United States. After some 30 years of use, it was found to be more dangerous than thought, and supposedly safe levels were found to be unsafe.

---

[19]Colburn, T., Dumanoski, D., & Myers, J. P. (1996). Hormonal sabotage. *Natural History,* (3), 45–46.

HIGHWAY 1
Read leading scientists critiques of Herrnstein and Murray's book, *The Bell Curve*. Learn more about the problems and biases built into race-based intelligence testing.
www.indiana.edu/~intell/bellcurve.html

HIGHWAY 2
Visit the American Anthropological Association Web site to read the discipline's statement on race. Also, see how professional anthropologists work to bring their intellectual framework into the realm of public policy through their response to Office of Management and Budget (OMB) Directive 15 on federal standards for the reporting of "racial" and "ethnic" statistics.
www.aaanet.org/stmts/racepp.htm

The implications of all these developments are sobering. We know that pathologies result from extremely low levels of exposure to harmful chemicals. Yet, besides those used domestically, millions of pounds are exported to the rest of the world (40 million pounds in 1991 alone).[20] It is quite possible that hormone disruptions are at least partially responsible for certain trends that have recently become causes for concern among scientists. These range from increasingly early onset of puberty in human females to dramatic declines in human sperm counts. With respect to the latter, some 61 separate studies confirm that sperm counts have dropped almost 50 percent from 1938 to 1990 (Figure 13.5). Most of these studies were carried out in the United States and Europe, but some from Africa, Asia, and South America show that this is essentially a worldwide phenomenon. If this trend continues, it will have profound results.

It is not that the experts who assure us of the safety of such things are deliberately misleading us. (Although there are cases of that too, one notorious example being the case of asbestos. As early as 1902 it was included in a list of dusts known to be hazardous. By 1933 it was well documented as a cause of lung cancer, yet in the 1960s, corporate executives denied ever hearing of the dangers.) For the most part, experts are convinced of the validity of what they say; the difficulty is that serious problems, such as those having to do with radiation or exposure to various chemicals, have a way of not being apparent until years, or even decades later. By then, of course, serious financial interests are at stake.

What is clear, then, is that cultural practices, probably as never before, are currently having an impact on human gene pools. Unquestionably, this impact is deleterious to those individuals who suffer the effects of negative selection, whose misery and death are the price paid for many of the material benefits of civilization we enjoy today. It remains to be seen just what the long-term effects on the human species as a whole will be. If the promise of genetic engineering offers hope of alleviating some of the misery and death that result from our own practices, it also raises the specter of removing genetic variants that might turn out to be of future adaptive value, or that might turn out to make us immediately susceptible to new problems that we don't even know about today.

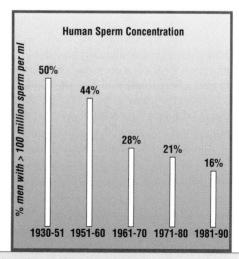

FIGURE 13.5

A DOCUMENTED DECLINE IN HUMAN MALE SPERM COUNTS WORLDWIDE MAY BE RELATED TO WIDESPREAD EXPOSURE TO HORMONE-DISRUPTING CHEMICALS.

---

[20]Ibid., 47.

Anthropology Applied

Studying the Emergence of New Diseases[*]

Ever since the Neolithic, humans have had to cope with a host of new diseases that got their start as a consequence of changes in human behavior. This has become a renewed source of concern following a recent resurgence of infectious diseases and appearance and spread of a host of new and lethal diseases. All told, more than 30 diseases new to medicine have emerged in the past 25 years, of which perhaps the best known is AIDS. This has now become number 4 among infectious killers of humans, with 5.8 million people infected in 1998 alone.[†] But there are others—like Ebola, which causes victims to hemorrhage to death, blood pouring from every orifice; hemorrhagic fevers like Dengue fever, Lassa fever, and Hantavirus; Invasive Streptococcus A, which consumes the victims' flesh; Legionnaire's disease; and Lyme disease. What has sparked the appearance and spread of these and other new diseases has been a considerable mystery, but one theory is that some are the result of human activities. In particular, the intrusion of people into new ecological settings, such as rain forests, along with construction of roads allows viruses and other infectious microbes to spread rapidly to large numbers of people. It is now generally accepted that the HIV virus responsible for AIDS transferred to humans from chimpanzees in the forests of the Democratic Republic of Congo as a consequence of hunting and butchering these animals for food. For the first 30 years, few people were affected; it was not until people began congregating in cities like Kinshasa that conditions were ripe for an epidemic.

To gain a better understanding of the interplay between ecological disturbance and the emergence of new diseases, anthropologist Carol Jenkins, whose specialty is medical anthropology, obtained a grant from the MacArthur Foundation in 1993. From her base at the Papua New Guinea Institute of Medical Research, she is following what happens to the health of local people in the wake of a massive logging operation, begun in 1993. From this should come a better understanding of how disease organisms spread from animal hosts to humans. Since most of the "new" viruses that have suddenly afflicted humans are in fact old ones that have been present in animals like monkeys (monkey pox), rodents (Hanta virus), deer (Lyme disease), and insects (West Nile virus), it appears that something new has enabled them to jump from their animal hosts to humans. A recent example comes from the Democratic Republic of Congo. Here civil war created a situation where villagers in the central part of the country were faced with starvation. Their response was to increase the hunting of animals, including monkeys, squirrels, and rats that carry a disease called monkey pox. Related to smallpox, the disease transfers easily to humans, resulting in the largest outbreak of this disease ever seen among humans. What makes this outbreak even more serious is an apparently new strain of the infection, enabling it to spread from person to person, instead of only from an animal host.[‡]

Large-scale habitat disturbance is an obvious candidate for such disease transfers, but this needs to be confirmed and the process understood. So far, it is hard to make more than a circumstantial case, by looking back after a disease outbreak. The work of Jenkins and her team is unique in that she was able to get baseline health data on local people before their environment was disturbed. Thus, she is in a position to follow events as they unfold.

It will be some time before conclusions can be drawn from Jenkins' study. Its importance is obvious; in an era of globalization, as air travel allows more and more tropical diseases to spread beyond the tropics, we need a fuller understanding of how viruses interact with their hosts if we are to devise effective preventive and therapeutic strategies to deal with them.

---

[*]Gibbons, A. (1993). Where are new diseases born? *Science, 261,* 680–681.

[†]Balter, M. (1998). On world AIDS day, a shadow looms over southern Africa. *Science, 282,* 1,790.

[‡]Cohen, J. (1997). Is an old virus up to new tricks? *Science, 277,* 312–313.

CHAPTER SUMMARY

In humans, most behavioral patterns are culturally learned or acquired. Other characteristics are determined by an interaction between genes and environment. The gene pools of populations contain various alternative alleles. When the environment changes, their gene pool confers the possibility for physical alteration to meet the change.

When a polymorphic species is separated into different faunal regions, it is usually polytypic; that is, populations differ in the frequency with which genetic variability is expressed. It appears that the human species has been polytypic at least since the time of *Homo erectus*. Gene flow, however, has prevented diversification into multiple species.

Early anthropologists classified *Homo sapiens* into subspecies, or races, based on geographic location and such phenotypic features as skin color, body size, head shape, and hair texture. The presence of atypical individuals and the nonconcordance of traits continually challenged these racial classifications. No examples of pure racial types could be found. The visible traits were found to occur in a worldwide continuum. No definite grouping of distinct, discontinuous biological groups has been found in modern humans.

A biological race is a population of a species that differs in the frequency of genetic variants from other populations of the same species. Three observations must be made concerning this biological definition: (1) It is arbitrary; (2) it does not mean that any one race has exclusive possession of any particular allele(s); and (3) individuals of one race will not necessarily be distinguishable from those of another. As a means for understanding human variation, the concept of race has several limitations. First, race is an arbitrary category, making agreement on any particular classification impossible; second, humans are so complex genetically that often the genetic basis of traits on which racial studies are based is itself poorly understood; and finally, race exists as a cultural as well as a biological category. Most anthropologists now view the race concept as useless for an understanding of human biological variation, preferring to study the distribution and significance of specific, genetically based characteristics, or else the characteristics of small breeding populations.

Physical anthropologists have determined that much of human physical variation appears related to climatic adaptation. People native to cold climates tend to have greater body bulk relative to their extremities than individuals who live in hot climates; the latter tend to be long and slender. Studies involving body build and climate are complicated by such other factors as the effects on physique of diet and of clothing.

In the United States, race is commonly thought of in terms of skin color. Subject to tremendous variation, skin color is a function of several factors: transparency or thickness of the skin, distribution of blood vessels, and amount of carotene and melanin in a given area of skin. Exposure to sunlight increases the amount of melanin, darkening the skin. Natural selection has favored heavily pigmented skin as protection against the strong solar radiation of equatorial latitudes. In northern latitudes, natural selection has favored relatively depigmented skins, which can utilize relatively weak solar radiation in the production of vitamin D. Selective mating, as well as geographic location, plays a part in skin color distribution.

Racism can be viewed solely as a social problem. It is an emotional phenomenon best explained in terms of collective psychology. The racist individual reacts on the basis of social stereotypes and not established scientific facts.

Notwithstanding the impossibility of defining biologically valid human races, many people have assumed that there are behavioral differences among human races. The innate behavioral characteristics attributed by these people to race can be explained in terms of enculturation rather than biology. Those intelligence tests that have been interpreted to indicate that European Americans are intellectually superior to African Americans are designed by European Americans for European Americans from similar backgrounds. It is not realistic to expect individuals who are not familiar with European American middle-class values to respond to items based on knowledge of these values. African and European Americans both, if they come from different types of backgrounds, are thus at a disadvantage. At present, it is not possible to separate the inherited components of intelligence from those that are culturally acquired. Furthermore, there is still no agreement on what intelligence really is, but it is made up probably of several different talents and abilities.

Although the human species has come to rely on cultural rather than biological adaptation for survival, human gene pools still continue to change in response to external factors. Many of these changes are brought about by cultural practices; for example, the shipment of powdered milk to human populations that are low in the frequency of the allele for lactase retention into adulthood may contribute to the death of large numbers of people. Those who survive are most likely to be those with the allele for lactase retention. Unquestionably, this kind of selection is deleterious to those individuals who are "selected out" in this way. Just what the long-term effects will be on the human species as a whole remains to be seen.

CLASSIC READINGS

Cohen, M. N. (1998). *Culture of intolerance: Chauvinism, class and racism in the United States.* New Haven, CT: Yale University Press.

This very readable book was written to counter political propaganda claiming that science affirms the need to shape the political order on the basis of inherent inequality and mutual disdain. In it, Cohen summarizes what scientific data *really* say about biological differences among humans; explores the depth, power, beauty, and potential value of cultural differences; shows how the cultural blinders of U.S. culture cause people in this country to misunderstand others as well as themselves; and looks at questionable assumptions in U.S. culture that promote intolerance and generate problems where none need exist.

Gould, S. J. (1996). *The mismeasure of man* (2nd ed.). New York: Norton.

This is an updating of a classic critique of supposedly scientific studies that attempt to rank all people on a linear scale of intrinsic and unalterable mental worth. The revision was prompted by what Gould refers to as the "latest cyclic episode of biodeterminism" represented by the publication of the widely discussed book, *The Bell Curve.*

Graves, J. L. (2001). *The emperor's new clothes: Biological theories of race at the millennium.* New Brunswick, NJ: Rutgers University Press.

Graves is a laboratory geneticist as well as an African American intellectual whose goal is to show the reader that there is no biological basis for separation of human beings into races and that the idea of race is a relatively recent social and political construction. His grasp of science is solid and up-to-date, and readers can benefit from the case he presents.

Jacoby, R., & Glauberman, N. (Eds.). (1995). *The Bell Curve debate.* New York: Random House.

This is a collection of articles by a wide variety of authors including biologists, anthropologists, psychologists, mathematicians, essayists, and others critically examining the claims and issues raised in the widely read and much discussed book, *The Bell Curve.* Included are pieces written to address many of the same issues as they were raised by earlier writers. For anyone who hopes to understand the race and intelligence debate, this book is a must.

Marks, J. (1995). *Human biodiversity: Genes, race and history.* Hawthorne, NY: Aldine de Gruyter.

In this book, Marks shows how genetics has undermined the fundamental assumptions of racial taxonomy. In addition to its presentation of the nature of human biodiversity, the book also deals with the history of cultural attitudes toward "race" and diversity.

"Absolute" or chronometric dates: In archaeology and paleoanthropology, dates for archaeological materials based on solar years, centuries, or other units of absolute time.

Action theory: The theory that self-serving actions by forceful leaders play a role in civilization's emergence.

Adaptation: A process by which organisms achieve a beneficial adjustment to an available environment; also the results of that process the characteristics of organisms that fit them to the particular set of conditions of the environment in which they are generally found.

Alleles: Alternate forms of a single gene.

Amino acid racemization dating: In archaeology and paleoanthropology, a technique for chronometric dating that measures the ratio of right- to left-handed amino acids.

Analogies: In biology, structures that are superficially similar; the result of convergent evolution.

Anthropology: The study of humankind, in all times and places.

Anthropomorphism: The ascription of human attributes to nonhuman beings.

Applied anthropology: The use of anthropological knowledge and methods to solve practical problems, often for a specific client.

Archaeology: The study of material remains, usually from the past, to describe and explain human behavior.

Archaic cultures: Term used to refer to Mesolithic cultures in the Americas.

Ardipithecus ramidus: Probable early hominine; lived about 5.8 to 4.4 million years ago.

Artifact: Any object fashioned or altered by humans.

Aurignacian tradition: Toolmaking tradition in Europe and western Asia at the beginning of the Upper Paleolithic.

Australopithecus: The first well-known hominine; lived between 4.2 and 1 million years ago. Characterized by bipedal locomotion when on the ground, but with an apelike brain; includes at least five species: *afarensis, africanus, anamensis, boisei,* and *robustus.*

Baton method: The technique of stone tool manufacture performed by striking the raw material with a bone or antler "baton" to remove flakes.

Blade technique: A technique of stone tool manufacture by which long, parallel-sided flakes are struck off the edges of a specially prepared core.

Brachiate: To use the arms to move from branch to branch, with the body hanging suspended beneath the arms.

Bronze Age: In the Old World, the period marked by the production of tools and ornaments of bronze; began about 3000 b.c. in China and Southwest Asia and about 500 years earlier in Southeast Asia.

Catarrhini: A haplorhine infraorder that includes Old World monkeys, apes, and humans.

Chromosome: In the cell nucleus, long strands of DNA combined with a protein that can be seen under the microscope.

Civilization: In anthropology a type of society marked by the presence of cities, social classes, and the state.

Clavicle: The collarbone.

Codon: Three-base sequence of a gene that specifies production of an amino acid.

Cognitive capacity: A broad concept including intelligence, educability, concept formation, self-awareness, self-evaluation, attention span, sensitivity in discrimination, and creativity.

Cold-blooded: Animals whose body temperature rises or falls according to the temperature of the surrounding environment.

Convergent evolution: In cultural evolution, the development of similar adaptations to similar environmental conditions by peoples whose ancestral cultures were quite different.

Cranium: The brain case of the skull.

Cultural anthropology: The branch of anthropology that focuses on humans as a culture-making species.

Culture-bound: Theories about the world and reality based on the assumptions and values of one's own culture.

Datum point: The starting, or reference, point for a grid system.

Dendrochronology: In archaeology, a method of chronometric dating based on the number of rings of growth found in a tree trunk.

Divergent or branching evolution: An evolutionary process in which an ancestral population gives rise to two or more descendant populations that differ from one another.

DNA: The genetic material, deoxyribonucleic acid; a complex molecule with information to direct the synthesis of proteins. DNA molecules have the unique property of being able to produce exact copies of themselves.

Domestication: An evolutionary process whereby humans modify, either intentionally or unintentionally, the genetic makeup of a population of plants or animals, sometimes to the extent that members of the population are unable to survive and/or reproduce without human assistance.

Ecological niche: A species' way of life considered in the context of its environment, including other species found in that environment.

Electron spin resonance: In archaeology and paleoanthropology, a technique for chronometric dating that measures the number of trapped electrons in bone or shell.

Endocast: A cast of the inside of a skull; helps determine the size and shape of the brain.

Entoptic phenomena: Bright pulsating forms that are generated by the central nervous system and seen in states of trance.

Enzyme: Proteins that initiate and direct chemical reactions in an organism.

Epicanthic eye fold: A fold of skin at the inner corner of the eye that covers the true corner of the eye; common in Asiatic populations.

Estrus: In primate females, the time of sexual receptivity during which ovulation takes place.

Ethnography: The systematic description of a particular culture based on firsthand observation.

Ethnologist: An anthropologist who studies cultures from a comparative or historical point of view, utilizing ethnographic accounts.

Evolution: Descent with modification.

Exogamy: Marriage outside the group.

Faunal region: A geographic region with its own distinctive assemblage of animal life, not precisely like that of other regions.

Flotation: An archeological technique employed to recover very tiny objects by immersion of soil samples in water to separate heavy from lightparticles.

Fluorine test: In archaeology or paleoanthropology, a technique for relative dating based on the fact that the amount of fluorine in bones is proportional to their age.

Foramen magnum: A large opening in the skull through which the spinal cord passes and connects to the brain.

Forensic anthropology: Field of applied physical anthropology that specializes in the identification of human skeletal remains for legal purposes.

Fossil: The preserved remains of plants and animals that lived in the past.

Fossil locality: In paleoanthropology, a place where fossils are found.

Gene flow: The introduction of alleles from the gene pool of one population into that of another.

Gene pool: The genetic variants available to a population.

Genera; genus: In the system of plant and animal classification, a group of like species.

Genes: Portions of DNA molecules that direct the synthesis of proteins. DNA molecules have the unique property of being able to produce exact copies of themselves.

Genetic drift: Chance fluctuations of allele frequencies in the gene pool of a population.

Genome: The complete sequence of DNA for a species.

Genotype: The actual genetic makeup of an organism.

Genus *Homo*: Hominine genus characterized by expansion of brain, reduction of jaws, and reliance on cultural adaptation; includes at least three species: *habilis, erectus,* and *sapiens.*

Gracile Australopithecines: Smaller, more lightly built members of the genus *Australopithecus.*

Grid system: A system for recording data from an archaeological excavation.

Haplorhini: A primate suborder that includes tarsiers, monkeys, apes, and humans.

Hardy-Weinberg principle: Demonstrates algebraically that the percentage of individuals thatare homozygous for the dominant allele, homozygous for the recessive allele, and heterozygous should remain constant from one generation to the next, provided that certain specified conditionsare met.

Hemoglobin: The protein that carries oxygen in the red blood cells.

Heterozygous: Refers to a chromosome pair that bears different alleles for a single gene.

Holistic perspective: A fundamental principle of anthropology, that the various parts of culture must be viewed in the broadest possible context in order to understand their interconnections and interdependence.

Hominid: Hominoid family to which humans alone used to be assigned; now includes African apes and humans, with the latter assigned to the subfamily Homininae.

Hominine: Member of the Homininae, the subfamily of hominids to which humans belong.

Hominoid: A catarrhine primate superfamily that includes apes and humans.

Homo habilis: Earliest representative of the genus *Homo;* lived between 2.4 and 1.6 million years ago. Characterized by expansion and reorganization of the brain, compared to *Australopithecus.*

Homologies: In biology, structures possessed by two different organisms that arise in similar fashion and pass through similar stages during embryonic development.

Homozygous: Refers to a chromosome pair that bears identical alleles for a single gene.

Horticulture: Cultivation of crops using hand tools such as digging sticks or hoes.

Hydraulic theory: The theory that sees civilization's emergence as the result of the construction of elaborate irrigation systems, the functioning of which required full-time managers whose control blossomed into the first governing body and elite social class.

Hypoglossal canal. The opening in the skull through which the tongue-controlling hypoglossal nerve passes.

Informants: Members of a society in which the ethnographer works who help interpret what she or he sees taking place.

Intensive agriculture: Intensive farming of large plots of land, employing fertilizers, plows, and/or extensive irrigation.

Interspecies gene transfer: Transfer of DNA as when retroviruses insert DNA into the cells of one species from another.

Isolating mechanisms: Factors that separate breeding populations, thereby preventing gene flow, creating divergent subspecies and ultimately (if maintained) divergent species.

Kenyanthropus platyops: Hominine contemporary with early Australopithecines; not certainly a separate species.

Lactase: An enzyme in the small intestine that enables humans to assimilate lactose.

Lactose: The primary constituent of fresh milk.

Law: Formal negative sanctions.

Law of competitive exclusion: When two closely related species compete for the same niche, one will out-compete the other, bringing about the latter's extinction.

Law of dominance and recessiveness: Certain alleles are able to mask the presence of others.

Law of independent assortment: Genes controlling different traits are inherited independently of one another.

Law of segregation: Variants of genes for a particular trait retain their separate identities through the generations.

Lemuriformes: A strepsirhine infraorder that includes lemurs and lorises.

Levalloisian technique: Toolmaking technique by which three or four long triangular flakes were detached from a specially prepared core. Developed by humans transitional from *Homo erectus* to *Homo sapiens.*

Linguistic anthropology: The branch of cultural anthropology that studies human language.

Lower Paleolithic: The first part of the Old Stone Age; its beginning is marked by the appearance 2.6 million years ago of Oldowan tools.

Maritime Archaic culture: An Archaic culture of northeastern North America, centered on the Gulf of St. Lawrence, that emphasized the utilization of marine resources.

Meiosis: A kind of cell division that produces the sex cells, each of which has half the number of chromosomes, and hence genes, as the parent cell.

Melanin: The chemical responsible for dark skin pigmentation, which helps protect against damage from ultraviolet radiation.

Mesolithic: The Middle Stone Age of Europe and Southwest Asia; began about 12,000 years ago.

Microlith: A small blade of flint or similar stone, several of which were hafted together in wooden handles to make tools; widespread in the Mesolithic.

Middle Paleolithic: The middle part of the Old Stone Age characterized by the emergence of archaic *H. sapiens* and the development of the Mousterian tradition of toolmaking.

Mitosis: A kind of cell division that produces new cells having exactly the same number of chromosome pairs, and hence genes, as the parent cell.

Mousterian tradition: Toolmaking tradition of the Neandertals and their contemporaries of Europe, western Asia, and northern Africa, featuring flake tools that are lighter and smaller than earlier Levalloisian flake tools.

Mutation: Chance alteration of a gene that produces a new allele.

Natufian culture: A Mesolithic culture of Israel, Lebanon, and western Syria, between about 12,500 and 10,200 years ago.

Natural selection: The evolutionary process through which factors in the environment exert pressure that favors some individuals over others to produce the next generation.

Neandertals: Representatives of "archaic" *Homo sapiens* in Europe and western Asia, living from about 130,000 years ago to about 35,000 years ago.

Neolithic period: The New Stone Age; began about 11,000 years ago in Southwest Asia.

Notochord: A rodlike structure of cartilage that, in vertebrates, is replaced by the vertebral column.

Oldowan tool tradition: The earliest identifiable stone tools.

Orrorin tugenensis: Possible hominine; lived 6 million years ago.

Paleoanthropologist: An anthropologist who studies human evolution from fossil remains.

Paleoindian: The earliest inhabitants of North America.

Paleolithic: The Old Stone Age, characterized by manufacture and use of chipped stone tools.

Palynology: In archaeology and paleoanthropology, a method of relative dating based on changes in fossil pollen over time.

Participant observation: In ethnography, the technique of learning a people's culture through direct participation in their everyday life over an extended period of time.

Pastoralist: Member of a society in which the herding of grazing animals is regarded as the ideal way of making a living, and in which movement of all or part of the society is considered a normal and natural way of life.

Pentadactyly: Possessing five digits (fingers and toes).

Percussion method: A technique of stone tool manufacture performed by striking the raw material with a hammerstone or by striking raw material against a stone anvil to remove flakes.

Phenotype: The physical appearance of an organism that may or may not reflect a particular genotype because the latter may or may not include recessive alleles.

Physical anthropology: The systematic study of humans as biological organisms.

Polygenetic inheritance: When two or more genes work together to effect a single phenotypic character.

Polymorphic: A species with alternative forms (alleles) of particular genes.

Polytypic: The expression of genetic variants in different frequencies in different populations of a species.

Population: In biology, a group of similar individuals that can and do interbreed.

Potassium-argon analysis: In archaeology and paleoanthropology, a technique for chronometric dating that measures the ratio of radioactive potassium to argon in volcanic debris associated with human remains.

Prehensile: Having the ability to grasp.

Prehistoric: A conventional term used to refer to the period of time before the appearance of written records. Does not deny the existence of history, merely of written history.

Pressure flaking: A technique of stone tool manufacture in which a bone, antler, or wooden tool is used to press, rather than strike off, small flakes from a piece of flint or similar stone.

Primates: The group of mammals that includes lemurs, lorises, tarsiers, monkeys, apes, and humans.

Race: In biology, a population of a species that differs in the frequency of the variants of some gene or genes from other populations of the same species.

Racism: A doctrine of racial superiority by which one group asserts its superiority over another.

Radiocarbon analysis: In archaeology and paleoanthropology, a technique for chronometric dating based on measuring the amount of radioactive carbon (C-14) left in organic materials found in archaeological sites.

Relative dating: In archaeology and paleoanthropology, designating an event, object, or fossil as being older or younger than another.

Ribosomes: Structures in the cell where translation occurs.

RNA: Ribonucleic acid; similar to DNA but with uracil substituted for the base thymine. Carries instructions from DNA to produce amino acids for protein building.

Robust Australopithecines: Slightly larger and more robust than gracile members of genus *Australopithecus,* with larger, more powerful jaws.

Sagittal crest: A crest running from front to back on the top of the skull in the midline.

Scapula: The shoulder blade.

Sickle-cell anemia: An inherited form of anemia caused by the red blood cells assuming a sickled shape.

Site: In archaeology, a place containing remains of previous human activity.

Soil marks: Stains that show up on the surface of recently plowed fields that reveal an archaeological site.

Species: In biology, a population or group of populations that is capable of interbreeding but that is reproductively isolated from other such populations.

Stabilizing selection: Natural selection as it acts to promote stability, rather than change, in a population's gene pool.

Stratified: Layered; said of archaeological sites where the remains lie in layers, one upon another.

Stratigraphy: In archaeology and paleoanthropology, the most reliable method of relative dating by means of strata.

Strepsirhini: A primate suborder that includes the single infraorder Lemuriformes.

Tarsii: A haplorhine infraorder that includes tarsiers.

Technology: The knowledge that people employ to make and use objects.

Tool: An object used to facilitate some task or activity. Although toolmaking involves intentional modification of the material of which it is made, tool use may involve objects either modified for some particular purpose or completely unmodified.

Transcription: Process of conversion of instructions from DNA into RNA.

Transhumance: Among pastoralists, the grazing of sheep and goats in low steppe lands in the winter and then moving to high pastures on the plateaus in the summer.

Translation: Process of conversion of RNA instructions into proteins.

Unaltered fossil: Remains of plants and animals that lived in the past and that have not been altered in any significant way.

Unconscious selection: The preservation of valued variants of a plant or animal species and the destruction of less valued ones, with no thought as to the long-range consequences.

Upper Paleolithic: The last part of the Old Stone Age, characterized by the emergence of more modern-looking hominines and an emphasis on the blade technique of toolmaking.

Vegeculture: The cultivation of domesticated root crops, such as yams and taro.

Warm-blooded: Animals that maintain a relatively constant body temperature.

BIBLIOGRAPHY

Adams, R. (2001). Scale and complexity in archaic states. *American Antiquity, 11,* 188.

Allen, J. S., & Cheer, S. M. (1996). The non-thrifty genotype. *Current Anthropology, 37,* 831–842.

Amábile-Cuevas, C. F., & Chicurel, M. E. (1993). Horizontal gene transfer. *American Scientist, 81,* 332–341.

Ambrose, S. H. (2001). Paleolithic technology and human evolution. *Science, 291.*

American Anthropological Association (1998). Code of ethics of the American Anthropological Association. *Anthropology Newsletter, 39*(6), 19–20.

American Anthropological Association (1998). Statement on "race." Available at www.ameranthassn.org.

Andrews, L. B., & Nelkin, D. (1996). The bell curve: A statement. *Science, 271,* 13.

Ankel-Simons, F., Fleagle, J. G., & Chatrath, P. S. (1998). Femoral anatomy of *Aegyptopithecus zeuxis,* an early Oligocene anthropoid. *American Journal of Physical Anthropology, 106,* 413–424.

Anonymous. (1998). The First Americans, ca. 20,000 B.C. *Discover, 19*(6), 24.

Appenzeller, T. (1998). Art: Evolution or revolution? *Science, 282,* 1451–1454.

Ashmore, W. (Ed.). (1981). *Lowland Maya settlement patterns.* Albuquerque: University of New Mexico Press.

Balter, M. (1998). On world AIDS day, a shadow looms over southern Africa. *Science, 282,* 1790.

Balter, M. (1998). Why settle down? The mystery of communities. *Science, 282,* 1442–1444.

Balter, M. (1999). A long season puts Çatalhöyük in context. *Science, 286,* 890–891.

Balter, M. (2001). Did plaster hold Neolithic society together? *Science, 294,* 2278–2281.

Balter, M. (2001). Fossil tangles roots of human family tree. *Science, 291,* 2289–2291.

Balter, M. (2001). In search of the first Europeans. *Science, 291,* 1724.

Balter, M. (2001). Scientists spar over claims of earliest human ancestor. *Science, 291,* 1460–1461.

Balter, M. (2002). From a modern human's brow—or doodling? *Science, 295,* 247–249.

Bar-Yosef, O. (1986). The walls of Jericho: An alternative interpretation. *Current Anthropology, 27,* 157–162.

Bar-Yosef, O., Vandermeesch, B., Arensburg, B., Belfer-Cohen, A., Goldberg, P., Laville, H., Meignen, L., Rak, Y., Speth, J. D., Tchernov, E., Tillier, A-M., & Weiner, S. (1992). The excavations in Kebara Cave, Mt. Carmel. *Current Anthropology, 33,* 497–550.

Barham, L. S. (1998). Possible early pigment use in south-central Africa. *Current Anthropology, 39,* 709.

Barham, L. S. (1998). Possible early pigment use in South-Central Africa. *Current Anthropology, 39,* 703–710.

Boehm, C. (2000). The evolution of moral communities. School of American Research, *2000 Annual Report,* p. 7.

Bednarik, R. G. (1995). Concept-mediated marking in the Lower Paleolithic. *Current Anthropology, 36,* 605–634.

Behrensmeyer, A. K., Todd, N. E., Potts, R., & McBrinn, G. E. (1997). Late Pliocene faunal turnover in the Turkana basin, Kenya and Ethiopia. *Science, 278,* 1589–1594.

Bermúdez de Castro, J. M., Arsuaga, J. L., Cabonell, E., Rosas, A., Martinez, I., & Mosquera, M. (1997). A Hominid from the lower Pleistocene of Atapuerca, Spain: Possible ancestor to Neandertals and modern humans. *Science, 276,* 1392–1395.

Berra, T. M. (1990). *Evolution and the myth of creationism.* Stanford, CA.: Stanford University Press.

Blumer, M. A., & Byrne, R. (1991). The ecological genetics and domestication and the origins of agriculture. *Current Anthropology, 32,* 23–54.

Bodley, J. H. (1985). *Anthropology and contemporary human problems* (2nd ed.). Palo Alto, CA: Mayfield.

Brace, C.L. (2000). *Evolution in an anthropological view.* Walnut Creek, CA: Brace, C. L. (1997). Cro-Magnons Я us? *Anthropology Newsletter, 38,* (8), 1, 4.

Branda, R. F., & Eatoil, J. W. (1978). Skin color and photolysis: An evolutionary hypothesis. *Science, 201,* 625–626.

Bull, J. J., & Wichman, H. A. (1998). A revolution in evolution. *Science, 281,* 1959.

Carneiro, R. L. (1970). A theory of the origin of the state, *Science, 169,* 733–738.

Cartmill, M. (1998). The gift of gab. *Discover 19*(11), 64.

Cavallo, J. A. (1990, February) Cat in the human cradle. *Natural History,* pp. 54–60.

Chambers, R. (1983). *Rural development: Putting the last first.* New York: Longman.

Chan, J. W. C. and Vernon, P. E. (1988). Individual differences among the peoples of China. In J. W. Berry (Ed.), *Human abilities in cultural context* (pp. 340–357). Cambridge: Cambridge University Press.

Chicurel, M. (2001). Can organisms speed their own evolution? *Science, 292:* 1824–1827

Ciochon, R. L., & Fleagle, J. G. (1987). *Ramapithecus* and human origins. In R. L. Ciochon & J. G. Fleagle (Eds.), *Primate evolution and human origins.* Hawthorne, NY: Aldine de Gruyter.

Clark, E. E. (1966). *Indian legends of the Pacific Northwest.* Berkley: University of California Press.

Clark, G. A. (1997). Neandertal genetics. *Science, 277,* 1024.

Coe, S. D. (1994). *America's first cuisines.* Austin, TX: University of Texas Press.

Coe, W. R., & Haviland, W. A. (1982). *Introduction to the archaeology of Tikal.* Philadelphia: University Museum.

Cohen, J. (1997). Is an old virus up to new tricks? *Science, 277,* 312–313.

Cohen, M., & Armelagos, G. (Eds.). (1984). *Paleopathology at the origins of agriculture.* Orlando, FL: Academic Press.

Colburn, T., Dumanoski, D., & Myers, J. P. (1996). Hormonal sabotage. *Natural History, 3,* 45–46.

Connor, M. (1996). The archaeology of contemporary mass graves. *SAA Bulletin, 14*(4), 6 & 31.

Conroy, G. C. (1997). *Reconstructing human origins: A Modern Synthesis.* New York: W. W. Norton.

Cornwell, T. (1995, Nov. 10). Skeleton staff. *Times Higher Education,* p. 20.

Corruccini, R. S. (1992). Metrical reconsideration of the Skhul IV and IX and Border Cave I Crania in the context of modern human origins. *American Journal of Physical Anthropology, 87,* 433–445.

Cowgill, G. L. (1997). State and society at Teotihuacan, Mexico. *Annual Review of Anthropology, 26,* 129–161.

Culotta, E. (1992). A new take on anthropoid origins. *Science, 256,* 1516–1517.

Culotta, E., & Koshland, D. E., Jr. (1994). DNA repair works its way to the top. *Science, 266,* 1926.

de Waal, F. (1996). *Good natured: The origins of right and wrong in humans and other animals.* Cambridge, MA: Harvard University Press.

de Waal, F., Kano, T., & Parish, A. R. (1998). Comments. *Current Anthropology, 39,* 407–408, 410–411, 413–414.

de Waal, F., Kano, T., & Parish, A. R. (1998). Comments. *Current Anthropology, 39,* 408, 410, 413.

de Waal, F. (2001). Sing the song of evolution. *Natural History 110*(8):76–77.

de Waal, F. (2001). *The ape and the sushi master.* New York: Basic Books.

Diamond, J. (1994). Race without color. *Discover, 15*(11): 83–89.

Diamond, J. (1996). Empire of uniformity. *Discover, 17*(3), 78–85.

Diamond, J. (1997). *Guns, germs and steel.* New York: Norton.

Diamond, J. (1998). Ants, crops, and history. *Science, 281,* 1974–1975.

Doist, R. (1997). Molecular evolution and scientific inquiry, misperceived. *American Scientist, 85,* 475.

Donnan, C. B., & Castillo, L. J. (1992). Finding the tomb of a Moche priestess. *Archaeology 45*(6), 38–42.

Durant, J. C. (2000). Everybody into the gene pool. *New York Times Book Review,* April 23, 11–12.

Fagan, B. M. (1995). The quest for the past. In L. L. Hasten (Ed.). *Annual Editions 95/96, Archaeology* (p. 10). Guilford, CT: Dushkin.

Fagan, B. M. (1998). *People of the earth* (9th ed.). New York: Longman.

Falk, D. (1989). Ape-like endocast of "Ape Man Taung." *American Journal of Physical Anthropology, 80,* 335–339.

Falk, D. (1993). A good brain is hard to cool. *Natural History, 102*(8), 65.

Falk, D. (1993). Hominid paleoneurology. In R. L. Ciochon & J. G. Fleagle (Eds.). *The human evolution source book.* Englewood Cliffs, NJ: Prentice-Hall.

Ferber, D. (2000). Superbugs on the hoof? *Science, 288,* 792–794.

Feder, K. L. (1999). *Frauds, myths, and mysteries* (3rd ed.). Mountain View, CA: Mayfield.

Federoff, N. E., & Nowak, R. M. (1997). Man and his dog. *Science, 278,* 305.

Ferguson, T. J. (1996). Archaeology for and by Native Americans. Paper presented at the 95th Annual Meeting, American Anthropological Association.

Fernandez-Carriba, S. and Loeches, A. (2001). Fruit smearing by captive chimpanzees: a newly observed food-processing behavior. *Current Anthropology, 42,* 143–147.

Ferrie, H. (1997). An interview with C. Loring Brace. *Current Anthropology, 38,* 851–869.

Folger, T. (1993). The naked and the bipedal. *Discover, 14*(11), 34–35.

Fox, R. (1968). *Encounter with anthropology.* New York: Dell.

Frake, C. O. (1992). Lessons of the Mayan sky. In A. F. Aveni (Ed.), *The sky in Mayan literature* (pp. 274–291). New York: Oxford University Press.

France, D. L., & Horn, A. D. (1992). *Lab manual and workbook for physical anthropology* (2nd ed.), New York: West.

Frayer, D. W. (1981). Body size, weapon use, and natural selection in the European Upper Paleolithic and Mesolithic. *American Anthropologist, 83,* 57–73.

Freeman, L. G. (1992). Ambrona and Torralba: New evidence and interpretation [paper]. 91st Annual Meeting of the American Anthropological Association, San Francisco.

Gabunia, L., Vekua, A., Lordkipanidze, D., Swisher III, C. C., Ferring, R., Justus, A., Nioradze, M., Tvalchrelidze, M., Anton, S. C., Bosinski, G., Joris, O., de Lumley, M-A., Majsuradze, G., and Mouskhelishvili. (2000). Earliest Pleistocene hominid cranial remains from Dmanisi, Republic of Georgia: Taxonomy, geological setting, and age. *Science, 288,* 1019–1025.

Gamble, C. (1986). *The Paleolithic settlement of Europe.* Cambridge: Cambridge University Press.

Gebo, D. L., MacLatchy, L., Kityo, R., Deino, A., Kingston, J., & Pilbeam, D. (1997). A hominoid genus from the early Miocene of Uganda. *Science, 276,* 401–404.

Gebo, D. L., Dagosto, D., Beard, K.C., and Tao, Q., (2001). Middle Eocene primate tarsals from China: Implications for haplorhine evolution. *American Journal of Physical Anthropology.* 116:83–107.

Geertz, C. (1984). Distinguished lecture: Anti-relativism. *American Anthropologist, 86,* 263–278.

Gibbons, A. (1993). Where are new diseases born? *Science, 261,* 680-681.

Gibbons, A. (1996). Did Neandertals lose an evolutionary "arms" race? *Science, 272,* 1586–1587.

Gibbons, A. (1997). A new face for human ancestors. *Science, 276,* 1331–1333.

Gibbons, A. (1997). Ideas on human origins evolve at anthropology gathering. *Science, 276,* 535–536.

Gibbons, A. (1998). Ancient island tools suggest *Homo erectus* was a seafarer. *Science, 279,* 1635–1637.

Gibbons, A., & Culotta, E. (1997). Miocene primates go ape. *Science, 276,* 355–356.

Gibbons, A. (2001). Studying humans—and their cousins and parasites. *Science, 292,* 627–629.

Gibbons, A. (2001). The riddle of coexistence. *Science, 291,* 1726.

Glausiusz, J. (1995). Hidden benefits. *Discover, 16*(3), 30–31.

Glausiusz, J. (1995). Micro gets macro. *Discover, 16*(11), 40.

Goodall, J. (1986). *The chimpanzees of Gombe: Patterns of behavior.* Cambridge, MA: Belknap Press.

Goodenough, W. (1990). Evolution of the human capacity for beliefs. *American Anthropologist, 92,* 597–612.

Goodman, M., Bartez, W. J., Hayasaka, K., Stanhope, M. J., Slightom, J., & Czelusniak, J. (1994). Molecular evidence on primate phylogeny from DNA sequences. *American Journal of Physical Anthropology, 94,* 3–24.

Gordon, R. (1981, December). [Interview for Coast Telecourses, Inc.]. Los Angeles.

Gould, S. J. (1985). *The flamingo's smile: Reflections in Natural History.* New York: Norton.

Gould, S. J. (1989). *Wonderful life.* New York: Norton.

Gould, S. J. (1991). *Bully for Brontosaurus.* New York: Norton.

Gould, S. J. (1996). *Full house: The spread of excellence from Plato to Darwin.* New York: Harmony Books.

Gould, S. J. (2000). What does the dreaded "E" word mean, anyway? *Natural History, 109*(1), 28–44.

Graves, J. L. (2001). *The emperor's new clothes: biological theories of race at the millennium.* New Brunswick, NJ: Rutgers.

Grine, F. E. (1993). Australopithecine taxonomy and phylogeny: Historical background and recent interpretation. In R. L. Ciochon & J. G. Fleagle (Eds.), *The human evolution source book.* Englewood Cliffs, NJ: Prentice-Hall.

Grün, R., & Thorne, A. (1997). Dating the Ngandong humans, *Science, 276,* 1575.

Halverson, J. (1989). Review of *Altimira revisited and other essays on early art, American Antiquity, 54,* 883.

Harrison, G. G. (1975). Primary adult lactase deficiency: A problem in anthropological genetics. *American Anthropologist, 77,* 812–835.

Hartwig, W. C., & Doneski, K. (1998). Evolution of the Hominid hand and toolmaking behavior. *American Journal of Physical Anthropology, 106,* 401–402.

Haviland, W. A., et al. (1985). *Excavations in small residential groups of Tikal: Groups 4F-1 and 4F-2.* Philadelphia: University Museum.

Haviland, W. A., & Power, M. W. (1994). *The original Vermonters: Native inhabitants, past and present* (Rev. and expanded ed.). Hanover, NH: University Press of New England.

Haviland, W. A. (2002). Settlement, society and demography at Tikal. In J. Sabloff (Ed.), *Tikal.* Santa Fe, NM: School of American Research (in press).

Holden, C. (1996). Missing link for miocene apes. *Science, 271,* 151.

Holden, C. (1998). No last word on language origins. *Science, 282,* 1455–1458.

Holden, C. (1999). A new look into Neandertal's noses. *Science, 285,* 31–33.

Hole, F. & Heizer, R. F. (1969). *An introduction to prehistoric archeology.* New York: Holt, Rinehart & Winston.

Holloway, R. L. (1981). The Indonesian Homo erectus brain endocast revisited. *American Journal of Physical Anthropology, 55,* 503–521.

Houle, A. (1999). The origin of platyrrhines: An evaluation of the Antarctic scenario and the floating island model. *American Journal of Physical Anthropology, 109:* 541–559.

Ingmanson, E. J. (1998). Comment. *Current Anthropology 39,* 409–410.

Jacoby, R., & Glauberman, N. (Eds.) (1995). *The bell curve.* New York: Random House.

Jolly, C. J., & Plog, F. (1986). *Physical anthropology and archaeology* (4th ed.). New York: Knopf.

Jones, S., Martin, R. and Pilbeam, D. (Eds.). (1992). *The Cambridge Encyclopedia of Human Evolution.* New York: Cambridge Univ. Press.

Kaiser, J. (1994). A new theory of insect wing origins takes off. *Science, 266,* 363.

Karavani, I., and Smith, F. H. (2000). More on the Neanderthal problem: the Vindija case. *Current Anthropology, 41,* 838–840.

Kay, R. F. (1981). The nut-crackers—A new theory of the adaptations of the Ramapithecinae. *American Journal of Physical Anthropology, 55,* 141–151.

Kay, R. F., Ross, C., & Williams, B. A. (1997). Anthropoid origins. *Science, 275,* 797–804.

Kirkpatrick, R.C. (2000). The evolution of human homosexual behavior. *Current Anthropology, 41,* 385–413.

Koufos, G. (1993). Mandible of *Ouranopithecus macedoniensis* (hominidae: primates) from a new Late Miocene locality in Macedonia (Greece). *American Journal of Physical Anthropology, 91,* 225–234.

Kramer, P. A. (1998). The costs of human locomotion: maternal investment in child transport. *American Journal of Physical Anthropology, 107,* 71–85.

Kunzig, R. (1999). A tale of two obsessed archaeologists, one ancient city and nagging doubts about whether science can ever hope to reveal the past. *Discover, 20*(5), 84–92.

Lawler, A. (2001). Writing gets a rewrite. *Science, 292,* 2419.

Leach, E. (1982). *Social anthropology.* Glasgow: Fontana Paperbacks.

LeGros Clark, W. E. (1966). *History of the primates* (5th ed.). Chicago: University of Chicago Press.

Leigh, S. R., & Park, P. B. (1998). Evolution of human growth prolongation. *American Journal of Physical Anthropology, 107,* 331–350.

Leonard, W. R., & Hegman, M. (1987). Evolution of P_3 morphology in *Australopithecus afarensis. American Journal of Physical Anthropology, 73,* 41–63.

Lestel, D. (1998). How chimpanzees have domesticated humans. *Anthropology Today, 14* (3) 12–15.

Lev-Yadun, S., Gopher, A., and Abbo, Shahal. (2000). The cradle of agriculture. *Science, 288,* 1602–1603.

Lewin, R. (1987). Debate over emergence of human tooth pattern. *Science, 235,* 749.

Lewin, R. (1987). The earliest "humans" were more like apes. *Science, 236,* 1062–1063.

Lewin, R. (1987). Four legs bad, two legs good. *Science, 235,* 969.

Lewin, R. (1993). Paleolithic paint job. *Discover, 14*(7) 64–70.

Lewis, I. M. (1976). *Social anthropology in perspective.* Harmondsworth, England: Penguin.

Lewontin, R. C., Rose, S., & Kamin, L. J. (1984). *Not in our genes.* New York: Pantheon.

Lorenzo, C., Carretero, J. M., Arsuaga, J. L., Gracia, A., & Martinez, I. (1998). Intrapopulational body size variation and cranial capacity variation in middle Pleistocene humans: The Sima de los Huesos sample (Sierra de Atapuerca, Spain). *American Journal of Physical Anthropology, 106,* 19–33.

Lovejoy, C. O. (1981). Origin of man. *Science, 211*(4480), 341–350.

Lowenstein, J. M. (1992). Genetic surprises. *Discover, 13*(12), 82–88.

MacLarnon, A. M. & Hewitt, G.P. (1999). The evolution nof human speech: the role of enhanced breathing control. *American Journal of Physical Anthropology, 109,* 341–363.

MacNeish, R. S. (1992). *The origins of agriculture and settled life.* Norman, OK: University of Oklahoma Press.

Marcus, J., & Flannery, K. V. (1996). *Zapotec civilization: How urban society evolved in Mexico's Oaxaca Valley.* New York: Thames & Hudson.

Marshack, A. (1976). Some implications of the Paleolithic symbolic evidence for the origin of language. *Current Anthropology, 17*(2), 274–282.

Marshack, A. (1989). Evolution of the human capacity: The symbolic evidence. *Yearbook of Physical Anthropology, 32,* 1–34.

Marshall, M. (1990). Two tales from the Trukese taproom. In P. R. DeVita (Ed.), *The humbled anthropologist* (pp. 12–17). Belmont, CA: Wadsworth.

Marshall, E. (2001). Preclovis sites fight for acceptance. *Science, 291,* 1732.

McCorriston, J., & Hole, F. (1991). The ecology of seasonal stress and the origins of agriculture in the Near East. *American Anthropologist, 93,* 46–69.

McGrew, W.C. (2000). Dental care in chimps. *Science, 288,* 1747.

McHenry, H. M. (1992). Body size and proportions in early hominids. *American Journal of Physical Anthropology, 87,* 407–431.

McKenna, J. (1997, October). Bedtime story, *Natural History, 50.*

Mellars, P. (1989). Major issues in the emergence of modern humans. *Current Anthropology, 30,* 349–385.

Meltzer, D., Fowler, D. & Sabloff, J. (Eds.). (1986). *American archaeology: Past and future.* Washington, DC: Smithsonian Institution Press.

Miles, H. L. W. (1993). Language, and the orangutan: The old "person" of the forest. In P. Cavalieri & P. Singer (Eds.), *The great ape project* (pp. 42–57). New York: St. Martin's.

Miller, J. M. A. (2000). Craniofacial variation in *Homo habilis*: An analysis of the evidence for multiple species. *American Journal of Physical Anthropology, 112,* 103–128.

Mintz, S. (1996). A taste of history. In W. A. Haviland & R. J. Gordon (Eds.), Talking about people (2nd ed., pp. 79–82). Mountain View, CA: Mayfield.

Mintz, S. (2002). A taste of history. In W. A. Haviland and R. J. Gordon (Eds.), Talking about people (3rd ed., pp. 87–90). New York: McGraw Hill.

Moffat, A. S. (2002). New Fossils and a glimpse of evolution. *Science, 295,* 613–615.

Moore, J. (1998). Comment. *Current Anthropology, 39,* 412.

Moscati, S. (1962). *The face of the ancient Orient.* New York: Doubleday.

Mydens, S. (2001). He's not hairy, he's my brother. *New York Times,* August 12, Section 4, p. 5.

Neer, R. M. (1975). The evolutionary significance of Vitamin D, skin pigment and ultraviolet light. *American Journal of Physical Anthropology, 43,* 409–416.

Normile, D. (1998). Habit seen as playing larger role in shaping behavior. *Science, 279,* 1454.

Normile, D. (2001). Gene expression differs in human and chimp brains. *Science, 292,* 44–45.

Nunney, L. (1998). Are we selfish, are we nice, or are we nice because we are selfish? *Science, 281,* 1619.

Oliwenstein, L. (1995). New footsteps into walking debate. *Science, 269,* 476.

Olszewki, D. I. (1991). Comment. *Current Anthropology, 32,* 43.

Otte, M. (2000). On the suggested bone flute from Slovenia. *Current Anthropology, 41,* 271–272.

Parés, J. M., Perez-Gonzalez, A., Weil, A.B., and Arsuaga, J. L. (2000). On the age of hominid fossils at the Sima de los Huesos, Sierra de Atapuerca, Spain: paleomagnetic evidence. *American Journal of Physical Anthropology, 111,* 451–461.

Parish, A. R. (1998). Comment. *Current Anthropology, 39,* 413–414.

Parnell, R. (1999). Gorilla exposé. *Natural History, 108*(8), 38–43.

Pickering, T. R., White, T. D., and Toth, N, (2000). Cutmarks on a Plio-Pleistocene Hominid from Sterkfontein, South Africa. *American Journal of Physical Anthropology, 111,* 579–584.

Pilbeam, D. (1986). *Human origins.* David Skamp Distinguished Lecture in Anthropology, Indiana University.

Pilbeam, D. (1987). Rethinking human origins. In *Primate evolution and human origins.* Hawthorne, N.Y.: Aldine de Gruytar.

Pimentel, D. (1991). Response. *Science, 252,* 358.

Piperno, D. R. (2001). On maize and the sunflower. *Science, 292,* 2260–2261.

Pitt, D. (1977). Comment. *Current Anthropology, 18,* 628.

Plattner, S. (1989). Markets and market places. In S. Plattner (Ed.), *Economic anthropology.* Stanford, CA: Stanford University Press.

Pope, G. (1989, October). Bamboo and human evolution. *Natural History, 98,* 48–57.

Pope, G. G. (1992). Craniofacial evidence for the origin of modern humans in China. *Yearbook of Physical Anthropology, 35,* 243–298.

Power, M. G. (1995). Gombe revisited: Are chimpanzees violent and hierarchical in the free state? *General Anthropology, 2*(1), 5–9.

Pringle, H. (1997). Ice Age communities may be earliest known net hunters. *Science, 277,* 1203–1204.

Pringle, H. (1998). The slow birth of agriculture. *Science, 282,* 1446–1450.

Puleston, D. E. (1983). *The settlement survey of Tikal.* Philadelphia: University Museum.

Rappaport, R. A. (1994). Commentary. *Anthropology Newsletters, 35*(6), 76.

Recer, P. (1998, February 16). Apes shown to communicate in the wild. *Burlington Free Press,* p. 12A.

Relethford, J. H., & Harpending, H. C. (1994). Craniometric variation, genetic theory, and modern human origins. *American Journal of Physical Anthropology, 95,* 249–270.

Relethford, J. H. (2001). Absence of regional affinities of Neandertal DNA with living humans does not reject multiregional evolution. *American Journal of Physical Anthropology, 115,* 95–98.

Rice, P. (2000). Paleoanthropology 2000—part 1. *General Anthropology, 7* (1), 11.

Richmond, B. G., Fleangle, J. K., & Swisher III, C. C. (1998). First Hominoid elbow from the miocene of Ethiopia and the evolution of the Catarrhine elbow. *American Journal of Physical Anthropology, 105,* 257–277.

Ridley, M. (1999). *Genome, the autobiography of a species in 23 chapters.* New York: HarperCollins.

Rightmire, G. P. (1990). *The evolution of Homo erectus: Comparative anatomical studies of an extinct human species.* Cambridge: Cambridge University Press.

Rightmire, G. P. (1998). Evidence from facial morphology for similarity of Asian and African representatives of *Homo erectus. American Journal of Physical Anthropology, 106,* 61–85.

Rindos, D. (1984). *The origins of agriculture: An evolutionary perspective.* Orlando, FL: Academic Press.

Rogers, J. (1994). Levels of the genealogical hierarchy and the problem of hominoid phylogeny. *American Journal of Physical Anthropology, 94,* 81–88.

Romer, A. S. (1945). *Vertebrate paleontology.* Chicago: University of Chicago Press.

Roosevelt, A. C. (1984). Population, health, and the evolution of subsistence: Conclusions from the conference. In M. N. Cohen & G. J. Armelagos (Eds.), *Paleopathology and the origins of agriculture.* Orlando, FL: Academic Press.

Rosas, A., & Bermdez de Castro, J. M. (1998). On the taxonomic affinities of the Dmanisi mandible (Georgia). *American Journal of Physical Anthropology, 107,* 145–162.

Rosas, A. (2001). Occurrence of Neandertal features from the Atapunerea-SH site. *American Journal of Physical Anthropology, 114,* 74–91.

Sanday, P. R. (1975). On the causes of IQ differences between groups and implications for social policy. In A. Montagu (Ed.), *Race and IQ.* London: Oxford.

Sanjek, R. (Ed.) (1990). *Fieldnotes: The making of anthropology.* Ithaca, NY: Cornell University Press.

Schepartz, L. A. (1993). Language and human origins. *Yearbook of Physical Anthropology, 36,* 91–126.

Schwartländer, B., Garnett, G., Walker, N. and Anderson, R. (2000). AIDS in a new millennium. *Science, 289,* 64–67.

Selim, J. (2002). Out of left field. *Discover, 23* (1), 30–31.

Sellen, D. W., & Mace, R. (1997). Fertility and mode of substance: A phylogenetic analysis. *Current Anthropology, 38,* 878–889.

Shearer, R. R. and Gould, S. J. (1999). Of two minds and one nature. *Science, 286,* 1093.

Shipman, P. (1981). *Life history of a fossil: An introduction to taphonomy and paleoecology.* Cambridge, MA: Harvard University Press.

Shreeve, J. (1994). Terms of estrangement. *Discover, 15*(11), 56–63.

Shreeve, J. (1995). *The Neandertal enigma.* New York: Willliam Morrow.

Sillen, A. & Brain, C. K. (1990). Old flame. *Natural History, 4,* 6–10.

Simons, E. L. (1989). Human origins. *Science, 245,* 1343–1350.

Simons, E. L. (1995). Skulls and anterior teeth of *Catopithecus* (primates: anthropoidea) from the Eocene and anthropoid origins. *Science, 245,* 1885–1888.

Simpson, S. (April 1995). Whispers from the ice. *Alaska,* pp. 22–29.

Sjoberg, G. (1960). *The preindustrial city.* New York: Free Press.

Solis, R. S., Haas, J., and Creamer, W. (2001). Dating Caral, a preceramic site in the Supe valley on the central coast of Peru. *Science, 292,* 723–726.

Solomon, R. (2001). Genome's riddle. *New York Times,* February 20, p. D3.

Spuhler, J. N. (1979). Continuities and discontinuities in anthropoid-hominid behavioral evolution: Bipedal locomotion and sexual reception. In N. A. Chagnon & W. Irons, (Eds.), *Evolutionary Biology and human social behavior* (pp. 454–461). North Scituate, MA: Duxbury Press.

Stahl, A. B. (1984). Hominid dietary selection before fire. *Current Anthropology, 25,* 151–168.

Stanford, C. G. (1998). The social behavior of chimpanzees and bonobos: empirical evidence and shifting assumptions. *Current Anthropology, 39,* 399–420.

Stiner, M. C., Munro, N. D., Surovell, T. A., Tchernov, E., and Bar-Yosef, O. 1999). Paleolithic population growth pulses evidenced by small annual exploitation. *Science, 283,* 190–194.

Stone, R. (1995). If the mercury soars, so may health hazards. *Science, 267,* 958.

Stringer, C. B., & McKie, R. (1996). *African exodus: The origins of modern humanity.* London: Jonathan cape.

Tardieu, C. (1998). Short adolescence in early hominids: Infantile and adolescent growth of the human femur. *American Journal of Physical Anthropology, 107,* 163–178.

Thomas, D. H. (1998). *Archaeology* (3rd. ed.). Fort Worth, TX: Harcourt Brace.

Thomson, K. S. (1997). Natural selection and evolution's smoking gun. *American Scientist, 85,* 516–518.

Tobias, P. V., & von Konigswald, G. H. R. (1964). A comparison between the Olduvai hominines and those of Java and some implications for hominid phylogeny. *Nature, 204,* 515–518.

Togue, R. G. (1992). Sexual dimorphism in the human bony pelvis, with a consideration of the Neanderthal pelvis from Kebara Cave, Israel. *American Journal of Physical Anthropology, 88,* 1–21.

Trinkaus, E., & Shipman, P. (1992). *The Neandertals: Changing the image of mankind.* New York: Alfred A. Knopf.

Weatherford, J. (1988). *Indian givers: How the Indians of the Americas transformed the world.* New York: Fawcett Columbine.

Weiner, J. S. (1955). *The Piltdown forgery.* Oxford: Oxford University Press.

Wheeler, P. (1993). Human ancestors walked tall, stayed cool. *Natural History, 102*(8), 65–66.

Whiting, J. W. M., Sodergem, J. A., & Stigler, S. M. (1982). Winter temperature as a constraint to the migration of preindustrial peoples. *American Anthropologist, 84,* 289.

Whitten, A, and Boesch, C. (2001). Cultures of chimpanzees. *Scientific American, 284*(1), 63–67.

Wills, C. (1994). The skin we're in. *Discover, 15*(11), 77–81.

Wittfogel, K. A. (1957). *Oriental despotism, A comparative study of total power.* New Haven, CT: Yale University Press.

Wolpoff, M. H. (1993). Evolution in *Homo erectus*: The question of stasis. In R. L. Ciochon & J. G. Wolpoff, M.H. (1999). Review of Neandertals and modern humans in western Asia. *American Journal of Physical Anthropology, 109,* 416–423.

Wolpoff, M.H., Hawks, J., Frayer, D. W., and Hunley, K. (2001). Modern human ancestry at the peripheries: a test of the replacement theory. *Science, 291,* 293–297.

Wolpoff, M., & Caspari, R. (1997). *Race and human evolution.* New York: Simon & Schuster.

Wong, K. (1998, January). Ancestral quandary: Neanderthals not our ancestors? Not so fast. *Scientific American,* pp. 30–32.

Wood, B., & Aiello, L. C. (1998). Taxonomic and functional implications of mandibular scaling in early Hominines. *American Journal of Physical Anthropology, 105,* 523–538.

Wood, B., Wood, C., & Konigsberg, L. (1994). *Paranthropus boisei*: An example of evolutionary stasis? *American Journal of Physical Anthropology, 95,* 117–136.

Wood, B. and Collard, M. (1999). The human genus. *Science, 284,* 68.

Woodward, V. (1992). *Human heredity and society.* St. Paul, MN: West.

Zeder, M. A. and Hesse, B. (2000). The initial domestication of goats *(Capra hircus)* in the Zagros mountains 10,000 years ago. *Science, 287,* 2254–2257.

Zilhão, J. (2000). Fate of the Neandertals. *Archaeology, 53* (4), 30.

Zimmer, C. (1999). New date for the dawn of dream time. Science, 284, 1243–1246.

Zimmer, C. (2001). *Evolution: the triumph of an idea.* New York: HarperCollins.

Zohary, D., & Hopf, M. (1993). *Domestication of plants in the Old World* (2nd ed.). Oxford: Clarenden Press.

PHOTO CREDITS

2 © Ancient Art & Architecture Collection; 3 © James Stanfield / NGS Image Collection; 4 © Giraudon / Art Resource, NY; 7 (top) The Granger Collection, New York; 7 (bottom) Smithsonian Institution Photo No. 56196; 8 Courtesy of Vice-Chancellor Mamphela Ramphele, © Shawn Benjamin; 9 AP / Wide World Photos; 11 (left) © Rhoda Sidney / PhotoEdit; 11 (right) © Laura Dwight / PhotoEdit; 12 © Roger Ressmeyer / Corbis; 13 Photographs furnished by the U.S. General Services Administration; 15 Peggy O'Neill-Vivanco; 20 © Mark Richards / PhotoEdit; 21 (top) © Bettmann / Corbis; 21 (middle) The Granger Collection, New York; 21 (bottom) Culver Pictures; 24 © Bettmann / Corbis; 27 AP / Wide World Photos; 28 Gordon Gahan / NGS Image Collection; 28 (top left) Wartenberg / Picture Press / Corbis; 28 (bottom) Alden Pellett / The Image Works; 29 © Paula Bronstein / Getty Images; 32 © Sisse Brimberg / NGS Image Collection; 35 AP / Wide World Photos; 37 Courtesy of Glenn Sheehan and Anne Jensen; 39 © 1985 David L. Brill; 40 Courtesy of Institute for Exploration; 41 © Mike Andrews / Ancient Art & Architecture Collection; 42 © James B. Petersen, Dept. of Anthropology, University of Vermont; 43 © G. Gorgoni / eStock Photo; 46 (both) © William A. Haviland; 47 Reprinted with permission from Kuttruff et al, Science 281, 73 (1998) fig. 1. Copyright 1998 American Association for the Advancement of Science; 48 From *Tikal, A Handbook of the Ancient Maya Ruins* by William R. Coe. University of Pennsylvania Museum, Philadelphia 1967; 49 © Andrew Lawler / Science Magazine; 51 University of Pennsylvania Museum; 54 © Kenneth Garrett / NGS Image Collection; 58 © UNEP-Topham / The Image Works; 61 (top left) © Morgan / Anthro-Photo; 61 (top right) © Michael J. Doolittle / The Image Works; 61 (bottom left) © Cleo Freelana Photos / PhotoEdit; 61 (bottom right) © Colin Milkins, Oxford Scientific Films / Animals, Animals; 62 © Layne Kennedy / Corbis; 63 © Bettmann / Corbis; 68 (top) © Photo Researchers, Inc.; 68 b © SuperStock; 70 © Biophoto Associates / Photo Researchers, Inc.; 73 © Meckes / Ottawa / Photo Researchers, Inc.; 75 (top) © 2002 Don Couch Photography; 75 (bottom) © The Image Works; 76 AP/Wide World Photos; 77 (top left) © George Obremski; 77 (top right) © Steve Elmore; 77 (bottom) © Lawrence Manning / Woodfin Camp and Associates; 79 (both) © E. R. Degginger/Color-Pic, Inc.; 80 (both) © E. R. Degginger/Color-Pic, Inc.; 82 Otorohanga Zoological Society; 86 © 1997 Tom Brakefield / The Image Works; 87 © Bojan Brecelj / Corbis; 88 © 1998 Jim Leachman; 90 © Bettmann / Corbis; 92 © James Moore / Anthro-Photo; 96 (both) © 1998 Jim Leachman; 97 (top) © Reuters / Getty Images; 100 (left) AP / Wide World Photos; 100 (right) © David Agee / Anthro-Photo; 101 © Michael Dick / Animals, Animals; 102 (top) © E. R. Degginger / Color-Pic, Inc.; 102 (bottom) © Peter Drowne / Color-Pic, Inc.; 103 (left) © Miriam Silverstein / Animals, Animals; 103 (right) © David Watts / Anthro-Photo; 105 © Irven DeVore / Anthro-Photo; 106 (both) © Anita de Laguna Haviland;

107 (top) © Bromhall / Animals Animals; 107 (bottom) © Amy Parish / Anthro-Photo; 111 © Bromhall / Animals Animals; 114 © David Bygott / Kibuyu Partners; 118 Illustration by Nancy J. Perkins; 121 (top) © 1999 Don Couch Photography; 121 (bottom left) © David Bygott / Kibuyu Partners; 121 (bottom right) © Donna Day / Corbis; 124 © O. Louis Mazzatenta / NGS Image Collection; 126 © Anita de Laguna Haviland; 127 © Martin Harvey; 129 © E. L. Simons / Duke Primate Center; 130 © Ollie Ellison / Duke University; 131 © 1985 David L. Brill; 137 © 1985 David L. Brill; artifact credit, Peabody Museum, Harvard University; 138 © Anup and Manoj Shah; 140 © National Museums of Kenya; 141 Irven DeVore/Anthro-Photo; 144 © 1998 David L. Brill \ Brill Atlanta; 146 AP/Wide World Photos; 148 1985 David L. Brill by permission of Owen Lovejoy; 151 © William H. Kimbel, Ph.D., Institute of Human Origins; 152 © Tim White, Department of Anthropology, University of California at Berkeley; 154 (left) Lee R. Burger, PURE, University of Witwatersrand; 154 (right) © Des Bartlett / NGS Image Collection; 155 © Melville Bell Grosvenor / National Geographic Society; 156 © National Museums of Kenya; 157 (top) © 1985 David L. Brill; artifact credits, (left) A. africanus, Transvaal Museum, Pretoria, (right) A. boisei, National Museum of Tanzania, Dar es Salaam; 157 (bottom) © 1994 Tim O. White / David L. Brill, Atlanta; 158 2000 © Philippe Plailly / Eurelios; 159 © Dr. Fred Spoor / National Museums of Kenya; 160 Photo by Dr. Rose Sevcik. Courtesy of The Language Research Center, Georgia State University; 161 © John Giustina; 166 © Michael Nichols / NGS Image Collection; 168 © John-Marshall Mantel / Corbis; 169 © Archivo Iconografico, S.A. / Corbis; 170 National Museums of Kenya; 176 (left) © National Museums of Kenya; 176 (right) © Kenneth Garrett / NGS Image Collection; 179 all David L. Brill, copyright © The National Geographic Society; 180 t © William A. Haviland; 180 (bottom) © J & B Photo/Animals, Animals; 182 © E. R. Degginger/Color-Pic, Inc.; 185 © Andy Freeberg; 186 © Sue Savage-Rumbaugh / Language Research Center; 187 © Anita de Laguna Haviland; 188 (top) © David Bygott / Anthro-Photo; 188 (bottom left and right) © 1993 Mary Ann Fittipaldi; 192 © Russell L. Ciochon, University of Iowa; 194 (top) Negative No. A11. Courtesy Department of Library Sciences, American Museum of Natural History; 194 (bottom) Courtesy of Dr. Phillip V. Tobias, South Africa; 196 © Russell Ciochon, University of Iowa; 197 (top) National Museums of Kenya; 197 (bottom left) Transparency No. 626. Courtesy Department of Library Sciences, American Museum of Natural History; 197 (bottom right) © 1985 David L. Brill; artifact credit, National Museum of Kenya, Niarobi; 198 © Antoine Devouard/REA/Corbis SABA; 199 Kenneth Garrett/NGS Image Collection; 201 National Museum of Kenya; 203 (right) © R. Potts and W. Huang, Human Origins Program; 203 (left) © R. Potts, Smithsonian Institution; 207 (top) © R. Potts, Smithsonian Institution; 207 (bottom) © 1985 David L. Brill;

208 Geoffrey G. Pope, Anthropology Department, The William Paterson College of New Jersey; **210** © 1985 David L. Brill; **211** (both) © Kenneth Garrett / NGS Image Collection; **212** © Alexander Marshack; **216** © 1995 David L. Brill\Atlanta, original housed in the British Museum; **219** (top) © Javier Trueba/Madrid Scientific Films; **219** (bottom left) © 1985 David L. Brill; artifact credit, National Museum of Ethiopia, Addis Ababa; **219** (bottom right) Zhou Guoxing, Beijing Natural History Museum; **222** ©1985 David L. Brill; **223** (top) Paul Jaronski, UM Photo Services. Karen Diane Harvey, Sculptor; **223** (bottom) Professor Wu Xinzhi, Bejing, China; **224** © Milford H. Wolpoff; **225** © Photo Researchers; **226** © Ralph S. Solecki; **228** (both) © Alexander Marshack, New York University; **229** Neandertal flute / University of Liege. Courtesy of Marcel Otte; **231** Negative No. 335658. Courtesy Department of Library Sciences, American Museum of Natural History; **233** Courtesy of Dr. Ofer Bar-Yosef and Dr. B. Vandermeersch. Item from Israel Antiquities Authority; **234** Iziko Museums of Capetown; **235** © Sally McBrearty; **240** Cliché Philippe Morel, Ministère de la Culture et de la Communication; **242** © 1985 David L. Brill; artifact credit, Musee De L'Homme, Paris; **244** © McBrearty / Anthro-Photo; **246** (both) © William A. Haviland/UVM Photo Service; **250** © Alexander Marshack, 1997; **251** (both) © Anita de Laguna Haviland; **252** (top left) Negative No. K15806. Courtesy Department of Library Services, American Museum of Natural History; **252** (right) Negative No. K15872. Courtesy Department of Library Services, American Museum of Natural History; **252** (bottom left) Negative No. K15823. Courtesy Department of Library Services, American Museum of Natural History; **253** © Jean Vertut; **255** © Randall White; **256** © Claudio Vazquez; **257** © Göran Burenhult; **259** (top) Peabody Museum; **259** (bottom) Joe Ben Wheat Photo, University of Colorado Museum, Boulder; **260** Courtesy of Anthropos Institute, Brno; **261** Jose Zilhao © Instituto Portugues Arqueologia; **262** (left) Professor Wu Xinzhi, Bejing, China; **262** (right) Drawing from Up From The Ape by Earnest A. Hooton, Copyright © 1931, 1946 by The MacMillan Company, New York; **266** AFP Photo Steven Jaffe © AFP / Corbis; **267** University of Pennsylvania Museum Image #T35-882; **268** Paul Conklin/PhotoEdit; **271** © William A. Haviland; **273** W. Fitzhugh; **274** © William A. Haviland; **275** (top left, top right) © Dr. W. van Zeist, Biologisch-Archaeologisch Institut, Rijksuniversiteit Gronigen; **275** (bottom) Dr. Dolores Piperno/Smithsonian Tropical Research Institute; **276** Illustration by W. C. Galinat. Reprinted with permission from W. C. Galinat, "The origin of maize: grain of humanity," Economic Botany Vol. 49, pp. 3–12, fig. 2A-C, Copyright 1995, The New York Botanical Garden; **278** AP / Wide World Photos; **281** © Mark Richards / PhotoEdit; **282** © Pierre Boulat / Woodfin Camp & Associates; **284** Courtesy of Zhijun Zhao; **285** © Mireille Vautier / Woodfin Camp & Associates; **287** © Bettmann / Corbis; **288** © BSIP / Chassenet / Photo Researchers, Inc.; **289** © Harvey Finkle; **290** Courtesy of the Oriental Institute of the University of Chicago; **291** (both) British School of Archaeology in Jerusalem; **293** (top) Ankara Archaeological Museum /Ara Guler, Istanbul; **293** (bottom) © John Kegan / Getty Images; **295** (both) © Alan H. Goodman, Hampshire College; **296** © Sepp Seitz / Woodfin Camp & Associates; **300** © Anita de Laguna Haviland; **304** © Arlette Mellaart; **305** © Richard Reed / Anthro-Photo; **307** (top) © William A. Haviland; **307** (bottom) © Enrico Ferorelli; **308** © Anita de Laguna Haviland; **310** The University Museum, University of Pennsylvania (neg. #T4-398); **311** (top) Peter D'Arcy Harrison; **311** (bottom) Ban Chiang Project, University of Pennsylvania Museum; **312** (top left, top right) © Ronald Sheridan/Ancient Art & Architecture Collection; **312** (bottom) Negative No. 330878. Courtesy Department of Library Sciences, American Museum of Natural History; **313** © Heather Angel / Biofotos; **314** © Getty Images; **318** (both) Dr. Christopher B. Donnan / UCLA Fowler Museum of Cultural History; **319** (top, middle, bottom left) Dr. Christopher B. Donnan / UCLA Fowler Museum of Cultural History; **319** (bottom right) Studied by Duccio Bonavia, reproduction by Gonzalo de Reparaz, Painting by Felix Caycho; **322** (top) © Anita de Laguna Haviland; **322** (bottom) © William A. Haviland; **325** (top) © James Mellaart; **325** (bottom) © Victor R. Boswell / NGS Image Collection; **326** © Mohenjo/Anthro-Photo; **327** Cultural Relics Bureau, Beijing; **330** © Terry Vine / Corbis; **334** (left) © Lauré Communications/Eliot Elisofon/National Museum of African Art; **334** (right) © Jean-Pierre Hallet / The Pygmy Fund; **335** AP / Wide World Photos; **339** © Laurence Dutton / Getty Images; **340** © Lawrence Migdale; **341** (both) Photo © Dinodia Photo Library; **341** (right) © A. Ramey/PhotoEdit; **342** AP / Wide World Photos; **343** AP / Wide World Photos; **344** © Steve Elmore; **345** (top) © Beryl Goldberg; **345** (bottom left) © Farrell Grehan / Photo Researchers, Inc.; **345** (bottom middle) © Richard Wood; **345** (bottom right) © E. R. Degginger / Color-Pic, Inc.; **346** Royal Anthropological Institute Photographic Collection; **349** (both) Dr. Cloyce G. Coffman / Texas A & M University; **351** (both) AP / Wide World Photos; **352** © Bill Clark / The Daily Progress; **353** AP / Wide World Photos; **355** (top) © VCL / Getty Images; **355** (bottom) AP / Wide World Photos.

LITERARY CREDITS

"Turnabout Map" © 1982, 1990 by Jesse Levine, (650) 494–7729.

Excerpt from E. E. Clark, *Indian Legends of the Pacific Northwest* © 1966. The Regents of University of California. Reprinted with permission.

Original Study: Based on The Strange Case of "Piltdown Man" from *The Piltdown Forgery* by J. S. Weiner (1955). Oxford University Press.

Original Study: "Whispers from the Ice." Adapted excerpt from "Whispers from the Ice" by Sherry Simpson, *Alaska*, April 1995, pp. 23–28. Reprinted with permission of the author.

Figure 2.1: Grid of ancient Mayan city of Tikal. University of Pennsylvania Museum (neg. #61-5-5).

Original Study: "The Unsettling Nature of Variational Change" from "What does the dreaded 'E' Word mean, anyway?" by S. J. Gould. With permission from *Natural History*, February 2000. Copyright the American Museum of Natural History 2000. Reprinted with permission.

Anthropology Applied: "Anthropology and the Ethical, Legal and Social Implications of the Human Genome Project" by D. E. Walrath (2001). Reprinted courtesy of D. E. Walrath.

Original Study: "Culture of Chimpanzees," by A. Whitten and C. Boesch, (2001) from *Scientific American*, 284(1). Reprinted with permission. Copyright © 2000 by Scientific American, Inc. All rights reserved.

Original Study: "Will the real human ancestor please stand up?" (2001) by D. E. Walrath. Reprinted courtesy of D. E. Walrath.

Original Study: "The naked and the bipedal," (1993) by Tim Folger. Used with permission.

Original Study: "Cat in the Human Cradle" by J. A. Cavallo. With permission from *Natural History*, February 1990. Copyright the American Museum of Natural History 1990. Reprinted with permission.

Figure 7.6: Flaked stone tool production. Reprinted with the permission of Simon & Schuster Adult Publishing Group from *Making Silent Stones Speak* by Kathy D. Schick and Nicholas Toth. Copyright © 1993 by Kathy D. Schick and Nicholas Toth.

Original Study: "Homo Erectus and the use of Bamboo" by G. C. Pope. With permission from *Natural History*, February 1989. Copyright the American Museum of Natural History 1989. Reprinted with permission.

Original Study: "African Origin or Ancient Population Size Difference." Reprinted with the permission of Simon & Schuster, Inc. from *Race and Human Evolution* by Milford Wolpoff and Rachel Caspari. Copyright © 1996 by Milford Wolpoff and Rachel Caspari.

Original Study: Excerpt from "Paleolithic Paint Job" (1993) by Roger Lewin, *Discover*, 14(7), pp. 67–69. Reprinted with permission of Roger Lewin.

Original Study: "History of Mortality and Physiological Stress," excerpt from "Population, health, and the evolution of subsistence: Conclusions from the conference" by A. C. Roosevelt in M. N. Cohen & G. J. Armelagos (Eds), *Paleopathology and the origins of agriculture*, pp. 572–574 (1984). Reprinted with permission.

Excerpt from "Editors' Summation" in M. N. Cohen & G. J. Armelagos (Eds), *Paleopathology and the origins of agriculture*, pp. 594 (1984). Reprinted with permission.

Figure 12.2: Grid-map of Teotihuacan © René Millon 1973. Reprinted with permission.

Original Study: "Finding the Tomb of a Moche Priestess," by C.B. Donnan & L. J. Castillo. Reprinted with permission of *Archaeology Magazine*, Volume 45, Number 6 (Copyright the Archaeological Institute of America, 1992).

Original Study: "Race without Color," by J. Diamond, *Discover*, 15(11), 1994, pp. 83-88. Reprinted with permission of Dr. Jared Diamond.

Abell, Paul, 152
Acheulean tool tradition, 199–205
Adaptation, 79–83
Aegyptopithecus, 130, 131
Africa:
    areas of early domestication, 283
    Australopithecus fossil sites in, 146, 147
    Bushmen of the Kalahari Desert, 287
    falciparum malaria, 3, 80–82, 296, 338, 352
    Homo erectus fossils, 195–196
    Homo sapiens fossil sites, 218
    human fossil remains sites, 40
    invention of bow and arrow, 245
    Lake Turkana *Homo erectus* fossil, 195, 197
    late Miocene vegetation zones, 165
    Neandertal fossils from, 223–224
    Olduvai Gorge, 53, 154, 155
African Americans:
    ethnographic studies of, 16
    intelligence testing of, 348–349
    rates of sickle-cell trait in, 81
Ainu, 259
Alleles, 70
Alva, Walter, 320
Ambrose, Stanley, 229
American Anthropological Association (AAA), 7, 24
American Association for the Advancement of Science, 18
American Sign Language:
    primate use of, 109
Americas:
    Archaic cultures in, 272
    areas of early domestication, 283, 284
    colonization by Upper Paleolithic peoples, 258–260, 263
    native civilizations and use of metal, 312
Amino acid racemization, 53–54
Animal domestication:
    areas of early development, 283
    diseases acquired from domesticated animals, 296
    early evidence of, 276
    of pigs, 282–283
    transhumance, pattern of, 281
    unconscious selection in, 275
    of wild sheep and goats, 280–282
Anthropology:
    archaeology, field of, 12–14
    contributions to contemporary life, 25–28
    cultural anthropology, field of, 10–12
    cultural comparison in, 22–24
    defined, 5, 6, 7
    development of, 7–8
    discipline of, 8, 10–17

ethics and obligations, 25
ethnohistory, 22–23
ethnology, field of, 14–17
European cultural values and, 8
fact, defined, 17
forensic anthropology, field of, 9–10
hypothesis, defined, 18
interacting with other sciences, 8
linguistic anthropology, field of, 14
museums of, 18
physical anthropology, field of, 8–10
relation to the humanities, 24–25
as a science and scientific work of, 17–22
subfields of, 8, 12
theory, defined, 18
using fieldwork, 6
Anthropomorphism, 60
Apes:
    hand and foot bone comparisons with humans and *Homo habilis,* 171, 173
    in primate order, 102–104
    trunk skeleton comparisons with hominines and humans, 150
    upper hip bone comparisons with hominines and humans, 153
    upper jaw comparisons with hominines and humans, 150
Applied anthropology:
    archaeology for and by Native Americans, 286
    in cultural resource management, 44
    economic development and tropical forests, 309
    ethical, legal, and social implications of the Human Genome Project, 69
    forensic anthropology and, 9–10
    forensic archaeology in, 227
    in primate conservation, 110
    stone tools for modern surgeons, 245–246
    studying the emergence of diseases, 357
Archaeological and Historical Preservation Act of 1974, 44
Archaeology:
    "absolute" dating, 51
    accurate and detailed excavation records, 48
    altered fossils, 39
    amino acid racemization dating, 53–54
    analysis of technology of a site, 50
    Archaeological and Historical Preservation Act of 1974, 44
    archaeology sites, defined, 33
    area of study, 5, 33–56
    artifacts of, 34
    as branch of cultural anthropology, 12–14

burial and cemetery sites, 40
chance circumstances and, 54–55
chronometric dating, 51, 52–54
cooperative efforts with Native Americans, 286
as cultural resource management, 44
dating remains, 33
datum point, 44
dendrochronology, 53
discovering sites, 42–43
electron spin resonance dating, 54
employment of archaeologists, 44
endocasts, 49
flotation, 44, 46
fluorine test dating, 52
fossil, defined, 35
fossil localities, 33–34, 40
"Garbage Project," 13
grid system, 43–44
Historic Preservation Act, 44, 286
"hit and run archaeology," 38
importance of context, 34–35
interpretation of fossils, 4
kill sites, 40, 247, 259, 260
methods of dating the materials, 51–54
methods of recovery, 34–40
National Environmental Policy Act of 1969, 44
paleoanthropologists and, 34, 35, 46–47
palynology method of dating, 52
potassium-argon analysis, 53
prehistoric, defined, 34
processing materials in the lab, 48–50
radiocarbon analysis, 52–53
relative dating, 51, 52
removing matrix, 47
respecting indigenous culture, 37–38
returning skeletons for reburial, 51
site and locality identification, 41–43
site excavation, 33, 43–47
sites, defined, 40
sites as nonrenewable resource, 48
social stratification studies, 317–322
soil marks, 41
sorting out the evidence, 48–51
state of preservation, 47–48
stratified site, 46
stratigraphy dating technique, 52
study of burials and grave goods, 317
unaltered fossils, 35, 39
village sites, 40
Archaic cultures, 272
Archaic *Homo sapiens,* 113
    appearance of *Homo sapiens,* 218–219
    Aurignacian tool tradition, 230, 231
    brain size compared to modern humans, 242
    cold climate adaptations, 225

Archaic *Homo sapiens (continued)*
　culture of, 224–230
　deliberate burials by Neandertals,
　　226–227
　development of hafting, 220
　"Eve" or "Out of Africa" hypothesis,
　　233–237
　evidence of physically disabled Neandertals, 226
　hypoglossal canal in Neandertals, 229
　Levalloisian technique, 220
　mass hunting techniques of archaic
　　Homo sapiens, 225–226
　Middle Paleolithic tools, 224–226
　"Mitochondrial Eve," 233–237
　and modern human origins, 230–237
　Mousterian tradition, 224–226
　multiregional hypothesis, 230–232
　Neandertals, 221–222
　spoken language in Neandertals,
　　228–230
　symbolic life of Neandertals, 226–228
　use of red ocher and yellow pigments,
　　221, 227
Ardipithecus ramidus, 157–159, 164
Armelagos, George, 297
Art:
　body ornamentation in Upper Paleolithic,
　　255–256
　cave art and engravings, 250–255
　entoptic phenomena, 250, 255
　Middle Paleolithic "crayons," 248
　rock art, 250–255
　in Upper Paleolithic peoples, 247–256
　Venus figures, 251, 252
Asiatic langur, 101
Asthma, 76
Aurignacian tradition, 230, 231
Australia:
　Arnhem Land study, 22
　colonization by Upper Paleolithic
　　peoples, 256–258, 263
　Murngin aborigines, 16
　rock art of entoptic motifs, 250–251, 253
　studies of Aborigines, 16, 22
Australopithecus:
　appearance of, 87, 145
　Ardipithecus ramidus, 157–159, 164
　Australopithecine predecessors, 157–159
　Australopithecus robustus, 154–155, 156
　bipedal locomotion in, 148, 151–154,
　　161–167
　Black Skull of, 155–156, 173
　dentition for eating meat, 176
　environment, diet, and Australopithecine
　　origins, 159–161
　Gracile Australopithecines, 146, 147–154
　Kenyanthropus platyops, 158–159, 173
　"Lucy," 147, 148, 151–152
　Orrorin tugenensis, 158
　plant/meat eating and brain size, 185

relations between *Homo habilis* and *Australopithecus,* 172–174, 175
　Robust Australopithecines, 146, 154–156
　sexual dimorphism in, 149, 151
　sites of fossil remains, 146, 147
　species of, 148
　Zinjanthropus boisei, 154
Australopithecus aethiopicus, 148, 155, 156
Australopithecus afarensis, 148, 149
Australopithecus anamensis, 148, 149
Australopithecus boisei, 148, 155, 172
Australopithecus garhi, 148
Australopithecus robustus, 148, 154–155,
　156

Baboons, 101
　behavior with leopards, 182
Barley, domestication of, 280
Behrensmeyer, Kay, 180
Bell Curve, The (Herrnstein and Murray), 349
Bible, 7, 8
Biological anthropology, 10
Bipedal locomotion:
　in *Australopithecus,* 145, 151–154,
　　161–167
　disadvantages of, 161
　in hominine evolution, 148, 151–154,
　　161–167
Birdsell, Joseph, 335, 344
Black, Davidson, 193, 231
Blade technique, 243
Blood types, A-B-O system in humans, 66,
　67, 70, 72, 332, 333
Blumenschine, Robert J., 181
Boas, Franz, 18, 335
Boehm, Christopher, 79
Boesch, C., 113, 115
Bonobos, 99, 103–104
　communication of, 109
　home ranges of, 109–110
　hunting activities of, 112
　individual interactions, 106
　sexual behavior, 106, 107
　social groups, 104–105
　use of objects as tools, 112, 160
Bow and arrow, invention of, 245
Brachiators, 97, 101, 102, 103
Braidwood, Robert, 278
Brain, C. K., 181, 206
Brewster, Karen, 36
Bronze Age:
　archaeological sites, 41
　period of, 311–312
Broom, Robert, 154
Bunn, Henry, 179
Bureau of American Ethnology, 7, 18
Burials/burial practices:
　indicating social stratification, 317–321
　of Maritime Archaic culture, 273
Burns, Karen, 227
Bush, George W., 26

Carneiro, Robert, 324
Carver, George Washington, 351
Caspari, Rachel, 242
Çatalhöyük, 303–305, 324, 325
Cayuse Indians, 6
Childe, V. Gordon, 277, 278, 279
Child-rearing practices:
　infants, sleeping arrangements with
　　parents, 11
Chile:
　Monte Verde site of Upper Paleolithic
　　remains, 258
Chimpanzee Material Cultures (McGrew), 113
Chimpanzees:
　behavior with leopards, 182
　communication of, 108, 109
　community social group, 104
　consumption of meat, 186
　cultural behavior of, 113–115
　genus *Pan,* 99
　grooming activities, 105–106
　handedness of, 188
　home ranges of, 109, 110
　hunting activities of, 112, 186
　individual interactions, 106
　infant mortality in, 165, 166
　learning abilities, 111
　play activity, 109
　sexual behavior of, 106
　use of objects as tools, 111–112
China:
　areas of early domestication, 283
　first cities in, 302
　Homo erectus sites, 192, 193–194
　Neandertal fossils from, 223–224
　sites of *Homo sapiens* fossils, 219
Chromosomes, 68, 70
Chronometric dating, 51, 52–54
Cities:
　and agricultural innovation, 310–311
　civilization in Çatalhöyük, 303–305, 324,
　　325
　and diversification of labor with growth
　　of, 311–313
　economic development and tropical
　　forests, 309
　in history of civilization, 302
　impact of warfare, 327
　internal stress of class system, 327
　Neolithic villages into towns, 302
　problems associated with civilization,
　　326–329
　sanitation and waste disposal problems,
　　326
　social problems associated with, 327
　social stratification with city growth,
　　316–322
Civilization:
　action theory of emergence of, 324–325
　agricultural innovation and growth of
　　cities, 310–311

ancient kings and government of, 315–316

appearance of the Bronze Age, 311–312

central government with growth of cities, 313–316

cities and associated cultural changes, 309–322

city of Tikal, 306–309, 310

collapses of, 327

competition for resources in emergence of, 324

defined, 302–306

diversification of labor with growth of cities, 311–313

economic development and tropical forests, 309

hydraulic theory of emergence of, 323

problems associated with, 326–329

sanitation and waste disposal problems in cities, 326

sites of early development, 303

social stratification with cities, 316–322

theories of civilization emergence, 322–325

trade and impact on emergence of, 323–324

writing and central government in cities, 314–316

Clan of the Cave Bear, The (Auel), 242

Clark, Ella, 6

Classification of living things:
analogies, 60
classification of humans, 62
early mammals, 125–126
genera/genus, 60
homologies, 60
mammalian order, 90–91
species, 60
theory of evolution, 61–65
warm-blooded *versus* cold-blooded, 126

Clavicle, in primates, 96–97

Clothing:
of Neolithic period, 292–293
of Upper Paleolithic peoples, 256

Cognitive capacity, in Upper Paleolithic peoples, 260

Cohen, Mark, 297

Color-naming, as impact of biology, 3

Convergence, 122–123

Coon, Carleton, 201, 335, 344

Corn (maize), domestication of, 275–276

Cotton, domestication of, 285

Crabtree, Don, 245

Crick, Francis, 65

Cro-Magnon:
rock shelter site in France, 242

Cross-cultural comparisons:
of infant sleeping arrangements, 11
time devoted to "housework," 16–17

Cultural anthropology:
area of study, 2, 5, 10–12

as branch of linguistic anthropology, 14

compared with sociology or psychology, 10, 11

divisions of, 12–15

Cultural diversity, impact of domestication and food production on, 296–298

Culture:
defined, 10

Culture-bound, 11

Cushing, Frank Hamilton, 7

Custer, George Armstrong, 9

Cystic fibrosis, 326

Czechoslovakia, Upper Paleolithic kill site, 247

Darnton, John, 221

Dart, Raymond, 146, 147

Darwin, Charles:
Descent of Man, The, 19

Darwin, Charles R.:
on biological evolution, 19
evolution as descent with modification, 60
human evolution theory, 120
theory of evolution and natural selection, 61–65
on unconscious selection, 275
voyage and studies on *HMS Beagle,* 63

Darwin, Erasmus, 63

Dating of archaeological materials, 51–54

Dawson, Charles, 19

Dendrochronology, 53

Deniker, J., 335

de Priest, James, 342

DeVore, Irven, 245

de Waal, Frans, 83

Diamond, Jared, 277

Diastema, 150

Dinosaurs, 124, 126

Disease and mortality:
AIDS, recent emergence of, 357
associated with civilization and growth of cities, 326–329
chicken pox, 326
Dengue fever, 357
Ebola, 357
Hantavirus, 357
HIV, 357
incidence of diabetes, 354
increase in Neolithic farming populations, 294–295, 296
influenza, 326
invasive Streptococcus, 357
Lassa fever, 357
Legionnaire's disease, 357
Lyme disease, 357
malaria, 80–82, 296, 338, 352
measles, 326
mumps, 326
pertussis, 326
polio, 326

rubella, 326
smallpox, 326
tuberculosis, 326

Divergent or branching evolution, 122–123

Dixon, Dean, 342

Dixon, Roland B., 335

DNA, 65
chromosomes of, 68, 70
codon, 66
ribosomes, 66
RNA, 66
structure of, 65–66
transcription process, 66
translation process, 66

Domestication:
beginnings of, 276–277
defined, 273–274
diseases acquired from domesticated animals, 296
evidence of early plant and animal domestication, 274–276
Fertile Crescent, 278, 279
"hilly flanks" theory of food production, 278
horticultural communities, 297
impact on cultural diversity, 296–298
intensive agriculture, 297
Irish potato famine, 287–288
oasis theory of food production, 277–278
in pastoralism, 297–298
population growth theory of food production, 278
spread of food production, 287–289
storage of food, 280
theories of transition to food production, 277–283
theory of chance convergence of natural and cultural elements, 279–280
unconscious selection, 275
vegeculture, 283

Dubois, Eugene, 192

Early primates:
adaptive radiation of early mammals, 125–126
Aegyptopithecus, 130, 131
and convergence, 122–123
divergent or branching evolution, 122–123
early apes and human evolution, 141
ecological niches of early mammals, 126
Eocene primates, 128–129
hominids, 132–136
hominines, 138
hominoid adaptations and late Miocene climatic change, 138–140
hominoids, 132, 136, 137
human origins and Miocene apes, 137–141
isolating mechanisms, 120–122

Early primates *(continued)*
  Kenyapithecus, 137, 139
  linear evolution, 123
  Miocene apes, 130–138
  move to arboreal existence, 127
  nondirectedness of evolution, 123–124
  Oligocene monkeys and apes, 129–130
  Paleocene primates, 127
  Proconsul, 131–132, 133–134
  races or subspecies, 120
  Ramapithecus, 135, 136
  rise of primates, 126–137
  Sivapithecus, 135, 136, 137, 138
  speciation, 120–124
East Timor, 28
Ebola, 357
Egypt:
  development of geometry, 312
  evidence of central government in cities,
    314
  Fayum depression, 129–130
  first cities in, 302
  native civilizations and access to trade,
    312
Ehrenberg, Israel, 335
Einstein, Albert, 351
Electron spin resonance dating, 54
Entoptic phenomena, 250, 255
Eoanthropus dawsoni, 19
Epicanthic eye fold, 344
Estrus, in primates, 98
Ethnographic Atlas, An (Murdock), 23
Ethnohistory, 22–23
Ethnology:
  area of study, 5
  as branch of cultural anthropology,
    14–17
  ethnography, 14
  ethnohistory, 22–23
  ethnologist, 14
  holistic perspective in, 14
  informants, 15
  participant observation, 14, 24
Eugenics, 335
Europe:
  Homo erectus fossil sites in, 196–197
  Homo sapiens fossil sites, 218
  Neandertal burial sites, 227
  Upper Paleolithic art, 251–256
"Eve" or "Out of Africa" hypothesis,
    233–237
Evolution:
  adaptation, 79–83
  convergence, 122–123
  as descent with modification, 60
  divergent or branching evolution,
    122–123
  early mammals, 125–126
  early primate evolution, 126–142
  evolutionary forces, 74–79
  gene flow, 76–77

genetic drift, 76
genetic mutation, 74–75
interspecies transfer, 77, 78
isolating mechanisms, 120–122
law of competitive exclusion, 156
linear evolution, 123
mutation, 74–75
natural selection, 62–65, 77–79
nondirectedness of, 123–124
selfish behavior benevolent, 79
sickle-cell anemia, 80–82
speciation, 120–124
stabilizing selection, 78–79
"survival of the fittest," 78
theory of, 61–65
transformational model of change, 64
variational theory of, 64–65

Fact, defined, 17
Falciparum malaria, 3, 80–82, 296, 338, 352
Farming:
  agricultural innovation and growth of
    cities, 310–311
  archaeological evidence in Mexico,
    284–285
  disease and mortality in Neolithic popu-
    lation, 294–295, 296
  horticulturists, 297
  impact on cultural diversity, 296–298
  impact on hemoglobin in response to
    malaria, 3, 81–82, 296
  intensive agriculturalists, 297
  narrow range of resources and risk of
    failure, 287–288
  slash-and-burn farming, 20
  time and labor involved in early farming,
    277
Faunal region, 332
Female Power and Male Dominance
    (Sanday), 23
Ferguson, T. J., 286
Fertile Crescent, 278, 279
Flannery, Kent, 324
Fluorine test dating, 52
Food foraging:
  contemporary populations of, 277
  theories for change to food production,
    277–283
Food production:
  "hilly flanks" theory of, 278
  impact on cultural diversity, 296–298
  increased fertility rates, 287
  Irish potato famine, 287–288
  oasis theory of, 277–278
  population growth theory of, 278
  risk of failure with narrow range of plant
    resources, 287–288
  spread of, 287–289
  storage of food, 280
  theories for transition from food foraging,
    277–283

theory of chance convergence of natural
    and cultural elements, 279–280
Forensic anthropology, 9–10
Forensic archaeology, 227
Fossey, Dian, 105, 155
Fossil localities, 33–34, 40
Fovea centralis, 94
Fox, Robin, 24
France:
  La Chapelle-Aux-Saints site, 221
  Les Eyzies Cro-Magnon rock shelter, 242
  Pech Merle Upper Paleolithic cave
    paintings, 252–254
  Upper Paleolithic kill site, 247
Freeman, Paul, 342

Galdikas, Birute, 105, 155
"Garbage Project," 13
Garn, Stanley, 335, 344
Gender:
  dominant roles of women, 23
Gene flow, 76–77
Gene pool, 73, 74
Genera/genus, 60
Genes, 65
  alleles, 70
  in DNA molecules, 65–70
  enzyme, 66
  genetic code, 66
  genome, 67
  Human Genome Project, 69
Genetic code, 66
Genetic drift, 76
Genetics:
  Fragile X syndrome, 75
  gene flow, 76–77
  gene pool, 73, 74
  genetic drift, 76
  genotype, 72
  Hardy-Weinberg principle, 74
  heterozygous, 72
  homozygous, 71–72
  Huntington's disease, 75
  interspecies transfer, 77, 78
  "jumping genes," 75
  "junk" DNA, 74–75
  law of dominance and recessive, 72
  mutation, 74–75
  phenotype, 72
  polygenetic inheritance, 72–73
  population, 73
  science of, 68
Genotype, 72
Gibbons, 102, 103
Gombe Chimpanzee Reserve, 105, 113, 115
Goodall, Jane, 104, 105, 106, 110, 113, 155
Gordon, Robert, 14
Gorillas, 102, 103
  "family" social group, 105
  home ranges of, 109
  individual interactions, 106

play activity, 109
sexual behavior, 106, 107
Gould, Stephen Jay:
anthropology and the scientific approach, 20
"golden barriers," 115
progressive advancement of life, 124
on variational change, 63, 64–65
Gracile Australopithecines, 146, 147–154
Guereza monkey, 101

Hammurabi, Code of, 315
Handedness:
in *Homo habilis,* 188
in humans, 188
Harcharek, Jana, 37, 38
Hardenbergh, Firmon, 246
Hardy-Weinberg principle, 74
Harpending, Henry, 236
Heizer, Robert F., 46
Hemoglobin, 3, 72, 81–82, 296
Heredity:
cell division and growth, 70–72
chromosomes, 68, 70
DNA, 65
gene pool, 73, 74
genes, 65
genetic code, 66
genotype, 72
Hardy-Weinberg principle, 74
homozygous and heterozygous chromosomes, 71–72
Human Genome Project, 69
law of dominance and recessive, 72
law of independent assortment, 65
law of segregation, 65
meiosis, 70–71
Mendelian genetics, 65, 68
mitosis, 70, 71
phenotype, 72
polygenetic inheritance, 72–73
sickle-cell anemia, 72, 73
transmission of genes, 65–73
Herodotus, 7, 314
Herrnstein, Richard, 349
Heterozygous, 72
Hispanic population, ethnographic studies of, 16
Historic Preservation Act, 44, 286
HIV/AIDS, 357
recent emergence of, 357
as a retrovirus, 66, 67
Hocquenghem, Anne Marie, 320
Hole, Frank, 46
Holistic perspective, 14
Home ranges of primates, 109–110
Hominids, ancestors of, 132–136
Hominine evolution:
Ardipithecus ramidus, 157–159, 164
Australopithecine predecessors, 157–159
Australopithecus, species of, 148

Australopithecus aethiopicus, 148, 155, 156
Australopithecus afarensis, 148, 149
Australopithecus africanus, 146–148
Australopithecus anamensis, 148, 149
Australopithecus boisei, 148, 155
Australopithecus fossil remains, 146–156
Australopithecus garhi, 148
Australopithecus robustus, 148
bipedal locomotion, 148, 151–154, 161–167
Black Skull, 155–156
environment, diet, and Australopithecine origins, 159–161
genus *Homo,* 151
Gracile Australopithecines, 146, 147–154
Kenyanthropus platyops, 158–159, 173
"Lucy," 147, 148, 151–152
"Millennium Man," 158
Orrorin tugenensis, 158
Robust Australopithecines, 146, 154–156
sagittal crest in, 154
sexual dimorphism in *Australopithecus,* 149, 151
trunk skeleton comparisons, 150
upper jaw comparisons, 150
Zinjanthropus boisei, 154
Hominines, 138
Hominoidea, 133
Hominoids, in the Miocene epoch, 132, 136, 137
Homo:
appearance of, 171
evidence of tool use, 170
fossil evidence of genus *Homo,* 170–174
hominine genus of, 151
Homo Rudolfensis, 170
KNM ER 1470, fossil of, 170
Homo erectus:
Acheulean tool tradition, 199–205
Africa, fossil finds in, 195–196
archaeological site of, 42
bamboo, use of, 201–204
baton method of percussion, 204
China, fossil sites in, 39–40, 193–194
construction of shelters, 207–208
culture of, 198–207
European sites of, 196–197
fire and cooking, use of, 206–207
Homo antecessor, 196
Homo heidelbergensis, 196
hunting live animals, 208–209
hypoglossal canal in, 210–211
Java, fossil sites in, 192
linguistic and language competence, 210–211
mandibular similarity to *Australopithecus,* 149
physical characteristics of, 197, 198
Pithecanthropus erectus, 192
red ochre pigment, use of, 210

relationship with *Homo habilis,* 198
Sinanthropus pekinensis, 193
symbolic artifacts, 209–210
tools for hunting, 208–209
Homo habilis:
cooperation and sharing, 187
dentition for eating meat, 176
earliest sign of culture with tools, 185–186
early representatives of genus *Homo,* 170–174
foraging for food and meat, 179–185
hand and foot bone comparisons with human and apes, 171, 173
handedness of, 188
language origins, 188
Lower Paleolithic tools, 174–185
meat eating and brain size, 185
Oldowan tools, 175, 176–179
relation between *Homo habilis* and *Australopithecus,* 172–174, 175
theft of tree-stored leopard kills, 179–182
tools, meat, and brains, 179–185
Homo Rudolfensis, 170
Homo sapiens:
anthropology study of, 6
Homosexual activity:
anthropological documentation of, 27
Homozygous, 71–72
Hooton, Earnest, 335
Horticulture/horticulturists:
communities of domestication, 297
Howell, F. Clark, 135
Human Genome Project, 69
Human Relations Area File (HRAF), 23
Hungary, Mousterian site in, 228
Hunting:
by archaic *Homo sapiens,* 225–226
by chimpanzees, 112, 186
by *Homo erectus,* 208–209
invention of bow and arrow, 245
in Upper Paleolithic peoples, 244–247, 263
Huxley, Thomas, 63
Hypoglossal canal:
in *Homo erectus,* 210–211
in Neandertals, 229
Hypothesis, defined, 18

Ibn Khaldun, 7
Inca empire and government, 316
Indus Valley:
evidence of cities, 313
first cities in, 302
Informants, 15
Intelligence:
considerations of race, 348–351
measurement of, 350–351
Intensive agriculture, 297
Interspecies transfer, 77, 78
Inupiat History, Language, and Culture, 36

Iraq:
  Neandertal burial sites, 227
Islam:
  proper burial practices, 227
Isolating mechanisms, 120–122
Israel:
  Neandertal burial sites, 227
  Qafzeh site, 232, 233
  Skuhl site, 232

Japan:
  Ainu people of, 259
Japanese macaques, 110–111
Java:
  Homo erectus fossil sites, 192
  Neandertal fossils sites in, 223–224
Jenkins, Carol, 357
Jensen, Anne, 36, 37, 38
Jericho farming community site, 290
Johanson, Donald, 39
Jungers, William L., 180

Kamin, Leon, 349
Keller, Albert, 23
Kenyanthropus platyops, 158–159, 173
Kenyapithecus, 137, 139, 173
Klickitat Indians, 6
KNM ER 1470:
  cranial capacity comparison with *Homo erectus,* 197
  relation to *Australopithecus,* 172, 173
Kroll, Ellen, 179

Lactase enzyme, 338–339, 353
Lactose tolerance, 353–354
Language:
  abilities in *Homo erectus,* 210–211
  Basque language, 289
  Black English (BE), 16
  "Ebonics," 16
  Neandertals and spoken language, 228–230
  origins with *Homo habilis,* 188
  primate use of American Sign Language, 109
Leach, Edmund, 16
Leakey, Louis, 43, 105, 155, 170, 172
Leakey, Mary, 43, 154, 155, 172
Leakey, Meave, 155, 158–159, 173
Leakey, Richard, 155, 170
Leavitt, George, 36
LeGros Clark, W. E., 94
Lemurs, 100, 130
Levalloisian technique, 220
Lewin, Roger, 251
Lewontin, Richard, 349
Linear evolution, 123
Linguistics:
  area of study, 5
  as branch of cultural anthropology, 5, 14
Linnaeus, 60–61, 63

Linton, Sally, 183
Lorblanchet, Michel, 251, 252–254
Lowenstein, Jerold, 67
Lower Paleolithic tools, 174–185
"Lucy," 147, 148, 151–152
Lyell, Charles, 63
Lyon, Patricia, 320

Macaques, 101
Mahale Chimpanzee Research, 113, 115
Maize (corn), domestication of, 275–276, 284
Malaria:
  development of sickle-cell anemia, 80–82
  human antimalarial genes and, 338
  human biological response to, 3
  persistence of, 352
  presence in farming regions, 296
Mammals:
  early mammals, 125–126
  ecological niches of, 126
  warm-blooded versus cold-blooded animals, 126
Man Makes Himself (Childe), 278
Man's Most Dangerous Myth: The Fallacy of Race (Montagu), 335
Marcus, Joyce, 324
Maritime Archaic culture, 272–273
Marriage:
  same-sex marriages, 27
Marshack, Alexander, 210, 228
Maya civilization, 26
  central government in Tikal, 314
  city of Tikal, 306–309, 310
  development of astronomy, 313
  economic development and tropical forests, 309, 310
  system of writing, 314–315, 316
  theory of emergence of civilization at Tikal, 324
  Tikal site, 21, 42, 43, 45, 46, 48, 51
McFarlane, Len, 245
McGrew, William C., 113
Meiosis, 70–71
Melanin, 344
Mendel, Gregor, 65, 68
Mengele, Josef, 9
Mesoamerica:
  first cities in, 302
Mesolithic period:
  Archaic cultures, 272
  composite tools of, 271, 272
  cultural diversity in, 271–273
  evidence of stress and disease in populations, 294–295, 296
  microliths in tool kit, 270–271
  Natufian culture, 272, 279–280
  tools and weapons of, 270–271
Mesopotamia:
  evidence of writing, 314
  first cities in, 302

Metal, Bronze Age period, 311–312
Mexico:
  Teotihuacan, 304, 305, 313
Microliths in Mesolithic tool kit, 270–271
Middle Paleolithic period:
  Qafzeh, Israel site of, 54
  tool tradition, 224–226
  use of "crayons" in art, 248
Middle Stone Age, 270
Miles, Hugh, 180
"Millennium Man," 158
Mintz, Sidney, 286
"Missing link," 19–20
"Mitochondrial Eve," 233–237
Mitosis, 70, 71
Monkeys:
  early ancestors of, 130
Montagu, Ashley, 335
Mousterian tradition, 224–226
Movius, Hallam, 201
mtDNA, in archaic *Homo sapiens,* 233–237
Multiregional hypothesis of archaic *Homo sapiens,* 230–232
Murdock, George Peter, 23
Murray, Charles, 349
Mutation, 74–75

Nash, Philleo, 15
Nation, 28
National Academy of Sciences, 354
National Endowment for the Humanities, 24, 25
National Environmental Policy Act of 1969, 44
National Institute of Health (NIH), ethical, legal, and social implications (ELSI) of the Human Genome Project, 69
National Science Foundation, 24, 36
Native Americans:
  Blackfoot Indians, 333
  Blood Indians, 333
  cooperative efforts with archaeologists, 286
  ethnographic studies of, 16
  frequency of blood types, 333
  return of skeletons for reburial, 51
  Snake River Indians, 6
Natufian culture, 272, 279–280
Natural selection, 62–65, 77–79
Neandertals:
  African, Chinese, and Javanese populations, 223–224
  culture of archaic *Homo sapiens,* 224–230
  deliberate burials by, 226–227
  "Eve" or "Out of Africa" hypothesis, 233–237
  mammoth tooth *churinga,* 227, 229
  "Mitochondrial Eve," 233–237
  modern human origins and, 230–237
  multiregional hypothesis, 230–232

"occipital bun" in skulls of, 242
skeletal remains of, 48
skull and bone features, 221–222
and spoken language, 228–230
symbolic life of, 226–228
Neanderthal (Darnton), 221
Negovanna, Silas, 36
Neolithic period, 270
    burial practices of, 317
    cultural changes with growth of cities, 309–322
    culture of Neolithic settlements, 289–293
    earliest farming settlements, 289
    evidence of stress and disease in populations, 294–295, 296
    housing and clothing, 292–293
    impact of domestication and food production on cultural diversity, 296–298
    Jericho farming community, 290
    manufacture and use of pottery, 291–292
    Neolithic culture in the New World, 293–294
    New Stone Age tools, 273
    social structure, 293
    tools and other technology of, 290, 292
New Guinea:
    colonization by Upper Paleolithic peoples, 256–258
New Stone Age, 270, 273
New World:
    Neolithic culture in, 293–294
    systems of writing, 314–315
Nez Perce:
    Coyote and Wishpoosh, 6, 80
    story of creation, 6
Nichols, Johanna, 258
Nicol, Mary, 155
Nishida, Toshisada, 113
North America:
    areas of early domestication, 283, 284
    colonization by Upper Paleolithic peoples, 258–260, 263
    land bridge between Siberia and Alaska, 258–259
    Maritime Archaic culture, 272–273
    Paleoindian sites, 259, 260
Notochord, 62
Nowak, Eva, 9

Obsidian:
    in evidence of long-distance trade, 289
    tools for modern surgeons, 245–246
    trade and control of in Mexico, 312
Oldowan tool tradition, 175, 176–179, 199
Old Stone Age:
    archaeological site of, 42
    dating of sites, 54
    Lower Paleolithic tools in, 174
    Paleolithic tool kits, 200
Olduvai Gorge, 53, 154, 155
    archaeological site of, 43

Homo erectus fossils, 195
Homo habilis site, 170
Paleolithic tools in, 174–179
On the Origin of Species (Darwin), 63, 154, 221
Orangutans, 102, 103
Original studies:
    African origin or ancient population size differences, 235–237
    arbitrariness of racial classification, 336–340
    culture of chimpanzees, 113–115
    on the Darwinian principle of natural selection, 64–65
    history of mortality and physiological stress, 294–295
    Homo erectus use of bamboo, 201–204
    leopards storing meat and hominine theft of, 179–182
    Miocene ape ancestors, 134–136
    Point Franklin archaeology project, 36–39
    recreating Upper Paleolithic painted art, 252–254
Orrorin tugenensis, 158
"Out of Africa" or "Eve" hypothesis, 233–237

Paleoanthropologists, 34, 35, 46–47
Paleobotanists, 274
Paleoindians:
    fluted points of, 259, 260
    in North America, 259–260
Paleolithic Age:
    tool kits by *Homo erectus,* 200
Palynology, 52
Pan:
    genetic differences and humans, 99–100
    Pan troglodytes, 113–115
Participant observation, 14, 24
Pastoralists:
    and domestication, 297–298
Patrilocal residence, 23
Pei, W. C., 193
Pentadactyly, in primates, 97
Percussion method of tool production, 176
Peru:
    first cities in, 302
    Inca empire and government, 316
    Moche kingdom and upper class burial, 317–321
    sociological and ethnographic studies in, 21
Physical anthropology:
    analysis of fossil man, 10
    area of study, 2, 5
    as field of anthropology, 8–10
Piggot, Stuart, 34
Pigments, use of:
    in archaic *Homo sapiens,* 221, 227
    in *Homo erectus,* 210

by Maritime Archaic culture, 273
in Upper Paleolithic peoples, 248
Pilbeam, David, 132, 135, 136
Piltdown fossil hoax, 146
"Piltdown Man," 19–20
Pithecanthropus erectus, 192
Plant domestication:
    areas of early development, 283
    early evidence of, 274–276
Point Franklin archaeology project, 36–39
Pokotylo, David, 245
Polygenetic inheritance, 72–73
Polymorphic species, 332
Polytypic variation, 332–333
Population, 73
Population genetics, 73–74
Potassium-argon analysis, 53
Pottery:
    appearance in the New World, 294
    manufacture and use in Neolithic period, 291–292
Powell, John Wesley, 18
Prehensile ability in primates, 98
Prehistoric, defined, 34
Pressure flaking, 244
Primate order:
    apes, 102–104
    arboreal, 92
    brachiators, 97, 101, 102, 103
    brains of, 92–93
    Catarrhini, 91, 100, 101–104, 139
    characteristics of, 92–100
    clavicle of, 96–97
    communication of, 109
    conservation of primates, 110
    cranium, 96
    dentition of, 94–95
    establishing evolutionary relationships, 99–100
    estrus, 98
    foramen magnum, 96
    fovea centralis, 94
    grooming activities, 105–106
    Haplorhini, 91, 100–104, 130
    home ranges of, 109–110
    human encroachment on home ranges, 110
    human evolution and primate behavior, 115
    hunting activities of, 112
    individual interaction, 105–106
    learning abilities, 110–111
    Lemuriformes, 91, 100
    modern primates, 100–104
    pentadactyly, 97
    Platyrrhini, 91, 100, 101
    play activity, 109
    prehensile ability, 98
    primate groups, 104–105
    reproduction and care of young, 98
    scaplua, 97

Primate order *(continued)*
    sense organs of, 93–94
    sexual behavior, 106–108
    sexual dimorphism, 108
    skeletons of, 95–98
    social behavior of primates, 104–112
    stereoscopic vision, 93
    Strepsirhini, 91, 100
    Tarsii, 91, 100, 101
    use of objects as tools, 111–112
Primates, 60
Principles of Geology (Lyell), 63
Proboscis monkey, 101
Proconsul, 131–132, 133–134
Putnam, Fredric Ward, 18

Qu'ran, 8

Race:
    and behavior, 348
    as a biological concept, 69, 336–341
    concept and categories of, 334–336
    defined, 333
    genocide and extermination of racial
        categories, 342–343
    human races, concept of, 341–347
    and intelligence, 348–351
    meaning of, 333–336
    racial categories of the U.S. Census
        Bureau, 342
    racial worldview and discrimination,
        342–343
    skin color and adaptation, 344–347
    social significance of race: racism,
        347–351
    as subspecies, 120
Races (Coon), 335
Racism, 347–351
Radiocarbon analysis, 52–53
Ramapithecus, 135, 136
Ramphele, Mamphela, 8
Rappaport, Roy, 24
Red ochre, 210, 221, 227
Reischauer, Edwin, 28
Relethford, John, 236, 237
Rickets, 345, 346
Ridley, Matt, 66
RNA, 66
Robinson, John, 154
Robust Australopithecines, 146, 154–156
Roosevelt, Anna, 294
Roscoe, Paul, 22
Rose, Steven, 349

Sagittal crest, 154
Same-sex marriages, 27
Sanday, Peggy Reeves, 23
Sarich, Vincent, 135, 136
Scapula, in primates, 97
Schliemann, Heinrich, 42
Selassie, Haile, 144

Selfish behavior benevolent, 79
Seligman, C. G., 15
Semenov, S. A., 49
Sexual dimorphism, 108, 149, 151, 263
Shea, John, 245
Sheehan, Glen, 36, 37, 38, 39
Sheets, Payson, 245, 246
Shreeve, James, 341
Siamangs, 103
Siberia:
    colonization by Upper Paleolithic peo-
        ples, 256–258, 263
    land bridge between Siberia and Alaska,
        258–259
Sickle-cell anemia, 72, 73
    human biological response to malaria, 3,
        338
    persistence in populations, 80–82
    presence in farming regions, 296
Sillen, Andrew, 206
Simmonds, Samuel, 38
Simons, Elwyn, 135
Sinanthropus pekinensis, 193
Sites, 33
Sivapithecus, 135, 136, 137, 138
Skara Brae site, 42
Skeletal material/skeletons:
    archaeological analysis of remains, 51
    comparison of *Homo habilis* foot bones
        with human and chimpanzee, 173
    comparison of *Homo habilis* hand bones
        with human and gorilla, 171
    cranium in primates, 96
    endocasts, 49
    evidence of stress and disease in
        Neolithic populations, 294–295, 296
    foramen magnum in primates, 96
    Neandertal skull and bones, 221–222
    returning skeletal remains for reburial,
        51
    trunk skeleton comparisons in
        hominines, humans, and apes, 150
    upper hip bones in hominines, humans,
        and apes, 153
Smithsonian Institution, 18
Snaketown, Arizona, site of, 47
Snow, Clyde C., 9–10
Social Structure (Murdock), 23
Soil marks, 41
South Africa:
    archaic *Homo sapiens* site, 234
    Australopithecus sites, 146, 152, 154
    Neandertal burial sites, 227
    Swartkrans *Homo erectus* fossil site, 206
South America:
    areas of early domestication, 283, 284
    changes in domestication and food pro-
        duction, 285
    economic development and tropical
        forests, 309
    farming as last resort of subsistence, 289

Inca empire and government in Peru,
    316
Moche kingdom and an upper class
    burial, 317–321
native civilizations and use of metal, 312
Southeast Asia, areas of early domestication,
    283
Southwest Asia:
    areas of early domestication, 283, 286
    Neandertal sites, 232
    spread of farming to other regions,
        288–289
Spain:
    Altimira Cave, 255
    site of *Homo sapiens* fossils, 218
Spear throwers, in Upper Paleolithic peoples,
    244, 247
Species, 60
Spencer, Herbert, 78
Spider monkeys, 101
Squash, domestication of, 284
Stabilizing selection, 78–79
State, 28
Stern, Jack T., 180
Stevenson, Matilda Coxe, 7
Stone Age, archaeological sites of, 41
Stonehenge, 42
Stratigraphy, 52
Strum, Shirley, 110
Sudden infant death syndrome (SIDS), 11
"Survival of the fittest," 78
Susman, Randall L., 180
Swanscombe site, 42

Tanner, Nancy, 183
Tarsiers, 101
Tay-Sachs disease, 326
Teeth:
    comparison of *Homo habilis* and
        Australopithecus, 175
    evidence of stress and disease in
        Neolithic populations, 294–295, 296
    sexual dimorphism in canine teeth, 151
    upper jaw comparisons of hominines,
        humans and apes, 150
Teotihuacan, 304, 305
Terrorism:
    attacks on the Pentagon, 9, 28
    attacks on the World Trade Center, 9, 26,
        28, 302
    "Operation Infinite Justice," 26
Textiles, appearance of, 292–293, 294
Thailand, *Homo erectus* fossil site in, 206
Theory, defined, 18
Thomas, Peter A., 44
Thrifty genotype, 354
Tomasello, Michael, 113, 115
Tools:
    Acheulean tradition, 199–205
    Aurignacian tradition, 230, 231
    baton method of percussion, 204

blade technique, 243

composite tools in Mesolithic period, 271, 272

development of hafting, 220

invention of bow and arrow, 245

Levalloisian technique, 220

Lower Paleolithic, 174–185

microliths in Mesolithic tools, 270–271

Middle Paleolithic, 224–226

Mousterian tradition, 224–226

obsidian tools, 245–246

Oldowan tool tradition, 175, 176–179, 199

Paleoindian fluted points, 259–260

percussion method, 176

pressure flaking, 244

scraper, Upper Paleolithic, 249

spear throwers, 244, 247

spokeshave, Upper Paleolithic, 249

stone tools for modern surgeon, 245–246

tools kits of Upper Paleolithic peoples, 230, 231, 243–247, 248, 249, 262–263

use by primates, 111–112

Torah, 8

Toulouse-Lautrec, Henri, 75

Transhumance, 281

Turkey, settlement of Çatalhöyük, 303–305, 324, 325

Tylor, Edward B., 23

Unconscious selection, 275

United States:

discrimination and notions of race, 26

Upper Paleolithic peoples:

blade technique in tool production, 243

body ornamentation, 255–256

bone flutes and whistles, 249

boneyards of kill sites, 247

carved Venus figures of, 251, 252

clothing of, 256

cognitive capacity of, 260

engravings and cave paintings, 250–255

as first modern humans, 242–243

gene flow and evolution of, 260–262

hearths and shelter, 256

hunting abilities of, 245, 247, 263

invention of bow and arrow, 245

net hunting innovation, 245

pressure flaking in tool production, 244

ritual burial of, 261

sexual dimorphism, presence of, 263

spear throwers, 244, 247

spread and colonization by, 256–260, 263

tool kits of, 230, 231, 243–247, 248, 249, 262–263

Upper Paleolithic art, 247–256

use of pigment, 248

Variation:

climatic adaptation body features, 339, 343

concept of human races, 341–347

continuing human biological evolution, 352–357

culture acting as agent of biological selection, 352–357

ecological encroachment and emergence of diseases, 357

epicanthic eye fold, 344

and evolution, 332

exposure to mutagenic agents and carcinogens, 354–356

faunal region, 332

fingerprint patterns, 339

gene flow between races, 340

geographic variation of traits, 336–340

and hormone disrupting agents, 354–356

human occupation of variable environments, 332

impact of ozone depletion on gene pools, 354

meaning of race, 333–336

melanin, 344

physical variables and body features, 332–333, 343–344

polymorphic species, 332

polytypic variation, 332–333

race and behavior, 348

race and intelligence, 348–351

races as a biological concept, 336–341

skin color and adaptation, 344–347

social significance of race: racism, 347–351

thrifty genotype, 354

Vegeculture, 283

von Königswald, G. H. R., 192

von Linné, Carl, 60

Walker, Alan, 131

Wallace, Alfred Russell, 62

Warner, W. Lloyd, 15, 16

Watson, James, 65

Weidenreich, Franz, 193, 231

Weiner, J. S., 20

Western Abenaki, 24, 25

What Happened in History (Childe), 278

Wheat, domestication of, 275

Wheeler, Pete, 162–164

Wolpoff, Milford, 242

Women:

dominant roles of, 23

in field of anthropology, 7, 8

food foraging abilities of, 183

Women's Anthropological Society, 7

World Bank, 25

World Ethnographic Sample (Murdock), 23

Wrangham, Richard, 115

Written word, in sites of early cities, 314–316

Yakima Indians, 6

Zihlman, Adrienne, 183

Zimmerman, Michael, 38

Zinjanthropus boisei, 154

Zuni Indians, 7

GN60 .H64 2003

Haviland, William A.

Human evolution and
   prehistory /
      c2003.

FEB 1 0 2004

FEB 1 0 2004

0 1341 0638796 9

2004 01 30